"Writing compelling fiction is an art, just as is writing archaeological and historical narratives for general audiences. We archaeologists have long distrusted fiction, much as we often place little value in writing for general audiences. Tom Layton shows us that thoughtful fiction backed by serious research can produce highly significant insights into the acts of historical figures known only from archaeological finds and incomplete written records. *The 'Other' Dixwells* **achieves what many have long felt was impossible—a marriage between academic inquiry and a lively, detailed fictional story based on it.** This is a brilliant achievement that could inspire an entirely new, rigorous approach to historical narrative."

> Brian Fagan, distinguished professor of anthropology, emeritus, University of California, Santa Barbara; author *The Little Ice Age: How Climate Made History 1300–1850* and co-author *Bigger than History: Why Archaeology Matters*

"As archaeologists we are taught so many valuable lessons about being great scholars. We learn to excavate, to plan projects, involve our colleagues, and write up our work as high-quality research. But **very few archaeologists are taught how to be great story tellers** that speak to both the public and our profession. It is a rare professional gift to possess the skill of easy narration—but this is a skill that we can all achieve if we take the time to learn how to be great story tellers. *The 'Other' Dixwells* can serve as a writer's masterclass in transitioning the pure pursuit of scholarly endeavors to the dreams and imagination of the public at large."

> Annalies Corbin, founder & CEO of the PAST Foundation; co-publications editor, Society for Historical Archaeology; co-author *Historical Archeology of Tourism in Yellowstone National Park (When the Land Meets the Sea)*

"*The 'Other' Dixwells* is imaginative, exciting, and brings to life a story that emerged from the soil, the sea and the archives. As the archaeologist who uncovered this story, Tom Layton has brilliantly and powerfully shared it in many ways. Using historical fiction, **he now takes readers back in time, using his meticulous research and years of inquiry to open a portal to the past**, populated by real people and events."

> James P. Delgado, senior vice president, SEARCH; author *Gold Rush Port: The Maritime Archaeology of San Francisco's Waterfront* and *War at Sea: A Shipwrecked History from Antiquity to the Twentieth Century*

"Thomas Layton takes us on a journey that begins with archaeological finds and leads the reader and author from Massachusetts to California to China. He interweaves a tale of complicated race relations, gender bias, family structures and struggles, and complex business arrangements that stretched the limits of socially acceptable behavior. These are social issues that plagued 19th-century United States yet have never left American society. **Archaeology and fiction have never been more relevant.**"

Rebecca Allen, preservation director, United Auburn Indian Community; co-author *New Life for Archaeological Collections*; former (and currently associate) editor, Society for Historical Archaeology

"Layton brings a global cast of characters to life by telling the fascinating story of the people behind the *Frolic*, a shipwreck off the coast of California that was transporting goods from China. Accessible to lay audiences and engaging to seasoned archaeologists, the book's eye-catching illustrations, maps, historical documents, and artifact photographs coupled with the author's 36 years of experience investigating the families embroiled in the *Frolic's* transnational trade make for **a compelling, unforgettable read**."

Stacey Lynn Camp, associate professor of anthropology, director MSU campus archaeology program, associate chair, Department of Anthropology, Michigan State University; author *The Archaeology of Citizenship* and co-author *Introduction to Archaeology*

"Bravo! *The 'Other' Dixwells* is **Tom Layton at his best, displaying again his awesome ability to transform the black-and-white worlds of the archaeological artifact to a technicolor past** of those whose lives touch the sherds that we archeologists dig up today. We need more like Layton, willing to wield a broad brush to colorize a dimly lit past."

David Hurst Thomas, curator of North American archaeology, American Museum of Natural History; author *St. Catherine's: An Island in Time, Archaeology,* and co-author *Archaeology: Down to Earth*

"Tom Layton has made **a ground-breaking contribution to the field of women's history.** For the first time, he has documented the direct connection between Judith Sargent Murray's work for women's equality in the New American Republic with the succeeding generation of feminists, suffragists, and abolitionists."

Bonnie Hurd Smith, author, editor, publisher, CEO History Smiths; founder, Judith Sargent Murray Society; author *Letters of Loss & Love: Judith Sargent Murray Papers,* and *We Believe in You: Twelve Inspiring Stories of COURAGE, FAITH, and ACTION from American Women's History*

Other Books by Thomas N. Layton

In My Father's House (with Min Yee), Holt, Rinehart and Winston, 1981

Western Pomo Prehistory, Institute of Archaeology, UCLA, 1990

The Voyage of the Frolic: New England Merchants and the Opium Trade, Stanford, 1997

Gifts from the Celestial Kingdom: A Shipwrecked Cargo for Gold Rush California, Stanford, 2002

The "Other" Dixwells: Commerce and Conscience in an
American Family

By Thomas N. Layton

ISBN: 978-1-939531-47-6
Library of Congress Control Number: 2020952067

Edited by Marianne Brokaw and Rebecca Allen.

Book & cover design by Knic Pfost & Tasheon Chillous.
Cover photo courtesy of Lauren Dixwell Rayfield.
Restored by Molly Perdue.
Author photo by Robert Bain.

Published by The Society for Historical Archaeology
13017 Wisteria Drive, #395 Germantown, MD 20874, U.S.A.
www.sha.org

The "Other" Dixwells:
Commerce and Conscience in an American Family

by Thomas N. Layton

A Society for Historical Archaeology Publication

To three remarkable women who deserve to be remembered:

Judith Sargent Murray (1751–1820)

Henrietta Sargent (1785–1871)

Hu Ts'ai-shun (ca.1848–1915)

The "Other" Dixwells

INTRODUCTION

Archaeology and Fiction Meet

Successful historians strive to find fresh perspectives from which to view the past. We archaeologists have it somewhat easier. A discarded artifact moves from its original, dynamic social context into the archaeological record at a uniquely specific time and place. When we excavate that artifact from the archaeological site, our first task is to reconstruct its last cultural context. We then work outward, connecting the local context to broader cultural systems with an opportunity for epiphany at every step.

That bottom-up approach describes the 36 years of research that led to this book. In the summer of 1984 my students excavated Chinese potsherds and green bottle glass from what I believed to be a prehistoric Pomo Indian village site. My first task was to determine whether these relics belonged to the Pomo or whether Chinese workers at a nearby logging camp discarded them in the early-20th century. When we found a porcelain sherd ground into what looked like a bead blank, together with an arrow tip flaked from green glass, we knew that our find was a Pomo assemblage. My attempt to explain how the Pomo could have acquired the porcelain and glass led me to the *Frolic* shipwreck and its cargo of Chinese manufactured goods. Suddenly, we connected a remote village site not only to a broader Pomo subsistence settlement system, characterized by seasonal movement from the interior to the coast, but also to a commercial venture linking California and China.

Still focused on the Pomo, I realized that I might be able to trace out the entire territory of this tribelet by looking for Chinese artifacts in other village sites, but first I would need to learn more about all the ceramic styles carried aboard the *Frolic*. The vessel's cargo manifest could include a fuller description of the imperishable remains of the cargo recovered by the wreck divers, but it could also identify the vast array of perishable cargo items made of wood, cloth, and other materials. It was at the Baker Library of Harvard University where I found the papers of Augustine Heard & Company, the Boston firm that had dispatched the *Frolic* and her final cargo from China to San Francisco in summer 1850.

However, the Heard Company papers contained much more than the *Frolic's* cargo manifest. Documents described how George Basil Dixwell, a company partner, had commissioned the *Frolic*—a sharp-built clipper—to be constructed in 1844 in Baltimore to haul opium from Bombay to Canton. The company records revealed all the details of the *Frolic's* 6-year life, ending with her fateful, final voyage to California in 1850.

A handful of Chinese potsherds, which were excavated from an archaeological site in a remote corner of Mendocino County, California, thus provided me with a starting point for a story linking Pomo Indians to Boston entrepreneurs, Baltimore shipbuilders, opium growers in the uplands of central India, Canton retailers, and, ultimately, to a worldwide commercial system balanced by the sale of opium. That was quite enough for one book, and so I wrote *The Voyage of the Frolic: New England Merchants and the Opium Trade*.

In like fashion, the *Frolic's* final cargo, recovered by 15 wreck divers, provided me with both a starting point and a vehicle for writing a second book that describes the beginnings of direct commerce between China and California—*Gifts from the Celestial Kingdom: A Shipwrecked Cargo for Gold Rush California*.

Still I was left with an intriguing, uninvestigated fact. In the Boston (Suffolk County) archives, I discovered the 1885 will of George Basil Dixwell, the Heard Company opium specialist to whose specifications the *Frolic* had been built—a will in which he left one-third of his $241,000 estate in trust to Teen Seng, alias Charles Sargent, his Eurasian son.

My search for Charley led me back to the Massachusetts Historical Society. While researching the *Voyage of the Frolic*, I had read through the Dixwell family correspondence but only up to 1850—the year of the *Frolic's* wreck. Charley, however, was born 18 years later in 1868. I wondered why George Dixwell left Charley Sargent a fortune but denied him the Dixwell surname. Had the upwardly mobile Dixwell family not been tolerant enough to accept a Eurasian into the family fold? I searched the more-recent family papers for any mention of a Charles Sargent and found none—not even a line in the family genealogy. It was as if he had never existed (see "Family Trees," Appendix B).

To untangle this mystery, I would have to learn more about the Dixwell family as well as about George Dixwell's life in China. His voluminous correspondence could provide me with that view of China, but I needed an equally engaged observer of the Dixwells in Boston. I found her in George's aunt, Henrietta Sargent, a prominent abolitionist and early supporter of women's rights. My search for the source of Henrietta's social activism led me back to her own aunt, Judith Sargent Murray. If I were to document the consequences of Aunt Judith's contentious ideas, I would need to push the story back a full three generations before Charley's birth.

Family Secrets

Leslie Dixwell thought it looked strange—the front third of a wooden sailing ship, sticking up out of the lawn. She walked under the skyward-aimed bowsprit to read the exhibit label: "A half-size reconstruction of the brig *Frolic*, wrecked near Point Cabrillo, August 25, 1850, with a cargo of China goods for Gold Rush San Francisco." In the distance she could hear the roar of waves breaking against the Mendocino headlands.

Her father's widow, Rose, had phoned to say that an archaeologist in California was writing a book about "a boat" owned by Great-Grandfather Dixwell in China. Leslie's father, Bazil Sargent Dixwell, had rarely spoken about his father or grandfather. It was like a hole in their family history. According to Rose, her father had not only corresponded with the archaeologist but also had saved the letters, which Rose forwarded to Leslie's older sister, Stephanie after Bazil's death.

Bazil Dixwell often spoke of their first American ancestor, Col. John Dixwell, the regicide. Bazil would tell how this great, great (he wasn't sure how many greats) grandfather had been one of the jurors who sentenced King Charles I of England to death. Yet, their closer relatives were a mystery. Leslie wondered if the genealogical gap had anything to do with her father's odd request that no obituary or notice of his funeral be published in the newspaper. Bazil said it was to "protect the names of his daughters"—but from what?

Leslie knelt to read the label on a rusted iron cannon, describing how a diver had raised it from the shipwreck. Why, she wondered, would her great-grandfather's ship have been armed with a cannon? She walked up the lawn toward a yellow Victorian house with white gingerbread trim. Hanging from the second-story window, a long triangular banner rustled in the breeze, and a flash of gold caught her eye—a coat of arms glowing in the morning sun. Red letters spelled *"Frolic"* on a field of white, edged in blue stripes that were studded with stars. Rather patriotic, she thought, as she entered the Kelley House Museum.

The docent gestured toward the main exhibit hall—an old parlor with lace curtains and glass exhibit cases along two walls. A large placard stated the theme of the exhibit: how the wreck of the *Frolic* had been the seminal event that led to the founding of the town of Mendocino. She skimmed the text. A man named Ford had come up the coast in 1851 hoping to salvage the *Frolic*'s cargo. Although he had found Indian women wearing silk shawls, there was no cargo left for him to rescue. As a lumberman, Ford did notice the giant redwoods covering the hillsides. A year later, he shipped a complete steam-powered sawmill around the Horn and re-assembled it less than a mile from this very spot. Another placard described how Eliza Kelley (of the Kelley House Museum Kelleys) bartered with the local indigenous peoples for a bolt of silk from the shipwreck to make dresses for her daughters.

Certainly redwoods and silks were not sufficiently compelling to have brought Leslie Dixwell from Salt Lake City to this country museum. Of the four Dixwell daughters, now scattered from Alaska to New Hampshire, she (the youngest) lived closest to California, so Leslie was delegated to visit the exhibit and investigate any Dixwell history for the others. So far, she had little to report. All she could see were relics of the *Frolic*'s cargo: nested brass weights and trunk handles, brass spikes that once held the vessel together, and a leather shoe preserved like a fossil in a rusty concretion.

Leslie quickly scanned the rest of the exhibit captions for any mention of her father's grandfather. At the far end of the case, in the section describing the construction of the *Frolic* in a Baltimore shipyard, she spied a photograph of a lanky, middle-aged man with a receding hairline, captioned, "George Basil Dixwell (1815–85)." The label told how he had written from Canton, China, in spring 1844, to his brother John James in Boston, asking him to arrange for the construction of a fast clipper to transport opium from Bombay, India, to the mouth of the Pearl River near Canton, China. Leslie laughed out loud. Opium! Was this the reason Father wouldn't talk about his grandfather?

She stared at the picture—the first she had ever seen of her great-grandfather. George sat with his legs crossed, in an ornate, overstuffed chair, his wide-brimmed, straw hat lying atop a balustrade. She searched the face for some trace of family resemblance. Shielding her eyes from the glare of the exhibit light, she tried to read his expression. There was no attempt to court the camera; his look was one of quiet introspection. How had this man come to marry her great-grandmother, the mysterious Chinese princess?

Bazil Dixwell, Leslie's father, had been an airline pilot. Once years ago, when he was away, Grandma Dorothy showed her a hand-tinted photograph of a young Chinese woman, seated beside a table and wearing a purple silk gown that was edged in azure and black. She wore two green jade rings on the second finger of her right hand. Standing on the other side of the table was a little boy in scuffed leather shoes, striking a jaunty pose. "See her big feet," Dorothy pointed to the woman. "The royal family were Manchus, and they didn't bind the feet of little girls like the other Chinese. And Charley, that little boy, grew up to be my husband and your grandfather!"

Leslie glimpsed her own reflection in the glass lid of the exhibit case. As a child, she often stared in the mirror, looking for evidence of her one-eighth-Chinese heritage. Was it her dark hair or her round face? Her sister Lauren's face was rounder, but she was a blonde. Stephanie's hair was darker, and Marcia showed their ancestry the most—she not only had dark hair but also Asian eyes, especially when she smiled.

It was a very nice exhibit, Leslie thought, but it wasn't telling her much about the Dixwells. She walked into the museum office. "My great-grandfather owned that ship," she told the woman at the desk and asked if they had any information about him.

The curator stood and motioned her to follow. "There's a whole book. But we didn't have space to present all the information or even all the artifacts. Let me get it for you." She gestured toward a table covered with jagged sherds of blue-and-white bowls.

Leslie looked at the archaeological debris scattered across the table. The waves that broke up the *Frolic* had reduced what was left of the cargo to smithereens. Of the 21,000 bowls that were loaded into the vessel's hold at Whampoa, only one was found unbroken. Leslie picked up a coarse potsherd. Her father used to have better Oriental things lying around their house! She recalled the hand-painted China jars and silk fans as well as the ivory netsukes from Japan—kimono toggles with tiny carvings of lions and birds and pot-bellied monks that had fascinated her as a child.

She turned the piece of porcelain in her hand and recognized that she held a partial foot-ring from a large bowl. Flipping it over, she found part of a Chinese character. She tried to imagine the whole bowl and wondered what the character meant.

"It means 'good fortune.' That's the "*fu*" character," said the curator from over her shoulder. She held a wrinkled, two-inch stack of paper with a broken plastic binding. Pink and blue sticky notes fluttered from its pages. "The book is full of information about the Dixwells, but we can't release it because it isn't published yet."

Leslie stared at the title—*Drug Runner: New England Merchants and the Opium Trade*—and winced. Opening her notebook, she carefully copied the name and address of the author.

I was that author. Two weeks later I received a letter from Leslie's sister, Stephanie Dixwell, asking how they might obtain a copy of my book, as it might contain historical information "that our father would not divulge, but that his four daughters, grandchildren, and great grandchild should know." I photocopied several pages from the manuscript and mailed them to Stephanie and began a correspondence with the four Dixwell sisters—Stephanie, Leslie, Marcia, and Lauren .

Meanwhile, my publisher objected to the title I had proposed for my book, and I renamed it: *The Voyage of the Frolic*. Having described the life of the vessel in the opium trade, I was now outlining a second volume that told the story of her final cargo of Chinese manufactured goods bound for Gold Rush San Francisco.

I knew that George Dixwell had made his first trip to China in 1841 and had lived there, off and on, for much of the next 30 years. During his time away, he corresponded with his family in Boston. I also knew that George had married a Chinese woman and had a son with her, Bazil's father. I had leafed through George's correspondence during an earlier visit to the Massachusetts Historical Society but only up to the *Frolic*'s life during the late-1840s.

A new idea had taken root that I might somehow use the story of the *Frolic* as a launching point to tell a broader story of America and China during the middle third of the 19th century. George Dixwell, the mercantile capitalist, could serve as my eyes and ears in China, but I needed an equally astute observer to present the contemporary events back in the States. With that in mind, I returned to Boston, hoping that somewhere in the Dixwell archive I might find that spokesperson. After two weeks of research, I found her in George's most prolific correspondent, his aunt Henrietta Sargent (1785–1871).

Through her letters, I could sense that Henrietta was a woman of high ideals, a committed member of the Boston Female Anti-Slavery Society and an early and ardent supporter of women's rights. A reference librarian suggested that I look for more about her in the Sargent genealogy published in 1923: *Epes Sargent of Gloucester and His Descendants.*

Turning first to the Dixwell section, I was disappointed. The marriages of George's two brothers were listed, together with all of their descendants down to the year 1923. George had only a one-line entry, stating his birth and death dates. Neither marriage nor children were mentioned. The family genealogist had preserved the racial purity of the Sargents and Dixwells by ignoring George Dixwell's Chinese wife and their son.

That genealogical entry helped explain not only why Bazil had been so hesitant to discuss his Chinese background with me but also why he had attempted to keep his daughters from that perceived stigma. With their father gone, the sisters came to me for information, and I hoped to be able to shed light into that hole in their past.

In addition, I was researching George's Aunt Henrietta, and as I flipped back the pages to the previous generation, I found a half-page summary of her life, taken from an appreciation written by George's brother Epes at the time of her death. He described Henrietta as a woman of strong character with a cultivated taste in art and poetry. She had been, he wrote,

> "... a pioneer in the cause of anti-slavery, and an ardent sympathizer of the colored race, before any movement for its freedom was publicly made. Later, when the anti-slavery party was organized and women took up the cause, she was found among the foremost to favor it. Even in the darkest days, when their meetings were dispersed by the over-zeal [sic] or determined hate of men of station in Boston, she was in the midst and did not flinch, but carried the spirit of martyrdom into her determined adherence to her party."

Henrietta, he went on to say, was an equally strong adherent of religious views, which she gained in her youth from the Rev. John Murray, the founder of American Universalism.

Again, I leafed backwards, looking for an ancestor from whom Henrietta might have received her inspiration. Her father, Epes Sargent, had been a delegate to the 1799 convention to draft the Massachusetts State Constitution. A competent public servant, he had been a customs collector and eventually became president of the Suffolk Insurance Company. I saw no evidence of social activism. I went back yet another generation. Henrietta's grandfather (another Epes) had, together with his brother Winthrop, convinced the Universalist Reverend John Murray to come to Gloucester, where in 1780 on family land the brothers built Murray the first Universalist church in America—no doubt the source of Henrietta's deep Christian faith.

Looking a few pages further, I discovered a magnificent portrait by John Singleton Copley, the pre-eminent artist of the day, who painted an image that could have graced the cover of any romance novel—a beautiful dark-haired woman in a diaphanous silk gown that barely clung to the curve of her breasts. The caption reads, "Mrs. John Murray." Born in 1751, Judith Sargent had married the Rev. John Murray, her second husband, in 1788. Most of her biographic sketch dealt not with her life but with his. Then one sentence caught my eye: "An industrious and tireless writer, she is now best remembered by her beautiful portraits by Copley and Stuart, for her prose and verse are as well forgotten as remembered."

I was stunned. If George's family had been ignored, Judith suffered worse. In her own family genealogy, she got an acknowledgement of her beauty and a crude dismissal of her literary life! Who was Judith Sargent Murray, and why were her intellectual achievements so denigrated by her family?

I soon learned that Judith was the first published feminist in America. She had written *On the Equality of the Sexes* about 1779 and published it in 1790. She was a popular and prolific professional writer whose craft helped support her family. In 1798, she published *The Gleaner*, a three-volume compilation of 100 essays she had written for American magazines. She was also a playwright. In 1807, her third play—*The African*—was closed after one performance at Boston's Federal Street Theater. We can only imagine the unpalatable and, quite likely, incendiary message presented in its now-lost script. Here was the antecedent for Henrietta Sargent's independence, her social conscience, her Universalist faith, her abolitionist fervor, and her radical spirit. Her mentor was none other than her aunt, Judith Sargent Murray—the grandmother of American feminism!

As a social activist, Henrietta represented a major counter-trend in 19th-century American culture, which stood in opposition to the expansionist mercantile ambition represented by her nephew, George Dixwell, a merchant motivated by monetary gain. She was a fearless and candid observer with as much mastery of her world as George had been of his. Now, within the limits of the data I could discover, I could write a more inclusive book than earlier seemed possible. Perhaps I would even be able to fill in the missing pieces of their family history for Stephanie and her sisters.

What follows, then, is a tale of America and China, told from the perspective of one family—a tale that presses to its limits the powers of this archaeologist to extract meaning from a mess of Chinese potsherds laid out on a table.

Technique

Although a bottom-up approach, linking a specific archaeological find to the social context in which it had once functioned, is guaranteed to provide a fresh perspective, each step outward to a broader framework yields a multiplicity of links to still other areas at an exponential rate of increase. The researcher must determine the focus and scope of the study and what themes will guide the narrative. As Wallace Stegner is reputed to have said about his style of writing, "First you learn everything about everything, and then you throw most of it away." You cannot fit everything into one readable narrative.

I also wanted to find a voice that would be more engaging than that used in an archaeological monograph like my *Western Pomo Prehistory* (1990). Successful teachers can make almost any topic memorable by personalizing it. Science teachers often accomplish this by describing the process of discovery. I employed that technique in chapter 1 of *The Voyage of the Frolic,* where I described how we discovered the Chinese potsherds and the way I traced them back to a story of Americans in the opium trade. For the body of that book, I then assumed the omniscient voice of a historian. I returned to my own, more personal, voice in an epilogue that described how my colleagues and I brought the story back to people now living on the coast.

My first draft of that book was so bloated with detail that the editor rightly asked for major cuts in order to preserve the narrative thrust of the text. For me that was a depressing prospect. I had worked hard collecting the data, and I didn't want to lose it. The problem was solved with two rather pedestrian discoveries: the endnote and the appendix. I learned that an endnote could contain not only a citation but also whole paragraphs of text, and that an appendix could hold even more. One full-page endnote allowed me to preserve the account of the first cargo of Massachusetts ice shipped to Calcutta, and I was able to move a long, detailed description of how the *Frolic* was built—drawings and all—into an appendix. My only real departure from scientific convention in *The Voyage of the Frolic* was a prologue written from the viewpoint of "Kitana," an imagined northern Pomo headman, standing high on a bluff and watching his people as they salvaged treasures from the *Frolic* shipwreck.

With that book completed and the wreck divers' collections in hand, I was ready to analyze the vessel's final cargo—14 cabinet drawers and 8 archival boxes that contained more than 2,000 pieces of things, which more *suggested* a cargo than represented one after almost a century and a half underwater. My task was to transport those things from an archaeological context on the ocean floor back to their behavioral contexts, including their manufacture in China and shipment to California. The meticulous analysis of thousands of things, however, seemed likely to result in more of a catalog than a narrative. Again I turned to the two literary devices that earlier had helped me to make *The Voyage of the Frolic* accessible to a broader readership.

Once more, I chose to personalize the text, this time with a firsthand account of my analysis of the cargo. Going several steps beyond my earlier vignette featuring the Pomo headman, Kitana, I decided to weave among the descriptions of my research a series of dialogue-driven vignettes. These scenes featured the actual people who had been responsible for the purchase and shipment of the *Frolic*'s cargo. I undertook this type of writing with some trepidation. We social scientists are adept at analyzing clusters of information and positing links between data points. But in order to write convincing vignettes, I would need to fill in the spaces among those data points, not only with dialogue but also with full descriptions of place. Further, if I was not sufficiently explicit about the sources of my data, my work might be dismissed as "creative nonfiction."

I wrote the vignettes only for times and places for which I had the actual documentation in correspondence or diaries of a major participant. At a more abstract level, I saw myself interpolating among closely clustered data points, while taking care not to extrapolate beyond them.

As I began drafting the first vignette, describing John Hurd Everett's 1844 trip from Monterey to Pueblo San Jose to collect payments from his customers, I found myself perched uncomfortably on the horns of a dilemma. As a social scientist trained to be critical of both data and interpretation, I intended the vignette to carry factual historical information; however, by employing the techniques of a novelist, I was inserting invented context that would ask the reader to suspend disbelief. I attempted to resolve that apparent contradiction by allowing the vignette to proceed for 20 pages, unimpeded by citations, to one endnote where I listed not only the historical sources but also specified exactly where I had inserted fictionalized context. Encouraged by the result, I wrote two more extended vignettes. *Gifts from the Celestial Kingdom* (2002), the result of that experiment in historical writing, was well received by professional reviewers and, to my surprise, was awarded a writing prize by the Society for Historical Archaeology.

As I began to draft the final volume of the "*Frolic* trilogy"—this present one—I faced a new challenge. I had already told the 6-year story of the *Frolic*'s life and of her final cargo as well as my own story of research and discovery. I needed a fresh approach to tell a much longer story of personalities and ideas in which the *Frolic* itself played only a very small part. In the *Gifts* volume, my voice as the researcher had been primary, and the vignettes were drafted to support my research narrative. I now reversed that emphasis, making the character-driven vignettes primary and the researcher secondary. I maintained continuity with the first two books by retaining my subsidiary voice in the prologue, epilogue, and a few places scattered through the body of the text.

I also rethought the purpose of the endnotes. Grouping all the citations for a long vignette into one endnote required at least one explanatory sentence for each. With a little tinkering, I discovered that those sentences could be transformed from a dense listing of sources into readable prose. By adding historical context, that prose could become a reflective narrative, running parallel to the main text of the book. In the *Gifts* volume, every nine pages of text required one page of endnotes. This volume required a four-fold increase in notes: one page of notes for every 2.4 pages of text. Finally, making a virtue of necessity, I rewrote the notes for continuity, and in so doing, they took on a life of their own.

Caveats

There is a slippery slope between fact and fiction, and historians are rightly suspicious of any style of writing that blurs the distinction. Throughout the "*Frolic* trilogy," I attempt to be explicit about the documented facts and exactly where I bridged among them. Still, any kind of crossover writing that intends to reach the general reader without losing the specialist is a tricky business. This volume is the story of people interacting with each other, and their historical interactions are the bones of the story. As a storyteller, I felt free to set the scenes at historically critical times and places, enabling the characters to fully experience the issues that I wanted to present as a historian. The historical effort thus resides within an artistic charade. If as an author I can sustain that charade, history will become the ultimate winner as it stealthily infiltrates the minds of the readers when all their defenses are down. Further, we hope to insure that no fraud is perpetrated because the endnotes will arm the reader with sufficient facts to become not only a confidante but also a behind-the-scenes co-conspirator.

While a poorly written story reaches no one, we social scientists generally expect to be judged by the validity of our research and only incidentally by the quality of our writing. If we borrow the techniques of the novelist—as I have done in this volume—the start-up cost of learning a new way of writing can be immense. To complete the first draft of *The Voyage of the Frolic*, I required a one-year sabbatical of full-time writing. To write, rewrite, and rewrite this volume required more than 15 years, most of them as a professor emeritus. Put bluntly, an academic had best be protected by tenure before undertaking this kind of writing. It can also cost money: for both the *Gifts* volume and this one, I hired a writing coach to read and critique my vignettes, one by one, as I wrote them.

Fools walk where angels fear to tread, and in this book, I have tread on a lot of unfamiliar turf—a problem that pervades anthropological research. We anthropologists view cultures as systems comprising interconnected parts, and we are trained to focus our attention on the connections. For this reason, I am never fully at home in any of the traditional disciplines; the locus of my professional niche is in the spaces among them. This focus on interconnections enables me to conceive of a story moving back and forth between China and America, spanning 200 years. That vision is ultimately grounded in a multiplicity of disciplines and subdisciplines that are occupied by other scholars who through years of focused study have mastered them.

Because I cross disciplines, I know that experts outside my field could read my work, and that they (not out of vengeance but because of their training) must automatically search my prose for anachronism and inaccuracy. Aware of the dangers of writing too independently while transcending disciplines, I sought out the help of those experts. They supplied essential context and tried to save me from the stupid mistakes of the amateur I am. The many acknowledgements at the end of this book testify to the help I have asked for and received.

Even as I sought a solid grounding in the historical record, I tried to remain open to intuition and insight—just as any novelist must. While I looked for opportunities to explore imaginative paths, I assumed the identity of every speaking character in this book. Thus, I stood in front of the South Boston house where George and Charley lived during the early-1880s and imagined Charley, newly orphaned, sitting alone on the marble doorsteps. On a summer Sunday morning, I walked from Epes Dixwell's house on Garden Street to the Unitarian Church in Harvard Square, where he once worshiped, to attend the service. I strolled through Mount Auburn Cemetery to visit the graves of George and Henrietta, and it was there on J.J.'s headstone that I spied the opium poppy capsule carved into the side—a wink and a nod to a storied past.

Amongst my research notes are these sentences that guide my writing:

"I sometimes find myself camped awkwardly with the paparazzi on the back steps of serendipity. I try to put myself into situations where serendipity can occur—and often it does. And I'm enough of an opportunist to always have a pencil and a notepad in my pocket."

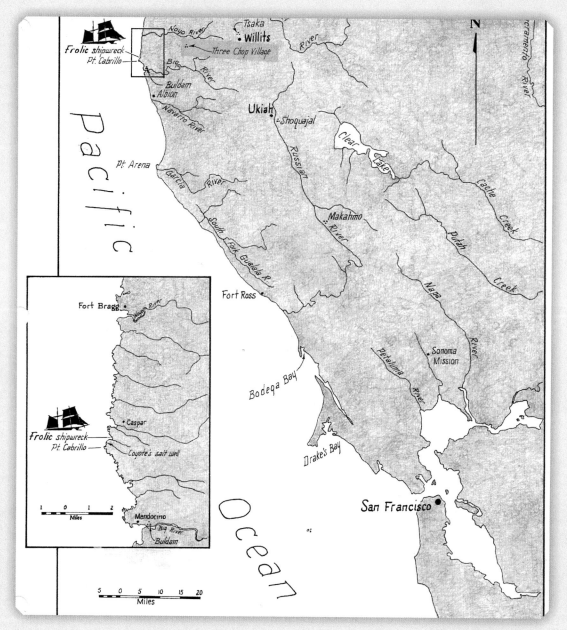

The *Frolic* wreck site [inset] at Point Cabrillo and Three Chop Village, Mendocino County, California. (Map by S. F. Manning.)

Historical archaeology incorporates many tasks. These include the identification of the artifacts and features that we excavate, the gleaning of contextual information from libraries and archives, interviewing experts, and recording oral histories from living descendants. To accomplish this, we archaeologists must plan adequate time for both research and critical thinking. The story found within the pages of this book evolved during 35 years of persistent and far-ranging inquiries. It attempts to provide alternate approaches for historical archaeologists who, after completing their essential site reports, wish to go *one step farther* and present their research results in a form that can reach the public

Reaching the public has become an essential task for historical archaeologists. We have come to understand that if we want the public and our legislators to value our work, we must produce a product that they will actually read. This volume attempts to take that further step. I have inserted fully formed characters (mostly real, a few invented) and their dialogue into the spaces among the fully documented, historical facts to provide a more easily accessible story.

The *Frolic* sailed from Hong Kong on June 10, 1850, with a full cargo of Chinese manufactured goods to be sold in San Francisco. She made good time across the North Pacific, covering 6,000 miles in 46 days, at 5.4 statute miles per hour and sighted Mendocino's coastal mountains on July 25, 1850. But the steersman was too late in sighting the mist-shrouded phalanx of surf-battered, offshore rocks that fronted the low coastal terrace. Captain Faucon ordered the vessel turned, but a strong swell drove the vessel backwards. The *Frolic* struck, stern-first, snapping her rudder and cracking her hull. As she filled with water, Captain Faucon ordered the two lifeboats lowered and the crew into them. Reaching shore in a protected cove the following morning, most of the crew elected to walk south to San Francisco. However, Captain Faucon, his officers, and four oarsmen boarded one of the boats and pulled south toward the Euro-American settlement at Bodega Bay.

The crewmen that Faucon left behind, returned to the wreck with the second boat to salvage whatever supplies they could find before the long walk to civilization. Meanwhile, indigenous people from the interior of California, who had come to the coast over thousands of years for summer shellfish gathering, were watching. After the *Frolic*'s crew departed, they began their own salvage.

San Jose State University anthropology students excavate House 1 at Three Chop Village in July 1984. (Photo by author 1984.)

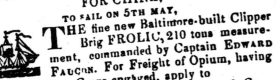

Bombay Times advertisement soliciting an opium cargo for the *Frolic* 29th April 1845.

Letters and commercial documents, packed in over 261 shelf-feet of archival boxes at Harvard Business School's Baker Library, enabled me to discover the story of an American firm's entry into the opium trade—a story later suppressed by the enriched descendants of those same opium traders. (Photo by author 1989.)

The archaeological discovery at the heart of this volume began in July 1984. While teaching a San Jose State University archaeological field school, I began excavation at a Native American site in ethnographic Pomo territory, with clearly visible house depressions that marked the locale of a village site near Point Cabrillo along the coast of northern California.

Shortly after my students began excavating House 1 at what we eventually called Three Chop Village, they recovered fragments of coarse Asian looking, "blue-on-white" painted stoneware. Clearly, the Pomo people at Three Chop Village had access to Asian-looking ceramics and green bottle glass, but from where? The local forest ranger told me that he had seen similar sherds on a beach 15 miles southwest at Point Cabrillo, and that his friend, an abalone diver, had collected more of them from a wreck out in the cove. That led me to a group of wreck divers who had pillaged the wreck. One of them had a fragment of a Chinese ginger jar, providing an exact match to our excavated sherds. That wreck, I realized, would provide a date for the Pomo occupation of Three Chop Village, if only I could identify the vessel.

More than half of an historical archaeologist's research occurs in archives and libraries. My research found a *Daily Alta California* news article that reported the wreck of the *Frolic* enroute from China to San Francisco. A search of the English-language *China Mail*, published in Canton, led me back to the *Frolic*'s first arrival in China from Bombay, where a *Bombay Times* classified ad told me she was built in Baltimore. The *Federal Ships Registry* for Baltimore listed the Gardner Brothers as the builders, and J. J. Dixwell (brother of George Dixwell) as the owner. J. J. Dixwell was well known as an associate of Augustine Heard & Co. of Boston and Canton. I then discovered that the Heard company papers were held by the Baker Library of the Harvard Graduate School of Business Administration, where the manuscript librarian told me that there was a small box, labeled "*Frolic*," containing 7-inches of documents, including a cargo manifest.

In summer 1989, I travelled to Harvard to study those 7-inches of documents relating to that final cargo and discovered that the Heard Collection occupied a full 261 shelf-feet. Scattered throughout was the story of the Heard firm's entry into the opium trade, with the *Frolic* as their primary clipper transporting opium from India to China. As I transcribed the Heard documents, I realized that I could tell not only the story of a cargo but also the story of a Baltimore clipper and the story of Americans in the opium trade—a chain of discoveries that would take me from the silent world of prehistory into the very noisy world of the historic period.

CHAPTER ONE

Judith Sargent Murray

Cambridge, Massachusetts
2001, July

I walked along Garden Street looking for number 58. To my left were the stately brick buildings of Radcliffe College. Across the street, on my right, a row of houses presented an awkward jumble of almost two centuries of architectural evolution.

On June 4, 1847, George and John James, the youngest and oldest of the Dixwell brothers, had given their middle brother Epes, headmaster of Boston Latin School, the money to purchase a lot in Cambridge and to build a house. Today, I was looking for that house.

I had just spent two weeks reading Dixwell documents at the Massachusetts Historical Society, and I needed a real-world fix—something solid and substantial. I almost blushed at my archaeologist's addiction. I needed an artifact!

Number 58 was behind a gigantic hedge. I got out my camera, advanced the film, and considered my problem. It was 8:45 am on a Sunday morning. The residents would probably be home. I would have to walk up their driveway and snap the picture without attracting attention—and I would have to do it fast because if the sun rose any higher, I would be shooting directly into it.

The gravel crunched noisily under my feet. I telescoped my lens to its widest angle and aimed the camera. The house didn't fit in the frame. I pushed aside a large branch and stepped backwards into the hedge. Instantly, every cupped leaf containing a droplet from last night's shower tipped downward, and I caught a full deluge down my neck. I gritted my teeth and aimed the camera. It wouldn't focus. I yanked up my shirt to get at the only dry spot, wiped the lens, and snapped the shot. As I retreated to the street, wet and disheveled, I felt like a voyeur—almost caught in the act.

Time is an unbroken progression, and so also, of course, was the story of the Dixwells. I needed to find a place to break into that continuum—to make time stop, even if only for a moment—so that I could begin to tell the tale.

The Massachusetts Historical Society was closed on Sundays, so I decided to visit some of the places where the Dixwells had lived. I imagined that on a summer Sunday morning like this in August 1849, Epes and his wife, Mary Ingersol Bowditch Dixwell, joined by Epes's Aunt Henrietta Sargent, would have walked this route from Dixwell's brand-new house to the Unitarian Church in Harvard Square. And so, this morning I was tracing what I imagined were their footsteps.

I walked through Cambridge Common. Now I was on more familiar turf—a landscape virtually unchanged from my own Harvard graduate school days. I passed Christ Church, built in 1759 to minister to Church of England congregants—most of whom, as Loyalists, had retreated to Nova Scotia during the American Revolution. [1]

I gazed at the slate gray tombstones in the Old Burying Grounds that separate this church from the Unitarian church about 100 yards beyond. My own memories came to mind. In 1966, when I had begun my graduate work in archaeology in the anthropology department at Harvard, I met students who, only a few years earlier, had been sent out by James Deetz to record the decorative elements and epitaphs on tombstones in cemeteries all over New England, including this one. When all of that data from 1680 to 1820 was tabulated, it demonstrated that these seemingly silent stone slabs tell a fascinating story of long-term changes in people's conception of their relationship with God.

In the late-1600s, these stones were adorned with death's heads—grinning skulls with hollow eyes, representing a grim, Puritan view of death in which only a very few members of the predestined "elect" would enjoy a happy afterlife. Then from 1730 into the 1760s, during the First Great Awakening, people began to develop a more personal relationship with God.

Henrietta's uncle, the Rev. John Murray who had introduced Universalism to America, was a major participant in this movement, preaching that not only did God love mankind but also that *all* people, by their own free will, could achieve salvation. Softened iconography on the tombstones of this period recorded this change with such motifs as cherubs, symbolizing resurrection.

This personalization process continued during the 1790s with the appearance of classical urns and weeping willows as decorations, along with epitaphs celebrating the individual's lifetime achievements. These memorials witnessed a more secular society, in which people were motivated less by divine principle than by earthly reward. Religion had become "worldly," as Henrietta Sargent would have expressed it—no doubt, wrinkling her nose for maximum effect! [2]

Deetz's insightful discovery was a major breakthrough in American archaeology, showing that the study of material things could reveal changes in world view, of which even the manufacturers and users of these items had not been conscious. I had always been a bit envious of Deetz. My own studies of prehistoric archaeology required me to spend most of my career merely trying to date the artifacts I had excavated from Native American archaeological sites. Deetz, however, as an historical archaeologist, often knew the exact dates of his sites almost from the start of his projects from documents and, as a consequence, was able to spend his time asking and answering more interesting questions.

I wondered if in August 1849, the earlier religious outlook symbolized by the many death's heads must have seemed outdated to Epes and Mary Dixwell as they had walked past Christ Church toward the Unitarian Church just beyond. [3]

As an upper-class defender of the underdog, Henrietta Sargent would have been painfully aware of not only the obvious differences of social rank and education between Unitarians and Universalists but also of the hubris and self-confidence of this particularly elite congregation, meeting directly across the street from Harvard University. Not only were these Unitarians increasingly discounting the word of God and finding non-Biblical sources for their inspiration, but in rejecting the Trinity, they had also seemed to demote Jesus Christ, her savior.

It was almost time for the service, so I climbed the steps into the church. A prominent sign reading "Unitarian-Universalist Church" yanked me unceremoniously back to the present. The Unitarians, I now recalled, merged with the Universalists in 1961. But in 1849 the differences between these denominations had still been substantial, and Aunt Henrietta would have been painfully aware of them as she took her seat next to her nephew Epes for a family Sunday.

As I walked down the central aisle and stepped into pew no. 14, I tried to transport myself back to 1849 and wondered which pew had been favored by the Dixwells. Casually dressed men and women entered and took their seats. Suddenly, the quiet was pierced by the crackle of static, and a deep sonorous voice seemingly coming from out of the walls began to ask frightening questions.

"Do you renounce Satan and all the spiritual forces of wickedness that rebel against God?

"Do you renounce the evil powers of this world, which corrupt and destroy the creatures of God?"

"Do you renounce all sinful desires that draw you from the love of God?"

Another blast of static was followed by an instant of dead silence. All around me was a buzz of whispered conversations. Had we really heard what we thought we had heard? A young man, his hair tied in a ponytail, walked to the lectern. He introduced himself by explaining he was a recent graduate of Harvard Divinity School and was the summer stand-in for the regular minister. Someone, he informed us, had apparently left the cordless microphone turned on, and we had just received a baptismal service broadcast from the Episcopal Church on the other side of the Burying Ground. "And," he added, "we heard about two things that we don't believe in. We don't believe in original sin, and we don't believe in Satan." [4]

Within the sanctuary of this liberal congregation, the Episcopal liturgy had sounded positively melodramatic and anachronistic. It reminded me that the orthodox, Calvinist religious substrate from which both Unitarians and Universalists had struggled to free themselves was still alive and well at Christ Church, only 100 yards away!

The young minister then struck four notes from a Tibetan chime, and our service began. We sang a hymn that didn't mention Christ or God—secularism had clearly won out over the divine. I imagined Henrietta Sargent next to me. Was she squirming in her seat?

What, indeed, would Henrietta have expected to find in this book? Certainly, readings from the sermons of Rev. John Murray, the founder of American Universalism. I checked the index and found only one reading by Murray. I found another by Hosea Ballou (1771–1852) who, even before Murray's death, had usurped his elder, becoming the de-facto intellectual leader of the denomination.

Whereas Murray had held onto the Calvinistic idea that there would be punishment after death for those who had sinned on earth, Ballou, beginning with his "Treatise on Atonement" (1805), had challenged this idea, first rejecting the idea of endless punishment and eventually taking the position that there would be no punishment after death at all. This stance, termed "ultra-Universalism," undercut the ideas of both Satan and Hell, the existence of which more traditional Universalists, like Henrietta Sargent, felt to be necessary deterrents against sinful behavior here on earth. [5]

Henrietta held Ballou in contempt not only for his ideas but also for the disrespect Ballou had shown to John Murray. The upstart ingrate had once preached his heresy as a guest in John Murray's pulpit. Ballou never adequately acknowledged John Murray's contributions in founding the church in America. Neither did this songbook. John Murray's single entry in the present-day hymnal seems to have been included as a historical curiosity—a pale, perfunctory, almost irrelevant acknowledgement of the origins of the sect.

Henrietta's discomfort with the church ran much deeper than the Universalists' dismissal of Uncle John Murray's contribution to her faith. Far more important to Henrietta was what she learned from Murray's wife—her Aunt Judith Sargent Murray whose public advocacy for the abolition of slavery and for the rights of women had become the guiding principles in her own life.

I imagined Henrietta closing her eyes as she remembered the events of a summer day 41 years earlier. And maybe that was the place to start my story.

The Sargent Home
65 Newbury Street, Boston
1806, August 27

With the curtains drawn against the August sun, the Sargents' back parlor was cool and quiet—except, of course, for the baby's howls. Esther Dixwell held the baby close as her sister, Henrietta Sargent, quickly ushered her into an armchair. "There," Henrietta sighed, putting an extra pillow behind Esther's back. "That should be more comfortable."

The baby stopped crying as he began to nurse. Early that morning, Dr. John Dixwell had brought his wife Esther and their baby over so that she could enjoy the company of her mother and sisters while he saw patients in his office. They were joined this afternoon by Mrs. Hunt, Dr. Dixwell's stepmother, who also wanted to see the two month-old baby.

The Sargent family tea service, fashioned for Grandfather by Paul Revere himself—polished this very morning by sisters Henrietta and Catharine—sat at a small table next to Mother. On the wall behind her, the famous artist John Copley's portrait of Grandfather, a dusting of white powder from his wig still fresh on his shoulder, gazed beneficently down on the gathering.

Mrs. Hunt sniffed as she lifted her teacup to her lips. "My, Mrs. Sargent! What a lovely aroma." Her deep southern accent sounded almost musical, so unlike the Sargents' clipped Boston tones. She took a tiny sip.

"It's the very first shipment from Canton of this year's crop." Mother tapped the red and gold lacquer tea caddy with her finger and poured. "Have you planned a full schedule of entertainments for the fall?"

"I do look forward to several concerts," Mrs. Hunt dropped a pebble of sugar into her cup and frowned slightly, "but we will probably forego the theater."

"But our theater is one of the great benefits of living in Boston." Catharine cut the teacake, placed a slice on a saucer, and passed it to Mrs. Hunt.

Henrietta nodded her agreement. For her, the family's move to Boston from New Hampshire five years ago had meant coming to a cultural Promised Land.

Mrs. Hunt poured a dollop of cream into her cup. "Aren't they opening with something called *The African*? Who in the world would want to see a stage play about nigras!"

A flush of color, noticed only by Catharine, came into Henrietta's cheeks. Catharine nudged her under the table. Dr. Dixwell stared coldly at his stepmother. Henrietta, mindful of Catharine's watchful eye, kept her voice mild. "I'm sure the play will properly present the most noble qualities that we all know among Africans."

Only the inner circle of the family, which did not include Mrs. Hunt, knew that *The African*, the play now being rehearsed at the Federal Street Theater, had come from the anonymous pen of Aunt Judith Sargent Murray—the family lightning rod. Everything she wrote attracted attention, more often condemnation than praise.

"I have always been accustomed to blacks," continued Mrs. Hunt, addressing

Henrietta, "and I do prefer them to attend upon me. Why, many of them are far from being disagreeable in their personal appearance."

"Oh, yes!" Catharine quickly agreed. "I see them walking to the African church every Sunday morning. They always look so elegant."

"Such colorful dresses," Mrs. Hunt drawled, "and many nigras are of excellent physical form. Why, I once had a young slave who was, without exception, the prettiest creature I ever saw."

"When you were a child?" asked Catharine.

"Oh, no, I was already the mistress of my first husband's plantation, and that girl tended table for us. Indeed a gentleman, who was often at our house, became dreadfully infatuated with her, so much so, that I asked him not to show attentions to the girl."

Henrietta patted her lips with her napkin to hide her expression.

Mrs. Sargent nodded her approval. "Yes, young girls do need to be protected."

"You're absolutely right about protecting one's girls," Mrs. Hunt leaned forward. "The inappropriate attentions of a man can upset an entire household. The young man desisted, but after a few weeks he came to me and said, 'I must have that girl! I cannot live without her!' He offered me a very high price, and I so pitied the poor fellow that I finally sold the girl to him!"

Henrietta's eyes widened, and she started to speak but stopped at Catharine's kick under the table. Mrs. Sargent's habitual smile seemed frozen. Even Catharine was at a loss for words. Dr. Dixwell broke the stunned silence, cleared his throat, and glared at his stepmother. "Ladies, please excuse us. We must be going." Ignoring his wife's puzzled look, he placed his napkin on the table and stood.

Mrs. Sargent half-rose from her own seat. "But, can't you stay just a little longer?

There was an edge to the regret in John's voice. "I wish we could, but I still have patients to see this afternoon." He bent to help his wife to her feet. She cast an apologetic look at her mother.

Mrs. Hunt, somewhat flustered, turned to Mrs. Sargent. "Thank you very much for having me. I am so sorry we must leave you so suddenly. It has been such a pleasure to see you and your charming daughters."

Dr. Dixwell hurried both women and the baby out the door, trying to hide his anger. He already disliked his stepmother for the shame her liaison with his father had brought on the Hunt family name. It had been more than 15 years since the Boston Selectmen (responding to citizen complaints) had given Mr. Sam Hunt three choices: to terminate relations with the young widow from South Carolina, marry her, or resign his position as schoolmaster. Bostonians had long memories for scandal. As Dr. Dixwell was also christened Sam Hunt, the same name as his disgraced father, he legally changed his name before marrying Esther Sargent. Resurrecting the honorable surname of his late mother, Mary Dixwell, he became John Dixwell. She was the last of the American descendants of Col. John Dixwell, one of the judges who had passed sentence on King Charles.

After seeing the Dixwells and Mrs. Hunt to the door, Henrietta returned to her mother's side and bent to kiss her cheek. "Why don't you rest for awhile. You know,

Catharine and I promised to take a piece of cake to Aunt Murray. I have a book to return to her, too."

Catharine followed Henrietta from the room. "I need some fresh air," Henrietta whispered to her sister, "after that dreadful woman."

A few minutes later, the two sisters were walking up Newbury Street. "I'm glad Father was at work." Henrietta's cheeks were still pink with indignation. "He would have died of apoplexy on the spot!"

Catharine, always the peacemaker, shook her head, "I'm sure Mrs. Hunt didn't realize what she was saying. The poor thing probably has no idea of how immoral—"

"—it is for one woman to sell another—like a *cow*?" sputtered Henrietta.

"But that's just how Southerners think." Catharine pursed her lips. "I suppose that's even how Uncle Winthrop thinks!"

Only a few years ago, before their father Epes Sargent, Jr., had found employment in Boston, Aunt Murray's brother, Winthrop Sargent (recently the Governor of the Mississippi Territory) had encouraged their father to move to Natchez and become a slave-holding planter. Father had firmly refused the offer, even though he had a house full of children to feed. As a Christian who read the Bible daily and as a man who had suffered for liberty, he could not bear any member of his own family supported by enslavement.

"Unfortunately, you are probably right about that." Henrietta paused. "Yet Mrs. Hunt has been in Boston for 15 years, and she cannot possibly remain deaf and blind to Christian morality. She would be horror-struck at the idea of selling a white woman into prostitution, even the poorest or most degraded one, but what can you expect from a woman of her—her moral character?"

Catharine sighed, "Henriet, we cannot change the world overnight."

The Murray Home
5 Franklin Place, Boston

The sisters turned into Franklin Place and stopped under the shade of an elm tree to admire Aunt Judith Murray's townhouse, which stood just to the right of the central arch of the Tontine Crescent—the most elegant row of residences in Boston.

Although the Rev. John Murray had been more used to the privations of a rural circuit, he had chosen this house to provide his wife the elegance to which she had been accustomed at her home in Gloucester. Judith had pledged a portion of her inheritance to purchase it; however, they still had to live on the reverend's inadequate salary, which, owing to the financial vicissitudes of his flock, arrived in small, irregular increments. Aunt Murray did her best to shield her husband from these earthly concerns, but the need for additional income had been a major impetus to her writing career.

Catharine shifted her basket to her other arm. "Look at the lovely roses beside Aunt Murray's doorway. That's one of the bushes she brought from her house back in Gloucester." Then she gasped, "Goodness, what a mess!" She suddenly noticed the pile of paper scraps at her feet. Torn and crumpled sheets littered the walkway and the formal garden.

Henrietta bent to pick up a page and stared at it in horror. "Catharine," she whispered, "this is from Aunt Murray's book!"

They followed the trail of paper to Aunt Murray's doorstep, where Henrietta picked up the leather cover of the first volume of *The Gleaner,* the collection of Aunt Murray's writings. Before Henrietta could pull the bell chain, her aunt appeared in the doorway, wiping a tear from her cheek with the back of her hand. Catharine rushed to her side.

"Who did this to you?" Henrietta shook the torn binding.

Aunt Murray stared blankly and walked slowly back to the front parlor. "Oh, it was Cousin Lucius. He slid the very page I autographed to his father under the door, so there would be no mistaking. But for the life of me, I do not know why he should suddenly hate me so." She sorted through the crumpled pages lying on her table. "Is it because I wrote that women are the intellectual equals of men, or does he hate Africans, or—"

"Now, Auntie!" Catharine interrupted, gently smoothing the pages and arranging them in a neat pile. "Lucius is too young to have ever read that article and as for Africans, not even the actors at the theatre know you are the author of that play."

"But why?" The hurt and bewilderment showed in the older voice as well as in her face.

"We all know there's no rhyme or reason to Lucius. He's, well, he's touched!" Catharine tapped her temple, "Batty!"

Henrietta looked sharply at her sister. "Oh? Perhaps it was just 'batty' of him to have poured India ink on his primary school teacher? Or to have written the libelous diatribe against the headmaster, for which he was expelled from Phillips Academy? Or his most recent outrage, which has gotten him expelled from Harvard? Not malicious? Certainly, publishing his *rhyme* attacking our dear aunt was a wanton act of evil."

Aunt Murray sighed, "Oh, Lucius's verse in the paper didn't disturb me. His intemperate words only demonstrate his mental aberration. It's obvious to any educated reader. I wish all my detractors could be so easily dismissed." She picked up the newspaper from her lap and shook it. "I don't mind criticism, but *this*—this is much more troubling. Not the content, but look at the way it is signed! This poem, supposedly in my defense, was written by someone calling herself 'Honora.'" She tapped the paper with her forefinger. "My pen name! And I *certainly* didn't write this!"

"What?" Henrietta leaned over her aunt's shoulder. "Who would do such a thing?" Everyone in Boston knew that while Aunt Murray had published *The Gleaner* as "Constantia," her more recent articles bore the nom de plume, "Honora Martesia."

Aunt Murray shook her head. "I don't know who wrote it, but somebody did and signed it 'Honora.' Now everyone will think me so vain as to have written these words myself."

"Let me see." Henrietta reached for the paper.

The offending stanzas were circled in pencil. She read aloud, "Why, MANLIUS, prostitute thy darling muse,—"

"Why, that means Lucius! It's his middle name!" Catharine exclaimed.

Henrietta continued reading.

"And female genius wantonly abuse;
Why wield the *bludgeon* with vindictive arm,
To bla't her numbers, and CONSTANTIA harm?
Say, does not beauty beam from every line,
And *wit* and *genius* in her strains combine?
What mind by *judgment* and *taste* inspir'd,
That has not read the *Gleaner* and admir'd?"

"Goodness, Auntie!" Henrietta folded the paper and waved it aloft as if to swat a fly. "You couldn't have bought a more artful defense from a Philadelphia lawyer!"

"But—"

"But nothing! You must draft a short note to the editor, simply stating that this 'Honora' should not be mistaken for 'Honora Martesia'—and let that be the end of it!" Henrietta stormed to the window and pulled aside the curtain. Outside, stuffed like white flowers between the few remaining red ones in the rose bush, were more crumpled balls of paper. "But this wanton destruction of your book is unforgivable—in this world or the next!"

"And someday Lucius must pay for his sin!" Catharine added.

Catharine was always the one to finish an unpleasant subject. Henrietta gazed fondly at her sister's sweet, soft-featured face, which contrasted so with her own sharp features and dark hair that shopkeepers at the market hardly knew them for sisters. Catharine, 11 years older, was clearly descended from Mother's people, while Henrietta resembled the Sargents, with the same dark hair that Aunt Murray had once had.

Auntie's front drawing room was pleasantly cool, its ceiling (over twice the height of a grown man) providing a welcome relief from the debilitating heat outside. On the far wall hung the portrait of the Reverend John Murray. Father had been among the first converts to Reverend Murray's message of hope—a rejection of the harsh orthodoxy that allowed only a few members of a predetermined elect to escape eternal damnation in a fiery hell. Universalist Murray described a compassionate God who, through the union of Christ and man, offered salvation to all.

"Now tell me about your brother, Eppie." Aunt Murray smiled, "Has your father accepted his decision?"

"Not exactly." Henrietta struggled to put the best face on an awkward situation. Without consulting the family, Eppie had committed to clerk for Mr. Perkins in his store for three years. At the end of which term, Mr. Perkins promised to send him to Canton.

"Father had his heart set on Harvard," Catharine put in, "and he is not at all happy that Eppie decided to go to China instead! Mother cried when she found out!"

"Of course, she cried!" Aunt Murray exclaimed. "That boy is so precious to her. Your mother was 40 years old when he was born and knew that little Epes was probably her last. That's why your father also named him 'Epes' to preserve the family name."

Epes was the second child that Father had named for himself. Seventeen years earlier, the first Epes had died at birth. Henrietta rose and walked to her aunt's side, gently touching her shoulder. That death was also a painful subject for Judith who had been almost the same age as Mrs. Sargent when her own first-born, also a son, was pulled lifeless from her body, hardly a month after Epes was born.

Four years younger than Henrietta, Epes had clung to his sister. Even though still a child herself, she had claimed him as her own. Despite the fact that they were grown, she still felt responsible for her Eppie's wellbeing. A distant church bell chimed the hour.

"Goodness!" Catharine said apologetically. "It's five o'clock. Father will be home soon, and we need to get ready for supper."

"Oh! Do linger just a bit. Mr. Murray will be bringing Julia Maria home from her music lesson." A kind God had given Aunt Murray a daughter two years after she had lost her little boy.

Henrietta bent to kiss her aunt, "I'm sorry. But we do expect to see all the Murrays at dinner on Sunday."

"My goodness. Imagine Eppie in Canton. We will miss him, but perhaps his auntie could be consoled with an embroidered cashmere shawl," chuckled Aunt Murray.

"Certainly!" Henrietta laughed, "And his sister with a silk one!" [6]

The Sargent Home
5 Poplar Street, Boston
1816, June 15

The 11-year-old at the reins gave a whoop as the sorrel mare broke into a trot, and the Sargent family carriage swayed around the familiar corner.

"Gently, Johnny! Pull up gently!" Epes Sargent cautioned his grandson. "Dobbin knows where we live."

They were in front of a modest red brick townhouse midway down Poplar Street. Quickly, Dr. Dixwell grabbed his little George by the coat collar as the squirming toddler wriggled out of his mother's arms. Grandfather Sargent reached down beside the driver's bench to set the hand brake, then took the reins from Johnny. "Go on in Esther. I'll drop John at the clinic and then go on to Judith's. We'll be back by dinner time."

Johnny reached for the reins, "Can I come to Aunt Murray's, too? Can I drive?"

"But, it's my turn," shouted little Epes Dixwell, two years younger than his brother.

"No, you'll both stay here. Grandfather needs some quiet to help Aunt Murray with her book." Dr. Dixwell stepped down, still holding George under one arm while helping Esther down with the other. He gave her a peck on the cheek. "I'm sorry to miss dinner."

"We'll keep a nice plate hot for you." Esther took George from his father's arms and set him on his feet beside her.

"Hello, my dears," Mrs. Sargent called from the front door. "That's my little Geordie!"

"Come along inside with Grandmother and me," Henrietta called, taking his hand.

Catharine added, "It's a blessing that Father and Auntie are working on her book together. It's good for both of them."

"Yes, they console each other," said Esther.

Their brother Eppie, the youngest of the Sargent siblings, died a year ago after returning from China. Only nine weeks later, auntie's husband, the Rev. John Murray, died after six years of paralysis.

Johnny and Epes finished a final circle of tag around the elm tree in front of the house and ran to the porch to their mother who handed them two nickels. "Now Johnny, I want you and Epes to go down to Grandfather Hunt's to say goodbye to him. You can take the Washington Street horsecar."

"But Father told us—"

"I know what your father said." Esther lowered her voice, "but Grandfather Hunt will want to see you."

As the boys ran up the street, Catharine held open the door for Esther. "When they're grown up, they'll remember. They'll be glad you sent them."

As they entered the sunny kitchen, George ran to his mother's side and clutched her skirt. Esther sighed and bent to pick him up, but Henrietta saw the fatigue on her sister's face. She put a hand on her arm and stooped down to the little boy and pointed to the back door. "Geordie, don't you want to go and see the chickens? I'll keep an eye on him," Henrietta called, following him into the yard.

"Thanks, that should keep him out of trouble." Esther joined her sisters at the table.

Catharine poured a cup of tea, "It's a pity John will miss dinner with us."

"He won't be home from the dispensary 'til evening," Esther spoke sadly. "He doesn't dare to refuse any work!"

"And he's right in doing so!" Catharine agreed, "There are doctors in this town who are too proud to treat paupers."

Dr. Dixwell's medical practice had not flourished during the recent war with England. The British blockade of Boston had deprived everyone of sufficient hard currency to pay a physician, and his only reliable source of income was work for the county, treating the poor.

On her way back into the house, Henrietta stopped to savor the warm sun on her back. A truly glorious morning, she thought. How much had happened since 1814, just two years earlier. That August, the British had captured Washington, DC, and burned both the Capitol and the home of President Madison. In December of that year, Esther gave birth to little Geordie. Yes, the country was indeed rising from its *own* ashes, and baby George was like a rebirth of hope to the Sargent family after the two awful deaths they had suffered in such close succession. She lingered on the marble step for a moment. As Henrietta entered the kitchen, Esther was questioning her eldest son who had returned from his visit.

"But Johnny," Esther prompted, "Grandfather Hunt must have said *something*?"

"No, he didn't say anything. He just climbed up to the driver's seat and jiggled the reins." The boy squinted down at the kitchen floor, trying to recall some salient fact to satisfy his mother.

Little Epes, however, missed no opportunity to upstage his older brother. "But Mother, that wasn't all! Grandfather came down from the carriage to shake our hands and he started to cry! And then he climbed back to his seat. Grandmother Hunt and Uncle Henry and Aunt Eliza were already inside."

"And all their trunks were strapped on top of the roof!" Johnny tried to reestablish his authority. "And there were two bay horses pulling and another tied to the back."

"They'll need more horses than that to travel all the way to Kentucky," Catharine observed. "But what did they finally do about their furniture?"

"Well, Mr. Hunt asked us what we wanted," said Esther, "but John didn't want much; we only took a few things that had been his mother's. They sold everything else. Mr. Hunt said carting it over the mountains to Lexington was too expensive."

Henrietta expounded, "Crossing the mountains will only get them to Pittsburgh. That's where the road ends. Lexington is another 400 miles down the Ohio River—they'll have to take a flatboat."

"At least they have family there to meet them," added Esther. "Mr. Hunt's son William—John's half-brother—is editor of the *Western Monitor*. I suppose they'll sell the carriage in Pittsburgh."

Catharine disagreed, "No, they're taking it with them on the flatboat. John says there are already too many carriages for sale there—so many other emigrants have left them."

Henrietta sniffed, "Yes, and Mrs. Hunt will need that fine carriage in Kentucky, to put on airs."

"Now, Henrietta!" Esther cast a glance toward the boys. Despite the bad feelings between her husband and his father's second family, Esther tried to maintain a semblance of civility for the boys' sake, avoiding the subject of Mrs. Hunt when they were present. "You boys go outside now but come back when Grandfather Sargent returns with Aunt Murray." She waited until the back door slammed before she finished her thought. "I hope their father won't be upset that I sent them to say goodbye."

Henrietta shook her head. "Oh, I don't think so. John's bad feelings are only towards his stepmother."

"How tragic for Mr. Hunt," Catharine mused, "to leave a lifetime of friendships and all the comforts of Boston at 71 years, to move into the wilderness, to live out his old age among strangers. Thank goodness Mother and Father are settled *here*."

"And let us hope," Henrietta added, "that Father may never again feel the need to move."

"Yes," Catharine nodded, "but how could they stay in the old house on Newbury St. after Eppie—"

Henrietta looked away, trying to hold back tears. "Poor dear," Catharine patted her shoulder. "You were always the little mother to him when you were children, and you hardly left his side when he was ill, until it was over."

Henrietta would never forget the long nights of coughing and gasping before her younger brother had finally succumbed to the consumption he had contracted in China. Eppie's death had brought Mother and Father from the cheery bustle of the old Belknap neighborhood to a new brick house on Poplar Street. With the loss of his namesake and only son, Father could no longer bear to live in that once joyful house. Henrietta had felt a double loss. Not only had she lost the brother she had tried to protect since childhood, but also the move had taken her and Catharine away from the little community of free Africans whom they had come to love.

"Working on Aunt Murray's book has done wonders for Father's spirit," said Catharine, turning to positive thoughts. "He was so pleased to be going over this morning to help her."

"Father may be pleased," agreed Henrietta, "but I doubt that Auntie's publisher will be, when he has to insert those new pages into the middle of the book and then renumber all the rest!"

Since her husband's death, Aunt Murray had sought to overcome her grief and loneliness by completing the memoir he had written only as far as his middle years. Her request for help had also been a godsend for Father. Editing her prose distracted him from his own grief over the loss of his son. Aunt Murray had insisted on adding details about a long-ago trip to Philadelphia and inserted a letter from George Washington, hoping those passages would attract enough new subscribers to help the book turn a profit. Having helped Father with the proofing, Henrietta was most familiar with the content of the book. Not only had she found paragraphs from an earlier edit that should not have been deleted, but also she had repaired much of the disfigurement caused by careless typesetters—apprentices or "printer's devils."

Catharine shook her head. "Poor Auntie has had a heavy cross to bear, losing Uncle Murray, and now she may lose Julia Maria as well if Mr. Bingaman has his way. Imagine, insisting little Charlotte be delivered to him in Natchez."

"That odious man!" Henrietta frowned. "Aunt Murray took him into her family while he prepared for Harvard, and he repaid her by taking advantage of Julia Maria and then abandoning her and the baby! He even tried to defraud Auntie out of the balance he owed for his board and room—"

"And now he wants Charlotte!" Esther interjected.

"Yes," Henrietta scowled. "Auntie talked to an attorney, but, according to the laws of both Massachusetts and the Territory of Mississippi, he has the right to take his child."

The voices of Judith Murray and Epes Sargent could be heard from the hallway, bringing the indictment to a halt. Catharine sternly held her finger to her lips. "Not another word of this."

"Hello Auntie!" Henrietta noticed the red marks on Auntie's nose where her spectacles had pressed against it during months of editing.

"Father," Catharine laughed. "What are you going to do with your mornings now that Auntie's book is finished?"

Epes Sargent hesitated, "I'm sure something will come up."

"Thank you so much, Henrietta dear, for helping your father find all those errors. If only we could replace those printer's devils with a few printer's angels!" grinned Aunt Murray.

"Printer's devils certainly are aptly named," Father agreed.

"At least now, with my scribblings off his desk, your father can return to his own memoir. He tells me he has decided to conceive it as an allegory set in China."

So, thought Henrietta, that's why he had gone to the Athenaeum and brought home those books about China! George rushed into the kitchen, followed by his grandmother. Henrietta knelt to embrace the little boy, and a wave of warmth coursed through her as he clutched her arm and cuddled against her breast—just as her baby brother Eppie had once done. When George was born, Esther had been so exhausted from looking after the two older boys that Henrietta had moved to the Dixwell's for a month to help her. It almost seemed as if God had replaced her lost younger brother with Geordie.

"I think he'll be the tallest of the three." Aunt Murray said as she leaned forward to pat the child on his bottom.

"Amie!" scolded little George.

"You mean Auntie!" Henrietta corrected him. "And I can smell some sugary cinnamon roll-ups ready to come out of the oven. Would you like one?" [7]

The Murray Home
1818, August 16

Henrietta sneezed as her fingers brushed a cloud of dust from the top of the portrait propped against the wall.

"Bless you! Here, use this." Catharine set aside the gown she was folding and handed Henrietta a dust rag before returning to her packing.

Father insisted that they use his leather-covered Chinese trunk to pack Aunt Murray's silk clothing—the camphor lining would repel moths and other insects. The sisters were helping Auntie prepare for her move to Natchez. Henrietta wiped off the picture and set it back against the wall. For a moment she studied Gilbert Stuart's portrait of Julia Maria, Aunt Murray's beloved only child. Julia's left hand was in the exact same pose as Aunt Murray's in her portrait by Copley. Henrietta wondered if it had been Stuart's homage to Copley or a sentimental idea of Auntie's. She glanced at the clock. Father and Julia would soon be back from India Wharf. They had gone to look for a crate large enough to hold the painting without removing it from its frame.

"Isn't Mama beautiful?" Six-year-old Charlotte joined Henrietta by the picture.

"Yes, she is!" Henrietta smiled at the curly haired child who had inherited the beauty of her mother and grandmother, although Henrietta noticed an unfortunate resemblance to her father around the jaw. Her father—Adam Bingaman—was the cause of this wrenching move. It was all happening so quickly. Auntie had just been planning to move to New York City, when the letter arrived from Mr. Bingaman in Natchez. It announced that he would soon be in Boston to take Julia Maria and Charlotte to Mississippi. Just as suddenly, Aunt Murray had decided to join them.

Catharine tucked the last of Aunt Murray's silk gowns into the trunk. Henrietta folded a China shawl. "I think there's room for this."

Henrietta inhaled the sweet pungent aroma of camphorwood. Her beloved brother Eppie had breathed the same scent from this same trunk as he packed for his return from China. Had his lungs already carried the contagion that took him away, hardly a year after he had come home? She closed the trunk and turned to consider the stack of letter books on the table.

Catharine pointed to a mound of bed linens, tablecloths, and napkins she had taken from Aunt Murray's cedar chest. "I don't think we should waste space with these. The Bingamans will have plenty."

Henrietta went over and picked through the pile, extracting an embroidered sampler.

"Let's pack this, though," she said, smoothing the cloth. "Grandmother Sargent made it, and Auntie will want to save it for Charlotte."

"My great-grandmother Sargent?" Charlotte peered at the cloth. "I know about her—she lived in Gloucester. Grandmama took me to see her house!"

"Of course she did!" Catharine took the sampler from Henrietta. "And family mementos are important. This one won't take any space at all." She opened the trunk and laid it in top of the clothes.

Aunt Murray came down the stairs holding two large packets of papers to her chest. "Mr. Murray's sermons!" she called, "Do find a place for them."

"Of course we will! reassured Catharine. "We'll put them in your cedar chest." She had a sudden thought as she packed the sermons and whispered, "Do you think Auntie would like Father to drive her past the Bennet Street church one last time?"

Henrietta glanced up sharply and rolled her eyes toward Charlotte. "You know better than that—and little pitchers have big ears!"

Aunt Murray had not set foot in her husband's old church since his flock had welcomed a new pastor who preached the heretical doctrine that hell did not exist.

"Why are you whispering?" Charlotte spoke from the table, where she was poring over the newspaper.

"Never mind, dear," said Catharine. "Don't you have any more packing to do, Charlotte?"

"I'm all done!" she replied, proudly.

"That's because you are such a good little girl," Henrietta said fondly.

Charlotte smiled modestly and turned back to the newspaper. "Aunt Henrietta, do you want to buy any superfine flour? Mr. Coolidge has two hundred beebles for sale—what is a 'beeble?'"

Charlotte's precocity always surprised Henrietta. Her mother and grandmother let the child read whatever she liked. "For heaven's sake, what are you reading?"

"There." Charlotte pointed to an advertisement.

Henrietta laughed, "That's an abbreviation. It's a shortened word, where you leave out some of the letters. 'Bbls' means 'barrels.'"

"That's silly! Words should be spelled properly, Grandmama says!"

"Well your grandmother is quite right, but why not read something nicer?"

Henrietta flipped back through the *Centinel* to find the daily poem on the front page. Pencil marks bracketing an article caught her eye.

> "Charleston, South Carolina ... By several acts of the Legislature it is positively forbidden that slaves or free people of colour should assemble for mental instruction ... every person of colour who shall keep a school to teach reading or writing, is subject to a *fine of thirty dollars* or to be *imprisoned ten days and whipped thirty-nine lashes.*"

Henrietta turned the page. It was all so morbid. There was nothing here suitable for a child to read, no matter what Julia Maria and Aunt Murray thought. "Charlotte," she said. "Would you run upstairs and see if Grandmamma wants us to save space for anything else? I'll watch your dolly."

Charlotte hurried up the steps, eager to undertake her important mission.

Seeing Henrietta's expression, Catharine peered over her shoulder and read aloud, "… we met with a schooner off the Berry Islands, having on board 73 Negroes, all Virginia born, smuggled from Virginia, bound for New-Orleans."

"Oh!" Catharine leaned back. "Poor Aunt Murray! To have to live in a place where such dreadful things happen! You don't suppose the Bingamans—"

Henrietta's mouth was set in a grim expression. "It's obvious they can't breed their own Negroes fast enough to pick all that cotton." She turned away from the paper, but she could not turn her mind away from the hateful subject. "They'll have to import even more of them—tearing husbands away from wives and paying Virginia breeders to despoil girls of twelve and thirteen."

Catharine patted her sister's arm. "Let's not think of it now, dear, but we need to think of Aunt Murray," she said resolutely. She turned back to the pile of linens to search for any more souvenirs.

Henrietta cast her eyes around the room. Catharine was right. They must think of Aunt Murray now. The stairs creaked, and Charlotte's little steps were followed by Aunt Murray's heavier tread. She smiled, "Auntie, is there any other small thing you want to take from here as a memento?"

Mrs. Murray glanced at the mantle, and then considered the stack of letter books on the table with their wallpaper covers. She held the topmost volume to the wall. Its feathered red and purple pattern exactly matched the wallpaper. "I think these will do just fine! Those green ones are from Mr. Murray's room, and those with the buds and flowers—" she smiled at Charlotte—"are from your mama's."

Henrietta lifted the books, four at a time, into the chest. "I count 19."

Mrs. Murray took one last letter book from the bookcase, and set it on the table. "Twenty!" She sat down to catch her breath, and her eyes fell on the *Centinel* lying open to the articles her nieces had just been reading.

Henrietta wished she had put the paper away. How would Aunt Murray's spirit survive in a place where human beings were property, to be disposed of at their owner's will, where every transgression by an African might be met with the lash? Auntie was a proud and independent New Englander—how would she tolerate an idle life, where her every whim would be anticipated by a hovering slave? They were already leaving the day after tomorrow!

Mrs. Murray struggled to her feet, then, jaw set, handed the last letter book to Henrietta without a word. Tears streaming down her cheeks, she slowly ascended the stairs. [8]

The Sargent Home
1820, August 4

"Here you are, Miss Sargent."

Henrietta thanked the delivery boy and gave him a five-cent piece. She clasped the four loaves of bread, still warm from the baker's oven, under one arm and inhaled their sweet, yeasty aroma as she closed the front door and turned back to the kitchen. Catharine was placing a bowl of roasted chicken in the smaller of the two baskets on the table. Henrietta laid two loaves on the counter and bent to place the other two in the larger basket. "Pastor Snowden didn't mention anyone else needing help this week, did he?"

"No, just Sari." Catharine placed a tea towel in the basket beside the bowl and carefully nested seven brown eggs, one for each day, into its folds. "I think Sari would like some of these, too." She pulled a burlap bag from beside the woodbin. Turning to the larger basket, she slid the bread to one side and counted out seven large, red apples.

Even after their move from Newbury Street, Henrietta and Catharine maintained their connection with their old Belknap neighborhood, hiring African women from there for housework and the men for yard work and, in the winter, for shoveling snow. Pastor Snowden, the former slave who led a small congregation there, let them know who in the community needed charity, and once a week the sisters delivered baskets of food. For the past few weeks they had been assisting Sari, who had until recently done the Sargent family's washing.

Henrietta glanced up at the clock. "We need to hurry. I told Mr. Finney to have his carriage here at exactly 9:00."

A few minutes later they were on their way. The carriage lurched sharply to the right as it bounced across the dried ruts of Chambers Street. Henrietta slid across the seat into her sister, catching the smaller basket between her feet. The larger one skittered across the floor. "Mr. Finney," she called, "Will you please slow down!" She lowered her voice, "He must think he's Colonel Jackson on the road to New Orleans."

"Oh, Henriet!" Catharine laughed. "He's doing his best."

Henrietta lifted the smaller basket and inspected it. No damage had been done. None of the eggs had broken nor had any juice from the chicken splashed from the bowl. Catharine was right; Finney was a good driver. Henrietta still felt annoyed with him—and even more annoyed with Andrew Jackson, for that matter. While she had cheered Jackson's rout of the British in Louisiana, she certainly did not approve of his making war on harmless Indians during his campaign to drive the Spaniards out of Florida.

Catharine nodded toward Henrietta's sleeve. "You're missing a button. Sari would have spotted that before she put it out to dry."

Henrietta laughed, glancing down at the broken thread, "Yes, and had it repaired before hanging it in the wardrobe." Washday was not the same since Sari had become too infirm to work. Henrietta missed her soft singing—the same spirituals she had so often heard when passing the African church.

"Goodness!" Catharine gasped and held her handkerchief to her nose. A vile odor filled the carriage as they passed the reeking fen that had once been Mill Pond. Henrietta winced and raised her own handkerchief to her face.

Long ago, ingenious Bostonians had created the pond by building a dam across the cove, so that the movement of ocean tides flooding in and out through a narrow gate could power a gristmill. But two centuries of built-up silt had reduced the tidal flow to a trickle. Further, the effluent from scores of privies built more recently along the pond's eastern shore had turned what little remained of it into an open sewer. Henrietta tried not to inhale until they were well past the malevolent air. There was no telling what diseases it might carry.

The carriage rattled across the ruts of the intersection where Chambers Street narrowed and became Belknap. Now, the houses were smaller and in various states of disrepair. Belknap was the main thoroughfare of Boston's colored community, and to Henrietta, it was her old home. She waved to a woman weeding her vegetable garden. "Look! There's Phoebe. And she still has her medicinals in the last row."

"Wasn't it she and Sari who taught you so much about roots and herbs?" Catharine mused, "That seems an age ago now."

Henrietta nodded. She had been 22, when Father had moved their family to the Belknap neighborhood. Her curiosity about the unruly patches of medicinals in the African women's gardens had been insatiable, and the women had eventually taught Henrietta many of their secrets. Now Henrietta was 35, and, whenever a relative or friend took ill, they would come to her for a poultice or an infusion—all, of course, except for Dr. Dixwell. Henrietta craned her neck to catch a glimpse of the dogleg in the street one block east. "There's our old house!" she exclaimed as they drove past Newbury Street.

Further ahead, Belknap diminished to a wagon track at Beacon Hill. Bostonians, viewing the chain of small hills from the other side, referred to this geographical feature as Beacon Hill, Mt. Vernon, and Mt. Pemberton. Less formally, this area where the African community had settled was called "Nigger Hill." Although Boston Africans were not slaves, they still did not receive the respect of their fellow citizens.

Catharine pointed at a horsecar loaded with sand and gravel. "Look! They've been digging there forever."

"Yes, before long, there won't be much left of Beacon Hill at all. If only they'd use what's left of it to fill that wretched pond."

Catharine laughed, then pointed to a plain wooden boarding house. "That's Sari's house."

"We're here!" Henrietta called out to the coachman. The carriage stopped, and Henrietta waved to a small figure peering from an upstairs window. "We'll be back in just a minute, Mr. Finney."

An aged African woman met them at the top of the stairs. Henrietta took the woman's swollen hand gently in hers. She noticed the green stain of a recently applied poultice across her knuckles and wrists. "We've missed you, Sari."

"I miss the both of you, too—I can't do no washin' no more."

"We can't stay just now," Catharine smiled, "but let us leave a few things on your table." She took Henrietta's basket in her other hand and stepped quickly into the room before Sari could object. A moment later Catharine reappeared, the empty baskets stacked one inside the other. "Now, Sari, you must promise to tell Pastor Snowden what you need for next week."

"God bless you, Miss Catharine, and you, too, Miss Henrietta." Sari leaned against the door frame for balance as the sisters started down the stairs.

The carriage rapidly turned the corner for the trip back toward Poplar Street, and Henrietta grabbed the velvet handhold. "I see Sari needs a new dress. I'll shorten and take-in my old blue calico."

Catharine nodded her approval, "Her shoes need to go to the cobbler, too."

A group of African children were playing hide-and-seek in a growth of willows in a vacant lot, and the sisters watched for a moment. "You know," Catharine broke the silence. "I saw in the *Centinel* that the topic of the speaker's address at the Union College commencement was 'The Equality of Talent between the Sexes.' It has *only* been 30 years since Aunt Murray published her essay on that very subject," she laughed.

"Well," Henrietta noted dryly, "the mothers and sisters of those graduates may have been flattered to be described as the equals of men in a commencement address, but the fact remains that they are still insufficiently equal to be allowed into any of the classes! But we must write Aunt Murray and tell her."

"Yes, it's been over a month since we've heard from her. Such dreadful news about Uncle Winthrop."

Henrietta nodded. It must have been such a shock—Aunt Murray's younger brother's sudden death aboard an overnight steamer to New Orleans.

Catharine raised her voice above the rattle of the carriage wheels. "Young Epes tells me he's spending his prize money on a flute." Both the sisters had been present for their nephew's winning recitation at the Latin School competition. "Perhaps," Catharine went on, "Father may still have a grandson at Harvard. Though it's a pity that Johnny is so dead set against it."

"He couldn't resist the offer of that apprenticeship," Henrietta tightened her lips. "Thomas Wigglesworth's counting house—quite prestigious—and now the commitment is made."

"Yes, of course," Catharine agreed. "He will certainly make a good living in the India Trade."

"A good living, indeed. Still, I cannot understand that his father raised no objection at all!" Henrietta replied.

Catharine nodded sympathetically, "I suppose, as Dr. Dixwell's practice has never done well, Johnny must have had his fill of genteel poverty, and John knows it."

Henrietta sniffed. "Their circumstances don't seem to suit John either. Clearly, that's why he's bringing his lawsuit—not that it will come to anything." Esther's husband had hatched a hare-brained scheme to sue for the English estates that Colonel John Dixwell abandoned when he had had been forced to flee England for America a century and a half ago. "I cannot believe," Henrietta continued, "that after such a bloody war, he could dare to be willing to sacrifice his American citizenship for a minor title in a morally corrupt monarchy. But, then, greed is a powerful force for evil."

She gazed glumly at a newly established dry goods emporium. Johnny's decision to forego education for trade disturbed her. She so hoped that all the Dixwell boys would become men motivated by Christian principle, not by avarice. A church bell chimed in the distance, and Henrietta turned toward the sound. "Goodness!" she said. "Geordie will be wondering why I'm not at home to meet him for his lesson." [9]

§

"Nineteen, plus two, plus one." Henrietta spoke slowly, penciling the numbers on a scrap of paper.

"Twenty-two!" The six-year-old boy grinned at his aunt.

"Geordie. Did you add those in your head? That's very good, but you need to copy them into your notebook in columns, one number beneath the other, and add the columns one by one."

"But that takes too long! Can I have another cookie? Grandmother makes the best cookies!"

"Now, Geordie, you've had two. You may have another when you finish your lesson." Henrietta moved the bolt of silk on the sewing table away from the scatter of cookie crumbs surrounding her favorite nephew. Esther had asked her to tutor little George for primary school, and Henrietta had come to treasure these special afternoons. George frowned, gripping the pencil as he slowly copied the numbers. "Good!" Henrietta patted his head. "Now draw a straight line across, underneath the column, to write the sum below."

The clock against the wall chimed the hour and the boy turned to look at it. "Aunt Henrietta, may I see the gears?"

At five and a half, George was mesmerized by clockworks and all other things mechanical. It was always his job to pull the chain that lifted the brass weight to power the clock for another day. So much younger than his brothers, the boy had also developed a stubborn self-sufficiency. Still, he had to learn to concentrate on a task. A peavine without a pole to guide its growth produced nothing but a tangle. Underneath George's unruly distractibility, Henrietta saw an unusual intellectual promise, not always apparent to the casual eye. She hoped that with persistence she could train the boy's mind toward worthy goals. The boy was very clever. He memorized his older brothers' lessons by listening to their recitations. Nonetheless, he would still have to learn the fundamentals.

"Let's do another sum." Henrietta picked up the pencil. "This one is a little bit harder—107, plus 387 plus 259."

"Those numbers are too big!" protested the boy.

"Now Geordie, an impossibly big job can always be done if you break it into its parts and then follow the right steps." As she penciled the numbers for him to copy Henrietta felt a twinge of doubt about giving the child such a difficult problem, but he needed to be challenged, she reminded herself.

Henrietta heard a knock at the front door and frowned at the interruption. Catharine was out. "Father!" she called, "would you answer the door? I'm doing lessons with little George." She leaned back to get a glimpse down the hall. Father was guiding Mr. Young, the editor of the *Palladium*, into his library.

George, his brow furrowed in concentration, mumbled the numbers as he added them. The shriek of a steam whistle sounded in the distance. "Auntie, you promised we could go to the river to look at the steamboats."

"Yes, I did," Henrietta nodded, "but you need to add that third column before you have a sum."

George hunched his shoulders in renewed effort. All three of the Dixwell boys had gone through a phase of being fascinated by steam engines, but each had shown a different bent. Where Geordie's brother Epes had become keen on music and Johnny on plants and seashells, George showed an insatiable fascination with gears and gauges. As she gazed at her nephew, it struck Henrietta that he—long-legged and slender with his bright, piercing eyes—was not so much a peavine as a sapling that she might train to become a well-formed tree with sturdy branches—a man to someday become a force for good.

She heard father say goodbye to Mr. Young, then felt a hand on her shoulder and looked up. Her father's eyes were watery; his expression stunned. He swallowed and cleared his throat. "It's your Aunt Murray. She's gone. Mr. Young came to tell us before we read it in the *Palladium*."

Henrietta gasped, "What happened?"

Mr. Sargent shook his head before he could speak again. "A fever. All Mr. Young knows is what appeared in the New York paper. He wanted to tell us personally. I expect we shall have a letter from Julia Maria soon."

Henrietta and her father looked at each other. It was so sudden. She felt overcome with grief. Her last memory of her beloved aunt was of her waving bravely from the upper deck of the steamer as it pulled away from the passenger pier.

"Seven, five, three!" George shouted. "That's the answer!" He held the paper across his chest. "Grandfather, I can do *big* sums now! Auntie, can I have my cookie now? And can we go see the steamboats? Do you want to come with us, Grandfather?"

It took Henrietta a moment to take in the boy's words. "Yes, you're right." She tried to control her voice. "That's 753." She handed him a cookie without noticing where the crumbs fell. As she rose to her feet, she held on to the edge of the table. "Father," she spoke firmly. "Will you join George and me for a walk to the river?" [10]

They walked slowly down Poplar Street toward its dead end at the riverfront—past the last house and the vacant lot where the brick sidewalk ended. George pulled away from Henrietta and ran ahead, returning in a minute with a rusty spike. "Grandfather! Is this from a ship?"

Mr. Sargent bent down to examine the broken piece of metal. "No, George. A good ship is fastened with copper—because copper doesn't rust."

Henrietta took her father's arm. He seemed even less steady on his feet than the last time they had walked together. They stopped at the riverbank. The tide was out, and seagulls were picking at the carcasses of stranded jellyfish.

From the landing just beyond came the thud of a shipwright adzing the broad end of a long timber. "What is he making?" George pointed.

Mr. Sargent shaded his eyes against the glare of the afternoon sun. "He seems to be squaring the foot of a mast."

Turning, George slid down the bank to the beach.

"Geordie, come back!"

"No, let him go, Henrietta!" Mr. Sargent smiled as the boy ran to join a group of workmen standing beside a beached harbor tug. He gazed at the little boy on the beach. "Henrietta, you are seeing the beginnings of a man."

"Yes," she agreed. "And I want him to grow into a good man, with a fine character."

A hawk hovered over the far shore of the river, then soared upward on the afternoon breeze. Taking his daughter's hand, Mr. Sargent spoke slowly. "Cousin Judith was my dearest friend, but her labors here are completed. She has passed through this vale of tears to join our Savior in everlasting life. That is what Mr. Murray taught, and that is what we believe."

Henrietta did not speak. Memories of Aunt Murray washed over her mind in a collage of color. How hard auntie had struggled to be heard, only to have her writing ignored and forgotten. Her play, *The African*, perhaps her most passionate work, had been ridiculed. Now she lay in a grave dug, most likely, by African slaves about whose condition she had written so movingly.

"She has a cracked piston!" George shouted as he clambered up the bank and ran to his grandfather, "but the cylinder is fine!"

"George!" Henrietta stepped back. "Your hands are covered with grease. Don't smear it on Grandfather's clothes."

"It will all wipe off, with a little whale oil." Mr. Sargent smiled, "Life goes on." He took the boy's hand and turned back toward Poplar Street.

"Grandfather, tell the story about Wangfo and his boat," begged George.

"Once upon a time, far away in China, there was an old man with five daughters and one little son."

"Like me?"

"Well, not exactly," the old man smiled.

Perhaps, Henrietta thought, she would buy Father some real China paper and ask him to write down the whole story as he had told it to her. She turned to look back at the river. Yes, life does go on, but Aunt Murray's work was not complete. Henrietta looked past the spires of Harvard to where the green-forested hills formed a distant horizon. Our allotted time on earth was three score and ten, and Aunt Murray's life had fallen just one year short of that span. God granting, she herself still had 35 more years—fully half her life—to bring Aunt Murray's ideas to light. She closed her eyes and prayed for the time and the strength to accomplish that commission. [11]

John Singleton Copley's portrait of Judith Sargent Stevens (later Murray) when she was about 21 years old (ca. 1772–74). Oil on canvas, 50 in × 40 in (127 cm × 101.6 cm). Terra Foundation for American Art, Daniel J. Terra Art Acquisition Endowment Fund, 2000.6. (Photograph Terra Foundation for American Art, Chicago.)

Gilbert Stuart's portrait of Judith Sargent Murray when she was about 55 years old (ca. 1806). The original portrait by Stuart is lost (perhaps in a private European collection). (Photo copied from Lawrence Park, 1926.)

We live in an era of revisionist history, and we archaeologists are right ask ourselves who has the right to reinterpret the past and what is the proper place of archaeology in that process?

I was shocked and appalled when I discovered that the intellectual career of Judith Sargent Murray (1751–1820), the "Grandmother of American Feminism," was denigrated and dismissed by her own family. Today her primary treatise *On the Equality of the Sexes*, written in 1779 and published in 1790, is recognized as the foundation document of American feminism.

A series of fictionalized vignettes enabled me to pull together the factual story of that denigration and how her writings were passed on to a younger generation of women's rights advocates during the 1830s.

Henrietta Sargent (1785–1871), abolitionist and women's rights activist at the age of 32 (1817), portrait by James Frothingham. (Courtesy of the Sargent House Museum.)

Henrietta was the forgotten intermediary, who in the 1830s introduced the ideas of her aunt Judith Sargent Murray to Sarah Grimké and Lydia Maria Child. My use of fiction brings together the documented facts of Henrietta's life and reestablishes her rightful place in the struggle for women's rights. Henrietta's 1840s letters to her nephew George Basil Dixwell, an opium merchant in China, introduce the conscience in the "conscience vs. commerce" debate underlying this book.

CHAPTER TWO

"Hyenas in Petticoats"

The Sargent Home
1835, August 11

The coach carrying Henrietta, her friend Maria Child, and a large amount of Maria's luggage pulled up in front of the modest two-story brick house. Henrietta stepped down and instructed the driver, pointing to the larger of the two trunks strapped to the rack. "That one goes upstairs in the first room on the right!" She hurried up the front steps, "Catharine, we're here!"

It had been a long morning. Henrietta hired the carriage to take her two miles down Boston Neck, the narrow strip of land that connected Boston to the rest of the continent, to pick up her best friend and all her remaining belongings at Le Paradis des Pauvres, the tiny rented cottage where Maria had just finished her book. Maria had written an encyclopedic *History of the Condition of Women*.

Last Saturday, the Childs had auctioned off all of their furniture and household goods. Mr. Child had gone ahead to New York to settle his business affairs, while Maria remained behind, with a borrowed bed and table to complete the final editing of her manuscript. Early tomorrow morning she would journey to meet her husband, and they would soon be on their way across the Atlantic. Maria, valise in hand, stepped awkwardly from the carriage. "I don't dare let my manuscript out of sight," she said, apologetically.

Catharine rushed to join the two women at the curb. "Maria!" We're so happy you're staying the night with us. Now, come right along with me. I have pastries in the oven!"

Henrietta waved Maria toward the house. She took a silver dollar from her reticule as the driver returned to lift Maria's second trunk, the one she would be taking with her to England. "Please leave that one in the front vestibule!"

"Ladies! Tea is ready!" Catharine called.

Maria dropped a large lump of brown sugar into her tea. "I shouldn't, but I am glad you have it," she whispered. "I have such a sweet tooth!"

For months, abolitionists had been discussing a boycott against slave-grown West Indian cane sugar, but as there was no available alternative, they had come to no decision.

"Oh Maria!" Henrietta interjected. "If you could only convince your Mr. Child to plant his field of beets, we might be able to sweeten our tea with a substance produced by free men earning honest wages."

"True," agreed Catharine, "but I am sure that while we are waiting, our use of a product tainted by human bondage can be justified by the strengthened constitution it provides us for our philanthropic labors. Still, Mr. Child's red beet sugar would be far more festive. It *is* red, isn't it?"

"I suppose so!" The corners of Maria's mouth turned up slightly, "But, you know, I've never actually seen beet sugar myself. I will have to ask my husband what color it is."

Maria's smile was tense. Poor thing, Henrietta thought. She had her trials lately, and her book was written as it was written—*a fait accompli*. Of course, she was worried about her book, Henrietta thought. Over the past months Henrietta had read it, chapter by chapter, to her growing disappointment, as Maria well knew. Henrietta would try to be philosophical about it. Maria was still her friend, and she was going across the ocean. Who knew how long it would be before they saw each other again.

Henrietta fished through the sugar bowl with the tongs, seizing the very largest chunk. She waved it aloft before dropping it in her cup. "You know, Maria," she said with a wink, "I may take a larger chunk of slave-grown sugar, but I do believe I've surpassed you in purging prejudice from my soul. I am willing to defile myself daily with this tainted stuff, so long as the energy I gain serves me to help free even one more unfortunate from the house of bondage."

"Oh, really! Maria drew herself up. "I see your sacrifice does not extend to your handsome cotton dress."

The friendly contest between Henrietta and Maria over who was most committed to freedom for Africans had gone on for years, and they especially savored the gales of laughter they elicited from Catharine as they vied with each other in their devotion to the cause.

"Perhaps I do still own one or two shabby old cotton things," Henrietta replied, chin raised, "but you should know that I have decided to ask Preacher Snowden to make the prayer at my funeral."

It *was* an amusing prospect. Henrietta could imagine the consternation of her Dixwell and Sargent relatives—few of whom had any tolerance for Africans, abolition, or abolitionists—as they stood around her coffin while an African officiated at the service. But no matter how the rest of the family or the world thought, here in their "mouse's nest," she and Catharine and Maria could plot and joke without fear of criticism. It was good to see Maria laugh as heartily as Catharine. Her woes had taken a toll; she looked older than her 33 years. Her bright, brown eyes still shone with the same light, but her thick, dark hair, parted in the middle and combed down to tightly pinned curls, seemed incongruously youthful against her lined, pale face.

Whatever the shortcomings of Maria's book, it was a miracle that she had completed it at all. The board of the Athenaeum had been so incensed by the publication of her *Appeal in Favor of That Class of Americans Called Africans* that they had rescinded her courtesy borrowing privileges! Even when the members of the Boston Female Anti-Slavery Society raised enough money to buy Maria's membership, the board rejected the application.

Of course, that money might better have gone for Maria's rent, as her improvident husband mired them even deeper in arrears. He used his own money to travel to Washington to appeal for the lives of a ship's crew he had defended in court and from whom he received no fee. Last Saturday, Maria suffered the final indignity when she and Mr. Child auctioned off what little furniture they had accumulated during the seven years of their marriage, just to pay their passage to England.

Henrietta took Maria's hand across the table. "We wish you weren't going so far away!" Maria was like another sister—a younger one, beloved, if at times maddening. Despite their disagreements, they were bulwarks for each other against the social disapprobation they and all the members of the Boston Female Anti-Slavery Society endured.

"You know, Henriet," Catharine touched her napkin to her lips, "we ought to see if Esther can come over for supper tonight. She does need to get out. She's been so lonely since Dr. Dixwell passed."

Over the past few years, death had been an all too familiar visitor to the family. First, Uncle Murray was taken and then Auntie. Only a few months later, Julia Maria wrote that little Charlotte had succumbed to a fever like the one that had taken auntie. Two years after that, Julia Maria herself died after giving birth to a little boy, and that was the year Father passed away. Then, death relented, until nine months ago when he returned without warning to claim Esther's husband.

"Yes, we could have a little party!" agreed Henrietta quickly.

"I would love to see Esther," Maria chimed in. "How are her sons?"

Catharine smiled proudly. "Epes is a clerk at Mr. Loring's law office, but he is hoping for an opportunity to teach at the Latin School if the headmaster retires. He's still in Boston, but Esther misses J.J. and Geordie terribly. Calcutta is so far away."

"Calcutta?" Maria looked up in surprise. "Both of them? I thought George was at Harvard!" Maria had been so busy, first with her book and then preparing to move, that she had missed all the gossip.

"No," Henrietta shook her head. "George couldn't get enough of J.J.'s stories of sailing with Captain Heard, and he insisted on following him into the East India trade."

"He's going out with J.J. as supercargo!" Catharine interjected. "Those stories were just too much to resist. Did you know that he once took a cargo of Massachusetts ice to Calcutta?"

"Ice?" Maria looked incredulous. "Around Africa, twice across the equator? Was there any left when he got there?"

"One hundred tons!" Catharine giggled. "And the Indians had never seen ice! Why, there was a Parsee who took a block of it home with him, and then wanted his money back the next day because it melted! And the best part was that with the money from selling the ice, J.J. bought a cargo of monkeys! A whole line of them were perched on the main sail yard when they docked at Central Wharf—and they sold like hotcakes!"

"Monkeys for ice!" Maria shook her head. "It must at least put Esther's mind at ease that George is making his first voyage with J.J. and with Captain Heard at the helm."

Henrietta noticed the color had returned to Maria's cheeks. Talking about something other than her book was a tonic for her friend, and she was glad to serve it. "Oh, no!" Henrietta shook her head. "Captain Heard would hardly ease her, if it were so. He was quite the daredevil, but he has retired from the sea now. He's gone to China for Russell and Company as a merchant and *that* is what puts Esther's mind at ease!"

Catharine added, "Yes, Esther had nightmares whenever J.J. told one of his Captain Heard stories—like the time they were caught in a tornado—"

"A typhoon!" Henrietta corrected.

"—Yes, well, the typhoon was driving their ship, the *Emerald*, toward a sandbar at the mouth of the Ganges River—"

"You mean the Hoogly!" Henrietta rolled her eyes. Catharine could never get details right.

Catharine gave her sister a sharp look. "Anyway—Captain Heard knew the *Emerald* was drawing 18 feet, and there was only a 14-foot clearance over the bar, so he sent all the sailors aloft and had them set every sail."

"In a typhoon?" Maria leaned forward. "Not in a typhoon!"

"Yes, that is exactly what he did! Then he turned the ship broadside to the sandbar, and the wind filled every sail, and the ship hove over until her port rail was actually underwater, and that lifted the keel just enough to slide across the bar to safety! And, you know, J.J. said that forever after, Mr. Heard never once even mentioned what he had done!"

Henrietta reached across the table to pat Maria's hand. "I trust your voyage won't be so eventful," she said reassuringly. "You and David will be safe in London well before the fall storms."

"I do hope so!" Maria was relieved. "Mr. Thompson has reserved our passage from New York on Monday after next. That will give David enough time to settle his affairs.

Henrietta nodded. To the extent they could be settled, she thought. The now-bankrupt abolitionist newspaper that David Child edited had cost him a good deal more than he ever earned from it, and it was only Maria's pen and public skills, not Mr. Child's, that brought the offer from Mr. Thompson to become paid anti-slavery agents in London. Henrietta hoped the couple could make a fresh start. With Mr. Child's propensity for flailing at any windmill that offended him, she wondered if they would ever be solvent.

Catharine glanced at Maria's valise. "And, what about your book? Is it ready for Mr. Ticknor?"

"As ready as it will ever be," Maria sighed. "I only hope he'll be able to read my hen-scratching."

"Well, if he can't decipher it, I can!" Henrietta pushed her cup to the side. "And you can tell him that when he comes to pick it up in exactly two hours!" Henrietta wanted so much to think the best of her friend on this, the eve of her departure, but the thought of the book brought a fresh wave of dismay over her. Yes, she could decipher Maria's handwriting but for what purpose? The volume was a compendium without a conscience, and it was beyond her power to insert a soul into its pages.

Maria rose and dragged the valise to her chair. She lifted an armload of pages onto the table. Scraps of white, pink, and blue stationery, cut and pasted together like ancient scrolls, spilled over the table's edge to the floor. "Oh, dear! Mr. Ticknor wants each of these chapters tied into a separate packet!"

"I'll get some twine!" Catharine hurried to the cupboard.

Maria looked down into her valise and extracted three leather-bound volumes and two frayed magazines from the valise, stacking them on the table next to the piles of manuscript pages. "Oh!" she gasped. "I almost forgot to return Mrs. Murray's books to you."

"I only wish you could have built upon her ideas." Henrietta blurted out.

"They are wonderful ideas," Maria frowned, "but, as I have already told you, I have my readership to think of. And we cannot demand everything all at once."

"I had such hopes for your book," Harriet said quietly.

"I know you are disappointed, Henrietta," Maria replied, "but please, let's not resurrect those old arguments."

Henrietta couldn't help herself. Seeing Aunt Murray's works again only reminded her of the optimistic expectations she had when she had loaned them to Maria for her research on her *History of the Condition of Women*. Now that Maria's manuscript was completed, there was no avoiding the fact that those hopes were dashed. Henrietta assumed that Maria would take Aunt Murray's argument to the next step, calling for the equal rights for women that Auntie had so meticulously justified. Despite her repeated urging, Maria failed her. How could she have written so much about the condition of women and then failed to draw the obvious conclusions?

Maria meticulously describes the lives of women throughout history and in scores of societies, from Amazons and Hottentots and Ancient Hebrews to modern Americans, but she stops short of calling for justice. She makes no mention at all of women's rights. Maria had made such eloquent appeals for the liberation of African slaves, but, even after reading Aunt Murray's article, she ignored the rights of women to equality before the law!

Henrietta's heart felt heavy. "If only you could have followed through to the conclusion," she said. "You squandered such a golden opportunity."

Maria looked exasperated. "Well, then, since that is your opinion, I'll have a copy sent just to Catharine."

Henrietta hesitated, then picked up Auntie's works. "I'll go put these back on Father's shelf." She went down the hall to Father's old office. She looked at the empty space in the center of the middle shelf of the mahogany bookcase where he had proudly displayed Aunt Murray's writings. To the left of the gap stood more old issues of *Massachusetts Magazine*, where she had published so many of her articles. To the right was Aunt Murray's last literary effort, the autobiography of John Murray that she completed after his death. Laying the magazines down on the desk, Henrietta slipped the first and second volumes of *The Gleaner* into their place. Maria had left a paper marker between the pages of Volume Three, and it opened to "Observations on Female Abilities," with Mrs. Murray's 10 numbered "Evidences of Achievement."

Henrietta smiled. Half of the "Evidences" that women were "in every respect equal to men" now appeared in Maria's table of contents, although changed under Maria's editorial hand. Aunt Murray's "They are equally brave" had become "Female Bravery," and "Literary achievement" had become "Learned Women."

Of course, Maria was a learned woman, too. It had taken real bravery to write her *Appeal in Favor of That Class of Americans Called Africans*. Maria knew from the start that her incendiary demand for the immediate abolition of slavery would bring a storm of censure that could easily destroy her career as an author of books for women and children. When that storm came, it had taken pluck and determination to continue her work, but Maria and David had gone forward, renting the tiny cottage where she wrote her history of women. It was a monumental achievement, but Henrietta felt a sadness in her friend's accomplishment when she wanted, instead, to share her pride.

Henrietta looked at the worn covers of the old magazines—March and April 1790. So much had happened since Aunt Murray published "On the Equality of the Sexes" in those two issues. Yet after 45 years, how little had changed for women! How could Maria not call for justice? They had always been so close, and now an awkward discord separated their hearts as much as the Atlantic Ocean would soon separate them physically.

The wound was still fresh. After simmering for months, the tension between them came to a boil two months ago. She had read Maria's chapter on English and American women and had pleaded again to her friend to make an appeal for women's rights. Maria's face had hardened, and her words were harsh —her *History* was fully adequate without any such "appeal." Weeks followed during which they did not exchange a note. Now the book was written. Well, there was no use crying over spilt milk, and Maria needed to be encouraged for what she still might accomplish, not chastised, yet again, for her dreadful failure. The Christian thing was to forgive her friend's betrayal. The sad truth is that in her desperate need for income, Maria censored herself, avoiding anything that might offend a reviewer or a potential reader.

It suddenly struck Henrietta that Aunt Murray had censored herself, too. How else to explain how she neglected to find a place for "On the Equality of the Sexes"—her most important and controversial article—anywhere in the 998 pages of *The Gleaner*? Aunt Murray, just like Maria, needed to earn a living from her writing, and that must have been why she didn't include the inflammatory article in her collection. She did not include anything that might limit the sale of the 1,000 copies she ordered from her publisher.

Thanks to Father, she and Catharine were left with enough, so that they would never be forced by financial necessity to stifle their voices. She set her lips in determination. Maria and Aunt Murray, too, might have fallen short, but there would be other opportunities. The natural equality of the sexes and the logical, moral consequences of that equality would not remain unspoken. Somehow, she would see to that! [1]

The Sargent Home
October 14

Henrietta slipped the notebook and pencil into her bag. Much would be discussed at the second anniversary meeting of the Boston Female Anti-Slavery Society. They were electing officers and reviewing correspondence with sister organizations. She had asked that the society consider holding a winter fundraising festival. The ladies would have a lot to say about that, and if she expected to record all the ideas, she would surely need to sharpen her pencil again during the meeting! "Catharine," she called, "where is Father's razor?"

"It's in his desk, the top left drawer!" Catharine peered into the room. She pointed at the black cape Henrietta had thrown across the back of the chair. "You're not going to wear that dowdy old thing, are you?"

"Well, it has at least *one* more winter's life left in it." Henrietta loved the old worsted garment she received when Aunt Murray moved to Mississippi. It seemed strange that Catharine had no memory of it. Her sister wasn't sentimental about material things.

"Well, if you insist on wearing it, at least let me brush off the lint!" Catherine folded the cape over her arm and mounted the stairs.

Henrietta rummaged through the drawer to find the familiar, old razor with its hinged blade folded back into the ivory handle. She always thought more clearly with a sharp pencil and doubly so if it had been sharpened with Father's razor. She slipped it into her bag and hurried upstairs to fetch her black winter hat. Standing on tiptoes, she retrieved it from the top shelf of her wardrobe and, turning to the mirror, adjusted it on her head at a slight angle. How could summer have gone so quickly?

A loud rat-a-tat sounded from the front door. Such an impertinent rhythm, she thought. Only a street huckster or repairman would knock in such a manner. Henrietta hurried down the steps. "Package for Miss Sargent!"

"It's a package for you!" Henrietta called.

"I haven't ordered anything! Catharine hurried down and tried the string. "It's too tight to untie!" Henrietta took the razor from her bag and cut the twine. She coiled the cord around her hand and repeated Mother's old saw: "Waste not, want not!"

"Why, it's a set of books!" Catharine squinted to read the gold leaf lettering. "It's Maria's new book! Two volumes! And, it's autographed! It says: 'To Catharine Sargent from the Author, L.M.C.' Oh, my goodness, Maria wasn't joking when she said she would send it just to me!"

Henrietta looked closely at the inscription. "Well, that's not her hand. The publisher must have sent it. At least Maria does what she says—as far as that goes."

"She certainly has written a great deal here." Catharine hefted the two volumes in her hands.

"Indeed," Henrietta agreed, "and it is a shame that she will be better remembered more for what she did *not* write."

"Yes, she failed to address women's rights, Catherine agreed, "but as you well know it's not the first time she stopped short of going the full mile. Remember how we had to drag her kicking and screaming into our Anti-Slavery Society?"

"But, she *did* join in the end. Maria has always been staunch against slavery."

Catharine nodded. "Of course she is, but she didn't want to join an association of mere women. She was very clear about that. 'A woman's organization is like half a pair of scissors.' That is exactly what she said! And you are always so clever—you explained to her that sometimes half a pair of scissors, well sharpened and firmly applied to the seat of a pair of broadcloth trousers, is far more effective in bringing about political change than two hinged parts working at cross purposes."

Henrietta smiled at the remembrance.

"It isn't right!" Catharine continued. "Maria failed you, and all of womanhood— and after you helped her so much. You gave her Aunt Murray's articles for this book. You gave her your secret remedies for her *Frugal Housewife*. You even gave her that horrid story about Elizabeth Gibbes selling the slave girl into prostitution, which she put into her *Authentic Anecdotes of Slavery* book. And even though she did thank you for it, I still think that publishing it, as she did, was a terrible disservice to the Dixwells, especially to Esther!"

"But Maria called the woman 'Miss G' and didn't use Elizabeth's married name."

"The letter G, plus an asterisk was not much of a disguise," Catharine scoffed, "especially when she explained the story was told in the house of a Boston lady, intimately known by the writer, by a Miss G. from South Carolina! You and Maria were both at fault about that. And now that young minister's story in *The Liberator* makes it worse. How can Esther hold up her head when everyone in Boston can recognize the name and see that Elizabeth Hunt's son is Dr. Dixwell's brother."

Henrietta had to admit Catharine was right. It had been a stunning blow to the family. Two weeks ago, *The Liberator* published the narrative of Amos Dresser, a divinity student who had gone to Tennessee to sell bibles to earn money for his tuition. A vigilance committee, suspecting him to be an anti-slavery agitator, seized his trunk and found within an abolitionist book. They immediately convened as a "court" and enacted a sentence of 20 lashes upon Mr. Dresser's bare back. Moreover, there in the published account, listed as a member of the vigilance committee, was Mrs. Hunt's eldest son and Dr. Dixwell's half-brother—William Hasell Hunt, editor of the *Nashville Banner*.

"Well, his *half*-brother," Henrietta corrected. "Not one drop of Dixwell blood flows in his veins, and, thank goodness, Dr. Dixwell was wise enough to change his name before marrying Esther."

"Those technicalities are beside the point." Catharine paused to let her words sink in. "*Our* concern is for *our* sister and *her* feelings."

"It *was* dreadful," Henrietta agreed, "but Maria didn't write that!"

"No" Catharine continued, "but I think Maria has done quite enough damage, by both commission and omission."

Catharine was passionately devoted to family, but Maria was still their friend. "Catharine," Henrietta said gently. "Maria didn't deserve what happened when she and David tried to board the boat for England. Imagine the shame, seeing her husband arrested and taken to jail in front of all her friends—and on a warrant sworn by his own partner!" It was awful to think of. Henrietta wished she had been there to comfort Maria.

"Well no, of course. That must have been dreadful for her." Catharine patted Henrietta's hand, "Let's turn our minds to something better. Here's your cape, as good as new—well, perhaps not quite as good as new," she smiled, "but quite presentable."

Henrietta was relieved to hear Catharine's humor return. "You've not even left a single speck of lint to mark its past."

Catharine pointed to the cape's lower edge. "That frayed hem adequately documents its service—as well as its impending retirement. We don't have time to mend it now. It's already 2:30, and the meeting starts in half an hour. We need to hurry if you want to arrive early."

"It's not that far," Henrietta smiled slyly. I happen to know that the Anti-Slavery Office is only 1,000 paces from our front door—exactly—and at 80 paces per minute we will be there in 12 minutes."

"Gracious! How can you possibly know such a thing?" Catharine was astounded.

"Geordie!" Henrietta laughed. "When he was little, I taught him to calculate distances, so we counted 1,000 paces and that took us to City Hall, and the Anti-Slavery Office is just around the corner. Then, to complete his lesson, we converted the paces to yards, and then to feet, and then divided by 16-1/2 feet per rod because the scale of the map was in rods."

"Amazing!" said Catharine, thinking how like Henrietta, to make a little boy's lesson so practical.

Anti-Slavery Meeting

A cool afternoon breeze caught the feathers on Henrietta's hat as she and Catharine turned the corner from Poplar Street. "You know," she said, looking back at the house, "we must have the windows painted before the weather changes."

"Yes, winter is almost here," Catharine agreed, "And we need to buy more firewood while Mr. Cartright still has a few dry logs. I wonder," she added, "is our Geordie celebrating the beginning of summer or winter in Calcutta?"

"Calcutta is in the northern hemisphere," Henrietta explained. "The same as we are. Remember? That's why J.J. had to cross the equator twice with his ice!"

"The last we heard, he was learning to talk Hindoo." Catharine ignored her sister's impatience. "Or whatever they speak in Calcutta. I do wish he would write more often."

"Now Catharine," Henrietta defended her favorite nephew. "J.J. keeps George busy all day bargaining with Parsees and Musselman cloth merchants. He spends his evenings studying the Hindoo language. And yet he still finds time to send us a letter by every ship leaving Calcutta for the States."

"I suppose you're right," Catharine quickened her step. "We do get more news from George than we do from Maria. I wonder if David will ever put his affairs in order, and if they'll ever sail for England.

"Let's walk on the sunny side of the street!" Maria's refusal to publicly acknowledge the oppression of women still rankled Henrietta, but she did not want to discuss her with Catharine anymore. She took her sister's arm and stepped from the curb, nodding in the direction of a boisterous group of well-dressed clerks, followed by some not-so-well-dressed men who looked to be workmen. "I wonder where all those young men are going?"

"Perhaps, there's an auction of some bankrupt merchant," Catharine surveyed the young men. "That always attracts a crowd looking for bargains."

The two women walked along Court Street past Bowdoin Square. A placard affixed to a light pole caught Henrietta's eye. She read aloud:

> "The infamous foreign scoundrel Thompson will hold forth this afternoon at the Liberator Office, No. 48, Washington Street. The present is a fair opportunity for the friends of the Union to snake Thompson out! It will be a contest between the Abolitionists and friends of the Union. A purse of $100 has been raised by a number of patriotic citizens to reward the individual who shall be the first to lay hands on Thompson, so that he may be brought to the tar kettle before dark."

"Oh, my goodness!" Catharine gasped, "but Mr. Thompson left town yesterday just to avoid creating a disturbance."

"Clearly, whoever printed this handbill doesn't know that."

The sound of loud voices rose. Hundreds of men filled Washington Street, blocking the entrance to the Anti-Slavery Offices. Taking Catharine's hand, Henrietta edged through the crowd. Clusters of men stepped aside as the two women approached.

A rough-looking man in tar-stained pants sneered at them from the entrance of the building. He gestured toward the door with his cigar. "I wouldn't go in there, Dearies!"

The sisters were used to this. Every Thompson speech drew an angry crowd of opponents. Ironically, the violent behavior of the mobs, in turn, provoked the establishment of new anti-slavery societies all over New England. Sometimes the atrocious behavior of ruffians finally overcame the natural reticence of good people to take a public stand against the enslavement of their fellow beings. Henrietta brushed past them and led Catharine up the stairs to the Anti-Slavery Office, still holding her hand. Was it possible to physically feel the loathing in dozens of hateful stares? As heavy footsteps sounded behind them, the sisters quickly entered the meeting room and closed the door behind them.

Henrietta acknowledged the nod of Mr. Garrison, the editor of *The Liberator*, who was conferring with Miss Parker and Mrs. Chapman. His shiny, baldhead seemed too old for his youthful, sharp-featured face. Taking her seat beside Catharine, she counted 14 women—a good turnout, considering the frightening scene outside.

The door opened, admitting harsh male voices. "Gentlemen!" Mr. Garrison's voice rose above the din. "This is a meeting exclusively for ladies. I am sure you would not be so rude as to thrust your presence upon them. If however, any of you are women in disguise, give me your names and I will introduce you to the rest of your sex!"

A titter of laughter rose from the assembled women, and the door closed with an abrupt clunk. Mr. Garrison slid the deadbolt to lock it.

President Mary Parker walked to the front of the room. "Will the meeting please come to order! Let us begin with a prayer."

As the women bowed their heads, the cacophony of voices outside the door reached a fevered pitch. Miss Parker looked uncertainly toward the door, but spoke firmly. "Amen! As you know, sisters, today is the second anniversary of the founding of the Boston Female Anti-Slavery Society. And as per our charter we must elect officers for the next year."

Henrietta found it hard to concentrate with the heavy pounding on the door. She admired Miss Parker, a young woman, who supported herself by operating her own rooming house.

Miss Parker cleared her throat. "But before we move to official business, Mr. Garrison has kindly agreed to address us with a few words regarding the health of our movement. Please welcome Brother Garrison!"

"Sisters in the Cause! I take great pleasure in addressing you on this auspicious occasion—"

"We want Thompson! Give us Thompson!" A harsh chorus came from just outside the door.

"Sisters in the Cause—" Garrison began again, but the pounding of fists on the door drowned out his words.

Miss Parker cupped her hands to speak to him, motioning him toward his office door at the end of the room. Suddenly, the din outside diminished, and there was a single firm knock.

"Ladies! This is Mayor Lyman. Please allow me to enter!" Miss Parker hurried to the door and slid back the deadbolt. Two uniformed policemen burst in, followed by the mayor, his face flushed, his top hat in his hand. He waved his hat aloft. "Ladies! Please go home! You must retire. It is too dangerous to remain! Do you wish to see a scene of bloodshed?"

Mrs. Chapman, her sharp nose pointing like a weathervane, rose to speak. "Mr. Lyman, the instigators of this mob are your own personal friends. And if this be the last bulwark of freedom, we may as well die here, as anywhere." Mrs. Chapman always had a touch of the melodramatic, Henrietta thought. Her husband was a rich, well-known merchant, but it was her own passion that brought to the cause many of the ladies present.

Catharine nudged Henrietta, "If our time has indeed come, I would rather be protected by Holy Scripture than by that cowardly politician!" She wrinkled her nose in disgust. Henrietta nodded her agreement. In any case, regular business was going to be impossible, and she did not want to witness a violent confrontation, much less be a party to it. The hooting and pounding on the wall resumed.

Miss Parker rose from her chair. "Mr. Lyman! May we pass safely from here?"

"If you leave now, I will protect you!"

"I move that the meeting be adjourned. Are there any—" Catcalls from the hallway drowned out her voice.

Henrietta and Catharine nodded at each other. Taking hands, they rose and, with the rest of the women, followed Miss Parker close behind the policemen. Enraged men, shouting and cursing, lined the staircase. The policemen jabbed at them half-heartedly with their clubs.

As she stepped out of the building, Henrietta felt a drop of something wet on her cheek. Strange, there had been no sign of rain. She looked up to see but one distant cloud against the blue afternoon sky. She reached up to wipe her cheek and saw, to her horror, shreds of tobacco in brown spittle. Before thinking, she wiped it on her cape. Turning, she saw her anti-slavery sisters behind her, grim and stolid, two by two, followed by a uniformed policeman, his silver sword held upright like the blade of a guillotine.

The mayor's voice boomed over the crowd. "Please go home! Mr. Thompson is not in this building!"

"Give us Garrison!" a single loud voice pierced the din. "Let's snake him out! Give us Garrison!" The crowd chanted, "Garr-i-son!"

Henrietta turned back to look. A man carried a rope coiled over his shoulder, dangling a noose. Catharine pulled her forward and around the corner. Henrietta felt a cold, clammy fear, thinking of Mr. Garrison's young wife and his little boy. Then she pictured Christ upon the cross. [2]

Boston, 5th Ward
1837, June 19

Catharine stopped at the brick walkway leading up to the porch and waited for Henrietta to catch up. "I think this is the last one for today—and the parlor curtains are open."

"That's always a good sign." Henrietta opened her notebook and glanced down the list of names and house numbers on Allen Street. Late morning was the best time to canvass the neighborhood. Husbands were away at work, and their wives would have a few minutes to talk. Unfortunately, most of the households on her list were marked with a large penciled "X," signifying that the man of the house had refused to sign.

The petition was addressed to the United States Congress, demanding the abolition of slavery in Washington, DC. A few names on the list bore a checkmark signifying a signed petition. Three more were circled to show that Henrietta and Catharine had left a petition with the woman of the house to present to her husband. It was one of these, the house of Mr. and Mrs. Robert Edgerton, at which the sisters now stood.

"Do you think Lucy was able to persuade her husband to sign?" Catharine shifted the heavy satchel containing the petitions.

"It's hard to say, remember, Mr. Edgerton is a member of the African Colonization Society. He deplores the condition of Negroes enough to want to send them all back to Africa, but that's hardly a vote to set them free in this country."

Catharine shook her head ruefully. "If only Lucy and all women were free to sign the petition ourselves, we would have had to order a second printing. It's an outrage to be circulating a petition that we have no more right to endorse than the Africans themselves."

Henrietta gritted her teeth. She never forgot the "woman question" for a minute.

It was an inequity so fundamental that it seemed it could well split the anti-slavery movement asunder. "Even more outrageous that our own brothers in the cause of abolition do not see that hypocrisy!"

The two women climbed the steps, and Henrietta sounded the knocker. "Mr. Edgerton!" Henrietta gasped in surprise. Instead of Lucy, a large burly man filled the doorway. She hesitated, organizing her thoughts. "My sister and I were wondering if you might have had an opportunity to look at the petition we left with Mrs. Edgerton?"

"A petition for what?" Mr. Edgerton's voice was hoarse; his eyes, red.

"Robert!" Lucy Edgerton, joined her husband in the doorway. "Miss Sargent left a petition for you to sign, to free the slaves in Washington, DC."

"Set them free?" Mr. Edgerton frowned. "Free to pilfer and plunder? Better to send them all back to Africa —every one of them!"

Henrietta took a breath and struggled for her warmest smile and sweetest tone. "But the real danger, Mr. Edgerton, arises from keeping the Africans in bondage. Set them free and they will at once be converted from dangerous enemies to grateful servants."

The man cocked his head skeptically.

"I feel confident," Henrietta continued, "that if good men such as yourself knew only a hundredth part of the barbarous cruelties exercised on poor unoffending Negroes, you would see plainly that the true savages are the southern slaveholders and that this savagery should not be tolerated in our good nation's capitol."

"But sending the Negroes back," Mr. Edgerton spoke carefully, "would be a great good for both Africa and America—it would civilize and Christianize Africa and, at the same time, free us from a public nuisance of lazy, ignorant brutes."

Henrietta kept her smile. Her adversary was about to be hoisted on his own petard. "Mr. Edgerton, I am sure you see the absurdity of sending a host of lazy and stupid vagabonds to civilize and Christianize Africa!"

The words rolled easily off her tongue, just as she had read them in Mr. Garrison's *Liberator*—just as she had memorized them and rehearsed them over tea with Catharine playing the devil's advocate. For each argument, Henrietta had practiced a disarming reply with some compelling fact that would turn the conversation to yet another elegantly expressed and unassailable truth.

The man drew back, his face reddened. She was using his very words, but somehow— "Madam, you know perfectly well," he sputtered, "that is not what I meant!"

"Now, Robert!" Lucy Edgerton put her hand on her husband's arm. "When Miss Sargent left off the petition, yesterday, I told her that I thought you would sign. Henrietta, I'll bring it to your house tomorrow morning. Now, come inside Robert. You must keep your neck warm or you'll have the grippe all summer." Mr. Edgerton, looking relieved, stepped back into the house. Henrietta and Catharine walked back to the street.

"You know," Catharine looked back to be sure that the Edgerton's door was firmly closed, "I'd give 50 cents to hear what Mr. Edgerton has to say about now."

"He's probably calling us 'hyenas in petticoats,'" Henrietta giggled. Aunt Murray had often liked to repeat the phrase some Englishman had used to describe Mary

Wollstonecraft after she published a book on the rights of women, a few months after Aunt Murray had published her own article on the same subject.

Catharine smiled in recollection. "Better to be a howling hyena than a shrinking violet! That man may not like you or like what you told him, but he will not soon forget that a mere woman, engaged him in intelligent debate."

Catharine was right, Henrietta thought. The issue was whether a woman had a right to say anything at all. Only a month ago, she and Maria had traveled to New York City for the first-ever national Convention of American Women. Representatives of women's anti-slavery societies from throughout the northern states convened, ostensibly to coordinate their efforts in the abolitionist movement. One unstated issue loomed larger than all the stated items listed on the official agenda—the *woman question*. Was it logical or moral to expect American women to champion the rights of enslaved Africans without demanding their own equal treatment before the law?

Long before the convention in New York City, conservative clergymen began a concerted opposition to women's rights, railing from their pulpits with contrived biblical interpretations that enjoined women to silence and submission. Of course, many of these men were—at best—lukewarm on the issue of abolition itself.

The noontime peal of a church bell filled the air. Catharine forced a smile. "That's Dr. Channing's Federal Street Church,"

Henrietta nodded. The Reverend Dr. William Ellery Channing's long-awaited book on slavery proved a disappointment—timidly, if carefully, crafted to avoid offending the merchant families whose wealth supported his church and paid his salary. He had even chided Mr. Garrison for advocating immediate emancipation!

Now the women heard the chimes from the other churches—those wealthy enough to have bells and vain enough to sound them—ringing discordantly, tuned to a multiplicity of different keys.

"They do seem to squabble," Catharine commented, "just like their small-minded ministers!"

"Yes," agreed Henrietta, "and considering that, we can be thankful our convention in New York was just for women. Had any of those ministers attended, we would not have accomplished anything at all. Bad enough that some delegations of women stayed home on orders from their pulpits!"

Catharine nodded, her lips tightly pressed together. "And to think that you had such a struggle to convince Maria to come!"

"Oh Catharine!" Henrietta scoffed, "we can't blame the ministers for that!"

Maria had written such a sad little letter describing her "vacillating and discouraged state of mind" and asking if she was wrong in deciding not to attend. Maria, once such a firebrand, had retreated from public life after the lukewarm reception of her book about women. She and her husband even planned to begin a new life as farmers in Mexico. Like most of David's schemes, that, too, had come to nothing.

Henrietta's reply to Maria's letter put the starch back into her friend and roused her from her despondency. Once the convention began, Maria burst forth from her cocoon, participating fully in the discussions. She was marvelous! An impressive convention surprise were the Quaker women whose speaking skills (honed in their meeting houses before gatherings of men and women) were revealed as equal if not superior to those of any male orator. The most powerful speakers among the Quaker women were the Grimké sisters, who had explicitly connected the rights of women to the abolition of slavery.

"Now, remind me," said Catharine, as if she knew her sister's thoughts, "is the Miss Grimké who wrote the resolution on women at the convention the one who is coming to see us at one o'clock?"

"Yes, that's Sarah Grimké, the writer. She's the younger one. Angelina, the lecturer, is going directly to the church. She'll speak at three o'clock, and I'll introduce you after her lecture."

"I can't wait to meet both. It is wonderful that Sarah is so interested in Aunt Murray's writings!"

Henrietta spoke with pride. "When I introduced myself to congratulate her on the resolution, she told me she wanted to write a series of articles on the woman question, so I told her all about Aunt Murray. And when Maria joined us, she not only confirmed everything I said, but she remembered all the details I forgot!"

"Well," Catharine said, "Aunt Murray would certainly have loved that resolution—especially the line about 'perverted application of Scripture!'"

Aunt Murray had always been eloquent about biblical misinterpretations that disparaged women. Henrietta had felt as if Aunt Murray were there beside her as she raised her hand in support of what, to her mind, had been the most important resolution of the convention. She had found the entire resolution worthy of memorizing. Now she began to recite it to Catharine:

> "Resolved, that as certain rights and duties are common to all moral beings, the time has come for woman to move into that sphere which Providence has assigned her, and no longer remain satisfied in the circumscribed limits with which corrupt custom and a *perverted application of Scripture* have encircled her —"

"Yes!" Catharine interrupted, "and what was the part about 'just duty of women?'"

> "Therefore, it is the just duty of woman, and the province of woman, to plead the cause of the oppressed in our land, and to do all that she can by her voice, and her pen, and her purse, and the influence of her example, to overthrow the horrible system of American slavery."

"It's a wonder you won a majority on that one!" Catharine laughed.

"Well, to be honest, it was more of a plurality. I am afraid that more than a few women abstained in deference to their pastors.

It's too bad Miss Grimké won't have time to stay for tea before her sister's lecture."

"Yes," Henrietta agreed. "But I am so happy she is coming over. I hope she will want to borrow Aunt Murray's writings."

The two women quickened their pace. Henrietta was ready for a cup of tea. Except for the visit to the Edgerton's house, they were finished with Allen Street, and in a few days, she could deliver the signed petitions to the Anti-Slavery Office. [3]

The Sargent Home

"I didn't know they could shoot water from their trunks!" Sarah Grimké leaned forward to examine the brightly colored picture of a mother elephant and her twin calves frolicking in a deep pool at the bend of a river, their keeper sipping tea in the shade of a palm tree.

Catharine joined the slim, Quaker woman at the mantle. "Our youngest nephew, George, returned from Calcutta last fall, and he brought with him a little Hindoo man to help him learn the language. When they visited us on Christmas Eve, the Hindoo gave us that picture! And the little Hindoo was standing right there," Catharine pointed to the floor beside Sarah, "in his scarlet turban, orange-colored mantle, and baggy white trousers, and I told Henrietta that Christmas at 5 Poplar Street had never looked so festive!"

"They've now both returned to India," Henrietta explained. "It's a pity that the Hindoos are so much more solicitous of their elephants than they are of their women! My sister and I are most interested to learn how you plan to address the question of women's rights when you next put your pen to paper."

Sarah peered more closely at the picture, and then turned to Henrietta. "Yes, and, in a way," she said, "that is why I wanted to meet with thee."

"Oh, yes!" said Catharine "The woman question! I had so much wanted to go to the convention with Henrietta and Maria, but I took ill with the grippe and had to stay home. But I did follow all the accounts in the papers—and, of course, Henrietta told me more!"

Henrietta smiled at her sister. "I *do* believe my account was *somewhat* different than what you read in the newspapers!"

"I should hope so!" Sarah laughed. "'Oratresses who put away their frying pans to debate weighty matters of state.' Indeed! They actually called our meeting an 'Amazonian farce!'"

Henrietta caught the twinkle in Sarah's eye. "Yes, and if the reporters had listened to one word of what they dared to call our 'gentle invective' and 'soothing indignation,' they'd have had their ears pinned back! But—," she looked at Catharine, "my sister and I want so much to hear *your* thoughts."

Sarah closed her eyes for a moment, then as if in prayer leaned forward. "My sister Angelina and I both believe, as thou dost, that commerce in human flesh is the major moral issue of our time. And we also believe that it is the duty, before God—of both men and women—to bring that scourge upon our nation to an end."

Henrietta nodded. It was unusual to hear a woman speak without introducing her subject with banal niceties. In the background of Sarah's Quakerly "thee's" and "thou's," Henrietta thought she could hear a faint souvenir of a South Carolina childhood in the inflection of her words, each syllable drawn out an instant longer. Even though almost everything about Sarah Grimké's appearance was unremarkable, there was something refreshing about her plain face, her unadorned plain black gown, and her plain words—forthright and to the point.

"Thus," Sarah continued, "as men *and* women both share the responsibility to bring slavery to an end, my sister and I believe the time has come to examine any stricture condemning women to silence."

"Yes," Henrietta agreed, "and so many of those strictures are derived from false interpretations of scripture!"

"Exactly!" said Sarah. "That is the biggest obstacle we face. The authority of the clergy and their distortions of scripture have stifled woman's voice for far too long. That is why I plan to write a series of articles in the form of letters to Mary Parker, who, like so many abolitionist women, has held back her voice regarding the woman question."

"It has been difficult for Mary," said Catharine. "It was natural, as she is the president of the Boston Female Anti-Slavery Society, to be elected to chair the Woman's Convention—but her pastor was outraged by the passage of the women's resolution. Poor thing, it put her in such a quandary!"

"Many women share her situation," Sarah continued, "and, for that very reason, I intend to base my exposition of the proper sphere of woman *solely* on the Bible, for I believe that almost everything that has been written on this subject has been founded on misconceptions of the simple truths revealed in scripture—and from what thee and Maria Child told me in New York City, I think thy Aunt Murray's treatment of that subject will be most helpful."

Henrietta held up a magazine from the stack on the table beside her. "Well, these are my aunt's writings! It was not only the *misconception* of scripture that Auntie objected to but also its *mis-translation*."

"Do you mean to say that she went back to the Hebrew and Greek texts?"

"Just hear what she had to say!" Henrietta opened the magazine and found her favorite passage, the one that she had bracketed in pencil so many years ago and read:

> "Some ignoramuses have absurdly enough informed us, that the 'beauteous fair of paradise' was seduced from her obedience, by a malignant spirit, in the guise of a baleful serpent; but we who are *better* informed, know that the fallen spirit presented himself in her view, a shining angel still; for thus, saith the critics in the Hebrew tongue, ought the word to be rendered."

"Oh, my!" Sarah was writing rapidly in her copybook.

Henrietta looked up. "There's no need for you to copy all of this," she said. "You are most welcome to borrow Mrs. Murray's writings for as long as you need them!"

"Oh, I thank thee! That will make my task so much easier! But how does she treat the original sin by Eve in the Garden of Eden? The clergy always use that as their great argument for the natural unworthiness and sinfulness of women."

Henrietta scoffed, "The evidence for that *alleged* sin is far too flimsy to support such an indictment. As my aunt put it, 'it took 'all the arts of the grand deceiver' to mislead Eve—whose only motivation was to improve her mind—while Adam, the 'pusillanimous father of mankind,' forfeited the happiness of all posterity without a second thought!'"

"I think thy aunt is right. Should anyone have been condemned, it should have been Adam. And, to think she wrote those words in 1790!"

Henrietta handed the magazine to Sarah. "Auntie actually wrote those words, in a letter, in 1780. She only published them in 1790."

"Clearly, her work deserves to be more widely known, and I would like to develop her line of reasoning. Indeed, Maria Child's *History* is a great work, too, also deserving more attention. I want to take up where she left off." Sarah flipped back through the pages of the article to the title and stared at it as if transfixed. "On the Equality of the Sexes," she whispered. "How simple and direct! Woulds't thou object if I took Judith Murray's title for my own?"

Catharine smiled warmly at Sarah. "Good idea! Is there a way that you could quote Maria's title, too? It would be a true tribute."

"You mean, call it *On the Equality of the Sexes* and *The Condition of Woman*? What a wonderful idea," Sarah agreed. "That would be a most memorable title!"

Henrietta beamed at her sister. Somehow Catharine always found a way to repair a worn sock—or a damaged friendship. "I think Maria and Aunt Murray would both be very pleased!" [4]

Lydia Maria Child (ca.1856) (1802–1880), Henrietta Sargent's close friend who wrote *History of the Condition of Women* (1835). (Courtesy of the Schlesinger Library, Harvard University.)

William Lloyd Garrison (1805–1879), the abolitionist editor of *The Liberator* (ca.1868). (Etching from Stowe 1868:153.)

Sarah M. Grimké (1792–1873) wrote the 1838 book, *Letters on the Equality of the Sexes and the Condition of Women,* a title that deliberately joined and memorialized Judith Sargent Murray's *On the Equality of the Sexes,* and Lydia Maria Child's *History of the Condition of Women.* (Courtesy of the Library of Congress, date unknown.)

During the 1830s, many anti-slavery activists believed that a public campaign for women's rights would be a divisive issue, undermining their more important campaign for the abolition of slavery. Although he was a strong supporter of women's rights, William Lloyd Garrison was one of those who believed that abolition should take precedence over women's rights.

Sarah Grimké met Henrietta Sargent at the 1837 New York Convention for American Women. Henrietta introduced Sarah to the ideas of Judith Sargent Murray. Sarah's sister, Angelica, presented the most controversial resolution of the conference: "The time has come for woman to move into that sphere which Providence has assigned her, and no longer remain satisfied in the circumscribed limits with which corrupt custom and perverted scripture have encircled her."

CHAPTER THREE

Travels by Water

Boston to Nantucket
1841, August 8

Henrietta followed Catharine down the narrow aisle of the passenger car and waited as Catharine slid their valise under the seat. Stooping to glance through the open window, she spotted their two trunks on the cart amidst a shower of ashes from the steam locomotive.

Catharine held up the soot-smudged handkerchief she was using to wipe off the brown leather seat pads. "Goodness! Could you please shut that window?"

"Oh, my! That *is* dirty!" Henrietta slid the heavy glass pane across the opening.

Catharine peered down the aisle "Not many familiar faces!"

"No, there aren't, are there. But then, what can we expect? We wouldn't even be coming ourselves if Maria hadn't asked me to write that article."

"Good morning! Miss Henrietta—and my dear Miss Catharine!" William Lloyd Garrison dropped his valise, took Catharine's hand, kissed it, and addressed Henrietta. "Mrs. Chapman tells me that you will be reporting again for Mrs. Child."

Henrietta hesitated. She did not want to feed the flames of the acrimonious debate between Maria's paper, the *Standard*, and Mr. Garrison's *Liberator*. She winked and smiled sweetly. "Why, Mr. Garrison! Catharine and I are off to see the famed palaces of New Bedford and the luminous isle of Nantucket!"

Garrison laughed, appreciating her diplomacy. "I'm sure it will be a wonderful article. And I look forward to reading your reports on the Phillips' return from England and the Chapmans' return from Haiti—and the soirée for Mr. Ruggles." He tipped his hat and started down the aisle toward a companion.

Two weeks ago, Henrietta had mailed Maria her "Welcome Home" article, which included several quotes from Mr. Garrison himself. It would be published in today's *Anti-Slavery Standard*. Now Maria gave her a more important assignment—to report on the three-day Anti-Slavery Convention on Nantucket Island. But just how should she write about it? Ever since Maria had moved to New York City to edit the *Standard*, Henrietta's old friend had been struggling to produce a journal that would not just preach to the already converted but would also reach out to the greater numbers of people who were uncertain about slavery and might yet be moved to join in the abolitionist cause.

Many long-time abolitionists criticized Maria's efforts. The new paper, they said, "lacked the fire" of Mr. Garrison's *Liberator*, and its gentler tone attracted only "half-and-half, milk-and-water" abolitionists who would leave the movement at the first sign of a crisis.

Henrietta reached into her handbag for her pencil and notebook. She could get started on her introduction now, writing, "Today I began an excursion with old organization anti-slavery friends to New Bedford and Nantucket." She shifted her notebook on her knees and continued, "I was *not* led from my peaceful home by curiosity to see the famed palaces of New Bedford, or the luminous isle of the ocean. I simply wished to know where anti-slavery lived out of the city, and how truth was welcomed in counties other than Suffolk."

The car jerked forward. Henrietta closed the notebook and looked out the window. The Boston-Providence Railroad station was on new ground at the edge of the tidal flats near the south corner of Boston Common, although "tidal flats" was a euphemism. Even as the old Mill Pond that had caused such a stench on Poplar Street was being filled, developers had engineered an even larger receiving basin. A causeway topped its dam, extending Beacon Street south from what remained of Beacon Hill to enclose a vast marshy area fully half the size of Boston.

The tidal flow through gates in that long barrier powered new gristmills, but after only 20 years, this receiving basin was rapidly becoming a bigger cesspool than the old Mill Pond. At first the effluent from Boston's sewers had been flushed out with every tide, but now new causeways, built to support the Boston & Providence and the Boston & Worcester railways, crossed and formed a big "✘" in the middle of the basin, blocking flow to over half of the tidal marsh.

Protruding out of the muck, an iron horseshoe dangled like a fishhook from the hoof of a dead horse. Still, Henrietta had to marvel at how fast Boston was changing. Already developers were imagining and even naming streets to build out into this morass.

Henrietta returned to her notebook and reread her opening sentence. "*Old organization friends*," she murmured, underlining the words. Maria's new readers would probably not understand the significance of that term and the three years of conflict it implicitly referred to.

"You look troubled," Catharine observed.

"More perplexed than troubled," Henrietta smiled, "over the consequences of our friend Sarah's five simple words."

"You must mean *the perverted application of scripture*?" Catharine laughed.

Henrietta nodded. That phrase in the Grimké sisters' resolution at the Women's Conference in New York had ignited a firestorm and caused a schism in the anti-slavery movement. Hardly had Henrietta arrived home from the convention when angry words over that phrase broke out among the members of the Boston Female Anti-Slavery Society. Before long, Boston's conservative ministers also reacted. From their pulpits they condemned not only women who would dare to discuss politics in public but also Mr. Garrison and *The Liberator* for condoning such behavior. In the end, the more conservative women in the society, in obedience to their pastors, demanded that the group terminate all financial support for *The Liberator.*

That same summer, Henrietta and the Grimké sisters proposed that the Boston Female Anti-Slavery Society host a public meeting in Boston to discuss the rights of women. Most society members voted down their proposal. After months of argument, the conservative women issued a final rebuke to Henrietta, Catharine, Maria, and the other Garrison supporters by voting to dissolve the society.

Henrietta fumed at the memory. "Every time I remember the shameless way they cheated on that vote it makes me—to think that they would count the votes of women who had never even participated in the organization and then ignore yours!"

"Now Henrietta," Catharine chided, "we *did* resurrect the society, and today we are embarked on a beautiful outing, and we should be thinking beautiful thoughts."

"I know, I shouldn't brood on old wounds. But some things are hard to forgive—and even harder to forget. That was the very day we became old organization!"

Henrietta could not get the pictures out of her mind. Only minutes after watching their conservative sisters troop out of the room, she and Catharine and Maria and the other radicals decided to reconstitute the old organization. The break had only been the beginning of a broader division. Soon afterward, the conservative members of the American Anti-Slavery Society resigned over the same issues and formed a new organization. Mr. Garrison too had become "old organization."

Henrietta stared down at her notebook. Poor Maria! Editing the *Standard* required that she steer a middle course between "old organization" and "new organization" people. That meant she had to bite her tongue. The snide comments of old friends did not make her task any easier. At least, Henrietta thought, writing this article, her second one for the *Standard,* was a public testament to her long friendship and continued support of Maria. Henrietta wondered if Maria would edit her provocative opening line. She read it once more. "I began an excursion with old organization, anti-slavery friends to New Bedford and Nantucket." No, thought Henrietta. Maria would respect the truth.

"Henrietta!" Catherine pointed out the window. "We must wave to our sister Anna."

Henrietta looked up. They were now on solid land, and to the west she could see Parker Hill rising above Roxbury. Anna's husband, John Parker, was reputed to be one of the wealthiest men in Roxbury, and their country estate covered most of the hill that bore his name. She waved dutifully to humor Catharine. She always found it an ordeal to visit Anna, having to listen politely to her contempt for abolition and abolitionists.

The rocking of the car made Henrietta sleepy. Her thoughts drifted. What would happen when they got off at Taunton to board the New Bedford train? She wondered if Mr. Garrison would take a seat in the colored car with the Africans or even urge the colored people into the white car and create a confrontation with the conductor, as David Ruggles had done only a few months ago. Perhaps he would wait until he had a larger audience at New Bedford.

§

Henrietta left Catharine to save their seats inside the main deck cabin of the steamer *Telegraph*, then stepped outside and walked to the rail. The heavy odor of whale oil filled the air. Next to the pier, 100's of barrels lay on their sides, draped with mounds of dark green seaweed to keep the barrel staves from drying and shrinking in the summer sun and leaking the precious liquid that made New Bedford the busiest whaling port in the world. She could feel the excited anticipation of the conventioneers, colored and white, as they gathered on the pier.

Near the boarding platform, Mr. Garrison huddled with three men. Two of them moved into the crowd, going from person to person. Now the third man came aboard with Mr. Garrison, and they stationed themselves at the foot of the steps that led to the upper deck. A colored woman was standing uncertainly by the stairway.

Henrietta heard the whispered instructions. "Everybody stay on the main deck!"

The first mate stepped aboard, pointing up the steps. "All Negroes please move to the upper deck! All Negroes move to the upper deck!" he bellowed again, more loudly.

Mr. Garrison joined Henrietta by the rail and turned toward the crowded deck. "Conventioneers!" he thundered. "I ask you to honor the captain's order—and to pray for his salvation. We will *all* join our colored brethren on the upper deck." He pointed towards the stairs. "Conventioneers! The upper deck is 10 feet closer to the warming, forgiving countenance of our Lord."

Henrietta walked quickly to the cabin to fetch Catharine. This would be an interesting trip!

The upper deck had no cabin. Henrietta hefted their valise onto the bench beside Catharine and then joined the circle of activists clustered around Mr. Garrison. He was saying that in addition to the 41 abolitionists aboard, another group of passengers had joined them on the upper deck—a known slaveholder from New Orleans and an Episcopal clergyman.

"I don't see his cloven hoof," said Catharine, "or his horns and tail!"

"Don't be fooled by a top hat, wool suit, and boots," whispered Henrietta. "The devil is quite at home in high society."

Mr. Garrison was quickly organizing the travelers into a meeting. Henrietta listened intently from her seat. Now that the steamer had begun to move, the nasty plume of smoke and ash was trailing behind. She opened her notebook and began to take notes. A resolution was bellowed out in a loud voice that "the holding of a fellow-being in bondage" was a sin and "prejudice on account of complexion" was likewise sinful.

In short order, four gentlemen, all abolitionists, asked for recognition to address the meeting. Henrietta stopped taking notes as the second man began to speak. His examples were the same old chestnuts, timeworn from countless repetitions at scores of abolitionist meetings and printed in every issue of *The Liberator*. It was nine-hours to Nantucket, and Martha's Vineyard was still only a big bump on the southeast horizon. The afternoon light danced on the waves.

Henrietta woke suddenly, as her pencil slipped from her grasp. A young gentleman retrieved it for her. Someone she did not recognize was asking if anyone else wished to speak. "Any objections to emancipation," he said, "will be heard with attention and respect." The offer was a pro-forma generosity repeated at most abolitionist meetings—a mere gesture toward an openness to discussion. After all, who would be fool enough to advocate slavery to an audience of abolitionists?

The Episcopal minister—the companion of the slaveholder on the deck—stepped forward. "I would like to say a few words on this subject!"

Henrietta sat upright and pulled a fresh pencil from her handbag. She had seen and heard many lukewarm ministers of the gospel, but she had never heard one defend slavery!

The white-haired divine spoke with clerical formality. "Of the 47 millions of sons of Ham now on earth, none are so well off, for time and eternity, as the 3 million American slaves! These dark brothers are well fed and well clothed, with honorable employment and comfortable homes. I regret, as you do, the existence of the institution of slavery in this country, but I assert that slavery is not a sin nor is it contrary to the laws of Providence or the divine decrees of God."

It was outrageous. When the clergyman had finished an hour later, she realized that his address had so disturbed her that she had forgotten to take notes. Satan had indeed revealed his cloven hoof. A cool evening breeze ruffled the pages of her notebook.

Catharine took two heavy shawls from the valise and arranged one over Henrietta's shoulders. "I think it's time for us to bundle up!"

"Thank you!" Henrietta gathered the wool garment around her neck and pointed at the distant island. "That must be why they call it the 'luminous isle!'" Nantucket seemed to stand atop the horizon, iridescent in the last rays of the setting sun.

"It *is* beautiful," Catharine agreed. "Just think! Our dear Georgie was perspiring in Calcutta when he bought these shawls made of real Kashmir wool, from the mountains of the Himalayas. I wonder where he is right now."

"Well, let's see," said Henrietta, "the latest news from China came aboard the *Akbar*—109 days in transit. We waved goodbye to George on June 22, almost 50 days ago, so I calculate George must be almost half-way there."

"He must be passing around the south tip of Africa?"

"I think he must be nearer the south tip of India," asserted Henrietta. "If they stop to take on supplies in Ceylon, he'll certainly send a letter home from there."

"Will *it* come all the way back around the south tip of Africa?" Catharine closed her eyes and tried to imagine a map of the world.

"No, of course not! George will put it aboard a steamer going up the Red Sea to Egypt, where they'll carry it overland to the Mediterranean, and put it on a steamer to England—where they'll put it on another steamer to New York, or Boston."

"You mean, George's letter will pass by the pyramids?" Catharine shook her head in wonder. "If only we could ride along with it—across the desert on a camel."

"I would much rather *we* meet George in Ceylon and convince him to come home."

"Now Henrietta," Catharine chided. "George could hardly refuse Mr. Heard's offer of a partnership in China, especially after J.J. recommended him."

"But why should George sail to Canton when the city has been evacuated—the shops closed, the streets deserted. And now we learn that the Emperor has issued an edict ordering the extermination of every Englishman."

"But that news is 109 days old," Catharine reminded her. "Certainly by the time George arrives, the British Navy will have bombarded the Chinese into smithereens!"

Henrietta started to answer but desisted. Catharine was right. The news was old by now. Undoubtedly, Mr. Heard had moved his business to Macao, as all the other merchants had done and would remain there, under the protection of Portugal, until the crisis subsided. She looked out across the water, where she could just make out the two windmills atop Nantucket's nearest hill. The ingenious Quakers of that island had devised gristmills that did not require tidal dams and their inevitable cesspools. Perhaps the clean ocean breeze would ease her mind and bring fresh vigor to this little band of conventioneers.

Nantucket Island
August 11

Henrietta surveyed the Nantucket Athenaeum. The pointed arches of two gothic windows and a central doorway were the only remaining signs that the building had once been a Universalist meetinghouse. Now they peeked uncomfortably from behind the new Greek portico and four Ionic columns that the city fathers had added in front.

"Really, Henrietta!" Catharine was growing impatient. "How can you possibly commune with a building?"

"I want to pay my respects before the crowd arrives. It's an affront to John Murray." Henrietta wrinkled her nose in disgust.

"Henrietta, Uncle Murray has been gone for 24 years, and he never much cared about material things even when he was alive."

All through the two days of meetings, Henrietta felt John Murray's presence. Over and over, her eyes were drawn to the northeast corner of the auditorium. Seventeen years ago—it seemed only yesterday—the Nantucket Universalists had asked for a souvenir of John Murray to place in the cornerstone of their new meetinghouse.

Just a few years earlier, Uncle Murray lay in his coffin in the parlor, and Henrietta remembered how Auntie had clipped a tuft of hair from his dear forehead. That lock of hair along with a few newly minted coins and the names of the church fathers were sealed in a bottle and placed beneath the cornerstone. The congregation had not thrived, however and neither had the memory of John Murray. None of the abolitionists seemed aware of the hallowed ground they stood on.

Catharine was growing impatient. "Henrietta, we've communed long enough! I do hope the proceedings are more lively today."

Henrietta agreed. The first two days had hardly been inspiring. The speeches were stale leftovers, stirred and reheated without any improvement of their tired flavors. The sisters went inside and took seats in the front row of the still-empty hall.

"I'd almost rather be at the temperance convention down the street," Catharine whispered. "They always have exciting speakers for their cause—people with experience, reformed drunkards offering their true testimony."

"Well, we do have the Grimké sisters," said Henrietta. "They speak with the authority of those who have lived among slaveholders. A reformed slaveholder would be a powerful crusader indeed, but I doubt we shall see any."

Catharine pondered. "No—but I suppose a reformed—I mean a former! —slave would be as good."

§

Henrietta was hungry. After three hours of resolutions and presentations—each duller than the last—she needed a cup of tea. The Nantucket abolitionists had been most generous in offering hospitality to the conventioneers. Yesterday she and Catharine had taken refreshment at the Macys' and today they were invited to the Gardners' home.

From the stage, a new speaker was being introduced. Henrietta suppressed a yawn. "And now I would like to introduce a young man who has lived in the shackles of captivity and who has felt the yoke of slavery on his neck."

The tall colored man who had sat quietly in the back of the auditorium for the past two days walked forward. He stood next to the podium while the introduction continued with the story of how the young man had escaped from bondage in Baltimore, where he had labored in a shipyard, and how the good people of New Bedford sheltered him. The young man shifted his weight uncomfortably, his hands clenched, his body tense, his eyes lowered. He glanced furtively around, lowered his gaze, and then, seemingly with great effort, raised his head and faced the audience directly.

Henrietta gripped the edge of her seat. Fear showed in his eyes as he struggled for words. His first words were awkward and formal. As he began to tell his story, his voice took on a tone of courage, remaining humble but ever more and more powerful. The audience was still, absolutely silent, as if a spell had fallen on the room. Mr. Garrison was staring in wonder.

A noontime chime in the distance broke Henrietta's concentration. The young man had spoken for a full hour. Now he offered thanks for the opportunity to address the convention. The audience remained stunned for a moment before breaking into a thunderous applause.

Henrietta had been too deeply spellbound to take notes while the African told his story. Now she wrote quickly to preserve the feeling of the moment: "One only recently from the house of bondage spoke with great power. Flinty hearts were pierced, and cold ones melted by his eloquence. Our best pleaders for the slave held their breath for fear of interrupting him."

She described how, as the ovation subsided, Mr. Garrison raised both hands to silence the crowd. "This speech," he announced, "would have done honor to Patrick Henry himself."

As abolitionists left the hall in an excited rush, Henrietta tried to remember a few more details. Henrietta nudged Catharine. "Did you hear his name?"

"I don't think they ever said."

No, thought Henrietta, of course not. Why aid the slave hunters and their spies by supplying a name?

§

Henrietta and Catharine thanked Mrs. Gardner for the tea and sandwiches and followed the other conventioneers back down the street toward the Athenaeum.

"So, his name was Freddy Bailey," said Catharine, "and now he calls himself Fredrick Douglass. Mr. Garrison says he should be hired as a speaker for the Massachusetts Anti-Slavery Society."

An afternoon breeze provided welcome relief from the summer heat. Henrietta touched her handkerchief to her forehead. "I do think we'll be hearing much more from that young man."

Catharine paused in front of the window display of a corner emporium. "Isn't that China tea set beautiful! I wonder what George will send us for Christmas?"

A blue-and-white porcelain tea service stood beside a large wooden tea chest, its sides covered in red and gold Chinese paper. Two bolts of rich green China silk, each unrolled a full turn leaned against the box. Since George had departed for China, Henrietta read everything she could find on the China trade.

"But you know, Catharine. Those pretty trifles are part of a much larger commerce that, if it were generally known, would trouble every abolitionist—indeed every person with a Christian conscience!"

"Why, whatever do you mean?" Catharine asked in surprise.

Henrietta explained. "Southern planters sell their slave-grown cotton to the English, and the English pay for that cotton with the silver they get from selling opium to the Chinese."

"But," Catharine looked puzzled. "J.J. buys his tea directly from China with New England coinage."

"Not exactly," Henrietta continued. "The same Southern slave owners use the English silver they earn from their cotton to buy our New England manufactures, and that's the very same silver we send back to China to pay for that box of tea, as well as," she pointed, "that tea service and those pretty bolts of silk."

Catharine gazed at the display. "Does Esther know that?"

Henrietta shook her head. Although she and Esther talked about their worry that George was on his way to a country in open warfare with all foreigners, Henrietta hesitated to discuss her growing revulsion with the entire China trade.

As Catharine digested Henrietta's words, her face took on an expression of dawning horror. "Does the Augustine Heard Company deal in opium?"

"Of course it does!" Henrietta replied with as much calm as she could muster.

The two women stood in silence. Catharine tried to control her emotions. "Then, they are contributing to the ruin of the Chinamen—and if George is engaged in such commerce—Henrietta—George listens to you. You *must* write him and explain the damage he may do to his *soul!*"

Two weeks later, as Henrietta wrote to warn George of the temptations he would face in China and the spiritual danger he faced, she was all too aware of her own spiritual quandary. She wrote first of herself, then alluded to the personal temptations that George would face. She ended by pointing to what she feared would be George's greatest vulnerability—greed. [1]

August 29, 1841

Dear George—

It is Sunday, an overcast muggy day, and I have concluded to stay at home and write to you at no sacrifice respecting public worship, for, unhappily for me, there is not a minister in town whom I wish to hear— and what service would it be to rue to be present [at] the teaching of one where doctrines I deem heretical, bigoted, or worldly, or of one bold enough to tear up all the land marks of my faith, to lay stumbling blocks in my way, and there leave me, like a midnight traveler without a lantern to his path, or a ship tossed by tempest without rudder or compass? …

You have not been absent but two months, yet it seemed a year since I saw you … George, I know not whether you are self reliant, or what is better Heaven reliant. I know not how you would resist the influence of a dangerous companion. Their way of undermining the principles of the young is often very insidious: they delight to reduce others to the same degradation as themselves. Ridicule is a powerful agent with them, and it is sometimes a stumbling block to find such, not without the apparent respect of the world. We must all go thro' a fiery trial and I trust you will be sustained thro' yours. The Widow's Son will not surely be without his shield, and our troubles, if well improved, serve to school our virtues.

Dear George. I pray you not be over anxious about lucre. "Man wants but little, nor wants that little long." Do not have an Eldorado the object of your pursuit, of your toil by day, and the disturber of your sleep by night. It is unphilosophical, it is unchristian. What was the wise man's prayer? "Lord give me neither poverty nor riches"—happiness, such as life affords is oftenest found in the mean—happiness does not want to be swathed and bandaged, and constrained by etiquette and fashion and aristocratic pride. She is free—she loves the free air of the forest and the upland—her head is not bent by a coronet of diamonds, but is wreathed with wild flowers. The feast, and the pomp and parade of the palace are little to her taste. She shuns not sorrow if she can alleviate it, ignorance if she can enlighten it, weakness if she can strengthen it. Her companion is perfect celestial freedom, which owns no Master but Christ, aspires no yoke but his, which is very easy to bear …

God bless you dear Nephew in all your thoughts, decisions and dealings with the Chinese. Pray remember they are men and do as you would be done by.

Henrietta Sargent

Aboard the *Masden*
Gulf of Canton
November 8, 5:30 am

The clank of anchor chain resonated through the walls of the aft cabin of the brig *Masden*. George Dixwell awoke and rubbed the sleep from his eyes. On Saturday, 136 days after boarding the *Coromando* in Boston, he arrived at Macao, China, to find the city overflowing with refugees. Yesterday morning, Monday, he boarded the *Masden* for the two-day voyage to Canton—the unfortunate city those refugees had fled. Halfway there, the captain dropped anchor for the night in the relative safety of open water, just outside the mouth of the Pearl River, and today they would begin the 50-mile ascent to Whampoa Anchorage.

George wriggled to the edge of his bunk, swung his feet to the floor, and felt for his shoes. He reached for the satchel that served for a pillow, struggled to his feet, and massaged the crick in his neck. Like the three other men in the stuffy cubicle, he slept in his clothes. The small bunk hardly accommodated his 6-foot frame. Quietly opening the cabin door, he descended to the deck and stretched. To the north, through the mist, he could make out the rock walls of the Chinese forts surmounting the heights on either side of the river's broad mouth.

"You must be Dixwell!" George turned to see the grey-haired gentleman who had been favored with a bed inside the captain's cabin. "The name's Ferguson—Dent and Company. I knew your Mr. Heard when he was out here for Russell and Company, and I raised a glass to him when he retired. What a surprise to find him back in the saddle!"

George offered his hand. "Delighted to meet you, Sir! Mr. Heard has always spoken highly of your firm. I must say he, too, was surprised to be called back into service."

"Maybe he just wanted to escape the clutches of all the old maids and widow women." Ferguson winked, "I barely survived my last visit to London."

"Well, Mr. Heard did have to guard his flank." George remembered how aunts Henrietta and Catharine had discussed which of their women friends might best suit a 56-year-old rich bachelor. Mr. Augustine Heard was a most eligible catch.

Ferguson chuckled. "Nonetheless, I never expected he would take over Canton!"

"I believe Mr. Heard would prefer to be described as caretaker of a litigated estate," George parried, "—a property that your esteemed monarch will repossess at her first convenience."

"Certainly, but in the meantime we, Her Majesty's loyal subjects, are forced to suffer the charity of upstart colonials in order to conduct our business." Ferguson wrinkled his nose theatrically.

George laughed. There was more than a grain of truth behind Ferguson's joke. Some two years ago, the Chinese emperor issued an edict forbidding the sale of opium. Commissioner Lin, sent to Canton to enforce the edict, seized 20,000 chests of the drug from the foreign merchants. Fearing for the safety of their countrymen, English officials summarily ordered all British subjects out of Canton. Despite being officially excluded from the Canton trade, British firms continued filling their ships with tea, employing American firms as their proxies. Jardine Matheson, the largest British firm of all, contracted with Augustine Heard & Company to manage all their Canton business.

It had been that turn of events, followed by the letter from Joseph Coolidge, Mr. Heard's partner, which begged for help with the sudden deluge of new business, that persuaded Mr. Heard to give up his comfortable retirement in Boston—and to offer George a one-third interest in the firm if he, too, would sail for Canton. Of course, Mr. Heard had no idea how serious the situation had become. Neither he nor George could have imagined that, within a week of their handshake, the Chinese would launch a sneak attack on the British warships anchored at Canton. The Chinese sent a flotilla of incendiary hulks downstream late at night on the ebb tide—barges linked together by long chains and loaded with oil-soaked bales of raw cotton—that were intended to entangle the British fleet in a web of fire.

"It's a good thing that your fleet wasn't incinerated by those fireboats," added George, sympathetically.

"Yes, despite the cowardice of their sneak attack," Ferguson shook his head, "we responded as civilized men by demonstrating what we could do without actually doing it! One row of siege guns atop the hill overlooking the city got their attention—and got us 6 million dollars to compensate for their savagery. It's a pity we couldn't stop the riot—and your Mr. Coolidge was lucky not to be murdered by that pigtailed horde!"

George shivered, imagining Mr. Coolidge surrounded by the riotous mob. He hadn't learned about any of that until a month ago in Singapore when he'd read a back issue of the *Canton Press*.

"Gentlemen, please tend your sterns!" The first officer waved George and Ferguson closer to the rail.

Two burly Indian lascars dragged an iron cannon past them toward the bow gunport. The officer pulled a wooden plug from the cannon's muzzle and slid a round cloth bag into the gaping hole.

"Keep that powder dry," said Ferguson. "We may need it!"

"I sincerely hope not." The officer turned to the lascar plunging the ramrod down the barrel. "Not so hard!" he ordered. "Now, the bucket!"

Hefting the rusty container to his knee, the bearded Indian tilted it against the cannon's mouth. George watched, mesmerized, as a tangle of iron nails poured into the opening.

Ferguson pointed to where the river narrowed. "That's the Boca Tigris—the Tiger's Mouth. Before the war, it was a safe passage up through here, but now that our blessed Majesty's fleet is keeping the emperor engaged in the north, the pirates are having a field day down here." He smirked, "One good volley of four-penny nails should take out a whole hive of the beggars. Of course, every crisis offers an opportunity. With the fleet off Chusan Island, and sailors' empty stomachs to be filled, there's money to be made—and this little brig will soon reach them with some fine delectables."

"The men should appreciate that, if your cargo is truly *delectable*." George replied.

"Certainly!" Ferguson laughed. "I've contracted for every jar of candied fruit, every bag of confectionary, and every last bottle of brandy from anywhere near Canton— and between English sailors, Punjabi Sepoys, Bengali light artillery lancers, black Cameroonians, and all their camp followers, I'll have my cargo sold before we even drop anchor!"

Every nation and race on earth was here in China. Each had its own function in an incredibly complicated system. Designated representatives appeared to be critical to all accomplishments. The emperor issued his edicts through Mandarins; foreign commerce was mediated though business merchants called "hong"; English and American captains commanded sailors known as "lascar crews"; the British waged war with colonials of every dusky complexion; and at the stern of this very vessel, George could see the first officer standing aside as a Chinese river pilot shouted instructions to the Indian steersman.

"Mark my words," Ferguson continued, "next spring you'll be able to follow the trail of those African bucks across China by the spawn they leave behind—if the Chinese don't get around to drowning all the little bastards!"

George ignored him. Up ahead, he could see a broad cove of glistening mud flats broken by narrow, ribbon-like channels.

Ferguson followed George's eye. "That's where the Chinese like to hide their war junks, but they can only get out at high tide. It's more dangerous upriver where they've run underwater chains and sunk old hulks as snags. That's why we need that Chinaman for a pilot." George watched the man, holding the wheel with one hand and pointing at the sails with the other. Ferguson spoke after a moment. "I imagine it will be a difficult task to reconstruct your ledgers."

George frowned, perplexed. "What about our ledgers?" Only a short note from Mr. Heard had awaited him at Macao with instructions to come immediately to Canton.

"Didn't they tell you? From what I've heard, all your records went up in flames, along with the building!"

George blanched. He watched the water rushing by the vessel's hull and tried to grasp the loss. It struck him that the river had taken on a brownish hue. A blast of cold wind penetrated his cotton jacket. Ferguson clenched his top hat to his head. "Let's sit behind the cabin."

George followed Ferguson around the deckhouse to a sheltered bench. The two men sat quietly, soaking in the warming rays of the morning sun. Ferguson addressed the

Chinese who approached them holding a steaming pot of tea and a basket of cups. "Yes, I want some!"

Wedging the basket against the deckhouse with his foot, the man extracted a small blue cup and filled it. George reached into his satchel for the Chinese dictionary he purchased in Macao. He found several useful phrases and practiced pronouncing their phonetic transliterations—but he had no idea how to voice the four tones described by the author. He opened the book to an underlined phrase.

"*Nah shur shummah?*"

The Chinese man stared blankly at him. George repeated his phrase, trying a different tone.

"Missa, You wannee tea?" The vendor spoke impatiently.

George blushed. "Yes, tea!" he mumbled.

Ferguson craned his head to see the cover of the book. "That won't help here—that's for the official language," he laughed. "Only Mandarins talk that. Everyone else speaks the Canton language or pidgin."

A lascar grunted as he lifted a blunderbuss onto its socket on the railing. George took a sip of tea. There was a lot he would have to learn about China![2]

Whampoa, Hong Kong
7:00 pm

The *Masden* drifted backward, then shuddered as her bow anchor clenched the river bottom. Shouts, muffled by the gusty wind, could be heard from aloft. George shielded his eyes against the evening sun to look up. Straddling the mainmast yard, sailors worked quickly to tie the flapping canvas into a long, snug roll. He lowered his eyes and looked impatiently toward the Whampoa waterfront, catching only a glimpse between the massive black-hulled ships that blocked the view.

"Take my word—" Ferguson took a deep draft of his cigar and slowly exhaled, "we're better off anchored out here where the peddlers won't pester us to death."

"It looks like they've already discovered us!" George pointed to the sleek, six-oared vessels racing towards them.

"Those are 'dollar boats'—hackneys—and we'll take the fast one. The peddlers arrive later." Ferguson glanced at George's two trunks stacked beside the cabin. "Are they ready to go?"

"Packed and padlocked!" George watched as the first boat pulled alongside.

Ferguson shouted to the steersman, "How muchee?"

The man waved his index finger in the air, "One piecee dollah!"

"Good!" Ferguson pointed aft where a sailor was hooking a ladder over the railing.

The oarsmen pulled the small vessel's squared nose beneath the ladder as Ferguson descended. George followed, accepting the steersman's steadying hand as he stepped aboard. He waited as a sailor passed his trunks down to another oarsman, who eased them into a compartment below deck. George hunched down and followed Ferguson into the passenger cabin.

Ferguson gestured around the room. "Somewhat nicer than the *Masden*, eh? We could have bargained him down, but he'd only waste our time finding more fares. This way, we've got it to ourselves."

George looked around the cabin, stunned by the opulence. Polished black wood benches, their backs carved in a latticework pattern of birds and flowers, extended around three sides of the compartment.

Ferguson slid his hat down the long smooth expanse of the left bench, sat down, and clicked open his pocket watch to consult its face. "Well, the tide is about to change, but with a little vigor we'll reach Canton in one and one-half hours, without having to fight the outflow."

George sat on the facing bench and raised the dark green window blind. The evening light caught the flapping flags of the ships in the harbor. "A lot of Union Jacks out there."

"Most of them are consigned to you! And they'll be pulling out of here, while the rest grow barnacles."

George cast Ferguson a questioning look. "Why is that?"

"Because," Ferguson answered with satisfaction, "when Mr. Lin stopped the trade in opium, Jardine Matheson and Company was smarter than everybody else. They waited until the market collapsed in India, where they grow the stuff, and then bought up the whole crop for a song!"

George looked perplexed. "But if they can't sell it in Canton ..."

Ferguson laughed. "Well, Jardine's was prescient, too! They'd bought a little fleet of fast schooners and brigs, so they could deliver drug to any rabbit hole up the coast—and for payment in silver. After the Celestials had to pay us those 6 million dollars in reparations, there wasn't much silver left in Canton. Meanwhile, a world of ships were already on their way to China from Liverpool and Lowell, loaded with enough trousers and shirts to clothe every last Chinaman three times over. With such a glut, the tea merchants refused to accept shirts for Souchong—and that is why half of those ships are now languishing out there, at anchor, while Jardine's hands their opium proceeds off to you, and you fill their ships as fast as you can scribble numbers on the tea chests."

Ferguson pulled a newspaper from his side pocket and folded back a page. "Look at the shipping list!" He handed the paper to George.

George ran his finger down the column. Seven of the 17 vessels listed were consigned to Augustine Heard and Company.

"And if you should ever wonder for what particular skill or expertise Jardine's chose your company to represent them, it was because you're too small to become a competitor!"

George nodded slowly. So that was why the Heard Company seemed to have so much more business than the other American firms. His head reeled a little from the effort of untangling the web of trade relationships. The compartment felt warm. "I'd like to get a view from the deck," he said, handing the paper back to Ferguson.

"Go ahead. I'll join you in a bit!" Ferguson flipped through the pages.

George climbed to the deck. Leaning back against the cabin, he breathed deeply. The breeze cooled the perspiration on his brow. The steersman shouted something, and the three port-side oarsmen dragged their oars. The vessel swerved around a sampan piled high with melons. To his right, a barber applied lather to the dark throat of a lascar. Slowing, the boat wended through a cluster of sampans surrounding a floating teahouse with charcoal glowing brightly in its braziers.

The steersman's scull groaned in its pivot as he eased the vessel past a muddy shallow into open water. The steersman sang out a chant, and as the oarsmen adjusted their strokes to his cadence, the boat shot forward. George felt something calming in the steady rhythm.

As they emerged from the protected lee of the island, a gust of northwest wind buffeted the little vessel. Cargo junks from far upriver, their segmented mat sails spread like batwings, were converging on the narrow entrance into the anchorage. A long, low tea packet approached, a mountain of green and red chests stacked on its deck. Close behind came a stately junk with an enormous eyeball painted on its bow, its deck piled high with bamboo furniture. Another junk with wicker crates filled with oranges followed close behind.

Once it had crossed the main channel, the boat turned upstream, skirting shimmering, water-filled rice fields and lush, green orchards. They snaked around fishing weirs, long fences of wooden stakes driven into the riverbed.

George's mind turned to the future. Where would he be living in Canton? Had the burned-out Heard building been repaired? Might there already be a packet of letters from home awaiting him, brought on a vessel faster than the *Coromando*?

"Not much like the Ganges!" Ferguson struggled up the steps. "But you won't find Canton much of an improvement over Calcutta. Down there, the Hindoos whimper and wail for a penny in their bowl, but the Chinese here are more likely to steal your purse!"

George felt for the precious lump deep in his breast pocket. "I'll keep my eye on it," he said.

A thin falsetto voice accompanied by the dissonant notes of a bowed instrument drifted from a garishly painted barge. A red-bearded man in a white linen suit leaned carelessly against the railing. In the pinkish light of a lantern, George could see a young, black-haired woman peering through the cabin window, an open fan in her hand.

Ferguson raised an eyebrow, then smirked. "One of the benefits of Canton service. Best pay extra for a young one—or you'll pay later, with interest."

George craned his neck as the woman pulled a translucent curtain across the opening. His eyes remained fixed on the curtain. Ferguson guffawed. George blushed and quickly looked away. He remembered the promise Mother insisted he sign, that he would not become a debauched man of the world.

The two men watched the passing panorama—like pictures in a gallery, thought George, except here the pictures did the moving. As they rounded a curve, the river was suddenly crowded with tiny sampans darting across their path. The steersman shouted and the boat slowed to a crawl.

Ferguson waved his arm at the shore in a sweeping gesture. "Canton!" George felt again for his purse. Ferguson laughed. "I wouldn't worry, Dixwell. By this time next year, you'll be a very rich man, indeed!"

George peered ahead with anticipation. They glided past row upon row of sampans, tied side-by-side, extending far out into the river. The little vessel turned into a slightly broader avenue between two of the rows and retracting his oar, one of the oarsmen stood up to pole it through the welter of mooring lines. They would be landing in a few minutes now. He could already see the facades of the foreign factories, which looked just like those in the watercolor at Aunt Henrietta's—the one Uncle Epes Sargent gave her before he died of the consumption he had caught in this very city.

It struck George that the long-ago artist had improved his rendering—omitting the sampans and drawing, instead, a Mandarin's 40-oared "fast crab," its banners flowing gracefully in the breeze. George's mind returned to the woman on the "flower boat." There would be much he would have to omit from his letters home. [3]

§

Henrietta glanced up at the watercolor of Canton harbor and began her letter to George. [4]

Boston
Oct. 30th, 1841

Dear Nephew,

I have been pausing to try and think of some news to tell you … By the way, perhaps you may like to know the fact—Miss Shattuck is not to spend the winter with us in Poplar St. What reason do you think she gives for depriving us of her company? Guess—you could—I know—not that we were dull—or out of the way—or were not polite or kind to her—not that she was not well fed and accommodated—no—you know the reason—but I love to write it—it gratifies me, flatters me—is it a weakness?—Forgive it. She could not stay with us because we were *Abolitionists*. Miss S. is not alone in feeling this repulsion.

As it respects engagements you care not. You have launched into the sea of speculation, money making, bah! For this you will leave your friends, your courting adventure, your precious health, of which you have little to spare —to have a house higher by some inches than your neighbors—a carriage for your wife to ride in who would be better off to walk afoot—a great sum to leave your children should you have any bestowed on you, who will thus stand a chance to be deteriorated in mind and body.

Are you not a great simpleton? I think you are. Depend on it. You have three great enemies, the World, Sin, and the Devil. Now you laugh and snap your fingers and think I write like a great fool—but is it for the World's opinion you want this great swad of money. Sin has got hold of you in the way of coveting your neighbor's goods. You mean to jockey the poor, simple Chinese. You know you do—and Satan has devised this temptation for you to lead you from the beautiful serenity, crowned with peace and temperance that the Christian enjoys. "He is a merchant—the balances of deceit are in his hands: he loveth to oppress" Hosea 12-7 "Woe unto you who are rich" Luke 5.

Now Aunt, perhaps you say, I am tired and you have on your white and are prosy, so we had better say good night and go to sleep. First tell me how Aunt Caty and I are going to dispose of ourselves. Well then, Aunt Caty and I have put in our wood and our winter stores, and the sun shines into our parlour and we have all things necessary for our comfort—abundance of Sleep—and a nice parcel of reading—and we remain at rest in our minds respecting the sufficiency of Christ to accomplish his work—even to save us. We are sturdy Abolitionists, believing that all men are brethren and the rule is "do as you would be done by." We are not anxious for length of days here but we anticipate a glorious *hereafter* through the mercy of our dear Lord who died that we might live.

Farewell

H. Sargent

Frederick Douglass (ca.1818–1895), ca. late 1840s. (Daguerreotype courtesy of the Library of Congress.)

George Basil Dixwell (1814–1885), ca. 1847. (Daguerreotype courtesy of Marcia Dixwell DiMambro.)

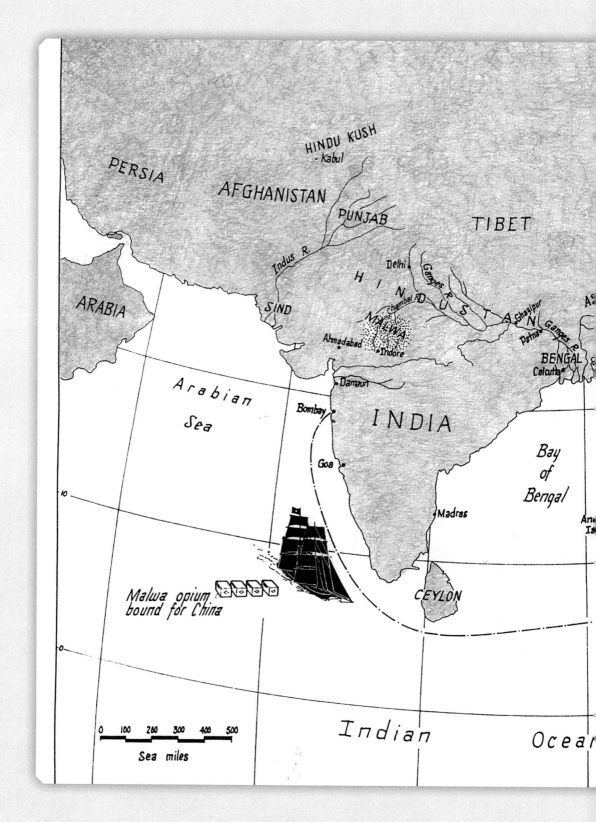

The South and East Asia opium trade. (Map by Sam F. Manning.)

Silver bullion and Sycee silver ingots from China in payment for Indian opium.

The Canton Factories before the 1841 fire, ca. 1840. (Oil on canvas, courtesy of the Peabody-Essex Museum.)

The actions and values of the male and female members of the Dixwell and Sargent families were often at odds with one another, yet the profits of international trade bound them together.

While archaeology often focuses on those who did not leave written records behind, my vignettes often do the opposite, presenting well-known personages but from perspectives that are not easily captured by academic writing alone.

From 1836 to 1838, the orator, editor, and writer Frederick Douglass worked as a slave in the Gardner Brother's Baltimore shipyard where the *Frolic* would be built six years later. In September 1838, Douglass fled north to freedom. Henrietta Sargent attended the 1841 National Anti-Slavery Convention on Nantucket Island as a reporter for Lydia Maria Child's *National Anti-Slavery Standard* and recorded the impact that Douglass's first speech had on her and the others. As I wrote that vignette, I was aware of the irony that in later years Henrietta would recall the power of Douglass's words, never realizing that the large scar on Douglass's face came from a beating he received at the same Baltimore shipyard where, six years later, the *Frolic* would be constructed and would become a major source of the wealth and reputation of her nephews. In 1841, as Frederick Douglas was addressing the National Anti-Slavery Convention, Henrietta Sargent's nephew, George Basil Dixwell, was sailing for Canton, China, to begin his partnership in Augustine Heard & Co. He would craft the Heard firm's commerce in opium and order the construction of the *Frolic* to transport the drug from India to China. George represents commerce in the "commerce vs. conscience" debate underlying this book.

By the 19th century, the Western world had become addicted to tea grown in China. But the West manufactured little that China wanted, so most of the tea was purchased with silver coinage, causing an unsustainable negative balance of trade with China, which the British and Americans tried to reverse with trade in opium. When the British defeated the Moghul rulers of India, they took over the opium monopoly and began shipping opium to China in exchange for silver, thus reversing their balance of trade. In 1838, the British allowed American vessels to transport Indian opium to China. In November 1841, George Dixwell arrived in Canton, China, to begin his residence in the narrow strip of land fronting the Pearl River where the "factories" of Western merchants were confined in order to prevent their interaction with any Chinese, except for a group of government-sanctioned "Hong" merchants who mediated all such transactions.

Cargo items included brass trunk handles in graduated sizes from nested China-export leather-covered camphor trunks. The nesting of large items, one inside another, reduced the amount of expensive cargo space needed aboard outgoing vessels. The camphor trunks themselves often became family heirlooms. Handles identical to those on these antique camphor trunks were recovered from the *Frolic*'s final cargo. (Photo by author.)

Canton pattern bowl. The *Frolic* cargo included at least one "Blue China" dinner set. The fragments of a long dish and lid from a dinner set of Canton pattern with rain and cloud border were recovered from the *Frolic*, shown here next to a Canton pattern heirloom piece. Upper sherd length 7 cm. (Photo by author.)

Chinese tinderboxes. Silversmiths fashioned tinderboxes that might be worn as neck or blouse ornaments—each containing a flint flake on a bed of tinder. Note the slot for the iron striker bar (horizontal length 3.6 cm). (Photo by author.)

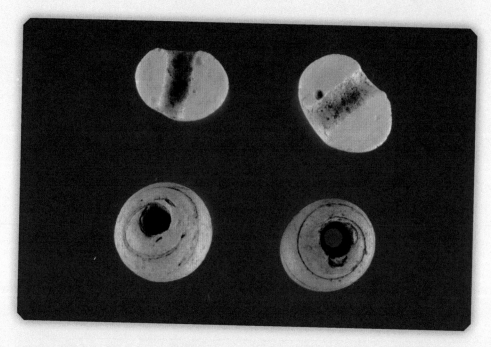

Coarse glass beads, the most abundant cargo item preserved at the *Frolic* wreck site, were so-called "false pearls," used for jewelry or as ornaments (lower left bead diameter: 7.4 mm). An 1863 *Chinese Commercial Guide* explained that they were wire-wound glass beads with an iridescent coating of fish glue and macerated fish scales, a covering that did not survive in the archaeological record. The Frolic's invoices revealed that she carried 6 (133 lb.) picules—over 600,000 of them. (Photo by author.)

Most of the *Frolic*'s final cargo, bound for San Francisco, was comprised of items manufactured in Western styles expressly for the Western market. My visit to the China export trade collection at the Peabody-Essex Museum in Salem, Massachusetts, greatly facilitated those identifications.

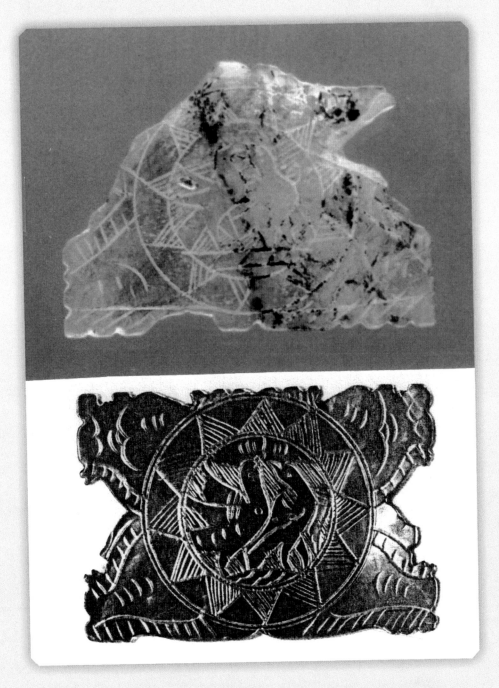

Mother-of-pearl wafer (2.8 cm. horizontal length). I originally identified it as a gaming piece, but Richard Kelton (Kelton Foundation Collection) re-identified it as a thread spool from a sewing kit manufactured for the Western market. (Photo by author.)

CHAPTER FOUR

The Fragrance of Opium

Augustine Heard & Co.
Canton, China
1842, December 6, 9:30 am

George Dixwell walked slowly between the rows of open wooden chests, admiring the perfect cubes. Almost knee-high, freshly garbed in bright green paper, they seemed to march from Footae's open warehouse across the broad verandah to the dock beside the river—a full platoon, in dress uniform, awaiting inspection before a reviewing stand.

George waited as the clerk inked numbers on the still-moist labels glued to the fronts of the chests. "Your arm must be getting tired!" he addressed the young man.

"I think that will finish this chop, Mr. Dixwell." Joseph Roberts stood and stretched. His red hair stood out against his cherubic complexion. "I'd best get back to Mr. Heard and Mr. Footae and add these to the inventory."

George nodded. He looked back past the massive balance scale that dwarfed the figures of the two gentlemen sitting at the table just beyond. Like salt and pepper, Augustine Heard, in his bushy white beard and white linen suit, chatted comfortably with Footae, garbed from head to toe in plain black silk. Appointed by the Emperor to act as intermediary in all transactions between Chinese merchants and foreigners, Footae had grown rich and fat on the commissions.

At the warehouse, some of Footae's men were pouring black congou tea into open chests. Others, barefoot, stamped down the tea leaves. Still others smeared glue onto square sheets of green paper before smoothing them onto the sides of the boxes. By mid-afternoon these last two batches, unloaded only yesterday from an upriver tea broker, would be boxed, weighed, tested, and put aboard the waiting lighters for transport to Whampoa. From there, the tea would be loaded into Jardine, Matheson & Co.'s ship *Prince William* for dispatch to England.

George gazed out across the river. It was a peaceful scene. Smoke drifted upwards from hundreds of tiny sampans, each arched over with a brown grass mat. The families within were brewing their morning tea. George, however, felt no peace. Last season they had shipped $10 million of tea—almost all of it for Jardine's. His share of the commissions was almost $25,000—more than 10 times what father had ever earned in a year as a physician. If he could match that this year and two years more after that, he would have his "lac"—a cool $100,000—more than enough to comfortably retire. In spite of Henrietta's tiresome sermons, he'd have enough capital to buy a respectable house for brother Epes, the schoolmaster, as well as more than enough to buy himself an elegant townhouse in a fashionable neighborhood *and* a country house besides. Never again would anyone pity the poverty of a Dixwell!

The gnawing foreboding he'd felt was looking more and more a certain prediction. As soon as the new treaty between England and China was ratified, the prospects of the Heard firm would change dramatically and not for the better. This season might see the last of Jardine, Matheson & Co.'s ships consigned to Augustine Heard and Co.

"Number 678 is light!" Augustine Heard nodded toward the scale.

Suspended from the 8-foot crossbeam, the left platform with the brass weights scraped the ground, while the right platform, which held the tea chest, swayed in the gentle morning breeze. Quarter-chests of congou tea were supposed to hold 63 *catties*—82 lbs—and a chest that was light or heavy was likely to contain a different tea of a different quality. If the discrepancy were not addressed now, it would be revealed later when an angry company of London grocers demanded their money back.

Footae flicked his finger, waving the chest back to the warehouse. "Hold that one!" Jardine's tea taster, Humpston, shouted from his table beside the stove. A workman hefted the chest to his shoulder and carried it to Humpston's table. George walked with him to the stove.

Digging deep into the chest, the taster scooped a measured ladle of black leaves into a small porcelain beaker. The gaunt, hunched-over man poured boiling water into the beaker up to a black line just below the rim and checked his pocket watch. "Four minutes!" Humpston said, placing the beaker on the table. "Well, look at that!" He peered into the beaker and grinned, revealing the brown-stained teeth of his trade. "Never trust an upcountry broker. See those woody leaves floating on top? That's a worthless, late-autumn fourth picking. When they've got a short chop, they'll mix in such trash—even twigs."

He took a sip, swirled it in his mouth and spat into a large brass pot. "Coarse and musty." He wrinkled his nose. "I doubt it takes a second infusion." Holding back the leaves with his strainer, Humpston emptied the tea into the waste pot, then refilled the beaker with boiling water and made an entry into his notebook. "Four more minutes. A good quality Congou should still be drinkable on the third infusion. Can you see the ink mark at the bottom of the cup?"

George looked down at the pale brown liquid and swirled the tealeaves, peering closely. "Looks like a zero."

"A proper third picking, properly roasted, should produce a second infusion dark enough to hide that zero completely," Humpston explained. "Of course, that says nothing about the taste, cherished by my countrymen." Humpston took another sip, wrinkled his nose, and spat it out. "We've tried sending better chops of green hyson, but we just can't sell it. Of course, that's all history now."

"History?—How so?" The usually laconic Humpston clearly wanted to talk, and George liked hearing any and all lore of the tea trade.

"Two centuries ago, when the denizens of our tight little isle first tasted tea, East India ships were so slow that only the most robust blacks could survive the trip—and they were the cheapest ones. We learned to soften the harsh taste with milk and sugar. And by the time we finally had ships fast enough to deliver the greens, our tastes were already formed, and we found the green tea too delicate to accommodate our favorite adulterants."

"Adulterants?" George laughed. He remembered Aunt Catharine pushing the cream pitcher toward Aunt Henrietta, as she dropped a second pebble of sugar into her cup.

"Yes, adulterants. And a thorough understanding of the subtleties of their interactions on an English palate ensures—most blessedly—that Jardine & Co. will always have an English tea taster."

"Time for breakfast!" Augustine Heard interrupted. "It will have to be a quick one, though. Footae expects our last shipment this afternoon."

"Hmm, breakfast," George winked at Humpston, "and a cup of good Sumatra coffee to clean the palate!" George hurried to catch up with his partner and followed him down the passageway to the rear of the Hong. Together, they walked out through the gate to 13 Factory Street. Looking back, he saw Roberts talking with Humpston. For the past few days, George had been preoccupied with the changes in their business that were likely to follow from the next news from London.

"Mr. Heard," he turned to the older man. "I'm worried about the treaty."

"Why so? The English fought the war—and, without spending one American cent, we've gained four new ports. Footae is the one who needs to worry."

Footae would indeed suffer under the provisions of the treaty. Foreign traders would soon be buying directly from the Chinese merchants, and Footae would lose his commissions as an intermediary.

"Of course," Heard continued, "it may be costly for us to staff a second factory in Hong Kong, but there are advantages in living under the predictable order of an English administration—as you saw full well in Calcutta."

"It's not our expenses I'm concerned about, it's our income. When that treaty's ratified, it may well be the last we see of Jardine's—and their business."

"And then we'll get back to our real business." Augustine Heard raised his voice over the din of a beggar banging on a brass pan. "We'll get back to filling orders from home, where there'll soon be more tea drinkers than in all of England."

"But," George persisted, "only if we have the silver, like Jardine's does, to pay for it!"

Heard placed his arm around George's shoulder. "May I remind you that we are a commission house, and by the terms of our partnership we provide market information to our clients. We bargain for their tea, we taste it, we pack it, we arrange for shipping and insurance, and we take a commission for each service. We do not risk our own capital—and in any case, operating a fleet of opium clippers, as Jardine's does, is another business, entirely."

George swallowed, forcing a deferential nod to his senior partner. It was not the first time he had raised the topic. Heard saw George's frustration. "I do like your scheme to import raw cotton from the States. I think we might build a good business here, bypassing the English mills and selling directly to the Chinese. Have you heard anything from your brother?"

George counted the months since he had written to J.J. asking him to investigate the idea with cotton brokers in New Orleans. "We should hear by the next ship from Boston."

The cotton business was, at best, a future possibility. To make any use of raw cotton, the Chinese would have to import mills and looms, and they were generally reluctant to make large capital investments. Regardless of what Mr. Heard thought about it now, the firm would soon need to attract consignments of opium in order to obtain the hard money to buy tea, and that would be difficult without a delivery fleet. For now, Mr. Heard's mind was made up.

George turned to pull the bell cord to the Dutch Hong. A coolie opened the gate. His stomach growled as he followed Mr. Heard up the passageway toward the Heard Company rooms at the front of the building.

10:30 am

George ran his fingers down the ledger columns. Each transaction was clearly rendered in neat schoolboy script. "You're doing a fine job, Roberts," he addressed the clerk. "You've got the hand of an accountant."

"Thank you, Mr. Dixwell. All I need now are those New York manifests."

Augustine Heard also peered over George's shoulder. "This record is probably as good as the one that burned. But don't tell Mr. Coolidge I said so," he chuckled.

The handwriting of Joseph Coolidge, the firm's prickly third partner, was so cramped and crooked that the other clerk, Mr. Heard's nephew John, had to recopy all his letters before they were sent to clients.

A loud metallic pounding echoed from down the hall. "Mistah Dik-wah," the company comprador, Kee Chong, called from his office.

George stepped inside, followed by Roberts. Two iron-bound boxes from Jardine & Co. stood open on the floor—one was filled with fist-size silver ingots; the other, with bags of silver coins.

Roberts bent to pick up a boat-shaped silver block. He turned it over in his hand. "Those ingots look like more trouble than they're worth. There's no telling what's inside them."

George nodded. Word had it that a shipment of Chinese ingots that Russell & Co. had sent to the foundry was found to contain rocks and pebbles. He turned to the comprador. "All same numba one dollah?"

Kee Chong laughed and raised his spectacles. "Mebbee numba one, mebbee all same no good. Mebbee Sun Kee know." He nodded across the room toward his nephew sitting at the shroffing table, testing money.

Like all the other foreign merchants, the Heard firm employed a Chinese comprador to manage their financial transactions. Piled high on Kee Chong's side table were bundles of documents recording months of billings and payments, bound together with black silk ribbons and each bearing Kee Chong's vermillion-stamped impression. Like most compradors, Kee Chong had hired a trusted relative Sun Kee as the shroff to test and evaluate all the silver received in payment for the merchandise shipped.

"All good dollah?" George addressed the shroff.

Sun Kee held up two coins. "Have some piecee no good! Betta you listen." George stepped closer. Sun Kee dropped the first coin onto the marble slab at the edge of his table, where it rang with a bell-like chime. He then dropped a second dollar. It sounded a dull clunk. "No good, no good,"

Sun Kee handed the coin to George who held the Spanish dollar up to catch the light from the veranda. "Clearly counterfeit."

Roberts bent to see the coin. "How can you tell?"

"Notice the yellow tint?" George handed the coin to the clerk. "They added a heavy dose of copper before making that one."

"It's a wonder we're getting any silver at all." Roberts returned the coin. "They must be running low after sending that $21 million to the Queen."

After laying siege to Canton, the British dispatched their navy up the coast, taking Chusan Island and then Shanghai. Finally, as they prepared to take Nanking, the Emperor avoided total defeat by agreeing to pay another indemnity—$21 million in silver—to reimburse the British for the cost of the campaign.

"Still, there's quite a lot of silver here," Roberts remarked, looking at the trunks. "I wonder how they'll manage to ship it all back to London. Do you think they can load it all into one cruiser?"

"Well, let's figure it out." George handed the young man the pencil and notepad he always carried in his coat pocket. "An unworn Spanish dollar weighs just short of one ounce avoirdupois. That should suffice for you to calculate the weight of $21 million in silver—first in pounds and then in tons."

The shroff heaved a dollar into the half-filled tea box beside his table and laid another on his anvil. Placing the chisel-like die that bore his mark just below King Carolus's ear, he struck a heavy blow with his hammer and handed the coin to George who looked at the engraved characters defacing the monarch's image. The mark represented Sun Kee's personal guarantee to replace the coin should it be found underweight or lacking in enough silver. George returned the dollar to the shroff's table.

"Mr. Dixwell, $1 million in silver should weigh 54,000 pounds. So $21 million should weigh close to 1,134,000 pounds. And that—," Roberts threw back his shoulders, "comes to a total of 567 tons of silver."

"And could you load that amount into the *Mary Ellen*?" George prodded.

"At 529 tons displacement," Roberts paused, "we'd fill the *Mary Ellen* to the gills, Captain Scudder would have to empty his pockets before boarding, and we'd still be leaving some 38 tons stacked on the dock." Roberts grinned. "Try me on another! That was easy."

Groping for a more complex problem to set the clerk, George paused, then continued. "All right, a stack of 10 Spanish dollars stands about 1 inch high. If the Emperor should lay a stack of Spanish dollars worth $21 million on edge, what distance would it cover?"

"In inches?"

"No," said George, smiling. "In miles." He stepped through the arched granite doorway and inhaled the cool, fresh air, surveying the sky. The winter monsoon had quickened since morning, but with only a few clouds to the northwest it looked like the weather would hold until all the chops at Footae's were loaded and sailed off to Whampoa. He peered up the river. Not a tea junk was in sight. It looked like they would be finished with this shipment before the next one arrived—.

"If $10, stacked, equals an inch, then $1,000 equals 100 inches—a little over 8 feet," Robert's voice interrupted his thoughts. "One million dollars would be about 8,000 feet—close to a mile and a half."

George pictured a rod of solid silver an inch and one-half in diameter, stretching from Aunt Henrietta's house, across Boston, and down the peninsula.

"However," Roberts continued, "the Emperor owes $21 million, and *that* stack of silver dollars would extend a full 31-1/2 miles!"

The two men silently pondered the enormity of the ransom to be paid to the British. Turning, they strolled to the fence between the Heard company veranda and the English Garden.

"What an untidy mess!" Roberts pointed, "Why, my mother would have those weeds pulled, and new flowers planted before church on a Sunday morning!"

"You're probably right." George agreed. "My Aunt Henrietta could do the same, although these look a little healthier than the medicinals she used to grow."

The English Hong, fully twice as wide as any of the other 12 foreign factories fronting the river, had remained vacant for the past 15 months since the mob torched it. Weeds had grown between the shrubs, flowered, gone to seed, and died. Now fresh ones sprouted among the dead stalks. Through the building's open door, Chinese workmen could be seen troweling creamy white plaster onto the fire-blackened walls.

"Maybe we should rent it," said Roberts.

George pointed to the broadsides glued to the pillars beside the doorway. "And have to reconstruct our books all over again? I don't think we want to occupy any building associated with the British. It's dangerous enough to live next door."

"But the Emperor *signed* the treaty." Roberts protested.

"Do you think that will stop a Chinaman from heaving a torch through the window?"

The clerk's naiveté was annoying. The local Chinese were seething with rage at the shame inflicted on them by the British. Every morning there were fresh broadsides glued to the walls, calling for revenge. Kee Chong had translated some of them for George.

The two men walked across the esplanade toward the waterfront, stepping aside to allow a troop of turbaned sailors—Indian lascars—to swagger past and turn into Hog Lane. George's eyes warily followed the men into the filthy alley. Their insolence would only be aggravated by the sham-shu (rice wine) they would soon be swilling. "There's a surly lot."

"Well, the Emperor's not in very good temper, either." Roberts offered, with a slight smirk. "Do you think that Jamaica ginger will help?"

"Perhaps," George grinned. He, too, had read the story in the *Canton Press* about the order from Pekin for Oxleys' Concentrated Essence of Jamaica Ginger. It was rumored that His Imperial Majesty "had got wind" in the belly. He added, "It would be better not to fill his order—much better, indeed, to have his Imperial Majesty 'making wind' in Pekin than fomenting it here in Canton."

"Perhaps it is better to keep the Emperor busy in Pekin—but he's unlikely to have any silver left to pay for his ginger. Of course," he added slyly, "if Mr. Coolidge should choose to make an advance to the Emperor ..."

"Now, now, Mr. Roberts." Even though it was cheeky of young Roberts to raise the topic, George savored the picture of the Emperor in an empty treasury, stifling his flatulence while petitioning Coolidge for a letter of credit.

Coolidge's sudden wealth had indeed become an awkward subject of gossip. After the Heard factory burned, Coolidge submitted a list of his *personal* losses—more than $10,000, plus a $10,000 surcharge for inconvenience. The claim was so grossly inflated that when the *Canton Press* published the sum, the entire foreign community was outraged. To everyone's disgust, the entire claim had been extracted from their closest Chinese colleagues, the Hong merchants—including Footae

George glanced at his pale-complexioned companion. During the past year he had supervised both Roberts and young John Heard as they reconstructed the company ledgers. There were few errors in Roberts's addition and subtraction or in his calculations of exchange rates for sycee silver ingots, Mexican dollars, and the older Spanish dollars for which the tradition-bound Chinese paid a premium. Roberts had proved himself a reliable subordinate. But the qualities commendable in a clerk were not exactly those desirable in a partner, and George wondered if the young man had the initiative to seek out opportunity and parlay advantage for himself, and, of course, for the firm as well.

John had shown equal competence in arithmetic. But where Roberts had immersed himself in the immediate tasks, John studied the broader structure of the trade. Now John coordinated the firm's shipping, dispatching thousands of tons of tea bound for England and America, but Roberts seemed to have achieved little perspective beyond the ledgers.

George surveyed the riverfront enclave reserved for foreign merchants. Near the far end stood the Dutch Hong—six buildings crowded one behind the next in a narrow strip going back from the waterfront.

The Heard firm occupied Number 1, the front building with the covered veranda. The English Hong with its much larger veranda was just this side of it, abutting Hog Lane. The tower of its newly rebuilt chapel jutted above the roofline. To the right of the Heard factory stood the Creek Hong, named for the fetid, sewage-clogged stream on its right, which marked the eastern end of the enclave. Across the creek, just beyond the Creek Hong, were the warehouse-like "go-downs"—belonging to Howqua,

Mowqua, Footae, and the other Hong merchants—in which they temporarily stored finished goods.

Now that system was about to end. George pursed his lips. Mr. Heard's continued unwillingness to discuss the consequences of the changing situation irked him. The flagpoles of all the foreign companies were bare now, but that would change when word arrived that the Queen and her ministers had approved the treaty.

Loud voices erupted from Hog Lane. A Chinese merchant in a pale blue tunic leaned across his counter, screaming at a lascar in a new straw hat. Roberts pointed. "I think that Hindoo stole something," he shouted over the commotion.

The lascar grinned insolently, waving an orange. The merchant spat a wet dip of snuff at him. The lascar looked down at the brown stain on his pants. Holding the orange high, he took aim and heaved it into the shelves of liquor bottles at the back of the shop. With a tremendous clatter, the wall of bottles crashed to the ground. The sailor's companions tried to restrain him as he lunged forward across the counter, sweeping the merchant's abacus, teapot, and cup aside. A Chinese porter, wielding a bamboo pole, struck the lascar across the back. Another sailor grabbed the porter's queue and yanked him to the ground.

Spectators crowded around, and George and Roberts were jostled aside as the alley suddenly filled with screaming Chinese. The lascars were trapped against the wall across from the shop. A brickbat crashed above their heads and a second.

"*Teeng ah!*" George shouted in Chinese. "Halt!" he repeated.

The crowd turned toward the strange, authoritative voice. George stepped forward, shouting at the Indians in Hindustani. "*Niklo uhanse!* Get out of there!" Clutching the trinkets they had purchased, the panicked lascars backed out of the alley in a cluster.

George's heart beat faster. Quickly he scanned the riverfront for a chop boat on which they could escape. There was none. A brick crashed to the ground in front of him and another. "*Mujhe karo!* Come with me," he ordered, pushing a lascar ahead of him. Another followed, blood streaming down his face, then the rest. Roberts huddled close behind him, covering his head with his arms.

A Chinese leapt atop a barrel. "*Fan ah! Yang koei ah! Sha! Sha!*" His voice sounded above all the others. George understood the words: "Barbarians! Foreign devils! Kill! Kill!"

This had gone beyond a fight over a stolen orange. It was Chinese vengeance against all foreigners. A hail of stones fell around them. A sharp pain seared George's ear as a cobble grazed it. He turned back to see the mob moving toward them. A man in front waved a knife.

The Creek Hong was vacant. It might be unlocked. George sprinted forward, Roberts and the lascars close behind. He pulled at the door and it opened, allowing the lascars to crowd inside. With a crash from above, glass rained down from a second-story window. For a moment, the Chinese seemed frozen at the sight of the jagged opening.

Seizing the instant, George turned and ran out, back to the Heard factory. He pounded on the door. "It's Dixwell!" he bellowed. The door coolies slid back the deadbolt. Rushing inside, George turned to find the ashen-faced Roberts just behind him. He had forgotten the clerk. "Roberts!" he shouted. "Run to Footae's—Get Mr. Heard—Take the pistols!"

9:00 pm

Acrid black smoke billowed from the muzzle of Augustine's musket and burned George's nostrils. Shrieks and shouts filled the air, rising in volume. Another volley of bricks and cobbles shook the wall. George steeled himself for the next assault. The mob pried loose the last bar from the window, and now an angry Chinese face appeared in the gaping opening—followed by the man's shoulders as he wriggled, fishlike, into the room.

George froze and shouted, "Mr. Heard!"

Augustine Heard emerged from the hallway brandishing a fresh musket. George braced himself for the explosion, but he lowered the musket. Waving back the house servants, he pulled a handkerchief from his breast pocket and draped it over the gun's muzzle. Gripping the barrel with both hands, he let it swing for a moment. In one smooth motion, he raised the weapon high over his head like an axe and plunged the wooden stock down on the back of the intruder's skull. George stared in horror, holding down nausea.

Augustine Heard's voice was grim. "We don't have powder to waste. Check the gate!"

He gestured toward Thirteen Factory Street and handed George the musket. George rushed down the covered passageway and stepped out into the uncovered alley leading to the gate. A hot blast of air struck his perspiring forehead. House servants were pushing against the massive wooden gate, bracing it against the heavy blows from the other side. Shadows flickered across their white jackets.

Flames like serpent tongues licked from beneath the eaves of the English factory. The sky glowed a pale orange. George took a deep breath and pulled back the hammer of the flintlock until it clicked. For a moment, he stared at the creamy flint flake clenched in the hammer's vice-like grip. Could he actually kill a man? A massive thud shook the gate.

"Mistah Dik-wah!" Behind him, George's houseboy, Ah Ten, motioned him back.

Another blow struck the gate. With a loud splintering of wood, it swung open. Rioters streamed in, clogging the passage. George raised his musket. No one should ever be able to say that George Basil Dixwell was a lesser man than Augustine Heard. The men in front seemed surprised to have broken through the gate—and shocked to be facing a musket. They tried to back away, but the mob behind pushed them forward.

George raised the musket to his shoulder. He aimed at the blue sash around the waist of the man in the center of the advancing line and squeezed the trigger. The explosion momentarily deafened him as the gun's recoil threw him backwards. The blast lit up the narrow passage, and the mob pulled away slowly, like a riverboat changing course.

Ah Ten handed George another loaded musket. "Mistah Dik-wah, Chinee barefoot. Break bottle!"

George waved the musket back and forth, taking aim at any man who stepped forward. "Get the bottles—fast!"

The kitchen boy emerged from the house, dragging a gunnysack. George reached in, grabbed an ale bottle by its neck and hurled it against the wall just beyond the gate. The rioters backed away.

George stepped through the gate, his musket leveled. The man he shot lay writhing on the ground on his side, clutching his stomach. There was a splotch of red above the man's kidney where the lead ball had passed through his body. George looked away. Heard Company servants rushed past him, smashing bottles against the cobble pavement.

George retreated through the shattered gate. Suddenly, the passage exploded with light. He looked up. The belfry atop the British Hong flared like a torch. From the other side, fire leapt from the upper windows of the Creek Hong. George hurried back into the Heard factory. "Top side on fire!"

Ah Ten ran down the stairs, coughing. Two houseboys followed, clutching empty buckets. The mob had built a fire against the front door, and the boys had poured down as many buckets of water as they could from the second-story veranda.

Augustine Heard stood guard beside the gaping hole of the window. Splashes of blood, trailed crimson down the wall from the sill. George wondered why he was continuing such a resolute stand against the rioters when fire now threatened to engulf them, not only from both sides but also from the front door, where the Chinese had set yet another blaze.

All the company ledgers had been sent out to a tea boat hours ago. All that remained inside were the house furnishings, their personal belongings, and the company treasury. The stone vault with its iron door contained $500,000 in silver, stacked in bags of $1,000 each. There was no way to transport those tons of silver through the mob and even less hope now! The only thing left, was to save their own lives, so why was Mr. Heard delaying? Thick black smoke drifted down the stairwell.

George felt his side pocket for the packet of letters Ah Ten had brought down from his room. He felt for his watch. No, it was upstairs on his bed stand.

Mr. Heard peered out the window, aimed, fired, then stepped aside, awaiting the inevitable return barrage of bricks. "We'll wait a little longer," he said, "till we're in full flame. Now, take our pikemen to the rear entrance. Two in front and two in back. No more firing. I want every musket and pistol fully charged."

The pikemen moved into position. The Heard Company men formed a smaller cluster between them. The guards waved their pikes—actually oars, with their blade ends hatcheted to jagged points. The old man had indeed thought of everything

"What about the vault?" George glanced toward the iron door.

Heard smiled grimly. "They'll fry before they get it open. And it'll stay red hot till morning."

George was astonished. While the rest of them were worrying about saving the building, their senior partner had already resolved to let it burn.

J.J. had often repeated stories about Augustine Heard's glacial calm in the face of danger —how when his ship was intercepted by a pirate schooner, he had lowered his ensign in apparent surrender, gently eased his vessel—still under full sail—toward the pirate, and then, suddenly, cranked his rudder to full port, crushing the schooner under his massive hull. As J.J. had told it, only the mast of the pirate vessel remained above water as Heard resumed his course towards Canton.

"Forward!" Mr. Heard shouted.

Ahead, the street was blocked by the enraged mob. Heard stepped forward, raising his musket to his shoulder slowly for maximum effect. The roiling crowd moved back to a safe distance beyond the reach of the leveled pikes.

George surveyed the 200-yard passage to Footae Hong. There seemed to be no way they could get through. Augustine aimed at the crowd and fired. The thunder of the musket echoed down the street. The Chinese shrieked and cowered back against the walls.

George handed Heard a fresh musket. "Move!" Heard ordered, and the company group started at a trot, the pikemen striding ahead, screaming at the crowd, and jabbing at anyone in their path. As they passed the Creek Hong, the gate opened, and the lascars came sprinting toward them. The first of them pushed past George to the safety of the pikemen.

George slowed. He swept his pistol back and forth, protecting the lascars' flank. The door to Footae Hong swung open. They were safe! From behind, a scream pierced through the noise of the mob. George turned to see the last lascar fall from view as the mob closed round him. [1]

§

Dear George—

I have nothing very special to communicate, and, as like as not if whim takes me I shall be prosy. You and I think and act differently, as if we were not branches from the same tree—members of the same family. Perhaps you have chosen the wisest course—perhaps not. I am not sufficiently acquainted with you to be accurate, but sometimes I think you are dreadfully shackled with fashionable society: fearful of not keeping a distinguished ... halo in the said class; willing to sacrifice health and life— anything but honor ... [to] live in a certain style, termed gentlemanly and aristocratic; to hold your head very high and look down on the canaille; fearful of an associate whose coat is not of a particularly fashionable cut—[or] of visiting except at a house lofty and well-servanted, whose doors are never opened but at conventional hours.

Is this so? Have I misjudged you? Are you manly and independent— not asking or wanting reflected lustre? ... Look at the picture and tell me it is a likeness of my dear George? What is your great object in life? Is it one that meets your approbation in your deep and solemn communication before God? I hope it is.

... I hope you will not go to smuggling opium. It would seem to me much like ... holding light to iniquity. I do not know that the design ever entered the mind of you or your partners. Pray do not be affronted with me for admitting the possibility. Many ease their consciences, similarly situated, by thinking that they may as well reap the benefit as another—and if they do not do it, others will. If this argument is sufficient for any wrong doing, it will serve in all cases. Why may I not rob another? If I do not, another will. Why may not I enslave a brother? If I do not, another will. Why may not I get drunk? Others do it without losing caste. Why should I ... ?—All sophistry—Touch not, taste not, handle not. Refrain from even the least semblance of evil ...

Your letter—Thank you kindly for it. I like it better because it is evidently unstudied, of course sincere. Thro' it I think I can look into your heart ... Now, although I am grateful for your letter and like its off hand sincerity, in itself I did not like the letter.

In this letter allow me to say you have trifled with the wrongs and sufferings of down trodden humanity ... Were you in cruel bondage under the lash of a task master would you respect the man calling himself a Christian who would not voluntarily espouse your cause, but avowed himself ready to do it for hire?—and this from my high minded nephew!!

Now, the Abolitionists have been cruelly taught many a useful lesson— and if I were to propose to them to send to you for shiploads of sugar— granting for the sake of argument they were able—and you guaranteeing to "Kick up a dust about the poor darkeys," they would reply to me, they never had an agent on similar terms ... who would not take a higher bribe from the slave holder to abandon or betray the cause? I have great pleasure in saying that altho' I should admire to have you stand with me in this cause, shoulder to shoulder, yet the cause has taken such a deep root, is so manifesting the evidences of a rich harvest, that I think you can be spared.

I do not like your sentiments "my good Nephew" ... You advocate gradualism. I hold to the true Christian doctrine—<u>NOW</u> is the time— Now is the day of Salvation. What would any sinner ask, but a reprieve— ... a further indulgence, more time. Is this other than betraying the citadel to the enemy? What has Henry Clay and all the host of slave holders ever required, but gradual emancipation? Grant them that, and they will join with you in deploring the evils of slavery.

I was <u>sorry</u>—Truly <u>sorry</u>—that you were about aiding these wretched sinners by opening a market for their bloodstained harvests of cotton among the Chinese. How singular it is, that while a large body of men are endeavouring to drive the slave holder to justice and mercy by persuading England to raise her own cotton in the vast fertile plains of India, where labor is abundant and cheaper far than slave labor—a plan is devised immediately to again rivet ... the chains of the poor slave by way of introducing, not merely the manufactured goods, but the raw material, fresh from New Orleans.

I am pleased with the idea that perhaps this abomination may be stopped the 23d day of April next—the day that has been adjudged as the one fixed and prophesied of—as the point of time when the world will come to an end!! ...

If this be true, what a pity it is you took your long voyage and left friends and country in quest of lucre when you might have remained at home, and have gone to parties, and ate ice creams and waltzed—and gone to lectures, and attended the great Box dinner.

I have no faith that it will be so—but I have no objection—for otherwise I should be delighted. [For] the thousand years you kindly pray Catharine and I may live, will then commence. And, as I believe, we are in the true faith, wholly trusting in Christ ... we may reign with him.

May such be your blest position prays your ... well wishing and affectionate

Aunt Henrietta Sargent

Aboard the *Frolic*
Macao, China
1845, June 15

"Why stow the cannon so far aft?" George addressed the *Frolic*'s captain, as he ran his hand along the rusty iron muzzle tied beneath the starboard rail. It felt warm in the noonday sun. It seemed a little strange to tour the actual vessel he had only been imagining when he had first sent the specifications to J.J.

"I moved them both aft before we cleared the Chesapeake." Captain Faucon pointed to the other cannon tied beneath the port rail. The short, wiry man tilted his hand, to show the angle of the vessel's hull as if balanced on a fulcrum. "All that weight forward under press of sail had her rudder near out of the water. Of course, if we'd been carrying a cargo—"

"You're right about that," George interrupted Faucon's peevish comment. It irked him, too, that J.J. had dispatched the clipper brig halfway around the world from Baltimore to Bombay, virtually empty except for her rock ballast. Faucon had reason to be concerned. He had purchased a one-fifth interest in the vessel, and he needed to earn his share of freight fees in order to pay off the loan.

Nevertheless, J.J. had done well to hire the best-known captain in New England—best known, at least, to those who had read Richard Henry Dana, Jr.'s, *Two Years Before the Mast*. Faucon's reputation was sure to enhance the Heard Company's prestige among the English and American firms in China.

As George moved along the rail, he admired the *Frolic*'s sleek lines. Even at rest, her massive raked-back masts gave the feeling of movement. He ran his toe across the triple row of shiny glass blocks set down into the deck. "Now, these are an innovation!"

"I had them installed in Baltimore," explained Faucon with some pride. "They're prismatic on the bottom, to spread out the light so the men can read the labels without lanterns."

Looking down through the glass blocks, George could see shadowy forms moving toward the open hatch. The captain's men were lifting burlap-covered chests out of the hold up to the deck and over the rail to the chop boat alongside.

"Keep the labels forward and the numbers consecutive," Faucon called to his second officer aboard the Chinese vessel. A broad stack of identical chests extended the full length of its deck. "Take those ashore—there'll be one more load."

The Chinese threw loose the mooring lines, dipped their oars, and began the quarter-mile pull toward the broad promenade of Praya Grande. The gentle arc of red tile roofs and arched windows and doorways seemed to cradle the pale green waters of the shallow harbor. George inhaled the rich odor of wood smoke. It reminded him of sandalwood. With what aromatic species had Faucon restocked his woodbin in Singapore? He turned to look toward shore. The chop boat was approaching the yellow sand beach.

Faucon nodded toward the tall, young man standing just forward of the hatch beside the iron stove. "I think your Mr. Endicott is about ready to start his testing. It looks like he's brought his own pots to cook the drug in."

It was truly serendipitous that the waterfront house on Praya Grande that George had rented two months ago, in order to escape Canton's summer heat, had come with an attached warehouse. No one could have anticipated that the British Consul would order the opium station out of Whampoa. In the resulting period of uncertainty, he would be able to bring the *Frolic*'s first cargo of Malwa opium almost to his door. The foreign merchants had already reestablished their storage vessels at Cumsingmun Anchorage, 12 miles north of Macao. That was sufficiently remote from official eyes to allow business to resume without interference. With that development, it was clear the Heard firm needed its own station vessel there as well from which the *Frolic*'s future cargoes could be sold—

"I'll need to cut more ports for ventilation. She's like a furnace in the tropics." Faucon's voice intruded on George's thoughts as he pointed to a tiny brassbound window into the cabin.

George nodded, absently, still working out his plans. The *Frolic*'s future cargoes would go directly to a receiving vessel at Cumsingmun, and he had just purchased the *Snipe* for that purpose. He needed an experienced man, who was familiar with all the dodges of the drug business to serve as her master. James B. Endicott, captain of Russell and Co.'s opium-receiving vessel, recommended his much younger brother, William, only 22 years old. George invited young Endicott aboard to evaluate his competency as an opium inspector. Of course, the cargo had already been inspected before being loaded at Bombay, but George wanted to see Endicott demonstrate his ability.

Faucon paused to lean against the hatch cover tilted up against the main mast. "Well, I think I've shown you the whole of the vessel. I do think she'll serve us well."

"I agree—and I thank you, Captain, for the tour," said George, bowing slightly.

"I think you were quite right to have the brig's bow built sharper. The added speed is well worth the loss of cargo capacity."

Two years ago, when J.J. sent him the wooden half-model of the proposed hull, George had whittled and sanded it even sharper.

The compliment was also a gentle reminder that Faucon just completed the year's fastest passage from Bombay to Macao, making better time—34 days—than any vessel in the entire opium fleet, beating out venerable captains who had plied the route for over a decade.

"Captain," George smiled, "your record time will provide the best possible advertisement for the brig. Every shipper will remember her name!"

William waved from the stove. "I'm ready, Mr. Dixwell! Select a chest, and I'll show you how I go about an inspection."

"How about that one?" George pointed to a chest lying beside the open hatch. "Over here!" he instructed the sailor.

William took a knife from his pocket, slit the burlap wrapping, and pulled the chest from its covering. Taking a small crowbar from his satchel, he pried loose the lid and brushed back the poppy-leaf packing. "You select the cake!"

George pointed to a fist-size cake lying at the top. He was already impressed by the young man's efficiency. William blew off the dried poppy leaves and turned the cake over in his hand. He shook his head. "This is *not* Number One drug," he said, handing it to George. "It's soft, it's moldy, it's misshapen—and if a Chinese broker spots it, he'll discount every cake in the box."

"But it *all* passed as Number One in Bombay—." George stopped himself before he revealed any more of his inexperience.

William laughed, "That's beside the point! Those inspectors work for the Indians. You've got to have your own man down there to check every single chest consigned to you before you take any of it aboard."

George stared at the misshapen lump. Unlike Patna opium, which was processed and guaranteed by the British East India Company, Malwa opium was produced by independent, unsupervised upland merchants, and it carried no guarantees. William was right. He had foolishly given the Indians the upper hand, and they would demand Number One prices for their drug, regardless of its actual grade. George pursed his lips and pitched the cake back into the chest.

William bent down to select a larger cake. Retrieving the knife from his side pocket, he cut a thin slice from its edge. "It's not enough just to look at the outside. Notice the rubbery skin? They've mixed-in some kind of gum." He took a sniff and winced, "Fish oil!"

George examined the slice. It looked like brown cream cheese. He held it to his nose and inhaled the putrid odor of rotten fish. William took back the sticky slice. "That's why you need *your own* inspector in Bombay! When the drug arrives up here, every Chinese broker will make you test it all over again. They'll pull every misshapen cake from the chest. Here, this is how we test it."

William took a small, narrow-mouthed brass pot and a spoon from his case and scooped a small dollop of the oily paste from the slice. Standing the spoon in the pot, he filled it with boiling water from the stove, then stirred vigorously with the spoon. "See how quickly it dissolves? Now, we pass it through the filter." He cupped a small square of cheesecloth into a funnel, slipped the funnel into the mouth of a second pot, and poured in the steaming liquid. George watched the brown fluid pass down through the gauzy fabric.

William peeled loose the encrusted cloth from the funnel and handed it to George who peered at the thick patch of greasy sludge. "What's this?"

"Well, a chest of Malwa opium is supposed to weigh 133 pounds net, so this might be anything the Indians decided to mix in to add to the weight. They have quite an inventory—mud, manure, vegetable gum, fish oil —" He paused, "And this particular cake doesn't even pass for Number Two."

George was speechless. Endicott pointed to the liquid that had passed through the filter. "And we haven't yet boiled down the filtrate. Your Chinese will expect a cup of tea while you boil that down to a paste, so that his man can smoke just enough of it to impugn its fragrance. Then, after drinking another cup, he'll haggle. He'll demand a discount for impurity. Then, he'll say the smoke was only of mediocre potency, and then—"

"Yes, I see." It was time for George to bring up the point of this exercise.

"Mr. Endicott," he cleared his throat. "You appear to be fully proficient in this business, and, as you know, we have just bought the *Snipe* for a station vessel. Will you be satisfied with her and willing to serve as her captain and supercargo?"

"Yes sir, completely. And, in the meantime, I can pull every bad cake from this batch. If you discount them here, they'll sell fast—without testing. And every chest I take aboard the *Snipe* will bring top price."

Faucon stepped from the cabin, a ledger sheet in his hand. He laid the sheet across the top of an up-ended chest and ran his finger down the columns. "Excuse me, gentlemen, the chop boat's ready for the remaining chests. We loaded 647 chests in Bombay, each paying $6 dollars freight. Of the 437 chests consigned to you, I've delivered 187 here. I transferred the remaining 250 onto the *Dart*, and they're off to Shanghai. We still have 105 chests aboard—all of which I'll be delivering to your brother. If this breeze holds, I should be at Cumsingmun by dinnertime."

"You'd best wait until *after* dinner," William winked. "My brother holds that ritual to be practically sacred."

George smiled at the young man's wry humor. The elder Endicott brother—all 300 pounds of him—was a man of voracious appetites, and food was but one of them.

George turned to Faucon, pleased with his sense of detail. "Next time up, we should have a full hold of Bombay drug—thanks to your fast passage."

"It may be the passage," Faucon stroked his thick, black beard, "but I think the Hindoos' share in the vessel will motivate them somewhat more than her speed—and we'll all benefit from that."

"Yes, we'll *all* share in her success."

George watched William adjust the lid on the open chest before nailing it into place. The Hindoos had purchased a two-fifths interest—which meant that the Heard firm controlled one of the fastest clippers in the business for an investment of only $8,000 dollars of company capital.

George turned to Faucon. "By the way, Captain, I want you to be the first to know that Mr. Endicott will be joining us as Master of the *Snipe*."

"Congratulations, and welcome to the fleet!"

William bowed slightly. "I look forward to your return. We'll have much to chat about."

Faucon squinted, looking upward at the top of the main mast, where the Heard company's red-white diamond flag flapped vigorously.

"If that breeze holds, and we get underway, we'll be alongside your brother well *before* his dinner! We've got everything out and aboard the chop boat." Faucon turned to his first officer, "Have the men drop the hatch cover."

George and William stepped back as sailors rocked the heavy wooden lid back and forth toward the opening. They tilted it forward and dropped it into place. Faucon nodded his approval and waved for the officer to join him at the helm.

William waited until Faucon was out of hearing before speaking to George. "At $6 a chest, he'll work hard to keep her filled. And if he runs her economically, he'll pay her off in a couple of years. But he only cares about filling her hold with as many chests as possible, paying $6 each—and that's not where our profits come from."

George's whole purpose in building the *Frolic* was to attract consignments for the firm to sell for a commission.

"I'm sure my brother will be most pleased when Faucon offloads those 105 chests," William continued, "but when he reads the freight list and sees that the Hindoos consigned the rest to you, he'll know that's a test—whoever gets the best price this time will get the larger consignment from them next time."

"Yes, and *that* is where the money is," said George. "Six dollars freight per chest may be enough to keep the vessel running, but a 2% commission on every $800 chest yields $16 profit on each—so those 105 chests represent lost profits of $1,700!"

Endicott nodded in agreement and pointed upward. The sailors were ascending the main mast shrouds. "Looks like it's time to get ashore."

The poor-quality opium was a disappointment, but George had learned from his mistake. Really, everything was working out according to his plan. He pictured the map of India and China with brigs and schooners flying the red-white diamond flag, coursing all the waters between them. The *Frolic* would sail from Bombay to China, offloading half her cargo onto the *Snipe* at Cumsingmun and the other half onto the *Dart* to run up the coast. He imagined the *Dart* stopping to sell drugs at every estuary and harbor, finally offloading what remained onto the *Don Juan* at Woosung Harbor, only a few miles from Shanghai. He had duplicated Jardine, Matheson & Co.'s opium strategy, and the Heard firm was now perfectly situated to barter Indian drug for enough Chinese tea and silk to supply all its American clients.

William walked to the rail and gestured for the Tanka boat woman to scull her sampan toward the clipper's rear ladder. He pushed his satchel under the bench and sat beside George. The boat woman's daughter pushed the little vessel away from the *Frolic*, and the mother began to work the oar. George looked back. The *Frolic*'s swept-back lines reminded him of a greyhound. The mainsail billowed as she moved forward, gathering speed.

"Isn't she a beauty!" William broke the silence.

"Yes, she is," George shook his head, "though Faucon thinks she's over-sparred for her weight."

"Not the boat." William laughed. "I mean the girl!"

George turned to glimpse the girl's bare leg as she knelt to tie down the scrap of canvas that served as a doorway to the tiny mat-covered cabin. The girl's mother held a monopoly on this section of waterfront just below his house, ferrying merchants out to boats anchored in the harbor, and for months, without quite admitting it to himself, George had been watching the daughter—and the gentle curve of her bosom. "Yes," he cleared his throat. "She's a beauty, too."

William smiled slyly, "Well, if you need a *housekeeper*, they're worth every cent. My brother James will testify to that, but you'll need to save your pennies. He tells me some Englishman has offered $500 for this one, but her mama's holding out for more."

"More than five hundred?" George waited for William to say more. In his most private thoughts, he had imagined intimate moments with an Asian woman. He glanced toward the small rise behind his house, where, only a short walk beyond, James had rented a house, hired servants, and, seemingly without embarrassment, established a household with a Tanka woman, Ng Akew.

"Are you staying with your brother?" he asked Endicott.

Endicott rolled his eyes upward. "Yes, and with two screaming babies. He's named the new one James Bridges after himself—at least for part of himself."

George joined in William's laughter. James had taken care not to compromise the Endicott surname, giving both of his little Eurasian sons the Bridges surname of his mother instead.

William continued, "And James is looking after Hunter's woman and her brood as well, until he returns from the States."

George had visited William Hunter's house, just a few blocks beyond James Endicott's, where the older man, recently retired from Russell and Co., had instructed George in reading Chinese characters. Anna Rosa, his precocious 5-year-old, would climb onto his lap and correct George's pronunciation. In Macao, where there were so many mixed-blooded children of Portuguese, Dutch, English, Tanka, and Chinese parentage in every possible fraction, any union seemed possible.

The sampan slid to a stop on the sandy bottom, and the girl, clutching her trousers above her knees, pulled its bow up onto the beach. George waited as William stepped ashore. He took a silver dollar from his pocket, handed it to the girl, and followed William up the steps to the roadway. The Chinese man he had hired to guard the warehouse scrambled to his feet. George gave the errant watchman a curt nod.

William returned to their conversation. "Word has it that Hunter's bringing back an American wife."

George wondered if Hunter had told the American woman about his Chinese household. "How in the world will he work that out?"

"It should work out just fine." William waved to two porters lounging beside their palanquin. "He'll set up a nice house in Canton for his three little ones and their mother. And, by Chinese standards, she's still wife number one. Maybe she'll even feel sorry for his new concubine. And he'll keep number two here."

The porters lowered the sedan chair to the ground. William placed his satchel on the floor and slid into the black lacquered seat. "I'll send over a stove and get started in the morning." The men lifted the carrying rails to their shoulders, and William waved as they turned the corner to ascend the hill.

The George Dixwell Home
Praya Grande, Macao

George leaned back in the wicker chair and reread the note from John Heard. His junior partner had a return cargo ready for Faucon: 8 tons of silver bullion, worth more than $270,000. He must send a note to Cumsingmun instructing Faucon to proceed to Whampoa. Taking the telescope from the table, he walked to the edge of the balcony and focused the glass on a small schooner rounding the point. A favorable gust revealed her Portuguese flag.

He pointed the telescope lower, to the beach, and focused on the girl in the sampan. She was laughing at something her mother had said. He imagined her smiling at him, beckoning. Forcing his eyes away, he returned the telescope to the table. Upstairs were his letters from Mother and Aunt Henrietta, tied in a packet, and now a few of Mother's choice phrases echoed in his mind. "Dear George, I have a promise, given under your hand, that you would not become a dissipated man of the world ... I beg you for my sake to keep a guard on the purity and simplicity of your early training ... for I assure you wealth would not compensate for the loss." How in the world could he have signed such a promise? Here in China, Mother's entreaties and Aunt Henrietta's endless admonitions seemed quaint and irrelevant.

Less than a year later, George traveled to Shanghai to open the Heard company's first branch headquarters. He purchased a building, hired staff, and remained there until the office was in full operation. We do not have any of George's letters to Henrietta, but it seems that he not only disagreed with her political views but also did so in a flippant and dismissive manner. Henrietta's replies express her disappointment, defiance, and barely suppressed anger. It was clear to her now that George had passed over a moral divide to embrace values contrary to her own.[2]

March 20, 1846

My dear Nephew,

What news shall I tell you? You make fun—you know you do—at my politics and my love of reforms. Well, you are welcome to make fun of me, or at me, if you will let it be good-natured fun—not bitter or sarcastic. You may laud our present government—if you like the institution that I dare not name. Very well. They want lauding. You may admire the Whigs and think them a glorious band of patriots. Very well. Admire them if you like, but I despise their sycophanting, their turncoat propensity, their subservience. They would sell their country as Esau did his birthright

Now, [I suppose] when you come home, I shall never hear your sentiments on church or state. In the first place, you will say I have ultra, wrong notions of men and measures, and, therefore, you will not take the trouble to enlighten me. Then, what should a woman know or care about such things. She has not (in our country) to vote, or hold office—let her mind on her knitting.

So, George, I am not going to write about wars or rumors of wars, of mad Presidents or truckling statesmen, of clergymen—blind leaders of the blind, dumb dogs that will not bark. No, I abjure such writing. In future my letters will be strictly feminine. "Let the shoemaker stick to his last."

Now you will say I am sensible, very clear, doing at last what I always ought to have done. But I do not profess to be altered in the least—only to have resolved not to intrude my opinions. It is hard holding in, tho', I confess ...

I anticipate your return before this time next year. Life is too short for you to remain longer absent.

Farewell, ever yours

Henrietta[3]

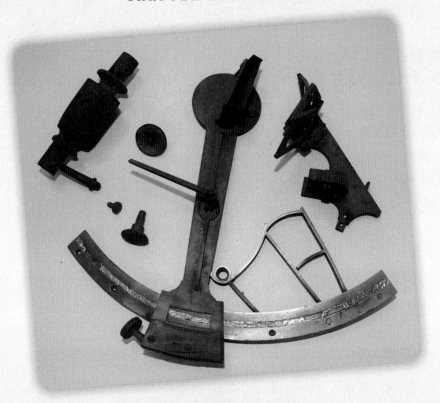

Captain Faucon's sextant, portrayed here beside an identical heirloom sextant.
(Original donated by Patrick Gibson; replicate from author collection.)

Leather shoe, recovered embedded in a concretion together with a cannon-ready charge of grapeshot (iron pellets packed around a wooden spindle in a cloth bag). Opium clippers were lucrative targets for pirates. The Frolic was armed for self-defense. (Donated by David Buller; photo courtesy of the Kelley House Museum.)

Prismatic deck light (length of fragment 13 cm) recovered from the *Frolic*. During the *Frolic's* construction, rows of prismatic glass blocks were set into her deck to diffract sufficient sunlight into her hold, allowing the markings on cargo containers to be read. (Donated by Bruce Lanham; photo by author.)

Although the *Frolic* shipwreck was discovered and pillaged by sport divers during the mid-1970s, most of them subsequently donated their collections to the *Frolic* repository at the Mendocino County Museum in Willits, California. Since most of those artifacts were heavily damaged, I attempted to locate and purchase identical heirloom pieces that could be exhibited next to the fragmented originals. Now, with the publication of this volume, those heirloom pieces will join their "cousins" in the *Frolic* repository.

Frolic's lift model (half-model). The model was sent to China for George Dixwell's approval. The lines were then taken from the lifts and chalked onto a platform, from which the frames were assembled. (Drawing by Sam Manning.)

Loading opium aboard the *Frolic*, Bombay, India, 1845. Two versions of this drawing show how my approach to illustrations has matured. For my 1997 volume, I rejected the deck scene collage in the second drawing as too artsy. I have now embraced Manning's imaginative approach—just as I hope readers will embrace my own. (Drawing by Sam Manning, author collection.)

The *Frolic* under sail. The Augustine Heard & Co "red-white diamond" flag flying from her main mast. (Drawing by Sam Manning.)

After over 150 years of steady battering by North Pacific waves, there was very little left intact of the *Frolic*, beyond her cannons, anchors, windlass, and cast-iron ballast blocks. A search of the Heard firm's archive produced an itemized account, listing the costs for each step of her construction and outfitting. I knew that, as a classic Baltimore clipper, a full description of the vessel would be important both to marine historians and to history buffs who would later visit her wreck site at Point Cabrillo. I also understood that my task an archaeologist and as a writer was to attempt to put the pieces back together. The best way to accomplish that was to provide a detailed description of how she had been constructed, and for this I would need professional help.

I located marine historian John Goldsborough Earle (1901–1992) in Easton, Maryland, provided him with the itemized listing from the Heard archive, and tape-recorded his detailed interpretation of how the *Frolic* was constructed.

Hoping to tell a more complete visual story, I contacted Sam Manning, a marine artist in Camden, Maine, whose artwork I had seen in other books. I gave Manning the Heard firm's itemized account, together with Earle's narrative, an 1840s map of the Fells Point district of Baltimore, and an 1850s photo of an actual Baltimore shipyard. Then I asked him to illustrate the major steps of the Frolic's construction. Together, Manning and I began to document the life of the *Frolic*—a process that required uncounted draft illustrations, each one corrected to better reach some approximation of truth. In an artist's hands and mind, the illustrations became another tool for me to re-imagine the past. Discussions with Manning, on how to fill-in the peripheral blanks on the canvas led me investigate the broader context of the *Frolic*'s life.

CHAPTER FIVE
High Fashion

When George Dixwell left China and his position with the Augustine Heard & Company in 1847, the company papers and correspondence no longer had any reason to refer to him. I lost my most important source of information. I knew that during the next few years George's ambition would gain him both increased wealth and social position—along with arrogance—but I had almost no primary documents for these years. Henrietta had no need to write him long, detailed letters when he was close by in Boston, and none of the letters she may have written him in London, Paris, New York, or California have survived.

Then, George's great-granddaughter Marcia Dixwell DiMambro came to visit me. For several months, I had been corresponding with Marcia, a nurse living in New Hampshire. She told me she was coming to see the *Frolic* shipwreck exhibit that I had helped stage at the Maritime Museum in San Francisco. As she later revealed, the real reason for her trip was to meet me in person and ascertain whether I was trustworthy enough for her to help me in my study of her family.

When Marcia arrived at the San Francisco airport, she was carrying a backpack. That evening, on the other side of the Bay, we barbecued a salmon at my sister's hillside home and watched the San Francisco skyline disappear into the sunset and reappear as a lattice of lights. My 82-year-old father pointed toward the narrow strait connecting the Bay to the Pacific Ocean and confided to Marcia, in his own inimitable way, that had the *Frolic* made it through that passage—over which the lights on the cables of the Golden Gate Bridge now glittered like a diamond necklace—there would have been no *Frolic* Shipwreck Project, "and Tom would still be measuring arrowheads from some hole in Mendocino County."

The next morning, as we finished breakfast, Marcia opened her backpack and laid a stack of leather-bound volumes on the table. "I think these will help you," she said.

I opened the top volume. It was George's diary for the year 1848. Each 8- by 14-inch page displayed one week's calendar with six dated spaces for Monday through Saturday. The Boston stationer had enforced the Sabbath day of rest by eliminating any space for Sunday appointments. Each diary volume comprised a full calendar year, and George had written an entry in every space—even dividing each Saturday rectangle to record his defiantly secular Sunday activities.

The diaries told a far fuller story than that conveyed in the Heard Company letters. While the latter contained lengthy discussions of the minutiae of the firm's business, George's diaries provided not only a virtually complete record of his commercial appointments by day but also his social engagements by night—all with telegraph-like brevity.

From the instant Marcia handed me George's diaries, I knew I would be spending the rest of the summer transcribing them. I made large photocopies of the pages and took them to my favorite coffee shop. On a good day, I could transcribe two weeks of entries. From reading and then transcribing George's record of his daily activities, I could discern both his personal and career decisions.

According to the diary, after Sophia Dwight rejected his marriage proposal in 1848, George retreated to London and then Paris, where he began to reinvent himself as a sophisticated *bon vivant* and dandy. He spent his days taking dance lessons and instruction in French. In the evenings he went out with other Americans to the opera and the theater.

In November 1848, George took the Grand Tour—five weeks down the Rhône to Marseilles, then along the Riviera enroute to Rome. Six months later, he traveled up the Rhine and into the Alps to view the lakes and glaciers of Switzerland. Along the way, he visited galleries and art dealers, purchasing oil paintings, prints, statuary, and cameos.

Finally, polished with a veneer of fashionable culture, George returned to the States, took a suite of rooms at the New York Hotel, decorated them with his newly purchased art, and began his assault on New York society. He had mastered the complicated moves of the "German Cotillion" and was able to direct a ballroom of guests through its figures. Socialites eagerly sought George's presence for their evening galas, and he found their parlors ideal for meeting young ladies appropriate to his new social rank.

I wondered how George would integrate his new sophistication into the staid world of the Boston Sargents and Dixwells. I thumbed through his diary, trying to make sense of the abbreviated words and stark initials that stood for people and places. The entry for Thanksgiving 1849 caught my eye.

"Thanksgiving at Epes'. Aunt P. Aunt C. Aunt H. Mother, Epes, Mary, their four children & JJ & Eliza with their two & Uncle Chandler formed the party. Evening drove the children & nurses home & then went to a little family party at Mrs. Grey's. Had a little music & a little dancing."

The Epes Dixwell Home
58 Garden St., Cambridge, Mass.
1849, November 29

"Aunt Henrietta!" George peered into the china pantry of his brother Epes Dixwell's new house. Behind the glass doors stood stacks of dishes with evenly spaced teacups hanging from hooks above. Four platters were propped side by side against the wall behind the counter, the largest pieces of the hand-painted Canton Blue set that George sent to Epes and wife Mary from China.

Henrietta hesitated. George had interrupted her just as she was about to deliver the rhetorical coup de grace to Uncle Chandler's argument. Cornered against the rear cupboard, the old merchant rolled his eyes upward and drew his hand across his brow. "I believe I shall return to the library," he said, maneuvering sideways around Henrietta's full skirts.

"And what was Uncle's offense?" asked George, observing Henrietta's withering look.

"He speaks of housing and libraries to benefit the workers in the mills of Lowell, but he refuses to see that the whole enterprise rests on the bondage of the African men and women who pick cotton in the broiling Carolina sun. On this Thanksgiving Day, Brother Chandler would have us thank his merchant friends for a few showy acts of generosity contrived to deflect our attention from the sordid truth. And, I am sure my poor sister turns in her grave every time he mouths such drivel."

George took his aunt by the arm. "I don't recall," he said, "that Aunt Dorcas ever voiced a strong opinion on that particular topic—which, I beg to remind you, we are enjoined not to discuss at this gathering."

Henrietta glared toward the library. "Holding her tongue all those years was a painful sacrifice Dorcas made to preserve peace with Mr. Chandler."

George gazed at Henrietta's face—plain as ever—framed on either side by a tightly braided coil of silvery grey hair. The color—"Dark like Aunt Murray's!" she had always said—had faded during his years abroad, but her flashing, darting eyes were the same with the excitement of a terrier ready to pounce on an unwitting rodent. Uncle had done well to escape.

George led Henrietta through the rear parlor, where her three older sisters sat in a tight circle. Their full black skirts practically filled the corner of the room—each one sewn from 12 yards of Nanking silk personally selected by him in China. At 75, Catharine was the eldest. She and Henrietta shared both their home at 5 Poplar Street and a passionate commitment to the abolition of slavery. Catharine looked feeble now, nodding to the conversation but saying little. George's mother, Esther, two years younger, giggled as Aunt Anna Parker, five years younger still, related a delicious piece of gossip. With Dorcas gone, Henrietta, at 65, was now the youngest of the Sargent sisters.

"—And," Anna concluded her anecdote about a local abolitionist, "when he had the impertinence to raise the issue at church, they ignored him."

George held to Henrietta's arm as she pulled toward the group. "That's not true at all," she blurted.

"Now, Henriet," Esther chided. "It's quite all right for Anna to see things differently."

"Mother's right," George laughed, "and besides, it's my turn to have your full attention."

He squeezed Henrietta's arm, opened the door to the sun porch and led her to the curved settee. There was hardly an underdog too obscure for Henrietta to champion nor an opinion too popular for her to condemn. He loved her for that combative spirit and shared her joy in a well-crafted argument—so long as she didn't meddle in his life. But Henrietta couldn't help meddling, and that was one of the reasons he had decided to pursue his career as a land-based merchant in New York rather than here in Boston.

George sat down beside his aunt. Only a few red and gold leaves still clung to the bare branches of the tall trees bordering the broad expanse of Epes's back yard. He and J.J. had bought the lot and provided the money to build the two-story clapboard structure with its one attic garret projecting from the mansard roof as a gift to Epes and Mary on the eighth anniversary of their marriage. As headmaster of Boston Latin School, Epes's low salary would not enable him to buy a house, while the $5,000 contribution by George, authorized from China, had hardly diminished his own capital at all.

"This house reminds me of Aunt Murray's in Gloucester," Henrietta mused. "You remember where she lived when she was still Mrs. Stephens—except that this has a widow's walk on the roof, where Auntie's house didn't, when she needed it." Henrietta paused, thoughtfully. "Thank heaven Mary will never have to search the horizon, as Auntie did for her first husband when he was already dead in the West Indies."

"Goodness," said George. "What a dreary thought! Epes says that little platform is the best vantage in town to see the July Fourth fireworks, and the whole family eats ice cream up there every year!"

"I'm sorry." Henrietta looked down at her lap. George nodded sympathetically. After all these years, Henrietta still missed her beloved Aunt Murray. "And, how are you, my Geordie? Are you still half a pair of scissors? Has any foray into courtship borne as much fruit as your commercial speculation? I heard your last investment of the heart was a poor one."

George, pricked by her needle, responded stiffly. "I am pleased to regard that affair as entirely closed. I was fortunate not to have been fancied by the lady."

"Oh, really?" Henrietta's eyes glinted.

"Yes. She had traits which would have made it a laborious duty to maintain that love a man should have towards his wife." George stopped abruptly, realizing that his formality might, paradoxically, reveal a depth of feeling he preferred to keep private.

Henrietta nodded knowingly. "I see the affair is closed, indeed, and so Miss Dwight's engagement to Mr. Wells of Springfield is no concern of yours."

George tried not to reveal his emotion. The Dwights were close friends of the

Sargents and the Dixwells, so when he first returned to Boston, Sophia Dwight's attentions encouraged him to propose marriage. Rather than decline his offer to his face, she had shown his letters to her friends. Humiliated, he quickly retreated to England, while an attorney friendly with both families arranged the return of his letters in exchange for hers.

At first, he felt despair at his loss, then anger. His escape into the anonymity of London, then Paris opened an expanded and less-constrained world, one that his position had not granted him access to either in China or Boston. That life, far from the propriety of the Heard firm and the meddlesome scrutiny of his mother and her sisters, confirmed his decision to reside in New York City rather than Boston.

George watched his brothers' children playing in the yard and wondered if he would ever enjoy the comforts of home and family or, indeed, if he even wished to. Fanny, almost nine, seemed suddenly to have outgrown her younger siblings. She chided little Johnny, 18 months old, for throwing handfuls of dirt at his sisters. Circling around Fanny, the little boy fell, spotted Henrietta, climbed to his feet, and ran toward her.

"Candy!" he pleaded, grasping for Henrietta's embroidered reticule.

Henrietta stroked the boy's hair. "Dinner first, my little regicide, then you and I will have a peppermint." She turned to George, "It's too bad that Johnny doesn't have a little cousin named George, Jr., to play with."

"Or an older one, named Henrietta, with whom to practice his litigation skills." George savored the rare victory. "Perhaps, had King Charles offered the first Johnny Dixwell a peppermint, our family history would have been different."

"Indeed," agreed Henrietta, "Charles would not have lost his head, and you would not have needed an invitation to visit your ancestral home at Broome Hall!"

George leaned back, relieved to have gotten Henrietta away from the subject of his romantic life. For years, his father had persisted in the hope that somehow, after almost two centuries, the Dixwell estates in England might be returned, if only the proper documents could be presented in court. George harbored no such fantasy, but connecting his family name to British aristocracy would give him cachet in New York society.

During his stay in England, he did hire attorneys to research what was known about Colonel John Dixwell, the regicide. The attorneys' report provided sufficient information for George to draft the inscription for a brass plaque to be installed on a monument to be built at John Dixwell's gravesite in New Haven, commissioned by George and J.J.

He gave Henrietta a broad smile. "Well, having seen the old place, I don't really regret letting our British cousins have it. I'm glad to be back in the States."

"Your mother tells me you have chosen the broad boulevards of New York over the beauties of Boston," Henrietta sniffed.

"Yes. I'll miss being close to our family, but sales of tea in Boston can only grow as fast as the city, and J.J. manages that business quite well. There's a huge potential market inland, up the canal from Albany, and I can manage that best from New York."

"At last you will have access to the interior of a continent—access the wise Chinese wouldn't allow you up the Yangtze. What will you do with the rest of your time—frighten horses with your contraptions?"

George flushed. Henrietta would never forget his schoolboy antics, like the flying apparatus he launched from the third-floor window at his family's house on Allston Street. A burst of wind did hold it aloft for a moment before it spiraled downward to splatter on the cobbled street, a pile of wrinkled paper and broken sticks.

George shook his head. She belittled his scientific interests only because she didn't understand them. "The future is not with wind power but with steam. I've secured the services of Mr. James Dorr, a patent attorney, to register my so-called 'contraptions.'" He hoped the mention of attorneys and registration might convince Henrietta of the seriousness of his purpose.

"And your Mr. Dorr is a reputable man?"

"Yes, he's quite a respectable fellow. His father was in Congress, and James went to Harvard just behind Epes."

Henrietta did not need to know that Dorr was well connected in New York society and had arranged for George to be invited into the homes of the men who controlled commerce in that city. Henrietta's disapproval of what she called the "merchants of plutocracy" was well known. Neither did she need to know that in anticipation of the spring social season, he and Dorr purchased a dozen dancing lessons at Monsieur Serracho's studio, just off Broadway.

"Supper!" called Epes from the direction of the dining room.

"Shall we go in then, Auntie?" George offered Henrietta his arm.

§

George looked at the 10 faces around the table: mother, his three aunts, Uncle Chandler, Epes next to Mary, Eliza next to J.J., and, across from him, little Fanny, sitting with the adults for her first time. Canton-pattern plates, matching the platters in the cupboard, were set in front of each family member. On the side table stood the silver tea service made for great-grandfather Sargent by Paul Revere. Epes stood at the head of the table with its centerpiece of golden oak leaves and acorns tied with a red ribbon.

"We feel deep gratitude on this Thanksgiving Day, and we give thanks that our dear George is safely home from abroad and that our family is once again together for this blessed opportunity to break bread in happiness and health." Epes turned and nodded toward the portrait of his father hanging on the wall, which he had moved in from the parlor so that the family would be complete. "Finally, Mary and I give thanks to George and J.J. for the gift of this beautiful house. I feel as rich as Croesus—for far more than material wealth, I have an inestimable treasure in the token and assurance of harmonious brotherhood for time and all of eternity!"

George lowered his eyes at his brother's lavish praise. He inhaled the medicinal odor wafting from the linen tablecloth, just removed from one of the camphor trunks he had sent Epes from China.

"Better his Croesus than your Midas!" Henrietta whispered in his ear.

"Perhaps," George whispered back, "But remember, it was Croesus who introduced gold and silver coinage to the world—the very foundation of commerce!"

"True. Although the wealth of Croesus produced public works that benefited his subjects, while the greed of Midas merely sustains the plutocrats of New York society."

George planted a kiss on his aunt's cheek. [1]

Henrietta was not the only member of his family who was unimpressed by George's new worldliness. In December 1849 Epes gently chided George for his pretensions in his annual Christmas poem:

> "But all the foreigners and folks that's got
> of foreign coloring here, and there's a spot
> Make it quite awful to plain folks like me
> what in the world the fashion next will be.
> One, always gadding, prates of home's romance.
> Another comes it over us with 'France.'
> Holds Yankee pork and beans much under par:
> Calls for Champagne and pâté de foie gras.
> And grows fastidious, though he dotes on home
> compares the Common with the Place Vendome."

This teasing doggerel made its point, but I was amazed at the speed at which George mastered the requisites of a New York society "swell." On Tuesday, January 15, 1850, with the ink hardly dry on Epes Dixwell's verse, George was at Serracho's for a dancing lesson in mid-afternoon; then with Dorr to Warren Delano's house in the evening; from there, on to Franklin Delano's, where he was introduced to Miss Astor; and finally to the Wetmore's party, where he danced the polka with Madame du Trobriand and was "introduced to Mrs. Edward King, Mrs. Williams, Miss Gerard, Miss Fering & two Miss Ludlows."

It was exhausting just to read George's calendar. Week after week, virtually every evening was crammed with engagements.

In March, George decamped with the younger set of New York society for a month in Washington, DC. There he called on President Taylor, enjoyed a festive gathering at the home of Mrs. Daniel Webster, and passed his evenings at elegant houses and hotel ballrooms for suppers, dancing, and champagne.

By the summer 1850, although George was still fully engaged in high society, his diary entries began to document a more serious interest. The first of May found him at the New York Mercantile Library, reading an article from the *Philosophical Transactions of Edinburgh* on "Flame and the Resistance of Fluids." Diary entries mentioning his scientific investigations then began to increase in frequency: "studying steam"; "inquire about supercharged steam"; "search Mercantile Library for information about wave-lines." A month later, George bragged of his visit to the laboratory of the steam engineer Jonathan Frost. "He thinks my idea in steam cannot be carried out," wrote George. "I persuade him that it can."

Summer 1850 was such a social and scientific whirlwind for George that the event, which had been so important to my own career and which had first led me to the Dixwells—the sinking of the *Frolic*—rated but a few words. George's entry for September 24, 1850, read: "Get Faucon's a/c of the loss of the *Frolic*." I checked the next entry, September 25, hoping for a reflective commentary: "Auction of tickets for Jenny Lind's concert. 1 ticket 625$! Average 8–10$."

Clearly, George had left China, the *Frolic*, and the opium trade far behind, but I could see that he had become interested in solving a technological problem that first came to his attention there.

The J. J. Dixwell Home
Jamaica Plain, Mass.
1851, August 17

George opened the cabinet door and surveyed the flasks, bent glass tubes, and thermometers. His suite of rooms in New York had no kitchen and was not a practical place to conduct experiments. J.J. let him use the buggy shed at Sunnyside for a laboratory. During several short visits, he had already completed a series of experiments there. He boiled ether, alcohol, and chloroform, then measured the gaseous volumes each produced when transformed from liquid to vapor—George wanted to invent a more-efficient steam engine.

The principle underlying the entire technology was, of course, the generation of steam from water and the transformation of the energy produced (by the expanded volume) into motive power. As engineers had long known, however, the condensation of water on the cylinder walls inside a steam engine dramatically reduced the working pressure and, thus, the efficiency of the engine.

While still in China, George had studied the problem from a practical economic interest. Steamships were revolutionizing passenger traffic across the Atlantic, but carrying freight was another matter. Ships had to carry so much coal for fuel that there was little space left for cargo, making their operation too expensive for bulky commodities.

In China, the situation was worse. Although coal existed somewhere up the Yangtze, there was not enough of it, and the quality was poor. More to the point, like all the other resources reputed to exist in the interior of China, coal remained out of reach for commercial development by Europeans and Americans. All the coal for fueling steamers on the China coast had to be transported from England, America, or Australia. A more-efficient steam engine would reduce fuel costs, and the patent on any key innovation to that end would be worth millions.

George had not set himself a simple task. He flipped open J.J.'s most recent issue of

Scientific American and reviewed the article titles for any mention of steam technology. In order to solve the condensation problem, he would have to learn what happened to the steam as it touched the surface of the iron piston and the cylinder walls. How, exactly, did the vapor return to a liquid state? Direct observation of the process was impossible because of the high temperature and pressure inside a working steam engine.

He had begun his experiments with ether, alcohol, and chloroform because all of these condense from gas to liquid at lower temperatures than does steam. He had even paid a mechanical engineer to generate steam at a lower than atmospheric pressure. These experiments did not yield the answer he sought. This morning, he rose early to study his notes before the summer heat—and the arrival of aunts Anna and Henrietta—rendered sustained concentration impossible.

George leafed through his records of steam patents. In the world of invention, precedence was everything. Two people might have the same idea for the same invention at the same time, but only the one who registered it first would reap the profit. It wasn't like normal commerce, where the first merchant to bring a cargo to port would get a higher price for his goods and the next merchant somewhat less. With patents, it was all or nothing. Great gains could be had from a steam engine that could power a cargo ship across the vast Pacific. Fortunately, Dorr was an expert patent lawyer, and George's discovery would be safely his—*if* he could only come up with it.

A clatter of hoofs sounded from the cobble drive. Aunt Henrietta would sniff him out in no time. George placed his notebooks back in the cabinet. He wondered if Henrietta had seen Dorr's pamphlet on the Fugitive Slave Act. He shuddered, anticipating her reaction.

Henrietta swept into the carriage house. "There you are! If I didn't talk to your mother, I would never hear anything at all about my Geordie. I knew more about your life when you were on the other side of the world than I do when you are here."

George kissed his aunt to quiet her scolding and lifted a newly acquired thermometer from its velvet-lined case. "Look at this! It goes up to 600 degrees, Fahrenheit."

Henrietta squinted at the mercury column, "A wonderful instrument, I'm sure. But I know of only one place with such temperatures, and I have done my very best to avoid the possibility of ever residing there."

His aunt had lost none of her fire. George led Henrietta from the buggy house, through the garden to a lone bench beneath a towering oak. J.J. had carefully placed the bench to provide a complete vista of both his impressive house and Jamaica Pond far below.

J.J.'s mansion was almost three times the size of Epes Dixwell's modest house. As a successful merchant and now the president of Massachusetts Bank, J.J. had accumulated a fortune. As befit his status, he purchased the entire promontory overlooking Jamaica Pond and renamed it Bowditch Hill in memory of his father-in-law, Nathaniel Bowditch. Now he was planting a botanical garden with rare species from all over the world, but it was the excesses of the interior of J.J.'s house that excited the most comment within the family.

"I prefer Epes's house," said Henrietta. "It doesn't demand so much of one's attention."

"Well, J.J.'s house is grand, but I'm sure Epes's house is equally suitable for his family."

"Yes, much too grand. And against all reason, your Aunt Catharine seems to approve of J.J.'s ostentation. Well, it's not really the house she admires so much. It's the water closet—which, after much reluctance, she was finally induced to use. It truly delighted her. Now *she* wants a water closet, too, just like J.J.'s. You should have heard her—'Just one pull on the chain and it was gone,' She declared she had 'never seen anything so complete!'"

George was astonished. Aunt Catharine's tastes were at least as austere as Henrietta's. "I'm sorry that Auntie could not join us today."

Henrietta looked serious. "She is indisposed. The poor dear has lost all the stamina she had only a few months ago. And she had the vigor of a woman half her age at the last Christmas Bazaar."

"Oh, the Christmas Bazaar! Don't the two of you always sell things at a table there?"

"I'm afraid the wares on our little table have been much diminished since you returned from the Orient, as we no longer have your exotic things, and our society still has a great need for funds to advance the abolitionist cause. This year, we will be selling copies of the *Liberty Bell*—perhaps you could write a few stanzas for us to publish there? I know, your poetry would be far better than mine."

"What have you written?" asked George, evading her request.

"I have a poem that tells the story of an olive tree."

"I'd like very much to hear it.

Henrietta reached into her handbag and extracted a stack of pages. "It has 27 stanzas, but I'll only read the last two." She straightened up to read:

> "Beauty for ashes then be given—
> For grief the Oil of Joy
> Chains from the toil-worn slave be riven,
> And Sin no more alloy.
>
> 'Twas Jesse's Godlike Son compared
> The Righteous man to Thee,
> Renowned type of Light and Life!
> Thou fair 'Green Olive Tree!'"

"I only wish my words might serve as more than flickering candles in a cold, dark cavern," Henrietta mused. "They may reveal the shadowy form of leviathan, but I doubt they could ever melt the icy heart of your Mr. Dorr."

George steeled himself and pondered the mélange of images. They must all somehow be related to abolition. So, Henrietta had discovered Dorr's treatise explaining the legality of the Fugitive Slave Law. "How is that, Aunt?" he temporized.

Henrietta glared at him. "Your Mr. Dorr's pamphlet supports an unjust, inhuman, unchristian law."

George didn't much care about the law—so long as the resulting conflict did not obstruct commerce. Still, he knew its passage had been a bitter defeat for Henrietta and her abolitionist friends. Under its terms, slave owners could now secure orders from southern courts identifying runaway slaves, and northern authorities were bound to return the fugitives without any further court proceedings. He chose his words carefully. "Mr. Dorr does not actually favor the law. He merely explains why, despite all its inequities, the law is *legal* under the Constitution."

Henrietta looked George in the eye. "It is an evil law. If it be constitutional, then the Constitution itself deserves the same epithet."

"Oh really, Aunt! That is an extreme view! If you had lived as I have, in an autocratic empire like China, you would have more appreciation and respect for our country's institutions. As for Mr. Dorr, he is an attorney. His analysis is an intellectual exercise based on the chain of precedent. And it is for those very skills as an attorney that I secured his services to protect my financial interests."

Henrietta's eyes bore into him. "Are you a simpleton? You have launched into a sea of speculation—moneymaking. You are so driven by ambition and greed that you have fallen prey to Mr. Dorr's specious sophistries. Satan has devised this temptation to lead you from the beautiful serenity, crowned by peace, that a Christian enjoys."

George sighed. "Surely you can appreciate that, as a legal advisor, Mr. Dorr's opinion must be based on the logic of precedent and not on religious abstractions."

"George! Have you lost your moral compass? You cannot believe what you are saying. Before God, no immoral law can be legal! It is a moral duty to disobey such laws. My sisters in the Boston Female Anti-Slavery Society have resolved that every slave catcher found on Massachusetts soil should be detained until one of our colored citizens, imprisoned in the South, shall be discharged in exchange for him."

Henrietta was clutching her handbag so tightly that her knuckles were white. While George had been away in China, the anti-slavery movement had become increasingly angry and radical, and, like Mr. Garrison, Henrietta now seemed unable to discuss the issue without denouncing the morality of anyone who disagreed. George wished Aunt Catharine had been well enough to come. Her cautionary "now Henriet," had always been sufficient to dissuade her disputatious sister from arguing a topic to the bitter end.

But he was on his own now. George opened his mouth to speak, but Henrietta interrupted him.

"—Your so-called law has obliged the God-fearing citizens of Boston to take justice into their own hands. Only African men were brave enough to snatch Shadrach Minkins from the courthouse before he could be shipped to the South. And our respectable"—Henrietta hissed out each syllable of the word—"our *re-spec-ta-ble* white citizens did nothing but talk when Thomas Sims was dragged in chains onto the boat for Savannah. Indeed, our African neighbors have shown far more courage than the white citizens of this so-called 'Bastion of Liberty.' And the situation becomes worse every day! Even as poor, dear Father Snowden lay dying, 13 more fugitives arrived at his door seeking asylum."

George knew the Reverend Snowden. For years Henrietta had threatened to have the old Negro preach at her funeral.

Henrietta put her hand on his sleeve. "George. If only you could see the human suffering, the families torn asunder—children sold from their mothers, wives torn from their husbands."

George nodded gravely—at a loss for words, as he often was when Henrietta's arguments turned emotional. "I can imagine," he murmured, though he preferred not to.

Henrietta softened her tone. "There are at least, sometimes, rays of hope. Only a few weeks ago, a girl, Miss Smith—nearly white—was at our office. A white gentleman had given her money to escape, and Reverend Parker married them. Now that was courage—and with a slave catcher already roaming Belknap Street, carrying a court order, threatening to kidnap the girl if the mayor did not order the police to do his dirty bidding."

"He *married* them?" George wondered at the Reverend Parker's temerity. He was a well-known abolitionist, but he was still a prominent member of the community. Uniting an African woman with a white gentleman in Christian matrimony was an act of defiance against the social order. "That was quite bold of Mr. Parker," George murmured. "but do you think such a marriage is wise?"

Henrietta smiled slightly. "Well, is not Miss Smith's marriage more honorable than the relationship of your Mr. Endicott with Miss Akew? Was there no minister in China as courageous as Mr. Parker to join *them* in Christian wedlock?"

George took a deep breath. Henrietta kept up with everything. The *New York Herald* had published a front-page article about James Bridges Endicott and Ng Akew, describing Ng Akew as "a shrewd, intelligent woman not troubled with those feelings of degradation which Europeans attach to females in her condition."

How could he best explain the complexities of *that* situation? "The Chinese have a different view of such marriage. White men do not marry Chinese women because the Chinese would be offended."

Henrietta appeared too absorbed in her outrage to hear him. "And your Mr. Endicott, did he tell his family in Danvers about his Chinese children or did they, like the rest of Boston, read about them in the morning paper?"

"Did you *read* the *Herald* article?" George spoke a little more loudly.

"No, but I have heard the matter discussed at length in more than one Boston parlor," replied Harriet defensively.

George sighed. "Well, Aunt, if you had read the entire article, you would have discovered that Mr. Endicott and Miss Ng are both well known in China and that their children are fully acknowledged there. If you had corresponded with Mr. Endicott you would know that for the past two years James and Henry, his two eldest boys, have been attending school in Georgetown, Kentucky. Moreover, you would know that just six weeks ago, their sister Sarah arrived here to receive an American upbringing."

George savored the look of disbelief on Henrietta's face. Rarely did he gain an advantage in a debate with his aunt. "If the local Endicotts do not know of this, it is because they do not wish to know."

Esther Dixwell came around the corner of the buggy house. "Geordie! We know you love to talk with Henrietta, but why won't you socialize with the rest your family?" Esther quietly complained to Henrietta, "He is already packing for Newport in the morning—to waltz all night with his friends at the Bellview."

"He is always off to somewhere," Henrietta agreed. "But I have his word not to depart until he has his daguerreotype taken. If he refuses to visit me, at least I can gaze upon his image."

Esther lowered her voice to a conspiratorial whisper. "Henrietta, did George tell you that Mr. Dorr has introduced him to the salon of Madame de Trobriand, and he has taken tea with Mrs. John Jacob Astor?"

"We have been discussing Mr. Dorr," Henrietta said stiffly, casting a pitying glance at George.

Esther's perplexed look darted back and forth between them.

"Well, I didn't mean to interrupt your tête-à-tête, my sweet ones, I only came to tell you that lunch will be served in 10 minutes."

Henrietta, freshly reminded of the perfidious Mr. Dorr, stared at George in silence. He struggled not to look away. "George, Mr. Dorr is doing you no favor with his introductions. Your Madame de Trobriand is nothing but a merchant's daughter wrapped in pretty paper. She was only Mary Jones before her advantageous marriage. The boorish manners of Mrs. Astor's lamented husband were a disgust to polite society until the glow from his pile of gold hid the little man sitting behind it."

"Auntie, times have changed. These are the most important people in New York—."

Henrietta barely paused, "Bah! You are all ambition. I hate a disposition that cannot accept an ordinary station. It is a part of wisdom to simplify our wants and never let them rise above an attainable height. Is it for the world's opinion you want this great wad of money?"

Henrietta stood. "'He is a merchant. The balances of deceit are in his hands.'" She walked toward the house and called over her shoulder, "Hosea: Chapter 12, verse 7."

George sat on the bench and took a deep breath. Henrietta always overstated things. What did she find so reprehensible in his desire for a comfortable life, a good social position, and—with grace—an estate to pass down to his heirs? He got up and joined Mother and Aunt Parker in the parlor, noticing that J.J. had framed the prints he sent from Paris, and the marble bust, a copy of a Roman original, now stood on a fluted stand.

"Geordie, you must fatten up if you're going to dance all night."

George smiled at his mother, took her arm, and bent close to whisper in her ear. "I beg you, Mother, hereafter, do not discuss my personal affairs in front of Aunt Henrietta." [2]

The fall 1994 *Frolic* shipwreck exhibit at the Kelley House Museum in Mendocino, California, featured a half-size model of the brig *Frolic* sinking into the lawn. (Photo by author.)

One of the cannons recovered from the *Frolic* shipwreck rusting on the lawn of the Kelley House Museum in 1994. (Photo by author.)

In 1844, the newly constructed *Frolic* sailed from Baltimore with two cannons, each weighing well over 2,000 lbs. and designed to fire 9-lb. iron balls. Captain Faucon realized that their combined weight at the gunports near the bow of the vessel might submerge the bow, possibly cartwheeling the vessel when under full press of sail. So, when he arrived in Bombay, he replaced the two 9-lb. cannons with two 6-pounders, each weighing about 1,100 lbs. In 1965, wreck-diver Jim Kennon was able to read the Cyrus Alger Company maker's mark on the trunnion of one of those well-preserved cannons.

Experienced maritime archaeologists do not remove iron artifacts from the ocean without a plan for the long and arduous process of their conservation. But in 1967, when Louie Fratis raised the first cannon from the *Frolic*, it sat for decades in his garage until he donated it to the Kelly House Museum, where it rusted on the lawn for six years before being placed on display inside the Point Cabrillo Lighthouse. In 2004, Dr. Charles Beeker transported that cannon to Indiana University for conservation. He immediately immersed it in a solution of distilled water and soda ash to halt the corrosion. A year later he introduced electric current to begin four years of electrolytic reduction to remove the chloride ions that had permeated the iron while it was submerged in the ocean. Beeker completed conservation of the cannon by applying multiple solutions of tannic acid to its surface to inhibit further corrosion and to render it impermeable to air and water vapor. That restored cannon is now on display inside the Point Cabrillo Lighthouse. In the late-1970s when the Lanham brothers raised the second cannon from the *Frolic*, they submerged it for years in a flowing freshwater creek, where some of the salt was leached out. That cannon, donated by Bruce and Richard Lanham, is displayed at the Mendocino County Museum in Willets.

The author and Linda Noel, who wrote and acted the part of the Pomo elder in *Voices from the Frolic and Beyond*. (Photo from author collection, 1994.)

Bazil Sargent Dixwell's four daughters: (*L–R*) Leslie Dixwell, Lauren Dixwell Rayfield, Stephanie Dixwell Quigley, and Marcia Dixwell DiMambro in Salt Lake City, 1990. This book could not have been written without the diaries, documents, photos, and letters generously shared by them. (Photo courtesy of Marcia Dixwell DiMambro.)

The story of a wrecked ship with a cargo of silk was well known along the Mendocino County coast. Some of the earliest Euroamerican settlers had told of receiving bolts of silk from the natives, but the name of that vessel and the location of the wreck were lost to history. When I began to give lectures linking the *Frolic* shipwreck to the local indigenous tribes, there was a surge of local interest

The Mendocino County Museum in Willits, the Grace Hudson Museum in Ukiah, and the Kelly House Museum in Mendocino asked for my help in staging exhibits at the three museums—each exhibit telling a different part of the story. Meanwhile, the Ukiah Players Theatre wrote and produced a play—*Voices from the Frolic and Beyond*—in which local actors, portraying Captain Faucon, a Pomo woman, an early settler, a wreck diver, and an archaeologist (me), each told the story of a potsherd from the *Frolic* from their own perspective. The exhibit at the Kelly House Museum featured a half-size model of the *Frolic* sinking into the lawn. Leslie Dixwell, the great-granddaughter of Hu Ts'ai-shun, visited that exhibit, hoping to learn more about her family.

Discussions with descendants often lead to more treasures. In 1998, when Marcia Dixwell DiMambro came to see me and the *Frolic* exhibit at the San Francisco Maritime Museum, she brought George Dixwell's diary. That diary would enable me to envision George's life in the United States from 1848 to 1854.

Epes Sargent Dixwell's house at 58 Garden Street, Cambridge, Massachusetts. Fanny Dixwell may have sketched this 1860's view of the house. (Drawing from author collection.)

When George Dixwell returned from China in 1847, he was a wealthy man. But his brother Epes was earning only a modest salary as headmaster of Boston Latin School. George, together with his brother John, gave Epes the money to purchase a lot and build a house a few blocks from Harvard. As Epes expressed it in a note to George, "I feel rich as Croesus since the anniversary of our wedding and your joint gifts of house and land ... " Antiquities dealers acquire many important 19th-century documents, and I purchased a trove of Epes Dixwell documents, including this sketch, probably by Fanny Dixwell Holmes, from a Connecticut dealer. Those documents also included the list of technical innovations (probably mostly assembled by George) that Epes presented at the Cambridge Scientific Club in 1881, as described in chapter 12.

CHAPTER SIX

California Gold

In summer 1851, Epes Dixwell resigned as headmaster of Boston Latin School. In October he opened Dixwell's School, where for the next 20 years he would prepare young men for entrance to Harvard. Meanwhile, Henrietta devoted herself to nursing her sister Catharine. When Catharine died in September 1852, Henrietta sold the house they shared at 5 Poplar Street and accepted sister Anna Parker's offer to move into Anna's city house on Tremont Street, facing Boston Common. Now 68 years old and no longer occupied with caring for Catharine, Henrietta threw herself back into the anti-slavery movement.

Having made his "lac" in China, George now turned to venture capitalism—combining his interest in science and technology with his desire to increase his fortune. By 1853, he was seeking out technical innovations with sufficient patent protections to justify his investment. Impressed by their tunneling machines, he had paid $20,000 for stock in two stone-cutting companies. Then, for $25,000, he bought a three-eighths interest in a Staten Island brickyard that his friend James Dorr wanted to develop using mass-production technology. George also filed a caveat, a preliminary notice with the patent office, for the gas regulator he invented for use on steam engines.

As George's business fortunes were rising, his diary revealed that his personal life was not going so well—Miss Kelsey rejected him. She thought George—barely middle-aged—too old. I stared at his portrait, a late-1840s daguerreotype that Marcia loaned me. I could see a receding hairline, and no doubt Miss Kelsey had seen it too.

Reading between the lines of George's diary, it seemed that the young lady's parents attempted to discourage him gently, but George had been oblivious to their hints and redoubled his efforts, even sending his friend Dorr to plead his case.

As I studied George's diary, I was puzzled by a number of coded entries. The first of these short, cryptic notations had appeared five years earlier—three days after George arrived in England, where he went after Sophia Dwight rejected him. The coded entries appeared regularly for a time and then stopped when he began to court Miss Kelsey. When he finally realized that she would not accept his suit, the frequency of coded entries increased dramatically.

I had to break the code. At first, I thought George might have been using a cursive form of some Asian language. He had studied both Bengali and Chinese, so I showed sample passages to university colleagues from Calcutta and Hong Kong. Neither had ever seen such writing. I examined the code upside down and reflected in a mirror, but it was still impenetrable. Then, one afternoon, my friend George Vasquez, a professor of history, stepped into my office to ask me to help him clear a paper jam in our copy machine. I showed him the script. He stared at it for a moment and said it looked like the shorthand notations he had seen on 19th-century documents. The next afternoon I sat in the special collections room of our library, wearing silk gloves and flipping pages in the 1857 edition of Benn Pitman's *Phonographic Manual*. Dixwell's "code" was, in fact, an archaic form of Pitman shorthand, invented in 1837. Even with the manual in hand, I couldn't determine where the words started and ended—much less sound them out.

I turned to the local business college for help, but they hadn't taught any type of shorthand for almost 40 years. A colleague suggested I look for a transcriber on the Internet. The next day I had an email response with a telephone number from the Pitman center in England. Mrs. Pamela Dunmore told me she supplemented her retirement income by translating Pitman documents for historical researchers, so I mailed her three sample inscriptions. I was not really surprised when she responded that the notes appeared to document visits to prostitutes.

The diaries contained more than 300 such entries, and I was faced with a dilemma. This was part of the record of George Dixwell's life, but Marcia DiMambro had entrusted me with personal information about the Dixwell family. What would she think of this revelation? I resolved not to sensationalize this material but to use it only to the extent that it explained other parts of George's story. I did not want these entries to become the story itself.

My readings on 19th-century social customs suggested that visits to prostitutes were commonplace for men of George's social class; this was the underside of the stylized, conservative courtship practices of high society that grew out of the idealization of feminine purity. George was unusual only in that he documented these assignations in his diary and that his diary had survived. Had these passages not been encoded, I was sure that George's executors would have quietly burned the journals rather than leave them in his estate to be passed on to his heirs. From the dates of the coded entries, it appeared that George avoided visiting prostitutes during his courtship of

Miss Kelsey, but when he finally acknowledged to himself that she had spurned him, he tried to get her out of his system with the same intensity he exhibited during his courtship.

Meanwhile, fortunes were being made in California. While the riotous rush for gold had subdued, George could see many opportunities out West for a prudent businessman with sufficient capital to invest. Furthermore, getting away from New York would help him forget Miss Kelsey.

George booked a first-class passage aboard the steamer *Northern Light*, bound for the Isthmus of Nicaragua on December 5, 1853. In the one and one-half weeks before his departure, he spent four nights with prostitutes—one of whom, he believed, was a virgin. [1]

Grass Valley, California
1854, April 8

A deafening thunder echoed through Boston Ravine as the Empire Stamp Mill roared into action. George pulled hard on the reins to hold his skittish horse. He watched, mesmerized, as the whirling cams lifted the massive iron hammers, which crashed down, crushing the jagged cobbles of rose-colored quartz that the workman heaved into the hopper.

"Too much capital outlay for too little return!" William Tiffany's breath formed puffs of white vapor in the cold morning air. "And we'd be in direct competition with four other mills, some with better equipment." He raised his voice above the deafening din, "The Baroness is a fine actress —"

"But her performance yesterday was mostly humbuggery!" George laughed and pulled the wool muffler tighter around his neck.

The Baroness—Miss Lola Montez, whose brief marriage to King Ludwig of Bavaria caused his overthrow, now had a romantic and business relationship with John Southwick, co-owner of the Empire Stamp Mill. George and his business partner had spent much of the previous day listening to their well-practiced spiel.

George looked back at the mill. A watery slurry of crushed rock washed through a coarse screen onto a broad, gently tilted table and across a series of riffles—long wooden slats, each trapping a pool of mercury. A workman poured a stream of the silvery metal from an iron bottle into the lowermost riffle, then pitched the empty canister onto a pile next to the company office, which was a rude shack of rough-cut, yellow pine planks that still oozed globules of honey-colored sap.

Tiffany followed George's gaze. "Any mill we invest in had better have rollers, in addition to the stampers. The ore needs to be pulverized enough so that every speck of gold can be captured by the quicksilver. And the mill has to have legal claim to its own ore. There's not much profit in crushing other people's rock. We'd have to meet the price of the cheapest competitor!"

George agreed and added, "We should move on if we want to see Laird's hydraulic operation before lunch. It's six miles to Nevada City." He turned his horse toward the rutted road and urged it forward with his boot heels.

Fresh tendrils of grass formed a thin carpet of green among the charred stumps of the trees that had covered the hillsides until recently. Patches of orange-red soil bled downward from test holes abandoned by miners seeking veins of gold-bearing quartz. A single strand of wire—the telegraph line from Marysville—angled across the road.

Tiffany cleared his throat. "I think our money would be better put to use building barges to haul lumber down the coast to San Francisco. We could anchor them in the bay and avoid the expense of a lumberyard." He gave George a sidelong glance. "Of course, if your underwater lots were dry, we'd have the harbor frontage for a full retail operation."

George pursed his lips. Tiffany might mock his investment, but it was only a matter of time before the San Francisco Bay waterfront would be filled in out to his property. Then his lots would indeed become prime real estate. Tiffany, his partner in the Bolinas Lumber Mill, located 20 miles north of San Francisco, thought the growth of the city held greater prospects for sustained profit than did gold mines and stamp mills. George respected the man's judgment. Tiffany knew the law as well as the judges. Thus he knew how best to protect his partners' financial interests.

"My feeling is," said Tiffany, "you'd do far better with a closer horizon—investing in provisions or making short-term commercial loans."

George nodded. He had thought along the same lines himself. "I've already done that—$46,000 in loans to San Francisco merchants, at 3% interest per month. I'll double that money in a little over two years. But gold is the foundation for the whole commercial edifice, and a prudent investor should take a position farther upstream from all the markets that depend on it."

It was all about the gold. The very reason for this trip was to seek out and observe the most advanced approaches to gold recovery: the Grass Valley stamp mills, extracting gold by crushing quartz ore, and the Nevada City placer operations, where ancient gravel deposits were hosed down to wash out the precious metal. As they came around the curve, Amos Laird's gigantic hydraulic mining operation loomed before them—a hill had been almost cleft in two and washed away. [2]

§

"So you spent all day yesterday with that young pup, Southwick! Boston Ravine, Rhode Island Ravine, Massachusetts Hill—you must'a thought you never left home!"

Amos Laird spoke in an accent of the Deep South. He gestured up at the wooden flume running atop the near-vertical face of the carved-out hill. Water sprayed from the cracks between its roughly sawed planks. "I was mining Georgia placer when Southwick was a Boston schoolboy." He grinned. "No one back then ever harnessed the full weight of water."

George looked up the hill and waved to Tiffany who had climbed to the top with

Laird's foreman. He counted three canvas hoses snaking down the raw exposure. "Looks like you cornered the market on fire hose."

"You bet!" Laird laughed. "It may look kind of funny, but you don't see no broke-down engines here like you will at the stamp mills. We rely on the power of gravity—the gift of the Almighty!"

"George watched as Laird's pick men undercut the base of the cliff. The waterlogged earth slumped down under its own weight. Hose men, clad in black India-rubber slickers and hats, washed the pile of gravel and clay into a wooden sluice box that sloped down some 50 yards toward the streambed.

"I see your main investment is in the flume." George lined up his thumbnail with a hose man to make a quick measurement. The wooden aqueduct stood a full 7 times the man's height above the bottom of the cliff. If the man was 5-1/2 feet tall, the flume was elevated about 38 feet. A one-inch column of water 33 feet tall produced one atmosphere—14.7 pounds of pressure. The calculation was a familiar one from his steam-engine research.

"So, Mr. Laird, why do you settle for a mere 15 pounds pressure?" The older man's expression changed as he realized that this potential investor was nobody's fool—he was an engineer.

"Well," drawled Laird, "truth of the matter, I can get any pressure I want. If I run a pipe from up Deer Creek, I can get a 300-foot head."

"That's 9 atmospheres," George noted, "130 pounds per square inch"

"Yep," Laird agreed. "But I can't buy pipe or hose to hold that kind of pressure—at least not yet."

George could see the problem. Glancing down, he noticed the pile of empty iron flasks next to the sluice. "Is your remaining expense for quicksilver?"

Laird's eyes flickered to the empty flasks. "Them? They run about $100 for a 76-pound bottle, and I use 2 or 3 of them a day." He spat on the ground. "That would be my main cost—if I had slaves, that is! But I have to pay wages here for 50 men."

George was startled for a moment, but then realized, the man was from Georgia. He pointed to the hill. "Looks like you could pay them in gold."

Laird laughed. "Not with mercury amalgam out of that sluice. It's like being on an ocean with nothing to drink. We're still waiting for the new government mint in San Francisco to crank out some $1 coins. Meanwhile, I boil off the quicksilver and ship the gold down to San Francisco, and Kellogg runs it through his press." Laird pulled a large gold coin from his pocket and handed it to George. "And they send me back a gunny of these 20-dollar slugs."

George examined the coin. It bore the familiar face of Lady Liberty, just like U.S. gold money. Instead of bearing the motto "Liberty," however, the coronet above her forehead read "Kellogg."

"Very nice," said George, handing back the coin.

"Nice, indeed, but what we need is dollar coins and 50-cent pieces. You can't buy a bottle or a shave with a 20-dollar slug, and nobody up here has enough small coin to make change."

George knew about that problem. California might have all the gold in the world, but the scarcity of coinage rendered commerce difficult. Almost all of the gold produced in the state was shipped east across the Isthmus to New York. He had paid a premium for enough coinage to make this trip—the five-dollar gold piece he had paid to rent his horse had been more a sacrifice of liquidity than of wealth.

Laird waved up the hill to the flume and pointed to the dark clouds coming in from the west. "The people that own the water are the ones who really make a killing. Water is the key to hydraulic mining—the more rain and snow, the better!"

George looked at the sky. The prospect of a storm seemed far more certain than that of profits from investing in placer mining. Further, what was good for the placer miner was not so good for the traveler. It would quickly turn the road back to Marysville into a river of mud, and he didn't want to be stuck in the quagmire. He had seen quite enough of stamp mills, flumes, and hoses.

Southwick and Laird each promoted a different method for extracting gold, but neither one seemed to George a good method for extracting much return from his capital. He looked again at the stack of quicksilver flasks next to the sluice box. They were identical to those he had seen at the Empire Stamp Mill. He turned one over with his toe to read the painted initials: "QSMC"—Quicksilver Mining Company, New Almaden. [3]

New Almaden, California
April 17

"I'm bushed," Whitcomb gasped. "I need to catch my breath!"

The three men stopped, and George stepped into the shade of a scraggly Manzanita rooted in the rocky upslope of the road to the mine. The sun was nearly overhead.

"I'm beat too!" Upton wiped his forehead. "We should have waited for the carriage."

A massive ore wagon crept down the road toward them, hugging the inside of the curve. Moving to the outer edge of the road, George glanced over the precipice and felt a wave of giddiness. Hardly a shred of vegetation impeded the drop to a creekbed far below.

Atop the ore wagon, the driver set his handbrake to lock the rear wheels. The iron rims screeched as they slid across the rocky surface. The pulling power of the four mules was superfluous on the downgrade, but their innate stubbornness provided some added braking power. Their real work would come when it was time to pull the empty vehicle back up the mountainside.

A blood-red cobble tumbled from the wagon. George bent to pick it up. It had the weight of iron shot. Quicksilver had some eight times the specific gravity of water, which explained how crushed quartz and placer gravels washed across it, while the heavier gold sank into its silvery embrace.

"It is my theory," said Upton, "that Dixwell thinks he's a modern Ulysses, beginning *his* odyssey in the wild Sierras, on a quest for the ultimate source—only to discover that stamp mills were a humbug, and hydraulics, a flimsy tangle of fire hose!"

George laughed. Upton might only imagine himself a classicist, but he was right.

Southwick's mill was probably losing as much gold in uncrushed pieces as it was capturing, and Laird's placer operation was completely at the mercy of water claims.

"You'd do better buying a piece of the Mountain Lake Water Company," Whitcomb commented, "It's right upstream from a thriving metropolis—and that city is going to grow!"

Upton guffawed. "If he really wants to invest upstream of San Francisco, he should buy up the barley and the hops!"

George grunted. His colleagues' good-natured arguments only thinly disguised their own economic interests. A. C. Whitcomb had become his partner, together with Tiffany, in the Bolinas Lumber Mill, and now Whitcomb wanted George to purchase more San Francisco real estate. G. P. Upton, on the other hand, had invested the money George had loaned him in provisions and was trying to corner the market in salt pork and beef.

On the face of it, the Mountain Lake Water Company looked like a profitable venture. San Francisco needed the water, and the engineers promised that the reservoirs, aqueducts, and distributing pipes to provide it would be completed in six months. It would, however, be a long time before the company could recover those costs—and trying to extract monthly payments from San Franciscans for water seemed a risky gamble.

As the men neared the top of the hill, George spied the mine. A vast expanse of waste rock, flattened to form a work area, flowed fan-like from its mouth. Miners pushed a small rail car filled with rock out through the portal to the edge of the flat and sent the rock tumbling down the slope. A second car emerged from the interior, and the workmen sprang into action, pitching the cobbles onto a platform and sorting them into piles.

A well-dressed man approached George and his companions. "Welcome to Mine Hill. I'll be showing you our operation. You're watching the boys grade the ore before we send it down to the smelter. We're ready to go inside."

The man spoke with the same practiced cadence as any Niagara Falls tour guide. It was a relief for George to be just an anonymous sightseer, like all the others who had made this trip out of curiosity. He was weary of the feeling that all the merchants of California—every last one of them—wanted to get their hands on his money.

The guide placed a wooden stairstep beside the track, and George followed his two colleagues up into the cart. George noticed the gradations of color among the piles. The first pile's cobbles were vermilion-red, while the rocks in the fourth had only a faint tinge of pink.

Pointing to the dark opening, the guide continued, "This portal is 330 feet below the top of the mountain. We'll first ride 1,100 feet horizontally into the mountain. Then we'll descend four levels on foot."

The cart rolled into total darkness. "Abandon hope, all ye who enter here," George was reminded of the contempt his Boston Latin teacher had expressed for Dante and the "vulgar Italian" in which the poet had written his *Divine Comedy*. A soft, chilling dampness enveloped him, and he saw a faint glow at the end of the tunnel.

The car stopped near a shrine, lit by an arc of flickering candles, which made George think of the votive offerings at the cathedral in Macao. "That's Nuestra Señora de Guadalupe," the guide announced—the Mexican-Indian Madonna.

The men got out of the car and descended a "ladder"—notches hacked into a redwood log—then passed along a narrow ledge and down a stairway chiseled from the cavern wall. The air became increasingly warmer as they descended. Dark-skinned wraiths, their bare chests glowing with sweat, emerged from the depths bearing sacks of ore suspended from tumplines across their foreheads.

The guide recited a litany of statistics: "Hardy *tenderos* carry our rich cinnabar ore 127 feet up from the diggings; we burn 60 pounds of candles in a 24-hour day."

The wave of heat rising from below was like a hot, humid summer night in Canton. A workman perched on a plank suspended over the abyss grunted as he twisted his auger into a dark pocket of ore. His candlelit face shone like a Rembrandt portrait. George was transfixed by the scene's sheer beauty. He imagined Dante's Lucifer in his abode far beneath the mountain, perhaps irritated by the incessant hammering from above. He couldn't help sympathizing with the King of the Underworld. Suddenly, he recalled Aunt Henrietta's ominous query: "Are you a son of light, or a son of Belial?"

The guide pointed to a map displayed on the wall, lit by a flickering lantern and showing the levels of the mine and their twisted passages, "Each sack contains 200 pounds of ore, and each man makes 30 trips a day from the bottom of the shaft up to the rail car."

"It's a Labyrinth," gasped Upton, "the home of Midas himself!"

George winced. Upton didn't know the difference between Midas and Minos, but his ignorance wasn't worth correcting. The guide gestured toward the steps, and they began their long ascent.

Out in the sunlight at last, George stood and looked north over the Santa Clara Valley, lush and green, its orchards white with blossoms. Just beyond lay San Francisco Bay, glittering indigo blue in the early afternoon sun. Crouching on the far horizon, just beyond the Golden Horn, lay a cottony bank of fog. Past the mine, George saw the carriage carrying Upton and Whitcomb descend into a smoky-blue haze rising from the smelting furnaces of the Quicksilver Mining Company. He turned and started down the path to get a seat inside the next carriage.

§

George's nostrils burned from the noxious fumes blown down from the chimneys by the afternoon breeze. It was difficult indeed to purge his mind from the vision of Dante's underworld, but he wanted to focus on practical matters, not poetry. Investment, like science, needed to be based on logic and mathematical calculation: the costs of production and transport, balanced against a dispassionate analysis of market conditions. He stared down at the pile of red ore heaped beside the closest furnace.

The guide pointed to the rows of low brick structures, "Our mine produces 125 tons of cinnabar ore every month, and each of our 13 furnaces will cook one ton, taking two days to heat and four days to cool. The vapors of sulfur and mercury, driven from the ore, pass from the furnace into condensers, where the sulfurous gases pass upward into those chimneys. The heavier mercury vapors sink and pass into that water-filled cistern, where the condensed quicksilver forms a rivulet flowing into this iron vat." The engineer dipped a ladle into the vat, lifted it high for all to see, and poured back a silvery stream of liquid mercury.

It was not the mercury itself that now drew his attention, but the byproduct he saw. George took out his notebook to record details as the tour guide spoke. Each oven contained 35,000 bricks, weighing 70 tons, all manufactured from clay deposits on the property and fired in company kilns.

George's mind raced. How could the Quicksilver Mining Company manufacture its own bricks in such vast quantities as a mere sideline? If they could do that, then the threshold for profitable brick production was apparently so low that virtually any entrepreneur with a little capital could produce bricks in quantity—and that would be just as true in New York as here! Against that kind of competition, even with the advantage of Dorr's brickmaking machine, the profit margin on their Staten Island brickworks would drop too low to repay their outlay for equipment and land.

A horrible sinking feeling gripped him in the pit of his stomach. He had just received a letter from Dorr, asking for another $8,000 to carry their Staten Island brickworks until production began. They had yet to produce their first run of bricks, but Dorr just bought a steamer to transport their future production and paid $8,700 from their joint capital. It was, George realized to his dismay, as if Dorr had been infected with the same mad euphoria as these people in California, forgetting that credits must eventually exceed debits. He had written Dorr by return mail that his $8,000 advance was to be used only to get bricks into production—not as capital to expand their potential capacity.

The unease George had felt for weeks now had a definite shape and, suddenly, a palpable urgency. With investments in New York stonecutting, Staten Island brickmaking, Bolinas lumber, and San Francisco real estate, and loans covering 1,000's of barrels of preserved meat, perhaps he was spread too thin. In addition, he had no idea what new commitments Dorr might be making with his money. He needed to return to New York and take control of his affairs. [4]

Within a week George booked passage aboard the steamer *Uncle Sam* for the Panama Isthmus. Four weeks later on May 24, he landed in New York, just in time to prevent Dorr from buying 10 barges to transport their bricks—of which, as yet, not one had been produced.

Unfortunately, that was the least of it. George soon learned that his investment in New York stonecutting companies had been a swindle, and he lost $20,000. Worse still, due to Dorr's reckless spending, his share in the Staten Island brick factory turned into a $95,000 debt. Desperate to pay off the creditors, George sold $48,000 in California notes at a discount for $32,000 and moved from his suite of rooms at the New York Hotel into a rooming house in order to reduce his living expenses.

When George sailed from New York for California in December 1853, he had estimated his assets at $160,000. By fall 1854, they were reduced to about $40,000.

Regardless of his losses, he could not renege on the obligations Dorr made in his name. In the world of business, a man's word is his bond, and there is no recovery from a lost reputation. He had to preserve his name as a man of honor and as a success. As George struggled to maintain an illusion of solvency, Captain William Endicott of Augustine Heard and Co. arrived from China, looking for a partner in a venture of his own.

On Board the *Palmetto*
November 24

George climbed the last rungs of the ladder from the engine room of the steamer *Palmetto*, inhaling the cold winter breeze blowing across the Hudson. "Well, she's tight and trim, but that doesn't answer the real question. The question is whether your brother just wants to run her along the coast or up the rivers, too."

"She'll make a fine coaster." Endicott ran his hand along the varnished rail. "And a Macao-Hong Kong-Shanghai run won't be much different from New York-Baltimore-Charleston."

"Perhaps," George raised an eyebrow, "but she's got a 12-foot draft—too deep to use her in the rivers."

"We don't want a river boat. My brother is quite clear on that. He wants a piece of the business up and down the coast. So long as the Chinese insist on warring on each other, that's the only local business there is. She'd be one of the fastest steamers on the coast,"

George shook his head. "That propeller worries me. It's too risky to use in China. If you lose a blade, you'd have to send to England or America for a replacement—and you'd be out of business for a year."

The latest reports had Taiping rebels attacking Canton, and they still held the old city of Shanghai. There was little hope of developing river routes into the interior of China as long as the country was in state of civil war, and there was not much hope that the war would end any time soon.

George felt sick. It had taken him more than 20 years of hard work in Calcutta and Canton to earn his fortune, and in a mere six months, Dorr had squandered three-quarters of it. But Endicott didn't need to know about of that. The young man only wanted to know whether George would buy a share in the *Palmetto*.

He could see that Endicott already pictured himself master of the sleek 180-foot vessel. It wasn't help with the $25,000 purchase price that Endicott needed—he could easily afford to buy the *Palmetto* outright. He wanted something more important—investors with sufficient self-interest in the vessel to generate a steady stream of paying cargo flowing into her hold.

Right now, George didn't need to buy a steamer. In fact, he was trying to sell one. He received a few nibbles concerning the *Pacific*, which Dorr had purchased without his agreement, but no solid offers. Endicott's brother James was too valuable a friend to risk offending.

Although there was no way George could afford to buy a share in the *Palmetto*, even less could he afford to reveal his financial straits to an old friend like Endicott. He had to go through the motions. Word would fly along the waterfront that he was looking at the *Palmetto* and that would confirm his solvency in the face of his losses. He would advise Endicott against buying the vessel on grounds of impracticability, not price. He'd still be disappointed, but George's financial situation would remain his private business.

Endicott saw that George's attention was drifting. He smiled mischievously, "My brother sends you his best wishes from Macao. He recommends you, too, should assume the bonds of holy matrimony."

George was relieved that Endicott had the good sense not to press a negotiation to an awkward conclusion and returned the younger man's smile. "Perhaps I'll take it under consideration. How is James?"

"Well, it's been two years since he brought Miss Russell out from England. Little Fidelia is one year old, and there's another on the way."

George envied James Endicott's productivity in the matter of heirs. In addition to these two, he had five older children by Ng Akew. Miss Russell's marriage to James was arranged at a distance, and they had never met in person. She must have been surprised at the sight of her fiancé—all 300 pounds of him—but no doubt even more surprised to discover his Chinese family. Yet the prospect of marriage to the richest American in Macao would have improved the mood of any spinster—and it was a long way home to London.

George turned to avoid the frigid wind. "And how was your trip to the South? I thought you and Roundy would stay through the winter there and avoid the cold." Two weeks ago, William and his friend Captain Roundy, recently returned from China, had decided to tour the southern states.

"Well, it was my idea to visit Kentucky and Roundy's idea to return. James wanted me to see how his boys were getting on at Georgetown."

"And how are they?" George tried to remember their ages. "James, Jr., must be 11 by now."

"Yes, and Henry is seven. They've both become little Americans. Of course, Hunter wanted me to see how *his* boys were doing, too."

"Hunter's boys? Are they over here?" George tried to picture Hunter's two sons by his Tanka mistress.

"Yes! My brother spoke so highly of the education his boys were getting that Hunter decided to send over William and James. At 12 and 14 he thought the boys needed some time in the States, and they arrived here a couple of months ago."

"Wasn't Hunter raised in Kentucky?" George recalled his friend's slow drawl—and his love of horses.

"That's right, in fact, when my brother separated from Ng Akew, it was Hunter who made the arrangements with his friends in Georgetown for the boys to board there. James was worried they might forget their Chinese, but with the Hunters in town they'll all keep fluent until they come home."

George struggled for years learning to speak even a poor Chinese. Little Anna Rosa, Hunter's eldest, often giggled at his mispronunciations. When the Hunter and Endicott boys grew up, they would be able to conduct business face to face with the Chinese without a translator. "I see why you wanted to go to Kentucky, but what about Roundy?"

Endicott grinned, "It was *his* idea to return. Roundy was most insistent about that. Before we left, I introduced him to my niece—and he fell in love!"

George had met Martha Endicott, a pretty, devoutly Christian 20-year-old with whose parents Endicott was now visiting.

"And to make matters worse, just before we left New York, Roundy talked with Mr. Griswold of Russell and Company about returning for another term in China, and Griswold convinced him that there was a better opportunity to be had investing in cheap land along the new railroad going south from Chicago."

George protested. "That's not a railroad—it's 700 miles of unconnected pieces."

"But it's begun," William replied. "Griswold asked Roundy to join him and two other retired captains in partnership to take 2,000 acres along the right-of-way, lay out a town and sell lots—and what better name for the town than Woosung? All the way to Kentucky and back, Roundy couldn't stop talking about Martha and owning a farm and building a town and —well, last night he proposed!"

George mulled this over. So, Griswold, the recently retired senior partner of Russell & Company in Shanghai, had convinced three of his captains to invest in railroad land in northern Illinois. Everyone in Boston knew that the principals at Russell were investing their China capital in American railroads. Word had it that Griswold was in line to become president of the Illinois Central. Of course why wouldn't the people at Russell see more opportunity in the interior of America than in the strife-torn interior of China?

"So, Roundy intends to buy a farm, sell city lots, and marry your niece. But what about his boy? What did he tell Martha?"

It was well known in Shanghai that Roundy had also fathered a son with a Chinese woman and sent the child home to Boston when the mother died.

Endicott smiled. "He told her he'd been married to the boy's mother, 'according to the custom of China,' so the boy is legitimate. After all, his name is Charles William Roundy. You know, Captain Anderson brought his own Chinese boy over about the same time, and then *he* married Roundy's niece!"

George tried to work out all the connections. It seemed that captains Roundy and Anderson, and the Endicotts, all with Chinese children and nephews, found it most convenient to marry within each other's families.

"Charley Roundy is a handsome little fellow at nearly six, although he shows his Asian blood a good bit more than my brother's boys."

Yes, Roundy had chosen well, thought George. Unlike almost any other woman in New York City—or all of America—Martha Endicott already had a clan of Chinese nieces and nephews. She could hardly fault Captain Roundy for giving her one little Chinese stepson.

George struggled against a rising bitterness. At least his colleagues had families and numerous children—whatever their race. He had to face the fact, however, that at the age of 40 he could not afford a family of his own. His negotiations with Dorr had broken down, and it seemed his only hope for restitution lay in the uncertainty of a lawsuit. [5]

Immersed in disappointment, George was unaware that 215 miles north in Boston, Henrietta was struggling with disappointments of her own. Since Catharine's death she had been able to fully resume her work with the Boston Female Anti-Slavery Society, but she was deeply disturbed by the new direction in which many abolitionists were moving.

For 30 years her friend William Lloyd Garrison preached the doctrine "moral suasion," based on the belief that rational people could be persuaded by the power of reason that slavery was wrong. She herself had come to the abolition movement from a Christian perspective that was always opposed to violent means. Now, a new faction had gained influence. Calling themselves "radical abolitionists," they advocated not only political action but also force of arms—and it seemed that they had seized hold of the entire movement.

On June 8, 1855, *The Liberator* reported that Amos Lawrence had donated $1,000 to purchase weapons—including 60 Sharp's rifles—for the free settlers of Kansas. Only a month later, Henrietta read a report of the Radical Anti-Slavery Convention in Syracuse, where Gerrit Smith read an appeal from a Mr. John Brown who lived with his five sons in Kansas and asked for arms, declaring "'fighting suasion' is the most important institution of the new territory"—whereupon the conventioneers had taken a collection to cover the entire cost of his demand, "pistols and all."

Henrietta had all these things in mind on a wet fall afternoon, as she climbed the steps to Stacy Hall for a program to mark the anniversary of Boston's 1835 pro-slavery riot.

Stacy Hall, Boston
1855, October 21

We had better weather 20 years ago, thought Henrietta as she stood before the entrance. She folded her umbrella and shook off the rain. Indeed, if it had rained on the afternoon of October 21, 1835, the 5,000 hooting and howling "gentlemen of property and standing" would have run for shelter instead of storming the hall. Mob'ocracy might have been doused by a simple act of God, and the ladies of the Boston Female Anti-Slavery Society could have conducted their monthly meeting in peace.

Unfortunately, it had not rained that day. The meeting hall had reverberated with the chants and howls of the rioters outside and then the screech of nails as the mob ripped the society's signboard from the front of the building. The hoodlums stomped the sign to pieces and then taken up the pieces to pummel the door.

Now she turned back to the hall to open the door—a new door. Indeed, it was a new building. So much had changed, but still the pernicious cancer of slavery continued to grow. She leaned her umbrella against the wall to unbutton her coat and then watched helplessly as it toppled to the floor.

Ellis Loring picked up the umbrella and lifted the wet overcoat from Henrietta's shoulders. "Miss Henrietta! Let me check your things. I just saw your advertisement in *The Liberator* for the Christmas Bazaar."

"The pledges are starting to come in," Henrietta smiled. "We may even have a collection of historic autographs to sell—but don't tell anyone!"

She watched as the elegant attorney checked her umbrella and coat at the booth, then left on another errand. Only a few months after the night of the mob's attack, she and the other ladies had hired—the same, very young—Mr. Loring to fight in court to free the slave girl Med. How they had rejoiced when the jury announced their victory. It seemed then that slavery had been dealt a signal blow, marking the first step of a long-awaited retreat. How wrong they had been.

Henrietta had arrived early. The meeting hall was still mostly empty, and she searched for a familiar face. Finally she sat alone near the aisle. Twenty years ago, she was sitting next to sister Catharine. They always sat together. Now dear Catharine was gone almost three years, and Henrietta attended meetings alone. She lived with sister Anna Parker. Although Anna, like most Bostonians, was nominally opposed to slavery, she felt only contempt for abolitionists like Mr. Garrison whose agitation Anna considered dangerous not only to commerce but also to the Union itself. Anna did have a point.

For more than 20 years Garrison even refused to vote. As a true Christian, unwilling to sanction the injury of any person, he at least had always advocated a reasoned appeal to people's better angels as the most effective means to achieve abolition. He had maintained that view, always, even in the face of violence.

The mob attack on the Boston Female Anti-Slavery Society that was so clear in Henrietta's memory had not been the only one. The threat of violence against abolitionist speakers, and even their occasional martyrdom, only brought new resolve to the movement. It was the threat of violence that brought a young, uncommitted Wendell Phillips—now conferring at the podium with Mr. Garrison—to the movement.

Twenty years ago Mr. Phillips stood outside this very building and watched the mob drag Mr. Garrison down Washington Street. In that moment he was reborn—to a lifetime commitment to the cause of the slave. Some good had come from that dreadful afternoon, but what if Mr. Garrison had not been saved from the mob? What if the rope looped round his body had next cinched tightly round his neck?

Henrietta felt an icy stab down her spine. Without sweet Catharine's soothing influence, her thoughts often took a dark turn. Maria Child's just completed tribute to Catharine would be published in this year's *Liberty Bell*. Under her breath, Henrietta recited her favorite lines:

> "A gleam of bright celestial love,
> Touching this earth from realms above."

Henrietta lifted her head and looked around the room. More people were arriving now. She looked out the window to see a tiny patch of blue among the fast moving clouds. Perhaps it was a gleam of celestial love from Catharine. She fished the envelope from her purse, unfolded the page, and read over Maria's familiar script. Words were smudged out and penciled in, like raisins scattered across a slice of teacake.

> "Not in the glare of noon-day sun,
> Thy kind and gentle deeds were done;
> And silently thy prayers did rise,
> With offerings of self-sacrifice."

A beautiful plaudit. Catharine's quiet resolve, measured in baskets of food delivered to the poor and the infirm, both African and white, awakened her and Maria to the true nature of charity. Catharine had always been bustling around the kitchen at Number 5 Poplar Street, preparing tea and tasty morsels, while Harriet sat across from Maria, explaining herbal recipes for Maria's *Frugal Housewife*.

> "While statesmen argued day and night,
> To settle whether wrong was right,
> Thou had no need of subtle art,
> Seeing truth with thy honest heart."

Maria's verse went to the heart of the dilemma facing the anti-slavery movement: whether to remain true to the principles taught by Christ (and so powerfully advocated by Mr. Garrison) or whether to contaminate that spiritual and moral effort by uniting with politicians who were all too willing to sacrifice principle to achieve any easy consensus. Mr. Garrison was right, there could be no compromise with slaveholders— or murderers—

A voice broke into her thoughts. "Good afternoon Miss Sargent, is that seat taken? We've missed you on Sundays," the woman chided gently."

"Why, Mrs. Pierce, please join me," Henrietta blushed. "I've been called upon to accompany my nephew Epes Dixwell and his children to church in Cambridge. You know how it is with children."

She felt embarrassed by her mistruth even as she uttered it. She joined Epes and his family, not so much for the children as to avoid the new Universalist minister at the old church on School Street. His theology derived more from Hosea Ballou—whose doctrine was a betrayal of Uncle Murray's—than from Uncle Murray himself. It was easier for Harriet (and for the spirit of Aunt Murray who she often sensed beside her) to listen to a Harvard Unitarian than an apostate Universalist.

Mrs. Pierce nodded understandingly. "'But as the twig is bent—'"

It was true. Her nephew's children, still pliable twigs, were receiving religious training, but it was of a cool and intellectual sort, devoid of the passion and fervor of Uncle John Murray. Without that fire, would they have enough faith to see them through life's setbacks?

She thought of nephew George. She had tried, gently, to bend that twig throughout his childhood. George, so blessed with brilliance and wit, should have grown up to be a great force for good in the world. Instead, he became a merchant, more interested in making money than in the state of his soul. She sighed inwardly. Even now, even though most of his wealth had evaporated, his passion for it had not. In fact, it now seemed to consume him.

"You know, Mrs. Pierce," Henrietta confided, "there is only so much that a great aunt can do for children, when their parents are so decided in their outlook."

Just as Mrs. Pierce opened her mouth to reply, three sharp raps of the gavel cut through the din of conversation. "The meeting will please come to order."

Henrietta's mind wandered all through the preliminary speeches offering thanks to the organizers and welcoming the audience. It was time to be thinking about this year's Christmas bazaar. Catharine had always decorated their table so prettily with festive pine fronds and holly boughs with glistening red berries. She blinked back tears.

Mr. Garrison's voice echoed in the distance, "So many of those brave ladies who met here two decades ago have gone to their heavenly home, but the stalwart who was then vice president of the society is present tonight. Will Mrs. Southwick come forward and take a seat on the platform?"

Henrietta looked around for "Thankful Southwick."

"I would rather not come forward," the old woman's voice trembled. "My mind is too much affected, seeing the few who yet remain with us."

"To the stage!" A shout came from the back of the room, then a roar of applause. Henrietta joined in the applause as Thankful's daughter walked her mother up the aisle between the rows of seats.

Henrietta closed her eyes. She so loved Mr. Garrison's sonorous voice. "We are doubly blessed to have another long-tried and most devoted friend of the slave. Will Miss Henrietta Sargent please join us?"

Henrietta sat, stunned. Mrs. Pierce nudged her shoulder, "Miss Sargent, that's you!"

Suddenly, Mr. Loring was at Henrietta's side, taking her arm and walking her forward. On the stage, he made a sweeping bow and then raised his arms to the audience as the crowd erupted again in applause. At three raps of the gavel, Henrietta sat down, beside Mrs. Southwick, feeling awkward at being on display.

Now came the customary readings from Scripture, selections from Psalms, a prayer, and finally, a hymn, written for the occasion by Mr. John Greenleaf Whittier, set to the "Old Hundredth." Mr. Garrison read out the words, and Henrietta joined in the singing. But the words of the last verse seemed to express a philosophy quite opposed to Mr. Garrison's:

> "Wake, dweller where the day expires!
> Your winds that stir the mighty lake.
> And fan your prairies' roaring fires,
> They're Freedom's signals!—wake!—awake!"

Roaring fires! How could Mr. Garrison lead them in those words? Did Mr. Whittier really advocate fanning the partisan flames now raging on the prairies of Kansas? The three parties of abolitionist emigrants the society dispatched from Boston now faced gangs of Missouri ruffians, but must they forsake the peace and gentleness of Christ? What had become of their movement, when a Quaker poet could lure the unwary into violence and sin?

Henrietta clutched her purse to her lap. It was her favorite one George had sent from China years ago. Suddenly she realized how old and threadbare it looked, and now it could be seen by the hundreds of critical eyes sweeping the stage! She placed it on the floor, behind a fold of her skirt, and immediately felt guilty—caught out in vanity. She retrieved George's gift from the floor and replaced it on her lap for all to see. George had sent so many things from China for those long-ago Christmas bazaars. Whatever his shortcomings, he had the virtue of generosity.

Every fall during his seven-year sojourn in China he had sent a box of silk, lacquer, and porcelain treasures for the Christmas Bazaar. Once he returned, first she and Catharine—and now, she alone—were left to their own resources: hand-knit scarves and embroidered napkins. Of course, it was far better to have George close to home, far away from the horrid wickedness of the Chinese.

Two weeks ago *The Liberator* quoted from a letter by young Mr. Heard, George's colleague in Canton. While walking through the city square, Mr. Heard witnessed the beheading of 161 Tai-ping rebels—Christians—in the space of two and one-half minutes. The article included all the gruesome details. The images were overwhelming: a man cut into 24 pieces, yet lingering alive; the wife of a rebel chief nailed to a cross and skinned alive. To what purpose did the minute description of these atrocities—supervised by Mandarin officials—serve the cause of abolition in the United States?

Anecdotes indicting the vicious behavior of slaveholders had helped to provide moral suasion, but why describe the violent horrors of a faraway land, acts beyond the power of men to forgive—before God himself the weight of these sins must preclude the redemption of the sinner.

In an effort to rid her mind of the hideous pictures, Henrietta gazed at Mr. Garrison for inspiration and tried to focus on his words. He was describing how 20 years ago, on the very afternoon of the Boston riot, a convention to form an anti-slavery society in Utica, New York, was similarly attacked, and how Gerrit Smith invited them to reconvene at his house, whereupon he joined the association.

Mr. Garrison was far too generous to Mr. Smith. He might be the richest man in western New York, having inherited the entire estate of his father, the partner of John Jacob Astor, but he was too unreliable and self-serving to be so praised, especially at a celebration of Christian nonresistance.

Mr. Smith had ridiculed Mr. Garrison's principle of "moral suasion" for years. He persistently pressed for political action instead, until his neighbors, trusting that his commitment matched his fiery words, elected him to Congress. Before even completing his term, he summarily resigned his seat, offering only the feeble excuse that he needed to meet the demands of his "large private business!" Mr. Smith was a hypocrite—advocating political action but unwilling to stomach the process that he preached.

Now, he had moved even further from "moral suasion." He styled himself a "radical abolitionist"—an advocate of violent force! To add insult to injury, he was calling a three-day convention this very week in Boston, right under Mr. Garrison's nose.

Mr. Smith did have one thing in his favor. He always supported the right of women to organize for political change. Two years after that mob attacked the meeting of the Boston Female Anti-Slavery Society, Henrietta traveled to New York City to attend the Anti-Slavery Society of American Women. There, with Maria Child, the Grimkés, and Lucretia Mott, she met Ann Smith of Peterboro, whose husband, the same Mr. Smith, allowed her to travel unaccompanied to the conference.

No longer was the role of women in public life only whispered about as the "woman question." A few weeks ago, Henrietta walked up Washington Street to attend the Women's Rights Convention, where she heard Susan Anthony. Sarah Grimké and Lucretia Mott, two of the most powerful voices 23 years ago at the Women's Anti-Slavery meeting in New York, were present again to address this audience. It only troubled her that Aunt Murray's name had not been mentioned even once at that convention.

Henrietta blinked. She had not been paying attention, and Mr. Garrison finished speaking. It seemed that the whole abolition movement was as distracted as she. No one seemed to have noticed that a new, more-violent campaign against slavery was gaining such momentum against their old, peaceful ways—it crept up, mostly unnoticed.

Good Christian men now endorsed bloody violence, and no doubt it was only a matter of time before they sank to the depravities of the heathen Chinese. Henrietta felt ill. Mr. Garrison's elegant oratory could apparently persuade only those who had the refinement and the leisure to listen and to reason. There would be no time for that once the pistols and Sharps rifles were aimed and fired. Moral suasion was dying, and there was nothing that she or Mr. Garrison or anyone else could do about it. [6]

Nor was there anything that Henrietta could do about George. His financial troubles compromised his health. That fall, as Henrietta considered the fate of the abolitionist movement, a catarrh settled in George's lungs. His physician ordered him to Havana in the hope that in the mild climate he might ward off pneumonia. He also had to ward off bankruptcy and the consequent loss of face within his circle. George Dixwell had to find a way to make a new fortune and quickly. Even before he steamed for Cuba, he hit on a new venture in the currency market in China.

The *Frolic* carried 676 rolls of stacked stoneware bowls decorated in six distinct patterns that had been popular in Mexican California prior to the 1849 Gold Rush. *(Upper row, L–R)*: *fu*; peach & fungus; bamboo. *(Lower row, L–R)*: snail; unidentified; rocks & bamboo. Of these six patterns, only the bamboo-pattern rice bowl continued to be imported after 1850, mainly to supply Chinese laborers. (Photo by author.)

Gold filigree jewelry, made by Chinese craftsmen for the Western market. A sharp-eyed diver recognized the outer edge of this ornament (5.2 cm in length) in a concretion on the *Frolic*. It was fully revealed after a bath in hydrochloric acid. (David and Steven Buller donation; photo by author.)

Sets of nested brass weights (5 drams to 3 lbs.), manufactured for the Western market (diameter of the largest cup: 10.8 cm.), even though the Chinese foundry men had little understanding of Western weights and measures. The one-pound weight cup from this set weighed 0.819 lbs.—18 percent too light. What controversy these weights would have caused had they been used in California commerce! (Larry Pierson and Steven Buller donations; photo by author.)

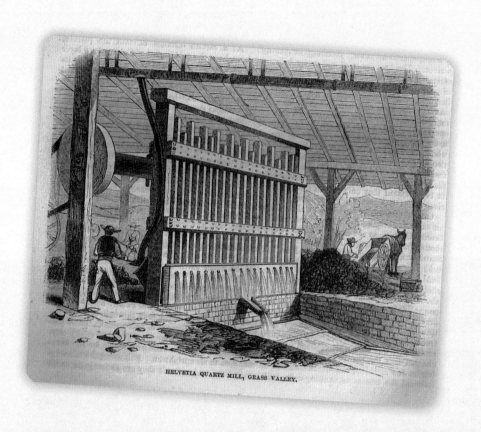

HELVETIA QUARTZ MILL, GRASS VALLEY.

Helvetia Quartz Mill (1860) in Grass Valley, California, similar to the Empire Stamp Mill that George Dixwell visited in 1854. (Image from *Harper's Weekly* 12 April 1860.)

In the years immediately following George Dixwell's return from China, he became a venture capitalist, seeking out new technologies—a rock-cutting machine for digging tunnels, a machine for mass-producing bricks, the technology for vulcanizing rubber. In spring 1854, he voyaged to California where he traveled into the Sierra Nevada Mountains looking for investing opportunities in gold production. Dixwell first visited the Empire Stamp Mill in Grass Valley to view its massive hammers crush quartz into a slurry for gold extraction. The next morning, he visited Amos Laird's hydraulic mining operation in Nevada City.

Amos Laird's hydraulic mining operation (1855). George rented a horse to ride the 6 miles from Grass Valley to Nevada City to visit this operation. (Drawing by Joseph Lamson; courtesy of the California Historical Society.)

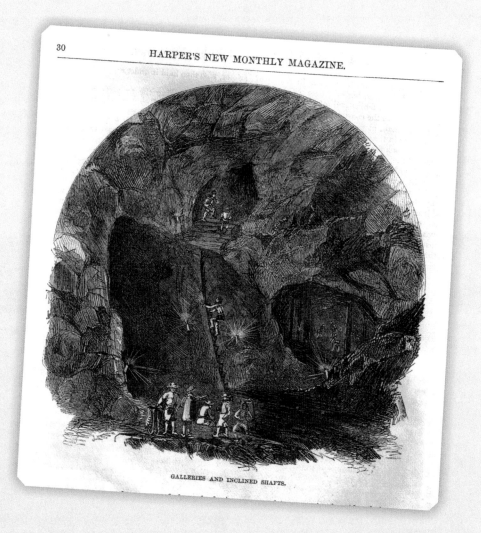

30   HARPER'S NEW MONTHLY MAGAZINE.

GALLERIES AND INCLINED SHAFTS.

Interior of the mine at New Almaden, 1857. (Republished by *Harper's Weekly* June 1863.)

Reduction works of the New Almaden mine, 1857. (Republished by *Harper's Weekly* June 1863.)

George noticed that the Empire Stamp Mill and Laird's hydraulic mining operation both required large quantities of quicksilver to coat and capture the fine particles of gold into an amalgam. So, he traveled to the Quicksilver Mining Company at New Almaden, near San Jose, California, to view mercury production. I wanted to write a vignette describing George's visit to New Almaden because I had taken my fall 1979 San Jose State University archaeology field class there to salvage what might remain in the interior of the burned-out, adobe-walled company store that the property owner planned to bulldoze away. Illustrations from *Harper's Weekly*, a magazine popular in George's time, helped me to reimagine the scenes that he encountered.

CHAPTER SEVEN
Old Heads

From his past experience as a trader in Canton, George knew that Chinese merchants preferred to be paid in "Old Heads"—Spanish dollars, bearing the familiar faces of Spanish monarchs. These coins were produced in Spain's silver-rich colonies, chiefly Mexico, in such quantities that they became the standard currency of world commerce. Even though the Chinese could not read the Spanish inscriptions, they had come to identify those heads and faces with authentic value. The problem was that the production of these coins virtually ended in 1821 when Mexico became independent. Although the newly minted, post-independence Mexican pesos—adorned with a snake dangling from the beak of an eagle—contained the same amount of silver, the conservative Chinese, particularly those in the tea-producing regions in the interior of the country, were loathe to accept them.

The Chinese had no silver currency of their own, and there weren't enough Old Heads still in circulation to sustain commerce. The coins were now worth a substantial premium over the actual value of the silver they contained. Therefore, a large profit could be reaped by anyone who could produce a new supply.

For almost a year, George had been investigating Spanish coinage, talking with bullion brokers and studying Jacob's *Historical Inquiry into the Production and Consumption of the Precious Metals*. In July 1855, a few months before sailing for Havana, he wrote to John Heard, outlining a project and urging the greatest secrecy. I do not have George's letter, but shortly after receiving it, John excerpted the basic points and sent them on to his uncle, Augustine Heard.

John agreed that Spanish dollars could be struck in China without violating any Chinese law. No actual fraud would be committed because the silver content of the new coins would be exactly equal to the standard. Yet, he did not feel comfortable with the scheme. "There is," he wrote, "something in the idea of coining, repugnant to my ideas, something in which I should not much like to be engaged, something which is suggestive of State's prison and penalties ... and whether right or not in the abstract, it had better be avoided."

George did not see this letter. Four months in Havana restored his health, and the enforced leisure allowed him to devote enough thought to his scheme to become fully convinced of its feasibility. In April 1856, he traveled from Havana to Mexico City, where many of the original Old Heads had been minted. During his month-long stay, he probably presented himself as a numismatist, a collector of coins and the memorabilia of coinage. The Mexico City mint had converted to steam-powered presses to produce silver pesos that were much more uniform than the old eight-reales Spanish dollars so highly valued in China. In order to replicate Old Heads that would pass the scrutiny of Chinese shroffs, George probably examined the old screw presses. He would need to use the older technology to produce coins that were not so uniform. Each one had to be slightly off-center in its own unique way.

Returning home, George took a steamer up the Mississippi and then a train to Boston. During his absence, John and his uncle Augustine further discussed the coinage project and agreed that they did not want any formal association with producing coins. They were respectable men of commerce with reputations to protect. Nonetheless, they agreed to help provide cover for George as a private tea merchant. It also appears that they secretly agreed to help circulate the coins by mixing them in with their payments for tea and other goods. On October 8, 1856, committing much of what remained of his wealth to the scheme, George Dixwell sailed for China.

While there, George was careful not to describe the progress of his project explicitly in writing, but his 14 letters addressed to Albert Heard in Shanghai contain many indirect comments upon which I could base an account. I deduced that George's overall plan was to mint the coins in Macao and then ship them north to Shanghai, where Albert Heard would mix them into payments sent by the Heard firm to tea merchants far up the Yangtze. Still I wondered, how did George accurately mint the coins? I, too, would have to familiarize myself with the Carolus dollar. [1]

§

I focused my 10-power magnifying glass on a section of the edge of the Carolus dollar and its border pattern of alternating circles and squares. I suspected that some 150 years ago George had peered through his own magnifying glass, carefully reverse-engineering each step of the coin's production in order to replicate the minting process. I noted that the Spanish masters of the Mexico City mint had wisely decorated the rims as well as the faces of these coins to discourage larcenous merchants from enriching themselves by shaving silver from the edges.

Rotating the coin slowly, I carefully followed the rim design along the narrow edge. The chain of circles and squares began near the numeral "1" of the date 1805 and continued unbroken to a spot exactly halfway around the coin. There, the chain ended and another identical one began circling around the rest of the coin back to the "1." The two chains overlapped at their beginnings and ends with a circle printed over a square or a square over a circle. It seemed this coin had been turned 180 degrees between two dies, each bearing the circle-and-square design, and the degree of overlap was a function of the skill or carelessness of the mint worker.

I examined two more Old Heads. On each, the edge pattern began within one-quarter-inch of the date. In order for the design to be stamped consistently adjacent to the date, the faces of the coin had to have been stamped into the blank silver planchet before the edge design was applied.

I felt encouraged by my observation. Although I might not be able to reconstruct all the steps of minting authentic Spanish dollars, perhaps I could deconstruct George's venture into counterfeiting them. [2]

Macao, China
1857, July 25

"These piecee chop velly old!" Ahwei laid four finger-size iron chisels on the table and resumed rummaging through the chest.

George pushed open a carved shutter to let in the morning light. Bright rays passed through the grillwork, throwing a lacy pattern across the table to the red tile floor and halfway up the pale plaster of the far wall. He gazed out at Macao. White houses glittered against the green foliage of a distant hill, surmounted by the crenellated walls of an ancient fort. He turned and picked out two of the chisels, holding their working ends to catch the light. Each bore a tiny raised design. He slowly extended his arms to bring them into focus.

"Yer'll either need bloody spectacles or longer arms to see them little marks." William Brown placed a stack of dollar-shaped silver disks on the table. The pile tilted awkwardly, the coins held slightly apart by the shaggy edges where the cutting die had not sliced cleanly through the milled silver strip.

"Maybe must hab long hand like monkey," Ahwei laughed.

George glanced up in surprise at the joke.

Brown gave the Chinese a sharp look. An English machinist, with long experience repairing steam engines for the British Navy, Brown knew his place, and expected the same of others. He turned back to George, holding up a shiny blank disk. "Edge to edge I c'n stamp nigh two dozen planchets from a 36-inch strip. But every strike'll squeeze the metal a eighth inch beyond. If yer want them coins the same thickness, the best yer'll git is 21."

That was all right with George. They would re-melt the wastage and roll out more strips. At this stage of production, the real work was Ahwei's. He would be the one to hand-file the edges of each raw disk to bring it down to the 27-gram weight of an authentic Spanish Carolus dollar. His most crucial work would come later when, as an experienced shroff, he would be the best judge of each coin's ability to "pass."

George turned his attention back to the chops, taking a hand lens from his side pocket and squinting through it. One chisel bore a dot encircled by eight rays, each of a different length and thickness; the other bore what looked somewhat like a Chinese character. George tried to mentally reverse the imprint, to imagine how it would appear when hammered into the face of a Spanish dollar. The lines of the design conveyed no meaning to an ordinary reader of Chinese, but its very idiosyncrasy was deliberate. Each unique mark or "chop" identified a particular shroff who would certify the coin as genuine and guarantee to replace it should the recipient later find its silver content to be deficient.

Ahwei removed two more chisels from their canvas wrappings and handed them to George. Their designs were so large, he hardly needed the magnifier. "Look-see new chop. Ol' time chop mark small, like ant mout'. New chop mark big, like numbah one ant."

George scrutinized the symbols. One of them was based on the character *fu*, signifying good fortune, but it was combined with several unfamiliar strokes. Ahwei's long years of experience meant not only that he knew as much about the coins used in Chinese trade as anyone but also that he knew the shroffs, themselves. There was no question that George needed his services. Nor was there any question of the man's loyalty—if not to George personally, then to Ahwei's older brother Tsun Atow, chief comprador of Augustine Heard and Co. in Hong Kong.

Hong Kong! George could not get used to attaching "Hong Kong" to the Heard Company name. For 15 years he had written to the Heards in Canton. To him that city's name became an inextricable part of the company appellation. Over a few short months, things drastically changed. While he had been enroute from Boston, years of smoldering tension between England and China again erupted into flames, literally— all the Western "factories" at Canton, including the Heard firm's, had been burned to the ground. Even before the embers cooled, virtually every American and English firm resumed business in Hong Kong on British soil.

Although everything had changed, the net result was no change at all. The Heard firm continued to dispatch cargoes of tea to New York and Boston, and Tsun Atow, with princely aplomb, continued to manage the firm's business with Chinese merchants. In addition to his official duties, he was fully informed regarding George's project and had already attended to a score of necessary tasks that George could not have accomplished himself without arousing suspicion.

The ongoing war had been particularly hard on Chinese merchants, and many moved their families and businesses from Canton to the security of the Portuguese territory of Macao, where the sudden increase in population made real estate prices skyrocket. George paid a premium to rent this building with its private courtyard. It was close enough to the inner harbor that the carts carrying the heavy crates containing the disassembled coin-press and rolling machines could pass quickly enough to avoid attracting attention. It would be impossible to proceed to full production without a tacit nod from the authorities.

Brown flipped a silver disk into the air, caught it, and slapped it into his open hand: "Well, 'eads er tyles?"

"You only make Ol' Head—no tail," Ahwei remarked.

George laughed. He was beginning to like the shroff's irreverent humor.

Brown weighed the coin in his hand. "If we myke 'em a hair overwyte, yer'll still have full value after we get some wear on 'em."

George frowned. A master craftsman like Brown was perfectly capable of minting Old Heads that were even better than the originals, but obviously Brown hadn't considered the subtleties of counterfeiting coins now one-half-century old. The formulas in Jacob's commentary described the amount of silver lost to wear.

"Think, Mr. Brown, if a standard Spanish dollar loses one part per 400 parts annually to wear, what would be the total loss of silver *today* from a coin minted 50 years ago in 1807?"

Brown stroked his chin, "Well, that's 50 parts of four 'undred .... a one-ayth loss a' wyte, or 12 and a half cents—that's a full Spanish real!"

"Maybe Missa Dikwah no likee eight-real dollah—you makee seben!" Ahwei's eyes crinkled in amusement.

"No," George replied, "Our dollars must be so ordinary that they attract no attention at all, positive or negative. So we can't make them either overweight, or underweight."

"But yer need 50 years a' wear?"

George examined the blank, "Not a full 50 years on every coin. Each coin needs to start at full weight and then receive enough wear to appear used, and each one with a different amount of wear. Ahwei's oldest chops should be hammered in before we apply the wear, and—"

"And, them new chops atop that wear," Brown completed his thought.

Ahwei looked incredulous.

Brown shook his head slowly, "A bloody pity. We'll be makin' perfict dollars just to grind off all the detail."

"Our goal is not perfect dollars. What I want is perfect dollars, perfectly worn, in all imaginable increments. I chose the years 1805 and 1807 precisely because they were so unremarkable—perfectly ordinary years at the Mexico City mint."

"Puttin' wear on 'em ain't a problem. Just toss 'em in bags wiv sand and gravel an' yer'll have yer wear, scratches an' all! Wot we need to start production is plenty a' good coin silver." He frowned, "Course, 50 year a' tarnish is another matter, ain't it?"

"Need Foochow chop. Makee good dollah," Ahwei put in.

George had the same thought, and he already instructed Tsun Atow to quietly buy up a stock of over-worn Spanish dollars, which the Chinese called by the derogatory name "Foochow"—maimed coins that a long succession of shroffs had chopped, scraped, cut, and punched until virtually all traces of their original designs were obliterated, giving these coins two important virtues: not only could they be purchased at a discount below their gross weight, but they also contained the exact ratio of silver to alloy George needed to mint the new dollars—the precise combination of metals would testify to their authenticity.

Ahwei held up a newly stamped blank, flipped it into the air, caught it, slapped it into his open hand, and winked at Brown. "Chinee money man head, tail all same, no mattah![3]

August 15

"Ayee! Missa Dikwah!" Ahwei shouted.

George ducked just before the iron crossbar powering the screw press whirled over his head.

"Fer Gawd's syke!" Brown grabbed for the bar and stopped its forward motion. Once the handle was pushed, the heavy weights at each end functioned as a flywheel. "Bastards!" he glared at Ahwei's nephews. "They damn near ruin't our dies!"

And they damn near crushed my skull, George thought. He put his hand on Brown's shoulder to calm him and to steady himself. "Ahwei," he spoke quietly, "tell your boys not to push that bar until they are told to. And never more than a quarter turn." He pulled the bar back one-fourth revolution. "Savvy?"

"An' never, ever, at all," Brown growled, "when we don't have a bloody planchet b'tween them dies!"

George breathed deeply. It had been a close call and not just for his head. Brown was right. In their enthusiasm, the boys had nearly crushed the new dies against each other. If that happened, the obverse die would gain design elements from the reverse one and vice versa, causing the designs for the two sides of the coin to be muddled together. It was an easy mistake; it had occurred at the Mexico City mint. On several coins among the hundreds he had studied, the face of King Carlos had been pockmarked with bits of the Spanish coat of arms from the reverse.

Brown grimly centered a blank planchet on the lower die. George leaned forward to watch the upper die engage the silver disk. "Quarter-turn," he called out. "Now another." He paused, "quarter turn."

Each boy pushed against his end of the crossbar. Nothing moved. The giant screw seemed frozen inside the threaded iron housing. The boys lunged, and the screw turned with a stuttering screech of iron against iron.

"Bloody 'ell! I want *steady* pressure," Brown shouted. "Git some grease on that screw."

"Ahwei," George called. "Tell your boys to grease the screw when it starts to bind." He pointed to the pot of petroleum lubricant on the floor next to Brown's toolbox. At Ahwei's command the boys scrambled to apply the grease to the screw.

"Not now!" shouted Brown. "Yer can't back off wiv a coin 'alf pressed. Another eighth turn'll do it."

George signaled the distance to Ahwei with his hands, and Ahwei instructed the boys. The screw screeched again. "Now, back off—two turns."

For a moment the coin seemed stuck to the upper die before it fell into Brown's outstretched hand. He looked at it closely and handed the coin to George who could see how the dies had squeezed the upper and lower surfaces of the coin outward.

"Not 'af bad, a mite less pressure and yer won't have them lips 'round yer edge. The edge dies'll flatten them lips when we stamp on the border."

"I think you've done a magnificent job." George beamed at the machinist. The test run had been a complete success. He passed the coin to Ahwei who examined it and shook his head.

"Chinee no need makee dollah wit' machine." He mimicked pouring metal into a narrow mold, "Chinee dollah edge more bettah."

George knew otherwise. He had seen Chinese-manufactured counterfeit coins. Cast in molds made from real dollars, they reproduced exactly whatever wear or scratches the original had accumulated during months or years of circulation. They were easy to detect, too, by their deficiency of silver. Contrary to Ahwei's assertion, the edges were not very good. There were always mold marks around the rim, which, when filed away, further defaced the circle-and-square edging.

Still holding the coin, Ahwei went to his chest and pulled out a battered volume. He opened it to a page marked by a black silk ribbon and laid the new coin between two line drawings.

George stared at the vaguely familiar images for some moments before realizing they depicted the front and back of a Carolus dollar—as seen by the Chinese. "What is that?"

"Big dress," Ahweh translated.

George pointed at the picture of the coin's reverse side. "And what do you call this?"

"Two stick." Ahwei turned the page, showing the image of Carlos's successor, Ferdinand. "*Hsiao yi*," he pointed. "Small dress."

George flipped the page back to Carlos. He did appear to be wearing a larger tunic than Ferdinand. He also looked more like a Chinese than a Spaniard. Not only did he have Chinese eyes, but his gigantic Habsburg nose with its beak-like hook at the end had been transformed into a short Chinese nose with a flat, almost concave arch. Moreover, the artist rendered the laurel wreath that crowned Carlos's forehead as loops of hair, like those worn by a well coiffed Chinese woman.

Ahwei was looking at the illustration of the coin's reverse side and asked, "Why two stick? Why no eight stick?"

George studied the coin. Ahwei seemed to think the two vertical lines were numerals, like the four capital "I's" after the name Carolus. The number eight would not only signify the reales of the coin's value but also it was a lucky number for the Chinese. To the Spaniard who had designed the coin, however, the "two sticks" represented the Pillars of Hercules, symbolizing the Straits of Gibraltar. The Chinese shroff who made the illustration of the coin drew scribbles for the tiny Roman letters on the banners furled round the pillars—*Plus* on the left and *Ultra* on the right.

"*Plus Ultra*," murmured George, "More beyond." More lands to be conquered—the motto of Spanish colonial expansion. George felt uncomfortable at the thought of explaining the iconography of imperialism to a sensitive Chinese. "I don't know what it means," he said. [4]

§

The day's work was done. From the street, George heard the sound of Ahwei sliding shut the heavy bolt to lock the courtyard gate. Thieves would have to scale a 14-foot wall to gain access, and all they would find would be greasy tools and heavy machinery.

Brown hefted the valise carrying the dies and the partially completed coins. "Too much ballast," he said, dropping his shoulder for effect.

George nodded. It was tedious to carry the heavy bag back and forth, but it seemed best to keep the dies separate from the press. There could be no chance of anyone else using them, and if for some reason the authorities raided the compound, they would not find these legally awkward items. Everything else could be explained away.

George closed one eye as if sighting through a sextant. "You do list somewhat to the left, but if you keep the breeze port side, you won't hove over."

Brown laughed. The two men turned the corner to the inner harbor and walked along the rock-paved Praia fronting the water. Sampans sat mired in the mud waiting for the incoming tide. Red, white, and blue bunting, left over from the recent Fourth of July festivities, drooped from the mainmast yard of an American ship that was anchored in deeper water. "Bloody 'ell! Look at that—"

George turned to see what Brown was pointing to—a louvered window spiked shut with heavy timbers. Brown wrinkled his nose in disgust. "'Uman flesh don't keep that well. They lose a lot to spilage. But it's the only payin' business them Portagees got."

Over the past weeks George had noticed gangs of Chinese men, some in manacles, off-loaded from junks and herded into the side doorway of the building. When British commerce had moved to Hong Kong, Macao bacame a backwater, not leaving much for the Portuguese to do. They were resourceful, though, and the coolie trade was now the best business going in Macao. Warehouses along the waterfront were being converted to "barracoons"—barracks holding hundreds of young men whose freedom had been gambled away, stolen by a crimp, or traded for an indenture. The Portuguese, of course, professed ignorance of the tactics used by their Chinese labor suppliers who provided the "merchandise."

Of course, that same moral flexibility was what made Macao the best place to manufacture Spanish dollars, providing one was sure to stay on the right side of the authorities.

Brown shifted the heavy valise to his right shoulder and gestured back toward the barracoon. "They've most of a cargo in there by now, likely four 'undred. But they'll only offload three 'undred an' fifty in Havana. An' none of the poor sods ever comes back."

George grunted an acknowledgement. He too had read the *China Mail* that none of the coolies shipped from Macao were ever heard from again, unlike those who emigrated from Hong Kong to California or Australia, and who often returned. It was an unsavory business. The local coolie brokers had a friend in Senhor Ferran, the government's chief coolie agent; they could purchase the toleration of the authorities. They paid standard fees by the head with a little *cumsha* under the table to expedite the paperwork.

Brown was shaking his head. "Yer can insure a chest a' opium or a box a' tea, but not a hold full a' Chinamen," he noted. "Keep 'em locked below an' they die like flies. Let 'em up on deck an' they murders yer crew."

George shuddered at what Henrietta would think of this place. His letters to her from Havana did not mention the coolies he had seen being auctioned off to plantation owners. He thought of the stack of articles Aunt Henrietta clipped for him. He did not want to discuss the coolie trade with her.

Brown sighed with the weight of the heavy valise. A Portuguese with Chinese features stepped from beneath a canvas sunshade. "Senhor! You wish a palanquin?"

"B'lieve I do," said Brown, shifting the valise again.

The Portuguese snapped his fingers, and four Chinese lounging under the sunshade jumped to grab the handles of their taxi, and in an instant lowered it beside Brown. Placing the valise on its floor he slid into the seat.

"And you, sir?" The Portuguese looked at George expectantly. George waved the man away.

He would rather walk home across the narrow peninsula. He needed to think about the project at hand. George pictured the coins they had stuck this afternoon. Once the circle-and-square edging was applied, the only remaining technical detail was tarnishing them. He thought he knew how. As a boy, his mother had rebuked him for eating his soft-boiled egg with one of her Sargent family silver spoons because the chemical reaction turned the silver black. She asked him, again, to use one of her cheaper white-metal spoons when eating eggs.

George brought three new, untarnished Mexican pesos back with him to Boston. Before he sailed for Macao, he repeated his childhood infraction as a scientific experiment, placing the coins in a bowl atop a gooey mess of soft-boiled eggs. Although the sulfurous, heavier-than-air effluent from the eggs was captured within the bowl, the tarnish it produced on the coins was uneven. The upper sides began to blacken within minutes (just as the spoon had), but the lower sides that were immersed in the eggs only had blotches of tarnish. Then he remembered the acrid, sulfurous fumes from the mercury furnaces at New Almaden in California, and the tour guide's remark on the blackened silver case of his pocket watch. "If you spend any time 'round here," he had said, "you'd best wear gold."

That remark solved the tarnish problem. A solution of liver of sulfur crystals from the apothecary gave the Mexican silver pesos an even coat of black, except over the greasy fingerprints they bore. George would tell Brown to scrub the finished coins with strong lye soap to remove any oils before bathing them twice in liver of sulfur between applications of wear to their faces.

Turning onto a quieter street, George climbed the gentle slope past William Hunter's old house. Like Endicott, Hunter was now living in a mansion on the hill overlooking Praia Grande and raising a second family with Rosalie, his American wife. Sarah Endicott was following Rosalie's example, showing a forgiving attitude and welcoming her husband's Chinese children.

Hunter and Endicott could *afford* families, but George did not want to dwell on that melancholy topic. The street rose more steeply as he approached the ruins of

São Paulo. He stopped below the ancient church and started up the broad steps. He would have a pleasant view of the town and perhaps catch a cooling breeze. As he climbed, George considered his project again. He had solved the technical problems, and today's test run finally produced credible coins. All they needed now to go into full production was a nod from the Governor Guimarães—of course, not from the governor himself but from an intermediary who would provide a cover of deniability for both Guimarães and himself.

The governor, whose term ended in December, seemed to be delaying a decision until he received word from Lisbon that he would be reappointed for another term. Although George believed he could produce a full run of coins by the end of the year, prudence would require slipping them into circulation gradually over a period of time. He could see Guimarães's point. If by some chance he was not reappointed (and who could fathom the politics of the Court at Lisbon), the new governor would be in a position to expose Guimarães and might blackmail him to extract a share for himself. In the meantime, word could arrive any day or it could be months. There was nothing George could do, except wait.

To calm his nerves, George counted the steps—66. He looked up at the ornate facade. There was no church behind it; the ancient edifice had long ago burned to the ground. He looked upward through the arched window opening to blue sky. It was like so much else in the *Cidade do nomo de Deos da Macão*—an elaborate front, with nothing behind it. Well, actually, a great deal was hidden behind the elaborate facade of Macao. Nature always abhors a vacuum. As Aunt Henrietta had often observed, the devil finds much mischief to occupy vacant minds, idle hands, and empty spaces.

George considered his own status in the ancient city. While watching the celebratory Fourth of July fireworks from the parade ground, Endicott had confided that gossips were speculating about why George was lingering so long in Macao. With the delay in negotiations, it was ever more critical that George preserve his cover identity as a tea broker. To avoid suspicion, he needed to present a facade of his own by making some conspicuous purchases of teas. Perhaps he would give a party, a ball, and invite everyone who mattered in Macao. [5]

October 23

"Mr. Dixwell!" Anna Rosa Hunter smiled, curtsied, and pointed at his signature. "My dance card arrived with your name on number four."

George bowed. "I knew that with such a popular young lady, I'd have to reserve a spot in advance, or there might be no dance at all."

William Hunter's 18-year-old daughter had the eyes and coloring of her Tanka mother and the cheery disposition of her father. George sent a dance card to each of the ladies who replied to his invitation. On certain of those cards, exercising his prerogative as host, he reserved a dance for himself. He examined Anna Rosa's card. Indeed, most of the 15 scheduled dances were already spoken for. Anna's father had reserved the second and his friend, Mr. James Bridges Endicott, the third. George looked up at the dark young man standing just behind Anna. "But I see that Mr. de Souza has taken the first dance."

The de Souzas were an old commercial family in Macao. The young fellow's father owned property all over the city. Like many old-time Macanese, the de Souzas also had intermixed with a few Chinese. George excused himself, and the two young people resumed an animated conversation in Portuguese.

The sounds of the two violins and cello tuning to the grand piano resonated across the white marble floor. The musicians would play the 15 dances on the program with at least five minutes between each to allow the men time to find their next partners. This was not New York or Newport, and George had taken care to choose old fashioned, familiar rhythms—sedate waltzes, a quadrille, a reel, and one polka for the younger folks. Later in the evening, the musicians would play whatever the dancers requested.

He looked around with satisfaction. The ballroom was a rainbow of silk gowns and embroidered shawls. For a bachelor without a hostess, he had not done badly. Rosalie Hunter and Sarah Endicott, George's neighbors from up the hill, had put their cooks to work preparing enough cakes, pastries, and sweets to last through a long, festive evening. Mrs. Mary Nye loaned the piano. George's houseboy stood beside a borrowed punch bowl filled with lemonade and glistening shards of Massachusetts ice. The men would find whiskey and cigars in the chamber to the rear, while the ladies could freshen up in the airy sitting room to the side.

All the important guests had arrived. George flipped open his pocket watch. Even by the relaxed standards of Macao, it was time to begin. He stepped toward a side table, rang the silver bell, and the room became quiet. George nodded toward a distinguished, white-haired man wearing a green-and-red sash across his chest. "I welcome his Excellency, Governor Guimarães. We are all grateful for his stewardship of this City of God, a welcoming haven for those of us whose homes are far away."

Guimarães stepped forward to the applause of the assembled guests. For an instant George met the governor's eyes, searching for a flicker of acknowledgement, some sign that the Old Heads project might proceed under his benign indifference.

"And in the absence of His Honor, the American Consul, I ask Mrs. Samuel Rawle to join me in the first waltz." George walked to the old woman's chair, bowed, and took her hand. "Thank you," he said, "for honoring this modest gathering with your radiant presence."

"And how gracious of you, Mr. Dixwell, to place your name on my card. My husband was most moved by your thoughtfulness."

George led Mrs. Rawle to the center of the floor to another round of applause. Mr. Parker, the former American commissioner, had sailed for Boston as soon as word arrived that he had been replaced. Mr. Reed, the new commissioner, was still enroute from New York. That left Mr. Rawle as the ranking American, but the aged Philadelphian lay paralyzed by a stroke. The small community of Americans came to Mrs. Rawle's aid, and everyone was happy to see her honored in her husband's place.

George signaled the lead violinist. As the music began, the floor filled with couples gliding counter-clockwise around the room. He heard a muffled "um, dois, três," as Senhora Bernardo Carneiro swept by, counting out the beat for her husband.

"How kind of you to invite Mrs. Drinker," confided Mrs. Rawle. "This has been a very hard time for her." She squeezed George's hand rather than speak of the poisoning.

Sandwith Drinker, co-partner in the firm of Rawle and Drinker, was dying of arsenic poisoning—the result of eating bread from a Chinese bakery in Hong Kong. Mrs. Drinker herself was still suffering from the lingering effects of the poison. The poisoned bread had frightened everyone. George had just breakfasted with John Heard in Hong Kong when Tsun Atow rushed in with the news. John immediately took a strong mustard emetic. George, who had only nibbled a little of his toast, decided to wait for clear symptoms before abusing his delicate stomach and bowel. Shortly thereafter it was determined that the loaves delivered to the Heard firm came from a different bakery. John had spent a painful morning retching for nothing.

Despite her best intentions, Mrs. Rawle could not avoid the subject. "And now they've let that vicious Chinaman out of prison," she blurted out.

George nodded in sympathy, not wanting to disagree with her. The white community jumped to the conclusion that Ah Lum, the baker, was the guilty party, but the Hong Kong court found no evidence to incriminate him. It now seemed more likely that the crime was the work of someone acting at the behest of Mandarin officials who seemed intent on undermining the European and American community in the colony. The incident only aggravated an already tense situation. The flotillas of British and French warships that assembled in the gulf during the 11 months since the conflagration in Canton now seemed to be only waiting for some new affront by the Chinese to justify a full assault on that ancient city.

"Such handsome young men," Mrs. Rawle nodded toward two officers from the United States warship *Portsmouth*. American policy was to remain neutral in China, and it was not certain that the American squadron would join forces with the British and French. The hard-nosed American merchants urged moderation and neutrality. It was their missionary brethren, despite laboring long years to impart the Christian virtues of mercy and forgiveness to the benighted Cantonese, who now demanded a full measure of Old Testament vengeance.

There was plenty of reason for the traders' embrace of moderation. Should a parliamentary directive arrive from London placing an embargo on British commerce with China, Yankee merchants would graciously accept whatever fees they could garner for representing their English colleagues. George considered the missionaries no more hypocritical than Aunt Henrietta's anti-slavery friends who saw no contradiction in sending arms to Kansas in support of their Christian ideals.

The piano boomed a final crescendo, and George guided a beaming Mrs. Rawle back to her chair. "My next dance is with Senhor Guimarães" she confided.

George saw that Anna Rosa, under the watchful eye of her stepmother, was chatting with the two young American officers. Her bright green gown glowed against their dress blue uniforms. [6]

§

"I'm too old to polka!" Hunter gasped, wiping his brow as he joined George at the edge of the veranda.

George leaned back against the balustrade. The evening was a success. Having completed the set list, the orchestra returned to waltzes that offered the predictability of a familiar step with some variation in tempo. Macao's perennial surplus of bachelors—foreign merchants, government officials, and military men—ensured that no woman, young or old, would lack for dancing partners.

Hunter held out his goblet. His houseboy, on loan for the evening, jumped to refill it from a crystal decanter.

"My dear Mr. Hunter!" Catharina Bonney swooped out onto the veranda with her missionary husband in tow. "Your sweet Anna Rosa has been so helpful at the school, and—"

Her eye fell on the boy with the decanter. Without looking at the dark hue of the contents, she extended her glass. Hunter stopped the boy from pouring.

"That's not for ladies," he warned her, "and how are your little scholars?" He turned to George. "Mrs. Bonney is a superb educator, Dixwell. She has made a proper young lady of Anna Rosa."

Mrs. Bonney blushed. "Well, I do my best; it's not like Canton here. There, I had 23 girls and my own schoolhouse, but I do have six little girls here."

"She's teaching them in Chinese," added the Reverend Bonney proudly. "They learn faster than in English, so we have primers and the four Gospels in Chinese. Our aim is to give the children a thoroughly Christian education without the least taint of idolatry."

George raised an eyebrow. "No Chinese classics, then?" he murmured. He marveled at the missionaries' optimism but wondered at the wisdom of a curriculum totally bereft of anything Chinese.

"Oh no, just the Gospel and good Christian literature." Mrs. Bonney smiled at her husband. "It is a mighty, although gratifying, undertaking. Unfortunately, now the landlord is taking our house for a coolie depot, and we have to move!" Mrs. Bonney's voice rose to an unseemly pitch.

"Now, now Catharina." Samuel Bonney, visibly embarrassed, placed his hand on his young wife's shoulder. "There's no need to burden Mr. Hunter—and our host—with our trials. We have faith that the Lord will provide."

George could see the frayed cuff of the missionary's shirt where it extended from beneath his dark coat. After the conflagration in Canton, all of the foreign missionaries retreated to the safety of Macao, further pressuring an already inflated real estate market. Now that the coolie trade was booming, brokers would pay even higher rents for any structure that could be used as a barracoon.

"Ah, yes, the coolie business," Hunter added absently. "Of course, our good Portuguese hosts do have the best interests of the Chinese at heart." He winked at George.

"That's not true at all!" Catharina Bonney's face flushed with indignation.

George remembered, she had been a New York Van Rensselaer before marrying her missionary husband, and she had retained the imperiously outspoken manners of her upbringing.

"The coolie trade is the most foul of occupations—an enterprise of kidnappings, imprisonings, and murder! They even dare to conduct that commerce aboard American clippers. Tell me, Mr. Hunter, with what justice can Northern ship owners taunt Southern slave owners for dealing in human flesh, while they themselves—"

Reverend Bonney interrupted her with another squeeze of her shoulder. "I believe Mr. Hunter is speaking ironically."

"Yes, indeed." Hunter now spoke with the mellifluous drawl he always used to recite his commentaries. "My dear Mrs. Bonney, Senhor Ferran, our esteemed coolie agent, has assured me that every Sunday in Havana the Celestial emigrants kneel in prayer beside their new employers." He sipped his drink. "I have it on good report that during their leisurely voyage to Cuba, they are taught good classic Latin so as to be prepared for future church attendance."

Mrs. Bonney, not amused, tried to regain her composure. The Reverend Bonney smiled and took her arm. "And with Mr. Hunter's generous support, we will strive to achieve a success at least equal to that of the teachers aboard the coolie boats—and in good Protestant teachings, too! But first we must sample Mrs. Hunter's famous tea cakes." With an apologetic nod to Hunter, he escorted his wife back into the ballroom.

At the balustrade, George caught a whiff of wood smoke on the night air and leaned over to see the view below. Along the path fronting his house, the paired arms of empty sedan chairs made a haphazard pattern. A street hawker had parked his portable teahouse with its charcoal brazier attached to one end of his shoulder pole and his basket of cups attached to the other. Red coals, the source of the smoke, glowed in the brazier beneath a steaming brass pot. A clink of porcelain sounded as the vendor picked cups from the basket. Some of the sedan men were already sipping their tea. Others were pitching copper cash against the rock wall, betting on whose coin would be closest. George looked out across the red-tiled roofs and walled gardens stair-stepping down to the Praya Grande. Far in the distance, atop Penha Hill, a beacon flickered to guide shipmasters, somewhere out on the black expanse of water.

James Bridges Endicott appeared on the verandah, interrupting George's thoughts. "Hello there, George, what a marvelous ball." He raised his glass, clinking his goblet against Hunter's and taking a drink. "Is that the life-giving essence of Scotland, or the nectar of Eire?"

"The nectar of Eire," responded Hunter. "But I'd prefer the simple bourbon of Kentucky."

"So, you must be missing your boys?" queried Endicott. "Did you get a letter on the steamer?"

"I got two. Anna Rosa misses them too!"

"Well, from what my boys tell me, yours are hardly suffering—they're riding the best horseflesh around. And now that my boys have seen the cavalry, they're not content to be foot soldiers."

"I'm sorry about that," Hunter shook his head in mock pity. "My boys are growing up too fast. Next fall Willie moves from the academy to the college. He writes he'll be taking Latin, Greek, algebra, and declamation. And next year, Jimmie will be in college too …"

George said nothing. What could he add to a discussion about children in college? He hadn't even the possibility of a wife without the means to support her, much less a family. He shook away his disappointment. The ball was grand, and the presence of Guimarães was a good sign. The governor was sure to be reappointed; it was just a matter of time. George would soon be minting Spanish dollars, and Albert Heard in Shanghai was ready to slip them into payments for the fall's tea purchases. Once his fortune was replenished, he would find a pretty young wife and start a family of his own. [7]

Coin press, early-19th-century example. The press used by George Dixwell
would have been similar to this. (Illustration clipped by an eBay dealer from an
1818–1830 English encyclopedia; drawing from author's personal collection.)

"Old Head" Spanish dollar. Illustration from an 1865 shroffs' manual. Every large transaction in China involving Western coinage required its examination by a Chinese shroff who, for a fee, would guarantee its silver content by hammering his unique chop mark into the surface of the coin, thus guaranteeing to replace the coin if it were found to be deficient in silver. (Illustration courtesy of Stephen Tsai.)

Iconography from "Old Head" coin. George Dixwell decided to counterfeit "Old Head" Spanish dollars because conservative Chinese merchants valued these coins above the actual value of their silver content. "Old Heads" featured the iconography of Spanish colonialism—the "head" side: *Carolus IIII Dei Gratia* (by the grace of God); the reverse side *HISPAN ET IND* (King of Spain and the Indies). The two columns on the reverse represented the "Pillars of Hercules" (the Gates of Gibraltar). The banners wrapped around each of the columns, inscribed *Plus Ultra* (more beyond), were to become the inspiration for the American dollar sign. (Photo by author.)

The relict facade of Macao's São Paulo Cathedral (1880's)—an elaborate front with nothing behind it! This image shows what George Dixwell would have seen from its 66-step staircase in 1857. George's metaphorical musings about it are a product of my imagination. (Photo from author's personal collection.)

By 1855, George Dixwell had lost most of the fortune he had earned in China, but he had a plan to earn it back. George knew that conservative Chinese merchants valued "Old Head" Spanish dollars at more than the value of their actual silver content. His plan was to counterfeit these antique coins with full silver content and to profit from their excess market value. He purchased counterfeit coin dies and shipped a coin press to Macau. John Heard, senior partner of the Heard, firm rejected any formal participation in the counterfeiting, although other members of the firm informally agreed to mix the counterfeit coins into their large payments for tea. George was able to produce credible silver coins, but for some reason the project was abandoned. The Heard firm in China then destroyed all correspondence relating to the project. One file of George Dixwell's letters survived in Boston, upon which this vignette is based.

A daguerreotype (ca. 1860) of Anna Rosa Hunter (1839–1923), the eldest of William C. Hunter's three children by an unidentified Tanka woman. Anna's marriage to John Endicott Gardner produced John Endicott Gardner, Jr. (1863–1943) who in 1915 was serving as Chinese immigration inspector in San Francisco. (Photo courtesy of Susan Briggs, Anna's great great-granddaughter.)

CHAPTER EIGHT

Reversals

A week after George's ball, Governor Guimarães received the long-awaited decree from Lisbon reappointing him to another three-year term, but this seems to have done nothing to further the Old Heads project. Although George had apparently overcome all the technical problems and was able to produce credible coins, the scheme never came to fruition. I do not know why. Perhaps George was unable to negotiate a suitable agreement with the Portuguese authorities. Perhaps, after seven months of negotiations, so many people knew about it and expected a percentage that there was no profit left. Perhaps rumors amongst the trading community had come to the Heard firm's attention, and they were no longer willing to cooperate, even tacitly, in circulating the coins. Word of the plan might also have spread through the closely-knit community of shroffs, so that George's coins would be easily recognized and rejected.

I only have circumstantial evidence for an awkward anticlimax. From March to November 1857, I can follow the progress of the Old Heads through oblique comments in George's many letters to Albert Farley Heard, but those letters end abruptly on November 24. A prodigious letter writer, George remained in China for another 16 months, but his letter file at the Heard Company is strangely empty for those months. It appears that sometime after the project's failure, the Heards purged their files of any embarrassing, perhaps incriminating, documents. The only letter of George's from this time that survives (probably only because it was sent to old Mr. Heard in Boston) is dated February 14, 1858. Here George expressed a hollow confidence at best. "My health has been very good," he wrote, "but the other objects of my visit have not been reached yet."

Worse was already in store. Even as the last of his ball guests said their farewells and George climbed into bed with the waltz music still echoing in his ears, the Panic of 1857 brought American commerce to a halt. Four letters were enroute from J.J. in Boston, describing the crash and its consequences for himself and George.

In the first, J.J. only mentions "a financial squall." That squall soon burst into a storm of immense destructive power. In the second J.J. wrote, "we are in the most appalling financial derangement since 1837." On the day of George's ball, J.J. wrote that the banks in New York had suspended payments in hard money and that those throughout the rest of the country "had been obliged to follow, in self defense." He cautioned George that tea purchased in China at July's prices could only be sold in New York at a great loss.

It would be eight weeks before the first of J.J.'s letters reached China. Unfortunately, George had been purchasing tea throughout the summer, some of it high grade and expensive, just the sort most difficult to sell during a depression.

In March 1859, George departed China for home, considerably poorer than when he had arrived, yet he had a new hope of recouping his fortune. Cousin George Barnard Sargent in Davenport, Iowa, had invited him to join the Cook and Sargent real estate and banking firm.[1]

Davenport, Iowa
1859, October 6

Barnard Sargent pointed to the map of Iowa that covered most of the table. "The plan is simple. We purchase large tracts along the railroad right-of-way. You find Eastern investors to purchase that land after a substantial markup. Then we subdivide it into smaller plots, mark up the price again, and sell it to farmers."

"That's right," Ebenezer Cook put in. "Since most farmers won't be able to pay cash, we'll make them loans out of our profits from reselling the large tracts to the investors."

George ran his finger along the inked right-of-way extending west from Davenport to the Nebraska border. "So we profit three times. First, on the sales to investors, then on the sale of subdivided land to the farmers, and finally on the interest the farmers pay us for their loans."

"And then," Barnard smiled, "we use the interest payments to buy more land. It's self-perpetuating! And we can cover any cash shortage with banknotes from our branch in Nebraska."

George had spent yesterday going over the figures himself. Barney was right and, better yet, they were related. Their grandfathers were brothers, and a deal within the family was bound to be trustworthy. As he looked back to the map, it suddenly struck him that the square tracts outlined in red ink along the railroad right-of-way looked like Christmas gift boxes. He looked out the window.

Outside, the timber trusses of the Chicago-Rock Island railroad bridge arched across the Mississippi River. Davenport, Iowa, was clearly the new portal to the West. Even though he would have to bear the expense of the new Boston office, George could easily sell enough land to take a healthy share of the company's profits.

Barnard pointed outside, "That bridge unites the two great oceans of the world. This very spot is destined to become the center of the globe, the grand highway and thoroughfare of nations! Our investors will be aboard from the very beginning."

George recognized the phrases from the text of the lecture Barney gave last year in Boston. Even if he himself didn't feel comfortable speaking in such hyperbole, he could have the speech reprinted for prospective investors.

Barnard turned to George with a smile. "I believe we have an agreement."

After his months of uncertainty in Macao, where every negotiation was characterized by excessive subtlety, even innuendo, George appreciated his cousin's directness. He offered his hand first to Barney and then to Ebenezer.

"Let's celebrate this evening at my house," said Barnard. "I'll see you off at the station tomorrow."

§

People and baggage poured out of the yellow passenger cars into the morning light. A woman pushed a roll of feather bedding out the window to a little girl standing below. George stepped out of the way for a man carrying a tool chest on his shoulder, followed by a boy clutching four saws bundled together with canvas straps.

The stationmaster emerged from his office and waved. "Well, halloo Mr. Sargent!"

"Halloo yourself! May I introduce my cousin, Mr. Dixwell, who is going to open our office in Boston."

The stationmaster stepped forward and extended his hand. "If you make all your connections, I guarantee you'll be takin' breakfast with your family in Boston, day after tomorrow."

"And I'll be talking about nothing but Davenport, Iowa, there," George laughed— "the hub of the nation!"

"And our magnificent bridge, from which all future rail lines will radiate, like the spokes of a wheel," Barnard interjected.

The stationmaster nodded, "You're right about that, Mayor—I mean Gen'ral, and there's nothin' the St. Louis City Council can do about it."

Cousin Barney had several careers before establishing Cook and Sargent. He had been surveyor general for the Iowa–Wisconsin district of the United States Land Office. After that, he was mayor of Davenport, and, like everyone else in the egalitarian West, he retained all his honorific titles. He carried his honorifics very well, aided by his massive beard that divided in the middle to make two identical tufts extending well down each of his lapels.

"Yes, St. Louis is dead." Barnard paused thoughtfully. "Our fair city is, by far, the best situated to be the gateway to the West. The river at St. Louis is too wide and has too soft a bottom ever to support a bridge. Railroads, not steamboats, are the future, and the bridge at Davenport is built. They'll never get it removed."

George agreed. St. Louis attorneys argued that the bridge at Davenport was a hazard to river navigation. True enough, the bridge had burned down once, ignited when a steamer crashed into one of its massive stone supports. Certainly, if the bridge were removed, Iowa property values would plummet, but that was a small risk—one he could accept balanced against the limitless possibility for gain.

George surveyed the stacked trunks and piles of personal belongings spread out on the platform. The stationmaster followed George's eyes. "The Gen'ral's circulars brings them all the way from Prussia and Schleswig-Holstein."

Barnard gazed at the immigrants clustered around their motley belongings. "A noble, hard-working race—the salt of the earth. Our circulars invite the farmers of northern Europe to throw off the shackles of serfdom for lands and fields and orchards of their own. And we encourage skilled mechanics and craftsmen to depart the wretched teeming cities of that tired continent to settle a new country where industry and perseverance reap handsome rewards."

Stationmaster added, "We've got New England abolition folks coming through here, too—two first-class cars yesterday, all wearin' fancy clothes and headin' for Kansas."

George thought of Henrietta. The Kansas-Nebraska bill had given the final decision on whether to allow slavery in those territories to the settlers living there. Abolitionist societies, bent on guaranteeing the outcome of that vote, dispatched contingents of settlers to comprise a lasting majority. But proslavery Southerners sent their own settlers—the ones Henrietta and her friends called "Missouri ruffians." Tempers ran high, and every news report out of Kansas described violent incidents between the opposing camps.

Cousin Barney was right. There was peace in Iowa, and Cook and Sargent owned vast tracts of potential farmland across the entire length of the state.

Before George boarded the newly arrived train, Barnard shook his hand firmly and looked him in the eye. "You'll do well with the Boston office, Dixwell, and I'll be out to help you before you open!"

The car jerked forward. George waved to his cousin and settled into his seat. The iron wheels screeched as the train twisted toward the waterfront. The throb of the locomotive slowed as it labored up the incline to the bridge. The smokestacks of Davenport's brickmakers, flourmills, and slaughterhouses lined the waterfront. Steamships tethered to the shore angled downstream like herring bones towards New Orleans and every destination along the way.

George followed the Mississippi-Missouri tracks up the bluff, past the six city blocks he now owned and beyond into the distance towards Nebraska. Underneath Cousin Barney's bombast was a basic truth—railroads were indeed the wave of the future, and Davenport was the gateway to the West. All western commerce would eventually have to pass through this portal.

His roll of maps rested in the overhead rack. George had just enough capital left to finance the opening of the Boston office. He leaned back and closed his eyes. All was well. The rhythmic clunk of iron wheels against the joints in the iron rails lulled him into sleep. [2]

The Parker Home
156 Tremont Street, Boston, Mass.
December 2

"For heaven's sake, Henriet, don't be so morbid."

Henrietta watched the minute hand click from 11:23 to 11:24. He would be walking toward the gallows now, she thought. Perhaps he was already standing on the scaffold. "For heaven's sake, indeed." Henrietta softly repeated her sister's impatient words. For all her lack of feeling, Anna Parker had come to the heart of the matter. It was, at bottom, an issue of Heaven or Hell. It was a question of whether John Brown was a Christian martyr doing God's work or a common murderer.

The minute hand clicked forward to 11:25. Would he be allowed to address the crowd? Had they already placed the noose around his neck? Henrietta pictured the hangman gently lifting Brown's long flowing beard over the noose. Like everything else in this strange world, it seemed a contradiction to treat a condemned man with solicitous respect just before taking his life. Perhaps she was being morbid, but she wondered what death by hanging would be like. Would Brown slowly suffocate? Would he twist and writhe in agony? She tried to elevate her thoughts. Mr. Emerson called Brown a "new saint," whose hanging "would make the gallows as glorious as the cross." Nice rhetoric, she thought, but a mockery of Christ's teachings.

Henrietta walked back to her table. It was not only futile to watch the clock, but it prolonged the ordeal. She looked out across Boston Common. Dark patches of frozen ground glowered between the snowdrifts. On October 16th, when the first news of the events at Harpers Ferry reached Boston, the elms and maples were still glorying, bright with yellow and red. Two weeks later, John Brown was tried, convicted, and sentenced. Today, only six weeks after that first news, the elms stood like skeletons, icicles dangling from their branches, and John Brown was about to hang by his neck until dead.

Right and wrong had seemed much more clearly distinguished before Harpers Ferry and even more so before the events that led up to the raid. As a Christian nonresister, Henrietta rejected violence, believing that slavery must be battled only with reasoned argument. She tried to come to terms with "Beecher's Bibles," the Sharps rifles that Boston abolitionists had sent to Kansas. It was right and proper for antislavery emigrants to defend themselves against proslavery thugs from Missouri. That was justifiable self-defense, but how could so wise and erudite a man as Ralph Waldo Emerson describe John Brown as a saint—a Christian martyr! Only three years ago that same Mr. Brown descended on his proslavery neighbors in the middle of the night, dragged a father and his sons from their beds and hacked them to pieces, while a wife—a mother—begged for mercy.

After such a brutal act, how could respectable antislavery men form a secret compact to fund Brown's attack on the arsenal at Harpers Ferry? It made her shudder. The letters that John Brown carelessly left behind clearly implicated men she knew well.

One by one, their faces came before her: Mr. George Luther Stearns, the husband of Maria Child's niece; Dr Samuel Gridley Howe, whom she had known for 30 years; and Gerrit Smith, the self-styled radical abolitionist, whom she knew well for the florid verbal excess of his incessant pronouncements.

These men, Brown's disciples, now disclaimed all knowledge of the raid. Their vehement denials were unconvincing, and their subsequent behavior did not speak well of their courage. Terrified by the prospect of prosecution for conspiracy, Mr. Stearns and Dr. Howe had fled to Canada, while Mr. Smith now cowered in a Utica lunatic asylum, perhaps, some charged, only feigning a well-publicized insanity.

Henrietta recalled the last words the disciple Peter spoke to Jesus. "Lord, I am ready to go with thee, both into prison, and to death." John Brown, although himself hardly a gentle Savior, might have borrowed Christ's reply. "I tell thee, *Samuel*, and *George*, and *Gerrit*, the cock shall not crow this day, before that thou shalt thrice deny that thou knowest me." How many times beyond thrice, she wondered, had these disciples publicly disavowed their pledge to John Brown?

Henrietta resisted her urge to look at the clock again. She stood and walked to the window, then sat at her table again. Biting her lip, she rearranged her scissors and letter opener and squared her inkwell and address book beside her blotter.

"Henriet, you're like Mr. Barnum's lion pacing around his cage." Anna Parker closed her account book. "Should we take a walk before lunch?"

Henrietta shook her head. She had already walked down to the Anti-Slavery Office on Cornhill Street to fetch her copy of *The Liberator*, so fresh off the press that the ink smudged her fingers. She smiled at her older sister. Despite the fact that Anna disdained her opinions and had only contempt for her abolitionist friends, Anna was trying to comfort her.

Henrietta placed the newspaper on her table. Its masthead had remained unchanged for years. Three images told the story of emancipation—at least as she and the other nonresistors had imagined it. To the left, an auctioneer shouted from a raised pavilion beneath a sign: "Slaves, horses & other Cattle in lots to Suit." In the background stood the Capitol; above its dome flew a banner emblazoned with one word: "SLAVERY." In the center stood Christ, clutching a cross like a staff in his left hand and pointing decisively with his right. The caption read: "I come to break the bonds of the oppressor."

Henrietta stared at the image. How, in all these years, had she never before noticed that the pose was just like Christ's in the familiar illustration of him driving the moneychangers from the temple! Before the figure of Christ, the auctioneer cowered on the ground, while a slave knelt in prayer. On the right side of the masthead, the third image showed a great heroic arch labeled "Emancipation." African men and women walked joyfully toward it. In the foreground lay a discarded shovel and hoe, and just beyond the arch was the Capitol, this time, with the banner "Freedom" flying above its dome.

It was a grand vision of the Cause: The Congress of the United States converted through the irresistible power of Christian moral suasion. No wild-eyed John Brown stood on the gallows; no so-called radicals shrieked denials from the Canadian side of Niagara Falls; no false friend hid in an insane asylum.

A church bell sounded in the distance: a faint cry in the wilderness. It was the African church. Henrietta glanced back at the clock. 11:31. It was over then. Mr. Brown's heart had ceased; his body was turning cold. The bell tolled a dirge—

"Judging by that lonely sound," Anna interrupted, "lamentations for Mr. Brown are hardly unanimous among our men of God."

"And when have our men of God been unanimous about anything regarding slavery?" Henrietta muttered under her breath. Mr. Garrison's Christ might proclaim emancipation, but not all Christians concurred with that image. So many years ago she sat next to Catharine aboard the little steamer filled with abolitionists bound for Nantucket, while the Reverend Mr. Robbins, also on board, lectured them on the wisdom and *benefits* of slavery. As with so many of the clergy, a polished boot barely hid a cloven hoof.

Anna's mouth tightened, "All of this has certainly kept your Mrs. Child busy. From what I see in the *Tribune*, she has written most impertinently to Mr. Wise, the governor of Virginia. Of course, that man's judgment falls well short of his surname—to contend publicly with such a virago."

Henrietta remained silent.

Anna sighed and returned to her correspondence at her own table. It was no secret between them that Anna loathed Maria Child almost as much as she did Mr. Garrison. When John Brown was arrested, Maria sent a private letter to the governor of Virginia offering to come and nurse the saber wounds John Brown sustained during his capture. Governor Wise, attempting to burnish his own reputation, released her letter to the press along with his hypocritically courtly response: "Coming as you propose, to minister to the captive, Virginia would be weak, indeed, if her State faith cannot be redeemed to the letter of morality and if her chivalry cannot courteously receive a lady's visit to prison."

Henrietta extracted a clipping from a folder on her table and ran her finger down the column to a paragraph circled in pencil. Silently she reread Maria's searing response:

> "Before I opened your civil and diplomatic letter, I looked thoughtfully
> at the State Seal of Virginia. A liberty-loving hero stands with his foot
> upon a prostrate despot; under his strong arm manacles and chains lie
> broken; and the motto is "*Sic Semper Tyranni*s, 'Thus may it ever be done to
> tyrants'... And, this is the blazon of a State whose most profitable business
> is the internal slave trade!"

Henrietta breathed a gentle sigh. Anna's mind was set. It had been 15 years since the two sisters agreed not to discuss the politics of abolition. Among the precipitating events then were the provocative words Mr. Garrison added to the upper-right-hand corner of the front page of *The Liberator:* "The existing Constitution of the United States is a covenant with death, and an agreement with hell. No Union with Slave holders."

Anna had made it quite clear that she wanted nothing to do with such treason. Her opinions had not troubled Henrietta so much as long as she and Catharine lived in their "mouse's nest" at 5 Poplar Street. There, Maria, Mr. Garrison, and other antislavery friends could gather. All of that changed after Catharine's death when Henrietta moved into Anna's mansion. Abolitionists knew they were not welcome in that parlor. Because of that, after tonight's memorial meeting at Tremont Temple, Maria Child would not be staying with Henrietta but at Mrs. Follen's house.

A crash of porcelain sounded from the dining room.

"Goodness!" Anna rushed toward the sound. "What has Biddy broken now?"

Henrietta tried to remember what she had been doing when she first turned to stare at the clock. On her table was a stack of printed invitations for the Anti-Slavery Subscription Festival. Last year, instead of their traditional Christmas Bazaar, the society staged a January Soirée. Each of the sponsoring ladies, armed with a subscription pledge book, served tea from her own table, on her own china.

How Anna had grumbled when Henrietta packed the Sargent family silver tea service for that soirée and fumed when she announced that she would "borrow" Bridget for the evening to help serve cakes baked by Eliza! But that precedent was established now. Thank goodness, from the very beginning of her residence with Anna, Henrietta insisted on paying half the salaries of the maid and the cook.

Recent events caused some uncertainty concerning the forthcoming festival. It had already been advertised for months when John Brown attacked Harpers Ferry. After so many fundraisings to support his legal defense, his family, and still others of his band yet to be tried, Henrietta worried that her friends might be less than eager to pledge yet again to support the Massachusetts Anti-Slavery Society. Weary donors might be disinclined to attend. Many respectable people might well stay away, repelled by the violent direction the movement had taken. Or would Brown's martyrdom attract even more supporters to the Cause?

The dinner bell sounded, Bridget's familiar tinkle. Henrietta straightened the stack of invitations. The bell sounded again, mimicking the tattoo of the Tremont Street horsecar. Anna was doing her best to bring cheer to this dismal day.

"Have some cream, Henriet." Anna poured a full tablespoon from the porcelain pitcher and took a sip. "Cats love cream!" She dabbed her lips with a napkin. "And if you insist on taking mother's Wedgwood to your soirée, you'll find you still have 12 saucers but only 11 cups."

Bridget blushed. [3]

Massachusetts Bank, Boston
December 16

"George, could you join me for a moment?" J.J. Dixwell, president of Massachusetts Bank, leaned into George's office, then stepped back across the hall to his own.

George set aside his correspondence. J.J. had been good enough to let him use this room, while the new Cook & Sargent office was being renovated a block away. Cousin Barney had taken a suite of rooms around the corner where he was promoting Iowa property to prospective investors. George was proud to be a principal in a growing firm. The workmen had already repainted the walls and were installing new gas lighting.

Stepping into J.J.'s office, George recognized Almon Hodges, the president of Washington Bank, and offered his hand. "Good morning Mr. Hodges."

The banker's grip felt strangely distant, and Hodges cleared his throat, "It's convenient, Mr. Dixwell, that you are so close by!"

George smiled expansively and nodded toward J.J., "I'm close enough to have afternoon coffee with my brother, even when I've moved to our new Cook & Sargent offices. We should be open by Christmas."

"That's what Mr. Hodges wants to talk about," said J.J., closing the door. "Yesterday, just before closing time, Mr. Sargent presented a large check to Mr. Hodges and took the whole amount in cash. The check was drawn on Mr. Sargent's personal account at Merchants Bank here in town—where there are, apparently, no funds."

George smiled genially at Hodges. "I sincerely regret your inconvenience. Sometimes, in his enthusiasm, Mr. Sargent forgets the distance between Boston and Iowa. A draft on his account at Cook & Sargent in Davenport is undoubtedly on its way, even as we speak, and we will of course gladly cover any surcharge caused by his miscalculation."

Hodges looked pained, "We are aware of the usual delays in transfers from the West, so we sent a telegraphic message to inquire. This is the reply."

George gasped as he read, "Cook & Sargent bankrupt—December 15—"

J.J. earnestly assured, "Of course, my brother will cover the deficiencies in Mr. Sargent's account, and I, personally, will endorse his note."

"Certainly," George mumbled, barely able to speak.

"Thank you." Hodges extended his hand to J.J., then to George as he left. "And, as you have requested, no word of this matter will pass outside this office. Good day, gentlemen."

J.J. put a hand on George's shoulder, whispering, "I'm so sorry."

George had no answer. He left quickly, not wanting his brother's sympathy, and hurried downstairs to the street. At the end of the block he crossed to the Cook & Sargent office. An iron chain held fast by a brass padlock was looped through the door pulls. He quickly strode around the corner to the hotel.

"Is Mr. Sargent in?" George addressed the desk clerk and waited as the man examined the guest register.

"Mr. Sargent checked out yesterday evening. He gives Davenport, Iowa, as his forwarding address."

George stepped out of the hotel, feeling sick to his stomach. For weeks, he and Barney had been urging Aunt Anna to increase her holdings of Davenport real estate. Only yesterday, over lunch, his cousin talked of opening a branch office in New York—all the while knowing the firm had already failed. The treacherous scoundrel! George remembered the map they had shown aunts Anna and Henrietta. The old ladies had been so pleased to see Parker, Bowditch, and Dixwell streets prominently marked. Now that shameless snake had slithered away. [4]

Music Hall, Boston
1860, January 25

Henrietta joined the other women walking onto the stage. Stopping beside the piano, she looked out at the crowd. No, it was not the same as the old Christmas Bazaar that she and Catharine had loved so much, but it was a gay gathering nonetheless. The drama of John Brown's execution seemed not to have dampened the antislavery sentiment in Boston one bit! The hall was filled and buzzing with animated conversation.

Henrietta raised her voice above the din and waved pages over her head. She and Maria had spent most of the morning writing out 30 copies of "The Hero's Heart" for a group sing. "Does everybody have the words?"

At the podium, William Lloyd Garrison rapped the gavel and waited for the room to quiet. "For 26 years, these brave and dedicated ladies have hosted an annual festival to support our holy cause. Tonight, before the good ladies adjourn, each to her own tea table, they will perform Mrs. Child's tribute to our fallen martyr of Harpers Ferry—a tribute that she dedicates to our stricken comrade from Peterboro, Mr. Gerrit Smith, for whose speedy recovery we all pray."

Henrietta lowered her gaze as a thunderous applause broke forth. Not too speedy a recovery, she thought, then chided herself for her lack of Christian charity. She surveyed the hall. Every seat was occupied, and more people stood around the edges. It was an astonishing crowd. Could they possibly have sent out that many invitations? She calculated: 27 women serving tea, each at the head of her own table, with seating for 9 guests. They would serve 243 people per sitting, a total of 729 for the three sittings. At least that many were here!

"Dear comrades ..." Garrison paused until the applause quieted. "When John Brown walked from the jail to the gallows, he stopped for a moment ... Yes, he stopped for a blessed moment to kiss a little colored child."

As if by signal, the piano thundered. At the far end of the line of women, Maria held her pencil aloft. Henrietta marked the first verse with her finger, cleared her throat, and began on the down stroke.

> "A winter sunshine, still and bright,
> The Blue Hills bathed with golden light,
> And earth was smiling to the sky,
> When calmly he went forth to die.
>
> The old man met no friendly eye,
> When last he looked on earth and sky;
> But one small child, with timid air,
> Was gazing on his silver hair."

Now the trumpet played a melodic interlude against the chords of the piano. Henrietta quickly read ahead:

"As that dark brow to his up turned,
The tender heart within him yearned;
And, fondly stooping o'er her face,
He kissed her for her injured race."

Henrietta frowned. Everybody who read the *Standard* knew the story about John Brown kissing the colored child as he walked to the gallows was not true. This morning at the Anti-Slavery Office, she had questioned Maria about the morality of bearing false witness. Maria answered without hesitation that the imagined story was far more faithful to the spirit of the man than were the actual facts. How could a falsehood possibly be more true than truth itself? Perhaps Maria meant that in a spiritual cause, it was spirit that mattered.

Not fully convinced, Henrietta sang with all the gusto she could muster.

"But Jesus smiled that sight to see,
And said, 'He did it unto me.'
The golden harps then sweetly rung,
And this the song the Angels sung."

To enthusiastic applause, Mr. Garrison returned to the podium at the end of the song to speak. "Dear friends of the Cause. Tonight we have an attendance far beyond anything we could imagine. Now, as each of you takes tea and cake with these fine ladies and signs their subscription books with a generous pledge, please enjoy their company for but one cup of tea, so that others may take the next sitting. Also, before taking your refreshment, please admire the display of busts and portraits of those who have labored in the vineyards of abolition. You may, however, pass one bald-headed bust without comment."

The crowd roared as Garrison dipped his shiny head and then joined the women near the piano.

Henrietta threaded her way through the crowd toward her table, passing the busts of Dr. Channing, Senator Sumner, Mr. Emerson, Mr. Phillips, and Mr. Garrison. A crowd gathered around Mr. Brackett, the sculptor, who was displaying photographs of his nearly finished bust of John Brown.

§

It was lovely to see the Sargent family tea service gleaming on its oval tray. Henrietta poured a test dribble of tea into the waste bowl. It had steeped to a chestnut brown. The half-chest George brought back from China brewed dark and rich with no bitter aftertaste.

"How kind of you to come to my table," Henrietta looked up at her guests. Every seat was taken, and more people waited behind each of the chairs for the next seating. "Dear Mrs. Shaw, how well you are looking," Henrietta said to the elderly woman to her right. "And how would you like your tea?"

"Not too strong — with sugar and cream, please."

Henrietta worked swiftly. Soon everyone had tea and cake, and three conversations mingled across the table. She sat straight and looked around the room. Clumps of people stood in front of each of the busts and pictures. A gentleman at the far end of the table was signing the ribbon-bedecked subscription book. Henrietta opened the lacquer caddy and added two measures of leaves to the teapot, as some dishes were cleared.

Mrs. Shaw rose from her chair, glancing over her shoulder. "Thank you, Miss Sargent. I see there are many others most eager to join you."

§

"My dear Miss Sargent, I waited for the last sitting." Dr. Henry Ingersol Bowditch nodded at Henrietta from the chair beside her. He waited while she poured the last cup of tea. There was a shadow of melancholy behind his smile. "How I wish my sisters were here with us."

Henrietta nodded in sympathy. "As I have wished for my own sisters."

With Catharine's death, the Sargent sisters had been reduced to three, and Esther, the mother of the Dixwell boys, had never shown interest in the Cause. It was at that genealogical node that Dr. Bowditch and Henrietta shared the same regret, for his sisters had married Epes and J.J. Dixwell. While the Dixwells were nominally opposed to slavery, they had no more sympathy with abolitionists than did Anna.

"I hear your nephew Epes has his hands full at the Scientific Club," Bowditch chuckled, "keeping Dr. Agassiz and Dr. Gray from coming to blows over Mr. Darwin's theory. From what he tells me, the Wednesday night meetings have become most lively."

"I imagine so. Mr. Darwin has called into question the whole nature of creation."

Dr. Bowditch frowned slightly. "Yes, and Dr. Gray is his great supporter."

"There was quite a large advertisement for Mr. Darwin's book in the *Transcript* yesterday, as large as our notice for our subscription benefit! I must confess I have not yet read the book, but from what Epes has told me, I'm not sure I care for its implications."

Bowditch was pleased to show his expertise. "Darwin believes that the species on earth are mutable—they change in tiny increments over long periods of time as they compete like common street vendors for advantage. In his view, all species have thus developed from lower forms of life."

Henrietta shook her head. "This theory allows slaveholders to justify their position that Africans are a lower form of life. That is terribly wrong! Surely there can be no justification in modern science for the barbarous custom of slavery!"

"Indeed," Bowditch nodded. "But the contrary view of the Catastrophists, like Dr. Agassiz, that there were earlier creations, which were wiped away by great sheets of ice, gives those same slaveholders the argument that Africans are an inferior remnant of some earlier creation before Adam and Eve were created in God's image."

Henrietta's eyes widened in disbelief. "Certainly Dr. Agassiz doesn't believe that!"

"I think he does. In his introductory essay to Nott and Gliddon's *Types of Mankind*, Dr.

Agassiz observes that the differences among the races of men are of the same kind or even greater than those that distinguish the anthropoid monkeys as different species."

Henrietta pursed her lips. "Every scientific theory seems like a Trojan Horse, concealing a multitude of morally offensive consequences." She stopped and looked quickly around the table. She had almost forgotten her guests, but they were all engaged in their own animated conversation as they rose to sign the subscription book.

"Henrietta," Maria Child stood beside her and whispered, "you must come with me before you leave."

Henrietta smiled at Dr. Bowditch. "Will you excuse me?" Maria took Henrietta's hand and led her toward the stage. From the podium, a young man was unfurling a canvas—a life-size depiction of the Virginia state seal—but in this version, Lady Liberty stood upon a prostrate, manacled slave. Maria beamed. "Isn't it wonderful? Now come with me to see Mr. Brackett."

They approached the sculptor, surrounded by a knot of admirers looking at a clay bust of John Brown. A sign noted that the sculptor, Mr. Brackett, was asking two dollars for a photograph.

Henrietta sniffed, "At least the sale of your pamphlets at five cents each will support the Cause. That man's proceeds only support his own pocket."

"Yes, but we must be nice to him," Maria whispered. "My dear Mr. Brackett," she addressed him, "the head looks like the best of the Hebrew prophets—like Moses, himself, seen in vision by Michelangelo. You must make haste to put this into marble before anything happens to you."

"My dear Mrs. Child," Mr. Brackett pulled at his mustachio. "I promise I will not die before I do. You need not fear."

Maria lowered her eyes slightly. "And, good Sir, you will *never* die, after you have!"

Henrietta looked at her friend's face to see if she was serious. Maria was capable of saying anything with a subtlety that made it difficult to distinguish drama from satire. Henrietta examined the noble-looking bust.

The world was topsy-turvy. Scientists vied over which view best proved the Africans subhuman; John Brown was now a saint; this huckster of a sculptor paraded as a gentleman; and bloody violence had brought this multitude of people to what had been a celebration of peaceful moral suasion for the past 26 years. [5]

The Parker Home
May 4

"Biddie, please serve Mr. George another slice of ham." Anna Parker dabbed a damask napkin to her lips.

"Geordie," Henrietta nodded in agreement, "you must keep up your strength."

George waved Bridget away. He felt enough like a cripple without his aunts' stifling solicitude. For weeks, the old ladies had carefully avoided any allusion to his financial collapse. Fourteen years ago (the year Annie was born) he had returned from China even richer than J.J. Now he occupied a spare bedroom in J.J.'s house. It was a stunning reversal from his suite of rooms at the New York Hotel, the lavish soirées at the Wetmores' and Astors', and his summers at Newport.

George's portfolio had been reduced to unsaleable land in Iowa; the uncollectible debt of James Dorr was mired in litigation that could take years to resolve; and he had a personal obligation to reimburse Washington Bank for Barnard Sargent's fraudulent overdraft. "Pride goeth before destruction, and a haughty spirit before a fall." The old proverb echoed in his head. He had been brimming with confidence during those fat years or had it been arrogance? Was this what Henrietta had meant so long ago when she warned him against "seeking an Eldorado"?

He looked around the little family table. J.J. sat at the head and Aunt Anna at the foot; Henrietta and little Annie across from him, and to his right, J.J.'s wife, Elizabeth. Family chat swirled around him.

"Annie, the flowers in your last watercolor practically jumped off the paper. I could almost smell their fragrance." Anna Parker addressed her namesake.

"Thank you, Auntie. Now I'm working on perspective."

"And she wants to work in oil," Elizabeth winced. "I'm afraid the air of Sunnyside will be permeated with spirits of turpentine."

"But, Mother!" Annie protested. "With oil I can have real texture in my brush strokes. If you're worried about the smell, we can put a studio next to Uncle George's laboratory in the carriage house."

"But dear, you mustn't strain your eyes, like your poor cousin Fanny." Anna Parker spoke with concern.

On doctor's orders, Epes Dixwell's daughter Fanny had greatly reduced her hours at her easel. Now she expressed her artistic talent with embroidery.

"J.J., you haven't said a word all evening." Henrietta looked down the table at her eldest nephew. "And you look so glum."

"He is worrying about what the war will do to commerce." Elizabeth patted her husband's hand.

J.J. fiddled with his napkin ring. "I think we are all on tenterhooks, especially since President Lincoln's proclamation calling upon the rebels to disperse. He gave them 20 days to return their allegiance to the Union. Monday will be the 20th day!"

Anna rolled her eyes. "Perhaps we read different papers. That proclamation was meaningless a week after Mr. Lincoln issued it once the rebels fired on Sumter."

J.J. nodded slowly. "Still, the day should not pass unnoticed as we 'let slip the dogs of war.'"

"Of course not." Anna's voice took on a motherly tone. "But those dogs have already slipped their collars. As you well know, Mr. Davis is now issuing letters of marque to Confederate privateers to seize Northern merchant ships on the high seas. More to the point for commerce, there is no insurance company in the world that will bond a clipper and its cargo of tea against wartime seizure."

Henrietta brushed away a stray breadcrumb. "Commerce aside, I, for one, am cheered by the fact that there are, at last, a North and a South. That first shot fired at Sumter told me that never again will a fugitive slave be returned to bondage. When the rebels are finally crushed and the Union reestablished, the stranglehold of slaveholders over our government will be crushed as well."

George cleared his throat and attempted to steer the conversation toward safer ground. "I am delighted to read in the *Transcript* that Aunt Anna is identified as the first donor to the fund for the protection of Boston against the rebels."

"And I," Henrietta turned toward Anna, "salute my dear sister for her generosity and patriotism."

George saw tears welling in Anna's eyes. For the first time in years the incompatible political views of his two aunts had converged. Regardless of whether the aim was emancipation or healthy commerce, they were finally in agreement that the rebellion must be quelled. All of Boston seemed to be united. His old China colleague Bennet Forbes had contributed $500 toward a Coast Guard gunboat for Boston harbor. Young Wendell Holmes, Fanny's beau, and his Harvard classmates were planning to enlist in the Army, Navy, and a host of new volunteer regiments. Wendell's father wrote a timely, new verse for the "Star Spangled Banner."

Anna regained her composure. "Tonight, at Annie's request, we will have a special dessert treat—vanilla ice cream and the season's first blackberries from Maryland."

And perhaps the last, thought George. The sentiments of most Marylanders were clearly with the rebels. To his relief, Henrietta did not ask whether the berries had been picked by slaves.

George gazed at his aunts. It was not only the Union they wanted to help. J.J. had revealed to him, in strictest confidence, that the aunts had changed their wills to put his share in trust, beyond the grasp of his creditors. In addition, J.J. revealed that Anna offered to advance a sum sufficient to pay off George's debts and provide enough capital for him to re-enter commerce.

This he could not accept. To be saved not by his own efforts but by the generosity of an elderly aunt would forever mark him as a failure, a pitiable charity, as well as a man of impaired judgment, too unreliable to include in any future mercantile venture. He urged J.J. to tell Anna that, on mulling over her kindly intended offer, he had not mentioned it to George and that it should never be spoken of again. It would not only destroy George's honor but also what remained of his credibility. George had a plan to restore himself by his own efforts.

He folded and refolded his napkin. He needed to tell the family his news before the cheery banter of dessert. George cleared his throat and arranged his words. "I have an announcement to make. I have decided to accept the offer of Augustine Heard & Company and will return to China in their employ. I plan to take the morning rail to New York to discuss the arrangement."

Henrietta broke the silence. "I have thought that you would go. It is a brave and honorable thing to do, but I am so selfish. God gives us but three score and ten. Your mother and Anna and I have well passed that mark. We must somehow clutch and cherish these last few moments, for we may never see you again." [6]

Three days later, George drafted a formal letter to Gus Heard, of Augustine Heard & Company.

New York
7 May 1861

Dear Heard

I was a good deal out of order yesterday partly from physical causes, partly from worry ... I felt that I had delayed too long answering the questions in yours of April 5th as to when I would go out in anticipation of the originally contemplated term & what I would consider as suitable compensation for the extra time ... .

This brings me to an avowal which is something like drawing teeth—to a sensitive man—an avowal of the fact that since the panic I have been exceedingly cramped for funds & am perplexed to divine where the means are to come from to pay my expenses of the overland journey, and such outfits as I must have to present myself becomingly as a representative of A.H. & Co. & also to pay such local charges as I must before going ... .

With $3000 cash or in notes I should see myself clear to do all these things, and if you felt that you could help me in the matter I would leave the sum to be charged against me in any way that John should decide. I should leave it entirely to him—as I ought—and should not bother him with any bargaining about this, that, or the other.

Don't do this if you think John will disapprove or if you see any objection yourself. I will in such case manage the best way I can & if I cannot do any other way will go by ship.

Is it not damnable that a man under the name of my friend—should have stripped me of $160,000 the whole of which he equitably owes me—should then have got his debt reduced to half that amount—& then interpose legal delays to collection of any portions of the reduced claim; & put me under the necessity of asking to have the future discounted? Yet such is the world we live in.

Yours truly,

G. B. Dixwell

The Heards advanced George enough money for clothing and a steamer ticket. On August 14, George boarded the *Africa* for Liverpool. Four days later, with George safely on his way, Aunt Anna Parker wrote him a farewell letter:

> "Let me say one word about your absence. When I first heard you were thinking of going away, I thought of proposing to you to stay with us—accepting a part of my resources—and mentioned it to some of your and my friends ... who all begged me not to mention the thing to you, as you would not like it ... The step to China was the most manly, and independent one—and the most likely to promote your health and prosperity ... Heaven grant it may be so! There's a divinity who shapes our course, 'rough hew it as we will.'"

Henrietta's farewell letter has not survived. [7]

Henrietta Sargent (ca. mid-1860s). Her reticule appears to have an ethnic provenance befitting her support for oppressed people. (Photo courtesy of the Massachusetts Historical Society.)

The front-page banner of *The Liberator*. For many years the banner presented the hoped-for trajectory of emancipation in three images: an auctioneer selling slaves, the auctioneer cowering before Christ, together with a slave kneeling in prayer, and finally, a group of emancipated slaves celebrating their freedom. (Drawing from author's personal collection.)

George Dixwell (ca.1860), essentially bankrupt and much aged. His brother John had guaranteed a loan from the Washington Bank that not only covered George's debts but also protected the Dixwell family name. On April 14, 1861, George sailed for China in the vain hope of recouping his fortune. (Photo courtesy of the Massachusetts Historical Society.)

CHAPTER NINE

Yangtze Trader

Chinkiang, China
1863, February 27

"No!" George shouted, pointing. "More to the right." He shivered in the cold. Checking his position just above the high-water mark on the Yangtze River bank, he squinted downstream to the pile of rocks that marked the edge of the Russell company property. He and William Cloutman, the Heard firm's Chinkiang agent, had hiked the whole riverfront, past the Dent, Jardine Matheson, Fletcher, and Russell companies' markers. All in a row, they formed the boundary of what might someday become a foreign bund. George envisioned a row of stately buildings rising along the riverfront, housing British and American companies. It seemed strange that "bund"—a Hindoo word—should come to describe a Chinese waterfront.

Some Mandarin speculator had already grabbed the 800 feet next to Russell's. George was measuring the future site of the Heard firm's Chinkiang agency house at this remove—if indeed the foreign community were to be established here on the north side of the river. To cover an alternate possibility, he spent the previous morning surveying another parcel over on the city side.

George gazed south across the broad expanse of brown water. Compared to the Mississippi at St. Louis, the Yangtze looked to be almost twice as wide. On the far shore, the ancient city of Chinkiang looked like a toy hunkered beneath a winter haze of burning charcoal.

George turned to Cloutman, "Make them pull it tight!" Cloutman's men obeyed, drawing the measuring line so taut that it vibrated in the frigid north wind.

The past three days had been busy ones. The Heard Company's steam tug, *Fire Dart*, had made the 140-mile trip up the Yangtze in 25 hours, despite having two salt junks in tow. Before she pulled upstream on the next leg of her 600-mile voyage to Hankow, George had borrowed the spare 20-fathom depth line to measure whatever property they might purchase. They could make do with the one-fathom (6-foot) knotted intervals, but a 100-foot rope would have been simpler. The Chinese speculators, eager to lure in foreign buyers, were now offering river frontage in multiples of 100 feet.

George grimaced. He suspected that Ahow—the tea merchant through whom the Heard Company channeled most of their Chinkiang business—was, along with Cloutman's comprador, in league with the speculators. In this particular matter, Ahow was working somewhat more for "Ahow & Company" than he was for the Heard Company.

George folded the sketch of the property and shoved it into his pocket. In the two years since the treaty, Western merchants had quickly established agencies at the three Yangtze river ports that were opened to foreign commerce. The Heard firm placed men at Chinkiang as well as at Kiukiang and Hankow. Now that tea was coming out of the interior to the upstream ports with some regularity, it was time to build a permanent Chinkiang agency house, with "godowns" secure enough to warehouse the opium they hoped to barter in exchange for tea.

"Pile some of those rocks here. And smear some paint on them!" Cloutman shouted, gesturing toward the sampan the men had towed across the river behind the eight-oared taxi. The young man seemed comfortable with his first independent posting. The workmen heaved ashore the heavy ballast rocks to mark the featureless river frontage. Covered with sticky white paint, the stones would be too conspicuous to be appropriated to mark someone else's parcel.

Cloutman joined George at the water's edge. "You're right, Mr. Dixwell, this is the better location. The winter waves. They'll all break over there. This side will make a better harbor."

Yesterday morning George directed the *Fire Dart* along both shores of the channel between Chinkiang and the island, plumbing the depth of the anchorages. Not only was the water on the far side too shallow for a side-wheel steamer to pull close to the shore, but the river bottom was too soft to build a wharf out from the shore or to set an anchor against a winter gale. This side offered a better anchorage, but they would still have to haul in a good 3 feet of fill before building a house and godown sufficiently high to keep the contents dry.

"Do you think Ahow is leveling with us about the property?" Cloutman nodded toward the water taxi where the tea merchant, elegantly clad in a quilted black cape and fur cap, sat chatting with its master.

"I suspect that all the frontage on both sides of the river is owned by his fellow compradors. Ahow is sure to reap a grand commission regardless of what we do."

§

George watched Cloutman's men lug his trunk towards the aft cabin of the *Independence*. His business here was completed, and it would be over a week before the *Fire Dart* steamed back from Hankow with, he hoped, a cargo of tea, a deck load of Chinese passengers, and a long string of junks in tow. Rather than wait for it, he bought passage aboard this vessel. Even though the sail-powered *Independence* would travel much more slowly, he was anxious to be on his way.

Cloutman joined George, shivering by the shore-side rail. He opened his valise and took out two bottles—one of English whiskey and the other of sherry. "These should keep you warm. Compliments of the Chinkiang Agency!"

George slipped the bottles into his own valise. Apparently, the young agent had the requisite breeding and manners to represent the company. "Thank you! May your fortune ever grow and may your shadow never diminish!" A somewhat awkward translation, he thought, but of course Cloutman wouldn't understand the Chinese.

George appreciated Cloutman's deference and show of respect. It was probably as much a response to his seniority in years as to his position as the Heard firm's managing partner at Shanghai. Cloutman wouldn't know that he, in like manner, now deferred to Albert Farley Heard, the firm's senior partner at Hong Kong.

Things had changed. Seventeen years ago, when Albert was only 9 years old, George was the Heard firm's senior partner in all of China. Without consulting anyone, he had purchased the Chinese compound and the land upon which it stood to house the firm's first Shanghai agency. But this time, he returned to China nearly a pauper, without even the resources to pay for his own ticket. Oh, he was the Russian vice-consul, but that was a largely empty honor.

Albert had been most gracious, never mentioning his reduced status, but it was understood that George would seek Albert's approval before committing the firm to any significant expenditure beyond normal operating costs. Young Cloutman only needed to earn the initial confidence of the Heard brothers, but George faced the greater task of earning it back from the deficit of his failure.

"And what have you decided, Mr. Dixwell? Will you bargain from Shanghai?"

"I have come to a decision," said George, "but how would you approach the negotiations?"

Cloutman gazed across the river, considering, "Ahow says none of the owners are in a hurry to sell. The best they'll do is take our bargain money for a right to buy at some price yet to be decided—by them. We've got to be hard. We can't let them push us around."

"Not quite. Your response to them should be a calculated indifference." George allowed Cloutman time to ponder his words. He had to admire the cagey negotiation style of the Chinese. They could read a foreigner's impatience in an instant and knew well that a corresponding delay would always yield a higher price.

"It may be frustrating for you, but these negotiations will have to run their course. And remember, any move to speed the process will add another fortnight to its length."

Cloutman raised his eyebrows. "But Ahow says Jardines' man has raised his bid on the city side—and Ahow is about to leave on his trip to Canton."

George placed a hand on Cloutman's shoulder. He spoke quietly. "Jardine's man is a fool. If we are such fools as to match his bid, he will bid again. That's just what the

Chinese want. They're itching for a bidding war. We'll simply offer to pay whatever Jardine Matheson pays, and if the sellers ask for more, we attack them from above."

Cloutman looked confused.

George explained, "I have confided to Ahow, in greatest secrecy, that I plan to address my concerns to the Chinkiang provincial official—the *taotai*—first as an American citizen through our consul, Mr. Seward, and then directly, in my capacity as Russian Consul. Ahow will, of course, reveal this development to his friends before he travels to Canton. Then instead of having their exorbitant gains so exposed, the sellers will be most happy to settle with us quietly for a fair profit they can keep all for themselves, rather than be squeezed by a greedy *taotai* for his lion's share of an excessive one."

"Mr. Dixwell, you're more Chinese than Ahow!"

George laughed. Some wisdom could only be acquired by long residence in China. He pointed across the river toward a parcel on the Chinkiang side. "Ahow told me those owners will offer us a 15-year renewable lease if we place the highest bid. I told him we will pay exactly what the other houses pay—not a tael more—or I provide those details to the *taotai*, as well. Meanwhile, I want you to erect a mat shanty on that ground and keep someone there in possession, so we can be in a better position to fight over the price—at our own convenience!"

Cloutman shook his head in admiration. Then, as something occurred to him, he frowned. "What do we know about Ahow's uncle? Will he know enough English?"

Ahow had written the Shanghai office that he planned to bring in his uncle to manage the Heard Company's tea purchases while he was in Canton.

George reassured him, "The uncle will know about as much pidgin as any Canton comprador. Further, he'll be guaranteed by three generations of Ahows—and all the dead ones, too. Just like our Ahow, he will put the business of Ahow and Company in the first place and that of Augustine Heard and Company in second place. He will also see to it that neither shall suffer during the absence of Ahow himself while he is in the South, where he is going in order to marry a wife and thus perpetuate Ahows."

"Is that what he wrote?" Cloutman was incredulous.

"Not exactly, but that was his meaning," said George, knowing his growing facility with Chinese was respected by the merchant community.

§

In perfect unison, four Chinese deckhands heaved against the capstan bars. Links of iron anchor chain, bleeding red rust, clanked through the hawsehole in cadence with the men's chant. Slowly, moving 5 feet with each turn of the capstan, the *Independence* moved upstream toward her bow anchor. George measured the forward motion against the cluster of sampans anchored between their portside and the teeming Chinkiang shoreline.

As the anchor broke loose from the bottom, George felt a new movement. The harbor pilot shouted at the helmsman to crank the rudder starboard. Caught by the current, the sailing ship slowly rotated away from the shore. Her Chinese sailors scrambled to set the jib. It billowed out, catching a gust of northwest wind. A cloud of brown river mud streaked from the flukes of the anchor.

Freed, powered by wind and current, the *Independence* moved downstream to the east. George crossed the deck to watch the old city slip past. Brick buildings with swooping red-tile roofs gave way to beached hulks and shanties with mat sides bearing signs in English and Chinese—rooming houses, brothels, and similar dives serving the needs of sailors and lowlifes of every stripe.

"Dixwell! Welcome aboard!" A burst of wind fanned Captain Crowell's cigar into open flame. He crouched down to shield the tip with his hand and took a deep puff.

"Captain!" George greeted him. "That was quite a slick maneuver."

Crowell looked up quizzically from his cigar.

"I mean the way you turned the ship downstream," George explained.

"Avoids a tug," Crowell grinned. "Which keeps down costs. Money's always tight." He gestured with his thumb toward the Chinese sailors ascending the mainmast shrouds. "That's why I use Chinamen. They work cheaper and better than foreign riffraff."

"True," George agreed, "but we at Heard's prefer lascars and Malaymen. They're more likely to take our side in a pinch." George looked at the billowing mainsail. "Feels good to be on a sailing ship, after the din of the *Fire Dart*."

"Well, I'm glad you like her—you'll have to spend two nights aboard. The owners insist we drop anchor between dusk and dawn."

"The owners?" queried George.

"Well, the insurance company. They think we'll lose the channel and snag a bar."

George was familiar with insurance practices. Steamers paid lower insurance rates all around, and they didn't lose their coverage when the sun went down. As long as visibility was good, they could continue along the river all night. Crowley pointed at two black lorchas anchored in a protected cove with sleek, European-style hulls, surmounted by mat sails that were rigged Chinese style, like a junk.

"Of course the real risk is over there. Look at them! If they pull anywhere near, you might just as well say your prayers. They may run up the 'Stars and Stripes,' but their crews are as bastard as they are. Those scum swarm aboard, steal everything, and murder the witnesses. Crowley spat into the river. "And the worst—some of them are white men!"

The Captain had good reason to be concerned. With the Imperial Government locked in its 15th year of warfare against the Taiping rebels, protecting foreign vessels on the Yangtze was not a high priority. Collecting duty on the transported goods was another matter, and to that end the Peking government had established the Imperial Maritime Customs Service, staffed by foreigners and thus immune to the squeeze of Chinese provincial officials. For most of this year a young Irishman had been acting inspector general.

"Presumably, as Mr. Hart's customs officers are checking all vessels for smuggled goods, they'll bring a little more security to the river," George ventured.

Captain Crowell snorted. "Security? Two of Hart's men already got themselves shot, right here in Chinkiang, trying to seize lorchas just like those. But you're right about one thing. If we was to be attacked by them pirates, tonight, I have no idea whose side my Chinamen would take." He laughed, darkly. "But let's go inside before we freeze to the deck. We can talk over tea."

George followed Crowell toward the aft cabin and started up the stairs to the pilothouse. He glanced back at the Chinese passengers riding steerage, crowded around the foremast and bundled against the cold. An entrepreneurial hawker was selling tea from his brazier. The lorchas were passing from view.

Word had it that Hart had brought James B. Endicott's nephew north as a customs inspector. The young man recently married Anna Rosa Hunter. How gracefully she danced in her green silk gown. Six years had passed so quickly, and he had nothing to show for it! He wondered if Anna Rosa was teaching her husband some Chinese. With luck, John Endicott Gardner would be assigned to Woosung or Shanghai and would never have to board a Chinkiang lorcha. [1]

Shanghai
September 23

"And I swear to tell the truth, the whole truth, and nothing but the truth, so help me God."

"Thank you, Captain Taylor." George F. Seward, U.S. consul at Shanghai, pulled his chair closer to the head of the table. The scraping sound echoed through the cavernous room. "And being duly sworn, I ask you to confirm your testimony taken yesterday." He flipped through a stack of papers, looking for his transcription of Taylor's statement.

George glanced up the table at his three fellow jurors. Charles Angel clicked shut his pocket watch and shifted in his chair. The New York commission agent had grown noticeably corpulent during the two years since George had returned to China. George wondered, running his fingers through his own thinning hair, if he also was aging so dramatically. Next sat James Wainright. The elderly tea broker removed his spectacles and commenced polishing them with his handkerchief. Last in line, Mr. Arthur Hayes, his beard a shade redder than his hair, gazed vacantly out the door in the direction of the chapel and cemetery he had built for seamen just across the harbor.

"Dixwell," Angel nudged George's arm. "Do you think we'll get the case this afternoon? I have cargo to load."

George shrugged. It was hard to predict how long the proceedings would last. Two sullen prisoners sat chained to their chairs. The attorney Seward had appointed to defend them was arranging his papers on a nearby table.

Yesterday, when Taylor had given his actual testimony, the room was filled with spectators when the pirates' attorney presented a rudimentary defense of mistaken identity. Today, other than the reporter from the *North China Herald* and the armed guard, the room was empty of all but the principals. Seward was rereading Taylor's statement at the request of the overly conscientious juror Wainright, who, George recalled, had been napping during the previous day's proceedings.

Behind Seward, an American flag drooped from the tacks affixing it to a rafter. George wondered how many of the 34 white stars could still be legitimately arrayed against its blue field. English correspondents of the *Herald* now spoke snidely of the "dis-United States."

"Yesterday, you swore that your name is John Taylor and that you are a citizen of the United States, and you testified to the following:" Seward began to read aloud. "I was born in New York and will be twenty-one years in a month. I am Captain of the paplico *Jupiter*, owned by Mr. Creamer of Frazar and Company—"

"No, not *paplico*, she's a *papico*," interrupted Taylor.

The court recorder looked up from his notes. "And how do you spell '*papico*'?"

"Begging permission of the court—" George addressed Seward, speaking with all the authority he could muster, "I believe, that *papico* is an adequate English corruption of *hua-pi-ku*—a Chinese sea junk, rigged Western, like a ship, with three masts and cloth sails."

He spelled the English version of the word to the reporter. The court did not need to know that *hua-pi-ku*, literally translated from the Canton dialect, meant "duck's arse." George wondered whether Frazar's purchase of a *papico* was a move to undercut the competition with a cheaper vessel or an abject admission that they were losing money on their steamers. Probably both, he thought. A converted junk, a mongrel crew, and a green captain would tie up very little company capital and cost little to operate—and the insurance premium for replacing such a vessel would be far below that for an expensive steamer.

"You stated," Seward continued, "that a short distance below Nanking, three white men came aboard and asked to see your papers."

"Yes, Sir, and then five more, and they acted like they were customs inspectors."

"Please, Captain Taylor," Seward spoke firmly. "We are simply confirming your testimony at the request of the jury, not taking new evidence."

He looked back at the transcript. "So, after you opened the hatch, two of the men ordered you below, together with your shroff, a Chinese passenger, and one of your sailors, to dig into the ballast for the money. Whereupon, one of these men—the one with the rifle and bayonet—said, 'Be quick!' and when the sailor laughed, he shot him in the head and killed him."

"Yes, that man over there, the one on the right."

George looked closely at the sallow, barefoot prisoner. The dirty rag wrapped round his ankle had fallen loose revealing a festering wound where the leg irons chafed. Of the eight pirates, only these two had been captured.

"Then," Seward continued reading, "the man with the sword, whose identity we do not know, shot the Chinese passenger, and when you came up with the money—$700 worth of sycee silver—another unidentified man with a revolving rifle shot the other Chinese, who was standing by the fore windlass."

George wriggled his toes in his boots, trying to regain some circulation. The consul was hardly 23 and owed his appointment to the influence of his uncle, President Lincoln's secretary of state. Week after week he had been conscripting the more respectable United States citizens of Shanghai in groups of four to serve as jurors in the adjudication of commercial disputes over ships and cargo and in the prosecution of low-level miscreants for theft, assault, and public drunkenness.

Usually these proceedings were rather casual, but this case was more serious. Piracy and murder were capital offenses, and a death penalty required a full written record for review by Mr. Burlingame, the American commissioner in China.

Seward continued, "You sent the dead men ashore, and the next morning you sailed the *Jupiter* for Kiukiang—without making a report."

"Well, I was going to make a report, but the shroff said, 'nevermind.' He was afraid."

George was disgusted. Taylor didn't deserve the title of captain. He hadn't acknowledged the crime until almost a month later when harbor gossip reached the American vice-consul in Hankow. Three men had been murdered in cold blood, and with his whining prattle, Taylor sounded like a schoolboy caught with declensions inked in his palm. George suspected his silence had been self-serving—providing him sufficient time to dispose of a smuggled cargo on which he hadn't paid customs duties.

Seward rose to his feet and closed his folder. "... Thank you, Captain Taylor. That completes your testimony. Thus, as United States consul, acting judicially, I hereby place this case in the hands of the jury."

George leaned back and stretched his legs, suppressing a yawn. Angel bent over. "This won't take long!" he whispered.

§

An hour later, George followed his fellow jurors across the small unkempt yard that passed for the grounds of the American consulate. The massive flagpole beside the modest two-story building was a pretentious facade. The seat of American government in Shanghai occupied rented rooms in the edifice whose other tenants were small-time brokers and commission merchants too poor to lease more prestigious space in the British concession. Angel waited for him by the gate.

"They got off *comparatively* easy!" said George.

Angel shook his head. "Well, perhaps the accomplice could have done with more than 10 years, but the murderer will hang."

George chuckled. "I meant easy compared to Chinese justice. My long-departed friend Mr. Sturgis once told me that when the mandarins finally captured the pirate Apootsae, they sliced him to pieces—slowly—so that he and the assembled crowd could fully enjoy the spectacle of the administration of justice to whatever deterrent benefit the performance might inspire."

"That's disgusting!" Angel's voice quivered. "It's a good thing we have the treaty. Even an American so base as to turn pirate against his own countrymen doesn't deserve that kind of barbarity. After all, he's still a Christian and as tiresome as these trials are, it's still our duty."

George nodded, "Yes, and tiresome they are. Next in the dock tomorrow morning is Pinder. I believe my colleague George Heard will be pressed into service for that one. Talk about one of our own!" Frederick W. Pinder, the United States marshall of Mr. Seward's consular court, was to be tried for selling arms to the Taiping rebels.

"I'll bet the Chinese would love to get their hands on him," Angel shuddered. "Think of his poor wife forced to watch him skinned alive or slowly torn limb from limb."

"Well," George said. "Pinder's an American, and he's got the protection of American justice. Indeed, he may be over protected. I understand the only eyewitness is Chinese, and no jury is likely to convict a Christian on the testimony of a heathen. But what are we to do with his great friend, Burgevine? Perhaps the Chinese will have their way with him. The *futai* makes a case that Burgevine has actually become a Chinese subject"

The Chinese had hired Henry Burgevine to lead Imperial forces against the rebels and given him the rank of general. The story of his defection from the Chinese Army to fight for the Taiping insurgents—the same rebels who had laid siege to Shanghai—was all over the pages of the *Herald*. Pinder's alleged crime of selling arms to Burgevine paled in comparison. The *futai*, Mr. Li, offered 3,000 taels to any person delivering the body of General Burgevine, dead or alive, to a representative of the Imperial Government.

George, along with the nine other treaty consuls, had drafted a joint reply, asserting that Burgevine, as the citizen of a treaty signatory, must be tried according to the laws of his home country. He himself had translated Mr. Li's official response: "As Burgevine has been invested with Chinese official rank, and has been employed as a military leader on behalf of the Chinese government, and having thus violated Chinese law, it is right that he should suffer the penalty attached by China to the crime."

"But that's preposterous," sputtered Angel. "Burgevine is an American, from North Carolina!"

George shrugged his shoulders and continued with Mr. Li's response: "General Burgevine has audaciously passed over to join the Rebels and appears as foe alike of China and the forces of the several powers engaged in the protection of Shanghai. Thus, having become one of the banditti, General Burgevine cannot be accounted as a citizen of your *honorable* nation."

George paused, "Furthermore," he smiled, "as a loyal North Carolinian, Burgevine can't be accounted a citizen of any honorable nation at all."

Angel pursed his lips. "It's true, I suppose, he's now a citizen of the Confederacy, and their privateers *are* ravaging our shipping, but the Union has steadfastly rejected the secession of the southern states. We don't recognize the Confederacy."

"True enough," George agreed. "Still, one wonders how an honorable citizen of the Confederate States can claim protection from a country with whom he is in open warfare, not only in China but at home as well."

George recalled how earlier in the year, Burgevine, wearing a uniform of his own invention, had strolled down the English Bund surrounded by his aides. He pitied the man. He might be an arrogant fool, but his motivation was only that of any merchant, selling his wares—in this case, his military skills—to the highest bidder. Greed was hardly a sin in China.

"You know," George assumed a confessional tone, "although General Burgevine is guilty of the most blatant treachery against his employer—the Emperor—we foreigners are all more or less complicit. We pay for our silks with silver, buying from merchants who in turn use that silver to bribe the rebels for safe passage across the territory they control. The rebels in turn use that same silver to buy arms and pay the soldiers who in the name of holy insurgency wage war against the Imperial government."

"But," Angel protested, "what can we do about it?"

"Nothing at all." George shrugged. "And thus, perhaps, just like you and me, Mr. Pinder and General Burgevine deserve a special dispensation for their sins."

As they crossed the Soochow Bridge, Angel gestured back at the narrow-rutted road. "I guess soon our Bund won't be pure American anymore."

George turned to survey the Shanghai harbor. For years, the center of the Soochow bridge and the fetid creek that flowed beneath it marked the boundary between American and British jurisdiction—as if one couldn't readily distinguish them by the abrupt shabbiness of the American side. "It's been some time since it was particularly *American*," George laughed. "And I wouldn't say it was ever particularly *pure*, either."

Professional policing and restrictive zoning mandated by the municipal council on the English side had driven the unsavory criminal element across the creek to the American side. The American side was changing. The old grog houses and brothels were being pushed out by grocery shops, apothecaries, and newly constructed tenements to accommodate thousands of Chinese refugees escaping the depredations of the Taipings.

Only a few days ago, the British and American concessions had joined to form an International Settlement. It was a godsend. Now the tax base of the larger British community would support the overwhelmed police and what barely passed for public works on the dismally rundown American side of the creek—much to the dismay of the English ratepayers.

George squinted down the British waterfront, its broad boulevard three times wider than the muddy track on the American side. The Heard headquarters stood out in the long line of agency houses, its three stories towering above most of its neighbors.

They reached Angel's street. He tipped his hat and nodded toward the British Consulate. Chinese servants were hanging bunting from the roof of the garden gazebo. "Well, good afternoon, my good Dixwell. Will we be seeing you at the concert?"

"I do believe you will," George smiled.

He watched as Angel turned onto the street fronting the creek. George quickened his step. He had to review the clerks' copy work before meeting Captain Endicott and going on to the evening festivities. [2]

§

The chimes of the vestibule clock echoed up to the third floor of the Heard firm's Shanghai headquarters. George removed his reading spectacles, rubbed his eyes, and gazed vacantly around his room. He had spent the early morning hours before his duties at court translating Tong Loong-maw's letter from Hankow. His penciled draft looked complete, except for the four spots where he was uncertain how to read the names of remote villages. In the morning he would show them to Chen Tzu Fang, his Chinese secretary for Russian consular affairs. Then he would dictate a reply for Chen to render into Chinese.

"Dixwell! Aren't you going to the concert?" George Heard stood in the doorway. "All work and no play makes Jack a dull boy!"

"But *no* work and *all* play..." George leaned back and squinted to examine his freshly shaved junior partner, the youngest of the Heard brothers. He smelled a whiff of pomade. "I do believe you've stepped directly from a *Harper's* fashion plate. Try not to frighten the ladies."

Young Heard leaned against the doorjamb, pensively polishing his boot against the back of his trouser leg. His tone became suddenly serious, "Carpe diem. For tomorrow we die."

The morbid sentiment reminded George that in the morning, young Heard would be sitting with the jury at Mr. Seward's consular court where his friend Pinder was being tried for capital treason. "I'll be along soon. Don't wait for me," George forced a smile. "I promised Endicott I'd wait for him to come ashore, and I need to finish translating this letter from Tong first."

"Ah, first things first, then. And just what does our old Foochow comprador report from his new digs. Does his tea brokerage keep him fat?"

"Well," George glanced back at his translation. "Tea is not the subject. Tong reports that Ahow and Mr. Lewis, the geologist, have returned from another prospecting trip in the coal regions. Quite an adventure—at one place the villagers thought they were looking for buried treasure! The major problem is that all the good quality coal is in hilly areas and so far from water that it has to be carried out in small pieces on men's backs."

Heard snorted. "They'd better keep looking then." He waved on his way out. "I'll see you later on."

It *was* frustrating. If they could only find a good source of cheap coal, Heard steamers could charge less than those burning fuel imported from Australia, and the resulting increase in their cargo business would more than compensate for the lowered rates.

George lifted the frayed cozy—a long-ago gift from Henrietta—from the teapot and poured himself another cup. He looked at his aunt's fine stitching. She and Mrs. Child were sewing bivouac caps and knitting stockings for the Union troops now. At 78, Henrietta was finally getting old. Her last letter, written in a quavering hand, reported that Wendell Holmes had been wounded yet again since the bullet through his neck at Antietam. He'd been courting Epes Dixwell's daughter, Fanny. George wondered how she was taking the news.

He took a sip of tea and peered out his window across the Shanghai waterfront. He chose this room at the northeast corner of the Heard headquarters, not only for the harbor view and the early morning light but also for its shelter from the stifling heat of the late afternoon sun. But summer was over, and the fleeting rays of evening light had crept so far up the main mast of the firm's station vessel, *Anne Walsh*, that the company's red-white diamond flag seemed specially illuminated. Captain William Endicott, who conducted the local opium trade from the vessel, would be coming ashore soon.

George clicked open his watch—7:25 pm. He had five minutes to get down to the wharf to meet Endicott. He slipped into his cotton jacket. In just a few weeks he would need his black wool suit for an evening outing. He grabbed his Panama hat and started down the broad marble staircase.

§

George stepped around the mound of soggy rope inconveniently coiled in the center of the wharf and watched Endicott descend the stairway from the *Anne Walsh* to the boat whose oarsmen would bring him ashore. Well, not quite all the way ashore. George looked across the 75 yards of glistening brown muck now exposed by the low tide.

Some of the city fathers had wanted the ends of the wharves to be built on pontoons, so they would float up and down with the tide. Loading heavy cargo ships, however, required rigid structures, and more practical heads had prevailed. A series of wharves had been built on rock supports. They sloped downward to the low waterline with pile buttresses angled into the riverbed to prevent their wooden walkways from washing away in a spring flood. As a result, even with an ordinary high tide, the last quarter of the wharf was submerged. This evening, with the tide out, the slimy green surface was almost fully exposed. A clatter of oars, then the small boat's bow slid up onto the walkway. William stepped gingerly onto the slippery surface. "Hello, Dixwell! You do cut a dapper figure."

George offered his colleague a steadying hand and glanced down. "I suppose we should have it scraped again or strewn with sand. It wouldn't look good for our good captain to go under before his vessel does!"

William grimaced. "I wouldn't want to be in that race. She's taking in a good five gallons an hour through those cracked planks."

For weeks, since the station vessel had been struck by an awkwardly anchored tea ship, William had been urging the Heards to find a good teak vessel to replace her. George remembered the last time William asked for a new ship. That time, they had both been younger men, standing on the foredeck of the steamer *Palmetto* with a frigid north wind gusting off the Hudson River.

It was a painful memory. While William waxed poetic about the prospects of carrying passengers and cargo between Hong Kong and Shanghai on a new steamer, George had been gazing across the sound to Staten Island, where Dorr's megalomaniac brick-making folly had entangled him in the financial snare that would lead to his inescapable ruin. Fortunately, that was finally over and done with. His lawyers had reached a settlement with Dorr, albeit for only pennies on the dollar.

Resolutely, George moved to a happier topic. "I hear your brother's boys are home from the States."

"True enough, and brother Jamie's sent James, Jr., to a clerkship in Manila, and he's made Henry the *Spark*'s shipping agent. *That* boy's the bright one," William said proudly. "He's picking up his Chinese again—almost like a native."

Well, he *is* a native and half-Chinese by ancestry, to boot, George thought. He wondered what Ng Akew, the boys' mother, was doing now that they were grown, having heard that James Endicott had bought her a building in the Chinese district of Hong Kong where she rented rooms to prostitutes.

William continued, "Henry lost a lot of his Chinese in Kentucky—he wasn't much over five when Jamie sent him there. He wanted Henry to become an American but not so American that he'd forget his Chinese."

George understood. Language had come so much more easily to him, too, when he was young. He sometimes wished J.J. had sent a Chinese home to Boston as a language tutor instead of a Hindoo. Of course, J.J. could not have known that the seat of family commerce would move so quickly and decisively from Calcutta to China. "I thought that was the reason your brother got Hunter to send his boys over, too. With the four of them all living together, you'd expect they would talk some Chinese among themselves."

William snorted, "Hunter's boys got so American that Jimmy joined the Kentucky Cavalry, fighting for the Union. Last we heard, Willy was about to enlist too. That's why Jamie brought his boys home. He was afraid they'd join up. Of course, ordering them to come home only brought a new worry—that their ship could be captured by some Confederate rebel privateer, waiting off the tip of Africa."

For the past year, the Confederate Captain Raphael Semmes had been prowling the Atlantic shipping lanes from the Azores to Newfoundland, capturing and burning vessels flying the Stars and Stripes.

"That could happen right here," George laughed. "I hear that Semmes is moving the *Alabama* to somewhere off our coast." He gestured across the harbor towards the ocean. "Now that the Atlantic is crawling with Union gunboats, all trying to capture him, a vacation off the coast of China would offer easy pickings with little risk. If he captured some coal hulk, he'd have enough fuel to take every last merchant ship bound for California or the Straits."

"You're right about that," nodded William. "Jamie wants me to ask what you're doing to cover the risk."

"There's not much we can do," George shrugged. "No insurance company will cover losses to Confederate privateers—it's an act of war."

"Jamie's not so concerned about that. He's more worried that if the British side with the South, they might seize the *Spark* at dockside in Hong Kong. He's thinking about reregistering her under the Union Jack."

George had thought about that too. "That won't work if she's still under American ownership, and I can't see your brother changing his citizenship. The only real way to protect the vessel would be to sell her. But even then, if she's carrying American cargo, it won't matter a whit."

"So," William mused, "maybe we should just go Chinese—change the Heard letterhead to 'King Kee.'" He chuckled. "At least Hunter would be happy. We could use his calligraphy. What do you think of his rendering?"

George laughed. Chinese merchants had called the Heard firm "King Kee" for years. Accepting the Chinese name, William Hunter rendered it in Chinese characters. Albert Heard, always punctilious about the firm's image, had written George to ask if Hunter's characters were sufficiently auspicious for the firm to use in their Chinese correspondence. "Well," George opined, "Hunter's first character is a compound of 'carnation' or 'precious gem' with 'metropolitan,' while Kee means 'to recollect.' So the result is something like 'rosy memory'—poetic but not very commercial. Although it would look handsome stamped in red cinnabar."

"Humph," William snorted. "I hear Hunter is most pleased with his first grandson. Jamie and I are, too, of course—our new little grandnephew carries *our* family name."

Anna Rosa Hunter's husband, John Endicott Gardner, was an Endicott nephew. If Anna was half-Chinese, the baby would be a quarter.

George raised his right hand, thumb, and forefinger poised, as if holding the stem of a champagne glass. "May Master John Endicott Gardner, Jr., be but the first of many "collaborations" between the Endicotts and the Hunters!"

The captain laughed, returning the salute.

George looked back at the Bund. The sun had fully set, but its waning twilight framed the tall buildings in a pale orange glow. A stream of well-dressed men and women strolled along the broad roadway. Snatches of voices and cheery laughter drifted through the heavy, humid air.

"Looks like Russell and Company is out in force," said William, pointing.

George followed his friend's eye and spotted George Tyson, surrounded by his clerks. Russell's had recently revealed that beginning with the New Year, Tyson would be their senior partner in Shanghai. George suspected that under Tyson, the competition among steamships on the Yangtze would become even more intense. Word had it that Tyson was finding investors for new steamers among Chinese merchants and compradors.

William laughed. "Perhaps someday we'll see yet another 'collaboration'—between the Tysons and the Heards!"

George started. How much did William know? Everyone knew that Tyson had fathered four children with the beautiful half-Chinese Lam Fong Kew. It was *not* public knowledge that Albert Farley Heard was consorting with her twin sister—Lam Kew Fong—and it wouldn't do for such gossip to find its way back to Boston.

"I do not believe ..." George paused to find softer words. He didn't want to sound harsh or defensive. "I rather doubt that there are any Chinese Heards behind the woodshed."

"Perhaps not," William smiled, "but I hear from Jamie that there's a handsome two-year-old named Richard Heard living very comfortably with his Tanka mother in Macao." William paused for dramatic effect, "—where the church register, for some reason, neglects to name his parents."

George's wondered if Albert could have fathered a child with a Chinese woman before becoming involved with Lam Kew Fong? Or could John Heard be the father—or even young George? It would not do to ask William the child's birthdate, but the next time he was in Macao ...

William shrugged. "Well, if you don't like a half-blood Heard collaborating with a quarter-blood Tyson, how about a quarter-blood Tyson with a half-blood Hart? That should test your fractions!" William grinned broadly and inclined his head in the direction of Robert Hart, Shanghai commissioner of the Chinese Imperial Customs Service. Hart, walking briskly toward the gathering, had not noticed the two men on the wharf. George smiled. Gossip had it that Hart had produced a son and a daughter by a Chinese woman. "In the next generation," William continued, "there'll be hundreds of Chinese with English names: Endicotts, Hunters, Tysons, Harts, Roundys." He winked at George. "Perhaps even some Heards and, hopefully, a whole clan of Gardners. That's how we'll finally civilize this country!"

There was truth in William's half-facetious prediction. Half-blood Chinese, raised Christian and speaking both English and Chinese, would have a large advantage in China over foreign-born merchants. Old-fashioned miscegenation might change China far more than all the conversions claimed by the missionaries. Fathering Chinese children seemed not to diminish a man's prospects for a subsequent marriage to a white woman. Endicott and Hunter were both proof of that. Indeed, George had heard that Tyson's new wife was enroute now from Boston.

Two uniformed Navy men walked briskly past, one with a gleaming brass trumpet under his arm. They were followed by a Chinese porter, balancing a large drum on his head that bore a brightly painted coat of arms. William adjusted his hat at a jaunty angle. "We'd best get going. We won't miss any of the music if we get there before the drum."

The two men stepped down onto the roadway and followed the musicians. George's thoughts returned to William Hunter. His rendering of "King Kee" wasn't bad, but for all of Hunter's years in China, George suspected the man had little idea of the deeper layers of meaning the characters held. To get past the surface denotations of commodities and prices, one needed to study the classics. True scholarship entailed a mastery of the poetic and metaphorical far beyond the capacity of an ordinary merchant, be he born in China or, like Hunter, in Virginia.

As he had come to that recognition, George formed an ambition—to become more than another cunning barbarian. It was no longer sufficient for him to court the fickle respect of common merchants to whom money was the sole measure of a man. He had asked Chen Tzu Fang to become his teacher, and the elderly scholar had agreed. Now, after two years of study, he could translate a business letter, but he wondered if he would ever be able to write one.

In the middle of the roadway, a Chinese stood on a ladder holding a burning punk to the wick of a newly installed, coal oil lamp. Four more were already lit, illuminating half the remaining distance to the English consulate where the crowd was gathering. George breathed deeply. With luck there would be another five or six festive Wednesday evenings before the northwest wind brought the first freezing rain and snow and ended the outdoor social season.

Beneath the farthest lamp, George spied Tyson in animated conversation with a circle of brightly dressed women. Had the man fathered his brood of Chinese children in Boston, he would have been ostracized by polite society. But here in China such a thing was a mere peccadillo, hardly worthy of note. Keeping a Chinese woman, albeit at a discreet distance, was far less damaging to one's reputation than being seen stepping from a brothel or a "flower boat." [3]

Chen Tze Fang's Studio
1864, December 22

"So, one by one, six of them ... Wang-fo lifted each perfectly formed vase into the boat." George glanced up as he searched for the proper words in Mandarin. He had asked his teacher if he was familiar with the old Chinese tale Grandfather Sargent had rewritten in English half a century ago. As he'd already explained to Chen, Grandfather had seen in the story an allegory for his own family tragedy. Now George wished he remembered more of it.

"I do not recognize your grandfather's story. However, your search for its original Chinese inspiration is most commendable." Chen Tze Fang laid his spectacles on the table. "The literature of China is a vast ocean of swirling tales, but my poor eyes see only as much of that sea as from a small boat bobbing between the waves."

It was typically kind of Chen to attribute his unfamiliarity with the tale, not to George's awkward telling but to his own ignorance. George looked at his teacher. In his plain black tunic, his white hair pulled fastidiously back into a braided queue, the scholar had a simple refinement about his appearance. George had never seen his teacher without his skullcap, edged with a single ribbon of satin silk.

George continued, "And despite the gnashing teeth of the icy north wind, Wang-fo handed his ragged cape to his wife to tuck down in between the vases so that no one of them would break against another."

He closed his eyes for a moment, imagining Grandfather Sargent sitting alone at the Athenaeum, a book of Chinese fables open on the table, and before him, the broad blank sheet of China rice paper purchased by his youngest daughter, Henrietta. He could see grandfather dipping his pen to copy out the tale.

George went on with the story. "Then, with his little boy watching from the bow, Wang-fo took up his eaglewood staff and pushed the frail craft out into the water once again."

Grandfather's house had been only a few blocks from the Charles River. As a little boy George had clutched the old man's hand as they strolled to the rope walks along the bank. Together, they watched the workmen twist hemp into cords and cables to rig the masts and booms of Boston's merchant fleet. He remembered the way the river had looked a few years later in the winter of Grandfather's funeral—black water studded with diamonds of floating ice.

George hoped that he was not embellishing the story so much that Grandfather Sargent wouldn't recognize it. He glanced again at his teacher. Chen's forehead was furrowed, listening. "Somewhere during that crossing, in that cruel darkness between sunset and the first blush of dawn, the river snatched away his little boy." As he spoke, George wished his Mandarin was good enough to convey the vivid images his grandfather's words painted in his mind.

"And the six vases," Chen nodded his understanding, "they were your grandfather's daughters. He was right to sacrifice his cape to wrap around his vases, for children are the greatest of treasures. But how cruel his fate, to lose his son! Did he write the story from his own grief?"

George paused. "My grandfather's son—his namesake—went out to Canton as a young merchant to work for Perkins and Company. His fortunes fell, and he had to return home. On the journey he took ill, and, sadly, he came home only to die." Henrietta often told him the story and wept when she spoke of her brother. "Geordie," she said, "you were but six months old, and I cradled you in my arms on the day that he died." By her words, George came to understand that Henrietta viewed him as Heaven-sent to fill the void in her heart.

"Yes, travel over the ocean is dangerous." Chen spoke sympathetically. "There are often epidemics on shipboard. I have heard of that company. Was it not the honored ancestor of Russell and Company?"

George nodded. He might have had his own career at Russell's had not disagreements among its partners forced Augustine Heard to authorize Mr. Coolidge to form a new company, bearing his own name.

"Mr. Dixwell," Chen continued, "you must cherish the thought of your grandfather's ragged cape as he cherished his precious children. It was his mark of honor. It reminds us of another truth, too—that there is nothing shameful or disgraceful in being poor. What is important is one's character. Honest poverty is redeemed by virtue, virtue is nourished by scholarship, and your ancestor was—above all else—a scholar."

That was Henrietta's Christian calculation as well: virtue and knowledge were worth far more than worldly wealth. George wondered what his aunt would think if she could hear her own wise counsel issuing from the lips of a heathen. He wondered at how his lessons with Chen had begun with only the most crass purpose—to help him translate the Heard firm's Chinese correspondence—but had evolved into something very different.

When he first presented Chen with Chinese classics, the old scholar had humored him, providing simple translations. George persisted with increasingly penetrating questions, and each of Chen's answers introduced a concept provoking a still deeper question, until George was led to see that Chinese language and literature and philosophy were so intertwined that a student could not master one without understanding the others. From that time, at the teacher's suggestion, George's lessons moved to Chen's house where the Heard staff would not be troubled by overhearing how "impractical" his studies had become.

As those studies progressed, George found a welcome refuge in the generosity of spirit that pervaded Chinese thought—a spirit totally alien to his fellow merchants at the Club. While many of them might be able to parrot Chinese prices in dollars or taels, they seemed blind to the deeper value of anything Chinese. George found himself avoiding their company. He was weary of their empty banter, the predictable pomposity of yet another "club chair general" expounding on how to turn the tables on General Lee and the rest of the Confederate armies.

Strangely, as he moved into the world of scholarship, George somehow came to feel more and more a comfort and even an identity with things Chinese. In retrospect, it seemed that at every opportunity Chen found a classical allusion—a maxim and a lesson—to repair the self-doubt that hung over George like a cloud, blighting his very being.

"Has your Chinese typeface arrived in Boston?" Chen flicked a silent signal to his manservant as he spoke. "I trust you will not be called to travel there yourself to show them how to use it."

"I have no plan to cross the ocean," said George. "But my brother Epes informs me that the society will now have the first press in America able to print Chinese characters."

"That is good." Chen leaned back as the servant returned with a steaming pot of tea and placed it on the table. "It is good that Boston people will be able to learn true things about China."

George agreed. Not only had the American Oriental Society acknowledged the donation, but at their May meeting in Boston, before adjourning to evening refreshments at Epes's house in Cambridge, the members had elected George, William Endicott, and the six other donors to lifetime membership in the organization. Still, George was doubtful of the society's claim that they would now have the only Chinese font in America—surely there was at least one Chinese printing house in San Francisco.

Chen's servant brought a lacquer tray with two porcelain cups—not the familiar ones he and Chen used during scores of other meetings over the past three years but, rather, two mismatched pieces, their delicate rims chipped from long use.

"We have been discussing ancient truths," Chen explained, "and these cups are more suitable." He poured the first cupful and with both hands placed it in front of George before filling the other.

George examined the exquisitely rendered cobalt blue monkey on the side of the cup. It reached out for a plump, round fruit hanging from a limb.

"Yes, he too wishes to steal the peaches of immortality." Chen looked into George's eyes. "Now, let us enjoy a refreshment together."

George sensed that with the telling of his grandfather's story, something had changed in his relationship with Chen. He waited for his teacher to take the first sip. George also noted the cup of "guest tea" set to the side and recalled the story of the missionary who had caused so much consternation at the *taotai*'s office. Upon sitting down with that Mandarin official, the missionary had taken a sip of the "guest tea" always placed at the side of the table and not intended for drinking. Unwittingly, the missionary had signaled his wish to depart immediately, precipitating a frantic rush by the servants to bring back his overcoat. It made George wonder what faux pas he himself might have ignorantly committed during his first years in China. At least he had not committed that most barbarian of offenses.

"Mr. Dixwell, your grandfather, despite his tribulations, raised a worthy family. A man of your status should likewise be the master of his own house and the father of sons." George, taken aback, could not respond. His teacher had alluded to this topic before but never spoken so directly. Chen broke the awkward silence. "Tell me the end of your grandfather's story." He took another sip and cupped his hands in expectation.

George was relieved to return to a less personal subject. "Wang-fo pulled his frail craft up onto the riverbank and looked back upon the water, and, for a moment, it seemed as if not a ripple disturbed its surface ..." [4]

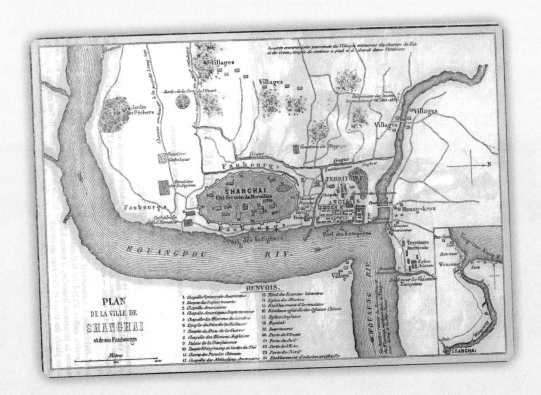

Map of Shanghai (ca. 1860). The Heard firm's branch office was located on a portion of the waterfront identified as *Port des Europeans*. Map from M. de Moges, *Voyage en Chine et Japon*, 1857–1858. (Author's personal collection.)

George Dixwell occupied the northeast corner room on the second story of the Heard firm's branch office on the Shanghai Bund. When George Dixwell returned to China in 1861, he became manager of the Shanghai branch office. From this room, he could survey all activity along the broad riverfront boulevard, buttressed against the tides by a timber bulwark, and watch cargo being loaded aboard Heard vessels anchored offshore. (Photo courtesy of the Peabody-Essex Museum.)

The Shanghai Bund wharves were constructed to extend beyond the broad muddy expanse exposed at low tide. Their outer ends, fully submerged at high tide, were anchored to the bottom to prevent their floating away. The bridge over Soochow Creek at the far end of the Bund led to the less prestigious American District where George would serve as a juror during court proceedings under the American Consul. (Photo courtesy of the Peabody-Essex Museum.)

The Heards' steamer (ca. 1863), *Fire Dart*. George's primary goal in Shanghai was to establish regular steam commerce up the Yangtze River from Shanghai to Hankow, with branch offices along the way to attract cargoes. She was among the first vessels assigned to that 600-mile route. (Photo courtesy of the Metropolitan Museum of Art.)

CHAPTER TEN

A Manchu Lady

The Parker Home
1867, November 18

"Now, Henriet," Anna Parker gently scolded her sister. "You must allow us some celebration. After all, you're almost as old as the country itself, and we had fireworks on the Common for that!"

Henrietta looked up from snipping the article from the *Transcript*. Outside the parlor window, she could see the trees that had been lush on July 4 now were bare silhouettes against a slate-gray sky. "Oh, I don't believe I'm so important as the country," she teased.

Anna Parker was sitting at her own table, identical to her sister's but for the geometrically precise order on its surface. Exactly 8 feet away from Henrietta's table, it faced the other parlor window with its identical view across Tremont Street to Boston Common. A sudden commotion in the vestibule drew the women's attention.

"Who can that be?" Anna rose from her chair.

"Happy birthday, dear Aunt!" Epes Dixwell burst into the room, his top hat still on his head. He bowed and handed Henrietta a single long-stemmed red rose.

"Oh Epes! You shouldn't have—it must be the last rose of summer!" Henrietta choked on her words.

Epes laughed, "Not this one. It's from Professor Gray's heated greenhouse. It opened just this morning to reveal its beauty—as if it knew that today you begin another blessed year."

"Now, Epes, don't make such a fuss over me. This week belongs to Suzie and Gat, not to us old folks!"

Susan Dixwell (Epes's third daughter) and Gerrit Smith Miller (grandson of the abolitionist, Gerrit Smith) had been making eyes at each other since that fall five years ago when Gat had first enrolled in Epes's school. Now they were to be married.

Henrietta continued, "I also happen to know that Dr. Gray hates to cut flowers from the university herbarium."

"True," Epes admitted, "almost as much as he dreads reading another article by Professor Agassiz. But years ago, when he took Suzie (way past her bedtime) to watch his night-blooming Cereus open, he promised her that when she grew up, he would give her a wedding bouquet from the greenhouse. For all these years as well, every time the Scientific Club has dined at our house, Suzie has reminded him of his sacred vow. Mrs. Gray insists now that he keep to it. Then, when I mentioned your birthday ... !"

Henrietta held the bud to her nose. The light fragrance brought her back to the roses at Aunt Murray's house and the single cutting that Catharine had nourished to life at Poplar Street. Now, that rosebush grew in J.J.'s garden at Sunnyside, awaiting winter pruning. "It is lovely, Epes," Henrietta smiled up at him. "Thank you."

Epes grinned, "And now, you have in fact received birthday greetings from two of your nephews."

"J.J. hasn't arrived yet," Anna protested.

Epes triumphantly pulled a pale blue envelope from his breast pocket. "No, but George has! He instructed me to deliver this in person on your birthday!"

"From George!" Henrietta clutched the letter to her heart, then slid her knife under the red wax seal bearing George's initials. Henrietta slowly unfolded the letter, savoring the surprise. "Well, it's dated September 19, and he says Happy Birthday, and he hopes that Epes will relay a special birthday kiss all the way from China."

"With pleasure," Epes stooped to kiss Henrietta's cheek.

Henrietta read ahead. "He also says he is mostly recovered from his rheumatism."

"I might have deduced that from the improved penmanship on the envelope," said Epes.

Henrietta, too, recalled the scrawled penciled notes during the months George had been too crippled to raise a pen high enough to dip into his inkwell. She wondered if her brandy and salt remedy had helped.

"Yes, yes," Anna said. "But what else does he *say*?"

Henrietta continued. "He says he studies Chinese every evening ... and while he was practicing calligraphy, he remembered Father's story of Wang-fo and how Father had written it on China paper. George hopes some day his brush strokes will be good enough to add Father's name to the bottom in Chinese characters."

"I'm sure that will be very nice." Anna cleared her throat. "But in two weeks he will be 53 years old, and he should be spending his evenings in company at dinners and such. There must be at least one lonely widow for him in Shanghai."

With a pang, Henrietta recalled her cautionary words to George from years ago. She wished she could take them back. When he had first embarked for China, she had warned him that by the time he finished his quest for riches, all his female contemporaries would be married or widowed, if not dead. If he were not to end his days as a solitary bachelor, he would find for a wife only a widow with a flock of children, an old maid of sour aspect, or (if he were truly a fool) a young girl who would count the days before she could erect a monument to his memory and reunite with some impecunious first love.

Henrietta sighed softly and went on to the second page. "George describes his day. The cannon fires every time a mail ship arrives, and he sends a junior clerk running to get the latest news before any of the other firms have a chance to act upon it. Then they have to hurry to have fresh letters to all their correspondents aboard before the ship leaves—but today my letter has taken precedence, over all the others."

"A cannon!" Anna exclaimed. "Wouldn't ringing a bell do it as well?"

"And as consul," Henrietta continued, ignoring her sister's commentary, "he has to entertain all the Russians—even at dinner—and translate their bad French into English. All day long the clerks interrupt him to make sense of what the Chinese merchants are trying to say, so that he feels like nothing but a dragoman—"

"What is it," Anna interrupted, "that George doesn't want to be?"

"A dragoman," Epes put in, "is an interpreter of Arabic."

"Well," Anna sniffed, "that makes about as much sense as studying Chinese. He should speak plainly. Using words like that will frighten away even the most desperate adventuress."

Epes assumed his most pedantic posture. "I'm sure George means dragoman in its more generic sense, as translator."

"And," Henrietta smiled at her sister, "he sends his love to you."

Anna was mollified. "When did he mail it?"

Epes squinted to read the date. "Two months ago, but I'll wager that two years from now, on your 84th, Henrietta, George will mail his letter by steamer across the Pacific—two weeks to San Francisco—and the new railroad will carry it over the mountains and across the deserts, and you'll have it in your hand in another week."

"Why, the ink will hardly be dry," mused Henrietta.

"I would be far more pleased to have that train cross the Mississippi at Davenport, Iowa," Anna interjected.

Henrietta waited for her sister to complete her thought with the usual condemnation of "that rascal nephew"—George Barnard Sargent.

Epes returned to the subject of the railroad. "Chinese coolies are already tunneling under the Sierra Mountains, and in a year they'll be crossing the salt desert."

"That's good! They'll be halfway to their new jobs in Louisiana," Anna laughed. "If the Africans won't pick cotton anymore, I'm sure the Chinese coolies will!"

Henrietta's drew herself up. "We did not labor to free the African slaves only to see the Chinese enslaved in their place."

Immediately she was sorry for speaking so sharply. It served no purpose to engage in combat with Anna on this subject. Every day, they could look out their windows upon the same prospect, and yet they saw such different worlds. Anna's views had always flowed more from commercial expedience than from any higher ideals or empathy with those who suffered.

"Now Henriet," Anna laughed dismissively. "It wasn't your abolitionists who freed the slaves. It was men of reason. Indeed, if anything, the tiresome tirades of Mr. Garrison and the rest of your friends only delayed the inevitable."

Anna was only repeating what was common knowledge about coolies going to Louisiana. Just months ago a cargo of them, transshipped from Havana, had landed in New Orleans. Plantation owners were only too happy to purchase coolie indentures for years of labor at only a fraction of what the price for an African slave had been.

"I was just thinking," Anna continued, "if the little, industrious Chinese marry large, indolent Africans, perhaps they'll produce an improved breed—strong, hard-working, and happy to pick cotton in the sun. Hybrid vigor!" She laughed at her own wit.

"I'm not so sure," Epes winked at Henrietta. "Dr. Agassiz and Mr. Darwin would probably both agree that it could just as likely come out the other way and produce a short, indolent race instead. But I'm told that in her new book, Mrs. Child has thoroughly mixed the races—and to their benefit."

"It cannot be to their benefit," Anna said firmly. "If God in his wisdom created the separate races, we cannot presume to flout that wisdom, even in a cheap romance."

"It's hardly a cheap romance!" Henrietta leapt to her friend's defense. "Mrs. Child has shown that a measure of goodness and hope can come even from an evil past, and that a new generation of fine people guided by the highest principles can descend even from African girls despoiled by their white masters."

"From what I have heard about the book," Anna snorted, "the Delanos will not be amused to see their good name soiled by association with such a menagerie of mulattos, quadroons, and octoroons."

Henrietta pursed her lips. In Maria's new book, *A Romance of the Republic*, the white son of a southern planter and his Boston-born wife is exchanged at birth for the planter's love child by his octoroon slave mistress. Unknowingly, the planter's wife raises the slave boy as her own, while her white son grows up as a slave.

Maria wove a complicated story of mistaken identities, spanning three generations of whites and Africans in mixtures of every possible permutation and every shade of political persuasion from fanatical bigotry to abolitionist fervor.

"From what I hear," Epes remembered, "the Delanos are not the only family that Mrs. Child has so abused."

Henrietta blushed. Maria admitted that she had based her abolitionist character on Ellis Gray Loring, whose legal skills had saved the slave girl, Med, from being returned to captivity so many years ago. Henrietta was certain that had Mr. Loring lived to read the book, he would have appreciated the tribute. But she hoped Anna would never actually read the book and discover that the white slave boy's mulatto wife who learns to write with a flowing hand and (by the end of the book) has become a lady was named Henriet. How many times in their "mouse's nest" at Poplar Street had Maria heard Catharine utter that pet name and with such love.

In the awkward pause, Epes remembered another purpose for his call. "Mrs. Dixwell has instructed me," he said, joining his hands in mock prayer, "to ask if we may borrow the Sargent tea service to assist the Dixwell urn at the reception?"

"Why, of course," Anna was relieved for the change of subject. It did not do to argue with Henrietta on her birthday. "I'm sure that we Sargents would be proud to gleam just as brightly as the Dixwells. Bridget will polish it this afternoon. Would you like to borrow her as well, to help with the service?"

"Then," Epes bowed, "I have for once surpassed Mrs. Dixwell's instructions. I know she will be most delighted to have the extra help—"

"What about cups and saucers, and confections, and —?" Anna took a fresh sheet of paper and a pencil from her table drawer and began a list.

Henrietta rose and tucked George's letter under her elbow and moved slowly toward the stairs. "Excuse me, please, you two have important things to talk about, and I need to rest a bit from all this excitement."

§

Henrietta took the book from her bed stand and lay down, leaning back against her pillow. How surprised she had been three years ago on her 79th birthday to open *Looking Toward Sunset*, Maria's book about growing old, to find the entire dedicatory page devoted to her name and Lucy Osgood's. This very morning, just as she had done last year on her birthday, she had leafed through its pages to reread her favorite two of Maria's essays. She suspected Maria had written "Letter from an Old Woman on Her Birthday" and "Unmarried Women" with Henrietta in mind. Maria's letter moved Henrietta to ponder again the double standard that gave the term "old maid" a more derogatory meaning than "old bachelor."

But Maria meant the words *Looking Toward Sunset* to be a metaphor for growing old, not as an excuse for postponing difficult tasks until the following day. Henrietta still had not yet written Maria to thank her for her copy of *Romance of the Republic*. What could she say? She had too much respect for Maria to be dishonest, but neither did she wish to be too critical. Yet despite her loyal defense of her dearest friend, she found the book profoundly troubling, or was it her own reaction that troubled her so? She had sincerely praised *Hobomuk*, Maria's novel about the marriage of an Indian to a white woman. Why did she not feel the same about a story of marriages between Africans and whites?

Of course, in *Hobomuk*, the intermarriage took place only in the heroine's imagination and with the woman's free will, not something forced on her by a brutal master. It was untainted with the sin of ownership. Still, Henrietta wondered, what if little Suzie asked her blessing to marry an African? How would old Gerrit Smith, who had an opinion on everything, really feel if his grandson proposed to take vows with a Negro girl and present him with black great-grandbabies with frizzy hair? Well, Smith had always been a hypocrite.

Smith's sins, however, were no excuse for her own. Why did it strike her as less repulsive for a white person to marry an Indian rather than an African? What if a white person married a Chinese? Was that better or worse than an Indian? She knew she was not being entirely logical. She could not think of a *reasonable* objection, but she could not deny that the thought of intermarriage among races made her queasy. It seemed unnatural, just as Anna had said.

She wondered what Catharine would have thought—probably that it was dishonest for her to criticize Anna's harsh views when in her own deepest heart, she herself harbored the same unseemly feelings. Although Anna's tongue might be sharper, her attitudes were no different from other Bostonians. Anna had a generous heart for those she loved. Hadn't she insisted on nursing Henrietta first through the typhoid and then the smallpox, even at the risk of her own life? No one could say she lacked courage or compassion.

What to write Maria? Henrietta closed her eyes. She would say that she was still reading the *Romance*, interspersed with chapters of *Rob Roy*. At least that was a true statement, but she was only buying time. Somehow, eventually, she would have to come up with the right words. She closed her eyes and lay back, putting the book aside. She wondered how many of Gat's family would come up from Peterboro for the wedding. [1]

The Epes Dixwell Home
November 21

"Such a nice young man, and his mother seems quite pleasant, not at all like—" Anna Parker braced herself as the carriage bounced across the frozen ruts of Garden Street into the circular drive of Epes Dixwell's house.

"—like her father?" Henrietta completed her sister's sentence and giggled. At the church, before the nuptials, they had exchanged a few words with Gat's mother, Elizabeth Miller. Despite all the rumors, they had found her to be quite pleasant, especially compared to her father, Gerrit Smith. One of the few things the sisters agreed upon was that Gat's grandfather was a self-righteous and vainglorious fool.

"It's a scandal that he didn't come to his own grandson's wedding," Anna snorted. "He was able enough to travel to Virginia to pledge bail for that traitor Jefferson Davis."

Henrietta laughed. "Scandal? Hardly, it's a blessing. Mr. Smith must always be the bride at every wedding, and the preacher in every pulpit."

"Not in any church I know of," Anna sputtered. "Why, his so-called religion doesn't even recognize the Sabbath."

Henrietta nodded in agreement. Years ago, Gerrit Smith had concluded that by tolerating not only slavery but also the consumption of alcohol, all existing Christian denominations had shown themselves to be the workings of Old Nick himself and the arch foes of truth and justice. He had seceded from the Presbyterian Church and established his own, the Free Church of Peterboro, where he now preached on the "true" Sabbath—Saturdays.

Over the years, Henrietta herself had lost patience with the established churches for the refusal of so many of their clergy to support abolition—at least until it became politically expedient. Smith went too far, however, in rejecting the divinity of Christ, although not, Henrietta suspected, his own God-like nature. He produced a steady stream of self-published, religious tracts promulgating his personal interpretation of the Bible—more diatribe than exegesis. Certainly he clearly relished all the notoriety his money could buy.

"What's taking so long? Is there someone in front?" Anna craned her neck to look up at the drive. "Suzie and Gat will be on their honeymoon before we even get to the front door."

Henrietta peered out to watch Gat's parents, Mr. and Mrs. Charles Miller, and his young sister, Nannie, descend from their carriage and climb the steps to the Dixwells' house.

Anna saw them, too. "Thank heaven, Mrs. Miller didn't wear those dreadful Turkish pantaloons," she remarked.

"You mean bloomers," corrected Henrietta. "Well, she did invent them, and I'm told they are quite practical for gardening or strolling in the country."

During her father's term in Congress, when she was still Miss Smith, people thought she had made a spectacle of herself by wearing her costume to official gatherings.

"I suppose," Anna mused, "Mrs. Miller's trousers caused somewhat less consternation in Washington than those cold-water Temperance dinners her father hosted."

Henrietta laughed. "We should be grateful indeed that Mr. Smith did not come up from Peterboro. Epes told me that if he had, they would have had to hide the champagne and toast Suzie and Gat with lemonade!"

§

"Thank you, Bridget." Henrietta accepted the gold-rimmed Wedgwood dessert plate with its slice of dark brown fruitcake. The creme sugar icing was hardly traditional, but the Dixwells were thoroughly modern. She looked for a place to sit down.

"I do hope they save a piece for their anniversary!" Elizabeth Miller joined Henrietta by the door. "It's a lovely old custom."

"I'm sure they will," Henrietta replied, although she wondered whether Gat and Suzie would wrap their anniversary slice in cheesecloth, liberally doused with brandy, the Dixwell fashion, or go with fanatical temperance views and nibble dry crumbs next November.

"My father regrets that he was too indisposed to travel," Mrs. Miller continued, "but he asked me to relay his best wishes, particularly to you—'a fellow toiler in the vineyards of truth and tolerance,' as he put it."

"Why, thank you Mrs. Miller. Your father is too kind, though. My contribution was small compared to that of many other ladies in Boston."

"That's not true at all, Miss Sargent," Mrs. Miller smiled warmly. "Why, Frederick Douglass himself told me that it was you who reported in the *Standard* on his Nantucket speech—the very beginning of his public career. When my dear cousin, Mrs. Stanton, heard our families were to unite, she told me that you attended the first women's convention in New York City, long before even she joined the cause."

"Yes, the papers called us an 'Amazonian farce' and told us to go back to our frying pans!"

"How little has changed," Mrs. Miller winced. "Even though, through our efforts, African men now vote in Alabama, we women are classed as those who cannot in the manner of criminals, paupers, and idiots." She lowered her voice. "And you know, it was largely because of *your* reputation that Mr. Miller and I entrusted Gat's education to your nephew Epes."

Henrietta was surprised at how thoroughly the Millers had investigated the Dixwell family.

"But with all that," Mrs. Miller continued, "I never expected that the Dixwells would give me their lovely Suzie for a second daughter."

"And I'm equally happy to have your fine son as a great-nephew," Henrietta smiled. "You know, every fall my sister, Mrs. Parker, and I watched Gat play football for the Dixwell School boys on the Common. We became most fiercely partisan, although we always prayed he would not be hurt."

"We worried too," confided Mrs. Miller. "We had hoped he would play baseball— it's less brutal. In fact, our Nannie," she nodded toward the tall, robust girl, "swings a bat as hard as any of the boys and wants to start a girls' team with real uniforms."

"My goodness!" Henrietta managed, thinking better of asking the designer of the bloomer costume what those uniforms might look like

"Oh! Please excuse me," Mrs. Miller flashed a broad smile. "I see my dear husband beckoning, so I must obey. Had I the prescience of dear Mrs. Stanton I, too, might have vowed only to love and honor him."

Henrietta had heard, of course, that Elizabeth Cady Stanton omitted the traditional "obey" from her marriage vows. "Yes," she agreed. "It does seem more in keeping with the principle of equity that both husband and wife pledge obedience to a mutually negotiated consensus."

"Yes, that's just as it should be," laughed Mrs. Miller, "although Suzie seems to have told Gat exactly what kind of plumbing she wants installed in the cottage, and Gat has obeyed her instructions in every particular. Indeed, with time and instruction, my Mr. Miller has become quite obedient, too!"

Obedient, indeed, thought Henrietta. Charles Dudley Miller spent most of his career in court extracting his wife's father from one legal quagmire after another. Ere the smoke had cleared at Harpers Ferry, Gerrit Smith, in a clear act of sanity before running off to hide in a lunatic asylum, dispatched his son-in-law to visit his co-conspirators and recover all documents that might link him to John Brown. Eight years after Mr. Smith's interlude at the Utica asylum, Mr. Miller helped negotiate a retraction and a settlement of his father-in-law's libel suit against the *Tribune* for intimating that Mr. Smith had only feigned insanity to avoid prosecution.

Henrietta joined Anna who was deep in conversation with the two artists of the family—J.J.'s daughter, Annie Dixwell, and Epes's daughter, Fanny.

"Look at the Chinese style, Aunt Anna," Annie was pointing at the Canton pattern platter in the cupboard. Anna and Henrietta peered at the familiar bridge and trees in the foreground and the awkwardly shaped mountains in the distance.

"Notice how rigidly the artist has rendered the scene," Anna continued. Now, look at the difference in Fanny's picture, how naturally the leaves hang from the branches. My teacher says it's how the Japanese painters do with brush strokes, but Fanny captures it in her stitching. Aunt Henrietta, you must remind Uncle George to send us some watercolor sketches the next time he visits Japan."

"I will do so in my next letter," Henrietta promised. "Will you excuse me? I'm going to sit down." She settled into the settee beside the fireplace and regarded the room. In the far corner, Suzie, the new Mrs. Gerrit Smith Miller, was chatting with her old friends from the sewing brigade she had organized during the war. How sweet that the girls still addressed her as "Colonel Suzie!" Henrietta had seen the beautiful linen napkins they embroidered for her trousseau—each with a flowing capital "M."

"It's a pity Fanny's given up her painting," Anna sat down beside Henrietta on the settee. "I don't see how doing tiny stitches is going to rest her eyes."

For once, Henrietta had more information about an important family matter than Anna, and she enjoyed it immensely. "It's because when she paints, she has to look back and forth between the canvas and whatever distant object she is painting, so her eyes always have to refocus, but when she sews on her embroidery frame, it's all at the same distance, so it's not so tiring."

"Well, maybe she should be fitted for spectacles," Anna smoothed a wrinkle in her black silk gown.

"Not at her age!" Henrietta objected.

"Now Henrietta, Fanny is 27, and with two younger sisters already married, she is quite nearly an old maid."

As they scanned the room for Fanny's foot-dragging suitor, a strident voice cut through the din as Wendell Holmes lectured two older men with a torrent of statute numbers and legal Latin. "There he is! What's wrong with that Wendell?" Anna whispered to her sister. "He pays no attention at all to Fanny!"

Ever since Wendell's days at Dixwell's school, he had been Fanny's closest friend. Everyone assumed that as the eldest, she would be the first married, but he still had not proposed. It was awkward for Fanny now, to have two younger sisters married and her own prospects still uncertain.

"Now that he's in practice as a lawyer," Anna continued, "he should do the honorable thing!"

"But isn't he researching a book?" Henrietta feebly tried to defend him. She liked Wendell. Even before the war, the young man had bravely advocated emancipation when his own father and Epes Dixwell still viewed ending slavery as an impractical dream, and abolitionists as rabble-rousing troublemakers.

"A book is no excuse! Goodness me, married men write books every day. His own father edits the *Atlantic Monthly* and still finds time for his social obligations. If young Wendell doesn't move quickly, he may lose the prize. Epes tells me that Will James has taken an interest in Fanny and is posting long letters from Europe. Really, Fanny should leave an envelope out where Wendell will be sure to see it. *That* ought to inspire him to act! If he fails to take the bait, young Mr. James should become the favored dinner guest in this house from the day he returns to Boston." Anna rose with a flourish, pleased with her scheme. "And that calls for a cup of tea!"

Henrietta didn't care for her sister's plotting. Fanny might marry Wendell Holmes or Will James as she chose—or no one. What was the harm in being single?

It was November, time to advertise the annual Anti-Slavery Subscription Festival, but younger women organized the festival now, raising money to support Freedmen's Bureaus. She herself no longer had the strength to even host her own table. The war was over, and the slaves were freed. The victory had been won, but, rather than triumph, she felt the loss of purpose and missed the camaraderie of the movement. Mr. Garrison had retired and closed down *The Liberator*. At least Maria's old paper, the *Anti-Slavery Standard*, still arrived weekly, even though the words "Anti-Slavery" had begun to sound out of date, relics from another age.

Henrietta looked down at her dessert plate. Everything was changing. For so many years the Dixwells used the blue-and-white Canton pattern that George had sent from China, but now it was stored in a display cabinet, rarely used. What was worse, in the six years of George's absence, his youngest nieces and nephews had virtually forgotten him. Ironically George had bought this very house so that his brother Epes might have a place to raise a family, yet George lived the life of a solitary ascetic in rooms upstairs from the office where he labored days without end. Although Epes never failed to acknowledge George's generosity, to the youngest of Epes and J.J.'s children their Uncle George was more a myth than a man.

"Well, Henriet, I and my horses are leaving. You can stay if you choose!" Anna announced with a flourish.

"You can hold your horses!" Henrietta smiled at her sister.

Despite all the changes in the world, Anna had not changed one whit. Without deviation, for all of the 15 years they lived together, Anna had used the same words of parting and Henrietta always made the same reply! Repeating those clichéd phrases brought such a sense of security and pleasure, of constancy and predictability. Henrietta struggled to her feet. It must be growing cooler in Shanghai. She wondered what George was doing. [2]

Chen Tze Fang's Studio
Shanghai

George watched his teacher's hand scribe the character in one smooth movement, without once lifting brush from paper. He treasured these weekly meetings as a respite from the grinding tedium of commerce, an ordeal to which he now saw no end.

Chen Tze Fang looked up from the page and smiled. He spoke slowly in a soft, almost self-effacing voice, his Mandarin elegant and musical.

"*Ts'ao shu*, grass script. It is an art, and a true artist must make that art his own. There are, of course, rules for all tasks, but the first rule of grass script is that it ignores the prescribed strokes of the conventional characters that you have mastered—"

A vase crashed outside in the courtyard, the shards skittering across the flagstones. Chen rolled his eyes. "That grandson is my treasure, but the rubber ball you so generously gave him seems intent on destroying every other treasure in its path."

George laughed. "Perhaps I should have given him dominoes, instead."

From the courtyard came a little boy's sobbing wail as his amah demanded the ball. Chen smiled and stepped outside. George could hear Chen's calming inflections as he talked to the boy, and slowly the sobbing subsided.

Over the time he had studied with Chen, George had come to feel like an uncle to the bubbling five-year-old. He remembered his own nephew, Johnny Dixwell, "the little regicide" as Henrietta still referred to him, who now stood six-feet tall and was about to begin his medical studies at Harvard. How could time have passed so quickly?

George heard the clink of potsherds outside as a servant swept them up. A vase could be replaced, he thought, but time was life and suddenly he was almost 53 years old. His hair, too, was turning gray. Somehow, his quest for fortune had devoured his youth. Growing older had not much concerned him during his first three-year partnership with the Heard firm. The happy prospect of earning back his fortune in short order still seemed promising, and he lived frugally, avoiding all extravagance, to pay off the last of his debts in Boston.

His main occupation, which had driven every other thought from his mind, had been to devise a way to capture steamer commerce on the newly opened Yangtze River. His strategy was to place agency houses with Heard men at every port and then convince Chinese merchants to invest in enough Heard steamers for him to schedule regular arrivals and departures along the 600 navigable miles of that immense river.

He had once imagined having a wife and a little boy of his own. For a while during those first three years back in China he still harbored that hope, but now that business had again taken a steep downward slide, George knew it would never happen.

It was unfair. His steamship plan had worked! Well, at least, it *had* worked until Russell's and Dent's and Jardine's and all the lesser firms copied his strategy. By the time of his second three-year partnership, the competition had siphoned off so much of the profits that Heard vessels were running at a loss.

In addition, who could have predicted that the final defeat of the Taipings would lead to a mass exodus of Chinese joyously returning to their ancestral villages from the safety of the Shanghai International Settlements? The result, of course, was a crash in real estate prices as hundreds of buildings suddenly stood vacant. Fortunes were lost, banks failed, and those Chinese merchants who had survived the collapse were now loath to loosen their purse strings for anything so uncertain as river steamers.

He had to remind himself that the Shanghai depression and the Heard firm's decline of fortune were *not* his fault. The defeat of the Taipings should have ushered in an era of prosperity instead of a depression, which so depleted Heard capital that this past spring they were forced to sell the *Kiangloong* to the monopoly of Tyson and Russell's steamship company. She had been their last steamer on the Yangtze, the last remainder of George's grand plan.

To add insult to injury, the Heard Company had been obliged to sign a promise not to place another vessel on the Yangtze for the next 10 years. George's chest tightened as he recalled lowering the red-white diamond flag from the *Kiangloong's* masthead. It was an excruciating loss of face.

George had to shake free of his self-recriminations and his habitual litany of failures. He glanced around Chen's sparsely furnished studio and rose to examine a scroll hanging from its silk cord on the far wall. The painted scene—a bridge spanning two points of land with tall mountains in the background—reminded him of the Canton pattern porcelain dishes he had sent home to Epes long ago. Five cinnabar chops were placed along the edges of the scroll, documenting the chain of owners over the generations, each one having stamped his chop mark onto the immortal masterpiece.

He shook his head and looked back at the table. Chen had silently returned to his seat and was staring at him quizzically.

"Do not worry, my friend, the errant ball will be soon be returned to the boy, and he will have learned to be more careful."

George smiled and wished his troubles were as simple as a confiscated toy. It served no purpose to mentally recount all of his defeats, one by one, like Macao Jesuits clicking the black beads of their rosaries. He brought himself back to what Chen was saying about grass script.

"Here, Mr. Dixwell. Now you try it." Chen turned the rice paper toward George and handed him the brush.

George struggled to duplicate the flowing line of the character as Chen had rendered it. The brush exaggerated the quaver that still lingered in his hand from the rheumatic fever.

"It is good that you wish to add your grandfather's name to his story of Wang-fo." Chen paused, considering his words. "The many pages over which your brush may travel in preparation are the true measure of the honor in which you hold his memory." Chen looked at George's face and stopped, a pained look flashing through his eyes. "I am sorry, Mr. Dixwell." The old man lowered his gaze. "You are still upset about the sadness of the boy."

George felt his eyes welling with tears. No, not exactly. It was his sadness at the thought that he would never have a boy of his own. The time for that had flown, but there was no point in going over his losses. He would spare his teacher that.

Chen waited for George to regain his composure. "How many brush strokes," the old man queried, "to render the character 'chia'?"

George pictured the character in his mind: a pig under a roof, designating "home" or "family" and suggesting economic success. "Nine strokes," he answered.

"Yes, nine." Chen wrote the angular character. "In grass script, it is but one."

Chen scribed the character again, its angles dissolving into graceful curves, the single line varying in thickness with his changing pressure on the brush—bold and broad as he pressed it down and fine as he lifted it up.

"But," Chen continued, "as you also know, there are but a few strokes separating 'home' from 'tranquility.'" Slowly, deliberately, Chen inked the character of a woman under a roof.

George looked at the figure of the woman beneath the roof. "Yes," he acknowledged, "Only a few brush strokes distinguish 'family' from 'tranquility.'"

Chen glanced at George and nodded. Again, he dipped his brush into the well of the stone ink-grinding slab and slid its tip along the rim, just enough to remove any excess.

"Mr. Dixwell, a successful home and tranquility are desirable, but they are not sufficient to a full life. A man must aspire to goodness and 'good' is only a few brush strokes more."

Once again, Chen wrote "woman," this time adding the brush strokes for "child."

George stared at the character. Another wave of sadness washed over him. Aunt Henrietta had been right all along. No one was left for him now but old maids and widows—if that.

"Mr. Dixwell," Chen continued gently, "if you have no woman, you will have no son. And if you have no son, there will be no one to carry on your name, and if your name dies, you may as well never have lived at all."

George avoided Chen's gaze. "It's not that I don't want a wife," he laughed dismissively. "I just haven't had the time to find one." He regretted his disingenuous words even as he spoke them.

Chen raised an eyebrow. "You have not had the time? His voice held only the gentlest hint of a scold. "Perhaps it is a pity that no wife has been found *for* you, as would be our custom." Chen placed his brush upright in its holder and turned to face George. "I know of a respectable young woman and inquiries could be made."

The blood rushed to George's face. He felt his heart thumping. So, it had come to this. There was no one else left in the entire world but Chen and Henrietta who cared enough to put truth into words. He stared for a moment at the elegantly scribed character, then back at his teacher. George nodded. [3]

Heard Headquarters
Hong Kong

George paused at the foot of the steps. A bustle of activity had greeted him upon his return to Heard headquarters, and this was his first opportunity to reflect on his morning with Chen. "Inquiries could be made"—the phrase echoed in his head. Just what had he committed to with his brief nod? What exactly, might Chen do? He pictured his usual manner of addressing any problem—the blank pages of a ledger. Never in his life had he made a decision in the heat of emotion without calculating the credits and debits, and he would not do so now. There would be debits, although only a few of them measurable in dollars—and the credits? Well, he hadn't agreed to anything. He recalled Henrietta's oft-repeated dictum: "Marry in haste, repent in —"

"Dixwell!" William Endicott emerged from the smoke-filled drawing room where the clerks were congregated for their afternoon break. He placed a finger to his lips, signaling he had business to discuss out of their hearing.

A coolie rushed to push open the massive front door. The two men walked through the small garden to the pillared gateway and onto the Bund. These were the best days of the year with cool breezes displacing the oppressive, sticky heat of summer. In a few weeks they would give way to frigid winds from the north, bringing freezing rain and slushy snow. The men paused for a carriage to squeak past, before crossing to the waterfront.

"I think we're done with Roundy," said Endicott. "I doubt there'll be any more bad chests of Malwa, and with luck, none of his creditors will sue. By now he should be home with Martha and no one there, the wiser."

It had come to light that Hervey Jencks Roundy, captain of the their opium-receiving vessel at Woosung, had been topping off the chests he traded on his own private account with opium from Heard Company chests. To conceal the crime, he had shipped 20 Heard chests to dealers in Hong Kong, each filled with a 133-pound picul of crushed rock ballast. Twenty chests of Malwa opium were stolen—worth upwards of $700 each. Fourteen thousand dollars was robbed from the meager profits of the firm!

George tried to control his indignation, "Sheer lunacy!" He shook his head. "That should put an end to it. We paid the customs on the 20 he sent to Hong Kong. How could Roundy think that an insurance company would cover such a loss without an investigation?"

William shook his head. "James and I appreciate the discretion with which you handled the matter. We did not relish the prospect of seeing Martha's husband dragged through the courts."

William's brother, James Bridges Endicott, the richest American in Macao, was a valued client of the Heard firm, and George had done his best to shield the family from embarrassment. George recalled the day, years ago, when William revealed that Roundy was to marry Martha Endicott, a niece to him and James. Roundy had purchased railroad land in Illinois and intended to sell building lots in a town he planned to name Woosung. When the Illinois venture proved unprofitable, Roundy had understandably returned to Woosung in China. At least Roundy—unlike himself—had been able to pay for his own ticket and arrived in Shanghai with the remainder of a nest egg in his pocket.

Perhaps the later injury to Roundy's back and the months of immobility caused the man to snap—there had even been the talk about suicide. Fortunately, William had confiscated the distraught man's pistol. It must have been insanity. Almost 30 years of loyal service to the firm and then this bizarre act. The attempted cover-up was far too clumsy for a truly criminal mind. It seemed almost as if Roundy had wanted to be caught.

George's outrage softened. For almost three full decades, Roundy had always completed his tasks reliably and without complaint. He had been the one who first suggested that the Heard firm unite their Yangtze fleet with the Dent's and Jardine's into one steam navigation company that would be large enough to face down George Tyson. They had *almost* achieved an agreement to unite, but the talks faltered over details. How Russell's must have gloated as its only competition fell back into squabbling disunity. By remaining divided, the companies had guaranteed Russell's victory. They did it to themselves without Russell's raising a finger.

George stared vacantly across the harbor. The broad, blue pennant of the Shanghai Steam Navigation Company—Tyson and Russell's monopoly—fluttered mockingly from the masthead of some new steamer.

Endicott followed George's eyes to the anchored vessels. "We should hold onto Roundy's share of the *Emily Jane* in case any remaining injured parties crawl out of the woodwork."

George nodded absently. Selling the vessel where Roundy perpetrated his fraud had pretty much cleared the slate, and they would withhold his share of the proceeds until the books were completely balanced. Yes, all things considered, Roundy had been right about his steamship strategy, and, aside from this one lunatic act, there had been goodness to the man. He had done right by his Chinese son—just as right as William Hunter and James Endicott had by theirs. He'd sent little Charley Roundy to the States for his education. Fortunately, the boy had been too young to fight for the Union.

If only Hunter had been so fortunate! His oldest boy, Anna Rosa's brother, fell to a Confederate bullet on some southern battlefield. At least Anna Rosa had presented Hunter with two healthy grandsons before her husband was taken by cholera. And Anna Rosa, now three years a widow —George brought himself back to the present. He hadn't been listening, while Endicott recounted each of Roundy's debts and its resolution.

"You've handled it well," George nodded his approval. "We've kept it out of the courts and out of the papers and nobody will lose face."

A side-wheel harbor tug, black smoke streaming from its stack, pushed a coal barge toward Russell's steamer. The two men stood watched the harbor traffic. Endicott broke the silence. "Henry seems to be doing well getting the ships out,"

"Yes, the best ever."

The Heard's shipping department was operating with a new efficiency since Henry, James Endicott's son, had joined the firm. With a Chinese mother and an American education in Kentucky, the young man was able to manage all things Chinese and English with equal facility. The Endicotts had a right to be proud of him. As George expected, Henry Endicott brought a large share of his father's coastal shipping with him to the Heard firm. At last report, James now lived comfortably in Macao with his English wife and a house full of their children. Both Chinese and white sides of the Endicott clan seemed to function without conflict or shame and to the benefit of all.

Their conference completed, the two men walked along the harbor's edge and then crossed back toward the Heard headquarters. George wondered what Roundy's boy was doing now in the States and if he could still speak any Chinese. He thought of the character Chen had written signifying goodness—the strokes for woman and child. Could the goodness expressed in his teacher's elegant brush strokes ever pass for goodness in Boston, if the woman were Chinese and the child a half-breed?

Last week's *Herald* had a remarkably apropos letter to the editor. The writer lamented that it was enough to make the angels weep to see the growing number of fine young men engaged in China commerce who, in the absence of eligible white women, were growing old and gray as bachelors, often becoming hardened profligates and debauchees. The correspondent argued that a properly trained Chinese girl was every bit as gentle, refined, and as faithful as a European woman, and that the missionaries should raise up a cadre of such girls to become the wives of these rootless American and British traders.

The writer's sentiments rang true to George. Only later had he noticed the snide postscript, supplied by the editor, to the effect that the correspondent's ideas of morality were, at best, Utopian! Of course, George realized that in Boston such a proposal would not even be regarded as Utopian; it would be miscegenation, plain and simple.

Was it a fantasy to think that he might somehow achieve the goodness scribed by Chen by abandoning the values of Boston? Or was that even important? Boston morality had always accommodated hypocrisy and relegated China to a separate universe, somewhere over the eastern horizon with its own rules. "The forbidden" could flourish conveniently "out of sight and out of mind." No one at home need ever acknowledge the existence of Albert Heard's Chinese woman or Tyson's—least of all, Tyson's pretty new wife from Boston. Youthful indiscretions, although hardly acceptable, could be tolerated so long as the Chinese mothers and their half-breed progeny never materialized on a Boston doorstep.

His situation was different. His would be no youthful indiscretion. It would be the reasoned decision of a man, more than a half-century old, one who had long ago lost hope of ever winning a rosy-cheeked Boston girl. His would not be a back-street liaison but a marriage, arranged by his teacher who stood as his father in all things Chinese, the closest bond in his adult life. There could be no going back on his word. He could never abandon the woman, as it would be a betrayal of that bond. And Henrietta? Although she might not encourage the union, once consummated, she would accept it and expect him to honor it for the rest of his life. His children would be Chinese, but they would be *his* children nonetheless. Were he to desert them, he could never again face either Henrietta or Chen—.

"I'm off to dinner with Charles at the Masonic Temple." Endicott gestured up the Bund.

George watched him walk away, still lost in his own thoughts, wondering if Chinese "live and let live" tolerance could ever take root in Boston. What was it that had made him receptive to his teacher's suggestion—the delicacy of the presentation or its underlying truth? What, if anything, had his nod signaled to Chen—a vague, general assent or a resolute agreement? What would his colleagues think? Had attitudes in China really changed? He recalled Delano's ugly epithet for Anna Rosa's mother: "Hunter's miserable Tanka mistress." Would there be snide discussion among the clerks of "Dixwell's concubine?" Would word reach Boston? What to do?

Perhaps, it was better to think about something else. Hard work left little opportunity for rumination, no time for brooding or self-doubt. He had letters to write and ledgers to audit. George passed back through the pillared gate, drawn to the shelter of predictability inside. [4]

Heard Headquarters
December 1

"Captain Endicott! You're up early!" George squinted as the morning sun flashed through the open door, reflecting off the hall mirror into his eyes. "Or are you just straggling in from last night's banquet at the Club?"

"My good Dixwell," William Endicott handed his hat to the door coolie and slipped out of his jacket, "a Sunday morning stroll is a tonic for both body and soul."

"For the body, perhaps, but you might have extended that stroll past a church to improve your soul." George cupped his ear to the morning chimes echoing in the distance.

"Well, I did contribute toward the purchase of one of those bells, but I must confess that with the Sabbath sun hardly up, my soul is already one entry to debit. I've already failed in my pursuit of temperance. They were pouring champagne for Tyson over at Russell's."

"For Tyson?" George scoffed. "Not at this hour! He spends Sundays with his wife."

"No, not for Tyson! Endicott's eyes took on a mischievous glint. "The bubbly was for his new baby boy, for whom, I am informed, Tyson has already chosen the most auspicious of names—Russell!"

"You're joking," gasped George.

"Well, Russell and Company has been good to Tyson, and he's going home a rich man. That boy can be eternally thankful he wasn't named for the Shanghai Steam Navigation Company!"

George forced a smile. Word had it that Tyson was about to announce his retirement.

Endicott continued, "He goes home with a fortune in the bank and a pretty wife on his arm—and a son with a name to grow into. Jamie tells me he's established a trust in Hong Kong to support Lam Fong Kew and her four little Tysons."

"Tyson's number one son must be eight years old, at least," George mused. "I wonder if young Russell will ever meet his brothers and sisters."

"That's hard to say," Endicott started up the stairs. "But I suspect that, in the presence of Mrs. Tyson, no one in Boston will ever identify Master Russell as son number three."

George laughed and continued down the steps to the Russian Consular Office where Chen was working.

"Chun-tzu, tsao an!" The greeting was perhaps overly flowery for the shabby office, but by wishing "morning peace" and identifying his teacher as a "princely scholar"—a man of complete virtue according to the Confucian ideal—George was able to show not only respect for his teacher but also his own erudition. After a week of talking Shanghai dialect to the silk merchants and Cantonese to the comprador, George relished the opportunity to address his teacher in the concise elegance of Mandarin. He peered over Chen's shoulder. The old man had almost finished drafting Admiral Popov's request to the taotai for a better anchorage and looked up from his work.

"The inner peace of a mere harbor pilot is of little consequence to an Admiral seeking safe passage through the shoals between him and his dinner."

"That may be true," George enjoyed the gentle jousting, "but while the taotai may perhaps begrudge the Admiral his rice bowl, he may yet marvel at the precision with which that pilot navigates among the reefs and around the rocks to reach the harbor."

"That humble pilot, though unworthy," Chen spoke softly, "appreciates the honor paid to his craft."

It was not the admiral George wanted to talk about. All week long the words "inquiries could be made" had gone round and round in his mind. He had always pictured a pretty, blonde Boston girl with a tiny waist and blue eyes, but now—

"My good teacher—" He searched for the neutral words that would not reveal the turmoil of his emotions, "you spoke of a young lady. Did you say she was an orphan?"

"It is true her parents, indeed, died some six years ago, in the disturbances at Hangchow. But she is hardly a beggar."

George remembered the *Herald* reports of the bloodbath in Hangchow, when the Taipings had overrun that ancient city.

"She lives with a highly respectable family and is well bred and of good character. Yes, she is modest, diligent and refined."

"But—" George stumbled, trying to find a more delicate way to put his question, "but what does she look like?"

Chen hesitated, then spoke slowly, as was his habit when expressing something of importance. "The classics tell us a man should marry a woman for virtue, not for physical beauty. For, as it is written, 'an ugly wife in the house is a treasure.'" Chen lifted one eyebrow and looked again at George. "And, remember, sir, that physical beauty without virtue is like a flower without a fragrance."

George pictured a chunky woman with a broad face and a flat nose—someone that no matchmaker had been able to unload. The old man was playing with him. George struggled to regain his dignity. "On the other hand, I would add, that virtue without beauty is like fragrance without a flower."

Chen chuckled approvingly at the riposte, then reached into his portfolio and handed George a photograph, face down. "Forgive me for teasing you, my esteemed friend; she has beauty both of character and of appearance. I do concur that a gentleman of refined taste should never be so prejudiced as to reject beauty out of hand!"

George stared at the cardboard backing, which bore the imprint of a Chinese portrait gallery. Only a few years ago the Chinese had tried to outlaw photography, believing that the Western barbarians used melted eyeballs plucked from Chinese babies to coat their glass-plate negatives. Now they were establishing their own photo galleries all along the coast. Still, George wondered how Chen could have procured the photograph of a respectable woman.

George turned over the card and stared at the sepia-toned image of a family group, posed in two carefully arranged rows. The center of the picture was dominated by the figure of a distinguished middle-aged man.

"The girl stands at the left end of the first row. The family is that of my friend, her uncle, whom I see often in regard to commercial matters."

George focused on the girl. She had the high forehead of a classical portrait painted on porcelain, a delicate nose, and finely chiseled cheekbones. Despite her full gown, he could tell that she was slim and willowy. Even though not more than a teenager, she looked confidently past the camera, her lips betraying neither smile nor frown but were slightly pursed, as if about to ask a question. There was a quiet elegance about her. She was beautiful.

"Maybe I gave you the wrong picture." Chen pointedly shifted his papers as if looking for a missing item.

George appreciated the generosity of his teacher in conjuring sufficient humor to soften the seriousness of the discussion. He looked again at the woman in the picture. The girl's slippered foot, although small and dainty, had not been bound and deformed into the lotus shape so loved by Chinese men.

"She is Manchu," Chen pointed out. "As you well know, the daughters of Tartary have not yet adopted the highest refinements of civilized life."

"Manchu?" repeated George, "but she can't be royal."

"No more or less than any of the Manchu banner regiments in Hangchow. Her name is Hu Ts'ai-shun, and she has served in the Forbidden City."

For more than 200 years a Manchu dynasty had ruled China. Nowadays, the brightest Manchu girls, as George knew, were invited to serve Manchu officials and their families in the royal precinct of Peking. Chen wrote the characters for Hu Ts'ai-shun's name and pointed to the surname, "Hu."

George understood. The syllable "Hu" could be written by several different characters, each representing a different meaning, but the character Chen had written had an additional connotation: Manchu.

George gazed again at the photograph. "My esteemed benefactor," George bowed his head in respect, "I would like to meet this Hu Ts'ai-shun." [5]

Interior of Epes Dixwell's house (ca. mid-1880s). (Courtesy of the
Massachusetts Historical Society.)

George Dixwell's life in China continued to affect the Dixwells back in Massachusettts.
George had contributed half of the cost to build his bother Epes's house in Cambridge,
Massachusetts. This interior photo of Epes's house shows a cupboard display of four
Canton-pattern platters sent by George from China. Nearby, a Japanese-influenced
drawing or embroidery (perhaps a window shade), likely created by Epes's daughter,
Fanny Dixwell Holmes, who became famous for her Japanese-influenced embroideries.

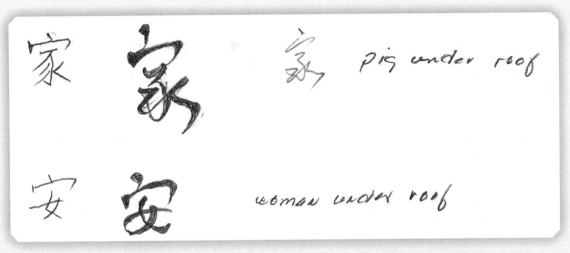

A demonstration of grass script or "grass writing," showing Chinese characters for "Family" + 2 strokes = "tranquility"— to "goodness"—and to grass writing. (Courtesy of Raleigh Ferrell.)

I have surmised that George Dixwell's Chinese teacher, Chen Tze Fang, arranged George's marriage to Hu Ts'ai-shun. My November 21, 1867, vignette placed in Chen's studio is, of course, imagined. My East Asian linguist cousin, Dr. Raleigh Ferrell, suggested the juxtaposition of the Chinese characters that I imagined could have convinced George to marry. With a shaky hand, Raleigh, then in his mid-eighties, attempted to demonstrate the grass-writing version.

CHAPTER ELEVEN
George and Ts'ai-shun

The George Dixwell Home
34 Hoihaw Road, Shanghai
1870, December 13

"My husband!" Ts'ai-shun leaned into George's office. "You ready for eat?"

"One moment, my dear." George looked up from his writing, returning her smile. Ts'ai-shun's Chinese was elegant, but she still struggled with her English.

He listened as she bustled back down the hall, then dipped his pen, trying to compose a stirring conclusion for tomorrow's speech to the Shanghai Volunteer Corps. He could hear his wife instructing the cook to delay dinner until the master arrived. How surprisingly comfortable these three years with Ts'ai-shun had been, despite some awkward obstacles to the marriage. Ts'ai-shun had insisted on a proper Chinese ceremony. His teacher, Chen, informally adopted George as a son, so the simple rite could take place in the correct manner with George's "family" represented.

Even though that day Ts'ai-shun had hardly raised her eyes, in the two years since Charley's birth she revealed a strong inborn confidence. While at first she and George felt but simple respect for each other, their shared laughter over their situation nourished an affection that had grown into a deep friendship, far more satisfying than the romantic love he imagined as a younger man.

"Jack!" Charley careened into the room waving the stuffed toy that was his constant companion for the past year. The little boy grabbed at his father's pant leg.

"And what does Jack say?" George put down his pen and lifted his son to his lap.

"Ruff, ruff!" Charley shook his cloth companion in George's face.

"And is Jack a chicken?" George bounced the boy on his knee.

"No!" Charley objected. "He dog!"

Ts'ai-shun reappeared at the doorway, followed by the amah.

"T'ien-sheng—Charley! Father must finish writing."

"He's doing no harm." George wiped his pen on a tuft of cotton and placed the cap on his inkwell.

The boy slid from his father's lap to hide under the desk. Ts'ai-shun squatted down and reached to extract her son, then clutched the squirming child to her hip with one arm.

Her husband is a good man, and she was glad she chose him. Some months after she had completed her service at the Forbidden City, a matchmaker proposed to her a marriage to the younger son of a Manchu merchant. Despite the misgivings of her uncle and after consultation with an astrologer, she decided to accept the offer made by Te-ch'en instead. He was such a grand man—more than 6 English feet tall, towering almost a full head above most of the Mandarins with whom he negotiated.

She still had trouble with English, especially pronouncing Te-ch'en's family name in English—George Dixwell—but she had not experienced a single moment of regret over the marriage. After all, she ran her own household with no mother-in-law to please. He gave her this house and a staff of her choosing. Further, with Te-ch'en there would never be a second or third wife to complicate her life. She had her own circle of friends—other Manchu women who had been in Imperial Palace service.

Of course, some disapproved of her marriage to a "barbarian." Official Manchu policy was to keep the bloodline pure, and marriage to any non-Manchu was strongly discouraged. But, then, most English and American people felt the same way about their own bloodline. She had done her duty too, giving him a healthy son—and such a lively one! She agreed with him that Charley needed to hear more English, and that dinner with his parents was a good time to practice.

She was so proud to have married such an important man, the chairman of the Municipal Council of the International Settlement, the vice-chairman of the Shanghai Chamber of Commerce, and the ex-officio commandant of the Shanghai Volunteer Corps.

She handed Charley over to his amah's embrace. "You finish speech for Volunteer Corps?"

"It's almost finished, except for the names of the winners in marksmanship." George shuffled the loose pages into a neat pile He rose to his feet. "How does this sound? … 'and, finally, I present the Portuguese Prize.'" George waved his arm in a broad flourish, as if toward the troops who would be standing before him in the morning.

> "When we reflect upon the fact that it was the illustrious Portuguese, Vasco de Gama, who first opened Asia to the maritime enterprise of the West, leading to the establishment of Europeans in China, and that his countrymen are still here today contributing to the continuance and safety of our residence; this association of ideas lends to this prize an interest quite peculiar unto itself …"

Ts'ai-shun nodded thoughtfully.

George stole a glance at his notes. "And now, Ladies and Gentlemen, I close this ceremony—which I hope has not been altogether devoid of either interest or utility—by expressing the hope that next year will bring forward many more accomplished marksmen to compete on equal terms with those who have had the good fortune and merit to carry off the prizes today."

It was good that George had taught her English and the workings of the English alphabet, but sometimes the speeches he rehearsed contained too many new words for her to fully understand. Later, she would ask him the meaning of "maritime" and "devoid." For now, Ts'ai-shun smiled at her husband. "Your words will give them honor. You ready eat dinner now?"

"Yes, my dear, I am ready for dinner."

"Dinner!" the little boy broke loose from his amah and raced down the hallway to the dining room.

Ts'ai-shun watched her husband follow the boy and listened to the boy's squeals of delight to have his father's full attention. She waited for her husband to seat her at the table. It still felt unnatural. A respectable woman did not eat with her husband but, rather, with the children, and only after the husband was finished. George, however, wanted their son to learn Western ways. She acceded to his wish that at dinner, the family would eat together in Western fashion and speak English. She waited as George took his seat across the table, and the amah lifted the boy onto the shipping box tied on the seat of the chair at the end.

"Stay close," she warned the amah. She signaled the maid to bring the food from the kitchen, then waited as her husband bowed his head and recited his prayer to the Christian god. The boy should hear English, and this particular prayer had lots of words in it.

George spoke slowly and clearly for Charley's benefit. "Give us this day our daily bread and forgive us our trespasses as we forgive those who trespass against us. With grateful thanks for all we receive, amen."

Ts'ai-shun thought the prayer strange. Why ask for bread when they never ate it? Despite the kind sentiments regarding *trespassers*, Charley kept a hired man at their gate at night to drive away such people. Her husband and the Municipal Council had just placed policemen at all the bridges crossing the Defense Ditch to prevent beggars from returning to the settlement once they had received food at the Christian Charity House. The Christians' religion seemed bizarre.

George's explanation that the prayer did not refer to real bread or real trespassers did not clarify anything. Christian prayers seemed to ask for nothing that one could actually use. It was far more logical to light incense sticks at the family altar to transmit one's wishes for important, necessary things. She waited to speak until George slipped his napkin from its silver ring and spread it on his lap. Ts'ai-shun then nodded for the amah to tuck the boy's napkin into his shirt.

"Husband, what is news from Peking?" She enjoyed hearing news from the Forbidden City. He always read her the newspaper reports, although the *Daily Herald* never seemed to get them right.

"You will recall," said George, "that on his trip to see the Great Wall, Mr. Seward, the American consul, requested a personal audience with Prince Kung in Peking and that Prince Kung, claiming illness, declined to see him."

Ts'ai-shun nodded. During the fourth or fifth year of her service at the Palace, Prince Kung had carried out the coup that elevated her mistress, concubine Yi, to the position of Empress Dowager Tz'u-hsi. Although she herself never personally served the empress, she knew some of the girls who had. She felt protective of Prince Kung who, as the Dowager's regent, was said to be responsible now for all Imperial dealings with foreigners. Ts'ai-shun knew also that Prince Kung's enemies accused him of opening China too much to the barbarians. He needed to avoid appearing too accommodating to any Westerner.

George continued, "Mr. Seward suspected that the Prince was not really ill and that he, the official representative of the United States of America, had been slighted. So he proposed to go himself to Prince Kung's house to see the ailing Regent."

Ts'ai-shun's eyes widened. "Mr. Seward dare go to Prince Kung's house? *T'a shemmo tou pu tung!*" She colored slightly. She often slipped into Mandarin when she was angry. "He understand nothing!"

George chuckled to himself at his wife's interpretation of Chinese politics.

The maid placed a platter of pork and another of vegetables on the table. Ts'ai-shun pursed her lips as she set down the next dish—long, flat noodles. How could she have forgotten to tell the cook! She looked down at her knife, fork, and spoon and back at the noodles. Rice might be eaten with such awkward instruments, but noodles were too slippery and required chopsticks.

She stole a glance at her husband. He smiled, understanding her predicament. "Go ahead," he said, "cut them into bite-size for Charley."

Ts'ai-shun instructed the amah and returned her attention to her husband's story. "How Prince Kung answer Mr. Seward offer to come his house?"

"Well, the Prince thanked Mr. Seward profusely for offering to take the great trouble to come to him and begged to decline, saying that his residence was mean and small, and he feared its condition might offend Mr. Seward. Thus, he would indeed call upon Mr. Seward, himself."

Ts'ai-shun giggled. "Husband, Prince Kung house almost so fine as palace of Empress. Sorry your Mr. Seward never see it!"

"True," George responded, "but the Prince sent many gifts to Mr. Seward as an apology—enameled fish vases, lacquer boxes, and a pair of enameled eagles."

Ts'ai-shun laughed. "Mr. Seward happy with gift? Those poor gift only good for low taotai."

Clearly, Mr. Seward was no match for Prince Kung. The U.S. counsel had been insulted yet a second time. He had lost face twice because of his lack of understanding of Chinese custom, and he didn't even know it. Ts'ai-shun waited as the maid spooned pork and vegetables onto her plate, but she waved away the noodles. She would eat those later in a proper way from a bowl with chopsticks. Poor Charley was starting to cry! There were noodles everywhere, and he was banging his fork against his bowl.

George suppressed a smile at the boy's consternation. "Maybe, we should let Charley master chopsticks first."

Ts'ai-shun gestured for the amah and changed the subject. "Husband," she said, "tomorrow morning I talk to carpenter about new altar." [1]

December 14

"Husband, I want show you something."

George rose from his desk and dutifully followed his wife down the hall. She had always objected to the inexpensive altar he purchased when they first moved into the house, far too modest for a man of his importance. As their ancestral hall had been used for propitiation of the ancestor spirits of another family (that of the previous owners), Ts'ai-shun cleaned it several times and burned incense until the air was thick with fragrant smoke. Who knew what pernicious spirit contamination might have lingered in the dimly lit room?

The house had been built for a comprador who was forced to sell after the late real estate crash. Like many of the houses that rich Chinese merchants built in the International Settlement, the wall, the columned gate, and the exterior of the house were of European style, while the interior was a hodgepodge of East and West. It included quarters for two concubines and their children, and, far to the back, accommodations for an army of servants. In any event, the house was sufficiently Chinese to please Ts'ai-shun.

There was one European-style room—the parlor, where Ts'ai-shun insisted they receive their European guests. It was elegantly furnished with blue velvet settees and a gilt-framed English landscape painting.

Ts'ai-shun waited for George to join her and admire the new ebony doors to the ancestral hall. She showed him the grillwork, which outlined a tortoise and an evergreen pine for longevity, two fish for abundance, and a pair of cranes for harmony.

Nodding his appreciation, George followed his wife into the dimly lit room. Against the far wall stood the family altar with three freshly lit incense sticks glowing in a porcelain urn. Faint wisps of fragrant smoke curled upward past the lithograph of his father, from the days when he was the grandmaster of the Boston Masons.

"That old altar not look good beside new doors," Ts'ai-shun frowned. "Your father must better—need one set ebony altar and table."

George agreed. He accepted her respect for his family, even if he did not share her beliefs. He had become accustomed to the Buddha standing in the middle of the shelf. To Buddha's left stood a statue of Kuanyin, the Goddess of Mercy. "I do like our Buddha," he said, reaching up to touch the bronze figure.

Ts'ai-shun clucked her tongue. "Husband, more good luck if give him something he eat." She demonstrated, moving the orange on the offering table closer to the Buddha.

George grunted his usual acknowledgement. He wasn't superstitious, hardly even religious, but Ts'ai-shun always smiled when he touched the Buddha. It reminded him of his visit years ago to the Vatican where, just like the other petitioners, he had reached up to touch Saint Peter's toe, even though he was no more a Papist than a Buddhist.

His eye fell again on his father's portrait. What would that conservative medical doctor—a good Unitarian who had hardly spent a night outside of Boston—think to see his image atop a pagan altar in Shanghai? Although Jesuits had long ago come to terms with ancestor *veneration*, the protestant missionaries who now flooded into China saw such practices as ancestor *worship* of the most heathen sort—an unpardonable affront to the monotheistic core of Christianity. It seemed a tempest in a teapot or in an incense urn to him. He certainly had no objection if Ts'ai-shun demanded a proper altar where, when her time came, her son could properly display her memorial tablet for at least the requisite three years.

He couldn't fault Ts'ai-shun. The connection to an ancestral lineage was important for him, too, and it troubled him that he had not given his own son Charley the Dixwell name. He had demurred, not out of deference to his father, gone almost 30 years, but because when he'd told J.J. and Epes of his marriage, they insisted he keep it secret from the rest of the family. That was before Charley was born. It caused him sadness that, by respecting his brothers' wishes, he felt obliged not only to continue the charade of bachelorhood but also to assign Charley the surname of Grandfather Sargent. It was a name so sufficiently common in Boston that no one in his family would be embarrassed by a connection to a half-Chinese child. With the passage of time, it was too late to expect the Dixwells to acknowledge his wife and son.

Ts'ai-shun took a fresh incense stick from the packet on the side of the altar and held its end to the flickering oil lamp on the offering table. "There," she said, brandishing the smoking wand. "For Prince Kung." Ts'ai-shun then poked the stick upright into the mound of sand filling the urn. "Here," she handed George a fresh stick. "For your father."

George held the stick to the flickering flame. Yes, family was important. Where he had once despaired of ever having a wife and son, he now worried about what would happen to them when he died. He hoped he could rely on the Fearons and Endicotts to look after his Chinese family. Those friends had blessed his marriage without apparent reservation or doubt. On that fall morning, they all stood together in a semi-circle in the Chen family house: first, Chen and his wife; then, Robert Fearon with Mary; and, finally, the two Endicott cousins, William and Charles. Fearon had grown up speaking Cantonese in Macao, and he knew China, while the Endicotts had between them quite a number of Chinese nephews and cousins. They all understood.

"Husband," Ts'ai-shun chided. "Put incense into urn. Is for your father, not for you! Mr. Fearon coming soon—almost time you give speech." With a regal sweep of her gown, Ts'ai-shun headed toward the kitchen to speak with the cook.

George walked back to his study. He still had to quickly revise the concluding sentences.

§

The bell at the gate clanged a familiar triple stroke, and George heard the maid welcoming Robert Fearon at the door. Ts'ai-shun interrupted her discussion with the carpenter to greet the junior partner from the Heard office.

George quickly reread his concluding paragraph. Perhaps a more stirring final flourish would come to him on his walk to the Public Garden with Fearon.

He joined his wife by the door and was just in time to see Fearon hand a glass jar to Ts'ai-shun. "Mrs. Fearon sends her best wishes and orders me to present this token of her affection."

"She make this herself?" Ts'ai-shun stared at the red fruit.

"Yes, English strawberries from her own garden," Fearon smiled.

George took the jar from her hand to examine it. Mary Fearon was among the few English women who had befriended Ts'ai-shun, and he appreciated her kindness. Although his wife was adept at managing their household, making fruit preserves was not a usual accomplishment for a Chinese lady.

Ts'ai-shun bowed. "Please tell Mrs. Fearon thank you for me and Mr. Dixwell."

"And, especially for Charley!" George laughed, handing the jar back to his wife. The two men stepped out into the chilly morning.

"Husband, please wait," Ts'ai-shun called from down the hall, hurrying back with his gloves.

George thanked her and slipped them on. Henrietta had mailed him the package two months ago to ensure its arrival for Christmas. The note inside was written in a shaky hand, more shaky than ever before. What would Henrietta make of his new family? George wondered how his indomitable aunt was doing now as he watched Ts'ai-shun hurry back to her meeting with the carpenter. His once-shy wife had proved to have a good head for business—after bargaining for another hour, over two cups of tea, the carpenter would be glad to settle on a price significantly lower than he had expected.

"K'an-k'an — look!" Charley dragged a small wagon, its bed piled with muddy leaves and pebbles, onto the walkway just in front of him. George narrowly missed tripping on it.

"T'ien-sheng—Charley—be careful! What have you got there?" He bent over to examine the contents of the wagon more closely.

The head of Charley's stuffed dog protruded from the mess.

"Make *fang-tzu* for Jack!"

"Oh, you made a *house* for Jack? Don't you think Jack would prefer a drier house?" George fastened a button on the boy's jacket and straightened up as Charley continued across the courtyard, dragging his wagon. "Charley's just learning to separate Chinese from English," he explained.

"He seems to be doing a fine job of it for such a little fellow. I see he demonstrates a proper English passion for gardening. Be thankful he hasn't discovered calligraphy. My boy's practice in our living room has not improved the wallpaper!"

Fearon's younger son, named Basil in George's honor, was only a few months older than Charley. He would have been named George Dixwell Fearon had not Robert's elder brother, Charles, now the Heard firm's agent in London, already pre-empted that name for his own boy. Reciprocating in kind, George named Charley after Charles Fearon.

Fearon became serious. "But on another topic, we just couldn't wait for an answer to our letter. I had to telegraph Hong Kong for an immediate advance to cover the teas. Twenty dollars for three sentences and as short as I could make them!"

"In cipher, I presume?" George had devised a secret code of letters and numbers to disguise Heard company messages, so gossipy telegraphers couldn't compromise the firm's credit by revealing their persistent shortage of capital.

"Yes, all in cipher, except for the company signature, of course. And I had Reding hand carry it to Woosung Harbor. That gained us half a day."

George had specified that the Augustine Heard & Company signature never be rendered in code because a coded signature at the bottom of a telegram would reveal 5 vowels and 11 consonants—more than enough for even the most incompetent snoop to break their code.

Fearon ran his hand along the brick "spirit wall" that blocked direct passage from the inner courtyard to the gate opening to the street. "It would have saved years of trouble to have installed one of these in Hong Kong and another in Shanghai and strung a copper wire between them!"

"A perfectly logical idea," said George, "if only the Chinese were perfectly logical."

It was well known that Chinese "bad spirits" always traveled in a straight line. To Ts'ai-shun's great satisfaction, this spirit wall just inside the gate shielded the courtyard from any bad influences from the street beyond. The same reasoning rendered Chinese officials unalterably opposed to any contrivance that appeared to point too definitely in any particular direction, thus providing a possible pathway for bad energy. As a consequence and despite the entreaties of the foreign community, the Mandarins successfully thwarted every attempt to string telegraph lines or lay railroad track atop Chinese soil.

Eventually, Western technology found a way around ancient superstition. There was nothing the Chinese could do to stop the creation of an offshore telegraphic cable that was laid on the ocean bottom from Hong Kong to Woosung anchorage and that emerged from the water at a station vessel anchored in the center of the harbor—thus never touching dry land.

"When Reding got to Woosung," Fearon continued, "he had to hire a sampan to ferry him out to the telegrapher who had just gone ashore for lunch! In any event, Reding says you should have held on to your carrier pigeons."

George laughed. He had kept the coop of cooing birds behind the Heard office on the Bund. His plan was simple. Whenever a Heard vessel or a mail steamer arrived at Woosung, Roundy would see to it that a pigeon was released with a note around its leg. The note contained any market information that might give the firm an early advantage over the competition. Unfortunately, his pigeons failed to return to Shanghai. Either their homing instincts were lacking or, as he strongly suspected, they were waylaid for Chinese stewpots.

Most concessions to fengshui were not so maddening as the problem with telegraph lines. Before he had agreed to purchase their house, Ts'ai-shun insisted they consult a fengshui specialist, who showed them a drawing of an ideal home site—cradled by low hills and open to the front with bold mountain peaks far in the rear to provide a shield against evil energy flowing from the north. Impossibly ideal in this flat landscape, of course, so in order to justify his fee, the specialist prescribed a somewhat wider bend in the curved pathway through the courtyard to the front door.

There were no mountains anywhere near Shanghai, not even a small hill. The previous owner had done the next best thing, selecting the most southeasterly facing lot on the road ringing the old racecourse and constructing the house with its back looming like the prescribed tall mountain.

George paused at the corner of Canton Road where the old arc of the racecourse, now transformed into city streets, turned north. How Shanghai had changed since his first visit in 1846, when all of this land was Chinese farmsteads. Sufficiently cheap that a few years later, Albert Heard and three other aficionados of fast horses were able to purchase enough of it to establish horse racing as a Shanghai tradition. The city's population had grown, and land values increased so much that the racecourse grounds had become too valuable for mere horses. The land was sold for development, and a new racecourse was built on the western outskirts of the settlement. The old racecourse was now crowded with new houses, including his own.

Albert Heard's life had changed in that time, too. He had become senior partner at the Heard headquarters in Hong Kong and, in turn, gone home to Boston, leaving his brother Gus in charge. Therein lay the problem that George needed to discuss now with Fearon. Only a year ago, Gus had urged George to retire, to give way gracefully to younger men. Then in a sudden reversal, Gus asked George to decide whether he himself or Fearon would go south to take over the Hong Kong office until another of the Heard brothers could return to China.

That wasn't the only unsettling change in Hong Kong. A month ago, James Bridges Endicott died suddenly. Even though James had three other Endicotts at the Heard Shanghai office—brother William, nephew Charles, and Chinese son Henry—the firm now faced losing the steady stream of paying cargo that James always shipped up the coast from Hong Kong aboard Heard vessels.

George searched for a way to broach the awkward subject of which of them would take Gus Heard's place there. "Have you talked with William since his return from Hong Kong?"

"Yes, and he says Mrs. Endicott is taking it very hard. I can only imagine how difficult it would be for Mary to be left alone with our little boys. As you can see with your Charley, boys, especially, need a father."

George silently cursed his own clumsiness. Already, he had botched this negotiation. Fearon spoke from the heart and, quite innocently, stole the advantage. He recalled his own words of warning to Albert Heard when Fearon first proposed to marry— that in order to retain his position, young Fearon would have to make matrimony subsidiary to business and be made to know that if he allowed a wife to draw him off from the office, he would have to give way to someone else.

Four years later, George had a wife of his own, and he was hoisted on his own petard. To send Robert to Hong Kong for a temporary appointment of uncertain duration would be judged a blatant act of selfishness, not only within the Heard firm but also in the eyes of the whole foreign community. His own wife and child would be irrelevant to that judgment. Despite his marriage having been formalized in a Chinese ceremony, all such un-Christian unions were ignored by the European community. Officially, George was still a bachelor

"J.B. leaves an estate sufficient to take care of Mrs. Endicott and the children, and I'm sure William will see that it is properly managed—just as my own brother would do for Mary, if I ..." Fearon's voice trailed off.

George frowned. He was only a couple of months younger than J.B., and the unexpected death of his friend was an unpleasant reminder of his own mortality.

Fearon went back to his earlier subject. "I think we should have word from Hong Kong on that cash advance by tomorrow morning."

George was hardly paying attention. It was clear he would have to go to Hong Kong—at least until the end of the current partnership in June. Ts'ai-shun could be made to understand but what about Charley?

Fearon tried again to maintain a conversation. "Endicott says the Reverend Vrooman's cotton-spinning machine has arrived in Canton. William went out to see it while he was settling J.B.'s affairs. He says all of the capital was put up by the reverend's Chinese friends."

George laughed sharply. "I seriously doubt that any Chinese would ever invest in anything simply out of gratitude to a missionary, even one of Vrooman's stature—all 6 feet, 4 inches of him. I assume the project has a strong likelihood of earning them a fat profit."

"Well, they only put up $20,000 to support that strong likelihood. William says all the machinery is second-hand and has seen a lot of use."

"And did William have any news of young Mrs. Vrooman?" Not long before Charley's birth, George had been delighted to learn that Anna Rosa Hunter ended her widowhood by marrying Daniel Vrooman.

"Endicott says Anna Rosa and her boys are doing well, and Vrooman has Johnny learning the Chinese classics. He says that boy will be the first American Mandarin!"

John Endicott Gardner, Jr., was now almost seven years old. His new stepfather, the Reverend Vrooman, knew enough Chinese to have translated and published a score of Biblical tracts for distribution in the interior of China, beyond the reach of missionaries. His mother was literate in both English and Chinese, too, so Johnny was certain to grow up bilingual.

George wasn't so certain about Charley doing the same. George wanted his son to grow up just as much American as Chinese, but Charley would hear hardly a word of English in his mother's house while George was in Hong Kong, and he was still too young for school. Even if he were older, it was not much consolation that Mrs. Bonney opened a school for children of mixed blood across the creek in the old American Concession. The school's very existence testified to a second-class status for Eurasians. Charley Sargent was not going to be second class!

Fearon gestured at two Chinese emerging from an alley, each carrying a pair of buckets, suspended from the ends of bamboo shoulder poles. He held his handkerchief to his nose. "I thought you'd banned those fellows from the streets. They've no right to be on the street at 10 in the morning!"

George paused to appreciate their graceful, lilting gait, choreographed to the rhythmic flexing of the poles, which ensured that not a drop of the pails' reeking contents spilled over the edge. "I'll raise the issue with the police." George sighed.

As chairman of the Municipal Council, he was subject to assault from the citizenry of the International Settlement with every petty complaint. True, it was long-established policy that the collection of excrement from privies was to be completed before sunrise and confined to the alleys behind the houses; however, the increasingly civic-minded foreign residents had begun to see their enclave, with its sanitary drainage and its broad streets all aligned in a grid, as a kind of model for how the Chinese might improve themselves. They saw the settlement as an example of Christian order, in stark contrast to the walled Chinese city only a few blocks to the south, with its warren of unmarked pathways and gutters overflowing with filth.

The two men continued toward the Bund. Wispy white clouds feathered across the deep blue sky. George tried to focus on a perfect salutation to greet the marksmen at the award ceremony.

The Public Garden

"Three cheers for Mr. Dixwell!" Captain Cann of the Shanghai Volunteer Corps waved aloft the rifle presented to him for having maintained the volunteer force in a semblance of readiness.

George stepped toward the edge of the pavilion and tipped his hat in acknowledgement. "And three cheers for the ladies!" George made a slight bow to Mrs. Goodwin and the bevy of wives who had subscribed to purchase the rifle.

He waited for the cheers and applause to subside before turning to look out across the expanse of the Public Garden. Although several maritime men had favored dredging, the council had instead authorized filling in an acre of the mud flats that festered beside the Bund where Soochow Creek flowed into the harbor. The newly planted park atop that reclaimed ground now provided an elegant venue for civic gatherings.

It was a site that called out for grand events, but the corps now assembled to attend the award ceremony numbered hardly 60. Despite the efforts of Captain Cann, now being celebrated, their professional demeanor had deteriorated markedly since the defeat of the Taipings, not that these men had contributed much to that effort either. The corps was beginning to function more as a fraternal order than a real bulwark for the defense of the city.

George signaled the leader of the band to commence the march that would end the formal festivities. The drums rolled. A few of the men snapped to attention.

The little parade marched across Soochow Bridge and up the American Concession waterfront. The Fife and Drum Corps led, followed by the volunteers, their banner held high. The volunteer firemen waved their helmets and axes aloft from their horse-drawn *mi huo lung* ("extinguish fire dragon"), the polished brass valves of its steam-powered pump gleaming in the noonday sun.

George caught a whiff of putrid air smelling of rotten eggs. The tide was out, exposing the mass of sewage that choked the waterfront.

"Mr. Dixwell, may I borrow your written remarks?" The reporter from the *North*

China Herald climbed the stairs to the platform. "You'd have got a better turnout if you had asked us to announce it!"

George smiled apologetically, handing the man his notes. Somehow that detail had been overlooked.

"Thank you! And have you decided on the agenda for the next council meeting?"

"Well, there is the Woosung mud bar, but, of course, that's really a Chamber of Commerce issue."

At low tide, hardly 12 feet of water flowed around the shifting shoal in the middle of the channel where the Whangpu joined the Yangtze. With so many related agenda items before the chamber and the council, George struggled to maintain the fiction of their separate jurisdictions.

"So, when will we see the bar dredged?"

George watched the little parade proceed into the distance, accompanied by sharp reports as the men fired their rifles into the air. The council issued them blank cartridges, not for show but for an afternoon of skirmishing exercises. The reporter followed George's gaze with his own and seemed intent on extracting some piece of news worth reporting.

"I'm sure we can rest well, knowing that they've frightened off all low-flying dragons, but what about the dredging?"

"As you recall, we passed a chamber resolution that the consuls should petition the taotai that the Woosung bar be dredged such that vessels of 24-feet draft can clear it at low tide, thus—"

"But the taotai has never raised a finger, even to remove any of the wrecks obstructing the Yangtze channel!"

George nodded seriously. "There is an old story, recorded, I believe, amongst the classics —" He stroked his chin as if trying to recall the details. "At one time, Chinese officials regularly removed all such obstructions to navigation along the whole length of the Yangtze, but then a devil entered into the river and moved all the wrecks and snags such that the Chinese could no longer find them to remove. We must be more charitable in our judgment." George tried to keep a straight face. "The non-removal of those wrecks may not be from any want of energy on the part of the Mandarins but simply a device of the devil to thwart them."

The reporter stared, incredulous, at the chief municipal officer of the Shanghai foreign community, unable to formulate a follow-up question. "Pardon me, sir," he blurted, suddenly turning away. "Mrs. Goodwin," he called out, "may I borrow your written remarks, too?"

George stood alone and watched the last of the dignitaries descend from the platform. The frigid breeze of the morning had stilled, and the sun felt warm against his back. He considered his shadow extending across the plank floor of the platform. For this moment, he was the pole of a sundial at midday. His shadow would grow by tiny increments for the next seven days until the winter solstice and then begin to shrink.

"May your shadow never diminish," he whispered the old Chinese salutation. He was already a full week into his 54th year, and his shadow could only diminish, along with the fleeting remainder of his allotted time on earth. What had he accomplished during the years of his life? He had earned a fortune, lost it, and now, after a full decade back in Shanghai, he had still not earned it back.

George turned toward the sun and squinted. According to J.J., sunspots were actually storms, tens of thousands of miles in extent, sweeping across the surface of the sun. His brother was taking a little time for himself to study the heavens with the new telescope he had helped purchase for Dartmouth College. Perhaps the rest would ease J.J.'s angina pectoris and strengthen his heart muscle.

George thought of the scientific instruments he had purchased years ago to research his hunch about superheating steam to prevent water condensation on the cylinder walls of steam engines. Conserving the heat loss from condensation would reduce coal consumption on ocean crossings, making them less expensive and leaving more space in the hold for cargo. Such an invention, if patented, could leave little Charley with a fortune.

George glanced back at the Public Garden—public but not for Chinese. Charley's amah knew better than to push his perambulator along its paths. George started down the steps. He still needed to thank Henrietta for the gloves. If the *Herald* published his remarks, he would include the clipping inside his letter. [2]

The Parker Home

Epes Dixwell tiptoed into the room, glancing at the bed. "How's Auntie doing?"

"She's sleeping," J.J. whispered to his younger brother by the door. "I don't know how she holds on without eating anything."

Anna Parker rose from her chair beside Henrietta's bed and joined her nephews, speaking in a lowered voice, "I am afraid my sister still has a great deal to endure. We Sargents have a great tenacity for life."

Henrietta listened, only feigning sleep. They thought her mind had gone, but it was only recent events that slipped away. Events of long ago were still crystal clear, although sometimes the past and the present combined in a strange mélange. At times she confused her younger visitors with friends who had been the same age 50 years ago. Her relatives clearly had concluded that she was dying. They were right about that, but it annoyed her that they acted as if she were deaf, too.

Henrietta lay still. With her eyes closed, she could hear an entire world: the bells on the horsecars pulling up and down Tremont Street; the clunk when Bridget turned on the faucet in the kitchen and the chattering squeal when she turned it off; the random popping of the iron pipes deep in the bowels of the house; and the burbling of her own bowels, about which she preferred not to think.

Instead, she listened to the ticking of the clock on the mantle, and suddenly it brought to her mind the ticking of the clock downstairs as John Brown had walked toward the gallows so many years ago. She pushed the unpleasant image away from her consciousness. A gust of wind rattled the window and whistled under its bottom edge. Henrietta opened her eyes. A frosting of ice glistened at its corners, while the bare, black branches of the elms in the Commons moved like bony fingers across the grid of its panes.

Loud voices and a discordant crash came from the street below. Anna hurried to the window. "My goodness, they've dropped a piano! I do wish they would take deliveries from the alley side. Lord only knows," she said, turning, "how a music store can make such dreadful noise. It's enough to wake—"

"—the dead!" Henrietta finished.

"Would you like something to drink? Perhaps a little broth?"

Henrietta shook her head. She had no appetite at all. She felt bloated and constipated, and the doctor seemed unable to do anything to relieve her. She wished she could still make the broth of greens that she used to prescribe to quiet Mr. Child's dyspepsia. If only she were strong enough to medicate herself. "If thou be the king of the Jews, save thyself." The verse from Luke leapt into her mind. She blushed, embarrassed by her unintentional comparison of her own discomfort to the ordeal of Christ. Gerrit Smith had had the disgraceful habit of elevating his notions to the level of eternal truths, and she did not wish to succumb herself to such conceit.

Epes came to Henrietta's bedside, "Hello, dear Auntie," he smiled.

"Your scarf!" Henrietta stared at the familiar red-and-white stripes.

"Yes, I wear it every winter because it reminds me of the very special aunt who made it."

Anna's voice overlapped. "Goodness, Henriet! You have more visitors."

Henrietta turned to see two young women at the door, their cheeks still flushed from the winter cold. They looked familiar, but she couldn't exactly place them. She watched as Epes kissed the taller one and stepped back to let them come closer to the bed. They couldn't be Mary and Eliza, the young sisters who had married Epes and J.J. But, of course! It came back to her. These were not the Bowditch sisters but were their grown daughters, Fanny and Annie.

"We made you a Christmas favor!" Fanny Dixwell unwrapped an evergreen bouquet, tied with a red silk ribbon. "Here, let me put it on your table." Annie leaned forward to give Henrietta a peck on the forehead. "The spruce came from the Dixwells in Cambridge, and I clipped the holly this very morning from our tree in Sunnyside."

Henrietta inhaled the piney fragrance. It brought back all the Christmas Eves of years past at Epes's and J.J.'s houses, when these women were toddlers, then little girls ... But was it Christmas already? Could she and Catharine have forgotten to make anything to sell at the Anti-Slavery Bazaar? She tried to remember if George might have sent a box of Chinese chow-chow things to display on their table. But, no, wasn't Catharine dead? And hadn't Mr. Lincoln freed the slaves? Of course, he had—and it had been many long years since the last Anti-Slavery Bazaar at the Music Hall. Nowadays, there was a New Year's Bazaar for Women's Suffrage. She smiled, proud that she had figured it all out by herself without anyone knowing how confused she had been.

Anna approached, holding a newspaper and handed the paper to Fanny. "I'm sure Henrietta would like to hear the news. Her *Standard* arrived in yesterday's mail."

Henrietta marveled at how either time or her own condition had mellowed her sister. Fortunately, the paper had changed its name. Even now, she thought, Anna would choke on the words "anti-slavery."

"Why, here's a poem by our own Mr. Whittier." Fanny began to read:

"He prayeth best, who leaves unguessed
The mystery of another's breast,
Why cheeks grow pale, why eyes o'erflow,
Or heads are white, thou need'st not know.
Enough to note by many a sign
That every heart hath needs like thine."

Henrietta considered the verses before responding. "Although Mr. Whittier seems to think that 'thou need'st not know,' I don't mind telling you—it's all the worrying we do about you young folks that turns our heads white. Now read me something of substance."

Fanny looked up in surprise. "Oh, Auntie, you're so droll."

"I'm sure Henrietta is interested in Mrs. Child's article, on page 8," said Anna.

Henrietta stole a glance at her sister. Anna had always loathed Mrs. Child. She must indeed be on her deathbed for Anna to have actually searched *The Standard* for something written by Maria.

"And, just what is Mrs. Child writing about this time?" Epes interrupted his discussion with J.J. to peer over Fanny's shoulder.

"Chalk, I believe." Fanny skimmed over the article. "She says that the white cliffs of Dover are part of a chalk bed hundreds of feet thick, extending across France and into North Africa."

"And how does Mrs. Child know anything about that?" Epes spoke dismissively.

"Well, she's reviewing a book by a Mr. Huxley."

"Thomas Huxley!" Epes smiled at Henrietta. "Now, that is something of substance!"

"Mrs. Child says there are myriads of microscopic skeletons, and it took myriads of years to make 1,000 feet of chalk."

"Read exactly what she says!" Epes said impatiently.

Fanny squinted and continued, "It's about all kinds of skeletons 'Those huge reptiles, the Ichthyosaurus and the Plesiosaurus—' I do hope I'm pronouncing them right. They 'swam in the waters that covered the earth thousands of years before man came into existence.' Here, you read it yourself."

Henrietta saw Fanny's squint. She must be too vain to wear glasses. She wondered if the girl was still waiting for Wendell Holmes.

Epes took the paper and read slowly, savoring the words, "They have been extinct from a period beyond the record of man, but their remains have been occasionally found in the chalk, showing the antiquity of that substance to be vastly greater than that of the human race."

"Goodness," remarked Anna. "Mr. Huxley sounds worse than Mr. Darwin."

J.J. spoke up from the doorway. "If only our own geology were so simple. Did you read the article in today's *Transcript*? Our Roxbury conglomerates, which form the foundation of Parker Hill, hardly extend beyond the Charles River."

"Well," Anna shook her head, "we won't even have them in Roxbury anymore, if they persist in removing my hill and your herb garden along with it, Henriet."

Henrietta's remembered her garden of medicinals behind Anna's summer residence atop Parker Hill, imagining how it would look now, undercut by a cliff of dirt with a steam shovel at the bottom. The picture in her mind's eye was remarkably like her memory of Mr. Bulfinch's Doric tower commemorating the Revolution, when she and father, with little J.J. in hand, had watched it teeter atop Beacon Hill as a train of horse carts, far below, lined up to dump the remains of that proud precipice into the Mill Pond. That was before George was born and years before father bought the house on Poplar Street. She recalled exactly how, decades later, on a hot summer afternoon, the pungent scent of sewage festering in the last remnant of that pond had assaulted her and Catharine and Maria as they emerged from their little "mouse's nest," where they'd been busily plotting emancipation.

Epes's mind was on modern science. "My son John informs me that Professor Shaler has examined all the sedimentary conglomerates to the north and south of Roxbury, and even though they are cut by similar dikes of intrusive igneous material, the microscopic *lingula* at Roxbury are clearly different."

Anna laughed. "So, now I have 'lingula' to worry about, along with fleas and lice?" She rolled her eyes. "I must say that the Latin of Linnaeus is Greek to me!" She smirked at Epes, proud of her joke. "But your Johnny must be too busy now with his medical studies to gaze at rocks with Dr. Shaler."

Henrietta was trying to recall exactly what Johnny Dixwell looked like, but all she could remember was handing the "little regicide" a peppermint from her reticule, long ago. How could he have grown up so suddenly?

§

Henrietta opened her eyes to see the Reverend Dr. Miner sitting by her bed. "We've missed you, Miss Sargent. None of our Sunday school teachers have your knowledge of the Scriptures."

"Mine is an old, old reading," Henrietta murmured.

"But you are our last active member who actually knew Mr. Murray." The minister took her hand in his.

Henrietta smiled at the minister. She knew she would be in the old church but one more time. So long ago, she sat beside Aunt Murray in her pew, listening to Mr. Murray preach. Dr. Miner was a proponent of a more modern view of Universalism, but at least he had never belittled Mr. Murray, as Mr. Ballou used to. Mr. Murray had lain on his deathbed, crippled by a stroke, while Mr. Ballou usurped his leadership of the church in America and denigrated his views. But Mr. Ballou went to his reward years ago. If he had been wrong and there was indeed a Hell—as she herself certainly believed—Mr. Ballou should have spent at least a sojourn there before proceeding to universal salvation.

Henrietta tried to make a connection with her present visitor. "You must be busy with the holidays."

"Never too busy to visit with you, Miss Sargent, although," Dr. Miner rose, "I am afraid I must steal away soon. I need to write a lecture on the current doctrine of probation for the Sabbath School Union this Sunday."

Henrietta chuckled, "I trust you won't change any of the requirements before I graduate! And after I have graduated, I hope you will visit me once in a while at Mount Auburn."

"Now, Henriet," Anna gave her sister a sharp look. "We'll all be at Mount Auburn soon enough, but we needn't dwell on it now."

"Perhaps we may rest eternally there," J.J. looked up from *The Transcript*. "But it's a different story in Virginia. There's a proposal before Congress to disinter the Union soldiers buried at Arlington and to return the property to General Lee's widow."

"What?" Epes was outraged. "That's preposterous!"

"Please!" Anna scolded.

Epes lowered his voice, but continued. "General Lee's estate was forfeited and sold at public sale for nonpayment of taxes! It was bought and paid for by the United States government."

"That vile man —" Anna searched for words. "Mr. Lee spat on our nation's flag, and then he prolonged a war he knew was lost. Every Union soldier buried there is a victim of murder, and the charge is laid at his door!"

Henrietta's lips curved. She didn't mind the morbid subject, and impassioned discussions amongst her relatives were far more familiar and comforting than the false cheer and fawning solicitude her fragile condition now seemed to elicit.

She gazed up at the ceiling. In all these years Henrietta had never noticed the swirl in the plaster directly above her head. She could see the long-ago workman, standing atop a ladder, carefully sliding his trowel across an expanse of wet plaster, sneezing. She closed her eyes. Henrietta was remembering how after one of Catharine's fainting spells, shortly before she died, she had described floating high above, watching as they tried to resuscitate her. Henrietta imagined herself, a fly on the ceiling, surveying the scene from her spot on that swirl. She could hear everything.

J.J. and Epes were now talking telescopes; Fanny and Annie were discussing art; and Anna and Reverend Miner were apparently talking about her. It was as if she wasn't there at all. Oh, she would love to look down as Reverend Snowden, from the African Chapel, stepped forward to preach her funeral. What wonderful consternation on Anna's face! She could not quite remember if she promised to contact Maria from across the ether or if Maria was to contact her.[3]

Boston Daily Transcript
1871

January 14, 1871
DEATHS,
In this city, 11th inst., Miss Henrietta Sargent.

§

Tuesy
March 7, 1871

Dear George,

I have before me two nice letters from you, one at Christmas, and the other at New Year—and one to Henrietta at New Year, written in a kind, and cheerful style, while she, at that time, was on her death bed. What will the advocates of sympathy, and spiritualism, say to this.

Mrs. Child has written another article for the *Tribune*, more personal, and bringing out my mother's infirmities of mind, and body, in a very improper manner. Why—I know not—except to tell that my sisters were very devoted to her—of course they were.

Thanks for the paper you sent from Shanghai, containing your speech &c.—why, it was grand, and your account of it in Henrietta's letter was very graphic. Who knows—maybe you will come back one of these days, and go to Congress!

Your quondam friend, Harleston P., is here in a new phase, as a man of fortune, and trying to inform himself, and conform himself to business habits. He sports a very pretty, modest equipage, means to settle down in Boston, and wants a wife, and talks a deal about the qualities he expects to find in one—beauty—good sense—good family, and good temper, and her whole thoughts, and time, devoted to him. I tell him he will never find such a piece of perfection as he is looking for. He says a man cannot live well, in Boston, without a wife. Granted—but he has lived so long in Europe, he will find it hard to find what he wants. And being about fifty, or so, the young fry won't like him, and he won't like the older ones.

There has been considerable "bother" and talk in Roxby, about cutting down Parker Hill. I am determined not to let it annoy me—even if they do, which I hardly think they will, for some time to come. J.J. looks out for me, and, as honest Abe says, "it is a big job to do." I have been busy looking over H's letters, and effects, and disposing of them—and then went to work on my own, to "set my house in order," and have made good head way. Oh! The notes, & letters I burnt. Good bye, dear.

Don't forget your poor old Aunty.

A P

[Anna Parker] [4]

Hu Ts'ai-shun (ca. 1848–1915) and her son, T'ien-sheng/Charles Sargent (1868–1934), taken ca. 1872. (Courtesy of Lauren Dixwell Rayfield.)

Detail of Charley Sargent's American-style boots. (Courtesy of Lauren Dixwell Rayfield.)

The families of George Dixwell's brothers (John J. Dixwell and Epes Sargent Dixwell) posed for a group portrait (1876) in Dresden, Germany. *Front row*: Arria; middle row: Carrie, Epes, Mrs. Miller, John J. and his wife Eliza; *back row*: May, Dudley Miller, Mary (wife of Epes), Annie (artist), Arthur (probably autistic, baseball fan), and unidentified person. (Photo courtesy of Caroline Dixwell Cabot.)

Hu Ts'ai-shun's gown and unbound feet confirm her Manchu identity, but the scuffed boots worn by her son reveal that George Dixwell, his father, wanted Charles raised as much as possible like an American boy. In 1874, following George's return to Boston, he wrote to a Shanghai colleague, "I am very much obliged to you for your report upon Charles Sargent ... I am greatly interested for the youngster. I do not want him spoiled and this was the chief reason why I put him at the school where he is rubbed against by other children and not corseted to death by his mother & half a dozen female servants." Charles Sargent/T'ien-sheng would never be publicly acknowledged by his American aunts, uncles, or cousins.

CHAPTER TWELVE

T'ien-sheng / Charles Sargent

10 Beacon Street, Boston
1875, April 29

George climbed the four marble steps to the identical pair of doors at 10 Beacon Street. The left door to the drugstore stood open beside an unwashed window displaying bottles of hair tonic and patent medicines. Leaning his roll of charts and diagrams against the iron handrail, George struck the hinged knocker on the right-hand door. He ran his fingers across the engraved letters on the shiny brass plaque affixed to the wall—John J. Dixwell, M.D.

A few months after Father's death, George removed an almost identical plaque from his mother's front door. It became awkward for her when patients continued to call, asking for Dr. Dixwell. George remembered the uneasy feeling as he pulled out the old nails, as if he were removing his father's memory along with the familiar plaque, but that was 37 years ago. This new plaque, announcing the new Dr. John Dixwell, seemed a fit remembrance as the young doctor opened the door.

"Come on in, Uncle George. I'm almost ready. I'll be with you in a minute." John disappeared up a narrow flight of stairs. "That's yesterday's *Transcript* on the table," he called back. "It's full of the Beecher trial.

For weeks the papers had been printing the court testimony as to whether the Reverend Henry Ward Beecher solicited an adulterous relationship with Mrs. Tilton and whether she had been coerced to retract her accusation. The late Gerrit Smith's cousin, Elizabeth Cady Stanton, apparently was the one who revealed the particulars of Reverend Beecher's affair with Mrs. Tilton. As a result of the revelation, the Reverend Beecher and Mr. Tilton—leaders of the country's two largest suffrage organizations—were now attacking each other's morals in court, to their mutual discredit.

"It was outrageous for Mrs. Woodhull to publish all the sordid details in her magazine. Suzy says that Mrs. Stanton told Mrs. Woodhull about the affair only in strictest confidence."

Unfortunately, Mrs. Woodhull, a proponent and rumored practitioner of free love, was one of the publishers of the *Woodhull and Clafklin Weekly*, which alleged that Reverend Beecher was secretly practicing free love while denouncing it on Sundays.

"Suzy says it's put the suffragists into a tizzy. She hardly knows whom she can seat at the table with Mrs. Stanton when she comes for dinner."

Mrs. Stanton was no fool. Everybody knew that Mrs. Woodhull was likely to embroider any salacious morsel to support her contention that free love was not just a peculiar theory but a common practice among prominent Americans. The only question was *why* Mrs. Stanton dropped *that* particular tidbit in Mrs. Woodhull's ear, and the obvious reason was troubling—this scandal could only strengthen Mrs. Stanton's leadership of the movement to secure voting rights for women, a leadership to which she as a woman felt justly entitled.

George's nephew reappeared in a light wool suit, a Panama hat in his hand. "You missed Professor Shaler's presentation at the Society of Natural History."

George would have attended the talk himself, had he not been spending every waking moment preparing his own lecture, which he would present exactly two hours from now at the Massachusetts Institute of Technology. The three-line announcement in the *Transcript* listed the day of the talk but omitted the time. He wondered how many people would attend tonight and if any would return in a fortnight for his second lecture.

"I think you would have found Professor Shaler's thesis quite relevant to your own work. He argued that when a glacier reaches a mile in thickness, the pressure of its weight generates an outflow of heat that causes melting at its bottom, and the flow of that water lubricates its movement." John waved his hand to indicate an undulating flow. "And *that*, dear Uncle, is the gist of how the great continental glaciers were able to flow south from Canada, scouring everything in their path."

George looked at his nephew. The "little regicide" not only knew enough chemistry and physics to evaluate scientific research and discuss it intelligently, but he had just opened his own medical practice here, a few doors up Beacon Street from where George had rented rooms for himself. Both George's brothers were touring Europe with their families and expecting to be abroad for another 11 months, so George rented a suite of rooms here in Boston where he could find a cooked meal nearby and be but a short walk from his laboratory.

Of course, the laboratory didn't belong to *him* but to the Massachusetts Institute of Technology. Thermodynamics was a new field requiring not only precise instrumentation but also a level of technical expertise unavailable in China. Perfection of George's invention would be impossible without trained technicians and specialized tools to accurately measure the changes in heat and pressure just above the piston of an operating steam engine. All of this, thanks to George—and Aunt Anna's money—now existed at the institute.

John touched his uncle's arm. "We had best get going if you want to talk to that reporter and still have time to review your notes. Let me carry that roll of papers."

George relinquished the awkward parcel and dutifully followed John to the door. The two men crossed Beacon Street and turned toward Park. "You know, Uncle George, the generation of heat by the pressure of glacial ice that Professor Shaler describes is almost exactly the reverse of the process that your new invention is designed to prevent."

George looked sharply at his nephew.

"It's really *quite simple*," John continued. "As you know all too well, when steam is injected into the cylinder of a steam engine, it expands to over twice its original volume as it drives down the piston. While a glacier *produces* heat from compression, the steam inside the cylinder of the engine does exactly the opposite. It *loses* its heat through expansion, causing all that expensive condensation of water on the walls of the cylinder, robbing the engine—by your measurements—of up to 17% of its power."

"Quite simple!"—the phrase was hardly fair to George's two years of experiments nor to the precise measurements derived from them. After all his years as a merchant, no one seemed to remember that, decades earlier, he had been an avid reader of scientific journals. He even invented and patented a gas regulator to maintain combustion at a constant uniform pressure in such devices as streetlamps. George suppressed his annoyance. "An elegant observation," he nodded. "You know, I once designed a refrigeration device based on that very principle." He thought better of expressing his next thought—when you were hardly out of diapers.

"But I thought you were always in pursuit of superheated steam." John laughed. "What in the world inspired a foray into refrigeration?"

"Necessity!—which *is*, of course, the mother of invention. I once had sufficient time and discomfort to raise the prospect of a cold drink to a holy grail. That was 22 years ago, when I had reason to cross the Isthmus of Nicaragua on the back of a mule in the broiling sun, only to discover that the steamer waiting on the Pacific side had used up the last of its ice. So, in an idle moment (of which I had many aboard that steamer), I designed a refrigeration device based on condensation."

"But you never patented it?"

George smiled at his nephew's admiring look. "No, and more's the pity." He patted his satchel to reassure himself that he had not forgotten to bring his lecture notes.

On that fateful trip to California, he was filled with optimism to the point of arrogance. He was so eager to invest the $100,000 of the fortune he had brought home from China. Then Dorr's boondoggle sucked away nearly all his fortune. George felt his stomach begin to churn at the memory. James Dorr was dead and gone, and George had successes to count, too. He *had* lived well in Shanghai. He *had* saved enough from his salary to pay off his debts, and when he sailed for the States two years ago, he left Ts'ai-shun with enough money for her and Charley to live comfortably until his return. He still had had enough money left over to work on perfecting his invention. Then only a month after he returned to Boston, Aunt Anna died. Suddenly, he once again became a man of means.

John's voice broke into his thoughts. "Father writes from Munich that he and Uncle J.J. wish they could telegraph themselves home just to hear your speech."

"Your father is a loyal brother, but I think that you will get far more from my talk, as a physician, than he would as a Latin teacher."

George wiped his forehead and slowed his pace. There was still plenty of time before his talk, and he didn't want to arrive perspiring. No, he would never again have to suffer over the loss of his fortune. Aunt Anna had left enough for Epes to sell his school and begin his retirement with a Grand Tour of Europe. His own portion—more than $100,000—was enough to allocate a modest sum to fully equip the new mechanical engineering laboratory at the institute, the very laboratory where he had carried out the experiments he would be discussing this evening.

"Mr. Dixwell—and Doctor Dixwell, too!" The young woman pushed a wicker perambulator to the edge of the sidewalk. "Why, we haven't seen you for weeks," she addressed George. "And my husband—Jack, come see Mr. Dixwell!—has been sorely derelict in not inviting you over for dinner." Mrs. John Heard beckoned toward the park bench where the senior partner of Augustine Heard & Company sat reading to his daughter.

"I'm sure the fault is mine," George mumbled. Heard rose from his seat, taking the little girl's hand, and walked slowly toward his wife. George wished he had taken another route across the Common, so as not to arrive here, directly across the street from the Heard's mansion. How much longer would John and Alice be able to live there? If the Heard firm failed, which was likely, they would lose the house, along with everything else held in John's name. Even those proceeds would be insufficient to pay off the firm's creditors.

It came as a complete shock to the Heard partners that Percy Everett, their Boston agent, had been selling bills of credit bearing the company's name in amounts far exceeding the Heard firm's $30,000-dollar credit limit. George spent months working with John, trying to balance the accounts. Only after they had saved Everett's reputation, did they discover the true size of the defalcation—more than a quarter-million dollars! This amount exceeded not only the company capital but also the combined assets of the partners! It was now clear that nothing would be recovered from Everett, who had spent all his ill-gotten proceeds on failed speculations and sham loans for his own benefit.

George forced a smile. "Good to see you, Jack! A wonderful day to be out and about." Heard's face looked pale and had a sheepish, almost apologetic, look. George sensed that his former partner wanted to talk seriously, but this was neither the time nor place.

"We do need to talk," Heard said. "I'll drop you a note."

"And I won't let him forget." Mrs. Heard adjusted the blanket over the baby sleeping in the perambulator.

George tipped his hat as she turned to follow her husband.

The two Dixwell men stood silent on the sidewalk. "Is it that bad?" John shifted the roll of charts from one arm to the other.

"Yes," George was grave, "I think it's pretty much over with the company, except for the formal announcement." George turned around to look at the Heard's mansion for a minute. Old Mr. Heard was said to have paid some $42,000 for 3 Park Street, and by the time the renovation was complete, he had spent over $100,000 more to make it one of the most magnificent of the grand residences that faced Boston Common. Unfortunately, instead of placing the house in a trust, he deeded it directly to the three Heard brothers. Now attorneys representing the company's creditors would seize the house for auction the instant the announcement of bankruptcy appeared in the *Transcript*.

Thank God, J.J. had the prescience to write Aunt Anna's will such that George's inheritance was held in a rock-solid trust. His Shanghai house and bank account were in Ts'ai-shun's name. He owned virtually nothing of value that the Heard firm's creditors could take.

"Do you expect any of Father's contingent to attend?" John inquired.

"I suspect your father's friends are somewhat more interested in abstract theories than in their practical application," George answered a bit harshly.

John had inadvertently touched a nerve, raising the awkward issue of why George funded a laboratory at the upstart Massachusetts Institute of Technology rather than at Harvard, where John's father was an alumnus, and the other members of the Cambridge Scientific Club were so closely affiliated. Young John himself was a Harvard alumnus.

George had no issue with the concerns of the Scientific Club but with those of Harvard itself. The university's overseers seemed oblivious, if not outright antagonistic, to technical coursework. They didn't support the idea that technical coursework, which applied scientific concepts to the solution of practical problems, should have any place in the undergraduate curriculum. They preferred to boast of no fewer than 23 elective courses in Latin and Greek. That effete snobbishness was the main stimulus to the establishment of MIT on the other side of the Charles River.

John, suspecting what lay behind his uncle's tone, changed the subject. "What part of your talk have you reserved for your second appearance?"

"Tonight, I'll review the overall problem of cylinder condensation and explain how my findings provide a practical solution. I'll save the actual experiments and the measurements for the concluding talk."

§

"Mr. Dixwell, would you describe your invention, and explain what it does?" The reporter waited, notebook opened in hand.

George hesitated and tried to organize his thoughts. It wasn't easy to boil down his theories in terms that anyone could understand, but if his discoveries were to become lucrative, he needed to be able to concisely describe their usefulness.

"Yes, we have long known that superheating the cylinder walls of a steam engine will substantially reduce condensation and the resulting loss of power when the steam expands to drive down the piston. We also know that sustained superheating will damage the working surfaces." George waited for the reporter to catch up. "What I have demonstrated is that the degree of superheating can be exactly regulated, allowing condensation to be safely reduced, thus saving one-fifth to one-half of the coal otherwise consumed to fire the boiler."

"So ... ," the reporter waved his pencil for George to stop. "It's the savings in coal consumption, especially by transoceanic steamers, that makes such an invention valuable?"

"Yes, exactly."

The reporter sat straighter in his chair, proud to have understood. "And you have perfected a device that accomplishes this?"

"Yes, through experiments here at the Institute, I have perfected one device that measures temperature inside the cylinder of an operating steam engine and a second that can maintain that temperature within the critical limits."

"You will be describing both of these, tonight?" the reporter queried.

"Tonight I'll describe my research into the thermodynamics of steam and how I arrived at my solution to the problem of power loss through condensation. Two weeks from now I'll present the exact measurements."

The reporter scribbled a few more lines and snapped shut his notebook. "Thank you, Mr. Dixwell. I'll get the other details from your talk."

George knew he had not really answered the reporter's question. He would indeed describe what his device was designed to accomplish, but in the competitive world of patents, success depended on being the first to file. The new science of electricity was moving forward so rapidly that he wanted his fourth, and final, application safely in the Patent Office before he revealed to the public exactly how the devices worked.

He designed a mercury thermometer linked from a galvanic battery to two circuits. If the mercury expanded above the desired temperature, say, 400 degrees, a circuit would close and activate an alarm bell. Likewise, if the mercury contracted below a previously set minimum temperature, say, 370 degrees, another bell would sound. These alarms would allow the engineer to adjust the valves that injected superheated steam into the jacket surrounding the engine. Thus, the temperature inside the cylinder could be maintained within a precise range—just high enough to prevent condensation while still low enough to prevent damage to the cylinder and piston.

George wished aunts Anna and Henrietta had lived to see his scientific ideas become more than mere "notions." Aunt Anna would be proud that her money had not been wasted. He missed Henrietta. She would have had no patience with the Dixwell's continued pretense that he remained a bachelor for the sake of appearances. She might even ask him in a whisper if he had heard how Charley was doing in school. He wished she could have met Ts'ai-shun. He turned toward the auditorium. The room was almost filled. Serious young men from the Institute occupied the first row. Many faces were familiar.

The president of the Institute's Society of the Arts waved as he stepped onto the podium. "Tonight we welcome our colleague and benefactor, Mr. George Basil Dixwell, who will lecture on 'Cylinder Condensation and the Means of Suppressing It.' Mr. Dixwell's attention was first drawn to this subject by an 1871 article in the *London Engineer*."

George quickly glanced through his notes, then looked up and tapped the loose pages into a neat stack. John had already hung his charts from hooks above the chalkboard. George surveyed the audience again—no Harvard contingent. Of course, as the *Transcript* had reported, the gentlemen at that august institution were otherwise engaged, debating whether the University's colors should be changed from crimson to magenta.

"Gentlemen of the Institute ... ," he began.

§

"There! I see what you mean!" George's nephew gestured toward the streetlamp. Once again, the flame flickered before it surged brightly. "That's exactly what your old patent was designed to prevent!"

George had just described the inner workings of his gas regulator. Now that the 17 years of patent protection had expired, most gas companies were installing similar devices—although, clearly, not enough of them. The flame surged again.

John shook his head. "So every time a lamplighter turns on a valve, you can see it in every lamp flame this side of the regulator."

George agreed. "Of course, it's most noticeable in the evening when everyone lights their lamps, and in the morning when they all turn them off." His invention came too early in the development of the gas industry to properly compensate him for that research. By the time they were ready for it, his patent had expired. His steam-regulating device, however, would improve an already established technology. He hoped that would facilitate not only its widespread adoption but also generate handsome royalties from the engine manufacturers who employed it.

God willing, his patents would escape the tentacles of the Heard creditors. After all, he had only begun the research *after* he left the company. He was no longer much concerned for his own financial security, but he wanted the proceeds from his invention to benefit his friends and not their creditors. More to the point, he dreamed of leaving Charley a millionaire.

John Dixwell seemed lost in his own thoughts as the two men walked home. Perhaps, thought George, some particular Boston beauty had caught his nephew's eye. His own mind was on Charley and Ts'ai-shun. After months of promises, his wife was probably wondering if he was ever coming back to China. It was also high time for Charley to begin his education in the States and to start feeling at home over here.

When could he return for them? It was more than a week by railroad via Omaha to San Francisco, where steamers departed for Japan once a month. It was a three-week passage across the North Pacific to Yokohama, and from there it was at least another week to Shanghai—a minimum of five weeks total, if he made all the connections. That was less than one-third of the time the voyage by sail had taken on his first trip, but it was still probably one and one-half months each way. George considered his calendar. If he could file his last patent application by the beginning of July, he could take the August steamer from San Francisco and be in Shanghai by mid-September. A fall return to Boston would risk winter storms on the Pacific and a railroad trip through blizzards or even avalanches in the Sierra Mountains. Ts'ai-shun would not be ready to travel before next spring. He couldn't bring her home to rented rooms. He would have to purchase a house. That would take time, which he didn't have if he was to get his patents filed and prepare to show his invention at the Centennial Exhibition next year.

The drone of cicadas echoed across the Common. A cool breeze rustled the branches overheard. For a moment, the cicadas fell silent—only to resume their symphony with fresh vigor. George breathed deeply. There was no way around it. He would have to delay his return to China until next summer, after the Centennial Exhibition in Philadelphia. Then he would hurry back to Ts'ai-shun and Charley. If Ts'ai-shun was willing, he would bring them both back to Boston. [1]

The George Dixwell Home
555 Shawmut Avenue, Boston
1881, April 22

George heard the front door slam, followed by a crash and then the hollow echo of hardwood rolling across the tiled floor of the vestibule. "Charley, is that you?"

"Yes, Father."

George walked to the head of the stairs. "Isn't it a bit early for baseball?"

"Oh, Father! Baseball season always starts in April."

George caught the exasperation in his son's voice, at his father's woeful ignorance of the obvious. Charley had taken the afternoon train home from the school where he boarded during the week with the Manson family, and within minutes went out to play baseball with his friends. Now he was starving.

"Mrs. Schmidt!" Charley called out. "Is there anything to eat?"

"*Ja* course, Charley *lieben*. I fix you a snack."

"Thank you, Mrs. Schmidt!"

George smiled in approval. His boy finally seemed to be acquiring the social graces. He wished, again, that the invitation from the Holmeses had included Charley. He imagined that they would be charmed by his son, if ever they acknowledged his existence.

George started down the stairs, pausing to nod at Kuanyin on her shelf above the hat rack. Despite his explaining that an American house had no place for an ancestral altar, Ts'ai-shun had insisted on bringing not only Kuanyin but also their Buddha, an urn, and an immense supply of incense sticks. Those other items now resided in the rear parlor. Guiltily, he realized that hardly a stick had been burned since he had returned home from accompanying Ts'ai-shun back to China.

Once again, George felt the familiar ache of loneliness. He missed the sound of Ts'ai-shun's voice and her persistent reminders that he honor his ancestors. George peered into the dining room. The boy had retrieved all the magazines from the discard box in the hall and strewn them across the table where he was hunched, reading, a plate of sandwiches by his elbow. George tried to recall if he had spread so much mess—or eaten so much—when he was 12. Well, he did have his flying contraption, fashioned from his mother's silk handkerchiefs, glued over a wooden frame and launched from his bedroom window over the busy street. Charley's interests were more literary.

George glanced beneath the table at his son's sprawled legs. How could it be that his trousers, newly tailored before the fall term, now hardly reached his ankles? Even when Charley was a toddler, Ts'ai-shun predicted that her son would be taller than a Manchu warrior and maybe even taller than George himself. It appeared that she was right.

"Father, would you save all the old *Harper's* for me? Mr. Manson doesn't subscribe to anything good."

"I won't throw them away if you promise to take them back with you—and the *Scribner's*, too, except for the last two issues."

George handed his son a folded blue sheet with Ts'ai-shun's cinnabar-red chop at the bottom. Once a month, just before the mail steamer departed Shanghai for San Francisco, Ts'ai-shun dictated two letters, one to George and the other to Charley, to a scribe who translated them into English. She, in turn, expected to find two letters aboard the return vessel. "We each have a letter from your mother. She asks me how we celebrated the New Year and what I bought for your present."

Again, George felt a twinge of guilt. Chinese New Year had passed unnoticed, almost three months ago.

"My present?" Charley looked up from his magazine. "I want a pocket watch and a violin."

"I think that *either* would make a fine gift," George ventured. Perhaps we can go shopping tomorrow, but have you written your mother? You know if she doesn't get two letters, we'll both be in trouble."

"I'll write tonight. I promise!"

"It looks like you need to be measured for a new suit, too. I suppose it won't be long—" George knew he was about to sound impossibly sentimental, "before you'll expect to be addressed as Charles."

"Oh Father!" Charley rolled his eyes, "My teacher calls me Mr. Sargent. So, can I buy a watch? A gold one—with a chain?"

"I'm sure your mother will be delighted, but I think that silver will be just fine—engraved with your name. And remember, Robert's mother has invited you to dinner at 6:30."

George wanted Charley to have everything he needed, but he did not want to spoil him with expensive luxuries. He, himself, had exercised restraint and modesty, buying a house here in the South End, a community of small merchants and tradesmen, not in the fashionable Back Bay with its broad boulevards and opulent mansions. He stepped into his office and glanced up at the framed photograph on the mantle of Ts'ai-shun wearing all the accoutrements of a stylish American woman.

Three years ago, when he had brought Charley and Ts'ai-shun to Boston, he wondered how they would adjust. He need not have worried about Charley. After all he had attended an English School in Shanghai. While Charley flourished in Boston, unfortunately, Ts'ai-shun had not.

How brave she was to come to Boston. She had practiced her English all winter before they sailed from Shanghai. Just before their departure, she purchased a fashionable English wardrobe. She and Charley had thoroughly enjoyed the railroad trip from

San Francisco in the Pullman Palace Car, and she even approved of the newly built, three-story brick house fronting on Shawmut Street.

Then Thanksgiving as well as Christmas had come and gone without a single invitation from any of the Dixwells, Sargents, or Bowditches. Further, the Christian women who invited her to one of their meetings offended her with their abject ignorance of China.

Worse still, it had been impossible to find a cook who would learn to fix any of the foods that she liked. They learned that no Irish maid would work for a Chinese. Eventually George found Mrs. Schmidt, an older German immigrant, to keep house for them, yet Ts'ai-shun still had had no one to talk to and missed playing mah-jongg with her friends.

Charley came in and laid the *Harper's Weekly* on George's desk, open to Thomas Nast's interpretation of the recently negotiated treaty with China. George looked at the full-page etching: A porcelain jar was encircled by a black dragon clawing its way upward toward the rim where, with three talon-like fingers, it appeared to be stuffing a document—the treaty—into the American Capitol dome turned upside down like a funnel.

Charley pointed to two of the crudely rendered details decorating a jar. "Father, I don't understand this cartoon. Why does the American flag have a clover leaf instead of stars—and who is that fat man?"

"Hmm." George gathered his thoughts. "That clover leaf is a shamrock, symbolizing all the Irish immigrants in America. And the fat man is John Bull—"

"John Bull?"

"Yes, you know the way Mr. Nast draws Uncle Sam in a cartoon with striped pants and stars on his hat? So, the fat man is John Bull, Uncle Sam's older brother, who symbolizes England."

"So, why does he have a cast on his leg with clover leaf on it?"

"It's a shamrock again, Charley, meant to show how Ireland weighs England down."

The whole cartoon made George cringe. He was grateful that Charley seemed to be ignoring the more offensive details, but the boy had to know about the hatred of Chinese laborers that was sweeping the United States and the growing movement to stop their immigration. There were hardly any Chinese in Massachusetts, but the papers regularly reported that yet another California mob burned yet another Chinatown. George had hoped to shield his son against the taunt of "Chinky, Chinky, Chinee."

Despite teaching him to be proud of both sides of his heritage, after only a few months in Boston, Charley suddenly refused to speak Chinese. George watched helplessly as the boy gradually suppressed anything that might connect him to China. It was hard to pinpoint when Charley's alienation began. Perhaps it was his embarrassment when Ts'ai-shun addressed him in Chinese in front of his friends. Perhaps it was a mistake to tell him that he was Manchu, not Chinese. He would never forget Ts'ai-shun's tears after visiting Charley's school and concluding that her very presence hurt the boy's claim to be an American.

Charley was now staring at the crude caricatures of Chinese men smoking opium at the base of the pot and two more hanging by their queues from the flagpole.

George tried to organize an answer around the underlying trade-and-treaty issues in terms of political economy rather than dwelling on the unfortunate consequences that the cartoonist had illustrated to such cruelly compelling effect.

"You've seen Mr. Nast's cartoons before. Well, this cartoon is about the new treaty between the United States and China. The well-formed china jar represents the stable, predictable relationship among England, America, and China under the old treaty."

Noting the crack at the base of the vessel, jagging upward that severed an arched banner, labeled "Opium Business," George quickly added, "For a long time, the opium trade was the basis of all Western commerce with China, and the new treaty breaks that old 'jar' by outlawing it."

"Then, what do the clovers—the shamrocks—have to do with it?" Charley pointed again.

Grateful he could avoid for now American commerce in opium, George continued. "The shamrocks are meant to show all the Irish immigrants who have come here as well as their electoral power when they all vote together. Many Irishmen are common laborers, just like the Chinese, but the Chinese are willing to work for less money than the Irish. So, the Irish and other ignorant people have politicked to keep more Chinese from coming to the United States. One provision of the treaty allows the United States to do exactly that."

"You mean like a protective tariff, only for people?"

George was dumbstruck. It appeared that Charley, who had never expressed a lick of interest when George had tried to explain his thoughts on trade treaties, had actually been listening.

"No, Charley. The work of immigrants, be they Irish or Chinese, increases the gross product of American manufactures. So, opening our doors to labor is a good thing, but opening our ports to cheap foreign manufactures robs those very laborers of a market for what they produce."

"What about things we *have* to import—like tea?"

"You raise an important point." George smiled. "And you make me very proud to have a son with such an analytic mind. The subject deserves further discussion."

He realized it was only a matter of time before Charley would ask about the opium trade too and would want to know whether his father had participated in that pernicious trade. George handed the magazine back to his son. "But now I need to dress; I'm going out later. Mrs. Schmidt is leaving early, too. Remember to be at Robert's house at 6:30. And be sure to thank his mother before you leave—and you can invite Robert to join us for ice cream tomorrow."

Suddenly, it struck George that those words were not his own but his mother's. He could imagine her and aunts Catharine and Henrietta and Anna all looking down from somewhere in the sky and laughing at him. [2]

The Holmes Home
10 Beacon Street, Boston
7:00 pm

"Johnny took away all his bottles and potions, but he did leave us that couch."

Fanny Dixwell Holmes pointed to the loveseat against the wall of what was now Wendell's crowded office—formerly Dr. John Dixwell's waiting room. The ancient loveseat sat for years in Epes Dixwell's rear parlor before he gave it to Fanny's brother when he opened his medical practice. Dr. John, in turn, left it for Fanny and Wendell when he vacated these same rented rooms for a spacious house of his own.

George ran his fingers over the threadbare upholstery, remembering Aunt Henrietta, sitting there primly beside Aunt Anna, and handing young Johnny a peppermint. He stooped to examine the stack of rough-cut pages on the seat.

Fanny reached over and handed George the topmost page: *The Common Law*, by O. W. Holmes, Jr. "Every single pencil scratch required Wendell's full attention. We really should throw these out now that the book is in print."

George picked up a page from the second stack. Its text was speckled with notations in two different hands. "It looks as if it required your full attention as well." He smiled at his niece.

"Oh, mine were only spelling and punctuation," Fanny blushed. "It was Wendell who wore himself out."

"I've almost finished reading the copy signed for me, and I must say it's a masterpiece of jurisprudence."

"You must be sure to tell Wendell that," Fanny whispered. "It's everything he's thought about for 10 years. It's been out almost two months now without a single review."

George understood. Wendell had not only sacrificed his own youth to his effort at making his name as a legal scholar. Having passed 40, this treatise was Wendell's last chance to become more than just another competent attorney. His work had exacted an even greater sacrifice from Fanny. Also past 40, it seemed clear that she would never become a mother. Poor Fanny, George thought, living above a drugstore, doing her best to entertain in crowded rooms that were furnished with dowdy hand-me-down furniture and that lacked even a properly equipped kitchen!

He took his niece's hand. "Your Wendell has not dashed off a novel or a mere book of verse. He has produced a philosophical work that presents all of jurisprudence in a completely new light. It takes time for a serious book to be read and to receive a serious review."

"Yet his father's last book was reviewed within weeks!" Fanny countered.

"My point exactly! Mark my words, Holmes, Jr., will be honored long after Holmes, Sr., has been forgotten ... but where is our fine legal scholar?"

Fanny gestured toward the steps, "He got home late from court; he'll be down as soon as he dresses."

"Well, why don't you show me *your* most recent creation?" George was eager to turn from the sensitive subject of father and son. Wendell was every bit as ambitious, self-centered and vain as his famous sire—the most public celebrity in all of Boston— and the young man chafed as "junior" under the name so wholly occupied by his father.

In the rear parlor, Fanny pulled a narrow wooden frame from behind the buffet. "I call this 'Twilight in Mattapoisset Harbor,' but I'm going to have to do it all over again."

"But why? It looks as good as anything ever produced in Japan—or China." George pointed at the dark trunk silhouetted against the glistening silk water. "That's a wonderfully ancient tree spreading above the rocky shore."

Fanny frowned. "I was in a hurry, and I thought I could do the water in pale blue, but then, when I'd almost finished, I realized the branches would be more dramatic if they were silhouetted against a *colorless* sky, as Hokusai might have done."

"Your Master Hokusai was reviewed in the *Transcript* a few days ago," George remarked. "I suppose now everyone will be copying him."

"I haven't *copied* him, Uncle George." Fanny's voice betrayed a hint of annoyance. "I've just drawn inspiration from him as well as from those wonderful scrolls you sent from China, and the prints you brought me from Japan. Here's my *improved* sketch." She pulled a thin roll of paper from behind the buffet and spread it flat on the couch. "You see how I've removed the tree but kept the tips of the branches—"

"George! I must say you're looking chipper." Wendell Holmes stepped into the room and glanced at the embroidery. "I trust we can drag you away from your writing to visit Mattapoisett for a few days this summer."

"I hope so," George spoke noncommittally. He had so far avoided Wendell and Fanny's invitations to their summer house on Cape Cod, as Charley was not included in these invitations, and he did not want to vacation without him.

The doorknocker sounded, and Fanny glanced down the hall, turning the embroidery to the wall. "That must be the Grays! Excuse us for a moment." Wendell hurried after his wife to greet their guests at the door.

George retrieved the rejected design, stood it against the buffet, and stepped back for a better look. The long, narrow shape of the frame recalled the painted scroll his teacher gave him when he married Hu Ts'ai-shun, although Fanny's composition was less symmetrical, like the prints he bought for his niece in Japan.

Where one of Fanny's earlier works had stitched the bold diagonal lines like her Japanese mentor to represent the driving fury of a Massachusetts snowstorm, this landscape encompassed a more static quality. George held up Fanny's sketch of the revised design for comparison. She was right. The busy detail of the rocks and the thick tree trunk in the first embroidery pulled the eye away from the fragile lines of the silhouetted branches. The new sketch depicted tendril-like twigs clutching a transient stillness about to dissipate in a blur of motion with the first breath of the evening breeze.

He looked more closely. Ruler-straight lines showed the actual lengths of the planned stitches. Viewed closely, they sprawled in jagged spans, like the strokes of a brush. Unlike the usual embroideries fashioned for decorative table covers and cushions, there was nothing measured or restrained here. George held the sketch at arm's length. Fanny's stitches, so awkward at close range, gave an entirely different impression at a distance. Fanny's style elevated her humble domestic craft to something much higher.

"Uncle George, you remember Professor Gray from the Law School and Mrs.

Gray." Fanny brought her guests into the parlor with Wendell following close behind. George still had the sketch in his hand.

"Oh! That's beautiful!" Nina Gray caught her breath. "It should be in your New York exhibit, too!"

"Yesterday," Mr. Gray addressed Wendell, "when the postman delivered *The Nation*, I found a truly magnificent review."

"You did?" Wendell leaned forward, expectantly. "I didn't think they would bother to review such a technical volume."

Mr. Gray looked confused. Nina Gray unfolded a sheet of paper from her purse. "I clipped the article for you in case you hadn't seen it."

She began to read aloud: "For some weeks Mrs. Oliver Wendell Holmes, Jr., has had upon exhibition at the rooms of the Ladies' Decorative Art Society a number of landscapes done in embroidery which are works of fine art, of a quality so far as we know, unique." Nina found her place and continued reading.

> "... Mrs. Holmes differs as widely from the classical formality of Japanese landscape embroidery. Her pictures are entirely free and individual, being in nothing more remarkable than in their avoidance of the semblance of conventionality, good or bad. In fine, she is an American artist of noticeable qualities ... This work alone would give Mrs. Holmes a place among her artist fellow-countrymen, few of whom show so much feeling for what is delicately poetic."

Nina looked up from the paper into an awkward silence. Fanny seemed frozen in her chair. Wendell looked grimly at his shoes. Poor Wendell, George thought. Nina couldn't possibly know how excruciating this was for him, but it was clear to George that there was room for but one celebrity in this household, and Fanny's fame was engendering more resentment than admiration from her husband.

Mr. Gray broke the awkward pause. "We've just heard from your boy, Kentaro. He writes that he's getting married."

"Yes, and to a Japanese girl." Nina added.

"Wendell received a letter, too," Fanny interjected. "We had thought he might wait and marry an American girl. After Wendell bought him swallowtails and a top hat, he attended every gala on Beacon Hill and turned more than a few fair heads!"

George raised an eyebrow. The young man must have become so much like an adopted son to Fanny that she apparently overlooked his race.

"Well, she is Japanese," Nina leaned forward. "And she's only 16!"

"Now, now," Wendell leaned back in his chair. "I believe Kentaro said they were only *betrothed*."

"Yes, *betrothed* as in the sense of a *contract*." Mr. Gray assumed his professorial tone, "and I have been convinced—as will be others who study jurisprudence—that Japanese law, like our own common law, may be best understood, not as a science based on universal principles but as a body of practices that respond to particular situations."

Fanny's relief was obvious. Mr. Gray had just summarized the thrust of the argument of Wendell's book and in Wendell's own words.

Wendell smiled appreciatively at him, "Thank you, John. But I confess that my *Common Law* may pale beside the thought-weighted verse of Emerson or the homely directness of Whittier, and it clearly falls short of the singing simplicity of Longfellow, but —"

"But, my dear Wendell, in the realm of 'learning-laden stanzas,' your prose leaves Lowell languishing in labored lugubriousity!"

"Touché!" Wendell slapped his knee and bellowed in laughter.

George joined Nina and Fanny in their applause. Wendell had begun by quoting the litany of superlative comparisons from the recently published review of his father's book, but Mr. Gray had cleverly paraphrased the finale for Wendell's benefit. The conversation returned to Kentaro.

"I suppose, as a samurai, Nao-tsugu, excuse me, Kentaro—" Fanny had inadvertently used Kentaro's childhood name. "I suppose he had to marry someone of his own station. He could hardly refuse the daughter of Governor Yamada. But we've worried about him as he must try to live as a Japanese, while he has learned how to think as an American. It was too much of a strain for poor Inoue." Fanny's voice quavered.

Inoue had hardly returned to Japan when the *Transcript* reported his death—a suicide. How hard for Fanny. George couldn't help but think that Inoue and Kentaro, along with all the other Japanese students that Wendell tutored and mentored, were the only children that the young Holmses would ever have.

Fanny rose to lead her guests to the dining room. "I do believe it's time for pie."

George followed the two couples down the hall. "Trying to live as a Japanese, while thinking like an American," Fanny's words echoed in his head. There was no way that Charley could ever return to China. He was far more American than any of the Japanese students who had found refuge in this house.

That was the bitter irony—Charley would never be welcome in this house—among his own flesh and blood! It had come to this: only he, a tired 66-year-old, stood between Charley and the lonely life of an orphan. How could Fanny and Wendell mourn the loss of their samurai boys and actually imagine Kentaro marrying an American girl without so much as acknowledging the existence of their own Manchu cousin, now a proper Boston boy. [3]

The J.J. Dixwell home
1881, October 24

George stepped from the carriage that had brought him up from the station, paid the driver, and turned to admire again the simple lines of J.J.'s house. High above the third-story dormers, atop the gray slate roof, the spindle balustrades and rails of a widow's walk were silhouetted against the deep blue sky. J.J. modeled that particular ornament after the one on Aunt Murray's old house in Gloucester. Now that J.J. was gone and Elizabeth alone, the widow's walk seemed the most distinguishing feature.

He walked across the yard to look down Bowditch Hill toward Jamaica Pond. J.J. loved trees and collected rare species from all over the world, turning the Sunnyside grounds into a botanical garden. Although the sandalwood he ordered from India had not survived, the ginkgo saplings he asked George to send from China now stood tall, their golden leaves brightly clashing with the orange-red foliage of the sugar maple.

He returned to the house. J.J. had been gone almost five years now. Before his heart finally gave out, he had asked George to promise to look after Elizabeth and their three grown children. It was Annie's urgent request that he help her decide what to exhibit at Mr. J. Eastman Chase's Gallery that brought him to Sunnyside this bright fall morning.

"Uncle George, you should have come right in!" Annie Parker Dixwell opened the door and stood on her toes to kiss her favorite uncle. "Lizzie and I have been laying out the pictures. Mother's upstairs, but she'll be down soon."

"How is your mother?"

"Mother still cries when we hardly expect it," Annie confided, "but I think she's getting better."

"And your brother?" George inquired. Arthur had been a strange child, slow to learn and obsessive about the few things that interested him. Although the boy had been an embarrassment, J.J. and Elizabeth did their best to train him to behave properly in company.

"Oh, Arthur's working for Mr. Wentworth. It's done him a world of good. He's mainly in the storeroom and not with customers."

"Hello, Mr. Dixwell." Lizzie Boott held out her hand. "Thank you for coming. We really need your advice. Mr. Chase wants us to choose our best for the show, and it's very difficult to decide."

"Forty-five of mine and forty-five of Lizzie's." Annie laid a second row of watercolors across the drawing room table.

"If only we can come up with enough different views. These are mine." Lizzie pointed to the upper row—images of ancient stone buildings with arched windows and pillared doorways.

"And these are yours?" George smiled at his niece and bent to examine a cluster of bright red blossoms and green leaves set against the weathered blocks of a wall tinted in the same tawny buff as Lizzie's renderings.

"What do you think, Uncle George? Do mine look different enough, or should I leave Alhambra to Lizzie and maybe show mine of Florence—then she could do Athens or Ravenna."

George considered. "If you hang your pictures on different walls, the patrons will be surprised and delighted that you've seen the same scenes so differently."

"We have etchings, too, and oils." Lizzie unwrapped a tall canvas and stood it against the wall. "But we need more space to lay them out."

George peered into the library. "I can clear some space on the desk and the top of the piano." He stepped into the book-lined room. He could still hear the two women discussing the relative merits of the paintings. He glanced up at the nude athlete, standing in his special alcove above the central bookcase, his bronze arms raised to acknowledge the cheers of a Roman patron. Elizabeth was horrified when J.J. first brought it home. How could she raise her daughters in a home where they could daily inspect a man's exposed private parts—and how could she face the mothers of their friends?

J.J. had always been a collector, and Annie and her sister Caroline grew up surrounded by art. When Annie first showed an interest in her cousin Fanny's drawings, J.J. arranged for private lessons. Then Annie asked to join the women taking instruction in Mr. Hunt's studio and met Lizzie Boott. Looking back over the years, it seemed inevitable that Annie would become an artist.

"Oh, you've cleared a lot of space!" Annie pointed up at the marble busts to the left and right of the athlete. "Father told me you bought those two heads in Paris."

"They're copies, of course." George smiled. He had gone all over Paris, scouring artists' studios, galleries, and auction houses for items suitable for his future mansion, where he would someday raise his family. Of course, there had been no mansion, and George gave his entire collection to J.J. to partially repay the money he advanced George to save him from bankruptcy.

"I painted all of these right here at Sunnyside." Annie spread out the pictures on the piano. "Do you think they will they look strange, with the others all from Europe?"

George bent to look at the watercolors. Here was one of Jamaica Pond with an expanse of lily pads by the shore; another was of the same view but with the pond's entire surface covered in ice; and there was the farmhouse he had passed near the foot of the hill, its front door rendered in a bolder blue than he remembered.

"I think if Lizzie exhibits some of her American scenes—perhaps from her trip to the Adirondacks—then together, they will provide a wonderful contrast to those done along the Mediterranean." George glanced back into the drawing room. "Where is Lizzie?" he asked.

"She went out for the etchings she left in the carriage."

"She seems to be in better spirits then when I last saw her," George ventured. "Is she still seeing Mr. Duveneck?"

"Yes," Annie put her finger to her lips, "but she doesn't tell her father. She's still in love with Frank," Annie went on to confide, "but our interlude in Europe has calmed her nerves."

Lizzie's rich father, Francis Boott, had been impressed with the power of Frank Duveneck's painting and delighted when Lizzie took lessons from him in Munich. Boott had even encouraged the young man to set up a studio near the Boott estate in Florence. Turned out Duveneck had more genius than breeding—he was born a hardscrabble Kentuckian. Boott became horrified when his refined Lizzie announced their engagement.

Lizzie had been devastated by her father's reaction, and Annie, frightened by her best friend's decline, rescued Lizzie from her father's disapproval. Annie spirited Lizzie, their easels, and their palettes away on a steamer bound for Spain. George knew the whole story—half of Boston probably did.

"Has Mr. Boott forgiven you for taking Lizzie off to the Alhambra, and—where else?"

"Oh, yes!" Annie giggled. "He wasn't amused when we announced our departure, but after three months on our own we joined him in Florence, and we all traveled home together."

"But how is it with Mr. Duveneck here in Boston?" George indulged his weakness for gossip.

"It has worked out perfectly," Annie smiled slyly. "Mr. Duveneck visits my new studio and so does Lizzie. But don't tell Mr. Boott!"

Annie took George's hand and squeezed it. "And if Mother sits for a portrait, that will give Mr. Duveneck another reason to spend the spring here in Boston. I need you to convince her to sit for him."

George raised an eyebrow, understanding Annie's scheme. So, it wasn't just for his advice on art for which Annie had requested his presence.

"George, is that you? Will you join us for tea?" Elizabeth Dixwell called from the drawing room.

He checked his watch. "I can't stay long. I have a meeting at the Institute."

"Well, I promise not to hold you for a second cup," Annie said softly. "But how is Charley?"

"He's doing well," George was happy to hear her ask. "He'll be home as usual on the weekend, and we'll celebrate his birthday. He's asked for a violin."

"Well, you must give him a birthday kiss from me!"

"Of course." George turned away, feeling tears stinging his eyes. Of all the Dixwells, only Annie and her cousin, Dr. John, had ever even acknowledged Charley's existence.

§

Elizabeth poured the first cup from the silver pot.

George glanced over at his niece Annie. Her light brown hair was pulled back into a bun, and a single silver strand glistened against her tortoise shell comb. It seemed odd to him that halfway through her 30's Annie was still a spinster—and her friend Lizzie, too. He wondered if they, too, would end up childless, like Fanny.

"Do have some cream, Henriet. Cats love cream!" Annie spoke to George, tapping her crystal goblet with her knife.

George grinned. Annie uttered the familiar phrase with the same clipped inflection as Aunt Anna Parker had used addressing Aunt Henrietta every day at teatime for all the years the two had lived together. "You know," he remarked, "I often wish we had good portraits of Aunt Anna and Aunt Henrietta."

"Well, for years John tried to convince the aunts to sit for portraits, but they could never agree on an artist. Of course, they could never agree on anything. John always said their portraits would have to face each other from opposite sides of the room." Elizabeth gazed up at the portrait of her husband. George saw the pain in her eyes. She still missed J.J. terribly.

"J.J. might have been right about the aunts," George touched Elizabeth's hand, "—but I think he looks lonely up there, without you."

"Do you really think so? Annie wants me to pose for that Mr. Duveneck."

Annie nudged his ankle with her toe. George felt like a co-conspirator. "I think Mr. Duveneck may be the greatest American portraitist of his generation, perhaps as great as Copley was in his." George nodded toward the portrait of Great-grandfather Epes

Sargent, looking down from the wall behind Elizabeth's chair, his elbow resting on the base of a column and a flounced cuff showing at his wrist. He pointed to a spot on the wall next to J.J. "And your portrait should go right there in place of that mirror."

"Perhaps … you're right."

"Then it's settled!" Annie ignored her mother's hesitant tone. "I'll ask Mr. Duveneck to come for tea so he can see Father's picture and think about a pose where you'll be looking toward him. Of course, he'll paint you in the same scale as father, so you can always be viewed together."

"You know," Elizabeth mused, "I sometimes think Great-grandfather Sargent is happier here in the dining room than he would be with Great-grandmother out in the parlor."

"You mean the austere, thin-lipped woman with the riding whip?" Lizzie Boott leaned forward. "Is that by Copley, also?"

"Yes, and with no horse in sight, John always wondered who felt the sting of that whip." Elizabeth laughed. "I wonder if she was really that stern, or if Mr. Copley just didn't like her."

"Well, Mr. Copley obviously liked Aunt Judith much more." Annie winked at George. "Aunt Henrietta always thought he should have painted Aunt Judith with more clothes. But, that picture was done long before she married the Reverend Mr. Murray."

"Hey, I want a scone, too!" J.J.'s only son had entered the room.

"Why, Arthur, dear, did Mr. Wentworth let you off early from work?" Elizabeth Dixwell handed the young man a plate.

"A customer bought two mirrors, so I went to see that they were properly delivered." The short, gnomish man bit into his scone and continued talking, to no one in particular. "You can't trust the newspapers to report the football scores."

"Do you have records of yesterday's scores?" Annie spoke solicitously to her younger brother.

Arthur pulled a worn notebook from his side pocket and opened it to reveal neat columns of numbers. "To get it exactly right, you have to attend the game yourself. Even if the papers do report a game, they never agree on the scoring."

No one knew exactly what was wrong with him, but he had always obsessed about sports and scores. Perhaps George's strange nephew was a throwback to some long-ago defect in one of the family lines, but which one? Arthur's maternal grandfather, Nathaniel Bowditch, certainly had an affinity for numbers, too. But he was a mathematical genius, and Arthur was far from that—there had never even been a thought of sending the boy to his Uncle Epes's Latin school.

George checked his watch. "This has been a great delight," he said, standing. "You two new American artists have more than enough for a wonderfully varied exhibition."

"Yes, and we didn't need your protective tariff either, dear Uncle!"

George smiled broadly at his saucy niece. It struck him that, in a way, J.J. had raised Annie to be his "son." Now that George had reworked his article on the tariff into a book, he would send Annie an autographed copy. [4]

The George Dixwell Home
October 27

Shawmut Street had been extended to the north. George could now ride the horsecar all the way to Boston Common, where he could board the Charles Street car direct to Cambridge. He settled into his seat and looked at the rough draft of the list of topics Epes planned to cover in his lecture to the Scientific Club: "Things introduced since my recollection." As one of the oldest members of the club, Epes succumbed to the conceit of recalling all of the discoveries, inventions, and innovations that had occurred during the 73 years of his lifetime.

George ran his finger down the list: "Water pipes in houses; gas illumination; horsecars and omnibuses." Yes, his own home, the house he had bought for Ts'ai-shun, had running water in the kitchen and toilet, gas lighting in each of the rooms, and the convenience of Shawmut Street horsecars passing at 15-minute intervals.

"Friction matches, free libraries, and card catalogues." George read on, "the use of chaoutchouc for other purposes than erasing pencil." He corrected the spelling to "caoutchouc" and penciled in "the vulcanization of India rubber." He pursed his lips. George had never succeeded in extracting royalty payments owed him by Mr. Goodyear—his share of the India rubber patents transferred to him by James Dorr in partial settlement of his debt. George penciled in "the establishment of a city-wide system of sewer pipes," then added, "a device for sharpening pencils." George turned the page to see Epes's next entry, "the telephone." Outside the car window he could see the wires of Mr. Bell's new system run helter-skelter from rooftop to rooftop.

"Dixwell, you're looking well!" Charles E. Endicott, George's long-time friend from the Heard Company, sat down next to him.

George reminded himself to stay off the subject of business. Endicott had lost his entire fortune to the Heard Company creditors. "You're looking well, yourself. What brings you up from Brookline?"

"Tonight I lecture to the Ancient Order of United Workmen." Endicott patted his valise.

"And you will exhort them to be satisfied with the generous portion allotted them by their taskmasters?"

"Not quite," Endicott laughed. "They heard my contrary opinions on that subject at my last lecture. Tonight, I discuss women's suffrage."

"To the A.O.U.W.? You'll be lucky to escape with your life!"

"Not so." Endicott leaned back. "It's my thesis that working women will always vote their common interest with working men, if given the chance."

Since his return from Shanghai, Endicott occupied himself publishing tracts that championed the cause of workingmen and assailed corruption in offices of public trust. It was Endicott who had first encouraged George to describe in a public forum how a tariff against cheap foreign manufactures protected working people and nascent industries.

"Thank you for sending me your *Premises of Free Trade*," Endicott continued, "What a wise move to reissue it as a book. Yesterday's *Wool Producers' Bulletin* is tomorrow's fish wrap, but those hardbound volumes will remain in libraries forever. And, how is Charley?"

"Well, it's good that he's become a 100% American, but it's a pity he's losing his Chinese."

Endicott nodded knowingly. "That's exactly why Cousin James sent his boys to Kentucky and then brought them back to China. He hadn't wanted them raised by Ng Akew, but he also worried they were forgetting their Chinese. Of course, he didn't want them enlisting in the Union Army either, like Hunter's boys." Endicott continued. "Yes, hiring young Henry Endicott was a brilliant move. You predicted he would bring us a lion's share of James's coastal shipping, but who would have guessed that he would build up such a profitable business with the Chinese shippers?"

"His fluency in Chinese was the key to that," George agreed. He was still disappointed that Charley had rejected Chinese, closing off that kind of opportunity for himself.

"Henry carried *all* that shipping business with him over to Butterfield and Swire— there was nothing the Heard creditors could do about that," Endicott laughed. "You know he's married a Chinese girl."

"I'm just glad Henry didn't take the business over to Russell's." George was surprised that even now, he felt such bitterness toward his old rival. It still pained him to remember watching the Heard firm's red-white diamond flag being lowered from the *Kiangloong*, their last Yangtze River steamer. "A pity about Tyson," George mused. It was bad form to think poorly of the recently dead.

"Yes, he was only 50," said Endicott. "At least he made careful provision for his family."

"Both families?"

"Both!" Endicott confided. "I believe you know my cousin Bill Endicott?"

George nodded. Bill Endicott was a well-known Boston merchant—an old abolitionist friend of Aunt Henrietta's who had served for two years as treasurer of the Institute of Technology.

Endicott lowered his voice, "Bill is one of Tyson's executors, and he told me that Tyson prepared a special codicil to his will, designating two friends to receive $20,000 to be used 'at their discretion in the adjustment of certain affairs in China of which they have cognizance.'"

"That would be Lam Fong Kew and her four children?"

"That's right," Endicott continued. "Now that Fong Kew has passed away, the money goes to her two sons and two daughters, and her twin sister, Kew Fong, who took over raising the children."

"She was Albert Heard's woman," George volunteered, "but I don't believe they had children."

Albert was rumored to be the father of little Richard Heard, who grew up in Hong Kong. Albert had long since died without ever acknowledging the boy, but George heard from friends in Shanghai that Richard seemed to have been well educated and now held a responsible position in Jardine Matheson.

"Do Fong Kew's children use Tyson's name?"

"No," replied Endicott. "Tyson loved those children, but after he married Sarah, he forbade their use of his name. Even so, he sent his oldest son, Chan Kai Ming, to college, and he's now official interpreter for the Hong Kong Magistracy."

Yes, with a second family in Boston, Tyson had good reason to reserve the Tyson name for his American children, but all the Chinese children in the Endicott-Gardner clan bore the names of their American fathers.

George's situation was different. When he married Hu Ts'ai-shun, he knew she would be his only wife. At the time, giving Charley the Sargent name, instead of Dixwell, seemed an acceptable compromise. In Boston, the Sargent surname was shared by a medley of unrelated families, from bricklayers to aristocrats. When Ts'ai-shun came to Boston, he did introduce her as Mrs. Dixwell and Charley as their son.

The Bowditch trustee of Aunt Anna's bequest assured him that Charley would inherit the remainder of George's own share, but George did not want to risk offending the man by changing Charley's name to Dixwell now. Everyone knew that Nathaniel Bowditch's daughters had married J.J and Epes Dixwell. Nevertheless, he was sorry he had been so considerate of his brothers' feelings.

"What news do you have of our other Chinese friends?"

"Do you recall my cousin John Endicott Gardner?" Endicott queried. "The one who married Anna Rosa Hunter?"

"Of course I remember. She married Reverend Vrooman after Gardner died."

"Anna Rosa writes that she and Vrooman have moved to Australia to missionize the Chinese in the gold fields. Vrooman has turned Johnny Gardner into a real Chinese scholar."

"He must be 18 years old now."

"Anna Rosa said they plan to sail for California in the spring," Endicott continued, "but of course that would be fall down there."

"Did she say anything about her father?" George always felt an affection for William Hunter. He was one of the few white men who could read Chinese when George first went to China and had helped him when George began his own study of the language.

"According to Anna Rosa, he is still living in Paris. I believe her Tanka mother died some years ago in Canton. She says Hunter is writing a history of Russell and Co., and I know for a fact that his old partners—Bennet Forbes, Warren Delano, and Tyson, too, before he died—have all warned him against saying too much."

George was not proud either of his participation in the opium trade. He'd heard that the Russell and Co. history omitted a great deal. Perhaps Hunter was right. It was best to let sleeping dogs lie.

The horsecar jerked to a stop at Boston Common. He watched a young woman guide a toddler along the sidewalk, just as Ts'ai-shun used to do with Charley. In her last letter, Ts'ai-shun once again complained that she was afraid that when she died, she would have no son in China to look after her tablets for the requisite three years. George wasn't in China, and he was not sure at his age that he could father a second son, and what if it was a daughter? Ts'ai-shun would still need a son.

She wrote that some childless friends of hers had adopted a little boy to raise up as their own. It was no accident that she now mentioned it again. Although she was only

33, she wanted an adult son in China before she grew old. Having kept Charley in America, George felt morally obliged to grant her that wish.

He extracted Epes's list from his pocket and reviewed the second page: "electrolytic plating, the stethoscope, the ice trade." He chuckled, remembering J.J.'s story of delivering the first cargo of Massachusetts ice to Calcutta, and how a turbaned Parsi complained that the frozen block he purchased only the day before had disappeared into a puddle of water.[5]

The Epes Dixwell home
6:30 pm

Epes Dixwell raised his goblet to the assembled members of the Scientific Club and took a sip of wine. "I have no scientific communication to make, and you do not expect one from me—but I am bound to say something that you may take in place of such a contribution." He looked up from the battered wooden lectern, one of the few items he had saved from Dixwell's School.

George and the five other men seated around the parlor shifted into comfortable positions. William Charles Eliot, president of Harvard University, raised his wine glass and winked at George. "My dear Dixwell, I suspect your humility is merely a ruse to take us all by surprise, for I believe I saw your brother slip you a page of listings. Knowing the catholic breadth of *his* interests, it may range from thermodynamics to political economy."

Joseph Lovering, the Hollis Professor of mathematics and natural philosophy, cleared his throat and waited for the laughter to subside. "But I trust that among the inventions and innovations you have borne witness to during your long and eventful life, you will choose to include in your discussion the protectionist tariff for which your brother, in the tradition of our own Professor Bowen, has become such an articulate advocate."

"Sufficiently articulate that it has crossed my mind to issue a revised edition of my *American Political Economy*." Francis Bowen, the Alford Professor of natural religion, moral philosophy, and civil polity, raised his glass toward George.

George acknowledged the toast with a nod. "I think we all agree that the tariff was an innovation long antecedent to the floruit of my esteemed brother."

"I must confess," Eliot spoke up, "that when Mr. Dixwell sent a copy of his new book to the university, I seized it and read it from cover to cover before relinquishing it to our library. I found his argument to be as innovative and scientifically logical as the topic itself is ancient. Moreover, I was delighted to read in Mr. Dixwell's very first paragraph his homage to Professor Bowen's writings on the subject."

"I have, in fact, drawn inspiration from your well-reasoned prose." George raised his goblet to Bowen.

"All true!" Epes adjusted his spectacles. "I confess, my brother provided me with several lists of modern discoveries and inventions, although he is too modest to have included any of his own. But most of those have already been introduced and fully discussed, while still in their nascent state, at meetings of this very club, which, I might add, now approaches the 40th anniversary of its founding."

"I trust you won't let modesty prevent you from mentioning the inventions and discoveries our own members have made." Dr. Morrill Wyman, medical doctor and Harvard overseer waved a handkerchief—one of several he kept close at hand.

"Nor should you overlook the premature *rejection* of such innovations by any of our members." Eliot addressed his comment toward the vacant seat from which the late Professor Agassiz had denounced evolution.

George considered the discoveries, inventions, and new theories generated by the men seated around the room. The handkerchief on Dr. Wyman's knee reminded him that this was the medical doctor who discovered the relationship of ragweed pollen and the symptoms of "autumnal catarrh," and who published the first pollen maps to guide sufferers how to escape polllen's debilitating effects.

To Wyman's right sat Bowen, founding editor and publisher of the *North American Review*, a leading advocate of currency reform, favoring paper money and the demonetization of silver and gold. Next sat Lovering with his unruly beard. Early in his career, this gaunt eccentric had published on terrestrial magnetism and the aurora borealis, even though more recently he characterized the growing interest in electricity as but "a spurt." Charles F. Choate, president of the Old Colony Railroad and the only non-academic in attendance, sat quietly on the loveseat.

George sat next to the man he considered the most important innovator in this small group. President Eliot had been drafted from his chemistry lab at the Institute of Technology to become, at 35, the youngest president of Harvard in its quarter millennium of existence. Despite fierce opposition from the classicists, he succeeded, in a mere decade, in bringing the physical and biological sciences into the undergraduate curriculum.

Epes cleared his throat. "I will not dwell on such well-known inventions as the telegraph but will instead point out some of the more interesting consequences of its introduction, for example, in meteorology. By the aid of the telegraph, this continent is surveyed daily and the weather reported for the whole area, so that the advance of storms and waves of heat and cold may be known, thus providing for the first time a rational basis for predicting changes in the weather."

"True, perhaps for a week or, at best, a fortnight," Lovering interjected, "but prediction in any longer term still eludes all but the groundhog."

"True," Epes continued, "and while telegraphs serve best for more urgent matters, the mail, too, has improved. It has become faster and cheaper. More amazing, it costs no more to post a letter to San Francisco than to Salem. Today's letter is written, not with a goose quill, as it was in my youth, but with a metallic pen and then placed into a mucilaged envelope."

"My dear Dixwell," Eliot paused until he had the group's attention. "Have you, perchance, apprised your son-in-law of those three innovations—the stylographic pen, the mucilaged envelope, and the one-cent postage stamp?"

Epes was spared the need to make an immediate reply by the applause and laughter of his club mates. "I must say that particular query concisely summarizes my last discussion with certain overseers of our august institution." Wyman leaned back and crossed his feet.

It was common knowledge that President Eliot had offered Epes's son-in-law—Wendell Holmes—a professorship at Harvard Law School and, after several weeks, was still awaiting a reply. Epes told George that Wendell was angling for a higher salary—enough to allow him to write and teach without the distraction of continuing to represent private clients before the bar.

Epes wrinkled his forehead in mock bewilderment, "I suppose, we'll have to wait until—Fanny makes her decision."

"She has been preoccupied," Bowen laughed. "I read in *Scribner's* that her embroideries have taken New York by storm—let me quote the critic, 'as true works of art, individual and unique, her imaginativeness of a poetic order, differing from a painter only in the material she uses.'"

George looked up at the empty space on the wall by the hallway where Fanny's landscape, "Drifting Snow," had hung before being borrowed for the exhibition. Of all her work, that was his favorite, with the diagonal slash of her unimaginably long stitches capturing the full fury of wind and snow.

"I trust when you treat the arts, Dixwell, you will mention Fanny's innovations." Professor Bowen hesitated, "As well as, of course, in its proper place, Wendell's magnificent treatise *The Common Law*, which stands alone in all of jurisprudence for its breadth and detail."

It was an odd twist of fate, George mused. Fanny's stitchery made her—next to Wendell's father, of course—the most famous Holmes in America. Cornelius Vanderbilt, Jr., was negotiating to purchase the embroideries she had exhibited in New York.

The rich aroma of Professor Bowen's pipe drifted through the room. It transported George back to the sweet fragrance of opium smoke wafting across the deck of the *Frolic* as Chinese merchants tested its quality. Somehow, as he grew older, the past was drawing nearer. He recalled Fanny, as a child, playing with her doll in this same room. Penciled on the doorjamb in the kitchen were the marks documenting the annual increments of her and her siblings' growth. He had bought this very house for Epes to raise a family on a schoolmaster's pay, paid for with proceeds from the opium he had sold in China.

Epes continued his lecture, punctuated by comments and laughter from his colleagues. George shifted in his chair. It was clear that the Dixwells' affair with China was over with and that he and Ts'ai-shun and Charley were but embarrassing souvenirs. Somehow, too, the empty place on the wall where Fanny's embroidery had hung resonated with the emptiness in his heart. Charley would never be a guest in Fanny and Wendell's house nor would he be welcome in this house either. He would seem to have no American kin.

George pulled himself back from his melancholy train of thought and returned his attention to his brother's talk. Epes was discussing innovations in medicine now and more categories of discoveries and inventions were yet to be addressed. It was no use. George stared down at the carpet. In three years, he would be 70, the full three score and ten that Henrietta always quoted as being man's allotted time on earth—the very age at which J.J. died. George had long ago taken care of Ts'ai-shun who collected rents from valuable properties held in her own name. Fearon's company could be trusted to manage the stocks and other accounts he set up for her. To be sure, next summer he would visit her in Shanghai, but what to do about Charley?

There was a rustle by the parlor door. Mary Dixwell waved to her husband and pointed toward the dining room.

"I will skip over recent advances in paleontology, embryology, and philology for the moment." Epes turned to the last page of his notes. "Perhaps we can discuss them over dinner. I would like to leave you with a concluding thought. Just as the man of 1807—the year of my birth—could not foresee or conceive of the advances to be made in the 70 years succeeding him, the mind is overwhelmed with the conjecture that prompts the question: In what direction will future advancement be made? And in what flood of light will the future historian stand when he looks back upon our time and calls it a dark age?"

Amid the applause, George wondered if in that future flood of light, a Chinese-American child might be as loved and cherished as any other.

He thought of Wangfo, Grandfather Sargent's sad allegory. Somehow with the passage of time, George felt he himself had become Wangfo. He, too, could feel that old man's desperation to protect his little boy as he poled his fragile boat across the river, only to turn and find that the torrent had snatched his son away.

George knew he faced a river of his own from which there would be no return, and, somehow, he had to protect Charley. He could, at the very least, protect him financially. George would instruct his attorney to rewrite his will, placing everything destined for Charley into a rock-solid trust, just as J.J. had done for George's share of Aunt Anna's estate.

Navigating the social world was something else again. Were George to die tomorrow, Charley would need a thoughtful man to guide him. Perhaps he should talk to Endicott—he would understand. In the meantime, tomorrow was Charley's American birthday, and on Saturday they would shop together for a violin. Ts'ai-shun would like that.

George rose and followed the other men into the dining room. [6]

Charles Sargent, age 12, already with the long legs of his father, boarded with a family while attending school outside of Boston. (Courtesy of Lauren Dixwell Rayfield.)

Thomas Nast's cartoon of the "New Treaty with China." (*Harper's Weekly* 12 Dec. 1881.)

Thomas Nast's cartoon incorporates all the elements of hatred that would bring passage of the Federal Chinese Exclusion Act of 1882. George Dixwell's deconstruction of the iconography for Charley is, of course, my attempt to describe the virulently anti-Chinese atmosphere in which Charley would grow up. In 1901, fearing that he might not be readmitted to the United States after living in France, Charley stated on his passport application that he was "born in Nagasaki, in the Empire of Japan."

Fanny Dixwell Holmes (1840–1929), ca. 1885. (Courtesy Harvard Law School Art Collection.)

Embroidery by Fanny Dixwell Holmes, entitled "Twilight in Mattapoisset Harbor" (ca. 1885). (Courtesy of the Peabody-Essex Museum.)

When Fanny Dixwell married Oliver Wendell Holmes, Jr., in 1872, she was already an accomplished artist. By 1881, when Wendell published *The Common Law* (initially to little recognition), Fanny was receiving rave reviews in national magazines for her Japanese-inspired embroidered landscapes. In order to preserve her marriage to Holmes, Fanny eventually discouraged any public recognition of her work, and late in life she appears to have destroyed all the embroideries left in her possession.

The dining room at John J. Dixwell's Sunnyside mansion (ca. late-1880s), featuring John's portrait together with Frank Duveneck's portrait of his wife, Elizabeth Bowditch Dixwell. (Courtesy of the Massachusetts Historical Society.)

George Basil Dixwell (ca. 1884) in Shanghai, China, during his final visit with Hu Ts'ai-shun. (Courtesy of Marcia Dixwell DiMambro.)

CHAPTER THIRTEEN

The "Other" Dixwells

The Chamberlin Home
Westford, Massachusetts
1885, April 12

Charley heard a knock at the front door. He looked up from his geometry. Memorizing theorems was easy but applying them to solve the problems in the textbook took more concentration than he could muster, especially after the sumptuous Sunday dinner Mrs. Chamberlin had prepared. He had done well on his written exams. Now he only faced the public exam that would establish his class ranking. Father would be proud if he could enter his final year at Westford Academy close to the head of the class.

There were voices downstairs. He recognized Mr. Frost, the school's headmaster, greeting Mr. Chamberlin and then quickly dropping his voice. Why, Charley wondered, would Mr. Frost ride out to the Chamberlin farm on a Sunday afternoon and whisper? He heard Mrs. Chamberlin gasp—then, only more muffled voices and footsteps on the stairs.

Mrs. Chamberlin appeared at his door. "Charley, would you join us in the parlor?" Her smile seemed strained. He got up and followed her downstairs.

"Hello, Mr. Frost." Charley smiled and offered his hand.

"Charley ..." Mr. Frost seemed confused. "Can we sit down? I have bad news." Mrs. Chamberlin led Charley toward the couch and sat beside him. "Charley I'm very sorry. It's your father. He passed away."

Charley sat, unable to absorb what he had heard.

Mrs. Chamberlin put her arms around him. "Oh, Charley!" He could feel the moisture of her tears on his cheek. Mr. Frost was talking, but Charley couldn't comprehend the words. How could it be? Two weeks ago, when he had been home, Father had a bad cough. Then last week had come a short note saying that with final examinations coming up, Charley should stay in Westford for the weekend and not come home and risk contagion from the flu.

"I need to go home." The words issued involuntarily from his mouth.

"Charley," Mr. Frost's voice cut though the rush of pictures and voices in his head. "it was Mr. Bowditch, your father's attorney, who telegraphed me with the news, and he says that under no circumstances are you to come home until you hear from him."

"But ..." Charley's voice fell off. He recognized the name. The Bowditches were relatives of the Dixwells, even though he had never met any of them, except for Cousin Annie and Dr. John. Why should those people have any say over when he could go home?

"Mr. Frost!" Mrs. Chamberlin spoke in her most authoritative voice. "We can talk about that later. Charley needs some air right now. We need to walk in the garden for a few minutes."

Charley felt the tug of Mrs. Chamberlin's hand, then her warm arm around his waist. His throat burned and constricted, and he wanted to cry. He wanted to be alone. He pulled away and ran to the stairway in a daze. [1]

Westford to Boston
May 10, 8:00 am

Charley grabbed the handrail and climbed aboard the railroad car, dropping his valise on the floor and sliding into his usual seat.

"I'm sorry about your father." He felt the conductor's strong hand on his shoulder. The man knew all the Westford students along this stretch of track and had long ago ceased asking to see Charley's annual ticket.

"Thank you, Sir."

Charley watched him walk forward from seat to seat, punching the tickets of the other passengers. Slipping off his jacket, Charley leaned back in his seat. The train jerked forward and crawled out of the station. He waved at the stationmaster and listened as the train picked up speed until the clack of the wheels against the junctions of the rails had reached a constant tempo. He recalled Father's calculation. Each rail was 20 feet long. The number of clacks in a minute, times 20, multiplied by 60, gave the number of feet per hour, which, divided by 5,280 feet per mile, gave the train's speed in miles per hour.

Whenever they traveled together, Father had posed questions and shown him how to calculate the answers in his head. Charley closed his eyes, sensing the familiar landscape beneath the train. He heard the hollow rumble as the train passed over the Pawtucket Canal and felt the car tilt slightly as it began its 32-foot descent into Lowell.

"Thirty-two feet"—what a lesson Father had made of that! Water diverted into the Pawtucket Canal from just above the great falls of the Merrimack River was then directed downward through massive turbines that turned all the shafts and belts powering the entire textile industry of Lowell. Charley glanced out the window at the immense brick buildings where bales of raw cotton disappeared into one end and emerged from the other as rolls of cloth.

He could still hear his father's voice. Water weighed 62.4 pounds per cubic foot. A 32-foot column of it weighed 2,000 pounds. Such a column of water, 3 feet squared at its base, exerted 18,000 pounds of pressure—enough to power a factory's worth of looms.

But Father was dead. After four weeks of postponements, Charley finally received word from Mr. Bowditch, allowing him to travel to Boston. Mr. Bowditch had certainly taken his time with everything. Father had died on a Friday, and his obituary appeared on Saturday. It was clear the Dixwells asked Mr. Bowditch to wait until Sunday afternoon after Father had been buried before sending the telegram to the Westford headmaster. They deliberately excluded him from his own father's funeral.

Charley braced himself as the train screeched to a stop at Lowell Station. The passengers on the platform crowded into the car. "May I sit here?"

Charley looked up at a matronly woman. Balls of red and yellow yarn pierced by knitting needles projected from her handbag. "Of course!" he mumbled, sliding closer to the window.

The woman sat down heavily and looked closely at his face. "You must be Japanese! I enjoyed Mr. Arikawa's lecture in Boston. He described thousands of students all over Japan, going to school in European dress and speaking English. Your people are so progressive," she confided and shook her head slowly. "So different from those wretched Chinamen."

Charley nodded noncommittally.

"How can they be so backward, living as they do right next door to the Japanese?" She paused, smiling warmly at Charley. "You must be a college student, too."

"I still have another year at Westford Academy," Charley replied. He was used to being taken for older than 17 because of his height.

"Oh, Westford! Did you know that Richard Henry Dana went there, too? It's in his book."

"Yes, *Two Years Before the Mast*." Charley seized the opportunity to demonstrate his knowledge. He was grateful to deflect the conversation away from Japan and China. Of course he knew about Dana. The headmaster never missed a chance to mention Dana or all the lesser-known luminaries who had ever attended Westford. He failed to mention that the great man spent but one year at Westford, then graduated from Boston Latin.

"Yes, of course," the woman said, a little sharply. She pulled her knitting from her bag and began to concentrate on counting stitches.

Charley watched the green, rolling hills move past his window. How simple it had been to become Japanese, he thought. He hadn't actually lied. The woman just assumed he was Japanese, and he had merely neglected to correct her. It was a lot easier to be a samurai than a coolie. He wondered if Father's relatives might have accepted him and his mother had he been born in Nagasaki rather than in Shanghai. He was glad to be going home to sleep in his own room and to smell Mrs. Schmidt's ginger cookies in the oven. [2]

The George Dixwell Home
10:00 am

In one practiced motion, Charley pulled the key from his pocket, slid it into the familiar brass-bound opening and twisted. A wave of pain shot from his index finger to his elbow. The key would not turn. Now, more gently, he jiggled the key and tried to turn it once more, first to the left and then to the right. The door remained locked. Frustrated, he sounded the knocker. "Mrs. Schmidt!" he called.

He glanced again at the lock. Streaks of blue green tarnish stained the mechanism. He looked down. Dried prints of muddy boots tracked across the marble landing. Charley dropped his valise and sat down on the top step. Suddenly, he realized the enormity of what had happened to his life.

"Mr. Charles Sargent?" Charley looked up at a youngish man, wearing a top hat. "I'm Mr. Bowditch, your father's attorney."

Charley scrambled to his feet and offered his hand. He followed Charles Pickering Bowditch's gaze to the key in the lock.

"I'm sorry for that, but as your father's trustee and executor I am obliged to secure the premises while we complete the appraisal of his personal estate." Bowditch pulled out Charley's key, inserted his own and opened the door.

Charley followed him into the vestibule. The air was cold and dank, and the parlor looked strangely unfamiliar. Round depressions in the carpet marked where the couch and armchair had once stood. It was as if he were looking at a diagram of a room that no longer existed. Charley peered into the dining room. The table where he did his homework was gone, the six mahogany chairs stacked in the corner. He felt disoriented, as if after a crazy, feverish dream.

"Charles?" Bowditch's voice came from his father's office.

It seemed unreal. Mr. Bowditch sat in his father's chair, and his desk, always neat and precisely organized, now stood against the wall—its drawers pulled open, its surface piled high with papers. Charley stared at the row of square pigeonholes where Father kept his correspondence. The opening to the far right where mother's letters had been kept was empty; the red silk ribbon with which Father had tied the packet lay crumpled on the floor.

Bowditch withdrew a document from his side pocket and unfolded it. "Please sit down! Your father was a thoughtful man. Accordingly, he made careful arrangements for your maintenance and support, appointing me as his trustee to act for him in loco parentis—that means, to act in his place as your legal parent until you reach your majority."

"In loco parentis"—did Mr. Bowditch think he was stupid? Didn't he know that Charley had completed three years of Latin and another of Greek? Mr. Frost had already explained to him that his school bills would be paid from the trust from now on, and Charley had already instructed a Lowell clothier how to address the invoice for his summer wardrobe to Mr. Bowditch.

Bowditch's voice droned on, like the repetitive sound of bow strokes when Charley tuned his violin. He looked around the room. Father's books on political economy were stacked on the mantle, their gold-leaf titles glistened from dark green bindings—five stacks of thin volumes and one of thicker ones—in which Father had republished everything as his collected works.

Charley craned his neck to peer into the rear parlor. Mother's incense burner and the scented sticks were missing from the buffet.

Bowditch noted Charley's searching looks. "I have placed personal items belonging to you on your bed. You may want to take some of them back to Westford. I have placed certain other items in the chest by the window, items which you may purchase from the estate, if you wish."

Charley was stunned. "Purchase them?" Weren't they his things? His father's things? Why on earth would he need to buy anything?

"Charley," Bowditch explained. "Your father left one-third of his estate to his brother Epes, one-third to the children of his deceased brother John, and the last third he left in trust for you. The only way to divide the estate equally into thirds is to inventory it and appraise everything of value. You will, of course, have first opportunity to purchase any of the personal items that I have placed in the trunk."

"May I look at them?"

"Of course," Bowditch checked his watch, "but remember Dr. Dixwell is to meet you at Harvard Square at one o'clock to take you to your father's grave."

Charley climbed the stairs two at a time and opened the door to his room. Everything seemed exactly as he had left it, except for the things on his bed. He flipped randomly through his collection of stereo-views—pictures of Yosemite, the smoldering ruins of the great Boston fire—Mother's photograph! He caught his breath and stared at the image, taken before she had returned to China. Father always kept it on the mantle in his office. Charley could feel her embrace. He heard her whisper "T'ien-sheng" as she had always done when she kissed him goodnight. He felt a wave of shame. Why had be been so impatient with her? He slipped the photo into his pocket. She should have received his letter by now. As always, he addressed it in care of Mr. Fearon. He pictured Mr. Fearon ringing the bell at Mother's gate. He tried to imagine how she would receive the news. He was glad that only a year ago Father was able to visit Mother in Shanghai.

"Charles!" Mr. Bowditch's voice echoed from below.

"Just a minute!" Charley opened the chest. Mother's bronze incense burner—someone had scrubbed it clean! He lifted out Father's silver tankard and tilted it to catch the light. Engraved on its side was the image of Father dressed as a Mandarin, shaking hands with a Hindu. Something rattled inside. Charley flipped back the lid and turned the tankard upside down. Father's gold watch slid into his hand, the links of chain clinking softly as they slipped through his fingers. He would ask Mr. Bowditch if he could take it with him today.

Charley rushed down the stairs. The open fireplace screen in the front parlor revealed a mound of ashes. A reddish tint caught his eye. Kneeling by the grate, he could distinguish the imprint of his mother's cinnabar seal at the edge of a charred page. So, her letters had been burned! Gently, he dragged Father's watch chain through the ashes. [3]

Mount Auburn Cemetery
Cambridge
1:30 pm

"Of course, that's just a temporary marker!" Dr. John Dixwell gestured toward the grave. "We're having a marker cut to match the others."

Charley stared at the wooden plaque with George Dixwell's name painted in black letters. The brown soil had sunk down in the spring rains, revealing the outline of the grave. Charley looked at the row of five headstones, thin square-ish slabs with gently arched tops.

John pointed down the row. "That's my uncle J.J.'s grave ... and my grandfather's— your grandfather's grave."

Next to Father's grave was a mound of fresh soil. Another grave? He looked at John questioningly.

"That's cousin Annie." John's voice cracked as he blinked back tears. He cleared his throat. "She was taken from us much too soon."

"Miss Annie? But she's in France!" Charley bent to read the marker: "Anna Parker Dixwell, 1847–1885."

"She died in Paris, about a week after your father."

Charley remembered when the cheery young woman had invited both of them to her studio. She had even kissed him, to his great embarrassment.

"We buried her yesterday, but it was just for family."

"Family?" asked Charley.

John started to say something but stopped. Charley understood. He wasn't really part of this family. They wanted Father all to themselves. They had seen to it that Father's obituary contained no mention of either Mother or him. Their Chinese blood was an embarrassment. With Father's death, that embarrassment was conveniently ended. They had no intention of sharing their ancestors with him.

Charley pulled Father's gold watch from his pocket. Mr. Bowditch would pay for it from his share of the estate. He wound the stem three full turns, held it to his ear, and listened to the same steady tick he always heard when Father hugged him. Charley felt his anger subside. Father wasn't here in this graveyard among these cold strangers. Mother was erecting his tablet on her altar in Shanghai. He could see her place three sticks of incense upright in a bronze censer. Little wisps of smoke curled upward past Father's portrait.

In the weeks following George's death, someone had sorted through his personal papers and destroyed every document linking the Dixwell family to Hu Ts'ai-shun and Charley—every document, that is, but the one beyond their reach: George's will. The evidence points to George's brother Epes, the senior surviving member of the Dixwell family. Charles Pickering Bowditch, George's executor, knew Epes Dixwell. He had prepared for Harvard at Epes's private school. It would seem natural for Bowditch to seek Epes's help in the disposition of George's papers. A further indication that Epes was responsible is that many letters written to George by his aunts Henrietta and Anna were preserved among Epes's papers.

Even as Epes Dixwell [or someone else] was wiping the record of George's life clean of any Chinese relations, Bowditch stepped into his role as Charley's legal guardian. It seems clear that before signing his will, George had secured private assurances that Bowditch would provide guidance to Charley as well as manage his inheritance. George's choice of guardian was inspired. Bowditch had an interest in the exotic; he was already undergoing a personal transformation that would bring him renown as a pioneer researcher in Mayan archaeology.

During Charley's final year at Westford, Bowditch saw to it that Charley had all the trappings of a young gentleman. In summer 1885, among Charley's first purchases were a horse, a saddle, and a buggy. As winter approached, he bought a sleigh.

In fall 1886, Charley moved from Westford to Boston, enrolled in Charles W. Stone's Classical School, and purchased a $300 violin. Charley's choices reflect an outgoing, self confident, sensitive young man. In 1888, he purchased two more items from his father's estate. The first was George's membership in the Boston Athenaeum. The second, perhaps more significant as a marker in Charley's search for identity, was a Mandarin scent box.

By 1888, billings for laboratory charges in addition to board, tuition, and music lessons suggest that Charley had begun preparing himself for a career in science or medicine. That summer, Charley booked a luxury rail tour across the United States with the Raymond Excursion Company. He enjoyed travel so much that the following summer, when he finished his studies at Stone's school, he planned a Grand Tour of Europe.

In July 1889, three months before his 21st birthday, Charley assumed his father's surname and became Charles Sargent Dixwell. In September of that year he boarded a steamer for England with 20 gold sovereigns in his pocket and an unlimited line of credit from Kidder Peabody and Company, a securities firm.

Although the Bowditches continued to manage Charley's accounts, their itemized record of his expenditures ended when he turned 21. Postmarks on the back of a forwarded envelope allow us to follow his travels from Paris to Rome to Cairo. A photo shows him in jodhpurs, posed with a tourist party beside elegant white tents with the towering minarets of a domed mosque looming in the background. A cabinet photo of a North African woman, bedecked in coin jewelry and smoking a cigarette, is signed "Fafaria Nov. 19, 1889, Biskia, Algeria."

Charley came back to Boston in June 1890. A little over a year later, in September 1891, he placed five cases of personal belongings, including a harp, into a Boston storage warehouse and returned to Europe as a student. Travel allows one to establish a new view of one's self, independent of one's past. Eight months as a gentleman touring Europe allowed Charley to see himself, not as a half-breed Chinese but, rather, as an exotic Eurasian.

I cannot trace Charley's movements during the next five years abroad; family lore has it that he studied medicine in Vienna. He almost certainly visited his mother in Shanghai.

The record of Charley resumes back in Boston on February 25, 1897, in the form of a passport application that gives his occupation as "student" and his birthplace as "Shanghai in the Chinese Empire." Three weeks later at age 29, Charley married Harriet "Hattie" Green Williams, a 39-year-old divorcee. Hattie was stunningly beautiful with red hair and fair skin, which she protected with a hat. She was also a talented pianist. Shortly after their marriage, Charley and Hattie moved to Paris where he resumed his studies, and together they embraced the salon society of American expatriates. A visit home to Massachusetts in spring 1901 was prolonged by the death of Hattie's mother. A letter of condolence from an artist friend, Henry Singleton Bisbing, suggests the character of Charley and Hattie's life in Paris.

> "I am writing this in the lightest possible attire in my studio, which went up to 89° today—hot *that* for Paris. The front of a café, and a cooling drink, is about the only thing now to do. The music at the Grand Café has improved. They've changed the orchestra, but somehow they can never fill my ideal until they invest in a base-drum [sic]. Nicol and all the 'boys' are round and hearty. We meet at Coleman's for dinner tomorrow night while the band plays 'there'll be a hot time etc.'"

In Boston, Charley found that the hatred of Chinese had reached a fever pitch. Congress was debating an even more stringent exclusion law, designed to make it more difficult for Chinese, even those claiming American citizenship, to re-enter the United States after traveling abroad. Charley and Hattie were planning a trip to China to visit his mother and his adopted brother, now 16 years old, and he wanted to avoid any problems with immigration officials when they returned. On December 5, 1901, when Charley renewed his passport, he changed his birthplace from Shanghai to "Nagasaki in the Empire of Japan." In explanation, he swore: "My father and mother were temporarily abroad at the time I was born, and subsequently returned to the United States to reside."

The next fall, cousin Fanny's husband, Wendell Holmes, took his seat as a Justice of the United States Supreme Court. In April 1904, while Charley and Hattie were still in China, Wendell, writing for the majority, held that Sing Tuck, who asserted he was an American citizen, could be denied re-entry into the United States by a summary procedure that virtually assured he would not be able to produce witnesses to swear to his U.S. citizenship. Charley's decision to amend his country of birth was wise. It had become much more than a mere embarrassment to be of Chinese birth. Holmes's opinion appeared so harshly shaped by racial prejudice that Justice Brewer, writing in dissent, remarked, "No such rule is enforced against Americans of Anglo-Saxon descent, and if this be a government of laws, and not of men, I do not think it should be enforced against American citizens of Chinese descent."

Charley continued in his effort to establish his new Japanese identity—an effort sufficiently successful that he was somehow able to solicit a formal invitation, dated November 7, 1904, from the Emperor and Empress of Japan to attend a chrysanthemum viewing party in the garden of Akasaka Palace.

After visiting Hu Ts'ai-shun in Shanghai, Charley and Hattie chose to live in the more racially tolerant atmosphere of Paris. Meanwhile, Ts'ai-shun had become a real estate entrepreneur. Charley corresponded regularly with her. The character of their relationship and her sense of humor is represented in a letter to Charley, probably dictated to a scribe, on March 8, 1906.

> My dear Charles,
>
> I have received a letter with three pieces of cards and a piece of handkerchief from both of you, and we were gladly receiving. You said about the rebuilding of the houses in the French Town. I have been told you all the things about it in my last letter … I got permission from Mr. Fearon on the month of May, from that time down to the end of last Sept. about four month and half for built them. Altogether built up twenty one houses cost about seven thousand four hundred taels, nearly three hundred fifty taels for each. The work was all finished last year without any trouble from the Municipal Government ... We are all well here, but only trouble is my feet. We said about the goose (Gandor) is old and strong as before.
> With love to both of you from all of us.
> Yours affectionate Mother
>
> *Hoo Ts'ai Shoon*
>
> [signed and then stamped with her seal]

On a visit home to the United States in 1906, Charley and Hattie decided to establish a foothold in New Bedford, Hattie's hometown. Charley joined the New Bedford Yacht Club and, two years later, purchased a large house on an acre of land. However, the charms of New Bedford paled beside those of Paris, and the house was rented out. Charley and Hattie maintained their primary residence in France as they continued to travel. Passenger ship records show them sailing first class from Cherbourg, France, to New York in 1909 and again in 1911. Rather than displace the tenant in their New Bedford house, Charley and Hattie kept a furnished apartment in the large residence of Dr. Frederick Ashley, a New Bedford dentist.

Charley may have finished his medical training, but he never practiced. Family lore suggests that he became a dealer in expensive jewels. Under the Bowditches' management, his trust account produced sufficient income for him and Hattie to spend most of their time in Paris, enjoying the pursuits of well-to-do expatriates. Charley bought fine jewelry for Hattie and collected netsukes—small, intricately carved ivory figurines used as fasteners for men's kimonos. Hattie collected silk fans. Charley joined literary societies and purchased collectors' editions of erotic art and literature. His personal bookplate—"Ex Libris CSD"—bore a drawing of a "printer's devil" with horns, pointed ears, and a tail, sitting atop a stack of books and reading a volume titled *Aretino*. The joke (sufficiently obscure to escape all but fellow insiders) referred to Pietro Aretino, who in 1516 wrote a mock "last will" for Pope Leo's recently deceased pet elephant in which the animal bequeathed his impressive genitals to a cardinal with a reputation for debauchery.

Late in 1913, with the prospect of war looming in Europe, Charley and Hattie (now middle-aged and childless) moved back to their New Bedford apartment in Dr. Ashley's house. They were still living there when on August 17, 1915, Charley received a telegram to come to China—his mother was dying. Hu Ts'ai-shun drafted and signed a new will on August 27 and died five days later. It was wartime, however, and the earliest steamer reservation Charley could secure from San Francisco to China was almost 5 months after receiving the telegram—January 8, 1916.

When Charley finally sailed for China, he was not accompanied by his wife Hattie but by Dorothy Elizabeth Ashley—Dr. Ashley's 18-year-old daughter. Their son, Basil, was conceived enroute. In order to avoid awkward explanations, Dorothy traveled using Harriet's name. The ship's register for their return voyage from Hong Kong to Victoria, British Columbia, listed Dorothy as "Harriet Dixwell, age twenty-two." The real Harriet, still living in New Bedford, was now 58. Charley returned to Boston with various keepsakes: photos of his mother's funeral cortege (which included over 20 carriages) and a photo of the "Dixwell Road" street sign, named after his father in the old American Concession.

Charley chose to remain with Dorothy, but he did not divorce Harriet. The official record of Basil's birth lists the parents as Edward J. and Elizabeth Dixon—fairly transparent aliases. Charley became a doting father. A 1917 photo, probably taken by Dorothy, shows Charley, sitting on the running board of their shiny new Studebaker roadster and holding up seven-month-old "Dixie" to "stand" on his unsteady legs. A second photo, probably taken by Charley, shows Dorothy balancing the little boy on the front fender.

Charley maintained a warm relationship with his adopted brother in Shanghai. This man was now the father of two young daughters, but his wife had died in the flu pandemic of 1918. Only one letter survives from this correspondence. It is dated 1919 and is from Charley's 12-year-old niece. In bold schoolgirl script she wrote:

My dear uncle,

I was very happy when I received your nice letter & generous gift. I wanted to write a letter to you always but my laziness overcame me ... My father wishes to write to you often but he can't because his body is unhealthy and always get a headache since the death of my mother. He will try to write you afterward.

I am studung at McTyier School. Preparatory second year now. If you like to know what kind of books I have studied. I will tell you as follow: Gramma, Peter Pan Story, Geography, Bible, Mandarine, Physiology, Arithmetic, Chinese and Chinese History ...

Your loving niece,   And my sister
Julia Vong Ying Woo   Helen Vong Tsue

That same year, Charley purchased a fashionable Dutch colonial style house for Dorothy in the village of Newton, a few miles outside of Boston. The 1920 Federal Census reports that Charley occupied rented rooms at a luxurious residential hotel in Boston, just down the hall from its owner, the retired songstress, Lotta Crabtree. Still mindful of anti-Chinese prejudice and with an eye on his son's future, Charley changed his birthplace for the third time and informed the census taker that he, Charley, and both of his parents had been born in Massachusetts.

By 1922, Charley gave up his hotel rooms and lived openly with Dorothy in Newton. When their daughter Eleanor was born that December, he felt comfortable giving her the Dixwell surname. Five months later, he drafted a will in which six-year-old Basil's surname was also given as Dixwell.

Charley and Dorothy lived quietly in Newton as their children grew up. In February 1930, they took a four-week vacation cruise to Barbados. When Dr. John Dixwell died the following year, Charley might have marveled at the irony that, after a lifetime of exclusion, he and his 14-year-old son were the only males remaining to carry on the Dixwell name.

Charles Sargent Dixwell died at home on July 15, 1934, from a carcinoma of the larynx, likely the result of a lifetime of smoking. Despite the fact that the United States was then in the depths of the Great Depression, his estate was appraised at $78,611.60. Most of this was still in the trust that his father had established in 1885. All contact with relatives in China ended with his death.

Although Charley seemed to accommodate the ambiguities of his mixed parentage and his unconventional relationship with Dorothy and Hattie, it was not so easy for his son. Hattie, his father's legal wife and widow, lived until 1939. The ever-present possibility of being revealed (as not only illegitimate but also as one-quarter Chinese) weighed heavily on the young man.

Almost six feet tall with brown hair and blue eyes, Basil Sargent Dixwell cut a dashing figure when he graduated from Newton High School in June 1935. He had already altered his stodgy first name to the more dashing "Bazil." His yearbook entry listed his nicknames as "Baz" and "Dixie." He completed the academic curriculum and was a member of the Aviation Club. His graduation wish was "to drive a Duesenberg [sic] at the Indianapolis Speedway Classic."

In 1939, Bazil married Barbara Southgate, a willowy blonde and former high school classmate. Pursuing his ambition to become an airplane pilot, he completed an Associate of Arts degree in Engineering at the Wentworth Institute and secured a job at Northeast Airlines. In August, he also received a "certificate of authority," which allowed him to take airway weather observations. He took his first solo flight in a Piper Cub in October 1940 and six months later received his Commercial Flight Certificate.

When the United States entered the Second World War, the U.S. Army contracted with commercial air carriers to haul cargo. In September 1942, Northeast Airlines assigned Bazil to the North Atlantic Wing of the Air Transport Command, authorizing him to fly the North Atlantic Ferry Route. Bazil's logbooks record repeated flights to Newfoundland, Greenland, Iceland, and Scotland. His personnel card states that in the event of his capture, he was "entitled to be treated as a lawful belligerent according to the law and usages of war."

By 1949, Bazil and Barbara had four daughters. In 1951, with the security provided by his salary as a senior pilot, Bazil was able to purchase a gentleman's farm in New Hampshire. He bred Angus cattle and eventually kept thoroughbred horses for his daughters to ride in dressage competitions.

Bazil was determined to protect his daughters from the stigma he had felt in his own youth. He rarely spoke about his father. His daughters heard about Ts'ai-shun only from their mother and Grandmother Dorothy. Harriet Williams Dixwell, Charley's first wife, was never mentioned.

On February 1, 1957, Bazil narrowly survived a deadly crash during take-off from La Guardia field in New York City, but he continued to enjoy his work and his leisure. Just as his own father had done, Bazil purchased a Studebaker sports car—an Avanti coupe—and he proudly joined the Avanti Owners Club. He remained a full-time pilot until he reached the federal age limit and retired on October 26, 1976, one day short of his 60th birthday. His only real regret was that since his own little boy had died a few months after birth in 1946, the Dixwell surname was fated to die.

Late in his life Bazil began to research his family origins. He asked Gus Loring (Charles P. Bowditch's son-in-law and successor at the Bowditch firm) for help in discovering what had become of his Chinese relatives. In this he was unsuccessful. He was able to locate J.J.'s granddaughter and Epes's great grandson with whom he exchanged letters. He began constructing a family genealogy that went all the way back to his first American ancestor, John Dixwell.

Even though Bazil had sufficiently overcome the embarrassment of Chinese ancestry to attempt to add that side of the family to his genealogy, he would never get over the shame of his illegitimate birth. It was too humiliating to reveal to anyone, and he resolved to bury that portion of his past and let it die along with him.

On January 2, 1991, he received a letter from an archaeologist in California who was researching the Dixwell family. Now 74 and legally blind, Bazil dictated a response to his wife Rosanna whom he had married after Barbara's death. I was that archaeologist, and my hands shook as I opened the letter—"<u>Personal!</u>" boldly scribed and underlined on the envelope. Bazil wanted to exchange information with me, but he was also frightened at what my work might uncover. His words were moving:

> "My father Charles Sargent Dixwell was not recognized by the families of John and Epes due to the fact that Charles' mother was a Chinese Princess of the Imperial Family, which makes a difficult subject no one wishes to discuss between any of the descendants (Chinese or English) ... My father Charles graduated from the University of Vienna Medical College, although he never practiced. He lived in Paris for 15 years or more and traveled around the world many times (spoke six languages). [He] collected jewels for Cartier. One stone he collected is in the English Royal Crown ... He spent much time in the desert with Lawrence of Arabia."

> "Please remember that I was 16 when my father passed away ... and we had not reached a point of good communication regarding family background. That is why I have bits and pieces. Please be aware this is an extremely sensitive subject! I have four married daughters who are not ready to receive my research, small as it may be—again, the Chinese background with all the stigma society and descendants place on it ..."

I continued corresponding with Bazil, mailing him transcriptions of George Dixwell's China trade letters. A year later, Bazil wrote:

> "I find your enclosures interesting and enlightening ... Regarding our exchange of information, I would like to point out that my sister and children and my children find this subject of the Dixwells most distasteful ... Because of their extreme distaste ... I was afraid you might want to contact them, which would break my heart ... therefore, not having reassurance from you I was hesitant."

I knew that Bazil was not leveling with me and that his real concern was not with the revelation of his Chinese ancestry but, rather, that (in my investigations of the Dixwells) I would discover or might reveal the unconventional circumstances of his birth. I respected his wish not to share that with me. I promised him I would not attempt to contact his daughters. I kept my promise, but still I hoped that one of them might someday contact me. Four years later, I received a letter from Stephanie Dixwell Quigley.

> "Dear Professor Layton,

It is with mixed emotions that I write this letter to you. I am the oldest of four daughters of Bazil S. Dixwell, who passed away February 10, 1995. It is only after his death that we have learned that you, through research, have found out certain information concerning our father's background. As a young girl, I remember my mother telling me about my great grandfather marrying a Chinese woman. My mother said the woman was a Chinese princess, but I do not think that was the case ... For whatever reason, my father, even though we asked, would not talk about his father or grandfather, and my mother is deceased ... I would like to know if you ever had the opportunity to talk to my father ..."

That long-awaited letter was like an answer to a prayer. This book is my answer to Stephanie's question.[5]

Charles Sargent was 17 years old, at the time of his father's death in 1885. Four years later, just before his 21st birthday, Charley assumed his father's surname and became Charles Sargent Dixwell, but he would never be acknowledged by the Dixwell family. (Courtesy of Marcia Dixwell DiMambro.)

Silver tankard presented to George Dixwell in 1844 by his business associates in Calcutta, India. Charles Sargent purchased this tankard from his father's estate in 1885. Apparently, attempting to retain some connection to his Chinese heritage, Charley also purchased a (now lost) "Mandarin scent box" from the estate. (Courtesy of Lauren Dixwell Rayfield.)

Detail on silver tankard, showing George Dixwell dressed as a Mandarin. (Courtesy of Lauren Dixwell Rayfield.)

Harriet "Hattie" Williams (1858–1939). She married Charles Sargent Dixwell in 1897, and they lived in Paris until World War I. (Courtesy of Marcia Dixwell DiMambro.)

Hu Ts'ai-shun, in Shanghai, China, ca. 1905. Charles and Hattie traveled to Shanghai several times to visit Ts'ai-shun. After George Dixwell's death, Ts'ai-shun adopted and raised a son, younger than Charley, who would remain with her in China. (Courtesy of Marcia Dixwell DiMambro.)

Shanghai march 8th 1906.

My dear Charles

I have received a letter with three pieces of cards and a piece of handkerchief from both of you and we are gladly receiving. you said about the rebuilding of the houses in the French Town. I have been told you all the things about it, in my last letter, on the last Nov. I suppose you have received or not. Now I write to tell you again about it. I got a permission from Mr. Fearon, on the month of May, from that time we began the work, until finished down to the end of last Sept. about four month and half for built them, Altogether built up twenty one houses cost about seven thousand four hundred taels, nearly three hundred fifty taels for each. The work was all finished last year and without any trouble with the Municipal Government.

I am gladly to tell the interest of the Gas Shares. On march 8th I received 371.25 Tls. from 75 shares and 257.88 Tls. on July 26th. So altogether I received 631.13 Tls. from the Gas Company, last year.

We are all well in here, but one trouble is my feet. we said about the goose (grandor) is old and strong as before.

With love to both of you from all of us.

Yours affectionate Mother

Hoo Tsai Shoon

1906 letter from Hu T'sai-shun in Shanghai to Charles Sargent Dixwell in Boston. Probably dictated to a scribe, the letter describes her construction of 21 houses. George Dixwell provided Hu Ts'ai-shun with sufficient wealth to allow her to become a successful entrepreneur in her own right. [Note: I use the modern transliteration of "Hu Ts'ai-shun" throughout this book, which is different from the "Hoo Tsai Shoon" used in the original documents.] (Courtesy Marcia Dixwell DiMambro.)

Charles Sargent Dixwell's personal bookplate featured a "printer's devil" with horns, pointed ears, and a tail, sitting atop a stack of books and reading a volume titled *Aretino*. As a wealthy expatriate, living in Paris, Charles enjoyed upscale café society. (Courtesy of Marcia Dixwell DiMambro.)

Charles Sargent Dixwell and his son, Basil "Dixie" Sargent Dixwell, with their Studebaker roadster, ca. 1917. Charles had separated from his wife Hattie and formed a lasting, unmarried relationship with Dorothy Ashley (1899–1982). They had two children, Basil (1916–1995), and Eleanor (1923–2001). (Courtesy of Marcia Dixwell DiMambro.)

Pilot credentials for Bazil S. Dixwell. By 1942 he was a pilot for Northeast Airlines, flying military cargo over the North Atlantic Ferry Route: Newfoundland, Greenland, Iceland and Scotland. He had grown up 100% American. As a Newton, Massachusetts, high school student, he changed his name from Basil to the more-flashy Bazil. His graduation wish was "to drive a Duesenberg at the Indianapolis Speedway." He took his first solo flight in 1940 and retired as a Northeast pilot in 1976. (Courtesy of Marcia Dixwell DiMambro.)

CHAPTER FOURTEEN

Epilogue

Mount Auburn Cemetery
2001, July 15

They are almost all here—the Dixwells, the Sargents, and the Bowditches—but I had put off visiting them at Mount Auburn Cemetery until I finished my research. Standing beside their graves would be the closest I would ever come to them physically, and I wanted the leisure to have a different kind of experience. I'm not religious or superstitious, but I hoped that by visiting their graves I might somehow bridge a century-and-a-quarter of time and perhaps receive an epiphany of understanding.

I oriented my map to the entrance gate and walked toward the massive statue occupying the fork in the road just ahead. Cast in bronze, Nathaniel Bowditch sat deep in thought atop his marble platform, a sextant and globe by his feet and a thick volume balanced on his knee.

Shortly after his death in 1838, a committee of Boston merchants had proposed a memorial for the man whose *Practical American Navigator* brought precision to the calculation of ship locations on the oceans of the world. The modest burial plot that Bowditch himself purchased for his family lay far back in the interior of the park—too obscure a site for a grand monument. Accordingly, the committee sought a better location, and in 1847 his statue was raised here at the foot of the hill, facing the main entrance gate. J. J. Dixwell, then a cemetery trustee, might well have stood at this very spot for the unveiling. He must have been immensely proud that he and Epes helped to achieve this most impressive homage to their father-in-law.

I could imagine Aunt Henrietta rolling her eyes at the Dixwell brothers' vanity and their need to validate their social position by attaching themselves to a Bowditch. They had reason to feel insecure. It was well known in Boston that their own father, who had been virtually anonymous as Samuel Hunt, MD, had publicly allied himself with his mother's more prestigious lineage. At the age of 28, to be sure to connect himself with the most prominent bearer of the name, Sam Hunt assumed not only her maiden name but also the Christian name of the original regicide—Col. John Dixwell—transforming himself into Dr. John Dixwell.

One hundred and ten paces brought me to the plot that aunts Catharine and Henrietta purchased in which to bury their parents, their siblings, and themselves. Tall marble slabs, each with a matching gothic arch, glistened in the harsh afternoon light. I could barely make out the lettering on Henrietta's stone. Oriented toward the north, it had felt the full brunt of one century-and-a-quarter of winter storms as well as the more recent ravages of acid rain. It seemed that nature somehow conspired with her own family, which had always found her politics an embarrassment, to efface her from history. I hoped that my book would give to her the recognition she deserves as a social reformer.

I hoped, too, to receive some sort of message from her. I closed my eyes and waited for her to speak. I heard the distant roar of an airplane, the closer rumble of traffic, and, closer still, birds chirping in the bushes, but Henrietta remained silent.

I stood there a moment longer, then looked back at my map. Fifty-five paces brought me to the shade of "*Ailanthus* Path." A small sign nailed to the trunk of the tree to my right identified it as a linden. As I turned to admire the manicured woodland, I noticed similar signs on each of the large trees. I recalled that way back in 1831, Mount Auburn had been conceived not as a graveyard but as a memorial park and arboretum—the first one in America—where lineages carved in stone could be visited in a garden setting.

There behind the linden tree, I spied the Dixwells, all in a row. It disturbed me that I wouldn't find Charley among them. In his will, he requested burial at Mount Auburn. His ashes lingered in storage here for three years until Ingersoll Bowditch had them removed to Forest Hills Cemetery about 10 miles to the south. Years later, Charley's son, Bazil, had them moved once again to the family plot he purchased in Exeter, New Hampshire.

I stared at the grave of Dr. John Dixwell, Charley's grandfather. A swath of oak leaves, symbolizing strength, was cut into the side and top of his marker. Beside him lay his wife, Esther. A flourish of carved ivy clung to her stone, just as a faithful wife should cling to her husband. J.J.'s stone bore a sheaf of ripened wheat, representing a full life. George's stone was decorated only with a generic wreath. Next to George, Annie's stone bore a bouquet of roses as a reminder of the briefness of life.

I paused to sketch a plan of the graves and record their inscriptions. I was not finding anything to enhance my story. Then, as I walked back along the headstones, I noticed that J.J.'s stone had a second motif carved up its other edge. Somehow, I had missed it. I knelt to identify the flowers and was shocked to see the bulbous seed capsules in their midst. Every botanical motif used on 19th-century gravestones had a symbolic meaning, and I had read that the opium poppy was sometimes used in a headstone decoration to represent the peaceful sleep from which one would awaken in the afterlife. It was a rarely used motif and one that would not be casually chosen by a sophisticated Boston family whose fortune had come from the sale of opium in China. J.J., tongue-in-cheek, must have specifically requested it!

Suddenly the cemetery seemed to come to life. I remembered a long-ago Berkeley High School production of Thornton Wilder's, *Our Town*. The last act of that play opens on a sparsely furnished stage on which all of the deceased characters from the first act engage in lively conversation amongst themselves. Now J.J. sat before me on his tombstone, debonair in a Panama hat, and acknowledged his headstone joke with a wink. George, a pencil in his hand, seemed to be editing a manuscript. Henrietta stood to the side amongst her sisters. I knew it still troubled her that her beloved Aunt Murray had not been buried here but lay far away in Mississippi.

I watched Henrietta take a peppermint from her reticule and hand it to a little boy. It was Charley! If only that could have happened in real life, how different this story might have been. [1]

John J. Dixwell's headstone with its opium poppy motif, Mount Auburn Memorial Park, Cambridge, Massachusetts. (Photo by author, 2001.)

This story has come to an end. I have pushed my research beyond the traditional limits of archaeological reporting. In my book, *The Voyage of the Frolic*, I wrote that we archaeologists must deal far more creatively with our data if we are to return it to the public in a meaningful form. I wrote this book as a challenge to myself as well as to archaeological convention and have, I hope, achieved a deeper understanding of the past.

Acknowledgments

I wrote this book to press the envelope of archaeological reporting—so much so, it turned out, that no academic press would touch it! At the same time, my attempt to hold close to documented facts undercut its potential as an historical novel. Thus, after eight years of writing, it sat on my desk for nine more years—a manuscript without a genre.

In 2019, I mentioned the predicament of my manuscript to Dr. Rebecca Allen, who was working the Society for Historical Archaeology book table at an archaeology conference. Rebecca said that she and Dr. Annalies Corbin were investigating ways for the society to reach a broader public and offered to take a look at the manuscript.

I thank Rebecca, Annalies, and the board of the Society for Historical Archaeology for daring to consider a book that so dramatically pushes the envelope of archaeological convention.

From the very beginning, Ruhama Veltfort, my writing coach, read and edited my prose, vignette by vignette, as she did for my two previous books, all now comprising the "*Frolic* Trilogy." Dr. Rebecca Allen helped me reorganize this text into the present narrative and shepherded it through production. Marianne Brokaw streamlined the text in her copyedit; Molly Perdue restored the cover photograph; Robert Bain took the author photo; and Knic Pfost created the unique design of the finished product.

This book spans over 200 years and reveals a story that ranges from Boston to Bombay; from Canton, China, to New Almaden, California; and from Macau to Davenport, Iowa. In order to write it, I have sought help from many specialists. I thank Bonnie Hurd Smith and the Rev. Gordon J. Gibson for information on Judith Sargent Murray; Dr. Carolyn L. Karcher, Dr. Debra Gold Hansen, and Dr. Jennifer Rycenga for help with women's history; the Rev. Carl T. Smith, Dr. R. Gary Teidemann, and Eric Politzer for information on Eurasians; Dr. H. A. Crosby Forbes, Dr. Jacques M. Downs, Dr. William R. Sargent, Dr. Patrick Connor, Dr. Robert M. Gray, and Dr. Paul A. Van Dyke for help with China Trade facts, images, and personalities; Dr. Raleigh

Ferrell, Dr. Stephen Kwan, and Terese Tse Bartholomew for help with the Chinese language; Dr. Annapurna Pandey, Dr. James M. Freeman, and Kathleen Zaretsky for help with Hindi; Dr. Adrian Praetzellis for help with English dialect; Dr. James Delgado, Dr. Annalies Corbin, Robert Schwemmer, John Foster, Daniel Foster, Dr. Sheli O. Smith, Samuel F. Manning, Mark Rawitsch, Daniel Taylor and Richard Everett for archaeological and historical advice; Dr. Shuo Wang, Dr. Linda Cooke Johnson, and Dr. Raleigh Ferrell for information on Manchu palace service; Salvatore Falcone and Stephen Tai for information on Spanish coinage and Chinese shroffage; Dr. Charles Beeker for information on iron conservation; Dr. Christine W. Laidlaw for information on Fanny Dixwell Holmes's embroideries; Edith Corinne Smith for help in researching Dixwell descendants; Dr. Timothy R. Mahoney for help with Iowa history; Marilyn Day for information on Westford, Massachusetts; and Janet Heywood for help with tombstone iconography and the history of burial plots at Mt. Auburn Cemetery.

None of these colleagues are to blame for the ways in which I have used their information.

Curators at several archives have guided me to important documents. I thank Laura Linnard, Timothy Mahoney, Timothy Driscoll, and Elise Thal Calvi for help with the Heard Collection at the Baker Library of Harvard Business School; Dr. Conrad E. Wright and Hannah Elder at the Massachusetts Historical Society for help with the Wigglesworth Collection; Dr. William W. Sargent, Karina Corrigan, Leslie J. Laufer, Clark Worswick, and Claire Blechman at the Peabody-Essex Museum; Anne Cooper and Karen McGrath at the Kelley House Museum; Debra Kaufman at the California Historical Society; Maria Quinonez at the Hoover Library, Stanford; Amy Groskopf at the Public Library of Davenport, Iowa; Stephen Hall of the Beverly Historical Society; and Maureen Melton of the Boston Museum of Fine Arts.

The descendants of several China trade families mentioned in this book have provided essential information. For the Dixwells, these include Bazil S. Dixwell, Stephanie Dixwell Quigley, Marcia Dixwell DiMambro, Lauren Dixwell Rayfield, Leslie Dixwell, Eleanor Dixwell Morrison, Douglas Dixwell Morrison, Bruce Morrison, Epes Dixwell Chase, Caroline Dixwell Cabot, Mason Bowditch Cabot, Anne Van Rensselaer, Natalie MacLachlan, and Dr. Douglas "Mac" MacLachlan.

For information on George Tyson and his Eurasian descendants, I thank Wilfred Tyson of Hong Kong. Daniel Fearon of London provided information on the Shanghai Fearons. Susan Briggs of Alameda, California, the direct descendant of William C. Hunter through his Eurasian daughter, Anna Rosa, provided important information on the Hunters, the Gardners, and the Endicotts.

Fifteen California wreck divers donated significant parts of their collections from the *Frolic* shipwreck to the *Frolic* Repository at the Mendocino County Museum in Willits, California. They include David Buller, Steven Buller, Cliff Craft, Louie Fratis, Patrick Gibson, Dale Hartesveldt, James Kennon, Vilho Kosonen, Vic LaFountaine, Bruce Lanham, Robert Lanham, Rick Lanham, Patrick Philpott, Larry Pierson, Dr. Kenneth Prewitt and Dr. Paul Selchau.

For computer help, I thank Jean Shiota, the faculty lab coordinator at the Center for Faculty Development and Support at San Jose State University.

Finally, for her steadfast encouragement and support, I thank my partner, Mabel Teruko Miyasaki.

Figure Captions

91   George Basil Dixwell (1814–1885), ca. 1847.

92   The South and East Asia opium trade.

94   The Canton Factories before the 1841 fire, ca. 1840.

96   Cargo items included brass trunk handles in graduated sizes from nested China-export leather-covered camphor trunks.

96   Canton Pattern bowl. The *Frolic* cargo included at least one "Blue China" dinner set.

97   Chinese tinderboxes.

98   Coarse glass beads, the most abundant cargo item preserved at the *Frolic* wreck site, were so-called "false pearls," used for jewelry or as ornaments (lower left bead diameter: 7.4 mm).

99   Mother-of-pearl wafer (2.8 cm. horizontal length).

121   Personal items recovered from the *Frolic* included Captain Faucon's sextant.

122   Leather shoe, recovered embedded in a concretion together with a cannon-ready charge of grapeshot (iron pellets packed around a wooden spindle in a cloth bag).

122   Prismatic deck light (length of fragment 13 cm) recovered from the *Frolic*.

123   *Frolic's* lift model (half-model).

124   Loading opium aboard the *Frolic*, Bombay, India, 1845.

125   The *Frolic* under sail.

140   The fall 1994 *Frolic* shipwreck exhibit at the Kelley House Museum in Mendocino, California, featured a half-size model of the brig *Frolic* sinking into the lawn.

140   One of the cannons recovered from the *Frolic* shipwreck rusting on the lawn of the Kelley House Museum in 1994.

141   The author and Linda Noel, who wrote and acted the part of the Pomo elder in *Voices from the Frolic and Beyond*.

142   Bazil Sargent Dixwell's four daughters.

143   Epes Sargent Dixwell's house at 58 Garden Street, Cambridge, Massachusetts.

163   The *Frolic* carried 676 rolls of stacked stoneware bowls decorated in six distinct patterns that had been popular in Mexican California prior to the 1849 Gold Rush.

Endnotes

1

~~~~~~~~~~~~~~~~~~~~~~~~~

MHS, N-114 = Massachusetts Historical Society, Wigglesworth Collection.

1.1 Cassara 1961:12.

1.2 Linden-Ward [1989]:134.

1.3 Cassara 1961:5; Robinson 1985:34–36. These fine works by Cassara and Robinson clearly describe the evolution of Universalism and Unitarianism and the doctrinal issues that both defined and sustained them as separate entities.

1.4 What we overheard, broadcast from Christ Church (Episcopal), was the "Presentation and Examination of the Candidates for Holy Baptism" from *The Book of Common Prayer* 2007:301–302.

1.5 Robinson 1985:5,215.

1.6 Our story begins with Dr. John Dixwell (née Samuel Hunt, Jr.) and his wife, Esther Sargent Dixwell, attending a tea hosted by Esther's mother, Dorcas Sargent, for John's stepmother, Mrs. Elizabeth Hunt, to meet Esther and John's infant son, Johnny Dixwell, later to be known as "J.J." Esther's sisters, Henrietta Sargent (age 21) and Catharine Sargent (age 35) live at home and assisted their mother with the tea.

Samuel Hunt, Jr.'s, petition to change his name to John Dixwell had been granted March 16, 1805 (reported in the *New England Palladium* 14 May 1805:1); (Secretary of the Commonwealth of Massachusetts 1805:13). Three months later, John married Esther in a ceremony performed by her "uncle," the Rev. John Murray.

Young Hunt had several reasons to change his name. First, with his mother's (Mary Dixwell) marriage to Samuel Hunt, Sr., in 1774, the Dixwell surname became extinct in America. When Mary died, on 4 Dec. 1783, her obituary stated: "She was the only branch of the family [of John] Dixwell, one of the Judges who passed sentence upon King Charles I and who retired to New England upon the restoration" (*Salem Gazette* 1 Jan. 1784:3). Samuel Hunt, Jr.'s, name change resurrected the Dixwell surname and also helped position him, as John Dixwell, to lay claim to the Dixwell estates in England.

Although the estates of the English Dixwells may have been on Samuel Hunt, Jr.'s, mind, a more pressing reason to change his name was the scandal attached to his father. Following Mary Dixwell Hunt's death, Samuel Hunt, Sr., became infatuated with Elizabeth Gibbes Shepherd, a young widow from South Carolina who was boarding with one of Hunt's relatives. Rumors were published that "greatly injured the moral character of Mr. Hunt ... and the Selectmen advised him to clear himself or quit the position of headmaster at Boston Latin School" (Williams 1990:264). Hunt married Elizabeth and retained his job, but the salacious story had sullied his name. In 1805, Samuel, Hunt, Sr., was still forced to resign his position at Boston Latin School because "his usefulness had become impaired" (Wigglesworth 1907:19).

Young Sam was further embarrassed to bear his father's name because the virulent, pro-slavery views of his stepmother, now Elizabeth Gibbes Hunt, were offensive to Epes Sargent, Jr., whose daughter Esther he hoped to marry. Years later, Henrietta Sargent, Esther's younger sister, recounted an incident illustrating Elizabeth Hunt's racist views to Lydia Maria Child who published the anecdote in her *Authentic Anecdotes of American Slavery*. Since I have based this vignette on Child's (1835) version of Henrietta's anecdote, I quote it as follows:

> "The moral influence [of slavery] ...was strikingly exemplified in a conversation that took place at the house of a Boston lady, intimately known by the writer. Miss G*****, of South Carolina had been invited to meet several ladies at the house referred to. The conversation turned on that never failing topic, the difficulty of procuring good domestics. One of the guests remarked,

> 'You are not troubled with these kind of difficulties at the south, Miss G.; but I think you should find it very unpleasant to be surrounded by so many negroes.'

> 'Not at all unpleasant,' replied the southern lady, 'I have always been accustomed to blacks, and I really like them to attend upon me. I assure you that many of them are very far from being disagreeable in their personal appearance. I had a young slave, who was, without exception, the prettiest creature I ever saw. She used to tend table for us, and almost always attracted the attention of visitors. A gentleman, who was often at our house, became dreadfully in love with her, and tried to make her accept handsome presents.

> 'One day she came to me, and asked me to speak to that gentleman, and forbid his saying anything more to her; for he troubled her very much about it; and I did so, telling him that his attentions were very unpleasant to my slave, and begged him to refrain from offering them in the future. For a few weeks he desisted; but at the end of that time, he came to me and said, "Miss G., I must have that girl! I cannot live without her!" He offered me a very high price. I pitied the poor fellow, and I sold her to him.'

> "Miss G. ... told the story with perfect unconsciousness that there was anything disgusting or shocking, or even wrong, in one woman's trafficking away another. Miss G. would have been horror-struck at the idea of selling into prostitution even the poorest or most degraded white woman."

Henrietta and Catharine Sargent's "aunt," Judith Sargent Murray, lived in a magnificent Tontine Crescent townhouse, designed by Charles Bulfinch (see Bonnie Hurd Smith 2005, illus. 12,13). Aunt Murray was, in actuality, their second cousin and first cousin to their father, Epes Sargent, Jr. I have Henrietta and Catharine address Judith as "auntie" because she was of their father's generation. Epes and Judith were such close friends and

1 confidants that in 1799 Judith designated her cousin Epes to raise and educate her daughter, Julia Maria, as a member of his family in the event of her death (Smith 2005:376–377). For a detailed biographical sketch of Judith Sargent Murray and a chronology of her life, see Smith 2005:309–403; see also Skemp 1998.

Epes Sargent, Jr.'s, daughters spent long vacations with Aunt Murray and were very fond of her, and the feeling was evidently mutual. Epes wrote in a letter to Judith (Epes Sargent, Hampstead, to Judith Sargent Murray, Boston, 20 March 1797, MHS, N-114, Box 1):

When you speak of my children, I sometimes am apt to conclude you see them with a poets eye, and write with a poets pen, but when they write of you, they tell me you perform all you say ... The time the girls have so delightfully passed with you has been mark'd to joy and will be [set] down I am persuaded in the Annals of their lives, some of their whitest hours, but life was not intended by its Author to be a uniform holiday; we have therefore intimated to them our wishes to return this day fortnight which will be the 3d of April ... your affectionate friend and

Cousin Epes Sargent

Epes Sargent had been an early convert to the Universalist creed as preached by Judith's second husband, the Rev. John Murray. The fundamental tenet of this creed was universal salvation, essentially bypassing judgment. As John Murray described it in a letter to Epes Sargent (John Murray, Boston, to Epes Sargent, Hampstead, 20 Aug. 1799, MHS, N-114, Box 1):

"Death, I cannot be afraid of. I am persuaded our Savior has abolished death, and left nothing remaining for us to pass thro' but the shadow of death, yet even this shadow is frightful. I stare at it, and am frequently afraid of dying tho' not of Death—and so, I fear I shall, till it comes—and then it will be gone—blessed are they who have left these fears behind them ..."

Judith Sargent Stevens Murray had been a professional writer since the early 1780s. In 1784 as Judith Sargent Stevens and using the pen name "Constantia," she published her first public work, "Desultory Thoughts upon the Utility of Encouraging a Degree of Self-Complacency, Especially in Female Bosoms." As early as 1798 Judith published *The Gleaner*, a three-volume compendium of her works. At the time of this vignette, Judith's play, *The African*, was in rehearsal for performance at the Federal Street Theatre. Unfortunately, the script of the play is lost.

Judith's 19-year-old nephew, Lucius Manlius Sargent, had already amassed a record of cruel, intemperate behavior (Sargent and Sargent 1923:194–196), before he derided *The Gleaner* in the *Columbian Centinel* and then tore out the pages of the volumes and strew them on Judith's doorstep (Smith 2005:384). An anonymous poem defending Judith, signed "Honora," appeared in the *Centinel* (27 Aug. 1806:2).

In 1850, Henrietta wrote a brief history of the Sargent family for her nephew, Epes Sargent Dixwell (Esther Dixwell's second son). She described her father's life, her siblings, their ties to the Rev. John and Judith Sargent Murray, and their moves from Gloucester to Hampstead, to Haverhill, and finally to Boston: "to us Boston seemed like the promised land to the Israelites." She described her younger brother, Epes Sargent, Jr.—his clerkship in the store of Col. T. H. Perkins, his dispatch to Canton, his return to Boston, and his early death from the "consumption" he contracted in China.

We can see from Henrietta's family history that she absorbed her unwavering anti-slavery stance directly from her father. She describes his horror at the invitation of Judith's brother, Winthrop Sargent (governor of the Mississippi Territory) in which he had suggested that Epes Sargent should move there "to become a planter, and represented to him certain wealth, and power, inseparably to be found in that mode of life, but your grandfather was a republican in deed as well as in word, and he was still greater, a Christian, and he rejected the proposal of investing his property in slaves, with unfeigned horror" (Henrietta Sargent, Boston, to Epes Sargent Dixwell, Cambridge, 7 Apr. 1850, MHS, N-114, Box 4).

1.7 This vignette takes place about the time that Judith's *Life of Rev. John Murray* (1816) was going to press. As Epes Sargent was Judith's closest intellectual companion, I have imagined that he and Henrietta helped to proof the galleys. The details of Samuel Hunt, Sr.'s, departure for Kentucky are taken directly from his grandson Epes Sargent Dixwell's description:

"I remember one summer morn'g going to the extreme south end of

Boston to see his departure. The old man was quite un-nerved at the sight of his two grandsons. He took our hands, gazed at us with tears in his eyes, said nothing and mounted his vehicle where sat the remainder of his family, and they drove off with their own horses and I never saw him again. He arrived at Lexington that autumn, was soon after taken suddenly raving and died in a few hours. The strain was too great upon his nerves."

Samuel Hunt died on 8 Oct. 1816 (*The Western Monitor* 11 Oct. 1816). Epes Sargent Dixwell noted that since "there was not a cordial feeling" between the Dixwells and Samuel Hunt's second wife, "there was little subsequent contact between the families." Further, "they were rank rebels in the Civil War, especially those in So. Carolina" (Wigglesworth 1907:12–13). Samuel and Elizabeth Gibbes Hunt had six children, five of whom lived to adulthood. One of them, William Hassel Hunt (1800–1841), later enters our story as the pro-slavery editor of the *Nashville Banner*.

1.8 On 16 Aug. 1818, Judith Sargent Murray was probably packing to accompany her daughter Julia Maria and granddaughter Charlotte Bingaman to Natchez, Mississippi. Judith's final letter from Boston is dated 14 Aug. 1818. What little is known about Judith's departure is summarized by Smith 2005:400–403.

Judith explained her refusal to attend services at the Bennet Street Universalist meetinghouse in an 23 April 1815 letter to [the redundantly-named] Rev. John Sylvester John Gardiner (Smith 2007:190):

1

"I cannot enter the house where I have been accustomed to unite with those of the persuasion of my adoption, without the intrusion of reflections painful in the extreme. When my eye is fixed upon the pulpit of my afflicted husband, the comparison of the present situation with what was in the days of other times, obtrudes upon my sorrowing mind, originating regrets almost too potent to be endured—Feelings of this nature it would, however, be my duty to surmount, had it not unfortunately happened, that the person officiating in our church, varies essentially from more than one of the fundamental principles in the faith which I have embraced; and I cannot believe it consistent, to sanction by my presence, in the congregation of Universalists, sentiments which my reason, and my conviction disdain, and thus am I, almost necessarily, precipitated upon the practice, of forsaking the assembling with those who ostensibly collect for the worship of Deity—."

Charlotte Bingaman was a precocious reader. On 23 March 1818, when she was four years, nine months old, Judith wrote: "Our little Charlotte can read any English book ... Taking up the News Paper she calls out 'Grandmamma do you want to buy any superfine flour? Here is some to be sold'" (Smith 2005:401). On 15 Aug. 1818, the *Columbian Centinel* advertised "Two hundred and twenty bbls, superfine flour" (p. 4); reported the South Carolina Legislature's act forbidding Africans to "assemble for mental instruction" and the penalties for teaching them to read or write (p. 1); and described "73 Virginia-born Negro slaves being smuggled for sale in New Orleans" (p. 2).

The John Singleton Copley portrait of Judith (ca. 1772–74) was left with relatives in Boston. The Gilbert Stuart portrait of Julia Maria (ca. 1805) was taken to Mississippi and retained by Bingaman descendants. Both portraits are reproduced in Sargent and Sargent 1923:50,54. Judith bound several of her letter books in bright wallpaper covers, probably left over from papering her Boston townhouse (Bonnie Hurd Smith, pers. comm.). She took 20 letter books with her to Natchez, where Rev. Gordon Gibson discovered them in 1984. See Gibson's introduction in Smith (2005:5–7).

Judith would have been fully aware that Natchez, Mississippi, was a major slave market. "The 'Forks of the Road' mart handled the largest volume of business in Natchez, but slave auctions were also held in other places around town ... Moreover, numerous slave transactions were negotiated at the landing, as attested by traveler Henry Fearon, who saw fourteen flatboats loaded with Negroes for sale there in 1817" (Clayton 1993:197). Judith may have read Henry Fearon's (1818:267–268) description of the Natchez slave market before her departure. We can only imagine her despair upon actually seeing it.

1.9 I have imagined Henrietta and Catharine's carriage ride to deliver food to a needy widow in the African-American community near Belknap Street. Henrietta's benefactions to "poor widows" and "destitute children" were described 50 years later in her obituary by Lydia Maria Child ("Another Friend Gone," *The National Standard* 28 Jan. 1871). Referring to Henrietta and Catharine,

Child wrote, "Few knew, and none can estimate the amount of good noiselessly performed by those excellent women. Their fingers were always busy making articles for Anti-Slavery Fairs, or converting piles of yarn and cloth into clothing for destitute children. Every Saturday, joints of meat and baskets of vegetables went to poor widows in the neighborhood." In Catharine's obituary (*Liberator* 1 Oct. 1852), William Lloyd Garrison wrote of her

"charities actively exercised, in behalf of the poor, the outcast, and the oppressed, without regard to color or race ... As the coffin containing her remains was carried out of the house, to be conveyed to Mount Auburn, a colored friend who was in attendance exclaimed aloud, with touching pathos, 'There goes one of the best friends I have found in the world'—and his eye moistened as he paid the grateful tribute. He related to us some of the many cases of distress which the deceased had alleviated through her charities, entrusted to his care, and by him faithfully applied."

The filling of the Mill Pond is described in Krieger and Cobb (1999:120) and is documented in their reproductions of Boston city maps of 1814 and 1826 (1999:191,193). See also the reproduction of Charles Bulfinch's 1808 map with his proposed street layout (Krieger and Cobb 1999:120). The progression of filling along the Shawmut Peninsula from 1630 through 1996, documenting the evolution of modern Boston, is illustrated by Krieger and Cobb in 8 computer-generated maps (1999:16–19).

Although the African Americans living in the Belknap neighborhood on the backside of Beacon Hill had established strong community institutions, some white Bostonians referred to their district as "Mount Whoredom." Whitehill and Kennedy (2000:70–71) quote an 1817 report to the Boston Female Society for Missionary Purposes.

" ... from this sink of sin, the seeds of corruption are carried into every part of town ... Five and twenty or thirty shops are opened on the Lord's days from morning to evening and ardent spirits are retailed without restraint, while hundreds are intoxicated and spend the holy sabbath in frolicking and gambling, in fighting and blaspheming; and in many scenes of iniquity and debauchery too dreadful to be named ... Here in one compact section of town, it is confidently affirmed and fully believed, that there are *three hundred* females wholly devoid of shame and modesty ... Multitudes of colored people, by these examples, are influenced into habits of indolence."

Various moves of Epes Sargent's family, including their residence in the Belknap neighborhood, are described by Henrietta in her "Recollections of Sargent Family History" (MHS, N-114, Box 4, 12 July 1858). Henrietta's friend, the Rev. Samuel Snowden (ca. 1765–1850), was one of several African American ministers active in the Belknap neighborhood. Born a slave in Maryland, nothing is known of his early life. At the time of this vignette, he was living on Belknap Street ("People of Colour," *Boston City Directory* 1820). Not long before this vignette, Snowden participated in the

1 "anniversary of the commencement of measures for the Abolition of the Slave Trade. Religious services were attended at the African Meeting House, in Belknap Street. The prayer was made by one of the black clergymen, Mr. Samuel Snowden" (*Manufacturers' and Farmers' Journal*, 17 July 1820 [1]57:2).

Henrietta probably began her study of herbalism while living in the Belknap neighborhood. By the 1850s she had become well known among family and friends for her concoctions.

On 29 January 1855, both David Lee Child and Lydia Maria Child sent letters to Henrietta acknowledging the efficacy of the remedies she had sent to David, who stated (David Lee Child to Henrietta Sargent, 29 Jan. 1855, in Holland and Meltzer 1979):

"I cannot sufficiently thank you for your great kindness in preparing and sending the homeopathic medicines. They have acted like a charm not only on the principal malady, but also on some other disorders, which have afflicted me, more or less, for a long time, so that I now feel as if I should be brought back in tune again. This is something, which a few weeks back, I did not look for in this world."

Henrietta's remedy of horseradish leaves wet with rum for David Child's rheumatism is mentioned in Lydia Maria Child's 2 Aug. 1858, letter to Henrietta Sargent (Holland and Meltzer 1979).

The Union College commencement orations of 26 July 1820, included "Equality of Talent Between the Sexes" (*Columbian Centinel* 2 Aug. 1820:2). Judith Sargent Murray's brother, Winthrop Sargent, the first governor of the Mississippi Territory, died 30 June 1820 (*New York American* 10 July 1820 [3]:3). Epes Sargent Dixwell took first prize for his "translation of Virgil's Pollio" at the Boston Latin School competition (*Columbian Centinel* 2 Aug. 1820:2). Second prize went to Edward Horatio Faucon, who would later become captain of the brig *Frolic* owned by George Dixwell and Augustine Heard & Co. At the time of this vignette, Dr. Dixwell's eldest son, John James, was training in the counting house of Thomas Wigglesworth on India Wharf.

The American Dixwells' claim on the English Dixwells' estates is a recurrent theme in Dixwell family history. On 31 May 1820, Dr. John Dixwell drafted a letter of "Instructions to James A. Dickson, in England, to make inquiries on the Dixwell estates." He explained (Dr. John Dixwell, Boston, to James A. Dickson, Esq., 31 May 1820, MHS, N-114, Box 1):

"The last named John Dixwell was my maternal Grand Father, and I have reasons to think should have been put in possession of Sir Basil Dixwell's estates. I have been informed Sir Basil left no children, and that the previous conditions of the will have not been complied with. If this claim in virtue of the said will is not valid, the Heirs of Col. John Dixwell had an equitable claim against the estate of Sir Basil for [the] property of the said Col. John Dixwell. My Grand Father John Dixwell left two children, a son & a Daughter, and one son was born after his death. The sons died young and my mother was the only child who lived to maturity, and I being the eldest Son have been authorized ["induced" is crossed out] to take the name of my Maternal Grand Father, in the hope of transmitting his name to posterity. I was born in the year 1777 previously to Great Britain having acknowledged the independence of the United States. I should, therefore, think by the laws of that kingdom that I might be considered entitled to the rights of a British subject and to inherit the estates of my ancestors unless some act of limitation has cut me off from that privilege."

1.10 I have imagined this vignette on the day Judith's death was reported in Boston (*New England Palladium*, Young & Minns, publishers, 4 Aug. 1820[3]:1):

"Died: At the residence of Mr. Bingaman, in Natchez, on the 6th ult, after a severe illness of seven days, Mrs. Judith Sargent Murray, relict of the late Rev. John Murray, of Boston. She was a lady of dignified and polished manners—of an excellent education, extensive erudition, and great literary application—and the public have read in periodicals and other publications many productions of her pen."

[Note that her death was published on 4 August, so "6th ult" or *ultimo mense* refers to an occurrence on the previous month or, in this case, July 6. "Relict" or *relictus* refers usually to the survivor of a marriage.]

1.11 By the time of this vignette **1** (1820), Epes Sargent had researched and written his story of Wangfo. The few details that survive from this story come to us via Henrietta Sargent's 13 May 1862 letter presenting the document to Epes Sargent Dixwell (MHS, N-114, Box 5, 13 May 1862). I have been unable to find a Chinese antecedent for the Epes Sargent story. It is possible that it was his invention. Marguerite Yourcenar's story, "How Wang-Fo was Saved" (1985:3–20, originally published in 1938) seems to be unrelated. Epes Sargent's manuscript is lost; however, since we return to his story of Wangfo later in this book, I present Henrietta's letter to her nephew, Epes Sargent Dixwell, verbatim:

Boston
May 13th 1862

Dear   Nephew!   [Epes   Sargent Dixwell]

I send you herewith your grandfather's Port Folio which I promised you, not even withdrawing some pieces of my own composery which pleased him. I have added Mr. Boylston's Medal, which my father valued exceedingly. I have slightly classified the extracts; as they were entirely without arrangement, the only papers he left that were not in perfect order. These extracts will answer the question, how did he pass his time at the Athenaeum?— they are a transcript of his mind. You see in them the Christian and the scholar. The story of Wangfo is an allegory—the literal meaning you will sympathize with. Wangfo symbolizes your Grandfather—the porcelain vases were his six daughters—the Eaglewood—the wakeful care—the exhausted resources—the trials and disappointments, the recrossing the river, with his vases, his wife, and his little boy—all run parallel with his own history—you too have vases of exquisite workmanship requiring nurture and care, you too have, like Wangfo, a tender Wife to share your watchful cares & you too have a little Boy. The paper on which the story was written was chosen for being <u>Chinese</u>, conformable with the story.

I trust by placing this treasure in your hand, you will appreciate it and take care of it.

very affectionately

your Aunt Henrietta

MHS, N-114 = Massachusetts Historical Society, Wigglesworth Collection.

2.1 Summer 1835 was a dreadful one for Lydia Maria Child. In early May, as she was trying to complete her *History of the Condition of Women* (1835), the Boston Athenaeum Board, offended by her *An Appeal in Favor of That Class of Americans Called Africans* (1833), withdrew her gratis borrowing privileges—then refused her request for a paid membership after her friends raised the money. On May 14, Maria returned the books she had borrowed. Then, unable to pay the rent on their South Boston cottage, "Paradis des Pauvres," Maria and her husband were forced to move. They sold their furniture and household goods at auction on August 6 (Karcher 1994:220–221,669,note 28).

We know Maria visited Henrietta at 5 Poplar Street, just before departing for New York, because she left several trunks there. Six months later, Maria wrote to Ellis Gray Loring: "I wish that you would pay for removing the trunks from Poplar St—also for a woman to repack one of them, according to the directions I sent to Henrietta" (Meltzer and Holland 1982:45). Maria was still in Boston on Aug. 11 when she wrote a thank-you note to the ladies of Lynn and Salem for the inscribed gold watch they gave her on Aug. 8. The inscription on the watch and Maria's note are published in *The Liberator* (29 Aug. 1835 [137]:3). I have imagined this vignette at Henrietta's house on the day Maria brought her trunks there.

Although Maria and David Child accepted George Thompson's offer to become anti-slavery agents in England, their departure from New York was delayed by David's arrest, and they were forced to eventually cancel the trip entirely. "God grant a fair breeze, that I may soon be wafted out of sight of this wicked city. I hope we shall sail tomorrow; but we may not; for Mr. Child has been arrested here at the suit of George Snelling, who is not content with leaving the whole burden of the Journal debts to his partner" (Lydia Maria Child, New York City, to Louisa Loring, Boston, Aug. 15, 1835, in Meltzer and Holland 1982:32). Snelling had been David's partner in publishing the *Massachusetts Journal and Tribune*, an anti-slavery newspaper that failed. Snelling eventually won a $9,750 settlement against David (Clifford 1992:127; Karcher 1995:213,242).

In fall 1836, David Child, on his quest to produce slave-free sugar, traveled to Europe to research the sugar beet industry (Meltzer and Holland 1982:53–54).

During the seven years since they first met, Maria had become Henrietta's closest friend and confidante. Twenty-nine years later, Maria recalled their long friendship in a letter to Henrietta (Lydia Maria Child, Wayland, to Henrietta Sargent, Boston, Feb. 11, 1864, in Meltzer and Holland 1982:437–438):

"How long ago it seems since I first went to your cosy little parlor in Poplar St. and was introduced to Dr. Howe, then a handsome, romantic-looking young man just returned from Greece with Byron's helmet! How many pleasant hours I afterwards spent with you and dear good Catherine! How she cared for me, and nursed me up, and made me comfortable! What lively chats we had together in the old days, when

2

the little band of abolitionists were a sort of apostolic church, fervent and united!"

Dr. Samuel Gridley Howe returned to Boston from Greece on Feb. 25, 1828 (Schwartz 1956:26). Henrietta was a friend of his family.

Henrietta and Maria's friendship was characterized by warmth and humor. Anne Warren Weston described visiting Maria at Henrietta's house (Anne Warren Weston to Debora Weston, Oct. 22, 1836, Boston Public Library, Ms. A.9.2.8, p. 63):

"Mrs. Child was agreeable & Henrietta more cunning than ever. Henrietta said to me, 'The other day Mrs. Child and I were talking about prejudice and Mrs. C said she had got over it very much. I told her I was got along farther than she, for I thought that I should like to have Father Snowden make the prayer at my funeral, and then I couldn't help laughing to think how my relatives would act. They would come into the room looking pretty sober & then they would look so, when they saw Father Snowden get up, all confounded, & then I'd look down & laugh.' So much for Henrietta."

In 1833, John James ("J.J.") Dixwell, then supercargo of the brig *Tuscany*, carried 180 tons of Massachusetts ice to Calcutta and returned with "one hundred male monkeys of the light faced species" (Fairburn 1945–1955:571–572; Layton 1997:194–195). J.J.'s ice cargo is described in the story of the Parsi who wondered what sort of tree the ice had grown on, and another customer who wanted his money back when the ice melted (Morison

1961:282). Augustine Heard's typhoon passage in the *Emerald* over the Hoogly sand bar is told by Waters (1916:28–29) and repeated by Morison (1961:89–90).

Maria Child had good reason for omitting an appeal for women's rights from her *History of the Condition of Women*. She desperately needed the income from sales of the volume and did not want to offend a large portion of the book-buying public. According to Carolyn Karcher (Maria's major biographer), Maria deliberately "confined herself to description and eschewed theory and polemic"—so much so that the resulting book is filled with "pregnant silences." Karcher argues that "The need to preserve her marriage at all costs complicated Child's responses to what came to be called 'the woman question' ...," making it impossible for her to "take the leadership role that her radical sisters expected of her in championing their right to equal partnership with men. Instead, she imposed uncharacteristic restrictions on herself, first as an anti-slavery activist and later as an analyst of the female condition" (Karcher 1994:220,215). Henrietta, with far less to lose, could afford to be more radical than Maria.

Although no correspondence survives in which Henrietta discusses Aunt Murray's feminist writings with Maria, there is compelling circumstantial evidence that Henrietta was the conduit. Not only did Henrietta have the writings of both Murrays in her possession (inherited from her father), but she had also made herself an expert on them. For example, she was sufficiently familiar with the details of Aunt Murray's three-volume compilation of John Murray's sermons (Murray 1812–1813) that she was able to answer a theological query from a Miss Howe with the specificity of a professor. "Give me leave my dear Miss Howe to direct your attention to Mr. Murray's view of the last supper, which you will find in the first vol of his works 233d page. If you do not own it I have it quite at your service" (Henrietta Sargent to Miss Howe, June 1827, MHS, N-114, Box 25, Epes Sargent Album 1820–1830).

I surmise that Henrietta loaned Judith Sargent Murray's writings to Maria, just as she had offered to loan Rev. Murray's to Miss Howe. Maria's borrowings are easily recognized. In volume three of *The Gleaner* Judith included her "Observations on Female Abilities" (first published in 1790), and in three subsequent essays expanded her argument, presenting a list of historical examples where women performed competently in roles that were usually reserved for men in late-18th-century Anglo-America. Murray organized her discussion by presenting 10 numbered "evidences" of women's achievements, which demonstrated that women were "in every respect equal to men" (Murray 1798 [1992], *The Gleaner* sections 88–91:702–731 [see page 711 for Murray's list of evidences]). Maria borrowed Murray's "evidences" to help conceptualize and structure her own *History of the Condition of Women*.

Although Maria took her title and many historical examples from William Alexander's *The History of Women* (1779), half of Murray's "evidences" appeared almost verbatim in her "Contents" (actually an alphabetical listing of topics by page number). In Maria's hands the fourth item on Murray's list—"They are equally brave"—became "Female bravery." Murray's "Fortitude & heroism" and "Patriotism" became "Military spirit in women." Murray's "capable of supporting, with honor, the toils of government"—became

"Offices held by women," and Murray's "literary achievement" became "Learned women." Maria incorporated Murray's other "evidences" into less specific sections of her book.

Henrietta would have been painfully aware that, after borrowing Aunt Murray's writings illustrating that women were the equals of men, Maria had stopped short of advocating their equal treatment before the law.

Of course, Judith Sargent Murray's ideas were not all her own. They too had antecedents. As Albert Rabil, Jr., (1996:xviii–xix) points out, from the 14th to 17th centuries there had been a "literary explosion" of works "enumerating the achievements of women," perhaps totaling as many as "several thousand titles." Clearly Murray had read some of this literature and was a product of that tradition. Murray freely acknowledged earlier scholars, mentioning the names of specific authors such as Mary Astell. Indeed, in Murray's text, we can directly trace her articulation to that tradition back to a specific work of the late-16th century. As Murray wrote in *The Gleaner* (1798 [1992]710), "Many centuries have revolved since the era, when writers of eminence, giving a catalogue of celebrated women, have made the number to amount to eight hundred and forty-five." Here, Murray referred to the exact number of women catalogued by Pietro Paolo de Ribera in the late-16th century (Rabil 1996:xix). It is unlikely that Murray actually read de Ribera; however, she clearly had read a published work containing information derived from that writer.

Judith Sargent Murray's (1790) title *On the Equality of the Sexes* also has a long prior history. It appears as early as 1676 in François Poullain de La Barre's, *De l'égalité des deux sexes* (Maclean 1988). Murray probably read either the English translation, published in 1677 (*The Woman as Good as the Man* or *The Equality of Both Sexes*), or some derivative publication.

Karcher (1994:221–224) documents Child's borrowings from William Alexander. These are recognized today in part because Child, in the fashion of that time, drew attention to them by deliberately incorporating part of Alexander's title into hers. The character of Child's borrowing from Alexander's text may be seen by comparing their discussions of Spartan women. Alexander (1779 [1]:71) wrote that "... they amused themselves with the masculine exercises of wrestling, throwing darts, &c. But this is not all: they were obliged to appear naked at some of their solemn feasts and sacrifices, and to dance and sing, while the young men stood in a circle around them." Child (1835 [1]:31) barely disguised Alexander's sentences: "Lycurgus ordered that maidens should exercise themselves with running, wrestling, throwing quoits, and casting darts, with the view of making them healthy and vigorous; and for fear they might have too much fastidiousness and refinement, he ordered them to appear on these occasions without clothing. All the magistrates and young men assembled to witness their performances, a part of which were composed of dances and songs."

In expanding her discussion of Spartan women, Child then presented a barely disguised example borrowed from Judith Sargent Murray. Murray wrote (1798:706), "... so highly did they prize the warrior's meed [reward] that they are said to have shed tears of joy over the bleeding bodies of their wounded sons!" Child (1835 [2]:33) wrote, "... those who received an account that their children were slain in battle, went to the temples to offer thanksgivings, and congratulated each other with every demonstration of joy."

It would be unfair to hold Child to modern standards of citation for her sources and ideas, although Murray was always concerned with proper attribution of her ideas and the ideas of women writers in general. Indeed, she discussed this very issue in *The Gleaner* (1798:805):

> "Rousseau has said that a female may ostensibly wield the pen, yet it is certain some man of letters sits behind the curtain to guide its movements ... A celebrated writer of the present century observes that 'a woman ought never to suffer a man to add a single word to her writings; if she does, the man she consults, let him be whom he may, will always pass for the original inventor, while she will be accused of putting her name on the works of others;' and surely the feelings of rectitude must revolt even at a suspicion of this kind."

Murray (perhaps anticipating the [1792] publication of Mary Wollstonecraft's book) had been careful to document that her "On the Equality of the Sexes" had been in manuscript since 1779 (Murray 1790:132). In *The Gleaner* (1798:727) Murray generously credited Wollstonecraft for "brilliancy of genius and literary attainments."

2.2 Maria knew that Henrietta would find her *History of the Condition of Woman* to be inadequate, and this appears to be the reason she requested that an inscribed copy be sent to

Catharine and, by implication (as I interpret it), not to Henrietta. "Remember me with my whole heart to good Henrietta & her sister. When the *History of Women* comes out, I want a copy sent to Catharine Sargent, from her affectionate friend L.M.C." (Lydia Maria Child, New York, to Louisa Loring, Boston, Aug. 15, 1835, in Meltzer and Holland 1982:32–33).

Maria's "half a pair of scissors" comment is taken from an 1839 letter explaining her ambivalence about female organizations (Lydia Maria Child, Northampton, to Lucretia Mott, March 5, 1839, Meltzer and Holland, 1982:106–107):

"I never have entered very earnestly into the plan of female conventions and societies. They always seemed to me like half a pair of scissors. This feeling led me to throw cold water on the project of the Boston Female Anti-Slavery Society ... This opinion has been confirmed by the two conventions already held. For the freedom of women, they have probably done something; but in every other point of view, I think their influence has been very slight."

The Narrative of Amos Dresser (1836), describing his flogging in Nashville in August 1835, was first published in the *Cincinnati Gazette* and then widely reprinted. Henrietta Sargent would have read it in *The Liberator* (26 Sept. 1835 [156]:2). Amos Dresser identified W. Hasell Hunt [Dr. John Dixwell's half-brother] as a member of the "Vigilance Committee" and described his participation in the outrage:

"... Mr. Hunt, Editor of the [Nashville] *Banner*, and as I am informed an emigrant from New England,

where he was born, set himself busily at work to secure in his own hands, my journal, sketch book, business and private letters, &c. By no one concerned in the whole proceeding was there so much exasperated feeling shown, as by Mr. H. It was now displayed in the pale death-like countenance, the agitated frame, the hurried furious air with which he seized the papers and tied them up in his handkerchief clenching them in his hands, and at the same time eyeing me with an intense yet vacant gaze, bespeaking not only rage, but a consciousness of doing wrong. Of my papers I have heard nothing since Mr. H. took them into his custody."

The Dixwells were not the only ones to be embarrassed by Maria's publication of this story. Lydia Maria Child wrote to Angelina Grimké, Dec. 26, 1838, responding to Angelina's concern that the "Miss G." from South Carolina might be confused with her and her sister Sarah. "You were a little disturbed lest the G. and the stars [asterisks] should be thought to indicate your name. The person was Miss Gibbes of South Carolina, I *think* of Charleston. She told the story in Henrietta Sargent's parlor in Poplar Street" (Barnes and Dumond 1965:730–731).

The topic of Miss Gibbes remained a sensitive one for Henrietta. Eleven years later, in 1852, when Harriet Beecher Stowe began working on a sequel to *Uncle Tom's Cabin*, a query was relayed to Maria Child via Ellis Gray Loring asking about that anecdote. Maria replied (Lydia Maria Child, West Newton, to Ellis Gray Loring, Dec. 16, 1852, in Holland and Meltzer 1979):

"The lady was a Miss Gibbs, I think, and she made the observation to Henrietta Sargent. I think it will be better to *speak* to Henrietta about it, than to write; and I will endeavor to do so, at Christmas time. I think she will be shy of having it quoted by Mrs. Stowe. She will be afraid of being called upon as authority for a story about *indelicate* matters. You know her virgin propriety is excessive."

The mobbing of the Boston Female Anti-Slavery Society on October 14, 1835, is told in Garrison's own words from original documents excerpted by his sons. These include the "Wanted" placard for Thompson, Garrison's "if any of you are women in disguise ...," and Mayor Lyman's words with the women (Garrison & Garrison 1885 [2]:4–15; see also *The Liberator* 7 Nov. 1835:178–179).

2.3 The Boston Female Anti-Slavery Society's 1837 petition drive to abolish slavery in Washington, DC, and prevent the annexation of Texas as slave territory, was announced in *The Liberator* (16 June 1837 [98]:4).

"Let every woman into whose hands this page falls INSTANTLY (for the work must be done before the extra September session) prepare four rolls of paper, and attach one of each of the annexed forms of petition; and with pen and ink-horn in hand, and armed with affectionate, but unconquerable determination, go from door to store 'among her own people' ... "

A week later, the society published a notice: "Members of the Committee on Ward and County petitions, appointed by the Boston Female Anti-Slavery Society, are requested to call *immediately* for blank forms ..." (*The Liberator* 23 June 1837 [103]:6).

Henrietta's attempt to convince Mr. Edgerton to sign the petition is fiction; however, the conversation is borrowed from sample dialogues printed in *The Liberator* (7 Jan. and 23 Jun. 1832).

Horace Walpole described Mary Wollstonecraft as a "hyena in petticoats" in a much-quoted 1795 letter (Walpole 1905 [15]:337–338, letter to Hannah Moore, Jan. 24, 1795).

Although the Reverend William Ellery Channing condemned slavery in his 1835 book (*Slavery* 1969), he also criticized anti-slavery activists such as William Lloyd Garrison for advocating immediate emancipation (Karcher 1994:203).

Maria revealed her reluctance to attend the 1837 Convention of American Women in a letter to Henrietta. "My Dear Henrietta, Do you think, and does Mrs. Chapman think, I do wrong in not going to the Convention? ... If so, tell me frankly. I have various misgivings. My reluctance to go is great, and it may blind my perception to duty. Besides I am in a vacillating and discouraged state of mind" (Lydia Maria Child, South Natick, to Henrietta Sargent, Boston, April 17, 1837, in Meltzer and Holland 1982:67–68). Although Henrietta's response is lost, her encouragement clearly convinced Maria to attend.

The Anti-Slavery Convention of American Women met May 9–12, 1837, in New York City. Their proceedings were published in *The Liberator* (16 June 1837:98). Angelina Grimké presented the most controversial resolution of the conference, which included the provocative sentence, " ... the time has come for woman to move into that sphere which Providence has assigned her, and no longer remain satisfied in the circumscribed limits with which corrupt custom and perverted scripture have encircled her ..."

2.4 The Boston Female Anti-Slavery Society scheduled an address by "The Misses Grimké, from South Carolina" at 3:00 pm on Monday June 19, 1837, at the Methodist Church on Church Street (*The Liberator* 16 June 1837 [99]:6). I have framed this vignette at Henrietta's house two hours before that address.

The description of George's "Hindoo" comes from a March 22, 1837 letter from Jane Wigglesworth in Boston to her sister, Mrs. Harry W. Fuller, in Maine (MHS, N-114, Box 2).

"Mr. Dixwell came in and brought some beautiful color engravings of scenes in India, and also brought his Hindoo servant who had come with him last fall. He brought him to this country because his brother, George had been taking a good deal of pains to acquire the Hindoo language when in Calcutta and wished to continue the study of it by conversation with a native. He will return to India this spring with George Dixwell."

The letter went on to describe the Indian's scarlet turban, orange colored mantle, and loose trousers.

The passenger list of the ship *India*, from Calcutta, records the Sept. 2, 1836, arrival at Boston of John J. Dixwell (age 30), Merchant, and George B. Dixwell (age 22), Clerk, accompanied by "Armen Khidmatghai" (age 25), of "Hindoostan" (Boston Passenger Lists, 1820–1943, Ancestry.com). This young "Hindoo" from Calcutta was almost certainly from a Parsi mercantile family. Parsis, of Persian Zoroastrian, origin were preeminent in commerce, education, and public works throughout the British Raj.

In India, surnames generally did not exist prior to British occupation but were required when dealing with British administration. The given name of George's servant/tutor is an anglicized rendition of the Persian-Arabic name "Aman" (peace), a name used by both Muslims and non-Muslims in modern India. *Khidmat* is also an Arabic via-Persian word, meaning servant. It is uncertain whether Khidmatghai was an established surname or simply the title of Armen's temporary occupation, used expressly for his visit to the United States (U.S. immigration authorities would not admit anyone without a family name).

Armen's Parsi identity would explain the ease with which he was able to accompany George on the long sea voyage to Boston. Parsis do not observe the strictures of the Hindu caste system, have no religious restrictions regarding food (as do both Hindus and Muslims), and are free to travel and associate with other races.

The major languages spoken in Calcutta at this time were the local Bengali and the closely related lingua franca, Hindustani. To British administrators and military officers of George's day, the informal Hindustani of the marketplace was the language of administration and communication. Some degree of fluency in Romanized colloquial "Hindoostani" was a requirement for service anywhere in India. Presumably this was the language

2

in which George addressed the Lascars [Indians] in Canton in 1842 (Layton 1997:36–37).

George assembled an impressive library of monographs on South Asian linguistics to assist him in learning the closely related Hindi and Bengali languages. In 1852, George and John J. Dixwell donated 15 of these monographs to the American Oriental Society, where they were individually listed in the *Journal of the American Oriental Society* (vol. 3, May 1852–March 1853:iv–v).

The *New York Advertiser* satirized the Convention of American Women as "an Amazonian farce," attended by "women who left their pots and frying pans to discuss weighty matters of state—'oratresses' ... [breathing] eloquence from their sweeter lips" (quoted in *The Liberator*, 2 June 1837:90 and by Karcher 1994: 245, note 102).

Between July 11 and October 20, 1837, Sarah Grimké wrote and published 15 individually numbered and titled open letters addressed to "Mary S. Parker, President of the Boston Female Anti-Slavery Society." In choosing an overall title for her series—*On the Equality of the Sexes and the Condition of Women* (1838)—Sarah paid homage to her literary predecessors, combining Judith Sargent Murray's 1790 title *On the Equality of the Sexes* with Lydia Maria Child's (1835) *History of the Condition of Women*. Sarah not only borrowed Judith's title, but some of her content, too.

Henrietta apparently first met Sarah Grimké at the Convention of American Women in New York City (May 9–12, 1837), and it was probably there that, upon learning of Sarah's passionate commitment to the "woman question," she and Maria told Sarah about Judith's writings. Two months later, on July 11,

1837, Sarah completed the first letter of her proposed series (*The Original Equality of Woman*) in which she concurred with Judith's concern about mistranslations of the Bible as well as with her reinterpretation of Adam and Eve's behavior in the Garden of Eden.

Regarding Biblical translation, Judith wrote in her *On the Equality of the Sexes* (Murray 1790:224–25):

"Some ignoramuses have absurdly enough informed us, that the beauteous fair of paradise, was seduced from her obedience, by a malignant demon, *in the guise of a baleful serpent*; but we who are better informed, know that the fallen spirit presented himself to her view, *a shining angel still*; for thus, saith the criticks in the Hebrew tongue, ought the word to be rendered."

Sarah expressed the very same idea, albeit a bit differently (Grimké 1838:4):

"I believe almost everything that has been written on this subject, has been the result of a misconception of the simple truths revealed in the Scriptures, in consequence of the false translation of many passages of the Holy Writ. My mind is entirely delivered from the superstitious reverence which is attached to the English version of the Bible. King James's translators certainly were not inspired. I therefore claim the original as my standard, believing that to have been inspired ..."

Of Eve's behavior in the Garden of Eden, Judith wrote (Sargent 1790:224–225): "Let us examine her motive. Hark!

the seraph declares that she shall attain a perfection of knowledge ... It does not appear that she was governed by any one sensual appetite; but merely by a desire of adorning her mind." Adam, in contrast,

"... could not plead the same deception ... What mighty cause impelled him to sacrifice 'myriads of beings yet unborn' by his unpious act? He was influenced by no other motive than a bare pusillanimous attachment to a woman! Thus it would seem, that all the arts of the grand deceiver ... were requisite to mislead our general mother, while the father of mankind forfeited his own, and relinquished the happiness of posterity, merely in compliance with the blandishments of a female."

Sarah likewise also reinterpreted the story of Adam, Eve and the serpent, but where Judith placed most of the blame on Adam, Sarah gave Eve an equal share of the responsibility for the fall (Grimké 1838:6–7):

"Here the woman was exposed to temptation from a being with whom she was unacquainted. She had been accustomed to associate with her beloved partner, and to hold communion with God and with angels, but of satanic intelligence she was in all probability entirely ignorant. Next, we find Adam involved in the same sin, not through the instrumentality of a supernatural agent, but through that of his equal ... Had Adam gently reproved his wife and endeavored to lead her to repentance instead of sharing her guilt, I should be much more ready to accord to man that

superiority which he claims; but as the facts stand disclosed by the sacred historian, it appears to me to say the least, there was as much weakness exhibited by Adam as by Eve. They both fell from innocence, and consequently from happiness, *but not from equality*."

Henrietta appears to have worked closely with both Grimké sisters during the summer of 1837, not only providing Sarah with Judith Sargent Murray's writings but also planning with Angelina to schedule a woman's conference in Boston to deal openly with the "woman question." As Sarah was writing her 10th letter (*The Intellect of Woman*), Henrietta and Angelina presented their proposal at the Aug. 4, 1837, meeting of the Boston Female Anti-Slavery Society. As Angelina described it (Angelina Grimké to Jane Smith, Aug. 26, 1837, in Ceplair 1989:286):

"Sister and I feel quite ready for the discussion of women, but our brothers Whittier & Weld entreat us to leave it alone for the present ... We know *our* views on this subject are quite new to the mass of the people of this State & think it best to throw them open for their consideration, just letting them have both sides of the argument to look at, at the same time. Indeed some of us wanted to have a meeting in Boston for us to speak on this particular subject *now*, & we went to town on the 4th day [Wednesday] on purpose to hold a conference about it at Maria Chapman's. Mary Parker, M C & S M G were against it *until* we came back in the fall, fearing that it would bring

2

down such a storm upon our heads that we could not work in the country, & so H Sargent & myself yielded, & I expect this is the wisest plan, tho' as brother Stanton says, I am ready for the battle NOW … The rights of the slave & woman blend like the colors of the rainbow."

MHS, N-114 = Massachusetts Historical Society, Wigglesworth Collection.

3.1 Henrietta Sargent's account of her trip to the anti-slavery convention on Nantucket Island appeared in the *National Anti-Slavery Standard*, August 26, 1841. While the railroad portion of the trip, from Boston to New Bedford, is my best-guess reconstruction, the remainder of this vignette follows Henrietta's written account. Henrietta described her reasons for traveling to the "luminous isle," the condition of "the colored people in New Bedford," and the confrontation with the captain of the steamer, as well as the hastily organized meeting on the upper deck, the presence of a New Orleans slaveholder, and the Reverend Dr. Robbins's pro-slavery speech. She reported on the meetings on Nantucket and Frederick Douglass's first public address. Henrietta's conversations with her sister Catharine are of course invented, but I have used words and phrases from Henrietta's writings where possible. For example, the conversation with Catharine about the temperance meetings is based on Henrietta's references to them in her description of the convention and Douglass's address:

> "Temperance meetings were held at Nantucket at the same time abolitionists were lecturing; and we indulged the hope that, as they had the testimony of reformed drunkards to sustain their glorious cause, so might we have some repentant slaveholder, or powerful slave to testify 'that which they themselves did know.' The morning of the 12th

instant fulfilled our hopes. One, recently from the house of bondage, spoke with great power. Flinty hearts were pierced, and cold ones melted by his eloquence. Our best pleaders for the slave held their breath for fear of interrupting him."

Henrietta's "Welcome Home" article reporting on the celebration of the Phillips' and the Chapmans' return from their travels, and the evening soirée for David Ruggles appeared in the *National Anti-Slavery Standard* (12 Aug. 1841). A Sept. 3, 1841, letter by Oliver Johnson to Maria Weston Chapman (Karcher 1994:278) describes the "half-and-half-milk-and-water" criticism of the *Standard*.

The "✗" configuration of the railroad tracks across the morass of the Back Bay receiving basin is documented and illustrated by Whitehill and Kennedy (2000:99,101). For a discussion of the history of the filling and the consequent sanitation problem, see Krieger and Cobb (1999:121–22,198–99).

Debra Hansen (1993) describes the political struggle leading to the dissolution of the Boston Female Anti-Slavery Society. Maria Weston Chapman in *The Liberator* (Extra Ed., 24 April 1840) describes the organization's demise and resurrection. Catharine Sargent's affidavit that she voted against dissolution and that her vote wasn't counted is published in this Extra Edition:

> "I the undersigned, am one of the earliest members of the Boston Female Anti-Slavery Society. My name is on the list of the Recording Secretary, and also on the copied list of Miss L. M. Ball. I answered in the negative, and Miss Ball responded

3

'no' after me, and *appeared* to check the list. My name is *not*, however, checked on the list, but is left without a mark, like those members who were absent. Catharine Sargent."

The *New York American* first published "The most recent news from China" (current through April 10, 1841), carried aboard the ship *Akbar* (109 days out of Canton), which was then immediately republished in the *Boston Daily Atlas* (6 Aug. 1841:2). The article described the evacuation of Canton, the Emperor's order to exterminate the English, and the deployment of 13 British men-of-war in the river both above and below Canton.

Alexander Starbuck (1969:337,597–582) describes the architecture of the Nantucket Athenaeum, its earlier life as a Universalist meetinghouse, and the bottle containing a lock of John Murray's hair.

Historian Jacques M. Downs (Layton 1997:92) first explained to me the international trade system linking American cotton, British-controlled Indian opium, and Chinese tea in which the Augustine Heard firm participated.

Henrietta's Aug. 29, 1841, cautionary letter to George Basil Dixwell, then enroute to China, is a long one and covers many topics. I have excerpted the passages presented here (MHS, N-114, Box 3).

3.2 Joseph Coolidge was forced out of Russell & Co. in 1839. Anticipating that eventuality, he secured prior permission from Augustine Heard to start a new firm bearing Heard's name. Coolidge announced the formation of Augustine Heard & Co. on Jan. 1, 1840. The exclusion of English merchants from the Canton trade provided the new firm

with a large business, representing Jardine, Matheson & Co. Downs (1997:190–198) and Layton (1997:27–40) summarize the formation of the Heard firm and its early years.

On May 18, 1841, Augustine Heard, accompanied by John Heard and Joseph Roberts, sailed from Boston for China aboard the *Mary Ellen*. They arrived at Macao, Sept. 8, 1841, after a voyage of 113 days (*Canton Register*). A month after Heard's departure, George Dixwell sailed aboard the *Coromando* (*Boston Transcript* 22 June 1841). He arrived at Macao Nov. 6, 1841, after a voyage of 140 days (*Canton Register* 9 Nov. 1841). His tenure as partner in Augustine Heard & Co. commenced on Nov. 15, 1841 (*Canton Press* 4 Dec. 1841).

I do not know the details of George's trip from Macao to Whampoa and Canton. The only documented passage from Macao to Whampoa during this period was that of the British ship *Masden*, consigned to Dent & Co., departing Macao after Nov. 6 and arriving at Whampoa before Nov. 13. Such a trip took at least two full days. For the purposes of this vignette, I surmise that George was a passenger aboard the *Masden*, Nov. 7–8, 1841. The *Masden* sailed for Chusan on Nov. 19, 1841 (*Canton Register* 23 Nov. 1841 [292]:1). Mr. Ferguson is my invention—an older merchant who can discuss the Opium War and its effect on foreign commerce.

For the names of British colonial regiments dispatched to Chusan, see, for example: "Synopsis of Events in China During the Year 1841," (*Canton Press* 1 Jan. 1842, Suppl. no. 14), wherein the entry for August 21, 1841, lists "The Bengal Volunteers," "Madras Artillery and Engineers," and the "Cameroonians."

On May 21, 1841, the Chinese launched a sneak attack on three British warships anchored just upstream from Canton—releasing a flotilla of fireboats "chained two by two, and filled with raw cotton soaked in oil." That day, the Chinese authorities captured Joseph Coolidge as he tried to escape from the Heard factory. A Chinese mob then pillaged and wrecked the factory. The British took their time to respond to the attack. They placed heavy artillery atop a hill overlooking the city and staged troops for an attack. On May 28, seeing their situation hopeless, Cantonese authorities raised a white flag of surrender. By evening they were delivering the first boxes of silver to pay the 6-million-dollar reparation demanded by the British (Fay 1976:289–299).

At the time of George's arrival in Macao, J. M. Gallery's *Dictionary on a Phonetic System of the Chinese Language; in Chinese, Latin and French*, in 2 vol., was for sale at the *Canton Register* office for $10. The *Register* reported, "This work contains 25,000 different characters and can be made use of as a method to learn the Chinese Characters, as well as a dictionary" (*Canton Register* 16 Nov. 1841 [1]:3).

3.3 The account of George's trip from Whampoa to Canton by "dollar boat" is taken directly from Osmond Tiffany's detailed description of his own trip in September 1844 (Tiffany 1849:21–25).

In 1839, when word reached India that the Chinese had acted to end the opium trade, the market collapsed. Jardine, Matheson & Co. already employed a delivery fleet of 12 vessels and began to develop a delivery business along the seacoast north of Canton, which was not patrolled. Jardine's Singapore agent quietly bought up much of the 1839 crop of

Malwa opium from Bombay brokers for only $200 per chest. They sold most of it in China for $800 per chest. The firm used some of the proceeds to purchase 10 more delivery vessels between 1840 and 1842 (Layton 1997:38).

Of the 17 British ships George saw anchored at Whampoa, 7 were consigned to Joseph Coolidge of Augustine Heard & Co. (*Canton Press* 6 Nov. 1841, Suppl. no. 6).

A Note on Pidgin

The conversation between Ferguson and the steersman of the "dollar boat" would have been in China pidgin (business)—the simplified jargon in which Westerners and Chinese conducted business. China pidgin developed following the Portuguese settlement of Macao in the mid-16th century. Since the Portuguese commercial world included India, this pidgin originally comprised words taken from Portuguese, Chinese, and the Indian languages spoken near Portuguese settlements on the west coast of India. The resulting trade language was already well developed by the mid-18th century when the British began active trade with China. By the mid-19th century, English vocabulary was the predominant ingredient of the China pidgin spoken by the British and Americans at Canton. For general discussions of China pidgin, see Hunter (1966:26–39) and Spence (1996:8). For a Pidgin-English vocabulary, see Leland (1904:119–136).

Replication of pidgin in dialog must be undertaken with care because in the late-19th and early-20th centuries, authors often employed it to ridicule Chinese people in a racist manner (Layton 2002, ch. 3, endnote 9). Throughout this book, I have used a much-simplified form of China pidgin, comprehensible to a modern reader. For the record, I present an example of pidgin in all its original complexity as expressed in an 1857 conversation between John Heard and the Heard Co. comprador (Chinese agent), Tsun Atow, as recorded by Albert Farley Heard (N.D.). I thank Heard descendant Robert M. Gray for his transcription of the hand-written document.

The dialogue begins with John Heard addressing Tsun Atow, followed by Tsun Atow's reply.

"Well compradore how fashion?"

"My hav' hear talkee this pigeon [sic], Missee H., juss' now no savey tlue how fashion. My tinkee no fear. My can secu allo man insi' tiss housee; tlue, he all good man. Suppose hav' got bobbely, he no got sha' insi'. My can secu!."

My translation of Tsun Atow's response is as follows:

"I have heard talk of this business [pidgin], Mister Heard, but just now don't know whether it is true. I think there is nothing to fear. I can guarantee [*secu*] all the men (Chinese employees) inside this building truly are all good men. If there's a ruckus [*bobbely*] (by outsiders), they can't get inside. I can guarantee it!"

3.4 I have excerpted Henrietta Sargent's Oct. 30, 1841, letter to George Dixwell, adding paragraph divisions and modern punctuation (MHS, N-114, Box 3).

Heard 1 = Heard Collection, Part One, Baker Library, Harvard.

Heard 2 = Heard Collection, Part Two, Baker Library, Harvard.

MHS, N-114 = Massachusetts Historical Society, Wigglesworth Collection.

4.1 The Heard staff spent the morning of Dec. 6, 1842, with Mr. Humpston, Jardine's tea-taster, "weighing tea" at Footae Hong (Heard 1891:41). My description of the packing and weighing process is taken from 19th-century images by Chinese artists reproduced in Christman (1984:80) and Kerr (1996:140). Details of tea production, transport, quality, weight, adulteration, and testing are taken from the *Chinese Repository* (1840:132–164). The tasks performed by Augustine Heard & Co. for its clients (as explained by Augustine Heard to George) are taken from studies of the firm by Lockwood (1971:17) and Layton (1997:91–92).

Since we do not know the names of the Heard company's Chinese staff in 1842, I have invented them: Kee Chong for the comprador; Sun Kee for the shroff; and Ah Ten for George's houseboy. The Chinese comprador was a central figure in the daily operation of a foreign firm. As John Heard explained (1891:33),

"It would be much shorter to tell what the comprador did not do, than what he did. Every money transaction, large or small, passed through his hands, and on each he levied a small percentage, which always came out of the Chinese at the other end of the string, so that you never felt the payment. He supplied the table of the house, kept all private accounts, in short, did everything there was to be done. Our compradore came to us without a cent in 1840. He died in 1846, leaving $70,000!"

The May 21, 1841, pillage of the Heard factory, Coolidge's capture by the Chinese, the loss of the Heard firm records, Coolidge's claim for reimbursement, Roberts's reconstruction of the records, and Coolidge's bad handwriting are all described by John Heard (1891:31–38). The outrage of the foreign community over Coolidge's excessive claim for his losses is reported in the *Canton Press* (2 July 1842).

The provisions of the Treaty of Nanking are presented in the *Canton Press* (10 Sept. 1842). Roberts's conversion of the $21-million indemnity paid by China to Britain, first into tons and then to miles (with the dollars laid on edge) are my invention to show the magnitude of the sum.

For a map of the foreign enclave at Canton, ca. 1840, showing the foreign hongs, Hog Lane, and Thirteen Factory Street, see Fay (1976:20). The Emperor's flatulence and his purchase of Oxley's Concentrated Essence of Jamaica Ginger are reported in the *Canton Press* (3 Dec. 1842).

My description of the Dec. 6, 1842, riot and destruction of the Heard factory at Canton is based on six sources. The events are described in great detail by John Heard, both in his memoir (1891:41–47) and in his Dec. 13, 1842, letter to his parents (Waters 1916:40–45). *The Canton Register Supplement* of Dec. 13, 1842, provides two first-person accounts. Edward Delano

(1841:133–137) provides an eyewitness account, as seen from the Russell & Co. factory, a few 100 feet from the Heard company. Finally, we have Robert Bennet Forbes's (1882:378–380) presentation of additional details told to him by Augustine Heard.

John Heard's letter to his parents described the events of the riot, from when Dixwell addressed the lascars "in the Indian language," to the final punishment of the rioters—"yoked together and exposed on the steps of Consoo house in a crowded thoroughfare and deprived of food and drink until they died." George would have addressed the lascars in Hindustani, the colloquial North Indian lingua franca from which both modern Hindi and Urdu developed. In place of Hindustani, I have used Hindi phrases supplied by Dr. Annapurna Pandey. It is possible that these Hindi words would have been pronounced similarly in the Hindustani of George's day. Dr. Raleigh Ferrell supplied the Chinese phrases.

Augustine Heard's strategy of delaying abandonment of the Heard factory until the flames would protect the company treasury, and the hong servants' suggestion—"He got no shoe ... suppose make broke bottley he no can walkee"—are both described by John Heard (1891:44–45). Robert Bennet Forbes (1882:379) reported that Augustine Heard told him that, in firing at the Chinese, he waited "to get two heads in line so as not to waste his lead." Several accounts describe Heard shooting one of the Chinese who gained entrance through the window and then clubbing another with the butt of his musket. I have left out the shooting and described the clubbing. Heard's use of the *Emerald* to crush a pirate schooner is described by Waters (1916:28)

and Morison (1961:89–90). Some 20 years after the riot, George recovered his pocket watch from a Canton pawnbroker (Heard 1891:47).

Henrietta's letter to George is excerpted from three long letters (MHS N-114, Box 3, Feb. 26, Sept. 4, and Oct. 6, 1842). Modern punctuation is added.

4.2 From May through September of 1845 George lived in Macao at the north end of Praya Grande in a house (with attached warehouse) rented from Russell & Co. The details of his stay come from his letters to Augustine Heard in Boston (Heard 1, EM 3-2, May 30 and July 27, 1845) and indirectly from John Heard's letters from Canton to Augustine Heard (Heard 1, EM 4-2, April 20 and Sept. 2, 1845).

Meanwhile, George was rapidly changing his business strategy. On June 22, 1845, John Heard correctly reported to Augustine Heard that Kessressung Khooshalchund had purchased a two-fifths share in the *Frolic*, but John was apparently unaware that George had stationed William Endicott and the *Snipe* at Cumsingmun (Heard 1, EM 4-2).

The *Frolic*'s first freight manifest lists 647.5 chests of Malwa opium. Of these, Kessressung Khooshalchund consigned 437.5 to the Heard firm and 105 to Russell & Co. The remainder was variously consigned by nine small-time shippers (Martin Murray & Co. [Bombay] to Augustine Heard & Co. [Canton] April 9, 1845, Heard 2, LV11, F16).

J.J. Dixwell's itemized listing of expenses for building and outfitting the *Frolic* is my primary source for the details of this deck scene (Heard 2, S18, F16, Jan. 11, 1845). For a full transcription of this listing, see

Layton (1997:187–188). The document lists "Costs of models transshipped," thus, I assume that a half-model of the *Frolic* was sent to George in China for final approval. Also listed are the *Frolic*'s two 9-lb. cannon, her outbound ballast ("18 Tons Iron Kentledge & 60 Tons Stone Ballast, Junk &c."), and her "skylights" (glass blocks set through the deck). The 9-lb. cannons, each weighing almost 2,000 lbs., were designed to fire a 9-lb. ball. Faucon replaced them with 6-lb. cannons, weighing about 1,100 lbs. each. Sport divers recovered two 6-lb. cannons and fragments of the glass skylights at the *Frolic* wreck site. Faucon complained about the lack of cross-ventilation in the *Frolic*'s cabin (Heard 2, S18, F14, April 27, 1846; Layton 1997:70).

Richard Henry Dana, Jr., depicted Edward Horatio Faucon (1805–1894) as the epitome of a good captain in his bestselling book, *Two Years Before the Mast* (1840). For a review of Faucon's career, see Layton (1997:59–70,147–155).

On her first voyage from Bombay to China, the *Frolic* was paired against Jardine Matheson & Co.'s brig *Anonyma* (formerly belonging to the Royal Yacht Squadron) in a widely publicized race. When John Heard read the news of the match, he wrote to Augustine Heard in Boston "I would give a great deal to have the *Frolic* beat the *Anonyma* ... it would be worth $5000 to her [in future cargoes] and more" (Heard 1, EM 4-2, June 8, 1845). The *Frolic* arrived at Macao on June 13, 1845, completing the 4,470-mile passage via Singapore in an impressive 34 days. Six days later, the *Anonyma* had still not arrived, and John Heard exulted: "The *Frolic* has beaten her!" (Heard 1, EM 4-2, June 20, 1845). Although John Heard states the *Frolic*'s elapsed time as 34 days, Fairburn (1945–1955:2584) records the

run as 35 days and as the fastest passage accomplished in 1845.

For a detailed discussion of Malwa opium production and adulteration in India and testing in China, see Layton (1997:76–80,97–99). William Endicott's commentary on opium quality—from mold to fish oil—is excerpted from several 1846 testing inventories written aboard the *Snipe* (Heard 2, S24, F3, N. Baylies; Layton 1997:100–101).

The Tanka boat dwellers of the Gulf of Canton were probably descended from landless farmers who expanded into an unoccupied niche. By the beginning of the 19th century, Tanka people maintained an active service industry from their small boats at virtually every anchorage in the Gulf of Canton. They provided ferry service and also operated floating brothels known as "flower boats." They were barbers, prostitutes, and small-time merchants, hawking fruits and vegetables.

Rebecca Kinsman (1950:139) described Tanka women as seen on Dec. 3, 1844, from her house overlooking the Praya Grande.

"At this moment, a little tankah-boat is before the window, looking almost like an egg-shell upon the waters, from its smallness and frailty of appearance. Here lives a family—here probably they were born, and perhaps will die. The mother has her baby fastened to her back, and as she pulls at the oar, the motion rocks the little one, who seems to enjoy it. I cannot see how many this boat contains, as it is covered or roofed over on one end, but frequently a mother, with one or even two grown up daughters, and two or three little children, live

4

on one boat, and sometimes two women join their means and take a boat together. They are managed entirely by women, whose husbands are either coolies on shore, or more probably fishermen of the larger boats. But it is really interesting to watch with what skill they manage these little cockle-shells."

George and William Endicott's discussion of the Tanka boatwoman's daughter is taken from John Heard's Sept. 26, 1844, letter to Charley Brown, as quoted by Downs (1997:50).

"The likeness of the Macao girl I sent you is a veritable portrait of one who is kept by an English gentleman there. She has a sister, also kept, who is nearly as good looking, and there is a little girl named "ayow"[sic] now about 15 years old who lives in a boat near our house [George's house], who is prettier than either of them. She is still virtuous & has refused an offer of $500. But I suspect will relent before long. These things are only looked upon here as amiable weaknesses, and there are a lot of bastard children kicking about Macao."

Both William C. Hunter and James B. Endicott formed long-lasting alliances with Tanka women. Ng Akew bore Endicott two sons. Carl T. Smith (1995:266–276) has summarized her life. Hunter's Tanka woman (we do not know her name) bore him two sons and a daughter. Hunter and Endicott remained close friends and looked after each other's Eurasian families. Although both men eventually married "white" women and started new

families, they continued to support their Eurasian children. Their Eurasian sons were educated in the United States.

Anna Rosa Hunter climbing onto George's lap and correcting his pronunciation is my invention. We will return to Hunter and Endicott's children in subsequent chapters.

I have framed the scene on George's balcony, replete with wicker chair and telescope, from Lamqua's ca. 1843 painting of Nathaniel and Rebecca Kinsman's house at the south end of Praya Grande, as reproduced in Crossman (1991:plate 28).

On June 20, 1845, John Heard wrote to Augustine Heard that the *Frolic* would "be dispatched for Bombay on the 25th having about three lacs on freight from ourselves, and we hope about $40,000 or 50,000 more (Heard 1, EM 4-2: one letter in three increments, dated June 8, 20, 22, 1845). The Hindustani word "lac," meaning 100,000, was widely used by merchants in the China/India trade. The *Frolic's* three bills of lading list 183,037 taels of sycee silver [ingots], 11,995 dollars, and 5,000 Cowchin dollars (Heard 2, S-18, F-12, June 22, 23, 26, 1845). A tael was worth $1.39. Thus, the *Frolic's* outbound treasure cargo comprised about $271,416, in silver. I've calculated the weight of this silver as follows: 26.8 grams of silver per dollar, times $1,000 per bag, yields 58.8 lbs. per bag. Thus 271 bags totals 15,958 lbs. or just under 8 tons.

George conflates moral reminders from two of this mother's letters:

" ... You can preserve your self-respect, and if by honest exertion you cannot lure fortune to make a favorite of you, you can, by keeping your desires simple, dispense with many of her favors. I have a promise, given under your hand, that you would not become a dissipated man of the world. Should you be thrown into circumstances of temptation, I beg you to think of this promise ..." (MHS, N-114, Box 3, Jan. 16, 1842). // "It is not your health I am most anxious about. That, with common care and discretion will be preserved, I trust—But this rude jostling in a world of out-of-the-way people, when [the] restraints of society are relaxed, if not wholly disregarded, is an ordeal, to which I would not willingly have a friend exposed. It proved too much for one dear friend of mine whose fate is often called up to my remembrance. I beg you for my sake to keep a guard on the purity and simplicity of your early training. Do not let ridicule affect it, nor example seduce, for I assure you wealth would not compensate for the loss" (MHS, N-114, Box 3, Aug. 31, 1841).

George traveled twice to Shanghai in 1846. His first visit is described in his May 9, 1846, letter from Shanghai to Augustine Heard in Boston (Heard 1, EM 3-2):

"This is going to be a great place," he wrote. "It has already beat Canton out of sight in the raw silk trade ... My plan at present is to induce C. A. Fearon to come up here as our Exclusive agent. We need such a person very much to sell our drug; for the Captains loose head and do not manage well ... The exports of teas this year are 8,000,000 lbs of blacks & 1-1/2 millions of green ... The other American houses except R&Co [Russell & Co.] cannot do anything here without great difficulty, for not being engaged in the opium business it would cost them much more to get funds here."

4.3 George's mother warned him in her June 11, 1843, letter, that both he and Henrietta "thrust and parry adroitly," and might in their play "wound too deeply" (MHS, N-114, Box 3). Henrietta's March 20, 1846, letter to George, excerpted here, confirms Henrietta's hurt feelings (MHS, N-114, Box 4).

~~~~~~~~~~~~~~~~~~~~~~~~

MHS, N-114 = Massachusetts Historical Society, Wigglesworth Collection.

GBD-D = George Basil Dixwell, Daily Journal, 1848–54.

5

5.1 This vignette is based on three main sources. The first is George Basil Dixwell's 1848–1854 diary (GBD-D), used by permission of Marcia Dixwell DiMambro. The second is Mary Catharine Dixwell Wigglesworth's unpublished typescript, "Only Glimpses, Nothing More" (1918), used by permission of her granddaughter, Constance Holden. Mary (1855–1951) was the youngest of Epes Dixwell's six children. Her memoir includes photographs (pasted into the typescript) of Henrietta Sargent and Anna Sargent Parker, as well as numerous interior and exterior views of Epes Dixwell's house at 58 Garden Street. Among these photographs is one of the china pantry and cupboard with the four Canton-pattern platters, a gift from George. Some of the dialogue is taken from the letters Henrietta Sargent and Epes Dixwell sent to George in China and London.

Henrietta's habit of badgering Abiel Chandler is described in Esther Sargent Dixwell's Nov. 3, 1844, letter to George in China (MHS, N-114, Box 4):

"Mr. Chandler and my sisters from Poplar Street passed the evening with me. It is a funny meeting whenever H[enrietta] and he come together. She questions him closely on all his concerns, which he by no means likes, teases him till he almost loses his temper, then she advances some of those extraordinary and startling opinions, which scares him almost out of his propriety. Then they gradually subside to the very best of friends, and nothing more."

Henrietta and Catharine (Kate) Sargent's increasingly radical stance on abolition is described in a Nov. 10, 1846, letter from Epes Dixwell to George in China (MHS, N-114, Box 4): "H[enrietta] and K[ate] are still as usual—red hot on the one question & that question is daily assuming in their minds the hue of violent hatred to the Union & the Constitution. That is the doctrine of their leaders now." On May 31, 1847, Epes would write (MHS, N-114, Box 4):

"Meanwhile the neighboring metropolis [Boston] has been thronged with the yearly visitors & busy with the numerous meetings of religious and philanthropic societies. Some of them are good—some indifferent & some very absurd. Prominent among these is the Anti-Slavery Society. Their meetings have been characterized this year by a greater absurdity than ever, which makes the judicious grieve. They now openly avow their hostility to the Union & their determination to repeal it if possible. They renounced all allegiance to it. They resolved that religion in America is the greatest obstacle to the abolition of slavery."

Epes Dixwell had been headmaster of Boston Latin School since 1837, but when a Boston city ordinance was passed in 1851 that required all of the city's public school teachers to live in Boston, Epes resigned his position and established Dixwell's School (1851–1871), where he taught until his retirement (Sargent and Sargent 1923:16). Even as George stopped in London on his way home from China, Epes was already teasing him about his wealth (MHS, N-114, Box 4, May 8, 1847):

"Dear Geordy, I have looked over all my paper & selected a sheet of the nicest to write the rich old cock who has made his fortune & is on his way home. I hope that this sheet will not offend your money bags for it is my greatest effort in the way of writing material & pray be satisfied when you know that I write with a gold pen."

The Fourth of July fireworks on Boston Common could be seen by Epes and his family from the fenced widow's walk on the roof of his house (Wigglesworth 1918:37). For a photograph of the Gloucester house of Judith Sargent Stevens (later Murray), see Bonnie Hurd Smith (1998:76). The "half a pair of scissors" line spoken by Henrietta in reference to George's bachelorhood is from George's diary (April 26, 1848). Regarding his failed romance with Sophia Dwight, George's overly formal response to Henrietta—"I am pleased ... to regard that affair as entirely closed"—is taken directly from his Oct. 15, 1848 letter to Theophilis Parsons (found folded into his diary). George recorded Sophia's engagement "to Mr. Wells a young lawyer of Springfield" in his diary (Dec. 5, 1849). Mary Dixwell Wigglesworth (1918:58) described Henrietta and "her reticule (a drawstring bag) [in] which she always had peppermints for me." The "little regicide" nickname comes from Epes Dixwell's reference to his infant son John (1848–1929).

"In the morning I take Johnny in his little waggon & drag him around the domain ... Then I carry the young regicide to his crib" (Epes Dixwell, Cambridge, Oct. 30, 1849, to George Basil Dixwell, London, MHS, N-114, Box 4).

George's attempt to research his Dixwell ancestry in British archives receives many scattered mentions in his diary. He visited Broome Hall as a guest of the Oxenden family, the descendants of the British Dixwells (GBD-D, Sept. 19–21, 1849). George did not share his father's hope that the Dixwell estates might be recovered, but his research provided sufficient information for him to draft the inscription for a brass plaque to be placed on the reconstructed Dixwell monument at New Haven. The full inscriptions were published in the *Boston Transcript* 31 Dec. 1849:

[North side, copied from the old gravestone]:

"J. D, ESQ, DECEASED— MARCH YE 19TH, IN YE 82D YEAR OF HIS AGE 1668–9

[East side]:

"JOHN DIXWELL, a zealous patriot—a sincere Christian, an honest man, he was faithful to duty through good and through evil report and having lost fortune, position and home in the cause of country, and of human rights, found shelter and sympathy here, among the fathers of New England. His descendants have erected this monument as a tribute of respect to his memory and as a grateful record of the generous protection extended to him, by the early inhabitants in New Haven. Erected, A. D. 1849.

[West side]:

"Here rest the remains of JOHN DIXWELL, ESQ, of the Priory of Folkestone, in the County of Kent, England, of a family long prominent in Kent, and Warwickshire, and himself possessing large estates and much influence in his country, he espoused the popular cause in the revolution of 1640. Between 1640 and 1660, he was colonel in the army, an active member of four parliaments. Thrice in the council of state and one of the high court which tried and condemned King Charles the First. At the restoration of the monarchy, he was compelled to leave his country; and after a brief residence in Germany, Came to New Haven, and here lived in seclusion, but enjoying the esteem and friendship of the most worthy citizens, till his death in 1688–9."

George's childhood interest in science and his attempt to build a flying machine was remembered by his mother in two letters (Esther Sargent, Boston, to George Basil Dixwell, Canton, MHS, N-114, Boxes 3 and 4). On July 30, 1843, she wrote, "None of your old bachelor pranks. No getting up at three o'clock to study nobody knows what—no setting the house in turmoil to carry forward some unsuccessful experiment. No flying machines with broken backs and unstable wings!!!" On Feb. 5, 1844, she wrote, "I was awakened from sound sleep by a mighty rushing sound—I thought of your flying machine. It was the wind playing pranks."

In April 1849, George began dance lessons at the studio of Henri Cellarius in Paris (GBD-D). Cellarius (1847) had published a dance manual with 83 figures for a series of dance games called "German Cotillion." George's proficiency in directing the intricate patterns of this popular dance (a refined version of the quadrille or square dance) served him well on his return to New York. To impress his friends, George sometimes wore the suit of "Mandarin dress" he had brought home from China (GBD-D, Jan. 12, 1851).

Attorney James Augustus Dorr (1812–1869), Harvard A.B., 1832, became George's closest business associate in New York. Dorr's father (1774–1844) was president of the New England Bank and, at various times, a member of both the U.S. House of Representatives and Senate (Register, Vol. 3, 1849:327; Vol. 25, 1870:17). George and Dorr began a package of 12 dance lessons at Serracho's on Jan. 7, 1850 (GBD-D).

Epes's heartfelt thanks to George for the gift of the house at 58 Garden Street, appears in his June 13, 1847, letter (MHS, N-114, Box 4):

"I feel rich as Croesus since the anniversary of our wedding, which J.J. made the occasion of announcing your joint gifts of house and land—no man in the community is so wealthy—for beside the value which can be expressed in $ Cts. & &ct I have an inestimable treasure in the token & assurance of harmonious brotherhood through all time & all eternity ... I shall be well advised ... before I take any steps in the matter of building. I trust that we shall secure solid conveniences & comforts such as you would approve rather than any vainglorious display of architecture or stylish living."

Henrietta's "Midas" response to Epes's "rich as Croesus" allusion is my invention.

I quote two stanzas of Epes Dixwell's Christmas poem, referring to George's newfound sophistication (MHS, N-114, Box 48, f. 4, Dec. 1849).

5.2 The August 17, 1851, family gathering at J.J. Dixwell's Sunnyside estate is based on George's diary entry for that date (GBD-D): "At S.S. [Sunnyside] Aunts P[arker] and H[enrietta] come to see us!" His Aug. 18 entry reads: "Into Boston with Aunt H[enrietta], Mother & Eliza. Dine at Tremont aftn having Daguerreotipe [sic] taken for Aunt H. PM go to Newport. Pleasant trip. Go to hop at the Atlantic."

The description of George's laboratory equipment for his steam experiments comes from a series of diary entries at Sunnyside, dated July 5–26, 1850: "read heat—gasses &c &c"; "order a thermometer of Huddleston to show degrees from 50–100"; "In to Boston. Order two glass tubes of Huddleston for experiments on vapours & steam"; "Order two more tubes of Huddleston & a thermometer going to 600°"; "Call Huddleston and get three bent tubes for experiment"; "Get some quicksilver of Huddleston. PM try my first experiments with ether"; "experiments on Ether, Chloroform & Alcohol"; "Athenaeum. Took out a number of the Journal of the Franklin Institute"; "see Phelps man about cylender [sic]." On Aug. 12, George visited James Frost's laboratory in Brooklyn to see "an instrument that shows the expansion of steam at temperatures under 212."

George's diary does not reveal exactly what he was seeking to discover by his experiments. However, on Feb. 21, 1853, he wrote, "Down to Mr. Keller's office with Dorr to sign caveats on air & Steam Engines." A caveat is a preliminary statement of a discovery, made to preserve precedence during the patent process. Two days later, George wrote: "Find that one [Mr.] Cable of St. Louis has been before us in the matter of water injected on wire gauzes!" Finally, on June 1, George wrote, " … think of method of cleaning the steam which has been formed by injection on wires on which flame had previously impinged."

I surmise that George's research was focused on finding a means to suppress cylinder condensation in steam and vapor engines through use of super-heated steam. This problem, with a very different solution, became the subject of George's research following his retirement 20 years later. In one of George's (1875a:1) patent statements he writes: "It is well known that the loss arising from cylinder condensation in engines using saturated steam is great, and that it becomes greater as the measures of expansion are increased ... Explain it as we may, the fact remains that the actual condensation in cylinders cutting off short is about five times the equivalent of that caused by radiation ..."

I suspect that George was already working on an aspect of this phenomenon in the experiments alluded to in his diary. On June 21, 1850, George wrote: "Went to see Jas. Frost at Brooklyn. Law of Mariotte. Give him 10$ to try steam at less than atmospheric pressure" (GBD-D). On June 22, 1850, George mentions going to the New York Mercantile Library to look up the steam engine patents of Haycraft,

Trevithick, Detmold and Frost. George's spelling of these names may be incorrect.

Several photographs of the interior of J.J. Dixwell's residence at Sunnyside have survived (MHS, N-114, Box 56). For the purposes of this vignette, I have Henrietta tell the story of Catharine's first use of a flush toilet, as described in Epes Dixwell's July 30, 1849 letter to George in London (MHS, N-114, Box 4).

5 Literary contributions for the *Liberty Bell* were assembled during fall 1852. The completed volume was available for sale at the National Anti-Slavery Christmas Bazaar. Henrietta's contribution was "The Olive Tree" (*Liberty Bell* 1852).

In his diary, George records going to James A. Dorr's office to read his draft opinion of the Fugitive Slave Bill on Nov. 10, 1850, and again on Nov. 19 to read the printed pamphlet (Dorr 1850). As we do not have Henrietta's personal response to Dorr's pamphlet, I have fabricated it from a resolution of the Boston Female Anti-Slavery Society (of which Henrietta was an officer), published in *The Liberator* (22 Nov. 1850).

> "Resolved that the Fugitive Slave Law is an unjust, inhuman and atrocious law; that, if it be constitutional, the Constitution itself deserves the same epithets ... Resolved, That we think both justice and reciprocity require passage of an act by the Legislature of Massachusetts ... and that such act in substance should provide that every slave-catcher found on this soil shall be detained until one of our colored citizens imprisoned in the South shall be discharged in exchange for him."

Despite George's protestations, as presented in this vignette, Dorr's sympathies were clearly with the South (Dorr 1856).

Henrietta's ("Are you a simpleton?") criticism of George's materialism is taken almost verbatim from a letter she wrote to him in China, Oct. 30, 1841 (MHS, N-114, Box 3).

Shadrach Minkins, a waiter, was arrested on Feb. 15, 1851, and was rescued when "fifty men of color entered the courtroom where Minkins was being held and bore him away" (Grover 2001:222). Thomas Sims, arrested in Boston only a month later (Apr. 4, 1851), was not so lucky. He was sent back to his owner in Savannah on April 12 (Grover 2001:227).

The Rev. Samuel Snowden's obituary, published in *The Liberator* (3 Jan. 1851) stated: "On the day of his death [age 85], Oct. 8th, 1850, thirteen fugitives arrived, asking that sympathy for which his name had become so famed ..." The story of the escape of the "nearly white" slave, Miss Smith, and her marriage to a "white gentleman," performed by Rev. Theodore Parker is discussed by Henrietta in her July 21, 1851, letter to Anna W. Weston (Boston Public Library, Weston Collection, Ms.A.9.2.25, p.105).

The story of James Bridges Endicott and Ng Akew was originally printed in the *China Mail* (29 Oct. 1849). George read it as reprinted on the front page of the *New York Herald* (21 Jan. 1850) and noted it in his diary (GBD-D): "Article in *Herald* about J.B. Endicott & Akew." Henrietta knew the Endicott family and would have read or heard about the scandal. The dialogue between George and Henrietta is, of course, my invention.

The *Herald* article summarized Ng Akew's sworn statement to the American Consul at Macao. As she told it, Endicott and Captain Langley (of the Heard company's receiving vessel, *Lady Hayes*) had bought, on private account, some of the opium salvaged from the wreck of the *Isabella* and had sold eight chests to Ng Akew on credit. She, in turn, shipped the drug up the coast, but somewhere along the way, it was stolen by pirates. Unfazed, she set out for the pirates' haunt at Tien Pakh, threatened their leader, Shap-ng-tsai, with vengeance from her foreign friends, and extracted a replacement cargo of betel nut. When the sale of the betel nut did not fully cover her losses, she went back to the pirates' lair (accompanied by six fully armed junks) and returned to Cumsing-mun, her two vessels laden with rice, sugar, and a multitude of other commodities. The port authorities, suspecting her goods to be the spoils of piracy upon British shipping, seized her vessels, but she (probably on Endicott's advice) quickly placed an advertisement in the newspaper—demonstrating a sincere, public-spirited effort to see if any owners could be found. When the case came before Consular Court, it was summarily dismissed. There was no evidence showing from whom, if anyone, the cargoes had been stolen—probably because the pirates had thrown the Chinese merchants (who owned the cargoes) overboard—avoiding the inconvenience of claimants or witnesses.

5

Mary Mason Jones, a New York merchant heiress, married Régis Denis de Keredern de Trobriand in 1843. In 1847 they took up residence in New York City (Johnson and Malone 1930:258–259). The awkward table manners of John Jacob Astor (1763–1848) were the subject of gossip among more-refined New York families (Simon 1978:75–76).

GBD-D = George Basil Dixwell, Daily Journal, 1848–54.

6.1 When George began legal proceedings against James A. Dorr, he published a summary of his investments from ~1848 to 1860 (Dixwell 1860). His gas-regulator caveat was filed on July 21, 1853 (GBD-D).

Miss Kelsey first appears in George's diary on March 17, 1852. By January 1853, he was actively courting her. That October, as she was trying to end the relationship, George redoubled his efforts. Although he never reveals Miss Kelsey's first name, he once refers to her as "Ch.K." Although many men of George's social class regularly visited prostitutes (Walkowitz 1982), George was unusual in noting these assignations in his diary. I attempted to translate these notations using the 1857 edition of Benn Pittman's *Phonographic Manual.*

George had been concerned about hair loss for some time. In London, on July 20, 1849, he ordered a wig. A month later, he wrote, "Went to Holmes' for my wig which was well made: but my hair meanwhile has grown so that the wig is scarcely needed." Some of George's hair loss may have been the result of an unspecified medical treatment (GBD-D).

George boarded the steamship *Northern Light* on Dec. 6, 1853, for the 10-day voyage from New York to the Nicaragua isthmus. After a four-day trip across the isthmus, first by river steamer and finally aboard a pack mule, he boarded the steamship *Sierra Nevada* on Dec. 19 for the 13-day voyage north to San Francisco (GBD-D).

6.2 George's visit to Grass Valley, California, is recorded in his Friday, April, 7, 1854, diary entry (GBD-D):

"Stage to Grass Valley. Mr. Tiffany & Mr. Clements in the stage ... At Grass Valley went at once to Mr. Southwick's mill. Met Lola Montez enroute. She has an interest in S's mill. Met Mr. Waddell. Saw Mr. Conway's mill Saw Mr. Meredith's & Mr. Walsh's Mill. Southwick's mill had Stampers only: the last had rollers also in which the quartz was reduced from pieces of the size of two fists to the size of a half a Nutmeg. The latter machine operated on 9 tons an hour. Southwick's mill had forty horse power & could crush 50 tons a day. 5–10$ got out quartz & carried it to the mill and 5–7$ crushed & amalgamated it. Some quartz had no gold but a great deal had from 30–90$ a ton. They all thought the supply of quartz to be inexhaustible. Labor was 4$ a day the laborer feeding himself which he could do at 1$ a day, the farmer having greatly reduced the expense of living. Freight from the plains 80$ a ton giving the farmer on the spot a great advantage. Water 1$ an inch. Water Cos the great enterprizers of the day. The Quartz mills acted as saw mills also & had used up nearly all the timber of the valley making me ask where they would get fuel by & by for their Engines. Sluices—long toms, cradles—rewashing—Water Cos—Claims &c &c &c."

George saw Lola Montez perform in New York on Jan. 15, 1852, and recorded his impression of her in his diary. "Evening go with Dorr to see Lola Montez. Born dancer, but the remains of a splendid woman." Montez kept a menagerie of animals at her Grass Valley home, including dogs, cats, a grizzly bear cub, and a parrot (Semour 1996:322; Ross 1947:245). Twenty-six-year-old, John W. Southwick of Massachusetts was one of Montez's partners in the Empire Mill. In 1853 he was "tinkering with a cylinder amalgamating device ... which was supposed to save at least 25% more gold than previous processes" (Varly 1996:171). As George does not mention seeing such a device at the Empire Mill, I have described the more traditional techniques for recovery of gold. However, it is likely that George and Southwick discussed amalgamating machines. Indeed, in his next diary entry, George writes, "Evening at Grass Valley with Mr. Meredith. Contrive an amalgamating machine."

Southwick had his spiel for investors well rehearsed by the time George heard it. An extended version was published in the *Grass Valley Telegraph* (22 Dec. 1853):

"Mr. Southwick, one of the Directors of the Empire Mill, furnished us with the following interesting statement concerning the business operations of their company, which, by the by, even under existing circumstances, will show that they are doing a good profitable business. This mill, the Empire, with only eight stampers, and at twelve hours per day, have crushed 1500 tons of quartz in four months, making a yield of $54,000. Cost of raising, hauling and crushing, $22,000, leaving a net profit of $33,000 for four months crushing. Now an investment of $50,000 would have bought

every ledge at that time, from which the rock was crushed. Had those ledges been owned by a mill, there would have been at least four times the work done in the same length of time; and instead of eight stampers, running twelve hours a day, there would have been twice that number running twenty-four hours per day, and consequently there would have been four times the work accomplished in the four months stated. The inference is a very plain as well as natural one. An investment of $50,000 would have produced a yield of four times $54,000."

6.3 My description of Amos T. Laird's hydraulic mining operation in Nevada City comes from two sources. George's April 8, 1854, diary entry states: "To Nevada [City]. Placer digging on a stupendous scale by Mr. Laird. A whole hill cleft in twain & washed away. Hydraulic washing by Hose & Pipe. PM back to Grass Valley." To augment George's description, I have borrowed detail from J. Lampson's early-1850s colored drawing of Laird's hydraulic operation (as reproduced in Andrist and Hanna 1961:142–143). Amos Laird, a native Georgian, got his start mining Georgia placer. Laird's discussion of Kellogg & Company's private gold coinage in San Francisco is my invention, based on Donald Kagin's (1981) study of private gold coins in America.

George fully understood water columns and pressures. While traveling north from the Nicaragua isthmus, he invented a cooling device employing similar principles.

"December 24 - Still hot. Calculate

power requisite for making ice through the medium of air ... // December 26 - Southern Lower California in sight. Conceive the idea of a machine for making ice without a condensing pump. A pump elevates water 35 feet into a reservoir. Thence it flows into a receiver thus condensing the air to say 2 atmospheres (an injection of water taking up the heat as it is evolved by compression). Then a valve lets the air pass through a chamber of water expanding as it passes" (GBD-D, Dec. 24, 26, 1853).

6.4 George visited the New Almaden mine and quicksilver reduction works on April 17, 1854, accompanied by his partners, G. P. Upton, Jr. (a speculator in provisions) and A. C. Whitcomb (a real estate investor). My primary source for this vignette is George's April 17, 1854, diary entry (GBD-D):

"Drive to the mines of New Almaden. Walk up the hill, a steep ascent of a mile, to the mouth of the mine & then in & down & around through dark & ugly passages. See the workmen digging by candles—a scene fit for Rembrant [sic]. Then to summit of Hill to gaze over the whole valley—stretching as far as the Bay & farther—a glorious sight. Then down Hill to dinner. Then to the Smelting House where the ore is smelted in long Brick chambers about 40 feet long & 12 square. 35,000 bricks in one of these edifices or 70 tons. 2000 lbs of ore smelted at once. 2 days to heat & 4 days to cool. At end of cooler a wooden box with a Stream of water passing through & above it to condense the fumes of sulfur & any quicksilver that may have passed over. Mine produces about 200–250,000 lbs per month. The ore averages about 28–30%—Some specimens give 70%—. Back to San Jose for supper. Evg Billiards."

The secondary source of information for this vignette is the magnificent description of the mine and furnaces by Mrs. S. A. Downer (1854), who made her visit there within a few months of George's. Not only is hers our earliest detailed description of the mine and smelting operation, but also it is remarkable for its almost anthropological detail. The mine inspired Downer to present several classical metaphors. Although the light across the miners' faces reminded George of Rembrandt, the references to Homer's *Odyssey* and to Dante's *Divine Comedy* are my invention.

George's California speculations were large and varied (GBD-D):

"January 12 - Drew 60,000$ on JJD 1/2 at 30 days & half at 60 days sight & deposited the proceeds 60,225$ with Mess Page Bacon & Co. Loaned 5,000$ on demand to Mr. Benson security of 5,600$ City scrip at 3% a month. Loaned 2,000$ on 15 days to Mr. Reece at 3% a month. // January 13 - Loaned 7,000$ on demand to Mr. Reece at 3%. // January 14 - Loaned 17,000$ through Mr. Reece on collateral security at 3%. // January 26 - Buy half a share (1/48) of a twenty year lien of the New Almaden—Mines for 1,000$—a flyer—... . Think about buying out the Bolinas

Mills with Whitcomb & Tiffany ... // January 28 - ... See Smith about the Bolinas Mills. He estimates the two Engines & Engine Houses & the Roads as worth 20,000$ the stumpage as worth 3$ a thousand &c &c ... // February 3 - ... Smith starts off to look at the Bolinos [sic] ranch & see how much wood is there. Talk with Upton about operation in Beef & Pork ... // February 4 - Look at Adelphi Theatre 14,000$. Property of 400,000$ offered me! at 100,000$ per annum. Evening play Billiards with Whitcomb & talk over investments. Hit upon ground rents as the best at 2%. Arrange Pork Speculation with Upton // February 5 - ... Complete the arrangement with Upton & [William L.] Chrysler [Provision Merchant] // February 6 - Upton & Chrysler buy about 1,000 Bbls at about 18$ ... // February 7 - Upton & Chrysler buy about 1000 Bbls more at about 18$— ... Smith gets back from Bolinos. Thinks the property there well worth 60,000$ ... Thinks 10,000$ should be applied to building barges which should be towed by steam. Thinks that 30$ a thousand will then cover all expenses of delivering lumber in San Francisco. Thinks that 40$ per M [thousand], here, the mills will clear themselves in 18 months if not sooner. Thinks lumber can be delivered from that point 5$ cheaper than from any other in California. // February 8 - ... Upton & Chrysler buy about 1000 Bbls more at about 18 1/2: —I buy half the Pacific St lots at 7,500$. The other half owned by Whitcomb ... // February 13 - Tiffany, Whitcomb & I buy into the

Bolinos at 33 for 365 and 30 for 155 shares. We conclude also to take the Mortgage of 9000$ at 6 2/3rd per cent compounding monthly ..."

Although George had planned to remain in California to manage his investments, James Dorr's letters, describing large expenditures on the Staten Island brickworks and the unauthorized purchase of a steamboat, frightened George into returning early. "Accordingly, I came to the conclusion that this was no case for correspondence; that I must return in person to see what Mr. Dorr was about. Great efforts and considerable sacrifices were necessary to enable me to do this; but by making these efforts and sacrifices, I got away from California about the first day of May and reached New York about the 28th" (Dixwell 1860:11).

6.5 William Endicott wanted to purchase the steamer *Palmetto* for use in China and hoped that George would take a share in the vessel. This vignette is framed around George's diary entry for Nov. 24, 1854, "Look at the *Palmetto* about three times with Endicott. Find she can be had for 25,000$" (GBD-D). My description of the *Palmetto* is taken from her listing in *American Lloyd's Registry* (1859:468–469). The vessel, built in 1851, was a single-decked, 532-ton, bark-rigged steamer, propeller-driven and powered by a vertical engine with two 44-inch cylinders. Her dimensions were 180 × 29 × 18 feet with a 12-foot draft. The paddle steamer, *Spark*, built in New York in 1849, was sent to China in pieces, where she was reassembled for James B. Endicott (Haviland 1956:162). James B. Endicott, in partnership with

James Cook and Thomas Hunt, operated a ships' chandlery, boatyard, and dry dock at Whampoa (Crossman 1991:139). We can follow George's frantic attempts to save the Staten Island brickworks, to sell the *Pacific*, and to avoid bankruptcy in his diary entries during summer and fall 1854 (GBD-D).

The conflict in China, now known as the Taiping Rebellion, and its deleterious effect on commerce was, of course, a constant subject of discussion among China-trade merchants. On Oct. 24, 1854, shortly after William Endicott's arrival in New York City from China, he met with George who noted the discussion in his diary. "Wm. Endicott comes in and I have a great deal of talk with him about China." During summer 1854, as Chinese Imperial forces battled the Taiping rebels, the international settlement at Shanghai endured a blockade. The rebels were finally forced from the walled Chinese city of Shanghai in February 1855 (Fairbank 1953:432).

William Endicott and Harry Roundy's trip to Kentucky is described by Robert Lovett (1961:65). Roundy's engagement to William Endicott's niece, Martha Endicott, is mentioned in his Nov. 25, 1854, letter to his sister. (Harry Roundy, New York City, to Mary Jane Roundy, Beverly, Massachusetts, Roundy Collection, Beverly Historical Society). John Griswold, formerly of Russell & Co., was elected to the board of the Illinois Central Railroad in fall 1854. He became president in January 1855 (Johnson & Supple 1967:140; Cochran 1953:343–344).

Roundy first revealed the existence of his Chinese son, Charles William Roundy, in a Sept. 14, 1853, letter from China to his brother George in Beverly, Massachusetts (Roundy Collection, Beverly Historical Society). As I have alluded to information contained in that letter, I present it here.

Sept. 14th 1853, Very Private

My dear Brother

I wish to make a confidant of you in a matter of delicacy & importance to me & leave it to your good judgment how to communicate it to Mother & Sisters Martha and Abby. I have a little boy about 41/2 years of age a son of mine by a Chinese girl who lived with me 5 years and who was an excellent girl. She died 18 months ago & I have made up my mind to send the child home to be educated. [I] Have engaged a passage in the ship "Celestial" of New York for him. My friend Capt. Johnson of Salem goes passenger and has kindly offered to take care of the little fellow. I am writing to brother John by this mail to get a place in Boston for him to live & to have him educated there. You know people in large towns don't know or trouble themselves so much about their neighbours "little affairs" as they do in small towns. So don't think I have thought you would not do every thing I could ask as well as John for I know you would. By the ship which I send the child I will forward an order for a sufficient sum of money to be paid from my funds annually for the expenses of his support and education, which please give your valuable attention to, & hand the amount to Bro John. I have told J. I should write you upon the subject so you can mention it to him. I call the boy Charles William Roundy and he cannot be considered illegitimate as his poor mother was married to me according to the custom of her country. At all events he cannot help his origin and I am determined he shall not suffer for any error if there is one in my being instrumental in bringing him into the world. He shows his Asiatic blood a considerable [sic] but is a pretty good looking chap and has a tractable kind disposition. Trusting you will look in as favorable a light as you can upon the matter I subscribe myself,

Your affectionate brother,

H. Roundy.

The 1860 Federal Census has Charles W. Roundy (age 10, born in China) listed next to John Anderson (age 13, born in China). The boys were living in Newton, Massachusetts, with R. R. Blaisdell, a teacher, and six other students—two of whom (Finomen and Raphael Rua) were from Cuba. The Blaisdell School may have specialized in taking children of color. As captains Anderson and Roundy were planning their Woosung, Illinois, land purchase, Anderson married Elizabeth Foster Roundy, the daughter of Harry Roundy's half-brother (Roundy 1942:354,421; Bicentennial History of Ogle County, 1976:451).

6.6 On Oct. 21, 1835, Henrietta and Catharine Sargent, along with fellow members of the Boston Female Anti-Slavery Society, were besieged by an angry mob. This vignette occurs at the 20th anniversary of that event. Henrietta attended and was called from the audience by William Lloyd Garrison to take a seat of honor on the stage. The entire proceedings, including the speeches by W. L. Garrison and Wendell Phillips, and the hymn by John Greenleaf Whittier, were published in *The Liberator* (2 Nov. 1855). Henrietta's responses are, of course, my invention, informed by the fact that she was a die-hard Garrisonian. The split between nonresistants (who advocated "moral suasion") and those advocating political action was an old one, but the radical abolitionists' advocacy of force ("fighting suasion") was a new development.

The National Anti-Slavery Bazaar, scheduled annually during Christmas week, was a major source of funding for the American Anti-Slavery Society. The first call for donations of items for the 1855 bazaar (the 22nd annual event) appeared in *The Liberator* (27 July 1855), bearing, as usual, Henrietta's name as a member of the organizing committee. The bazaar funded nonresistant activities. The donation of an autograph collection for sale at the 1855 bazaar was formally announced in *The Liberator* (21 Dec. 1855).

Lydia Maria Child's, "Lines: Suggested by a Lock of Hair from our Departed Friend, Catherine [sic] Sargent," was published in the Christmas 1855 edition of the *Liberty Bell* (1856:159–160). The *Liberty Bell* always bore the date of the forthcoming year.

"That little lock of silvery hair
Reminds me of what friendly care!
And gratefully my memory pays
Its tribute to departed days.
Thou good old friend, so
kind and true!
Thy worth was known to very few.
Not in the glare of noon-day sun,

Thy kind and gentle deeds
were done;
And silently thy prayers did rise,
With offerings of self-sacrifice.
Not for thy goodness unto me
Do I revere thy memory;
But for the love that never failed,
The courage, too, that
never quailed,
When the poor orphan
breathed a sigh,
Or slaves required thy sympathy.
While statesmen argued day
and night,
To settle whether wrong was right,
Thou hadst no need of subtle art,
Seeing truth with thy honest heart;
Religion was not unto thee
Any recondite mystery.
God loves all, was the simple creed,
Which served thee in each
hour of need.
Guileless thy life, serene they death;
And when had passed thy lat-
est breath,
From thy attendant angel's glance
A light fell on they countenance;
A gleam of bright celestial love,
Touching this earth from
realms above."

William L. Garrison read all 14 stanzas of John Greenleaf Whittier's (untitled) hymn and, as reported in *The Liberator* (2 Nov. 1855), "a portion of it was sung by the audience." We do not know the tune to which the hymn was set, but the meter fits the "Old Hundredth."

A detailed description of the executions at Canton filled an entire column of *The Liberator* (28 Sept. 1855). The article incorporated a letter from an unidentified Boston supercargo relating "Heard's" description of the executions. This was

Gus Heard, the nephew and namesake, of Mr. Augustine Heard, founder of the Heard firm.

Gerrit Smith was elected to Congress in 1852. His June 27, 1854, letter, entitled "To My Constituents" and that announced his resignation from Congress, stated: "To separate myself from my large private business, for so long a time, and to war against the strong habits formed in my deeply secluded life, seemed well-nigh impossible" (*Liberator* 7 July 1854:106).

In a blatant show of contempt for the Garrisonian nonresistants, Smith and the radical abolitionists scheduled an in-your-face, three-day conference in Boston to convene on Oct. 23, two days after the 20th anniversary celebration of the Boston Female Anti-Slavery Society's moral triumph over the 1835 mob (*Liberator* 29 Sept. 1855).

The Anti-Slavery Convention of American Women, convened in New York City, May 9–12, 1837. The proceedings of that first-ever, public political meeting of American women are now available with explanatory notes by Dorothy Sterling (1991). The attendees included Ann C. Smith (Mrs. Gerrit Smith), Lucretia Mott, Lydia Maria Child, Sarah and Angelina Grimké, and Henrietta Sargent. Although Henrietta was obliged to leave the conference early, she was appointed to the Boston Central Committee to handle correspondence with persons in all parts of the country (Sterling 1991:24).

In 1851, Gerrit Smith's daughter, Elizabeth Smith Miller, designed an outfit of Turkish trousers (extending to the ankle), worn with a skirt coming four inches below the knee. Elizabeth wore this to Washington, DC, receptions during her father's term in Congress. The style was later taken up by Amelia Bloomer who publicized it in a women's magazine that she edited (Stauffer 2002:214–215).

I cannot confirm that Henrietta attended the Women's Rights Convention in the Meionian Hall (the lower level of Tremont Temple) Sept. 19–20, 1855. As Tremont Temple was only a short walk from her residence on Tremont Street, and both William L. Garrison and Wendell Phillips were scheduled speakers, it is highly likely that she did attend. The proceedings were published in *The Liberator* (28 Sept. 1855). Phillips concluded his speech with the humorous observation, "After the cause is won, the Conservatives will say that they were Women's Rights men twenty years before you were. God grant they may soon have a chance to say so!" Garrison stated that the Women's Movement was

> "less a reformation than a revolution ... Wherever the rights of one human being are defined, there are defined the rights of every other human being on the face of the earth ... all the objections made to the woman's cause are identical with those urged against the cause of the slave; and belong to the community of oppression. Whoever is not for Women's Rights is not for Human Rights."

The *New York Herald* (19 Sept. 1855) took the proceedings somewhat less seriously. "It is hoped they will propose some plan of relief for their poor sisters at the Great Salt Lake. One husband for forty women! Let them make a dead set at Brigham Young."

Henrietta's five-dollar donation to the Massachusetts Anti-Slavery Society was acknowledged in *The Liberator* (8 June 1855). In the adjacent news column, *The Liberator* announced Amos Lawrence's purchase of arms. "A. A. Lawrence, of Boston, has subscribed $1,000 to furnish arms to the free settlers in Kansas, and it is said that a quantity of arms and ammunition has been forwarded, including sixty Sharp's rifles."

The Radical Anti-Slavery Convention in Syracuse, New York, was called to order June 27, 1855, by Gerrit Smith (*Liberator* 6 June 1855):

> "The Convention read an appeal this morning from a Mr. John Brown, who had five sons in Kansas, and who was desirous to join them. They had written home for arms and means of defense, and declared in their letters that fighting suasion was the most important institution in the new Territory. A collection was taken up to aid the father in the objects, pistols and all."

Henrietta had good reason to be concerned about the tilt toward violence. On Aug. 4, 1855, *The Liberator* reported: "The last news from Kansas represents that every settlement was forming a rifle brigade, running bullets, making cartridges and going through the drill exercises. From this species of industry, it is not difficult to surmise what the crop will be."

～～～～～～～～～～～～～～～

Heard 1 = Heard Collection, Part One,
Baker Library, Harvard.

MHS, N-114 = Massachusetts Historical
Society, Wigglesworth Collection.

GBD-D = George Basil Dixwell, Daily
Journal, 1848–54.

7.1 Carolus III 8-reales silver coins (Spanish dollars) were minted in Mexico City from 1760 to 1789, followed by Carolus IV (1789–1808) and Ferdinand VII (1808–1822). Mexico declared independence from Spain in 1821. The first peso, bearing the eagle and snake, was minted in Mexico City in 1823 (Krause & Mishler 1985:1246,1272). Spain continued to mint Ferdinand VII dollars, but these coins could not be produced in insufficient quantity to meet the needs of Chinese merchants. Spain had lost her Mexican silver mines. On August 27, 1853, the premium on the Carolus dollar rose to a record 86% over the value of its silver content (Fairbank 1953:404). George's first mention of his "Old Heads" scheme is a cryptic diary entry on Oct. 24, 1854. "Planning about Old Heads." We can follow his research over the next month (GBD-D): "Nov. 1 - Introduced by Goodhue to Bullion Broker // Nov. 5 - Studying coins & bullion all the morning // Nov. 19 - Reading Jacobs // Nov. 26 - Read Jacobs on Precious Metals."

George described his proposal in a July 2, 1855, letter to John Heard who excerpted the details, added his own commentary, and sent it on to his uncle Augustine Heard (Heard 1: EM 3-2). George prefaced his proposal with a statement of his financial condition. "I left California about a year ago with nearly 2 lacs [pidgin for $200,000] of dollars, partly invested there and partly left to be invested here. Unluckily, my N. York agent here invested 4 times as much as he was authorized to and let me in for nearly a total loss, & I find myself with only about half of the sum I counted on when I left China." John did not forward all the details of George's proposal. Instead, he wrote:

"Without going into all of Dixwell's details I can give you in fewer words an idea of his plan, with regard to which he had urged upon me the most profound secrecy. It appears that observing that Old Heads were worth 30 or 35% more than the same weight of silver in other forms, he has the idea of establishing a coining machine in China, for the purpose of throwing a large quantity of the dollars so manufactured into circulation, and bagging the profit. To manufacture them in America or Europe would be contrary to law, but the machine could be made in America & the dollars struck in China without interfering with any law. He says that he is in possession of all the details necessary to carry it out, but that it is so minute and difficult to obtain that he is certain that no one else could compete with him without studying the question for a year or two, so that he is secure from opposition."

John then quoted George's summary statement, verbatim:

"I think it can be done & that a full 20% can be cleared after paying all charges, if I go out myself [to China] & attend to it ... I have hesitated and delayed, partly because I found any move toward China, not with an avowed connection to A.H.&Co., would cause more gossip about my doings than was desirable & partly because it seemed as if I must join some house to secure that full employment which a residence in China would render necessary to me ... If Gus is getting tired of his labors, and you hate to go out again, and Albert is too young to be put in charge ... then I would undertake to pilot the House for the next term for a moderate share and would throw into the house a share of the other speculation (or if it should be thought better that the House should be able to say that it had no share in it) I would share it with such & such persons ... In such case it would be better to organize it separately and there are some reasons why it had better be in the hands of an Englishman. Could we have a better man than Fearon?"

George's Oct. 8, 1856, departure for China from Boston via Liverpool, England, was recorded by Epes Dixwell (Extracts from the Diaries of E.S.D. 1833–84, MHS N-114, Box 17). George arrived in Macao in spring 1857.

7.2 I thank numismatist Salvatore J. Falcone for answering my numerous questions regarding Spanish colonial coinage. My description of the Old Heads counterfeiting project is based on short passages in 14 letters (March 20–Nov. 24, 1857), written by George in Macao to Albert Farley Heard in Shanghai (Heard 1, HM 28-1). One of these, dated Sept. 4, was addressed to John Heard who was then visiting with Albert in Shanghai. Because this chapter relies so heavily on George's brief allusions to the project, I quote the relevant passages verbatim:

"March 20, 1857 - The *Nimrod* [probably carrying the coin press] does not make her appearance and I am beginning to be a little anxious about her: but I trust she will turn up all right. There is a great deal to be done after she gets in before any result will appear. It is even possible that on careful survey of Macao I may not think it best to operate here! But even if this should be the final determination, much may be done here in preparation. I am bound to do the thing somewhere. I think the invoice of duty dollars will turn out well. I have not heard yet from Hongkong how many there are. // March 27, 1857 - We are delayed here by the negotiations with the authorities (sub rosa) which were upon the whole deemed necessary. If they fail, another move will be I fear unavoidable. // April 15, 1857 - I am occupied in getting ready for operations: arranging machines: coquetting with the authorities &c—delays which are vexing but unavoidable. I hope & trust that I shall get it so settled that I may go ahead here for the place is very convenient in many respects. Please do not write me anything on the subject except in notes of which you yourself keep the copies. So long as the clerks can be kept ignorant of the enterprize it is better that they

7

should be kept so. I have a letter from Secher Torre & Co which, on the whole, does not look badly for future treasure business. // April 28, 1857 - No 'positive result' yet: no positive arrangement: but I am not losing the time and think it perhaps fortunate that events prevent my rushing into the fight—half armed. Be patient ... The 1000 duty dollars have been of vast use to me. // June 26, 1857 - There is no 'positive result' here. But the prospect is in reality a great deal brighter now than ever before. We did not know where we stood and found an immense deal of work to be done before any positive result could be attempted with any chance of success. I have been working harder this passed three months than ever before, and it looks as if there might be another month of it. No body can stand any chance of success with less work: they can be sure of failing with a twentieth part of it! // July 11, 1857 - It looks as if I was getting near to some positive result and I regret not having long since asked you to send me information about how long it took funds to go to the Tea country & the hill country & to get back to Shanghae & whether we could do that 'pigeon' [business] with some profit. // July 24, 1857 - You will have a specimen before long: probably several thousand by the 12 August Steamer. // August 14, 1857 - In the other pigeon there has been so much delay and disappointment & difficulty that I am out of patience & thoroughly disgusted. Just as I expected to send you a specimen, B fell ill & was good for nothing for a fortnight; & as soon

as he got about, I was made nearly useless with boils. so you got no specimens by the Mail Steamer as I intended; & though there are 1000-2000 nearly ready—indeed quite ready except shroffing & packing & a little cooking; —Yet we cannot get them off by the *Antelope* unless she is detained ... I am almost ready to say that I wish I had never undertaken the affair—and yet it is now that almost if not quite all difficulties seem vanquished. // September 4, 1857 [to John Heard] - I have translated to Amoo your messages about Foochow dollars & am very glad to be of any service in the matter—in any way. He says in reply that he is not asleep, but that none have arrived: that the Portuguese & Carlowitz have been offering 52 for them—in vain: that when any come he is sure to get them &c. // Sept. 7, 1857 - I am going on here doing a little good each day but there is a great deal to be done. // Sept. 29, 1857 - The job here is an everlasting one. I don't know that we shall ever get to the end. I am disgusted and almost tired out. The delay makes me doubt whether any thing will ever come of it: — but I will try a little longer. // October 26, 1857 - I have your of the 1 & 7th which I ought to have replied to sooner: but I have been giving a Ball which knocked my ideas so into chaos that I have done nothing in the way of business except growl at JH [John Heard] because the teas by the *Skylark* were so high a grade. // November 24, 1857 - I look for John immediately [his return from Shanghai]. I have had the American embassy living with me and Mugford which makes it quite jolly. My ball which you refer to went off splendidly. Plenty of young ladies as well as old & they staid till half past three in the morning having come at half past eight & been gay all the time. I don't want to give another one though! Nothing new to tell you yet—Don't know that I ever shall have."

7.3 I have framed this vignette on July 25, 1857, in order to describe some of the many production issues George had to resolve prior to his letter of Aug. 14, in which he writes that he and his colleague, "B," had "1000–2000 almost ready—indeed quite ready except shroffing & packing & a little cooking." George took pains to preserve the anonymity of "B," so I have created an identity for him as William Brown, a skilled English mechanic and diesinker.

I have assigned George's shroff the name Ahwei and made him the younger brother of Tsun Atow, who was, in fact, the Hong Kong comprador of Augustine Heard & Company (Hao 1970, Appendix A:227).

For my discussion on the use and abuse of pidgin, refer to "A Note on Pidgin" in ch. 3, note 3 of this book.

As reported in the *China Mail* (30 Apr. 1857 [70]:1), Tsun Atow demonstrated his loyalty to the Heard Company by remaining at his post even after being threatened by Chinese authorities with arrest.

"The persecution of such that disobey the mandarin's orders to return to their native places have been latterly resumed; and Chinese

of respectability detained in the colony in fulfillment of contracts previously undertaken, together with others whose residence here has rendered them obnoxious to their own authorities, are now, with their families, threatened with loss of liberty, if not life. Fuh, the Sub-Prefect of Caza Branca, has issued warrants against Cheong-Achew, the well-known carpenter; Tsun-Atow, Messrs Augustine Heard & Co.'s comprador ... and Wei Akwong ... interpreter in the Supreme Court."

William Jacob (1831 [1]:140–142) calculated silver loss from Spanish dollars, subjected to normal wear, to be one part per 400 annually.

George mentions an invoice for "duty dollars" on March 20 and then on April 27, "The 1000 duty dollars have been of vast use to me." I have not been able to find a contemporary description of "duty dollars" but suspect they were sufficiently maimed and chopped so that they were worth no premium above their gross weight, and, thus, these coins were reserved for paying import and export duties. Maimed coins were more frequently termed "Foochow dollars" (Kann 1927, Appendix 3:511). Dixwell mentions Foochow dollars in his Sept. 4 letter: "I have translated to Amoo your messages about Foochow dollars ... ." For the purposes of this vignette I have referred to "Foochow dollars" rather than "duty dollars." Note that the passage quoted above confirms that George had maintained or regained some fluency in Chinese. Amoo was probably the Heard's shroff in Hong Kong.

7

7.4 Manuals to assist Chinese shroffs in identifying foreign silver coinage were widely available in China. Numismatist Stephen Tai kindly copied a manual [written in Chinese] from his private collection, 4th ed. (1865), of *Various Essays on Silver*, by Huang You-Sung and Liang An Tzer (1st ed. 1826). Drawings of the Carolus III and Ferdinand VII Spanish dollars from this (and earlier manuals) provide the basis for this vignette. The terms "big dress" and "small dress" for, respectively, Carolus III and Ferdinand VII; the term "ant's mouth" for a small chop; and "two sticks" for the Pillars of Hercules come from this volume. Regarding "ant's mouth," the authors noted that this small chop was more frequently used in the North around Shanghai than in the South. Stephen Tai and others recognize a shift from small chops to larger chops through time, and I have incorporated this idea into the vignette.

7.5 The 1857 Fourth of July celebration at Macao, sponsored by Dr. Peter Parker, was reported in the *China Mail* (9 July 1857 [110]:3).

> "In Macao ... the day was kept as a holiday—the men-of-war and many of the merchant vessels being gaily decorated. In the evening, his Excellency Dr. Parker, the U.S. Commissioner, entertained the Governor of Macao, and the heads of Foreign Legations at dinner; and the night was wound up by a display of fireworks, &c, at the Parade Ground."

George's freshly minted Carolus dollars would require both wear and tarnish to appear credible. In his August 14, 1857, letter George refers to "cooking" the coins. I interpret "cooking" to refer to aging or tarnishing. As George provides no other details, the discussion of tarnishing with eggs versus liver of sulfur is my invention. I attempted to tarnish a freshly cleaned Carolus dollar with a soft-boiled egg and had the same problems with consistent application of tarnish that I attribute to George. Modern silver workers still use liver of sulfur (produced by heating potassium carbonate with sulfur) to apply tarnish to silver.

In a Letter to the Editor, of the *China Mail* (21 May 1857 [82]:3–4), a reader asked why Chinese laborers embarking from Macao seemed never to return.

> "It is odd," he wrote, "that there are thousands and tens of thousands of Chinese who have been to California and Australia, to easily be found; but I never saw a single one who had been to either Cuba or Callao—nor do I believe did the 'Macao authorities' either, unless it may be the crimp's agents who accompany the 'free emigrants' in the capacity of interpreters."

The editor went on to write that by the last mail he had received the *New York Herald*, whose Cuba correspondent reported the arrival of the ship *Cora* in Havana, said to have carried 600 Chinese from Swatow of whom 305 died during the passage.

7.6 Our entire record of George's ball comes from two short passages in his letters to Albert Farley Heard (Heard 1, HM 28-1): "October 26, 1857 - I have your[s] of the 1 & 7th which I ought to have replied to sooner: but I have been giving a Ball which knocked my ideas so into chaos that I have done nothing in the way of business ... // November 24, 1857 - My ball which you refer to went off splendidly. Plenty of young ladies as well as old & they staid till half past three in the morning having come at half past eight & been gay all the time. I don't want to give another one though!"

I have guessed that the ball took place on Friday, October 23, 1857, shortly before George's letter of October 26, in which he cites the ball as the reason for his lapse in correspondence. Although George does not provide us with a guest list, I have assumed that his friends and colleagues, both American and Portuguese, would have been present. The details of the ball—those present and the topics discussed—are my invention, informed by reading the *China Mail* and the letters of others then resident in Macao.

This task was made considerably easier by William B. Reed, who replaced the Rev. Dr. Peter Parker as American Commissioner in China. Reed arrived in Macao on Nov. 20, 1857, about a month after George's ball. In addition to meeting with government officials, Reed made social calls to most of the Americans in town and recorded these visits in letters home to his wife. Reed's dated, diary-like descriptions reveal the closeness of the small American community, and I have placed the core of that community at George's ball. These include Mrs. Samuel Rawle, Mrs. Sandwith Drinker, William C. and Rosalie Hunter, James B. and Sarah Endicott, Gideon and Mary Nye, Samuel and Catharina Bonney, plus officers from the Portsmouth, and, of course, Governor Guimarães. I have excerpted key passages from Reed's Nov. 20–26 narrative to document the close social ties among the Americans in Macao and their personal situations alluded to in this vignette (William B. Reed, Diary of April 1857–March 1859, Mission to China as Envoy Extraordinaire, Library of Congress, MMC-1650).

"Friday Nov. 20, 1857- ... On landing I went ... to wait on Governor Senor Guimarães, a very well looking youngish man with snow white hair. He speaks English perfectly, as if he thought in English. I then went to Mr. Forbes's, an old Portuguese house on the Praya with a garden and high wall in front ... I found the Russian admiral staying with Mr. Forbes ... which compels my party to separate, Washington and Mr. Neeley going to Mr. [George] Dixwell a Boston merchant who had on my arrival offered me the use of his house ... I went to see the Rawles ... Mrs. Rawle looks very well indeed ... and Mr. Rawle, a wretched wreck. He has had two attacks of paralysis and can neither walk nor talk. His mind is clear and he writes on a slate readily ... We thence went to Mrs. Drinker's ... // November 21 - ... Went with Mr. Perry to make some visits—first to the missionaries and their wives—Mr. & Mrs. French and Mr. Preston—all full of war and punishment of Canton whence they have been lately driven with loss—as they say, of all ... —Thence to Mr. & Mrs. Bonney.—They took me into their school where four or five Chinese little girls were learning to read out of some sort of Chinese primer ... We then called on several American Ladies, Mrs. Endicott, Mrs. Nye and Mrs. Hunter, the last a

7

very nice person who sails for America next month ... The houses here are nicely furnished and very pretty with gardens and fine views of the roads [outer harbor] ... // Nov. 25 - ... Went with Mr. Williams to look at Mr. Nye's house, an old Portuguese palace ... breakfasted at Mr. Endicott. ... This evening paid a visit to Mrs. Hunter, who now promises to see you in Philadelphia."

Anna Rosa Hunter (1839–1923) was the eldest of William C. Hunter's three children by a Tanka woman (whose name we do not know). Judging from a series of Anna Rosa's letters, written in 1882–83, it is clear that she was well educated (Anna Rosa Vrooman, San Francisco, California, to Catharina Bonney, Cherry Hill, New York; Historic Cherry Hill, Bonney Collection, Box 24, F.5). I have surmised that at the time of this vignette Anna Rosa Hunter would have been living in Macao. As a sophisticated, eligible, 18-year-old, she would have attended George's ball with her father and stepmother. In addition to English and Chinese, Anna Rosa was fluent in the Portuguese of her native Macao (Anna Rosa Vrooman, 1920 Federal Census, San Francisco, California). Anna Rosa's birth and death dates (Aug. 3, 1839–May 25, 1923) are taken from her Territory of Hawaii, Certificate of Death, no. 49, filed July 2, 1923. This certificate lists Anna Rosa's birthplace as Macao; her father as William Charles Hunter, born in Alexandria, Virginia; and the name and birthplace of her mother as "unknown."

Young Mr. de Souza's presence at the ball, although quite possible, is my invention. He came from a prominent Macanese family, and by 1860 he was an employee of Augustine Heard & Co.

in Shanghai. De Souza's 1860 portrait, taken together with the staff of the Heard firm's Shanghai Office, suggests that he was largely Chinese by descent (Peabody Essex Museum, PH6.4).

James B. and Sarah Ann Endicott enjoyed so close a friendship with William C. and Rosalie Hunter that they named their daughter (b. Oct. 4, 1854) Rosalie Hunter Endicott. The child died on March 13, 1856 (Ride and Ride 1996:111–112).

As many as 400 foreigners may have suffered or died from eating arsenic-poisoned bread from the Esang Bakery. Sandwith Drinker (b. 1808) succumbed to its lingering effects on Jan. 17, 1858. "After his death, his wife [Susanna] left for Baltimore and died the same year, probably of the same cause" (Ride and Ride 1996:118–119).

George narrowly escaped the poisoning. I have excerpted the details from Albert Farley Heard's [N.D.] account.

"My brother's [John Heard's] experience had in it an element of absurdity, which, taken in contrast with the possible tragic consequences, was irresistibly funny. He and a friend D [probably George Dixwell] partook as usual of their early breakfast on the verandah ... Suddenly their equanimity was disturbed by the abrupt entrance of the butler ... 'Hi, yah! Misse H [Heard], look see!'— he explained, presenting a huge placard, on which was inscribed in large letters: 'Caution! The bread is poisoned. Antidote, powerful mustard emetic and white of eggs. Harland, Surgeon-General.'

"The two victims, as they supposed, stared blankly at each other and the remains of their morning meal ... They sent for the compradore, and ordered the mustard and eggs ... My brother [John], of an excitable and nervous temperament, swallowed the noxious draught, but D [Dixwell], more skeptical and phlegmatic, demurred. 'I don't half believe the story,' said he, 'anyway, I feel perfectly well, and I'll wait before I make myself sick.' ... The antidote [however] had begun its work, and H. was [already] in the agonies of its operation ... when there was a violent commotion below and the Portuguese major domo came rushing up the stairs. 'It is all right Mr. H,' shouted de Lanca as he burst in ... 'Our bread is all right ... I had a row with Ah Lum a week ago ... and for the last three days we have had our bread from Ah How.' [There was] a loud laugh from D [Dixwell] ... but Misse H. was in a state of collapse."

7.7 The Reverend Samuel and Catharina Bonney were close friends of the Hunters, and Catharina clearly had an important role in Anna Rosa's education. Catharina confirms this in an account of her 1869 reunion with former students (Bonney 1875:487).

" ... I had a charming visit of a few days in Canton, which was truly refreshing and comforting ... The cordial greetings and courtesies of social life were not confined to missionary families and foreigners, but the crowning act of kindness and a greater surprise was the grateful memory of the Chinese.

The Chinese lady teacher formerly connected with my school together with many of my old pupils came, bringing their husbands and babies, to see me, with joy depicted on their countenance. The meeting with Anna [Hunter], now the wife of Rev. D. Vrooman with her three children; and Ahá wife of a native assistant belonging to the English Wesleyan Mission with her husband and chubby boy were charming re-unions."

The Bonneys' situation in Macao is taken from a Nov. 21, 1857, letter from Samuel Bonney to the Rev. R. Anderson (probably in Boston). Bonney describes Catharina's Chinese students, the exorbitant rents, and the impending loss of their schoolrooms and chapel for a coolie depot and a mercantile store. The Bonney's educational philosophy is taken from Samuel's 1857–58 Report to Rev. Anderson (Papers of the American Board of Commissioners for Foreign Missions, Unit 3, South China Mission, microfilm reel 259).

"Our constant aim in their [the little Chinese girls] training has been to give their whole education a thoroughly Christian character, rejecting every thing that has the least taint of the idolatry of their relatives and countrymen. For this reason they are not taught the Chinese Classics, which are used in all native schools."

William C. Hunter's humorous description of the kind treatment and educational benefits received by the coolies enroute to Cuba (not his own words), is borrowed from the *China Mail* (18 June 1857 :98).

"The picture drawn of 'the passengers [coolies] going with the natives [Cubans] to church, like brothers to pray' is quite affecting! Surely after this it becomes the duty of the Macao authorities, lay and clerical, to forward this [coolie] trade by every means in their power? We have to add to this statement—one we vouch for as being equally true—that all the passengers, in anticipation of their 'going to church to pray,' were taught good classic Latin during the voyage to Havana."

7   Catharina Bonney's angry response to Hunter (not her own words) is borrowed almost verbatim from the same page of the *China Mail* where the editor asked—rhetorically—by what means Governor Guimarães and other influential parties in Macao "had been induced to sanction, nay to encourage, by every means in their power, this horrid traffic? If so," he wrote,

"they are doing so with a full knowledge of their falsehood, and lay themselves open to the charge, often made, that they aid and abet, for the most sordid consideration, all the kidnappings, cheatings, imprisonings, transportings and murderings, inseparable from this most foul occupation ... Meantime ... we hear of recent engagements of American ships for this business: we had hoped that the Waverly would have been the last clipper so employed. 'With what justice,' asks a correspondent, 'can Northern Ship-owners taunt Southern Slave-owners with being dealers in human flesh.'"

At the time of this vignette, Henry and James Bridges (about 14 and 12), the sons of James Bridges Endicott and Ng Akew, had been boarding for at least seven years with Nicholas and Mary Long in Scott County, Kentucky. We first find them living with the Longs in the 1850 Federal Census. William and James Hunter (aged approx. 17 and 15), the sons of William C. Hunter and a Chinese mother, had probably been living with the Longs since their 1854 arrival in the United States. The 1860 Federal Census confirms that all four boys were still living with the Longs in January of that year—the three eldest boys all designated as "Student-College."

Dr. Glen Edward Taul, Archivist of Georgetown College, reports that, according to the college catalogues, the Hunter brothers from Canton, China, entered the Classical Academy of Georgetown College in 1858. In the 1859–1860 school year, William Hunter became a freshman in the college, while his brother remained in the academy. In 1860–1861, William was a sophomore, while James became a freshman. William was enrolled in Latin, declamation, Greek, and trigonometry, while James took Latin, Greek, algebra, and declamation. The spring 1861 session ended abruptly on April 23 because of the beginning of the Civil War. I thank Dr. R. Gary Tiedemann for making the initial contact with Georgetown College.

For the purposes of this October 1857 vignette, I have the eldest Hunter boy preparing himself for a final year at the academy in anticipation of the college curriculum. Although William C. Hunter [the elder] was fond of horse racing and imported several horses to Macao for that purpose, the discussion of his sons' horses in Kentucky is my invention.

On March 30, 1858, Mrs. Rosalie Hunter (listed as age 30) arrived in New

York aboard the ship *Contest* from Macao with 5 children: Paulina, age 12; Rosalie, age 8; Jane, age 9; Richard, age 5; and Alfred, age 2. Traveling with her were Mary Nye with her two children and a servant [Port of New York, Passenger List]. Mrs. Rosalie Hunter was actually somewhat older than indicated on the passenger list. The 1850 Federal Census for New York listed her as 26, which would have made her about 34 in 1858.

7

Heard 1 = Heard Collection, Part One, Baker Library, Harvard.

Heard 2 = Heard Collection, Part Two, Baker Library, Harvard.

MHS, N-114 = Massachusetts Historical Society, Wigglesworth Collection.

GBD-D = George Basil Dixwell, Daily Journal, 1848–54.

8.1 Eight days after George's ball, Isidoro Francisco Guimarães was reappointed Governor of Macao. The *China Mail* reported (5 Nov. 1857 [178]:1): "It appears that what we mentioned in our issue of the 22d October, about a new Governor for Macao, was not correct, for we observe in the *Boletim do Governo* of the 31st October, a Decree nominating Sr. Guimarães, Governor of Macao for another three years."

John James Dixwell described the onset of the Panic of 1857 in four letters to George, dated: Sept. 10, Sept. 24, Oct. 12, and Oct. 23, 1857 (J.J. Dixwell, Boston, to A. Heard & Co., Hong Kong, Heard 2, Case LV-2, f.51). The final surviving allusion to the then still-unresolved Old Heads project is George's Feb. 14, 1858, letter from Hong Kong to Augustine Heard [the elder] in Boston (Heard 1, EM 3-2).

8.2 While still in China, George apparently negotiated an agreement to join his cousin (their grandfathers were brothers) George Barnard Sargent at Cook & Sargent in Davenport, Iowa. This

agreement is mentioned in "Extracts from the Diaries of ESD [Epes Sargent Dixwell], 1833–84, taken by himself," (MHS, N-14, box 17): "1858, Oct. 21 Geo. B. D. accepted offer to join in the business in Davenport." Assuming that this decision must have been preceded by at least one full exchange of letters between George and his cousin, eight weeks in each direction, George seems to have given up on the Old Heads counterfeiting scheme sometime before June 21, 1858.

I do not know the exact date of George's return to the United States. He wrote (1860:29) of his return from China "in the latter part of 1859." George then traveled to Davenport, Iowa, to join Cook & Sargent. Although I have found no correspondence describing this trip, George had already become well acquainted with the place in December 1854 when, in anticipation of completing the bridge across the Mississippi River at that location, J.J. had dispatched him there to purchase investment property. During that two-week visit, George purchased enough land through Cook & Sargent to become a significant player in local real estate. His diary entries for that trip [punctuation added], describe the extent of those purchases (GBD-D):

"Dec. 9 - Spend the day at the office of Cook Sargent & Co. // Dec. 11 - Looked at the lots near the depot and at Cook & Sargent's addition &c &c &c. Evening called on Mrs. Eben[eze]r Cook & on J. P. Cook and talked with them about Bridge Bonds &c &c. // Dec. 14 - Get a letter dated 9th from JJD [John James Dixwell] about 25,000 at M[assachusetts] B[ank] currency. Buy 800 acres of land viz all of Section No

31 and NW 1/4 Section 28 Town[-ship] 79 North, Range One (1) West—at 5$ less 21/2%—3900$ due 14th Jany at Massachusetts Bank to Cr[edit] of Cook & Sargent // December 15 - Bought lots 3, 4, 5, in Block 76 in Davenport fronting on 3d St. and corner of Farnam St. at 1250 ea = 3750 + 4 mos int & 2& tax. 3881.17 due at Mass Bank April 15th/18th 1855. Went twice to auction of lots."

The specifications of the Rock Island Railroad Bridge are described in Wilkie (1858:122). An organized opposition to the Rock Island Bridge was mounted by competing downriver interests in St. Louis, "which hitherto had enjoyed a monopoly in Western Commerce, [and] was rampant in its opposition to the scheme." The St. Louis Chamber of Commerce "Resolved" that a bridge was unconstitutional, an obstruction to navigation, dangerous, and that it was the duty of every Western State, river city, and town to take immediate action to prevent the erection of such a structure (Wilkie 1858:118). For a full discussion of the clash between railroad and steamboat interests over the bridge, see Pfeiffer (2004:40–47).

Biographical details regarding the career of George Barnard Sargent are taken from Ross (1947) and Sargent & Sargent (1923:34–35). His bifurcated beard is shown in an 1857 photograph (Downer 1910). I have borrowed phraseology for George Barnard Sargent's hyperbolic descriptions of Western land and the Rock Island Bridge from his 1858 "Lecture on the West," presented at the Tremont Temple in Boston (George B. Sargent 1947 [1858]). Sargent touted Iowa land in ornate prose, replete with metaphor.

For example: "Every wheat harvest, that waves its yellow signals in the summer glory over our prairies, is a pledge and prophecy of permanence ... Then shall be built up a Republic, stretching from ocean to ocean. The noblest empire the sun ever saw, founded in Justice, Liberty and Love."

For several years, detachments of abolitionist emigrants had been traveling to Kansas to ensure that the territory would become a free state. See, for example, *The New York Herald*, "Another Detachment for Kansas" (4 Sept. 1854).

8.3 I do not know how Henrietta spent the morning of December 2, 1859. The *New York Daily Tribune*'s Boston correspondent reported (3 Dec. 1859 [3]:4) "John Brown's execution to-day attracted considerable crowds about the newspaper offices as the evening editions were issued, and several individuals promenaded the streets with crape attached to their persons. Religious services were held in several of the colored churches the most part of the day. Otherwise there were no manifestations unusual to every-day life in this city." The *Boston Evening Transcript* reported (2 Dec. 1859 [2]:5), "Today the shops of the colored people are generally closed, and the day is observed as a Fast, with religious exercises in the Southac Street Church."

I have assumed that Henrietta, aged 75, conserved her energies in order to attend the formal meeting scheduled that evening at Tremont Temple, where she would see her friend, Lydia Maria Child. Maria confirmed she would attend in a November 28, 1859, letter to Maria Weston (Meltzer & Holland 1982:331): "I expect to go to Boston on Thursday to help Garrison a little about the meeting he is getting up on

Friday evening, to commemorate Capt. Brown's execution."

During the December 1859 period of this vignette, Anna Parker's political views were so contrary to Henrietta's that antislavery activists were unwelcome in Anna's house. Seven months later, Lydia Maria Child referred to this in a letter to Henrietta (L. M. Child, in Wayland, to Henrietta Sargent, Boston, July 25, 1860 (Holland & Meltzer, 1979 microfiche):

"I trust you will have a room of your own, where you can freely receive old friends. It does not seem right that your circle should be narrowed, as it was last winter. For, after all, there is nothing you enjoy so much, as the society of old abolition friends. They are so much more alive, and impart so much more life, than the world's people. Your old friends feel it as a privation, also, not to be permitted to see you more. Mrs. Garrison almost wept while she talked about it."

Ralph Waldo Emerson presented a lecture, "Courage," at Tremont Temple in Boston, on Nov. 8, 1859, where he referred to John Brown as, "The Saint whose fate yet hangs in suspense, but whose martyrdom, if it shall be perfected, will make the gallows as glorious as the Cross" (*Liberator* 11 Nov. 1859 [178]:5).

The *New York Daily Tribune* (12 Nov. 1859) reported that on Nov. 7 Gerrit Smith entered an insane asylum in Utica, New York. Whether or not he had truly lapsed into insanity was debated then and now. As Edward Renehan (1995:223–224) describes it:

"Always unstable, Smith's mind gave away—or at least he gave the very strong impression that his mind had given away—within two weeks of Harper's Ferry. But, interestingly, in the midst of his mental collapse, he managed a few key sane and sensible acts. He sent his son-in-law to Boston to find and destroy letters that might further incriminate him ... and then, with all the housekeeping of self-preservation completed, he suffered a breakdown."

On November 14, 1859, as Samuel G. Howe fled to Canada, he mailed a letter to a Boston newspaper, disclaiming any prior knowledge of John Brown's plot. Two days later, the *New York Daily Tribune* printed the letter with a short explanatory introduction (16 Nov. 1859 [6]:6): "The following letter is published by Dr. Howe in the Boston papers. It will be seen that he denies all knowledge of Cook, Brown's lieutenant, who in his confession, hinted at Dr. Howe's direct complicity with Brown. The particular statement of Cook was that weapons had been given to Brown by Dr. Howe, sometime previous to the invasion." It is my invention to have Henrietta castigate these fair-weather friends of John Brown, employing the words Jesus addressed to his disciple Peter (Luke 22:33–34).

A simple boldface banner, "*The Liberator,*" graced the weekly newspaper's first issue, on January 1, 1831. Four months later (April 23), the image of a slave auction was added, just above the banner. An image of African slaves marching toward emancipation was added on January 6, 1843. Although these images were modified over the years, their messages remained the same. The central image of Christ was added on May 31, 1850. The most provocative change occurred on January 3, 1845, when six statements were added just to the right of *The Liberator*'s masthead engraving. The first asserted, "All men are born free and equal." The fifth identified slaveholders as "a race of monsters unparalleled in their assumption of power, and their despotic cruelty." The last, and most provocative, a paraphrase of Isaiah 28:18, asserted, "The existing constitution of the United States is a covenant with death, and an agreement with hell. No Union With Slaveholders."

On October 26, 1859, Lydia Maria Child wrote to Governor Wise of Virginia asking permission to nurse John Brown. I have quoted from the response of Governor Wise, dated October 29, and from Child's caustic [undated] reply, as it appeared in the *New York Daily Tribune* (19 Nov. 1859 [5]:5). Note that I have Henrietta slightly reorder the phrases in two of Child's sentences. The actual phrases, as Child wrote them, are "... where could he [John Brown] read a more forcible lesson than is furnished by the State Seal of Virginia. I looked at it thoughtfully before I opened your letter."

The entire correspondence was published in various daily and weekly editions of the *New York Tribune* during October and November of 1859. The letters attracted so much attention that the American Anti-Slavery Society reissued them as a pamphlet (Child 1859) that achieved a circulation of more than 300,000 copies. See *The Liberator*'s (27 Jan. 1860: 14) review of *The Correspondence between Lydia Maria Child and Governor Wise and Mrs. Mason, of Virginia*.

Mrs. Mason had published a scathing letter to Child, urging her to show a modicum of concern for the needy of the North before extending her unwanted charity to the South. She wrote: "Did you ever sit up in the wee hours in order to complete a dress for a motherless child, so she might appear on Christmas day in a new one? ... And do you soften the pangs of maternity in those around you by all the care and comfort you can give?" Child responded, "My dear Mrs. Mason, I have never known an instance where 'the pangs of maternity' did not meet with requisite assistance, but here in the North, after we have helped the mothers, we do not sell the babies!"

Aunt Anna's, "Cats love cream!" is as remembered by Mary Catherine Dixwell Wigglesworth (1918:57): "A meal announced, Aunt Parker would rise from her window, fold her little withered hands, and timing it exactly would repeat, 'For all we are about to receive, thank God,' at the end of which she would be seated, and Aunt Henrietta from her window also. At once, with no break, 'Have some cream, Henrietta. Cats love cream,' and [Anna would] put a teaspoonful into her own mouth."

8.4 Cook & Sargent failed on December 15, 1859 (Mahoney 1990:618). The *New York Herald*, quoting a Chicago paper, initially attributed the collapse to the "failure of their Boston house" (18 Dec. 1859:4). A week later the *New York Herald*, quoting the *Dubuque Herald*, presented a more detailed explanation (26 Dec. 1859:8).

"Our readers are already aware that Cook & Sargent, of Davenport, the principal owners and issuers of the Nebraska wild cat paper, have failed and shut their doors. This is the final winding up of the swindling

Nebraska wild cat banks which this paper warned the public against years ago, and incurred the wrath of the friends of the infamous concerns in so doing ... In Davenport the result has been not only the consternation and ruin of many poor persons ... but mercantile houses appear to be going down like the pins in a bowling alley."

Six years later, George was still attempting to reimburse Washington Bank for George Barnard Sargent's dishonest withdrawals. The vignette presented here is based on George's 1865 statement (George B. Dixwell, in Shanghai, to Albert Farley Heard, in Hong Kong, Jan. 6, 1865, Heard 1, HM 31-2):

8

"There remains in Boston an obligation of mine to the Washington Bank given after the failure of Cook & Sargent to patch up a transaction of G. B. Sargent's [that] was too fishy—(it was making good on his account at the Washington Bank just at 2 o'clock by depositing a check on Merchants Bank where there were no funds & which check could not be made good the next day!) ... I think it would be better for me to pay up my half. This may shame Sargent (who though a great rascal is very fond of reputation) into paying his half and so make it unnecessary for me to fork out further ..."

Although Almon D. Hodges was the president of Washington Bank, the details of this vignette, beyond those described in George's letter, are as I have imagined them.

8.5 Henrietta helped to stage the 26th Annual Anti-Slavery Subscription Festival and Soirée, Jan. 25, 1860, at the Music Hall in Boston. My description of the evening is drawn mainly from the detailed report in the *National Anti-Slavery Standard* (11 Feb. 1860 [2]:6–[3]:1):

"The ladies who extended the invitation presided each at her own separate tea table and did its honors with all grace and hospitality ... and subscription-books, gayly adorned with ribbons, lay invitingly open alongside of the tea-equipage, ready to record the free-will offerings as they were made. A hollow square of tables was arranged in the center of the Hall, with the intention of making that the nucleus of the meeting when the speaking should set in. But the attendance was so great that this idea had to be given up, and the presiding and speaking done from the platform ...

"[The] Music Hall was very fitly decorated for the occasion, and ... over the platform stood the busts of Messrs. Garrison, Phillips, Emerson and Sumner, and Dr. Channing. But the decorations in this kind which attracted the most interest that evening were the splendid photographs of Brackett's magnificent bust of John Brown. I have not yet seen the bust itself ... The head looks like that of an ancient bard or philosopher, or rather like one of the best-looking of the Hebrew prophets. Moses himself seen in vision by Michael Angelo, could scarce surpass in majesty of countenance the man who deemed himself (and, perhaps, justly) his appointed successor. It is no wonder that [an artist] exclaimed on looking at it, 'What a shame that the old cuss should make us look so mean along-side of him!' A more willing, but not less gratifying, tribute to the artist's success was paid by an anti-slavery lady ... Mrs. Lydia Maria Child, then, who was looking at the clay model and said to Mr. Brackett, 'You must make haste to put this into marble, before anything happens to you.' 'You need not fear,' replied he; 'I shall not die before I have put that bust into marble.' 'And you will certainly never die after you have!' said she. ... Copies of the bust will soon be offered for sale, and the photographs are already to be had at the low price of two dollars each. I trust the sale will be as remunerative as the artist deserves ...''

The Liberator reported (10 Feb. 1860 [22]:2):

"Our thanks are unitedly tendered to all who kindly aided our preparations to convert the Music Hall into a saloon of reception for the occasion, and helped us to decorate it in a manner befitting the object, with the busts and pictures that consecrate our homes, and make the friends of freedom of both races, both hemispheres, and North and South alike, a kindred band ... The conversations during the evening were of surpassing interest, covering the whole ground of the Cause in all its history, purposes, collateral bearings and tendencies. The occasion was too nearly a private one to permit us to reproduce them ... The following lines, sung by a volunteer choir of friends, were written for the occasion by Mrs. Lydia Maria Child ...''

The full text of Child's song, "The Hero's Heart," as sung by the "volunteer choir of friends," was published in *The Liberator* (3 Feb. 1860 [20]:1). I have surmised that the tune was borrowed from a familiar hymn.

An article, "John Brown Kissing the Negro Child," appeared in the *National Anti-Slavery Standard* (24 Dec. 1859 [3]:3): "The statement that John Brown, while on his way to the scaffold, stooped down and kissed a negro child has been discredited by some persons as improbable, and by others positively declared to be false." The article also reported a letter from a Maryland gentleman affirming the truth of the statement in the most positive terms, the only error being "to the place where the incident occurred, which was within the jail, not outside thereof."

Henry Ingersoll Bowditch, MD (1808–1890), professor of medicine at Harvard, was the third of Nathaniel Bowditch's eight children. His younger sister Mary (no. 6) married Epes Sargent Dixwell, and the youngest, Elizabeth (no. 8), married John James Dixwell. (Williams 1990:104). The life-size bronze figure of Nathaniel Bowditch (1773–1838), seated beside a globe and a sextant, still confronts every pedestrian entering Mount Auburn Cemetery via Central Avenue (Linden-Ward 1989:236–237).

The *Boston Evening Transcript* (24 Jan. 1860: 3) published the announcement of the "Twenty-Sixth National Anti-Slavery Subscription Anniversary" in column 1. The somewhat larger advertisement for

8

Charles Darwin's, *On the Origin of Species, By means of Natural Selection,* appeared in column 3.

The discovery of extinct fossil life forms, sealed within geological strata, did not fit easily with a literal interpretation of the biblical story of Creation. The French paleontologist Georges Cuvier (1769–1832) proposed an explanation—"Catastrophism," suggesting that God directed a series of creations, each followed by a destruction in which all life forms were exterminated, and that the living species of the world were those that survived the final destruction by boarding Noah's ark. Louis Agassiz, Cuvier's student, accepted this general model, adding that the force of world glaciations explained earlier—pre-Adamic—destructions (Dupree 1959:226).

Agassiz wrote an introductory essay to Nott and Gliddon's *Types of Mankind,* asserting (1854:lxxv–lxxvi):

"I maintain distinctly that the differences observed among the races of men are of the same kind and even greater than those upon which the anthropoid monkeys are considered as distinct species ... Now, there are only two alternatives before us at present: 1st. Either mankind originated from a common stock, and all different races with their peculiarities, in their present distribution are to be ascribed to subsequent changes—an assumption for which there is no evidence, whatsoever ... [or] 2nd. We must acknowledge that the diversity among animals is a fact determined by the Creator, and their geographical distribution part of a general plan which unites all organized beings into one great organic conception; whence it follows that what are called human races, down to their specialization as nations, are distinct primordial forms of the type of man."

Building upon Agassiz's argument, Nott and Gliddon concluded (1854:79):

"The laws of God operate not through a few thousand years but throughout eternity ... Nations and races, like individuals, have each a special destiny: Some are born to rule, and others to be ruled ... No two distinctly marked races can dwell together on equal terms ... Those groups of races heretofore comprehended under the generic term Caucasian, have in all ages been the rulers; and it requires no prophet's eye to see that they are destined eventually to conquer and hold every foot of the globe where climate does not interpose an impenetrable barrier. No philanthropy, no Missionary labors, can change this law! It is written in man's nature by the hand of the Creator."

8.6 We do not know exactly when Fanny Dixwell began to suffer from eyestrain, but by 1867 she was about to give up painting entirely. By 1869 her embroidery was already drawing critical acclaim (Laidlaw 2003:44).

The Liberator (3 May 1861 [71]:1), quoting the *Traveler,* reported: "The Proclamation of President Lincoln calling upon the rebels to disperse, gave them twenty days to return to their allegiance. This period expires on the 5th of May, after which, as the command will probably not be complied with, the Administration will be in a condition to 'let slip the dogs of war.'"

Jefferson Davis's April 17, 1861, proclamation, inviting Confederate sympathizers to apply for letters of marque, was published in the *New York Tribune* (26 April 1861, [67]:4–5).

Henrietta's observation that "at last there is a North & South," is taken from W. L. Garrison (*Liberator* 3 May 1861 [70]:2). Her comment that, "the first gun fired at Fort Sumter announced the fact that the last fugitive slave had been returned," is taken from an April 27, 1861, speech by Gerrit Smith, as published in the *New York Tribune* (3 May 1861 [6]:5).

Anna Parker's gift of $100 to the City of Boston for the Military—"the generosity only being exceeded by the prompitude"—was acknowledged in the *Transcript* (26 April 1861 [2]:4). Five hundred dollar contributions "to the Coast-Guard Gun Boat" by Forbes, Delano, and Sampson & Tappan, were reported in the *Transcript* (1 May 1861 [3]:2).

The senior Oliver Wendell Holmes's new verse to the "Star Spangled Banner," appeared in the *Transcript* (27 April 1861 [2]:1).

"When our land is illuminated by
liberty's smile,
If a foe from within strike a blow at
her glory,
Down, down with the traitor that
dares to defile
The flag of her stars and the page
of her story!
By the millions unchained when
our birthright was gained,
We will keep her bright blazon forever unstained!
And the Star-Spangled Banner in
triumph shall wave

While the land of the free is the
home of the brave!"

In order to protect George's inheritance against his creditors, aunts Anna (Jan. 5, 1860) and Henrietta (Jan. 7, 1860) drew up new wills, placing George's share of their estates in a trust, to be controlled by his brothers (County of Suffolk Probate Court: Henrietta Sargent no. 51244; Anna Sargent Parker no. 54256).

8.7 George's letter to Augustine [Gus] Heard, Jr., agreeing to return to China and asking to borrow $3,000 to cover his expenses (Heard 1: GM 1-9, May 7, 1861), survives as a press copy of a transcription by Gus Heard, along with an addendum by Gus, in New York City, addressed to John Heard, in London. George's letter appears in the text of this chapter. The addendum by Gus is as follows:

Dear John [Heard]

I saw him [George] afterwards & arranged to advance him say £200–£300 [pounds sterling] here & my notes at 8 mo for $2000, to be arranged in China as you choose & he is to go out in August. Sooner if he can.

I believe this says all that is necessary in this except that AH&Co must remit in time to take up these notes of which I will be advised.

Yrs truly

AH Jr.
[Augustine Heard, Jr.]

George is listed as a passenger aboard the Steamship *Africa,* departing New York for Liverpool, Aug. 14, 1861 (*New York Tribune* 15 Aug. 1861 [8]:6). Aunt Anna addressed her letter to George four days after his departure (Anna Parker, Parker Hill, Roxbury, Massachusetts, to George B. Dixwell, Hong Kong, MHS, N-114, Box 5, Aug. 18, 1861).

8

Heard 1 = Heard Collection, Part One, Baker Library, Harvard.

MHS, N-114 = Massachusetts Historical Society, Wigglesworth Collection.

9.1 This Chinkiang vignette is based on George Dixwell's detailed report to Albert Farley Heard in Hong Kong (Heard 1, HM 28-3, March 3, 1863). Additional detail regarding Ahow, his uncle, and the "perpetuation of Ahows" is taken almost verbatim from George's April 20, 1863, letter to Albert (Heard 1, HM 28-3). George details his visits to the two properties on opposite sides of the Yangtze and describes how he will respond to the Chinese land speculators. Cloutman was the Heards' Chinkiang agent, but his first name is never mentioned in the records. For the purposes of this vignette I refer to him as "William."

Details regarding the placement of boundary stones and measurement with a depth line (marked in fathoms) are my invention. To give some sense of the detail provided by Dixwell, I quote several sentences from his March 3, 1863 letter:

"So I went up the river and found that D&Co JM&Co Fletcher&Co & R&Co had secured lots pretty much all together. I tried to get the next lot—side by side with R&Co but a native Mandarin had got it and it was a case of no can for the present. So the best I could do was put down our marks about 800 feet above R&Co's lot for a space of 300 feet front. The land here is so high as to require only 2–3 feet filling and this solely under the house or godown. The ostensible managers agreed that we should have this lot at the same price paid by the others for adjacent land:— and this was the closest I could get to the settlement. I tried coaxing in vain, and finally came away in the Bullying & am telling Ahow that if they do not settle at the same price as R&Co ... that I would come up there and complain to the Tautae (as Consul) that a parcel of speculators had forestalled all the land and were squeezing foreigners. I did this because I guessed from sundry little things that the company of nations who have got hold of the land—are compradors—perhaps our own & Ahow included. I told Cloutman when I left Chinkiang in the Independence to put up a mat shanty on the ground and keep someone there in possession so that we could fight over the price advantageously ... if nothing can be done without, I can address the Tautae either through Seward as an American or direct as Russian Consul."

The loss of face and self confidence that George felt when he returned to China virtually bankrupt is expressed in his July 12, 1864, letter to Albert Farley Heard (Heard 1, HM 31-1): "... when I arrived out [in China] I had just met with great reverses which shook every body's confidence in my judgements & my own as well—and I was in no position to demand or obtain much influence."

Of his trip back to Shanghai, Dixwell wrote, "I had a rum time living three days on the Ham & potatoes in the Independence." The ambience aboard the

Independence is my invention, based on the vessel specifications listed in the "Shipping in Harbor" section of the *North China Herald* (26 Sept. 1863): "Am. Ship, Frazar & Co., 827 T, Capt. Crowell."

The discussion of nighttime insurance coverage on the Yangtze is my invention, based on Dixwell's April 8, 1863, letter to Albert Farley Heard (Heard 1, HM 28-3). Apparently, sailing vessels were not insured for nighttime use on the Yangtze. Only a month after his return from Chinkiang, Dixwell complained that insurance brokers were trying to impose the same restriction on steam-driven vessels, and they were having trouble reinsuring their steamer *Fire Dart* for use at night. "Can't you make the people in Hongkong put the Yangtze Insurance pigeon on better footing. I [illegible] very much when a policy comes in from the [illegible] requiring the Steamer to anchor from Sunset to Sunrise. It is a swindle almost."

The shooting of several Chinkiang Customs House men is noted in George's letter to Albert (Heard 1, HM 28-3, Feb. 16, 1863): "Several Custom house foreigners have been shot about Chinkiang—in trying to seize Lorchas ..." During spring 1863 (while his superior was absent in England), Robert Hart's official title was acting inspector general, Chinese Imperial Maritime Customs Service (Bruner, Fairbank, and Smith 1986:251).

The marriage of John Endicott Gardner (b. Aug. 3, 1823, at Rio de Janiero; d. Nov. 22, 1864, in Canton) to Anna Rosa Hunter (b. Aug. 3 [sic], 1840, at Macao) took place on Oct. 2, 1862, in Canton. These dates for John and Anna Rosa are taken from genealogical forms sent to their eldest son (John Endicott Gardner, Jr.) by William G. Endicott on Aug. 15, 1920. John filled out the forms but apparently

did not return them to Endicott. I suspect that Anna Rosa's Aug. 3, birthdate—the same day as her husband's—is a guess, supplied by her son. I thank John's great-granddaughter, Susan Briggs, of Alameda, California, for allowing me to copy these documents from her family archive (hereafter cited Gardner-Hunter Family Archive). John Endicott Gardner [Senior] is listed in the *China Directory for 1863* as a "Tide Waiter," living in Shanghai, employed by the Chinese Imperial Maritime Customs' Service.

9.2 This vignette is based on the September 23, 1863, proceedings of the United States Consular Court in Shanghai (United States vs. Carroll and Williams for Murder and Piracy). Capt. John Taylor confirmed his affidavit made on Sept. 11, 1863, and the case was presented to the jury, which comprised George Basil Dixwell, Charles H. Angel, James E. Wainright, and A. A. Hayes (all commission brokers). In 1856 Hayes, of Olyphant & Company, established a church and cemetery for seamen just across the harbor from the Bund. A description appears in the *Boston Transcript* (10 Dec. 1870 [2]:1). The number of stars on the American flag had been changed to 35 on July 4, 1863, but the American Consulate in Shanghai would not have received the new flag by the Sept. 23, 1863, date of this vignette (Dr. Scot Guenter, 2009, pers. comm.). The jury sentenced David Williams to hang and Henry Carroll (as accessory after the fact) to 10 years imprisonment. I have taken the details of the crime and Captain Taylor's behavior directly from his testimony as reported in the *North China Herald* (3 Oct. 1863 [159]:2–5). As Taylor's vessel, the *Jupiter*, is twice misidentified as a "paplico," I have contrived Taylor's correcting of the spelling to "papico" and George Dixwell's etymological connection of the term to its Chinese antecedent. This flourish, of course, does not appear in the court record. The *hua-p'i-ku* (corrupted to papico) was a style of junk built near Foochow for trade up and down the China coast (Worcester 1948:64-65,fig. 29). Valentin Sokoloff (1982:33) reports that "*Ya-p'i-ku*" translates as "duck buttocks," but he mis-identifies the vessel form as a lorcha.

American Consul George F. Seward was the nephew of Secretary of State William H. Seward. The American Consulate seems to have been located on the American concession waterfront, about 100 yards from the bridge over Soochow Creek. I base this conclusion on two 1862–1863 photographs showing a two-story building at that location with a large American flag flying from a very tall pole in the front yard (Peabody Essex Museum images: PH5-40 and PH6-34). George F. Seward's letter to Washington, DC, confirms that the consulate operated in rented rooms: "The expenses of the Consular Court consist of items for jail rent, rent of Court room, hire of jailor, and necessary servants in Jail and Court room ..." (George F. Seward, Shanghai, to C. M. Walker, Auditor of Treasury, Washington, May 17, 1864, Dispatches from United States Consuls in Shanghai, 1847–1906, Microfilm Roll 7, National Archives: No. 112). The shabby character of the consulate is described in the *Shanghai Recorder* (8 Feb. 1864, news clipping reproduced in Consular Dispatches cited above) "We hope that Mr. Seward will use his endeavours to obtain very shortly the erection of a commodious building, with jail attached,

worthy of the Nation which he represents, as it is at present absolutely a reproach to the Flag which waves above it."

Dixwell and Angel's discussion of Pinder and Burgevine is my invention, based on reports in the *North China Herald*. Frederick W. Pinder, marshall of the United States Consulate at Shanghai, was tried on Sept. 24, 1863, for aiding and abetting the Taiping rebellion by furnishing arms and provisions to the rebels. More specifically, he was charged with carrying supplies to Burgevine and helping him to escape capture. Pinder was acquitted by a jury (which included Heard junior partner George Heard) because of insufficient evidence, the court being unwilling to convict him based on the testimony of a Chinese (*North China Herald* 26 Sept. 1863 [457]:1–5).

The 3,000-tael reward for Burgevine, dead or alive, was issued by "Le-Hung-Chang, Futai and Imperial Commissioner" on August 12, 1863. On August 20, George Dixwell, as Russian vice-consul, joined nine other "Consuls of Treaty and non-Treaty Powers" in a response to the *futai*, arguing,

> "The undersigned are aware that according to American Law the act of General Burgevine in taking up arms for the insurgents is an offence than which none could be greater, but they are also aware that the punishment therefor as provided in the American Treaty, and similarly in all others, can only be inflicted by the Representatives of his own Government, and further that were there no treaties in existence, he ought only to be punished according to the rules of civilized warfare."

9

Both letters are published in the *North China Herald* (22 Aug. 1863 [134]:5).

The *futai*'s very different assessment of Burgevine's status was addressed to the consuls on August 24 (*North China Herald* 5 Sept. 1863 [142]:3–4):

"In reply I observe that Burgevine has been invested with Chinese official rank, and has been employed as a Military leader on behalf of the Chinese Government; and having violated Chinese law it is right that he should suffer the penalty attached by China to the crime ... Burgevine has now ... passed over to join the rebels at Soochow and appears as the foe alike of China and of the several Powers engaged in the protection of Shanghai. Thus, Burgevine, having become one of the banditti cannot be accounted as a citizen of your honorable nation."

The American and British concessions united on Sept. 21, 1863, to become the International Settlement. The British Concession ratepayers' Sept. 29, 1863, protest over the cost of improving the American Concession was reported in the *North China Herald* (17 Oct. 1863 [167]:3–4).

The Public Garden (complete with gazebo) between the British Consulate and Soochow Creek was constructed ca. 1868. I thank Dr. Patrick Conner for providing me with a photograph and the date. For the purposes of this vignette I have guessed that there may have been an earlier gazebo on the British Consulate grounds to accommodate the Wednesday evening concerts, which had resumed at the Bund, as reported in the *North China Herald* (5 Sept. 1863 [141]:4).

"During the past week, no events of importance have occurred within the limits of Shanghai. We can only chronicle ... the re-establishment of music on the Bund ... We congratulate the denizens of Shanghai on the pleasant Wednesday evenings in store for them during the autumn; and we trust that the Bund will again, for at least one evening in the week, resume its old lively aspect."

9.3 During the spring and summer 1863, George maintained an active correspondence with five or more Chinese merchants up the Yangtze River. George forwarded his English translations of 20 of these letters to the Heard headquarters in Hong Kong (Heard 1, HM 30–2). One of the most frequent correspondents was Tong Loong Mow, formerly the firm's Foochow comprador. The extant file of letters ends with Tong's letter of July 13, 1863, in which he discusses the coal-hunting expedition of Ahow and the geologist, Mr. Lewis. I suspect the correspondence continued but was not preserved in the Heard archive—probably because George ceased sending his translations to Hong Kong. For this vignette, I have George struggling with issues raised in two letters: Ahow's letter of July 9, 1863, where he mentions that the coal has to be carried out on men's backs, and Tong's July 13 letter (received by George on August 26, 1863) describing the suspicions of the local village people that "the foreigners were seeking for treasures."

Throughout the Civil War, Henrietta Sargent and Maria Child worked to supply the needs of Union soldiers. In February 1864, Maria wrote to Henrietta: "I sent you some needle-books and bivouac caps. I made the caps rather differently from your pattern, because I was told that the soldiers like to have them come down in the neck, to keep the cold winds out" (L. Maria Child, in Wayland, to Henrietta Sargent, in Boston, Feb. 11, 1864; Holland and Meltzer 1979, doc. 1536). Wendell Holmes was shot three times during the Civil War. On October 19, 1861, near Leesburg, Virginia, he took a shot in the chest. He was shot through the neck at Antietam, Virginia, Sept. 17, 1862; and on May 3, 1863, near Chancellorsville, Virginia, he received a shot through his heel (White 1993:52–60).

At the time of this vignette (September 23, 1863), George had already completed two years under the tutelage of Chen Tze Fang. This was to become a very close relationship of student and teacher. Indeed, the first bequest in George's 1885 Last Will was to Chen's family (Suffolk Probate Court, Boston, Massachusetts, Vol. 567:54, dated March 6, 1885, filed April 16, 1885): "First. I give to the family of Chen Tze Fang, of Shanghae, China: the sum of two thousand dollars to be paid to them in said Shanghae. From 1861 to 1873 the said Chen Tze Fang was my Chinese teacher, as also the Chinese Secretary of the Russian Consulate. All persons connected with me in Shanghae know of him."

I have described the setting for Dixwell and Captain William Endicott's discussion on the wharf just outside the firm's' Shanghai headquarters as depicted in two (ca. 1863) photographs (Peabody Essex Museum, PH 6.3, PH 6.34). These photos clearly show the Heard firm's Shanghai headquarters, details of wharf construction, their receiving vessel *Anne Walsh*, the mud flats at low tide, the clustered sampans, and the streetlamps along the Bund.

William Endicott's wish to replace the leaky *Anne Walsh* comes directly from George's letter of August 7, 1863, to Albert Farley Heard (Heard 1, HM 29-2): "The other day a cargo boat got athwart hawse of the Anne Walsh and her bow [has] begun to weep again, and Endicott thinks she should be replaced before many months are over ... He says the only comfortable reliable thing for a receiving ship is an old teak vessel. Cannot one be got either at Whampo or at one of the Indian Ports?"

George had apparently already received his settlement from James A. Dorr. The settlement is recalled in a later letter from George to Albert Farley Heard, in Hong Kong. "Since I have been out here [in China] I have recovered money from J. A. Dorr, but this has been applied to paying off encumbrances on property not now convertible into money ..." (Heard 1, HM 31-2, Jan. 6, 1865).

Both sons of James Bridges Endicott and Ng Akew went into commerce. James worked for Peel, Hubbell & Co. in Manila (Carl T. Smith, 22 Aug. 2002, pers. comm.). Henry worked for his father as shipping agent for the *Spark* before becoming shipping agent for Augustine Heard & Co. After her separation from James Bridges Endicott, Ng Akew engaged in many commercial ventures, including "the brothel business" (Smith 1994:231).

James Hunter of Macao, China, enlisted as a private in the Union Army at Louisville, Kentucky, on Nov. 6, 1861. He mustered into "C" Company of the 6th Kentucky Cavalry on Dec. 23, 1861. James's older brother, William C. Hunter of Macao, China, enlisted on July 21, 1863, at Winchester, Tennessee, as a 2nd Lieutenant. On that same day, he joined his younger brother by mustering into

9

"C" Company of the Kentucky 6th Cavalry. I thank Gordon Kwok for gathering information on Asians who served in the Civil War.

Captain Raphael Semmes and the C.S.S. *Alabama* eventually did prowl as far east as the South China Sea. However, at the time of this vignette, during late September 1863, his movement around the tip of Africa and into the Indian Ocean is mostly speculation. The *Daily Alta California* (10 July 1863 [1]:2) imagined Captain Semmes steaming unimpeded into San Francisco Bay, a captured coal boat in tow for fuel, "run[ing] her sharp bow, at ten-knots-an-hour-speed, into the midship port of Uncle Sam." Throughout summer 1863, George investigated various means of protecting Heard vessels and cargoes against capture by Confederate warships and privateers. In his Aug. 7, 1863, response to Albert Farley Heard's query about registering Heard vessels under the Portuguese flag, George wrote, "What use would it be? The nation has not power enough to compel the flag to be respected. Semmes would not care a straw for it ... He would take upon himself to decide the case by the torch" (Heard 1, HM 29-2).

George's discussion of William Hunter's rendering of "King Kee" into Chinese characters is taken almost verbatim from his May 14, 1863, letter to Albert Farley Heard. (Heard 1, HM 29-1 [Note: Dixwell incorrectly dated this page April 14]).

Anna Rosa Hunter Gardner gave birth to John Endicott Gardner, Jr., on July 6, 1863, in Canton (Gardner-Hunter Family Archive). Anna Rosa had apparently returned from Shanghai to Canton (where her Chinese mother lived) near the end of her pregnancy. At the time of this vignette, baby John Endicott Gardner, Jr., was 11 weeks old.

The relationship of the Gardners to the Endicotts is as follows: Maria Cecelia Endicott Gardner (1797–1880) was the mother of John Endicott Gardner, Sr., and also the half-sister of James Bridges Endicott and Capt. William Endicott. Thus, baby John Endicott Gardner, Jr., was the Endicott brothers' grandnephew (Endicott family file, pp. 26–27, New England Historical Genealogical Society, Boston).

Between 1859 and 1863, George Tyson (1831–1881) fathered four children with Lam Fong Kew (1842–1871). Albert Farley Heard's liaison with her twin sister, Lam Kew Fong (1842–1925), produced no children. The twin sisters were born from the union of a European father (Bartou) and a Chinese mother (Lam) (Hall 1992:199).

Our information on Richard Howard Heard (born in Macao in 1861 of unknown parents) comes from the notes of Rev. Carl T. Smith, who has compiled a massive record of Chinese-European liaisons and their descendants. Smith (2002, pers. comm.) suspects but cannot prove that Richard was the son of one of the Heard brothers of Augustine Heard & Co. Although I have worked from hard copy sent to me by Smith, his entire archive [hereafter cited as the Rev. Carl T. Smith Archive] has now been microfilmed by the Church of Jesus Christ Latter Day Saints [aka Mormons] and is available through their family history centers.

In the late summer and fall of 1860, during which time Richard Howard Heard was conceived, three of the Heard brothers were in China. John Heard (1824–1894) directed the Hong Kong office and spent much of his spare time in Macao. Albert Farley Heard (1833–1890) directed the Shanghai office and had already begun his childless liaison with Lam Kew Fong.

George Heard (1837–1875), the youngest of the Heard brothers, had come to China as secretary to John Ward and traveled to many locations during this period. Since Albert was in Shanghai and already had a Chinese mistress, I suspect that Richard Howard Heard's father was either John or George.

Richard Howard Heard (b. 1861, Macao; d. April 9, 1913, Shanghai) was apparently well cared for and educated. He eventually followed a business career in Shanghai (possibly with Jardines). Richard married Mary Purcell (b. 1858, Ireland) at the Roman Catholic Cathedral in Hong Kong (Sept. 2, 1882). They had five children. I thank Rev. Carl T. Smith for this information.

The 1921 obituary of Richard's wife Mary Purcell Heard (clipping from an unidentified Shanghai newspaper) states:

"The funeral of the late Mrs. R.H. Heard took place yesterday afternoon at Bubbling Well Cemetery ... Mr. A.J.P. Heard, the deceased's only son, was chief mourner. The late Mrs. Heard was born in Ireland and came to the Orient via the Cape more than 60 years ago, marrying Mr. Heard, then a principal in the old firm of Augustine Heard & Co. Deceased is survived by her son, Mr. A.J.P. Heard, and [married daughters] Mme. Chapeaux and Mrs. W.L. Gerrard, now on holiday at home."

Although Mrs. Richard Howard Heard's obituary incorrectly asserts that Richard worked for Augustine Heard & Co., it clearly confirms that the Richard Howard Heard family claimed a connection to the Heards. The Heard Company failed in 1875, so Richard, then 14, could not have been a "principal" with the firm. The many mourners at Mrs. Heard's funeral included the "Foreign Staff, Ocean Shipping Department, Jardines" and the "Chinese Staff Ocean Shipping, Jardines." This suggests that Richard Howard Heard worked for Jardine, Matheson & Co. I thank Frédéric Grangier, the great grandson of Richard Howard Heard, for this clipping. There is no memory of a mention of a Chinese ancestor among any of Richard's descendants.

Robert Hart took up permanent residence in Shanghai on September 8, 1863. His official title was commissioner of customs, but he was already functioning as inspector general. That title would be formally bestowed on November 15. At the time of this vignette (Sept. 26, 1863), Hart's liaison with Ayaou had already produced two children: Anna (born in late-1858 or early-1859) and Herbert (b. 1862). A third child, Arthur, was born in 1865 (Bruner, Fairbank, and Smith, 1986:230–231,258).

9.4 The story of Wang-fo, as told by George to his teacher, is my expansion of the few details preserved in Henrietta's May 13, 1862, letter of summary and explanation (MHS, N-114, Box 5). See Chapter 1, note 6, for a verbatim transcription of Henrietta's letter.

George's grandfather, Epes Sargent, IV (1748–1822), was educated at Harvard (1766). His first son, named Epes (1772–1773), died in infancy. Attempting to preserve the name (in his line) for another generation, he named a second son Epes (Sargent and Sargent 1923:12–13). This young man (1789–1815) went to China to complete the four remaining years of his apprenticeship to Col. Thomas Handasyd

Perkins. Henrietta's 20-page historical account of her family, addressed to her nephew Epes Sargent Dixwell, reported that the War of 1812–1814 was very injurious to the prosperity of the family and that her brother Epes (four years her junior) "returned home destitute and ... in a consumption, taken in the China Seas, on his return passage," and that he died June 24, 1815, in Boston (MHS, N-114, Box 4, April 7, 1850, p. 18). I surmise that Henrietta viewed George's birth during her brother's final illness as a special gift to her. This perhaps explains the special affection that Henrietta had for George—more, by far, than for any other member of her family.

The genealogy of China trade firms leading to Augustine Heard & Co. is as follows: Perkins & Co. (1803–1830), for whom George's uncle, Epes Sargent, went to China, was absorbed by Russell & Co. In 1840, Joseph Coolidge was forced out of Russell & Co. and founded the firm Augustine Heard & Co. George joined Coolidge and Heard as the new firm's third partner in 1841 (Downs 1997:364–366).

Herbert Giles (1911:226–228) is my source for the etiquette of "guest tea," as well as Chen's discussion of poverty and scholarship. As Giles expressed it:

"Honest poverty is no crime in China, nor is it in any way regarded as a cause for shame; it is even more amply redeemed by scholarship than is the case in Western countries ... If a foreigner can speak Chinese intelligibly, his character as a barbarian begins to be perceptibly modified; and if to the knack for speech he adds a tolerable acquaintance with the sacred characters which form the written language, he becomes transfigured, as one in whom the influence of the holy men of old is beginning to prevail over savagery and ignorance."

I believe that George was similarly transfigured through his study of Chinese language and culture. I thank Dr. Raleigh Ferrell for directing me to the Giles volume.

The *Journal of the American Oriental Society* (1866:xvii–xxv) reported the proceedings of their May 18–19, 1864, Boston meetings, at which it was announced that " ... eight American merchants, residents of Shanghai, had contributed the sum of 525 taels, or about $680, for the purchase of a fount of Chinese type for the Society, no such fount being hitherto anywhere to be found upon the western continent." The eight donors, including "Mr. George B. Dixwell, of Shanghai," were elected to corporate membership in the society, after which the attendees recessed for a social gathering at the residence of Epes Sargent Dixwell in Cambridge. In the larger listing of Corporate Members (p. xlii), George's name is followed by a small cross, designating life membership. The American Oriental Society's Chinese font was certainly not the first in the United States. The *Oriental*, a bilingual English-Chinese newspaper began publication in San Francisco, on Jan. 4, 1855. This paper was published for about two years and was soon followed by others in California (Ko and Lai 1977:2–3).

Heard 1 = Heard Collection, Part One, Baker Library, Harvard.

MHS, N-114 = Massachusetts Historical Society, Wigglesworth Collection.

10.1 This vignette is set on Henrietta Sargent's 82nd birthday, Nov. 18, 1867. Her sister Anna Parker had celebrated her 85th birthday five days earlier on Nov. 13 (Sargent and Sargent 1923:12,24). Mary Dixwell Wigglesworth (1918:57) described Henrietta's and Anna's worktables, looking out across Tremont Street to Boston Common.

The discussion of Professor Asa Gray and his flowers is taken from Wigglesworth (1918:26).

"Dr. Asa Gray would call us to the Botanical Garden to see the Night-blooming Cereus open. Dr. Gray was a very real person in our lives, as he was a warm friend of our father's, and both were members of the Scientific Club ... He never liked to pick flowers for amusement, so on my wedding day, when he brought me two sprigs of very white flowers, it was considered a wonderful recognition of the day. How full of boyish spirits when he turned up at ... Gat's [Gerrit Smith Miller] in Peterboro, having been off on a botanical hunt ..."

For this vignette, I have assumed that Dr. Gray provided flowers for Susan Dixwell's marriage, just as he later did for Mary. The red rose for Henrietta is my invention as is the rosebush transplanted from Aunt Murray's house.

George Dixwell's birthday letter to Henrietta, although undoubtedly written and mailed, has not survived. In July 1865, George suffered a crippling attack of rheumatic fever. On Sept. 6, he wrote Albert Heard in Hong Kong that he could stand for but a moment on his legs and was virtually helpless, the disease having taken half of his left arm and three-quarters of his right. "I can write a little as you can see ... but the right hand ... will not put the pen in the ink stand—so that the left paw does this!" On Sept. 18, George informed Heard that he "must use a pencil and [I] have taken passage in the *Glengyle* for Nagasaki to sail tomorrow" (Heard 1, HM 31-3, Sept. 6, 18, 1867).

Almost a year later, Epes Dixwell wrote George, "I am sorry that you have not overthrown your enemy the rheumatism. It must be very wearing. I have great faith in the efficacy of brandy & salt rubbed into the skin. Have you ever tried that?" (MHS, N-114, Box 5, June 17, 1866). As Henrietta was a recognized expert in medical remedies, I have guessed that Epes probably learned of the brandy-and-salt concoction from her. By the time of this vignette [November 1867], George had apparently recovered from the most debilitating effects of the illness.

The story of Wang-fo, as rewritten by Henrietta's father, Epes Sargent, as a metaphor for his own life, is discussed in Chapter 1, note 6, herein.

Henrietta's July 21, 1841, letter to George, describing the long-term consequences of his focus on the pursuit of wealth, was prescient (Henrietta Sargent, Boston, to George Basil Dixwell, Canton, July 21, 1841. MHS, N-114, Box 3):

10

"You are too ambitious I fear. You will risk years of comfort for a dashing establishment in your old age— all your contemporaries of woman kind will be dead or married or widowed and you will be between the horns of a dilemma. You must remain a bachelor in solitary grandeur, or wed a widow with a troop of children at her heels—or an old maid with rigid habits and sour aspect—or be such a fool as to marry a young girl who will long to erect a monument to your memory—that she may have her dower and connect herself with some first love."

George's letters to Albert Farley Heard in Hong Kong describe the constant interruptions to his work and the ongoing necessity (as Russian vice-consul) to provide simultaneous translations of dinner table conversations. The following excerpts from George's 1862–63 correspondence provide a sample of the intensity of this persistent activity:

"Dec. 6, 1862 - [Commodore] Popov seems disposed to make me Drago-man and I told him that if the matter was not intricate I perhaps could get through with the assistance of the Chinese teacher // Dec. 13, 1862 - Unfortunately for the progress of his acquaintance with the Russians, neither Benjamine nor his secretary can speak French. However that makes us all the more necessary as go betweens. // March 16, 1863 - I am writing in the midst of fifty thousand interruptions—only if it be half bad French, half bad Chinese & ... half bad English—do not be surprised ... If this sort of thing keeps up I expect

to talk no language—but a compromise between English, French and Chinese!" (Heard 1, HM 28-3).

Anna Parker was unabashedly outspoken in dismissing the labors of the abolitionists in bringing about emancipation. As the relationship of Anna and Henrietta existed against the background of Anna's total contempt for Henrietta's life work, I quote from the brutally frank letter Anna sent to George on May 23, 1865 (MHS, N-114, Box 5).

"I was writing about the War and I had not room to say what I wanted to, about the Abolitionists as they were and as they are. You remember when they were a disgrace, and so they were. They kept back the wheels of emancipation. The South began the war, not caring about the Abolitionists one jot. The first year of Abe's administration they tried conciliation—but it was no go. After then—and the affairs in Kansas— the whole nation rose up, en masse, and became abolitionized, the sword was drawn in earnest & the scabbard thrown away, and Abe's emancipation proclamation issued. Then it was that the old anti-slavery folks began to crow, that they had done it—but this was soon put down— and they now behave pretty well, considering. Garrison has behaved remarkably well, and Phillips and he are not on good terms—P[hillips], some think, is half-crazy. —G[arrison] gives up his anti slavery paper—no more need of it—the work is accomplished. There is some fear that the blacks will be pushed on by mistaken friends, to claim a

10

social position, as well as a political, such as equal place at the Theatre, Cars—lecture room & churches—schools decidedly so. Well, all will come right in time, I suppose. So much for the Abolitionists."

A *New York Tribune* article "The Coolie Trade in the South" was reprinted in the *Standard* (10 Aug. 1867 [1]:2). It described how

" ... Chinese coolies, who have been kidnapped or betrayed by false promises, are sold to the highest bidders for seven years, and paid nominal and minimal wages. At the end of this term they find themselves in debt to the planters and are forced to renew their contract. ... This is the system which is to be the substitute of slavery in the Southern States. Coolies are now employed on the plantations of Louisiana, and the other day a ship-load arrived at New Orleans from Cuba. The United States Vice-Consul at Havana has informed the government that he has reason to believe 'that an extensive scheme is on foot for the introduction of Coolie labor in the South.'"

For an excellent synopsis and discussion of *Romance of the Republic*, see Carolyn Karcher (1994:501–531). Karcher identifies five abolitionists (including Father Samuel Snowden) whom Maria Child mentions by name and four more whose characters appear in "fictional disguise." Karcher argues convincingly that the character, "Royal King," was a nostalgic portrait of the late Ellis Loring, whom Child expected his widow, Louisa Loring,

to recognize. I believe that the African character, "Henriet," was named as a tribute to Henrietta Sargent, employing the childhood nickname that Child would have heard used by Henrietta's elder sisters (especially Catharine).

Looking Toward Sunset, Child's book on aging, was published in early November 1864 (Karcher 1994:48), just in time for Henrietta's 79th birthday. Karcher (p. 483) notes that Child's most candid contribution to the book, "Letter from an old woman on her birthday," was addressed "to an audience of intimate aging friends like Lucy Osgood and Henrietta Sargent," to whom the book was dedicated. Child [in a letter now lost] apparently asked Henrietta how she had responded to the various contributions in the book—a request that Henrietta took quite seriously, prompting a Jan. 8, 1865, letter from Child: "Dear Henrietta, You wrote as if you were going to re-read 'Toward Sunset,' as a critical job. I beg of you not to trouble yourself to do that. I merely wanted you to tell me what happened to strike you most pleasantly, as you read" (Holland and Meltzer 1979, letter 1614). Henrietta's letter has not survived.

Hobomuk: A Tale of Early Times (1824), published anonymously "By an American Lady," was Child's first major publication. Although the novel pushed the limits of acceptability, it was positively reviewed—possibly because the marriage it described between a white woman and an Indian occurred only in the woman's imagination. For a synopsis and discussion of the book, see Karcher (1994:16–37).

Henrietta's bouts with typhoid and smallpox are mentioned in Child's Dec. 31, 1865, letter to her: "God bless your, dear, good old soul, and your dear feeble old body! How glad I am that they

10

insist upon keeping together, and that they won't let typhoid, or small-pox, or anything else pull them apart! ... I don't believe that I could survive such repeated attacks of severe illness as you do" (Holland and Meltzer 1979, letter 1699). The "typhoid" mentioned by Child may have been cholera. In a July 27, 1864, letter to George, Anna Parker described Henrietta's survival of a "<u>violent</u> attack of cholera morbus" three weeks earlier on July 4 (MHS, N-114, Box 5).

Henrietta's discomfort with *Romance of the Repub*lic was apparently evident in her letter (now lost) to Child. Fortunately, we do have Child's August 11, 1867, letter to Eliza Scudder in which she mentions Henrietta's lukewarm response—remarking that Henrietta was reading the book a few pages at a time, interspersed with Walter Scott's *Rob Roy* (Holland and Meltzer 1979, letter 67).

10

10.2 No first-person description of Susan Dixwell and Gerrit "Gat" Smith Miller's wedding reception has survived. I know that the Rev. Dr. Newell married the couple in Cambridge on Thursday, Nov. 21, 1867 (*Boston Transcript* 25 Nov. 1867 [3]:5). I have assumed that the ceremony was conducted at Rev. Newell's Unitarian church in Harvard Square and that the reception was held in Epes Dixwell's house a few blocks away at 58 Garden Street. Gat's parents, Charles and Elizabeth Smith Miller certainly attended the wedding, as they had just returned from England where they purchased the wedding rings (Ernenwein 1970:57). Winthrop Scudder (1924) summarizes Gat's schoolboy career in football.

Great aunts Henrietta Sargent and Anna Parker were much involved in the lives of the Dixwell daughters, including Susan. Mary Dixwell Wigglesworth (1918:56) recalled that following Susan's engagement to Gat, Aunt Parker became anxious that "Sue's letters [to Gat] would not reach their destination unless kept for Uncle John to post. She also disapproved of Sue's wearing her engagement ring all the time. She was sure Sue would loose it and wished her to put it in its box and carry it in her pocket."

In May 1867, Gerrit Smith traveled to Richmond, Virginia, to petition the governor for Jefferson Davis's release from prison. "The bond under which Davis was admitted to bail, dated November 8, 1867, was signed by Gerrit Smith, Cornelius Vanderbilt and Horace Greeley" (Harlow 1939:444–445).

On Nov. 1, 1867, three weeks before the wedding, an anonymous journalist described a visit to Peterboro ("Gerrit Smith at Home," *Anti-Slavery Standard* 30 Nov. 1867 [4]:1–2). He noted that Gat was managing the remaining 500 acres of his grandfather's farm and that the original mansion "had recently been enlarged and improved, modern conveniences introduced ... with all the comforts a household could desire." I have assumed that Gat did the same for the cottage that he and Susan were to occupy. Regarding Gerrit Smith's strong views on religion and temperance, the journalist wrote:

> "To us he gave a happy description of his life in Washington, and his anti-wine dinner parties given to his associates in Congress, who found no fault with the dinner, save that the abundant supply of cold water slightly chilled their ardent spirits ... . In religion Mr. Smith is a liberal Christian. He has built a small

church where the people gather twice on the Sabbath ... [at the afternoon meeting] Mr. Smith usually speaks. Since his withdrawal from the Presbyterian Church, that society has ceased to hold any service ..."

Ralph Harlow (1939:204) quotes Gerrit Smith that Christian sectarianism was "the mightiest foe on earth to truth and reform, to God and man; and in its features and spirit, one of the most marked children of its father, the Devil." John Stauffer (2002:264) states that by the end of the Civil War, Smith had not only rejected all supernatural acts in the Bible, embracing instead the laws of nature, but now "lamented 'how much the world has lost by the deifying of Christ!'" Like Gerrit Smith, Henrietta had long felt contempt for much of the professional clergy for not embracing the abolition movement, but, unlike Smith, she felt no need to explain away the Bible. During the 1860s, Henrietta conducted a Bible class at Rev. A. A. Minor's Universalist Church in Boston (Sargent and Sargent 1923:13).

In 1851, Elizabeth Smith Miller designed an outfit of Turkish trousers gathered at the ankle, under a skirt extending a few inches below the knee. The costume was popularized as "bloomers" when Elizabeth's friend, Amelia Bloomer featured it in *The Lily*, a woman's magazine that she edited. Elizabeth wore her bloomers to Washington, DC, social events throughout her father Gerrit Smith's term in Congress (Ernenwein 1970:8; Stauffer 2002:212–214).

By the time of this vignette, Nannie Miller was already organizing a girls' baseball club. Nine months later, wearing their "bloomer" uniforms, the girls played their first public game, attended by Elizabeth Cady Stanton who wrote a description and was quoted in the *Cazanovia Republican* (19 Aug. 1868 [4]:4): "we were delighted to find here a base ball club of girls. Nannie Miller, a grand daughter of Gerrit Smith, is the captain, and handles the club with grace and strength worthy of notice. It was a very pretty sight to see the girls with their white dresses and blue ribbons flying, in full possession of the public square, last Saturday afternoon, while the boys were quiet spectators of the scene." The girls' bloomer outfits were more accurately described in the *Rochester Evening Express* (8 Sept. 1868) as: "... short blue and white tunics, trimmed, white stockings, and stout gaiter shoes, the whole thing forming a combination that is at once, easy and exceedingly beautiful."

Elizabeth Smith Miller's allusion to criminals, paupers, idiots, and women being denied the ballot is borrowed from an article published one week earlier in the *Standard* (16 Nov. 1867 [3]:2):

10

"Miss Dickenson gave a very excellent lecture on 'Idiots and Women.' She said that the distinction thus made was retained in practice only as far as the last of these classes: the criminals of the Southern rebellion have been largely admitted to the franchise; the poor whites of the South, who for a year past have been living on government rations for the want of power to support themselves, have still their vote; and so have the idiotic politicians who maintain this state of things while they insist upon excluding women. It is quite time to try the experiment with the last of these classes also."

Henrietta's support of women's suffrage is clearly implied in Child's, Oct. 13, 1860, letter to Henrietta (Holland and Meltzer 1979, letter 1258):

"Did you read, in the *Standard*, Mrs. [Elizabeth Cady] Staunton's [sic] wide-awake Speech to the Wide-Awakes? It seems to me a very great speech; one of the noblest that ever came from the lips of a woman. How absurd it seems, that any tipsy, ignorant fool, with a hat on, can vote, while such a woman is disfranchised. Oh dear! What a labor it is, to get this world right side up!"

Ralph Harlow reports (1939:453) that "On July 27, 1867, the *Tribune* announced a settlement of the Gerrit Smith libel suit—and in doing so once more reprinted the libel in full. But the paper did express regret for its implied charge that Smith feigned insanity, and admitted that competent medical testimony proved that he had really been insane." We can only imagine the belly laughs at the *Tribune*.

An undated photograph of the interior of Epes Dixwell's house shows Chinese Canton-pattern platters on display in a pantry cupboard and what appears to be one of Fanny's embroideries hanging in the hall (Wigglesworth 1918, page unnumbered) Although none of Fanny's early embroideries have survived, Sheldon Novick (1989:117, note 9:17), who has studied Wendell Holmes's diary (Harvard Law School, B19, F2), reports that Holmes received a Japanese lacquer glove box for Christmas 1866, and then: "On New Years Eve Wendell visited Fanny in Cambridge where she lent Holmes an embroidered picture for his room, which he would return the following New Year's Eve. Before midnight, as 1866 ended, Holmes was back in his room alone, hanging his new embroidery, morning glories on a gilt background, and making the year's final entry in his diary."

By the late 1860s "Japanism" was already exerting a strong influence on artistic taste in Boston. Fanny Dixwell's innovative embroideries clearly reflected this influence (Laidlaw 2003:42–68). On Dec. 15, 1867, Holmes wrote to his friend, William James, that Fanny's eye problems had interfered with her painting (Laidlaw 2003:44).

Will James first met Fanny Dixwell in March 1866 and immediately wrote his friend Tom Ward that he was captivated by her. "... I made the acquaintance the other day of Miss Fanny Dixwell of Cambridge (the eldest), do you know her? She is decidedly A1, and (so far) the best girl I have known." A week later Will wrote to his brother, "Miss Dixwell ... is about as fine as they make 'em. That villain Wendell Holmes has been keeping her all to himself out at Cambridge for the last eight years; but I hope I may enjoy her acquaintance now. She is A1, if anyone ever was" (William James quoted in Bowen 1944:223).

Although Anna Parker's plot for Fanny to snare Wendell is my invention, the family was concerned by Fanny's continued spinsterhood. Only a few months earlier, Epes Dixwell had written to George, reviewing the family: "Annie [Dixwell] is a nice hearty tall girl, a little [illegible word], or playful rather—very well educated & much given to study. A.P. [Anna Parker] is bright, brick erect.—H.S. [Henrietta Sargent] is bent, tamer, evidently older—feebler than you remember her at all ... Fanny [Dixwell] about as you remember her, only getting to look a little old maid-ish" (MHS, N-114, Box 5, June 17, 1866).

In this vignette, Henrietta somewhat overstates her defense of Wendell Holmes. In November 1867, Holmes—though perhaps contemplating writing a book—was only writing book reviews for the *American Law Review*. In a few months he would begin the more arduous task of writing summaries of State Court proceedings (Novick 1989:119).

Soon after the start of the Civil War, women organized into volunteer sewing bees to provide clothing for the soldiers. On Nov. 1, 1861, 16 teenaged girls met to sew in Epes Dixwell's house. They named themselves "The Banks Brigade" (after Major-General Banks) and elected Susan Dixwell as colonel. After the war, the girls—now bonded for life—renamed themselves "The Bee." Their history, dedicated to Susan Hunt Dixwell (Miller), was published by Mary Towle Palmer in 1924.

Anna Parker's oft-repeated phrase to Henrietta—whom she always addressed as "Henriet"—was remembered by Mary Dixwell Wigglesworth (1918:58). "I had to grow way up before I realized that the stern voice with which Aunt Parker ended a call on us by these words, 'Well, I and my horses are going, Henriet. You can stay as you choose,' was meant as humor and not hatefulness."

10.3 The placement of this vignette at Chen Tze Fang's house is, of course, my invention. The issues discussed are real. During the 1860s, Heard partnerships were of three years' duration. George returned to China in fall 1861 during the second year of the Heard 1859–1862 partnership. George waited more than eight months before becoming a junior partner in the next Heard partnership of June 1, 1862, to May 31, 1865. [See George's letter of Sept. 17, 1867, to George F. Heard, in Hong Kong, for a discussion of partnerships and proceeds (Heard 1, JM 1-3).] The Heard firm began to experience serious losses during 1864, the second year of George's first term (1862–1865) as partner.

F. L. Pott (1928:79–80) describes the financial collapse in Shanghai that resulted from the final suppression of the Taiping Rebellion in 1864 and the consequent mass exodus of Chinese returning to their home villages from the safety of Shanghai.

> "Whole streets of newly built houses became vacant, buildings were stopped halfway in their construction, long lines of godowns [warehouses] along the river front ... became disused, and recently constructed wharves stood deserted ... The over speculation in land and buildings and the financial collapse, had a disastrous effect on banks. Six out of eleven suspended payment and the world-wide monetary crisis of 1866 made its effect felt in Shanghai also, and added further to the financial depression."

On Feb. 3, 1867, Augustine Heard & Co. signed away its right to operate steamers on the Yangtze River for 10 years, thus guaranteeing Russell & Co.'s Shanghai Steam Navigation Company a monopoly of Yangtze steam commerce (Heard 1, EL-6, as cited by Liu 1962:188, note 73). A week later on Feb. 12, the Heard firm concluded the sale of the *Kiangloong*, their last Yangtze River steamer, to Russell & Co. for 212,000 Taels (Liu 1962:62).

I thank Dr. Raleigh Ferrell for suggesting the series of characters—for home/ family, tranquility, and goodness—by which Chen Tze Fang illustrates George's need for a family. The relationship of teacher to student can become an intimate one, and Chen seems to have become the most influential person in George's adult life. Not only was he George's teacher for 11 years (1861–1873), but also he is the first person listed by name in George's will. I have guessed that it was Chen who encouraged George to consider marriage to a Chinese woman.

10.4 Dixwell describes Capt. Hervey Jencks Roundy's fraud in three letters addressed to Heard headquarters in Hong Kong—all dated May 6, 1867 (Heard 1, HM 31-3):

"It seems that Roundy has been in the habit of filling up his own opium [chests] when he shipped it off—to full weight—so as to save on duty. This spring he has thus accumulated 20 empty chests. Then he thought he should have trouble with the Customs House in closing accounts so he had them packed with a picul of Granite chips taken from the EJ's [*Emily Jane*] ballast—taped—sealed with the seal of Augustine Heard & Co. Shanghae and shipped down to Hongkong to some opium brokers ... We intend to put [William] Endicott on board [*Emily Jane*] for a few days and to get the drug out of the ship ... and then let her lay until we get an offer for her ... This is a very melancholy thing. It would seem that the hurt to his spine must have affected R's mind for had he been originally

dishonest he must have had plenty of chances during this past thirty years ... The defense of lunacy might or might not be satisfactory to assessors. At all events it would be dragging the man through purgatory to contest it ... Meanwhile Roundy bemoans his wife & children—says he shall die before many days ... Noble said yesterday he—R—had a revolver in his pocket."

Roundy appears to have been the first to propose that the Heard firm unite their Yangtze River steamer operations with Dent's and Jardine Matheson's in order to compete successfully with Russell & Co. Roundy's letter of Nov. 30, 1865, to Albert Farley Heard, stated: "If James Whittal [Jardine Matheson] and John Dent favor a proper combination of three houses, or a joint stock company, 'we can defy the world ...'" (Heard 1, HM-58; see also Liu 1962:188, note 60). Roundy's wife, née Martha Mansfield Endicott (b. 1834; m. 1855), was the daughter of James B. and William Endicott's half brother, John Endicott (William C. Endicott ND [~1920]:27).

William C. Hunter's oldest son, William C. Hunter, Jr., died while serving as a Union soldier in the Civil War. I do not know the exact cause of his death. His military record includes the following information: William C. Hunter, Macao, China, residence not listed; Enlisted 7/21/1863 at Winchester, TN, as a 2nd Lieutenant. On 7/21/1863 he mustered into "C" Co. KY 6th Cavalry; he died on 12/16/1864 at Louisville, KY. I thank Gordon Kwok, who has compiled a record of Asians who served in the Civil War, for supplying this information.

At the time of John Endicott Gardner's

death on Nov. 22, 1864, in Canton, he had fathered two children by Anna Rosa (Hunter) Gardner: John Endicott Gardner, Jr., (1863–1943) and William James Gardner (1864–1911). Most of this information comes from Endicott genealogy worksheets sent by William C. Endicott to John Endicott Gardner (Jr.) on Aug. 15, 1920. Gardner filled in the information but apparently never returned the sheets to Endicott. I thank Susan Briggs, the great-great granddaughter of Anna Rosa (née Hunter) Endicott for giving me copies of these important documents.

Henry Bridges Endicott (1844–1895), son of James Bridges Endicott and Ng Akew, was employed for many years as chief shipping clerk for Augustine Heard & Co. in Shanghai. Fluent in Chinese, he managed all commerce with Chinese charterers, shippers, and brokers (Liu 1962:119; Marringer and Hyde 1967:74–75).

"A New Field for Missionary Enterprise" was the title of a long letter to the editor of the *North China Daily News* (8 Nov. 1867:3511). The correspondent, "S," suggested that if the missionaries as "... the professed instructors of religion and morality were to make arrangement for education and bringing up a number of Cantonese girls with a view of ultimately making them the wives of Europeans, they would be doing a greater service to the souls of their countrymen and the cause of Christianity, than they could ever do preaching to Chinese coolies." All of the details as remembered by George—including the characterization of bachelor merchants as "hardened profligates, and abandoned debauchees"—are quoted virtually verbatim. I thank Eric Politzer for directing me to this letter.

10.5 Russell Tyson, son of George and Sarah Howland (Anthony) Tyson, was born in Shanghai, Dec. 1, 1867 (Harvard University, Class of 1890, 1915:256). On Jan. 4, 1867, soon after his marriage to Sarah, George Tyson purchased a residence in Hong Kong (Sec. B, Imperial Lot 450) for Lam Fong Kew (1842–1871), the mother of his four Eurasian children. Following the instructions in Tyson's will, this property was transferred to his eldest son, Chan Kai Ming (1859–1919), on July 23, 1889. I thank Rev. Carl T. Smith of Hong Kong for providing me with this information.

Hu Ts'ai-shun

This vignette introducing Hu Ts'ai-shun is my invention. Our only authoritative document regarding her life before marrying George is her will, dated 27 August 1915, in which she states: "I, the undersigned HOO TSAI SHOON [characters], am a native of Tong Kar Jaw [characters] of Jaw Sz Tsung District at Hangchow [Hangzhou], China, aged 67 years ..." I thank Marcia Dixwell DiMambro, Ts'ai-shun's great-granddaughter, for providing me with a copy of this document. [Note: I use the modern transliteration of "Hu Ts'ai-shun," which is different from the "Hoo Tsai Shoon" used in earlier documents.]

We have one other clue regarding Ts'ai-shun's past. Her son, Charles Sargent Dixwell, told his son, Bazil Sargent Dixwell, that Ts'ai-shun was a "Chinese Princess of the Imperial Family" (Bazil S. Dixwell, 3 Jan. 1991, pers. comm.). Although Ts'ai-shun was certainly not a Manchu princess, Bazil's phrase might be interpreted as a gloss for another scenario that, as was true for many Manchu girls, she performed

10

palace service in the Forbidden City—not as a court lady but in a special category of privileged maidservants.

Ts'ai-shun's stated age in 1915 indicates she was born ca. 1848. Her city of birth, Hangzhou, was the base for a number of important Manchu Banner garrisons, and Ts'ai-shun herself was Manchu. Her feet are unbound and her dress, as shown in all her many photos, dating from ca. 1873 to 1910, is typical of that worn by Manchu ladies of her day. I thank Dr. Linda Cooke Johnson and Dr. Shuo Wang for their analysis of Ts'ai-shun's clothing—and bearing—and their conclusion: "Manchu, and proud of it!"

In our speculative reconstruction, Ts'ai-shun would have entered the Forbidden City about 1857 when she would have been 10 *sui* by Chinese reckoning of age. While she was in palace service, her parents, living in Hangzhou, were likely killed along with 1,000's of other banner families when that city fell to the Taiping rebels in 1861. In addition to the 1,000's killed outright, an estimated 30-40,000 people starved to death during the two-month siege of the city, and another 10,000 men, women, and children killed themselves when the city fell (Crossley 1990:132,133). Ts'ai-shun, now an orphan, would have left the palace ca. 1867 after completing her approximately 10-year obligation. George Dixwell's long-time tutor Chen Tze Fang, or some other Chinese colleague, probably arranged for Ts'ai-shun to marry George late in 1867. Their son Charles T'ien-sheng Sargent [Dixwell] was born the following year.

Our reconstruction of Hu Ts'ai-shun's youth does not require palace service. In a possible alternative reconstruction, Ts'ai-shun could have survived the fall of Hangzhou as an orphan from a good Manchu family—thus without a dowry—and then married George. I have chosen the possibility of palace service as a serving girl in part because it reintroduces a vocation in which many Manchu girls were engaged that has been largely ignored in the literature.

During the Ch'ing (Qing) Dynasty (1644–1912), the privilege of palace service was reserved for daughters of Manchu "bannermen" (petty lords). All Manchus—Tungusic speakers from northeastern China who ruled China during the Ch'ing dynasty—belonged to one of eight warrior-administrator "banners." Han Chinese women were excluded from palace service. Scholars have focused primarily on the smaller number of Manchu girls who entered the palace as *hsiu-nü* (*xiunu* "elegant ladies") candidates for the position of imperial concubine. For an overview of that process, see Wang (2004).

Hu Ts'ai-shun would have been among the much larger number of girls from lower-ranking families who, as early as age 10, entered the Forbidden City as serving maids. An English- and French-educated Manchu girl Yü Der-ling, aka Princess Der Ling, who served as first lady-in-waiting to the Empress Dowager from 1900 to 1903, wrote (Der Ling 1911:100,101):

"Now regarding the servant girls, they are a much better class of people than the eunuchs. They are the daughters of Manchu soldiers, and must stay ten years at the Palace to wait upon Her Majesty, and then they are free to marry. One got married after my first month at the Court. Her Majesty gave her a small sum of money, five hundred taels [equivalent to 500–1,250 ounces of silver]. This girl was so attached to

Her Majesty that it was very hard for her to leave the Court. She was an extremely clever girl. Her name was Chiu Yuen (Autumn's Cloud). Her Majesty named her that because she was so very delicate looking and slight. I liked her very much during the short time that we were together. She told me not to listen to anyone's gossip at the Court, also that Her Majesty had told her she was very fond of me. On the twenty-second day of the third moon she left the Palace, and we were all sorry to lose her. Her Majesty did not realize how much she missed her until after she had gone. For a few days we had nothing but troubles. It seemed as if everything went wrong. Her Majesty was not at all satisfied without Chiu Yuen. The rest of the servant girls were scared, and tried their best to please Her Majesty, but they had not the ability, so we [court ladies] had to help and do a part of their work … ."

Der-ling also interpreted for American artist Katherine Carl while the latter was in the palace painting the Empress Dowager's portrait. It was no doubt through Der-ling that Carl learned some of the additional details she provided: "[The serving girls] live off the fat of the land, have beautiful clothes and many advantages. They wear … blue gowns, with their hair plainly parted at the side and braided in a single long braid (tied with silk cords), which hangs down the back. They wear bunches of flowers over each ear," and stay in the private quarters of the ladies they attend. After serving for 10 years they are free to return to their families, often with a generous endowment from the Court, allowing them "to make much better marriages than they would otherwise do" (Carl 1907:47).

It should be noted here, that two early-20th writers, intent on discrediting the Manchu court for their own purposes, attempted to cast doubt on Der-ling's account of palace service (Bland and Backhouse 1910; Backhouse and Bland 1914). More recently these writers' own accounts have been revealed as fraudulent (Seagrave 1992; Trevor-Roper 1976). The topic of palace service, especially at the lower level, deserves a fresh examination.

Ts'ai-shun certainly knew Wu, the Chinese dialect of the Shanghai area and Hangzhou, her home city. Whether she was conversant in Manchu is problematic; by the mid-19th century many ordinary Manchu families were more at home in local Chinese dialects.

While official Ch'ing records were kept in both Manchu and classical literary Chinese, by the mid-19th century the everyday language in the imperial palace was the Kuan Hua (*guan hua* "official language" or Mandarin) based on the Beijing dialect. During her stay in the Forbidden City, Ts'ai-shun would have become familiar with Kuan Hua. She probably used Kuan Hua with George, who was fluent in both Cantonese and Kuan Hua but most likely not the Wu dialect. With her household servants and in the marketplace, Ts'ai-shun would have used the Wu dialect, but she would have seen the advantage of her son growing up to speak Kuan Hua like his father.

I thank Dr. Raleigh Ferrell for suggesting the possibility of Palace Service and explaining the broader cultural context. The way I have structured that information in this chapter is my own.

10

Heard 1 = Heard Collection, Part One, Baker Library, Harvard.

Heard 2 = Heard Collection, Part Two, Baker Library, Harvard.

MHS, N-114 = Massachusetts Historical Society, Wigglesworth Collection.

11.1 George Dixwell's business activities during 1870 are well documented in his Heard Co. correspondence. His civic activities as member of the Shanghai Chamber of Commerce and as chairman of the Municipal Council are reported in the *North China Herald*. This vignette, dated Dec. 13–14, 1870, is structured around George's Dec. 14 remarks at the Shanghai Volunteer Corps award ceremony, as reported verbatim in the *North China Herald* (21 Dec. 1870:444–445). Although the vignette is framed by George's professional activities, my real purpose is to describe his domestic relationship with Ts'ai-shun and Charley.

We know little about George's marriage to Ts'ai-shun, except that it probably occurred nine or more months before Charley's birth on Oct. 28, 1868. Chen Tze Fang's role is a guess, based on his prominent mention in George's will. The involvement of the Endicotts and Fearons in the ceremony is also a guess. Charles E. Endicott is mentioned by name in George's will as knowing Charley. "The said Teen Seng, or in English, Charles Sargent, was born on the 28th day of October 1868 and is well known to C. E. Endicott, Esqr. of said Boston ..." Robert Fearon and his successors helped Ts'ai-shun manage her financial affairs until her death in 1915 and then helped to settle her estate.

Ts'ai-shun's 1915 will gives the address of her main home as 34 Hoihow Road in the Shanghai International Settlement. I have assumed this was the house George occupied with her. I do not know the architectural style of the house, but I have described it as Chinese in organization, built around a courtyard, with all the usual fengshui considerations (Bruun 2003). Our evidence for Ts'ai-shun's belief system comes from instructions in her will that her younger son—her older son Charley was then living in the United States—have use of the residence "because according to Chinese law and custom ... [he] must establish or put up my tablet and perform the regular ancestral worship after my death for three years, and his residence in this house will prevent the removal therefrom of my tablet and will ensure the ancestral worship being duly carried on."

George's relationship with Ts'ai-shun appears to have been mutually affectionate. This is suggested in his April 3, 1874, letter from Boston to Robert Fearon in Shanghai (Marcia Dixwell DiMambro, family archive):

" ... no letter came from H.T.S. [Hu Ts'ai-shun] by the mail that brought yours on Feb'y 14, although you say or intimate one was written. I am naturally disappointed, as I (as naturally) like to hear what is going on in that quarter ... I will enclose a letter to H.T.S. in this ... At the same time it is rather rough upon me and upon H.T.S. who no doubt has her times of thinking that Low Fuk Chen [probably a pet term by which Ts'ai-shun refers to George] does not mean to come. If that steam [George's invention] should turn up trumps—that little fellow [Charley] may be a millionaire before he is of age: although that is not of half so much importance as being a good and intelligent fellow. But enough of this. Help H.T.S. if you can in the matter of the repair of her houses. [Note that George refers to the houses as *hers*!] I don't think she will need any assistance beyond getting the necessary money out of the Bank. She may not know how to do this."

The ambience of life in George and Ts'ai-shun's house is suggested by George's June 3, 1874, letter from Boston to J. E. Reding, a Heard & Co. colleague who, along with Fearon, was looking after his affairs in China. "I am greatly interested for the youngster [Charley]. I do not want him to be spoiled and this was the chief reason I put him at the school where he is rubbed against by other children and not corseted to death by his mother & half a dozen female servants" (Marcia Dixwell DiMambro, family archive).

I borrow Ts'ai-shun's pronunciation of *Dixwell* from Tong Loong-maw's rendering of the name in Chinese—Te-ch'en—in his April 1, 1863, letter to George Dixwell (Heard 1, HM-60). The original letter is reproduced as an illustration by Hao (1970:38). Although the Lord's Prayer is seldom, if ever, used as a dinner grace, I have George repeat it here as a teaching device to enable Charley to hear more English.

The Municipal Council had "placed native policemen at the bridges crossing Defense Ditch, to prevent beggars from returning to the [International]

Settlement after they had been relieved at the Refuge" (*North China Herald* 21 Dec. 1870 [439]:1).

Prince Kung's refusal to see American Consul Seward, on Nov. 7, 1870, was reported as the incident unfolded. I have taken the salient details from a summary of their correspondence published in the *North China Herald* (21 Dec. 1870:445–446). Prince Kung had good reason to avoid publicly accommodating foreigners. Eight years earlier George noted this in a letter to Alfred Heard (Heard 1, HM 28–3, Dec. 10, 1862):

"Muirhead also told me that he thought from the recent appointments of Mandarins to office who were decidedly against foreign intercourse—that there was great reason to think that Prince Kung was fooling the foreign ministers in examining with them the idea that foreign intercourse was getting the upper hand—with his being the friend of the foreigners &c &c."

11

11.2 There were three Fearon brothers: Samuel (1819–60), Charles Augustus (1820–82), and Robert Inglis (1837–97). Samuel apparently learned Cantonese as a child in Macao and became the first professor of Chinese at King's College in London. Charles served as a Heard partner in China before becoming their agent in London. He named his eldest son (b. 1851) George Dixwell Fearon. Robert, probably also fluent in Cantonese, named his second son Frank Basil (b. 1868), apparently in honor of George Basil Dixwell (Fearon, 1972, tables 3 and 5).

In 1865, Chinese concerns about

bad fengshui prevented completion of a telegraph line from Woosung to Shanghai. To clinch their case, the Mandarins "produced the body of a man who had died in the shade of one of the poles." In 1870, foreign investors sidestepped part of the problem by laying an underwater telegraphic cable from Hong Kong to Woosung, where the cable emerged from the water at an offshore hulk. A landline from Woosung to Shanghai was finally completed in 1878 (Pott 1928:104–106).

In spring 1865, George had decided that the rapid transmission of news from Woosung to Shanghai via carrier pigeons might give the Heard firm an advantage. On Feb. 19, he reported to Albert Heard in Hong Kong: "The Carrier Pigeon man goes to work at once and will train the birds down to Yangtze Cape as soon as possible" (Heard 1, HM 31–2).

Well before 1865, George anticipated the widespread use of telegraphy in China and developed a cipher for Heard Co. messages. On Jan. 17, 1865, he mailed an explanation of his system to Albert Heard in Hong Kong. "I send you in a separate envelope legible press copies of 23 pages of Telegraphic Phrases made up by me years ago and abandoned as you know ... If you use letters to indicate numbers in telegraphic scheme, better use all consonants and such consonants that look as little as possible like any of the vowels" (Heard 1, HM 31–2).

Robert Fearon's June 28 and Aug. 10, 1871, letters to George reveal that telegraphic messages between Shanghai and Hong Kong were not only uncertain and insecure but also expensive. "We have made the note you speak of on our telegraphic code. What a nuisance that the Hongkong cable is broken again! ... We telegraphed Everett the day before

the cable stopped working (in cipher of course)"; "I feel morally sure to have thrown away $20 in telegraphing ..." (Heard 2, Case LV-22, Folder 22). Early in 1870, the Chamber of Commerce (of which George was a member) established its own cipher code for telegrams (*North China Herald* 22 Nov. 1870 [378]:3).

Hoihow Road is a short street following the southeastern section of Shanghai's second racecourse. Although the first racecourse was laid out in 1850, it is the second racecourse, purchased in 1854, that was preserved in a broad circle as Shanghai city streets. In 1860, Albert Heard and three friends purchased the land inside this racecourse to provide a field for cricket and other sports. This land was sold and subdivided in 1862 (Pott 1928:83).

On Dec. 26, 1869, Augustine "Gus" Heard asked George to consider retiring from the firm. Two weeks later George replied (Heard 1, HM 31–3, Jan. 9, 1869):

"Many thanks for the kind tenor of yr note of the 26th. I have thought much on the subject & although China is not a very bad place I am sorry not to be in a position to give way gracefully to younger men. As it is I do not see that I can help holding on to the Celestial Empire for some time longer. I do not feel much discouraged by the last seven years, for their unsuccess has arisen from causes beyond my control & moreover I feel as though there were lots of life left in me & almost a certainty of making up losses—sooner or later."

George's relationship with Gus Heard was, at best, awkward. As George later described to Albert, "When ... Augustine

[Gus] came out in 1868 he fell foul of me in not very gentle style ..." (Heard 1, HM 31–3, March 21, 1873).

Two years before his marriage to Ts'ai-shun, George had written a cautionary note to Albert Heard regarding Robert Fearon's imminent marriage (Heard 1, HM 31–2, July 11, 1865):

"With respect to his [Fearon's] position I think this is the best place for him—provided he makes matrimony subsidiary to business & not vice versa. I think you had better give him a trial here letting him understand that if he allows his wife to draw him off from the office so as to make him less of use than he is now—he will have to give place to someone else."

George's generous decision to go to Hong Kong in place of Robert Fearon is acknowledged in Fearon's letter of Sept. 21, 1871 (Heard 2, Case LV, Folder 2):

"I return the press copy of Charles's [Charles A. Fearon's letter] ... The first paragraph ... confirms what I have all along suspected, as to your generosity in sacrificing yourself for Mrs. Fearon's & my sakes—when the question arose as to which of us should go to Hongkong. I should have told you before how deeply we felt & appreciated your goodness ... Few men would have acted as you have, I am sure—but then, very few have your unselfishness. It is better for the House, I believe, that you should be at Hongkong than here [in Shanghai] while AH [Augustine "Gus" Heard] is away & I trust you may not suffer in health while

at the South ... Mrs. Fearon is well but I am sorry to say expects to be confined in November —*entre nous*. Children are welcome when money is flush, but otherwise every addition to one's family is an additional source of anxiety."

James Bridges Endicott (b. Aug. 16, 1814, in Danvers, Massachusetts) died of typhoid in Hong Kong on Nov. 5, 1870. A marble memorial tablet was installed inside the English Chapel at Macao (Ride and Ride 1996:263–264).

Rev. Daniel Vrooman began his missionary work in Canton in 1852. In 1860, he published a detailed map of Canton, and in 1863 he published an alphabet he devised to present Cantonese phonetically (Ride and Ride 1996:114). Vrooman's plan for a steam-powered, cotton-yarn-spinning plant was already underway by Dec. 1870. It was first reported in the *North China Herald* on April 12, 1871 ([260]:20). The $20,000 of capital that "he successfully persuaded his Chinese friends to invest" is discussed by Hao (1986:225). Albert Heard, apparently inspired by rumors of Vrooman's effort, proposed that the Heards establish a cotton factory of their own. George advised Albert against doing so—it was risky and would "absorb too much ready cash" (Heard 1, HM 31–3, Oct. 9, 1870). I thank Dr. R. Gary Tiedemann for informing me of Daniel Vrooman's height—6 feet, 4 inches—as recorded in Vrooman's Oct. 1, 1851, passport application (Passport Applications, 1795–1905, U.S. Dept. of State, Record Group 59, National Archives).

Mrs. Catharina Bonney established a school for Eurasian children in the Hongkew district of the Shanghai International Settlement late in the summer

11

1870 (*North China Herald* 22 Nov. 1870 [371]:1). Children of mixed blood were considered intellectually inferior. Pott (1928:119) implies this belief. "As far back as 1869, the *North China Herald* pointed out the necessity of providing boarding schools for this class, so that the fact of their mixed parentage might not be a handicap to them in competition with pure whites."

By 1870, buildings close to the Bund were piping their sewage directly into the harbor. Houses further from the harbor had privies. George refers to such a privy in a letter to Albert Heard (Heard 1, HM 31–2, July 8, 1865):

> "There is a report that Loriero (disguised, more or less) went on the 6th in the evening to Dent & Co's and took away two ledgers and a journal—and was seen by some boy or boys whose attention was attracted by the noise made in opening the safe (Dent being out dining)—[and] that the books or portions of them were [later] found in L's privy—and one story has it that L. is going down to Macao in irons to be tried."

George leaves the condition of these ledgers to our imaginations.

At the Nov. 16, 1870, meeting of the Chamber of Commerce, George voted with the other members: "That the Chamber memorialize the Taotai, through the Foreign Consuls at Shanghai, on the condition of the Bar of the Whangpu at Woosung, which, by ordinary dredging, might be made easily navigable to up to 24 feet draught ..." (*North China Herald* 22 Nov. 1870 [377]:1–2). The story of a devil taking up residence in the river channel and moving the wrecks so that Chinese officials couldn't find them is reported in the same issue of the *North China Herald* ([370]:2–3).

The first steam-pump fire engine in Shanghai was imported from the United States in 1863. The *Mih-ho-loong* [destroy fire wagon] voluntary fire brigade service was organized in 1866. (Pott 1928:70).

George's eldest brother, J. J. Dixwell, had a long-standing avocational interest in photography and astronomy. In 1840 he learned to make daguerreotypes (Hale 1917:72–73). By 1869–71 he was attempting to secure donor support for the astronomical observatories at Harvard and Dartmouth. He traveled to Shelbyville, Illinois, with his daughter Anna Parker Dixwell to view the sky during the solar eclipse of Aug. 7, 1869 (J. J. Dixwell to Epes S. Dixwell, MHS, N-114, Box 5, April 8, 1869). About the time George was addressing the Shanghai Volunteer Corps, J.J. was writing "Spots on the Sun" for the *Atlantic Monthly*, where he described observations of protuberances bulging outward 130,000 miles from the sun (J. J. Dixwell 1871:500–504).

George closely followed the development of steam technology. He described this passion in an April 24, 1862, letter to Augustine Heard [the elder] (Heard 1, EM 3–2):

> "Luckily for me, steam has been one of my hobbies ever since I was a boy, so that I feel quite comfortable in the midst of valves & pistons & cylinders & boilers & shafts & propellers & paddle wheels; and not at all confused among discussions as to cutoffs & superheating & expansion &c &c &c ... Without joking, my previous reading in mechanics is now coming into play and is of no little value."

11

George was particularly interested in the problem of energy loss due to water condensation on the interior surfaces of steam engines. Following his return to Boston, in 1873, he would conduct two years of laboratory research on the problem (Dixwell, 1875e:1–54).

11.3 Henrietta Sargent died of "old age" Jan. 11, 1871 (Massachusetts Vital Records, Boston, Deaths, Vol. 240, p. 7). This vignette is framed 28 days before her death on December 14, 1870.

Henrietta's physical condition was in decline for several years. On Oct. 14, 1868, Anna Parker wrote to George. "Your Aunt H. is just now sick in bed, with Dr. Russell to prescribe for her, and Mrs. Colby to help us nurse her. She grows more feeble every year, and if it was anybody but her, I should think they would not live long, but she belongs to a family of great tenacity of life, and I think has a great deal to endure" (MHS, N-114, Box 5).

Although written in a shaky hand, Henrietta's last extant letter to George, six months before her death is quite coherent—including her description of a memory lapse (MHS, N-114, Box 5). There is no hint that she was aware of George's marriage to Hu Ts'ai-shun or the birth of his son, Charles.

Roxbury
July 5, 1870

Dear Nephew,

Yesterday was a glorious day for our celebration of Independence. It was a National holiday—our country looked lovely, our harvests very promising. I am living with your Aunt Parker at her [summer] place [in Roxbury], which is pleasant, and from which I can see dear Boston. I hope when you return you will make it your home. Then we shall see you often, eight months of the year. [Anna and Henrietta always spent the four summer months at Anna's country house on Parker Hill in Roxbury.]

Yesterday I was called down to see a visitor, a tall young man who I had no recollection of. I soon learned that he was from Cambridge, and I asked him if he knew our nephew John Dixwell. Why, he replied, I am John Dixwell—what was my surprise!! He is six feet in height, with fine teeth. He kissed me while I was in ignorance of who he was, but we soon became acquainted. He is to go a short voyage to the Azores, return by the first of September, and then begin his medical studies, with his uncle [Dr. Bowditch at Harvard]. He seemed very happy, unembarrassed about his resources.

About six weeks ago looking over my accounts, I found I had a sum that I could spare. I decided to share it between my 3 nephews. J.J. and Epes expressed themselves very handsomely by their share, but I do not know what to do with yours—five hundred dollars! I think it had better be reserved for you against your return. What do you say? We do not know how you may be situated at that time. Think of it!!

Your Aunt Parker is in excellent

11

health and gives me a home very kindly. I am feeble, but keep about. All the members of your Father's family are prosperous, as are your Uncles [illegible].

I am afraid to urge you to return for fear you could not stand our winters. Therefore recommending you to our Heavenly Father I remain your affectionate Aunt

Henrietta Sargent

For several years, Anna's neighborhood on Tremont Street was changing from residential to commercial. On June 17, 1866, Epes Dixwell wrote George that "a warehouse & salesplace of an organ factory" had been erected next door to Anna Parker's house (MHS, N-114, Box 5).

The *National Standard* reported (31 Dec. 1870 [2]:2) that the Women's Suffrage Bazaar was scheduled for New Years Day at the Music Hall. Luke (23: 57) provides the verse: "If thou be the king of the Jews, save thyself."

"The Prayer-Seeker," by John Greenleaf Whittier, appeared in the *National Standard* (10 Dec. 1870 [8]:1), reprinted from the *Atlantic Monthly* of December 1870. Fanny Dixwell reads the eighth (final) stanza.

I quote directly from Maria Child's review of Thomas Henry Huxley's book, *Lay Sermons, Addresses and Reviews* (1870) in the *National Standard* (10 Dec. 1870 [4]:4–[5]:1). The Roxbury shale and Dr. Shaler's research are discussed in a *Boston Transcript* article reporting the proceedings of the Boston Society of Natural History (14 Dec. 1870 [4]:6). Young John Dixwell's geological training under Dr. Shaler is described in his April 22, 1931, obituary.

"His hobby was geology, which he studied under Professor Shaler, and followed with keen interest all his life" (Harvard Archives clipping file, name of newspaper missing). Anna Parker discusses the possible removal of Parker hill in her March 7, 1871, letter to George (MHS, N-114, Box 5). Henrietta's memory of the removal of Beacon Hill is based on an 1811 print "Cutting Down Beacon Hill" showing Bulfinch's tower at the top and the waiting horse carts at the bottom (Whitehill & Kennedy 2000:81–82,fig. 42).

During her later years, Henrietta taught Sunday School in the Universalist church of Dr. A. A. Miner (Sargent & Sargent 1923:130). Maria Child's obituary for Henrietta confirms that she remained conservative in her religious outlook to the very end. Referring to Henrietta and her sister Catharine, Maria wrote: "Even their religion was of an old-fashioned type. On those subjects they always thought just as their father had done; and he was a convert to the doctrines of the famous Mr. Murray, who taught the universal restoration of all human souls, though he retained many of the features of orthodoxy" (Child, "Another Friend Gone," *National Standard* 28 Jan. 1871 [1]:2–3). On Dec. 18, 1870, the Rev. Dr. Miner presented a lecture on "The Current Doctrine of Probation" (*Boston Transcript* 17 Dec. 1870 [1]:2).

The United States Senate debate regarding removal of Union soldiers' graves from Robert E. Lee's estate, in Arlington, Virginia (seized by the United States for nonpayment of taxes), and to restore the property to Lee's widow is reported in the *Boston Transcript* (14 Dec. 1870 [4]:2). That General Lee "continued the war after he had virtually confessed his defeat and when every death was a murder to be charged at his door," appears ([2]:1) in the same issue of the *Transcript*.

Henrietta's "view from the ceiling" in this scene alludes not only to her fantasy of watching Father Snowden give the prayer at her funeral (see Ch. 2, note 1) but also to the extracorporeal experience of her sister, Catharine, described in Maria Child's "Spirits" (1862:581). Child apparently used this story again over the years. Three years after Henrietta's death, the same extracorporeal experience now attributed to Henrietta herself, was published by William Denton (1874:19).

11.4 I present Anna Parker's, March 7, 1871, letter reporting Henrietta's death verbatim (MHS, N-114, Box 5). The *Tribune* article by Lydia Maria Child to which Anna objects is not in the *New York Daily Tribune*. It may possibly have appeared in the *New York Weekly Tribune*. Note Anna's disparagement of "spiritualism," a subject that engaged both Henrietta and Mrs. Child.

11

Heard 1 = Heard Collection, Part One, Baker Library, Harvard.

MHS, N-114 = Massachusetts Historical Society, Wigglesworth Collection.

GBD-D = George Basil Dixwell, Daily Journal, 1848–54.

12.1 On March 12, 1873, George Dixwell departed Shanghai for Yokohama aboard the Pacific Mail Steamship *Oregonian*. There, he would board the company's steamship *Colorado*, due at San Francisco on or about April 16th (*North China Herald* 13 March 1873 [1]:2; *North China Daily News* 12 March 1873). George probably bought one of the $415 through-fares advertising,

"First class passengers purchasing tickets to points beyond San Francisco, are allowed 250 pounds of Baggage Free. Through passenger trains run daily between San Francisco and New York, making the Trip in Six Days and Twenty hours. Distance 3,312 miles. The Silver Palace Sleeping Cars are run daily ... . These Drawing-room Cars by day and Sleeping Cars by night are unexcelled for comfort, convenience and elegance" (Pacific Mail advertisement, *North China Daily News* 12 March 1873 [230]:5).

There are several reasons why George, now approaching his 60th birthday, returned to the States. First, Augustine Heard & Co. was no longer a profitable enterprise, and the Heards were now recalculating the losses on company-owned steamers over the previous decade. They were charging a share of those losses to former junior partners (George included), even though these men had had no share in their ownership. George had already engaged in a testy correspondence about this with the Heards company's office in Hong Kong. Indeed, George's disagreement with the firm had reached such an ugly impasse and weighed so heavily on his mind that during his Yokohama layover, en route to the States, he wrote a long letter to Albert F. Heard in Hong Kong, once again disputing the firm's accounting, concluding, "If I am wrong in any of these matters I am ready (& anxious even) to be convinced, or to submit myself to the decision of impartial friends—but where two parties have opposite pecuniary views, neither has the right to decide the case" (Heard 1, HM 31–3, 21 March 1873).

Although the correspondence has not survived, a second motive for George's return to Boston may have been advice from his brother J.J. who had been managing Aunt Anna Parker's fortune. By spring 1873, Anna, now almost 91, was beginning to weaken. Over the years, J.J. had influenced her to leave the bulk of her fortune to the three Dixwell brothers, rather than to the Parker relatives of her deceased husband. J.J. may well have urged George to come home to reestablish his relationship with Anna (and thus his claim to a share of her estate) in person. Anna died on July 12, 1873, about a month after George's arrival in Boston. We get a sense of the awkwardness surrounding this issue in George's August 14, 1873, letter to his brother Epes: "John James is going up to the Hills on the 18th, and I hope he will have a good rest there

... What we inherit from Aunt Parker we owe in a great measure to him and to the assiduous care which he has taken of her and her affairs ever since Uncle Parker's death. Had it not been for him and his attention, there might have been little or nothing to divide or it might have been otherwise left" (MHS, N-114, Box 5).

A third reason for George's return to the States was to research his improvement to the steam engine. George found the technical expertise he needed to conduct this research in the person of Channing Whitaker, a young assistant professor at the Massachusetts Institute of Technology. George provided the money to equip a mechanical engineering laboratory for Whitaker, where he carried out his experiments from late-1873 to early-1875. John D. Runkle, president of MIT, described the importance of George's contribution in his *President's Report 1873–1874* (Runkle 1874:xv–xvi):

"In my last report Professor Whitaker gave the plan of the kind of laboratory which it was thought desirable to build up to aid in the instruction in this department, and also adapted to the solution of any new problems that might arise in relation to steam and power, and such other questions as are involved in their use. I have now great pleasure in calling your attention to Professor Whitaker's report showing what has been done ... This marked and substantial progress is mainly due to the aid of Mr. George B. Dixwell, who has not only furnished us with a large part of the means, but what is far more important, has set us a definite problem of the highest scientific as well as practical importance to solve, thus

imposing conditions of a very high order, and at the same time aiding us with the knowledge and experience gained by years of study and reflection upon the nature of steam."

On April 29, 1875, George presented the first of two lectures reporting his research to the Society of Arts at the Massachusetts Institute of Technology. The *Boston Evening Transcript* announced the lecture on April 28 ([1]:2) but neglected to note the time. The *Transcript* did, however, send a reporter and printed an extensive account of what George had to say (6 May 1875 [6]:2–3). The second lecture, presented on May 13, seems not to have been reported. George himself published a 54-page pamphlet fully describing his research (Dixwell 1875e). The most concise discussions of all four of George's inventions appear in his patent applications (Dixwell 1875a–d).

During this period, Harvard was more concerned with educating gentlemen than training engineers, proudly increasing its Latin and Greek offerings from 17 to 23 courses, while the students and faculty argued whether the university colors should be changed from crimson to magenta. That question was resolved at a meeting of the university departments by a vote "decidedly in favor of crimson, magenta being a fading, miserable, mongrel color ill adapted to wear with other colors" (*Transcript* 10 May 1875 [4]:4).

The 1876 *Boston Directory* (assembled in late 1875) lists George as living at 23 Beacon Street and his nephew, the newly established John Dixwell, MD, living and conducting his medical practice a few doors away at no. 10.

The day before George's talk, the *Transcript* published its daily update of

12

the Henry Ward Beecher trial—almost two full columns of salacious testimony regarding Rev. Beecher's attempt to cover up his alleged adultery with Mrs. Theodore Tilton. The testimony once again referred to Mrs. Elizabeth Cady Stanton's denial that it was she who had given Mrs. Woodhull the details of the adultery that were published in Mrs. Woodhull's magazine (28 April 1875 [8]:3–4). Stanton considered it an outrage that the two major women's suffrage organizations were presided over by men (Beecher and Tilton) (Banner 1980:117). A suspicion remains that Mrs. Stanton deliberately leaked the information to Mrs. Woodhull in order to embarrass and discredit both Beecher and Tilton (Lyon 1959).

The Dixwells were fully aware of the scandal. Epes's daughter, Susan was married to Gerrit ("Gat") Smith Miller—the grandson of Gerrit Smith. Mrs. Elizabeth Cady Stanton was Gerrit Smith's cousin and a frequent guest at the Peterboro estate that Gat and Suzy now managed for Grandmother Smith. George visited Gat and Suzy in August 1873, some time after news of Mrs. Stanton's role in the scandal had been exposed in the papers (MHS, N-114, Box 5, Aug. 14, 1873).

Professor N. S. Shaler's paper, describing how continental glaciers were able to move great distances, was presented at the Boston Society of Natural History on April 7, 1875. Dr. John Dixwell had been one of Shaler's students at Harvard and, as a close personal friend, probably attended the talk. I have taken the details of Shaler's thesis directly from the *Transcript* article of 28 April 1875 ([6]:3).

George seems not to have made any money from the gas regulator that he co-invented with James A. Dorr (Dixwell and Dorr 1854). George's refrigeration device is described in a Dec. 24, 1853, journal entry—penned aboard the *Sierra Nevada* as it steamed north from the Nicaragua Isthmus (GBD-D).

On April 28, 1875, the day before George's lecture, Augustine Heard & Co. declared bankruptcy in Hong Kong, placing all Heard properties in all parts of the world in the hands of trustees (Heard 1, EQ-7; Hao 1986:318, notes 60,61). Although George Dixwell and John Heard anticipated this outcome, official word would not reach them for several weeks.

John Heard recounted the story of his life, including the events leading to the collapse of Augustine Heard & Co., in a personal memoir (Heard 1891). It is here that he not only reports the purchase price and renovation cost of the Park Street mansion (p. 160) but also provides our most complete account of the bankruptcy (pp. 168–170). Since the decline and fall of the Heard Co. is central to George's career, I've excerpted key passages from John Heard's typescript:

"In 1873 began the troubles which oppressed us for the next three years. I had long seen that [Percival] Everett was a very careless agent, but I always had implicit confidence in his honesty. For a long time he had bills of exchange sent him from China, with permission to use as much of them as was required to cover any indebtedness to him of the house in China ... during the spring of 1873, I heard from China that remarks had been made in regard to the amount of these bills that seemed to be afloat ... He [Everett] made a statement to me of his affairs, showing that he had [been] running our bills at £63,500, or at the exchange of the day, $361,500. Of this, he had a right to have running, by our understanding, rather less than $30,000! The rest he had absorbed for his own benefit. I made him give me a statement of it, and found that it had been put into all sorts of straw loans and speculations. It was difficult to say how much could be realized, but by his own showing, and he was of course anxious to make the best showing possible, he was short some $30,000. I knew very well it would be much more than that. It turned out eventually, when everything had been realized, to be about $245,000.

"The question I had to decide was what course to pursue ... One, and the proper one, was to shut him up at once, the other was to try to pull him through. I thought I could do it, as I had not only all that could be realized from his estate, but Uncle Augustine's property, the Park Street house, and the power of drawing on London ... I determined to risk it. About the position of the China house I felt considerable uneasiness. If I caused Everett to fail at once, I could not tell what would be the effect on the China house, and, at any rate, I must be prepared to take up all the bills he had sold. It was very doubtful if I could do this, and the shock to our credit would have been almost, if not quite, fatal. For nearly two years, I maintained the fight ... but the house in China was obliged to succumb. It was almost a relief when the crash came, for I doubt if I could have stood the strain much longer ... James Sturgis was appointed assignee of our personal

estates in America, and Messrs. Whitehall & Linstead in China."

Before departing Shanghai for Boston, George arranged for his colleagues J. E. Reding and Robert I. Fearon to help Ts'ai-shun, as needed, during his absence. Their letters and George's answers reveal not only George and Ts'ai-shun's deep affection but also Ts'ai-shun's confident, entrepreneurial spirit. (The four letters comprising the Reding-Fearon-Dixwell correspondence are held by Marcia Dixwell DiMambro). On Nov. 26, 1873, Reding wrote:

"My friend went the other day with Hoo-Tsai-Shoon to the school to ask the mistress to take care of Charlie; and, to give better effect to this demand, I intend going to see him at school. No doubt an occasional inspiration will keep the schoolmistress up to mark. Hoo-sai-Shoon wishes me to see whether the lot of ground next to Hayes' Bungalow, Hangkuo, might not be sold. I will see Mr. Fearon about it. Land in general has risen considerably & perhaps now it may be disposed advantageously."

On Jan. 12, 1874, Reding reported:

"I went to see Hoo-Tsai-Shoon and C. Sargent. They are looking well and evidently they are well provided with everything. Hoo-Tsai-Shoon invites you back by next spring. She says the houses want repairing, and you have to be consulted about it ... Charles Sargent complained of having had cold at school; and Bridges and myself went to see him there on

12

a Monday at 11 o'clock while he was in the schoolroom. I looked into his bedroom & his bed. It looks clean and comfortable enough. His complaint of cold is explained by the fact that we had for 2 weeks unusually cold weather. Two or three nights the thermometer was about 20° below freezing point Fr't. We examined into the knowledge of Charles. His knowledge of writing the alphabet is rather small. He writes: 1. 2. 3. 4; but he is not quite certain whether four is written '[4 backwards]' or '4'; and whether '5' or '6' follows '4' he is equally persuaded. He persists in reading '<u>si</u>' for '<u>is</u>.' In the whole he seems to have learnt very little. No doubt this is due to his slender age. [Charles age was 5 years, 2 months.] With a little patience and time his knowledge will increase more rapidly than it has done so far. When I was 10 years old I had scarcely an idea why & what I was learning ... When Charles is 2–4 years older he will like me suddenly wake up to the importance of knowledge. To encourage him I will frequently go to see him."

On April 3, 1874, George replied to a letter from Robert I. Fearon.

" ... no letter came from H.T.S by the mail that brought yours of Feby 14th although you say or intimate that one was written. I am naturally disappointed, as I (as naturally) like to hear what is going on in that quarter. I have an old letter from the Lim Leung ... to which I will reply and [will] enclose ... one to H.T.S. As I just hear the steamer

does not leave San Francisco before the 18th, I have several days yet to write. If it were not for this damned Steam project I would go back with James and take a run about China. But the thing seems to be of too stupendous importance to be left between Heaven & Earth. I don't need it myself and should probably let it all go for a while—out of sheer fatigue—if it were not for others whom I would very much like to benefit. At the same time it is rather rough upon me and upon H.T.S. who no doubt has her times of thinking that Low Fuk Chen [George refers to himself] really does not mean to come. If that Steam [patent] should turn up trumps—that little fellow may be a millionaire before he is of age: although that is not of half so much importance as being a good & intelligent fellow. But enough of this. Help H.T.S. if you can in the matter of the repair of her houses. [Note that George refers to the houses as *hers*!] I don't think she will need any assistance beyond getting the necessary money out of the Bank. She may not know how to do this."

On June 3, 1874, George replied to Reding.

"I have before me your letter of March 25 and am very much obliged to you for your report upon Charles Sargent ... I am greatly interested for the youngster. I do not want him to be spoiled and this was the chief reason why I put him at the school where he is rubbed against by other children and not corseted to death by his mother & half a dozen female servants ... I am detained here longer than I expected & cannot say now when I shall start for Shanghae. As soon as I can—and no mistake."

George delayed his return to China so that he could exhibit his research results at the May 10–Nov. 10, 1876, United States International Centennial Exhibition in Philadelphia. On July 23, 1876, he wrote to Albert F. Heard in New York, "The Russian Commissioners to the Centennial carried off a half a dozen of my pamphlets" (Heard 1, HM 31–3). George was apparently forced to postpone his return yet again when his brother J.J.'s health began to fail. J.J. died Nov. 15, 1876.

12.2 The June 10, 1880, Federal Census lists Charles Sargent, age 11—his father English, his mother Chinese—"at school," boarding with George and Lucy Manson at Hudson, Middlesex County, Massachusetts (28 miles west of Boston). Our earliest American photo of Charley, taken in Boston [undated] shows a long-legged 11- or 12-year-old (Marcia Dixwell DiMambro Collection). We do not know the date of Charley and Ts'ai-shun's arrival in Boston. I have not found their names in the departure columns of the *North China Herald*. In addition, the 1870s San Francisco passenger ship registers were destroyed in the 1906 earthquake and fire.

There are several lines of evidence showing that Ts'ai-shun came to Boston. Marcia Dixwell DiMambro remembers, as a teenager, peeking into her father's desk and finding a photograph of Hu Ts'ai-shun taken at a Boston photographic studio (Marcia Dixwell DiMambro, 11 Jan. 2007, pers. comm.).

"I remember it because she wore a fur stole, with a very smart suit and high heels. She carried a clutch-style purse. I was fascinated by that fur stole and her fancy hat. I can recall this photo clearly because my sisters and I were sneaky and found the photo in my father's desk (off-limits to us). My mother confirmed that it was 'your great grandmother.' My mother also told us, as I recall, that her stay in the U.S. did not last, due to her reception in the Boston area."

Marcia's cousin, Douglas Dixwell Morrison, recalls that that particular photo was taken in a studio on Washington Street. The earliest Boston photo of Charles (at age 11 or 12) was taken at the Partridge Studio, 2832 Washington Street.

George's granddaughter, Eleanor Dixwell Morrison spoke of a conversation with Augustus P. Loring, the Dixwell family attorney and executor/trustee of Charley's estate. Gus Loring told Eleanor that Hu Ts'ai-shun was of "a well-to-do family," that she lived "a few years" in Boston, disliked it, and returned to Shanghai (Eleanor Dixwell Morrison, 20 April 1993 [telephone interview] pers. comm.).

Thomas Nast's full-page cartoon satirizing the new treaty with China—"A Diplomatic (Chinese) Design Presented to U.S."—appeared in *Harper's Weekly* (12 Feb. 1881). George's discussion of the cartoon with Charley is, of course, my invention. In early 1881, George presented a lecture on free trade at a Boston literary club. A member of the National Association of Wool Manufacturers heard the talk and convinced George to publish it in the Association's *Bulletin*. Later in the year, George republished the article as a hardbound book (Dixwell 1881).

12

12.3 In fall 1874, Wendell and Fanny Dixwell Holmes moved into modest rooms above a drugstore at 10 Beacon Street (next door to the Athenaeum). The apartment had a "gas ring but not a proper kitchen." Fanny and Wendell tended to invite friends over *after* dinner "for drinks, smokes and talk" (Novick 1989:146–147). The apartment had been vacated by Fanny's brother, Dr. John Dixwell, but sufficiently late in fall 1874 that it was still listed in the 1875 *Boston Directory* as his office and residence. The hand-me-down loveseat in Wendell's office is my invention. Considering how awkward it must have been for Fanny and Wendell to entertain, I have imagined that they had use of Wendell's parents' cook for this particular week while Dr. and Mrs. Holmes (who lived several blocks down Beacon Street) were out of town.

April 23, 1881, was an awkward time for Wendell and Fanny. Wendell's *The Common Law* had been published on March 3, 1881, five days before his 40th birthday, but it still languished unreviewed (Novick 1989:159,163). Meanwhile, Fanny's embroideries, then on exhibit at the Ladies Decorative Art Society in New York City, had just received a rave review in *The Nation* (21 April 1881:286). I have Nina Gray quote directly from that review. I have Wendell quote directly from the November 1880 (pp. 158–159) *Scribner's Monthly* review of *The Iron Gate*, his father's recently published volume of poetry.

The Nation review rightly compared Fanny's embroidery "to the analogous embroidery of the Japanese." Fanny's lifelong study of Japanese art and her familiarity with the woodblock prints of Hokusai and Hiroshige are described by Christine Laidlaw in "Painting with Silken Threads: Fanny Dixwell Holmes and Japanism in Nineteenth-Century Boston" (2003:42–68). Only four days before this vignette, the *Boston Transcript* (19 April 1881 [3]:3) published an article on art criticism in Japan, reprinting the "preface to the first volume of the 'Manguun,' or rough sketches by Hokusai."

I have described "Twilight in Mattapoisett Harbor" because it is the only extant example of Fanny's embroidery. Since this work is thought to have been completed ca. 1885, I have imagined an unsuccessful first attempt in order to provide George and Fanny an opportunity to discuss and critique her technique. Fanny's "Drifting Snow," then on display in New York, appears to have borrowed the bold diagonal lines of Hiroshige's woodblock print, "Sudden Shower at Tokaido" (Laidlaw 2003:46–47).

Professor John Chipman Gray, Jr. (1839–1915), of Harvard Law School, and his wife, Nina, were close friends of Wendell and Fanny and well acquainted with the Japanese students that Wendell prepared for admission to the Law School. Wendell tutored Inoue Yoshikazu (1852–1879) for five months in 1872 and Kentaro Kaneko (1852–1942) from September 1876 until his graduation in 1878. Kaneko's 1880s correspondence with Fanny and Wendell is lost. His November 28, 1878, letter to the Grays describes his struggle "living as Japanese—but thinking as American" as well as his name change (dropping his childhood given name, Nao-tsugu). Kaneko wrote to the Grays on March 15, 1881, to announce his betrothal. "I go married to Miss Yamada. She is only sixteen, so our marriage is only for the sake of betrothal. I know you—particularly Mrs. Gray—will be surprised to hear that I am at last married to a Japanese maiden, after telling all those things while I was in America" (Kanda and Gifford 1982:41–45,57–58,66).

Inoue Yoshikazu's suicide was reported in the *Boston Transcript* (20 March 1879). George's vacation plans with Charley are my invention.

12.4 On October 24, 1881, Annie Parker Dixwell and her friend Elizabeth "Lizzie" Boott had just painted their way from Spain to Greece and were planning a joint showing at the J. Eastman Chase Gallery in Boston. I begin at Sunnyside, J.J.'s home and botanical garden atop Bowditch Hill in the Jamaica Plain suburb of Boston. My description of J.J.'s house—the widow's walk, its interior rooms, and the art on its walls—is taken directly from a series of mid-1880s photographs (MHS, N-114, Box 56). The species of plants, their provenance, and the gong at J.J.'s door are my invention.

J.J. had a long-standing interest in trees. His collection of them on his Sunnyside estate became

"between 1860 and 1870 one of the most important and interesting in New England. He was one of the three trustees to whom James Arnold ... gave one and a quarter of the twenty-four parts into which he divided his residuary estate ... With the money thus entrusted to them, Mr. Dixwell and his associates, with the President and Fellows of Harvard College, established the Arnold Arboretum" (Sargent and Sargent 1923:14).

Under pressure from her father, Lizzie Boott ended her engagement to Frank Duveneck. The trip to Europe—her first without her father—was probably instigated by Annie Dixwell, "a staunch believer in women's independence, as well as an enthusiastic Hispanophile" (Osborne 1996:18). On August 9, 1881, Annie and Lizzie returned home from their three-month foray in Europe aboard the *Gallia* (Ancestry.com, New York Passenger Lists, 1820–1957). In January 1882, they exhibited together at the J. Eastman Chase Gallery (Osborne 1996:33). [Note: Martha Hoppin (1981:43) gives the date of their exhibition as March 1882.] Lizzie presented 44 works—31 oils and 13 watercolors—including paintings of the Alhambra and various other scenes from Spain and Italy (Osborne 1996:18). I have guessed that Annie exhibited an equal number. Although Annie's specialty was New England farmhouses and flowers (Hoppin 1981:43), the etchings from her 1881 trip with Lizzie included the Proplyaea and Parthenon in Athens, the tomb of Caius Sestus in Rome, the Peneta in Ravenna, and the Ponte Vecchio in Florence (Museum of Fine Arts 1887:10).

It was almost certainly Annie who arranged for Frank Duveneck to paint her mother. That oil portrait, dated 1882, now hangs at the home of J.J.'s great granddaughter, Caroline Dixwell Cabot. Annie was sufficiently independent that soon after her return from Europe she arranged to live on her own. The 1882 *Boston Directory* (assembled in late 1881) lists Annie as an artist, boarding at 98 Mt. Vernon, with her studio at 48 Boylston Street.

We do not know what was wrong with Annie's younger brother, Arthur (1853–1924). An 1876 portrait of the family suggests that his growth was somewhat stunted. He was not educated at Epes Dixwell's school. Although he continued to live at home, he was sufficiently

12

competent to be employed as a clerk from 1876 to 1881 at 63 Franklin Street. The 1883 *Boston Directory* lists Arthur as an "art, furniture and interior decorator" at 4 Park Avenue. This may have been something of an overstatement. Arthur later gained fame for his obsession with baseball statistics. Supported by a trust fund, he provided gifts and loans to Boston baseball players and became something of a team mascot, known as "General Hi Hi Dixwell" ("Baseball Cranks, General Dixwell of Boston," *Grand Forks Daily Herald* 3 June 1891).

12.5 George's activities on the evening of October 27, 1881, are remarkably well documented. The archives of the Cambridge Scientific Club record that he was present at his brother Epes's lecture: "Things introduced since my recollection" (Harvard University Archives, Cambridge Scientific Club, Box 1, meeting notes Oct. 27, 1881). Serendipitously—almost beyond belief!—Epes's handwritten notes for that talk (11 pages) and the complete handwritten text of the talk (30 pages) were listed for sale by a Connecticut documents dealer, and I was able to purchase them. The scientific specificity of the notes, well beyond Epes's competence, and the fact that George was invited to attend the meeting suggest that he helped Epes structure the technical parts of the talk. All the innovations read by George (from friction matches to the telephone) are listed on the first two pages of the notes.

George's and Charles E. Endicott's discussion aboard the Shawmut Street horsecar is my invention. Endicott (1832–1887) and George knew each other well, as they were Heard Co. colleagues in Shanghai

from 1860 until the firm's collapse. The attitudes attributed to Endicott in this vignette are taken from his obituary (*Brookline Chronicle* 31 Dec. 1887 [426]:1), where we read that after losing his fortune to the Heard creditors, "He went much among the working people, carefully studying their customs and conditions, and he was their champion both with voice and pen. His sympathies were ever on the side of the wronged and oppressed. He was outspoken in favor of the cause of Ireland and was an ardent supporter of suffrage for women."

Not only were George and Endicott close friends, but also they were both outspoken supporters of a strong tariff to protect American industry (Dixwell 1882a, b, c; 1883a, b). Endicott is mentioned by name in one of George's obituaries as having written a "loving tribute" and as having been "one of his [George's] worthiest disciples in economical studies ..." The obituary goes on to state:

> "The first public expression of his [Dixwell's] views on economical questions was the reading of a paper before a literary club in Boston on the 'Premises of Free Trade,' a paper which we suspect, won more admiration for its ability than sympathy with its views. A conviction that he would find more sympathy with the editor of this journal led him to place this paper, without the thought of its publication, in our hands for examination. It was only with our earnest solicitation that he consented to rewrite and enlarge it for publication in this Bulletin. It appeared in vol. xi (occupying 35 pages) ..."

The obituary also reveals that George borrowed the printer's plates for the article and reprinted it as a book, *The Premises of Free Trade Examined* (Dixwell 1881) [*Bulletin*, National Association of Wool Manufacturers 1885, Vol. 15:1, p. 96]. We do not know the name of the Boston literary club where George gave his protectionist lecture or if Endicott was involved in the arrangements.

Since Charles E. Endicott was a first cousin of James Bridges Endicott, I allow him to update George on news of all the Chinese Endicotts. Following the collapse of the Heard Co., Henry B. Endicott (1844–1895), the son of James Bridges Endicott and Ng Akew, was hired by Butterfield and Swire, where he "proved to be a valuable contribution to the company's success, [his contribution to the success of the firm] being second only to that of John Swire. He spoke Chinese fluently and had a thorough knowledge of every aspect of Chinese shipping as well as the psychology of handling Chinese shippers" (Marriner and Hyde, 1967:74–75).

By the time of this vignette, the Rev. Daniel and Anna Rosa Hunter Vrooman were planning their April 1882 move from Australia to San Francisco. Anna's 17-year-old son, John Endicott Gardner, Jr., was already demonstrating his scholarly bent as assistant teacher in an Australian high school. Within months of "Johnny's" arrival in San Francisco, he was "teaching four classes in different places to the Chinese in English," another "to an American in Chinese," and working part-time as a "court translator in nearby towns" (Anna Rosa Vrooman, San Francisco, to Catharine V. R. Bonney, Albany, N.Y., Historic Cherry Hill Collections, Box 24, F5, Sept. 9 and Oct. 20, 1882).

During fall 1881, several books-in-progress existed by Americans who had retired from the China Trade. These included Robert Bennet Forbes's *Personal Reminiscences* (1882) and William C. Hunter's *The 'Fan Kwae' at Canton before Treaty Days* (1882). Rumor had it that Hunter was also writing a history of Russell & Co. (De Vargas 1939:92). The former partners of Russell's were concerned that these books would expose their participation in the opium trade.

Shortly before his death in January 1881, George Tyson added a codicil to his will, discreetly directing his executors, (the brothers William Endicott, Jr., and Henry Endicott of Boston—cousins of James Bridges Endicott)

"to set aside from the assets of my estate the sum of twenty thousand dollars ... for John M. Forbes, Jr., of Russell and Company of Hong Kong China and ... [another friend in Massachusetts] ... to be used in their discretion in the adjustment of certain unsettled affairs in China of which they have cognizance" (Register for the Probate of Wills, Philadelphia, Pennsylvania; [and] The Supreme Court of Hongkong, Probate Jurisdiction, Probate No. 123, 1888).

Biographical information on Chan Kai Ming, Tyson's eldest son, comes from his obituary (*South China Morning Post* 12 Dec. 1919). I thank Wilfred Tyson of Hong Kong for providing me with a copy of George Tyson's will and codicil and Chan Kai Ming's obituary. For a full genealogy of George Tyson and Lam Fong Kew's children, see Peter Hall (1992, Pedigree Chart 35:199).

Although Ts'ai-shun's correspondence

with George has not survived, the adoption of a second son, during George's lifetime, would have been discussed. Ts'ai-shun's 1915 will mentions her "younger son named Hoo Zung Sung [characters]" as 31 years old. This would place his birth in 1884 before George's death. This child was certainly adopted as an infant, so that Ts'ai-shun could be sure of having a son in China during her old age.

12.6 The October 27, 1881, minutes of the Cambridge Scientific Club are brief: "Club at Mr. Dixwell's. Subject. Reminiscences: comparison of times when he [Epes Dixwell] was a boy with the present in regard to comforts and conveniences of life: science, art, literature, philosophy, theology."

In addition to "Dixwell's brother," the six members present were Francis Bowen, William Charles Eliot, Joseph Lovering, Epes S. Dixwell, Charles F. Choate, and Morrill Wyman (Harvard University Archives, Cambridge Scientific Club, Box 1, meeting notes Oct. 27, 1881). The biographical information on these men is taken from Vaille and Clark (1875), and Morison (1963). The publications mentioned are Francis Bowen's (1870) *American Political Economy* and Morrill Wyman's (1872) *Autumnal Catarrh*.

The several passages of Epes's lecture are quoted verbatim from his handwritten text. The dialogue is, of course, as I've imagined it. At the time of this vignette, President Eliot was waiting for Wendell Holmes's response to his offer of a professorship in the Harvard Law School. On Nov. 1, 1881, Wendell tentatively accepted the offer, contingent on a higher salary and the right to abandon the position should he be offered a judgeship (White 1993:198–199).

The superlatives in *Scribner's Monthly*'s May 1881 (pp. 697–709) review of Fanny's embroideries surpassed those expressed in the *Nation*'s April 21 rave. *Scribner's* illustrated six of Fanny's landscapes, including "Drifting Snow." I allow Francis Bowen to quote from this review. We know that Cornelius Vanderbilt II eventually purchased several of Fanny's embroideries. One of these was her landscape "Orchard," illustrated in the *Scribner's* review (Laidlaw 2003:61).

12

13.1 In spring 1885, Charley was completing his junior year at Westford Academy, a coeducational school located 30 miles northwest of Boston and 8 miles west of Lowell. He boarded with the Henry Chamberlin family on Francis Hill, about 2 miles from the school.

Westford Academy was established in 1792 with a proviso "that the English, Latin and Greek languages, together with writing, arithmetic and the art of speaking should be taught" as well as practical geometry, logic, geography, and music. Further it was stated that the "school should be free to any nation, age or sex." By 1880, special attention was given to those students who wished to go on to college "with apparatus provided for experiments in natural philosophy and chemistry." A public examination was held at the end of each term with "the rank, deportment and attendance of each scholar ... exhibited to parents and visitors." The town of Westford prided itself on being "remarkably free from everything which can tempt the young to evil habits and neglect of studies, and easy of access from all directions by railroad" (Abbot 1880:781–785).

13.2 Apparently sensing that his persistent chest cold was becoming something far more serious, George drafted a new will and signed it on March 6, 1885, five weeks before his death. He appointed attorneys Charles Pickering Bowditch and Alfred Bowditch as his executors and trustee. They were close relations of the Bowditch sisters who had married Epes and J.J.

George maintained an active correspondence with Hu Ts'ai-shun. His trip to visit her in Shanghai, probably in summer 1884, is documented by a portrait of an aged George Dixwell, taken by a Shanghai photographer (see page 302).

George died of pneumonia on Friday, April 10, 1885. The next day, his obituary, which included so much detail and elegant phrasing that it had to have been penned by his brother Epes, appeared in the *Boston Evening Transcript* [11]:6). The notation in the "Deaths" column ([4]:5) made no mention of a funeral, stating only, "Friends are kindly requested not to send flowers." George was buried on Sunday, April 12, 1885 (Janet Heywood, Director of Interpretation, Mount Auburn Cemetery, 20 Aug. 2000, pers. comm.).

The Bowditches maintained an itemized ledger listing Charley's expenses (by month) from 1885 until shortly after he turned 21 in 1889. Among the earliest entries, for May 1885 are tuition payments to William Frost, headmaster of Westford Academy; the cost of a telegram; and train fare from Westford. For the purposes of this vignette, I have placed that trip from Westford to Boston on Friday, May 10, 1885. The ledger also records Charley's board payments to Henry Chamberlin. I thank Marcia Dixwell DiMambro for providing me with photocopies of the ledger pages.

Shigehide Arakawa presented a lecture in Boston—"Japanese Manners and Customs"—on April 23rd (*Boston Evening Transcript* 24 April 1885 [2]:4).

13.3 George's will instructed his executors to send $2,000 to the family of Chen Tze Fang, his Chinese teacher in Shanghai and give the pictures of his mother and brother to Caroline Dixwell (J.J.'s younger daughter).

He directed that the balance of his estate be divided into three equal portions: one-third to the children of his deceased brother J.J.; one-third to his brother Epes; and the final third to be held in trust for "Teen Sung [characters], or in English Charles Sargent."

In their June 1885 summary of Charley's expenses, the Bowditches listed four purchases from his father's estate: a Silver Tankard for $25.00, a gold watch for $30.00, a Bronze Incense Burner for $125.00, and $9.00 for books.

13.4 We do not know who took Charley to see George's grave. Charley's daughter, Eleanor, remembered in a phone interview that when her father took her to Mount Auburn, he spoke affectionately of Dr. John (Eleanor Dixwell Morrison, Feb. 1993, pers. comm.). It is my invention that Dr. John took on this awkward task, for which he was well suited. Dr. John Dixwell had been employed in Boston as "General Agent for Lost or Stolen Children" (*Boston Directory*, 1880).

Anna Parker Dixwell was taking instruction in painting in Paris when she died on April 21, 1885 (only 11 days after George). She was buried next to George on May 9, 1885. At the time of George's death, the row of Dixwells comprised five headstones (Janet Heywood, Director of Interpretation, Mount Auburn Cemetery, 20 Aug. 2000, pers. comm.).

13.5 The Dixwells were devastated by Annie's unexpected and premature death so far from home, so much so, that her death completely overshadowed George's. When her uncle Epes, sitting in the home that George had bought for him, penned his annual Christmas poem, George did not get a single line! A copy of the poem, typeset and printed for distribution to the family, is preserved at the Boston Athenaeum.

"Annie, why tardy thus at
festal scene?
First hitherto with heart and face
so bright,
Our daughter, sister dear, our
heart's delight,
Long, mid our feast in frolic
foremost seen!
Brief absence was your purpose,
and to glean
Some laurels Art allured you from
our sight.
Why linger still beyond the deep
to-night?—
Return, we pray, return with
brow serene!
Dear Annie, yes you steal
among us here:
Undying love to love undying speaks.
We feel your spirit breathes
upon us near;
Your loving kisses meet our loving cheeks;
Your smile beams out; your pressing
hand is warm;
Your heart throbs nigh us; nay, we
see your form!"

Charles Pickering Bowditch (1842–1921) graduated from Epes Dixwell's school in 1859 (Wigglesworth 1907:64). He and his brother, Alfred Bowditch (1855–1918), managed George Dixwell's trust for Charley until World War I. At that time Charles Bowditch passed the responsibility to his son, Ingersoll Bowditch

(1875–1938), who, in turn, passed it on to his son-in-law, Augustus P. Loring, Jr. Charley had such confidence in Bowditch and Loring that when he drafted his own will in 1924, he named them as the trustees of his estate. Years later, Bazil asked the successor trustee, Augustus P. "Gus" Loring, III (1915–1986), for help in his unsuccessful attempt to locate his Chinese relatives. It was Gus who had told Bazil's sister Eleanor, that Hu Ts'ai-shun had come to Boston, found it unfriendly, and returned to China.

The Raymond Excursion Company offered a multitude of Western trips. The excursion, scheduled closest to the August 1888 payment recorded in the Bowditch ledger, departed for Yellowstone National Park on August 20 with "All Railway Travel in Palace Sleeping-Cars" (*Boston Transcript* 28 July and 10 Aug. 1888). Charley's trip cost $275, plus another $150 for pocket money. At that time an elegant five-room suite in Boston's Back Bay could be rented for $30 per month (*Boston Transcript* 10 Aug. 1888 [5]:6).

Charley, of course, was not at all concerned with the Dixwells after George's death. The most public of his father's surviving relatives was J.J.'s son, cousin Arthur—the baseball crank. A January 5, 1891, article in the *Philadelphia Inquirer* caught the essence of Arthur "General Hi Hi" Dixwell: "The dumpy little gent sits in blissful ignorance of all his surroundings, gazing only at his favorite players who seem to be inspired with unusual activity when they hear his familiar yell, so dear to them, but 'Oh: how annoying to the opposing players.'"

Marcia Dixwell DiMambro supplied many of the documents used to illuminate the lives of Hu Ts'ai-shun, Charles Sargent Dixwell, and Bazil Sargent Dixwell.

These documents include the following: photocopies of the Bowditch trustees' ledger, detailing Charley's 1885–1889 expenditures; the 1889 envelope forwarded to Charley from Paris, to Rome, to Cairo; the autographed 1889 cabinet photo of an Algerian woman entertainer; a photo of Charley with a tour group (probably in Egypt); an 1891 storage receipt for Charley's five cases of belongings (and an attached 1898 receipt for removing one trunk and a harp from storage); Henry Singleton Bisbing's July 13, 1901, letter; the Japanese Emperor's Nov. 7, 1904, invitation to attend a chrysanthemum viewing party; Hu Ts'ai-shun's March 8, 1906, letter to Charley; Charley's "printer's devil" bookplate; Fearon, Daniel & Company's telegrams regarding Ts'ai-shun's death; Ts'ai-shun's Aug. 27, 1915, last will; photographs of Ts'ai-shun's funeral procession, and a photograph of the Dixwell Road street sign in Shanghai; 1917 photos of Charley's Studebaker roadster; Julia Vong Ying Woo's Dec. 21, 1919, letter to her Uncle Charles Dixwell; Bazil's Nov. 29, 1963, letter to J. J. Dixwell's granddaughter, Anna Dixwell Knauth; a Jan. 9, 1984, letter to Bazil from Epes Dixwell's great grandson, Epes Dixwell Chase; a rough draft of Bazil's 1984 Dixwell family genealogy.

13

Marcia Dixwell DiMambro and Lauren Dixwell Rayfield provided the documents and dates for the events of Bazil's professional career with Northeast Airlines, the growth of his family, and his retirement years.

Helen Pierce searched the New Bedford city directories and city records for details of Charley and Hattie's life there. She located and interviewed Mrs. Marian Chase, the 90-year-old daughter of Hattie's sister (Mrs. Mary Arnold Houston), who remembered Hattie as "Beautiful, with flaming red hair and lovely skin, [who] always wore a hat and veil to protect her skin—a stunning woman, a very good pianist, with beautiful clothes and jewelry. She owned the house where the Houstons lived." Mrs. Chase described Hattie's collection of fans, and jewelry and said that Charles Dixwell was "a good man" and very kind to her when she was a child. Mrs. Chase thought Charles bought the house in Fairhaven as a present to Harriet in "atonement for his shenanigans with Dorothy." The house was actually purchased more than seven years earlier in 1908.

Charley's passport applications no. 8038 (May 25, 1897), claiming birth in Shanghai, and no. 49455 (Dec. 5, 1901), claiming birth in Nagasaki, are archived by the Passport Division, Department of State.

Oliver Wendell Holmes, Jr., authored the *United States v. Sing Tuck* decision (194 U.S. 161-1904) for the Supreme Court, reaffirming a bureaucratic procedure that made it virtually impossible for Chinese to produce witnesses to confirm their American citizenship (White 1993:344–45). Justice Brewer's dissent, suggesting that racial prejudice lay behind the willingness of the court to subject American citizens of Chinese descent to such "harsh and arbitrary" measures, is quoted and discussed by Lucy Salyer (1989:114).

Charley's passenger ship records are taken from the ancestry.com database. Although these records are incomplete, they record passages from Cherbourg to New York in June 1906; July 1909 and June 1911; a passage from Hong Kong to Vancouver, B.C., April–May 1916; and a round trip from New York to Barbados in February and March 1930.

Charley and Hattie never divorced. He continued to support her financially for the rest of his life and provided for her in his will. Hattie may already have been mentally disturbed when Charley left her. His Jan. 26, 1924, letter to her suggests that she had been judged mentally incompetent. "When you were taken away from 282 Union ... I did not know anything about it ... Then, as you were judged not quite right, I wanted Ingersoll Bowditch appointed your guardian, but they [her relatives] protested to the judge, so I did not insist and they had the judge appoint Mr. Crowley." This letter and several others written by Hattie to Charley in 1924 are held by Marcia Dixwell DiMambro.

Charley's bookplate celebrated Pietro Aretino (1492–1556) who achieved fame in 1516 with the "mock last will" he wrote for Hanno, the pet elephant of Pope Leo X, in which the pachyderm bequeathed his most impressive genitals "to one of the lustier cardinals." Aretino went on to become one of Italy's "lewdest and wittiest writers ..." (Zacks 1994:149).

Charley used fictitious names when registering the Oct. 27, 1916, birth of his son. Boston Birth Register entry no. 16096 lists Edward J. and Elizabeth Dixon as the parents of Basil S. Dixon (Index of Births: 1916. Boston, 1920:82). When Eleanor Sargent Dixwell was born in Newton, Dec. 15, 1922, Charley listed her parents as Charles S. Dixwell and Elizabeth Dixon (Massachusetts Registry of Vital Records and Statistics, Newton, Middlesex County, birth record no. 786, p. 321).

Charley's will, dated May 1, 1923, instructed his trustees to apply the income from one-third of his estate to support his wife, Harriet G. Dixwell, during her lifetime. The income from the remaining two-thirds was assigned to Dorothy Ashley until Basil and Eleanor both turned twenty-one, after which Dorothy would receive half the income. The other half was equally divided between Basil and Eleanor. The estate was valued at $78,611.60 on May 6, 1935. The final accounting of the trust valued it at $75,229.59 on Dec. 15, 1954.

Bazil S. Dixwell was co-pilot (first officer) aboard Northeast Airlines Flight no. 832 when it crashed on Rikers Island during takeoff from LaGuardia Airport, on Feb. 1, 1957. Twenty of the 101 passengers were killed. The wreck was attributed to pilot error. Dixwell was found blameless (Civil Aeronautics Board Accident Investigation Report, 10 March 1958, File No. 1–0081).

13

14.1 I visited Mount Auburn Cemetery on July 15, 2001. I had a plan of the Dixwell burial plot, found among the papers of Bazil Sargent Dixwell by his daughter Marcia.

Janet Heywood, the Mount Auburn Cemetery historian, told me where Henrietta Sargent was buried. The cemetery map showed all the paths and the location of the Nathaniel Bowditch monument. The first Bowditch statue was dedicated in 1847. Six years later the trustees, noting that the "design is better than the execution," appointed a committee of one to have the statue "repaired by stopping the holes and painting the whole of a bronze color." The statue was eventually recast (Bigelow 1860:52–53; Linden-Ward 1989:236–37). J. J. Dixwell was a Mount Auburn Trustee from 1847–1851 (Bigelow 1860:256) and is certain to have attended the original unveiling.

On Sept. 14, 1835, Catharine Sargent purchased Burial Lot No. 107 at Mount Auburn for the Sargent family. The following year she and Henrietta had their parents moved from Boston to Mount Auburn (Mount Auburn Burial Lot Register, Vol. 1:151).

I recall reading one of the parts in *Our Town* (Wilder 1957) in 1960–61 in Florence Schwimley's drama class at Berkeley High School. It must have been Miss Schwimley who impressed on me that Thornton Wilder (1897–1975) was a fellow Berkeley High School student, class of 1915.

Mount Auburn Cemetery records show that Charles Sargent Dixwell (aged 67 years, 8 months, 13 days) was cremated on July 17, 1934, two days after his death. Ingersoll Bowditch signed for his cremation. Charley's remains lay in storage at Mount Auburn for three years before Bowditch signed for their removal to Forest Hills Cemetery in Boston (Janet Heywood, Director of Interpretive Programs, Mount Auburn Cemetery, Aug. 26, 2000, pers. comm.).

Although no records survive, I suspect that during those three years Bowditch negotiated unsuccessfully with the Dixwell descendants for permission to bury Charley's ashes close to his father's grave. The last Dixwell to be buried in the family lot was J.J.'s great grandson, Oliver Dixwell Knauth, whose cremated remains were placed there on Oct. 31, 1968.

14

Bibliography

Abbot, Julian
1880   Westford Academy. *The American Journal of Education* 30:781–785.

Alexander, William, MD
1976   *The History of Women, from the Earliest Antiquity, to the Present Time; Giving an Account of Almost Every Interesting Particular Concerning that Sex, among All Nations, Ancient and Modern. With a Complete Index*, 2 vols. AMS Press, New York, NY. Orig published in 1779 by W. Strahan and Cadell. London, England.

American Lloyds
1859   *Registry of American and Foreign Shipping*. E. & G.W. Blunt, New York, NY.

Andrist, Ralph K., and Archibald Hanna
1961   *The California Gold Rush.* American Heritage Publishing Co., New York, NY.

Backhouse, Edmund, and J.O.P. Bland
1914   *Annals and Memoirs of the Court of Peking.* Houghton Mifflin, Boston, MA.

Banner, Lois W.
1980   *Elizabeth Cady Stanton: A Radical for Woman's Rights.* Addison, Wesley Longman, New York, NY.

Barnes, Gilbert H., and Dwight L. Dumond
1965   *Letters of Theodore Dwight Weld, Angelina Grimké Weld and Sarah Grimké, 1822–1844.* Peter Smith, Gloucester, MA. Originally published in 1934 by the American Historical Society.

Bigelow, Jacob
   1860   *A History of the Cemetery of Mount Auburn.* James Munroe and Co.,
             Boston, MA. Reissued 1988 by Applewood Books, Cambridge, MA.

Bland, J.O.P., and Edmund Backhouse
   1920   *China under the Empress Dowager.* William Heineman, London, England.

Bonney, Mrs. Catharina V. R. [Van Rensselaer]
   1875   *A Legacy of Historical Gleanings,* Vol. 2. J. Munsell, Albany, NY.

Book of Common Prayer
   2007   *The Book of Common Prayer and Administration of the Sacraments
             and Other Rites of the Church, According to the Use of The Episcopal
             Church.* Church Publishing, Inc., New York, NY.

Boston Directory
   1880   *Boston Directory: Embracing the City Record, General Directory
             of the Citizens, and a special directory of trades, professions, &c.,
             with an almanac... .* George Adams, Boston, MA.

Bowen, Catherine Drinker
   1944   *Yankee from Olympus: Justice Holmes and His Family.*
             Little, Brown and Co., Boston, MA.

Bowen, Francis
   1870   *American Political Economy: Including Strictures on the
             Management of the Currency and the Finances since 1861.*
             Charles Scribner's Sons, New York, NY.

Bruner, Katherine F., John K. Fairbank, and Richard J. Smith (editors)
   1986   *Entering China's Service: Robert Hart's Journals, 1854–1863.*
             Harvard Univ. Press, Cambridge, MA.

Bruun, Ole
   2003   *Fengshui in China: Geomantic Divination between State Orthodoxy and
             Popular Religion.* Univ. of Hawaii Press, Honolulu, HI.

Carl, Katharine A.
   1907   *With the Empress Dowager of China.* The Century Co., New York, NY.
             Reprinted 2004 by Kessenger Publishing Co., Whitefish, MT.

Cassara, Ernest
   1961   *Hosea Ballou: The Challenge to Orthodoxy.* Beacon Press, Boston, MA.

Cellarius, Henri
   1847   *La Danse des Salons.* Chez l'auteur, Paris, France.

Ceplair, Larry
    1989   *The Public Years of Sarah and Angelina Grimké: Selected Writings*
              1835–1839. Columbia Univ. Press, New York, NY.

Channing, William Ellery
    1835   *Slavery.* James Munroe and Co., Boston, MA.
              Reprinted 1969 by Arno Press, New York, NY.

Chapman, Maria Weston (editor)
    1852/1856 *Liberty Bell.* M. W. Chapman, Boston, MA. [The *Liberty Bell*
              was published annually throughout the 1840s and 1850s,
              generally published in December but always bore the date of
              the subsequent year; it was assembled by the Friends of Freedom
              for the National Anti-Slavery Bazaar as a gift book.]

Child, Lydia Maria
    1824   *Hobomuk, A Tale of Early Times*, By An American Lady.
              Cummings, Hilliard, Boston, MA. Reprinted 1986 as
              Hobomuk, and Other Writings on Indians, Carolyn L. Karcher,
              editor. Rutgers Univ. Press, New Brunswick, NJ.

    1833   *An Appeal in Favor of that Class of Americans Called*
              Africans. Allen and Ticknor, Boston, MA.

    1835a   *Authentic Anecdotes of American Slavery.* Charles
              Whipple, Newburyport, MA.

    1835b   [Mrs. D. L. Child]. *The History of the Condition of Women in Various*
              Ages and Nations, 2 vols. John Allen & Co., Boston, MA.

    1859   *The Correspondence between Lydia Maria Child and Governor Wise and Mrs.*
              Mason, of Virginia. American Anti-Slavery Society, Boston, MA.

    1862   Spirits. *Atlantic Monthly* 9(May):578–584.

    1865   *Looking toward Sunset. From Sources Old and New, Original*
              and Selected. Ticknor and Fields, Boston, MA.

    1867   *A Romance of the Republic.* Ticknor and Fields, Boston, MA.

Chinese Repository
    1840   Description of the tea plant. *Chinese Repository* 8:132–164. Reprinted
              [no date] by Krause Reprint Ltd., Vaduz, Liechtenstein.

Christman, Margaret C. S.
    1984   *Adventurous Pursuits: Americans and the China Trade.*
              Smithsonian Institution Press, Washington, DC.

Clayton, James D.
    1993   *Antebellum Natchez.* Louisiana State Univ. Press, Baton Rouge.

Clifford, Deborah P.
  1992   *Crusader for Freedom: A Life of Lydia Maria*
             Child. Beacon Press, Boston, MA.

Cochran, Thomas C.
  1953   *Railroad Leaders, 1845–1890: The Business Mind in*
             Action. Harvard Univ. Press, Cambridge, MA.

Crossley, Pamela Kyle
  1990   *Orphan Warriors: Three Manchu Generations and the End of the*
             Qing World. Princeton Univ. Press, Princeton, NJ.

Crossman, Carl L.
  1991   *The Decorative Arts of the China Trade: Paintings, Furnishings, and*
             Exotic Curiosities. Antique Collectors Club, London, England.

Dana, Richard Henry, Jr.
  1840   *Two Years Before the Mast: A Personal Narrative.* Reprinted
             1911 by Riverside Press, Cambridge, MA.

Delano, Edward
  1841   Diary [typed manuscript.]. Delano Papers, Franklin D.
             Roosevelt Library, Hyde Park, New York, NY.

Denton, William
  1874   *Is Spiritualism True?* [pamphlet]. W. Denton, Colby & Rich, Boston, MA.

Der-ling, Princess (Yü Der-ling)
  1911   *Two Years in the Forbidden City.* Moffat, Yard and Co., New York, NY.

De Vargas, Philip
  1939   William C. Hunter's Books on the Old Canton Factories.
             Yenching Journal of Social Studies 29(1):459–485.

Dixwell, George Basil
  1848   The Journals of George Basil Dixwell, 1848–1854. [The
             original bound journals are held by Marcia Dixwell DiMambro;
             for a transcribed and edited version, see Layton 1999.]
  1860   *Statement by George Basil Dixwell Concerning His Business Relations with*
             James A. Dorr, Esq. Knowles, Anthony & Co., Providence, RI.
  1875a   Improvement in Pyrometers for Steam-Engines, Specification forming
             part of Letters. U.S. Patent No. 160,400, filed Dec. 19, 1874.
  1875b   Improvement in Pyrometrical Indicators for Steam-
             Engines, Specification forming part of Letters. U.S.
             Patent No. 160,401, filed Jan. 12, 1875.

1875c   Improvement in Reciprocating Engines, Specification forming part of Letters. U.S. Patent No. 166,688, filed May 22, 1875.

1875d   Improvement in Reciprocating Steam-Engines, Specification forming part of Letters. U.S. Patent No. 160,311, filed Nov. 25, 1874.

1875e   *A Paper on Cylinder Condensation, Steam Jackets, Compound Engines, and Superheated Steam.* Read before the Society of Arts at the Massachusetts Institute of Technology, Boston, April 29 and May 13, 1875. Rand, Avery, & Co., Boston, MA.

1881   *The Premises of Free Trade Examined.* Reprinted from the *Bulletin of the National Association of Wool Manufacturers* by John Wilson and Son, Cambridge, MA.

1882a   *Progress and Poverty: A Review of the Doctrines of Henry George.* John Wilson and Son, Cambridge, MA.

1882b   *Review of Professor Sumner's Speech before the Tariff Commission.* John Wilson and Son, Cambridge, MA.

1882c   *Reviews of Bastiats Sophisms of Protection; [and of] Professor Sumner's "Argument Against Protective Taxes"; [and of] Professor Perry's "Farmers and the Tariff."* Reprinted from the *Bulletin of the National Wool Association* by John Wilson and Son, Cambridge, MA.

1883a   *Review of Bastiat's Sophisms of Protection.* John Wilson and Son, Cambridge, MA.

1883b   *Reviews of Bastiats Sophisms of Protection; [and of] Professor Sumner's "Argument Against Protective Taxes"; [and of] Professor Perry's "Farmers and the Tariff"; [and of] Professor Sumner's Speech Before the Tariff Commission; [and of] Progress and Poverty.* John Wilson and Son, Cambridge, MA..

Dixwell, George Basil, and James A. Dorr
1854   Gas-Regulator, Specification of Letters. U.S. Patent No. 10,786, filed April 18, 1854.

Dixwell, J. J.
1871   Spots on the Sun. *Atlantic Monthly* 27(162):500–504.

Dorr, James A.
1850   *Objections to the Act of Congress, Commonly Called the Fugitive Slave Law, Answered, in a letter to Hon. Washington Hunt, Governor Elect of the State of New York* [pamphlet]. n.p., New York, NY.

1856   *Justice to the South! An Address by James A. Dorr, A Member of the New York Bar, October 8, 1856* [pamphlet]. n.p., New York, NY.

Downer, Harry E.
1910   *History of Davenport and Scott County, Iowa*, 2 vols. S. J. Clarke Publishing Co., Chicago, IL.

Downer, Mrs. S. A.
　1854　　The Quicksilver Mine of New Almaden. *The Pioneer;
　　　　　or California Monthly Magazine* 2(Oct.):220–228.

Downs, Jacques M.
　1997　　*The Golden Ghetto: The American Commercial Community at
　　　　　Canton and the Shaping of American China Policy, 1784–1844.*
　　　　　Associated Univ. Presses, Cranbury, NJ.

Dresser, Amos
　1836　　*The Narrative of Amos Dresser.* The American
　　　　　Anti-Slavery Society, New York, NY.

Dupree, A. Hunter
　1959　　*Asa Gray: 1810–1888.* Harvard Univ. Press, Cambridge, MA.

Endicott, William C.
　1920　　Endicott Family Genealogy [manuscript and loose notes, ca. 1920].
　　　　　New England Historical Genealogical Society, Archive, Boston, MA.
　　　　　[Endicott never completed his manuscript. The typed, numbered pages
　　　　　bear numerous hand-written additions. This collection also includes
　　　　　correspondence and many unbound genealogical worksheets.]

Ernenwein, Raymond P.
　1970　　*The Borough of Peter.* Heritage Press, Sherburne, NY.

Fairbank, John King
　1953　　*Trade and Diplomacy on the China Coast: The Opening of the Treaty
　　　　　Ports, 1842–1854.* Harvard Univ. Press, Cambridge, MA.

Fairburn, William A.
　1945–55 *Merchant Sail.* Fairburn Marine Educational
　　　　　Foundation Center, Lovell, ME.

Fay, Peter Ward
　1976　　*The Opium War: 1840–1842.* Norton, New York, NY.

Fearon, Henry B.
　1818　　*Sketches of America.* Longman, Hurst, Rees,
　　　　　Orme and Brown, London, England.

Fearon, S. P.
　1972　　*Pedigrees of the Fearon Family Trading in China* [pamphlet, 26
　　　　　pp.]. Privately printed, Axbridge, Somerset, England.

Forbes, Robert Bennet
　1882　　*Personal Reminiscences,* 2nd ed. Little, Brown, and Co., Boston, MA.

Garrison, Wendell Phillips, and Francis Jackson Garrison
1885   *William Lloyd Garrison: 1805–1879, The Story of his Life, Told by His Children.* The Century Co., New York, NY.

Giles, Herbert Allen
1911   *The Civilization of China.* H. Holt & Co., New York, NY.

Grimké, Sarah M. [name not listed on title page]
1838   *Letters on the Equality of the Sexes, and the Condition of Woman: Addressed to Mary S. Parker, President of the Boston Female Anti-Slavery Society.* Isaac Knapp, Boston, MA.

Grover, Kathryn
2001   *The Fugitive's Gibraltar: Escaping Slaves and Abolitionism in New Bedford, Massachusetts.* Univ. of Massachusetts Press, Amherst, MA.

Hale, Edward E., Jr.
1917   *The Life and Letters of Edward Everett Hale.* Little, Brown, and Co., Boston, MA.

Hall, Peter A.
1992   *In the Web.* Peter Hall, England.

Hansen, Debra Gold
1993   *Strained Sisterhood: Gender and Class in the Boston Female Anti-Slavery Society.* Univ. of Massachusetts Press, Amherst.

Hao, Yen-P'ing.
1970   *The Comprador in Nineteenth Century China: Bridge between East and West.* Harvard Univ. Press, Cambridge, MA.

1986   *The Commercial Revolution in Nineteenth-Century China: The Rise of Sino-Western Mercantile Capitalism.* Univ. of California Press, Berkeley.

Harlow, Ralph Volney
1939   *Gerrit Smith: Philanthropist and Reformer.* Henry Holt and Co., New York, NY.

Harvard University, Class of 1890
1915   *Harvard University, Class of 1890, 25th Anniversary Report, 1890–1915.* Privately printed by Plimpton Press, Norwood, MA.

Haviland, Edward K.
1956   American Steam Navigation in China, 1845–1878. *American Neptune* 16(3):151–179.

1957   American Steam Navigation in China, 1845–1878. *American Neptune* 16(4):243–269; 17(1): 38–64; 17(2):134–151; 17(3):212–230.

Heard, Albert Farley
[1885]   Poisoning by Wholesale: A Reminiscence of China Life. [Heard
         descendant, Dr. Robert M. Gray, loaned me a photocopy of
         this hand-written document. For a different version of this
         story, see *The Poisoning in Hongkong: An Episode of Life in China*, by
         Augustine Heard [the nephew of Augustine Heard, Senior],
         Heard Collection, Part One, GQ 2-1, Baker Library, Harvard.

Heard, John
1891   Diary [memoir of Heard's life; manuscript (183
         pp.)]. Peabody Essex Museum, Salem, MA.

Holland, Patricia G., and Milton Meltzer
1979   *The Collected Correspondence of Lydia Maria Child, 1817–1880* [microfiche].
         Kraus-Thomson Organization Ltd. KTO Microform, Milkwood, NY.

Hoppin, Martha J.
1981   Women Artists in Boston, 1870–1900: The Pupils of William
         Morris Hunt. *The American Art Journal* 13(1):17–46.

Huang You-Sung, and Liang An Tzer
1865   *Various Essays on Silver* (in Chinese) [Kuangtung: Da
         Mao Tang], 4th ed. [See also: Yang Der Shen, 1876,
         Amendment to the Essays on Silver (in Chinese), 1st ed. Wang
         Bao Yuan, Chao district of Kuangtung Province.]

Hunter, William C.
1882   *The 'Fan Kwae' at Canton before Treaty Days, 1825–1844*.
         Reprinted 1970 by Ch'eng-wen Publishing Co., Taiwan.
1885   *Bits of Old China*. K. Paul, Trench, & Co., London, England.
         Reprinted 1966 by Ch'eng-Wen Publishing Co., Taipei.

Huxley, Thomas Henry
1870   *Lay Sermons, Addresses and Reviews*. MacMillan & Co., London, England.

Jacob, William
1831   *An Historical Inquiry into the Production and Consumption of the
         Precious Metals*. John Murray, London, England. Reprinted
         1968 by Augustus M. Kelley Publishers, New York, NY.

Johnson, Allen, and Dumas Malone (editors)
1930   *Dictionary of American Biography*. Charles Scribner's Sons, New York, NY.

Johnson, Arthur M., and Barry E. Supple
1967   *Boston Capitalists and Western Railroads: A Study in the Nineteenth-Century
         Railroad Investment Process*. Harvard Univ. Press, Cambridge, MA.

Kagin, Donald H.
  1981   *Private Gold Coins and Patterns of the United States.*
            Arco Publishing, Inc., New York, NY.

Kanda, James, and William A. Gifford
  1982   The Kaneko Correspondence. *Monumenta Nipponica* 37(1):41–76.

Kann, Eduard
  1927   *The Currencies of China,* 2nd ed., rev. Kelly &
            Walsh, Ltd., Shanghai, China.

Karcher, Carolyn L.
  1994   *The First Woman of the Republic: A Cultural Biography of
            Lydia Maria Child.* Duke Univ. Press, Durham, NC.

Kerr, Phyllis Forbes
  1996   *Letters from China: The Canton-Boston Correspondence of Robert Bennet
            Forbes, 1838–1840.* Mystic Seaport Museum, Mystic, CT.

Kinsman, Mrs. Nathaniel (Rebecca)
  1950   Life in Macao in the 1840's. *Essex Institute Historical Collections*
            86:15–330 [four sequential installments] Salem, MA.

Lo, Karl, and Him Mark Lai
  1977   *Chinese Newspapers Published in North America, 1854–1875.*
            Center for Chinese Research Materials, Assoc. of
            Research Libraries, Washington, DC.

Krause, Chester L., and Clifford Mishler
  1985   *Standard Catalog of World Coins,* 11th ed. (1984).
            Krause Publications, Iola, WI.

Krieger, Alex, and David Cobb (editors)
  1999   *Mapping Boston.* The MIT Press, Cambridge, MA.

Laidlaw, Christine W.
  2003   Painting with Silken Threads: Fanny Dixwell Holmes and Japanism in
            Nineteenth Century Boston. *Studies in the Decorative Arts* 10(2):42–68.

Layton, Thomas N.
  1990   *Western Pomo Prehistory: Excavations at Albion Head, Nightbirds' Retreat,
            and Three Chop Village, Mendocino County, California.* Institute of
            Archaeology, Monograph 32. Univ. of California, Los Angeles.

  1997   *The Voyage of the Frolic: New England Merchants and the
            Opium Trade.* Stanford Univ. Press, Stanford, CA.

  1999   The Journals of George Basil Dixwell, 1848–1854 [manuscript].
            Transcribed and edited by T. Layton; also see Dixwell 1848.

2002   *Gifts from the Celestial Kingdom: A Shipwrecked Cargo for Gold Rush California*. Stanford Univ. Press, Stanford, CA.

Leland, Charles G.
1904   *Pidgin-English Sing-Song, or Songs and Stories in the China-English Dialect, with a Vocabulary*, 7th ed. Kegan Paul, Trench, Trübner & Co., London, England.

Linden-Ward, Blanche
1989   *Silent City on a Hill: Landscapes of Memory and Boston's Mount Auburn Cemetery*. Ohio State Univ. Press, Columbus.

Liu, Kwang-Ching
1962   *Anglo-American Steamship Rivalry in China, 1862–1874*. Harvard Univ. Press, Cambridge, MA.

Lo, Karl, and H. M. Lai
1977   Chinese Newspapers Published in North America, 1854–1975. *Center for Chinese Research Materials, Bibliographical Series No. 16*. Assoc. of Research Libraries, Washington, DC.

Lockwood, Stephen C.
1971   *Augustine Heard and Company, 1858–1862: American Merchants in China*. Harvard Univ. Press, Cambridge, MA.

Lovett, Robert W.
1961   American Merchant Roundy. *Essex Institute Historical Collections* 47(Jan.):61–78.

Lyon, Peter
1959   The Herald Angel of Woman's Rights. *American Heritage* 10(6).

MacLean, Gerald M. (editor)
1988   Introduction in *The Woman As Good As the Man Or, the Equality of Both Sexes* by François Poullain de La Barre, trans. by A. L. Wayne State Univ. Press, Detroit, MI. [Based on the English translation of *De l'égalité des deux sexes*, 1673.]

Mahoney, Timothy R.
1990   Down in Davenport: A Regional Perspective on Antebellum Town Economic Development. *The Annals of Iowa* 50(5):451–474. [See also, part 2 of this article, 1990, Down in Davenport: The Social Response of Antebellum Elites to Regional Urbanization, *The Annals of Iowa* 50(6):593–622.]

Marriner, Sheila, and Francis E. Hyde
1967   *The Senior John Samuel Swire, 1825–98: Management in Far Eastern Shipping Trades*. Liverpool Univ. Press, Liverpool, England.

Meltzer, Milton, and Patricia G. Holland (editors)
  1982   *Lydia Maria Child, selected letters, 1817–1880.* Univ.
            of Massachusetts Press, Amherst.

Morison, Samuel Eliot
  1961   *The Maritime History of Massachusetts: 1783–1860.*
            Houghton Mifflin, Boston, MA.

  1963   *Three Centuries of Harvard: 1636–1936.* Harvard
            Univ. Press, Cambridge, MA.

Murray, John
  1812–1813 *Letters and Sketches of Sermons,* 3 vols. Munroe and Francis, Boston, MA.

  1869   *The Life of Rev. John Murray, Preacher of Universal Salvation, Written
            by Himself. With a Continuation by Mrs. Judith Sargent Murray,* A
            New Edition, with an Introduction by Rev. G. L. Demarest.
            Universalist Publishing House, Boston, MA. Originally
            published 1816 by Francis and Munroe, Boston, MA.

Murray, Judith Sargent [Constantia]
  1784   Desultory Thoughts upon the Utility of encouraging a degree of Self-
            Complacency, especially in Female Bosoms. See Judith Sargent Stevens.

  1790   On the Equality of the Sexes. *The Massachusetts
            Magazine. or, Monthly Museum of Knowledge and Rational
            Entertainment* 2(3):132–135; and 2(4):223–226.

  1798   *The Gleaner. A Miscellaneous Production, in Three Volumes.* I.
            Thomas and E. T. Andrews, Boston, MA. Reprinted as
            one volume 1992, with an introductory essay by Nina
            Baum by Union College Press, Schenectady, NY.

Museum of Fine Arts, Print Department
  1887   *Exhibition of the Work of the Women Etchers of America,* Nov. 1
            to Dec. 31, 1887. Alfred Mudge & Son, Boston, MA.

Nott, J. C., and George R. Gliddon
  1854   *Types of Mankind,* intro by Louis Agassiz. Lippincott,
            Granbo & Co., Philadelphia, PA.

Novick, Sheldon M.
  1989   *Honorable Justice: The Life of Oliver Wendell Holmes.*
            Little, Brown and Co., Boston, MA.

Ogle County American Revolution Bicentennial Commission (editor)
  1976   *Bicentennial History of Ogle County.* Ogle County American
            Revolution Bicentennial Commission, Oregon, IL.

Osborne, Carol M.
    1996   Frank Duveneck & Elizabeth Boott: An American
                Romance. *Duveneck: Frank Duveneck & Elizabeth Boott Duveneck*
                [exhibit catalogue]. Owen Gallery, New York, NY.

Palmer, Mary Towle
    1924   *The Story of the Bee*. Privately printed, Cambridge, MA.

Park, Lawrence
    1926   *Gilbert Stuart: An Illustrated Descriptive List of His Works.*
                William Edwin Ridge, New York, NY.

Pfeiffer, David A.
    2004   Bridging the Mississippi: The Railroads and Steamboats Clash
                at the Rock Island Bridge. *Prologue*, Quarterly of the National
                Archives and Records Administration 36(32):40–47.

Pittman, Benn
    1857   *The Phonographic Manual*. Phonographic Institute, Cincinnati, OH.

Pott, F. L. Hawkes
    1928   *A Short History of Shanghai*. Kelley & Walsh, Ltd, Shanghai, China.

Rabil, Albert, Jr., (editor)
    1996   Introduction. *Declamation on the Nobility and Preeminence of
                the Female Sex* by Henricus Cornelius Agrippa, translated
                by Albert Rabil, Jr. Univ. of Chicago Press, IL.

Renehan, Edward J., Jr.
    1995   *The Secret Six: The True Tale of the Men Who Conspired with
                John Brown*. Crown Publishers, Inc., New York, NY.

Ride, Lindsay, and May Ride
    1996   *An East India Company Cemetery: Protestant Burials in Macao*,
                abridged and edited by Bernard Mellor from the Rides'
                manuscripts. Hong Kong Univ. Press, Hong Kong.

Robinson, David
    1985   *The Unitarians and the Universalists*. Greenwood Press, Westport, CT.

Ross, Earle D.
    1947   George Barnard Sargent: Western Promoter. *The Iowa
                Journal of History and Politics* 45(1):115–132.

Ross, Ishbel
    1972   *The Uncrowned Queen: Life of Lola Montez*. Harper & Row, New York, NY.

Roundy, Everett Ellsworth (compiler)
1942   *The Roundy Family in America.* Privately published, [Dedham, MA].
          Reissued 2000 by the Shadrach Roundy Family, privately published.

Runkle, John D.
1873–1874 *President's Report, 1873–1874.* Massachusetts Institute of
          Technology, Archives, Collection AC 11, Vol. 4, 1873–1874.

Salyer, Lucy
1989   Captives of Law: Judicial Enforcement of the Chinese Exclusion
          Laws, 1891–1905. *The Journal of American History* 76(1):91–117.

Sargent, Emma W., and Charles S. Sargent
1923   *Epes Sargent of Gloucester and His Descendants.*
          Houghton Mifflin, Boston, MA.

Sargent, George B.
1947   Lecture on the West, delivered at the Tremont Temple,
          Boston, Massachusetts, February 24, 1858. Luse, Lane
          & Co., Davenport, IA. Republished 1947 by *The Iowa
          Journal of History and Politics* 45(1):139–174.

Schwartz, Harold
1956   *Samuel Gridley Howe: Social Reformer 1801–1876.*
          Harvard Univ. Press, Cambridge, MA.

Scudder, Winthrop S. (editor)
1924   Gerrit Smith Miller, an Appreciation [pamphlet]. *The Nobleman,*
          Supplement. The Noble and Greenough School, Dedham, MA.
          Part of this pamphlet was reprinted 1924 as "The First Organized
          Football Club in the United States," *Old Time New England* 15(1):7–13.

Seagrave, Sterling
1992   *Dragon Lady: The Life and Legend of the Last Empress
          of China.* Alfred A. Knopf, New York, NY.

Secretary of the Commonwealth of Massachusetts
1972   *List of Persons Whose Names Have Been Changed in Massachusetts:
          1780–1892.* Genealogical Publishing Co., Baltimore,
          MD. Originally published 1893 in Boston.

Semour, Bruce
1996   *Lola Montez: A Life.* Yale Univ. Press, New Haven, MA.

Simon, Kate
1978   *Fifth Avenue: A Very Social History.* Harcourt
          Brace Jovanovich, New York, NY.

Skemp, Sheila L.
1998   *Judith Sargent Murray: A Brief Biography with Documents*. Bedford Books, Boston, MA.

Smith, Bonne Hurd
2007   *"Mingling Souls Upon Paper": An Eighteenth-Century Love Story*. Judith Sargent Murray Society, Penobscot, ME.

Smith, Bonnie Hurd (editor)
1998   *From Gloucester to Philadelphia in 1790. Observations, Anecdotes, and Thoughts from the 18th-Century Letters of Judith Sargent Murray with a Biographical Introduction*. The Judith Sargent Murray Society, Cambridge, MA.

2005   *The Letters I Left Behind: Judith Sargent Murray Papers, Letter Book 10*. Judith Sargent Murray Society, Salem, MA.

Smith, Carl T.
1994   Protected Women in 19th-Century Hong Kong. In *Women & Chinese Patriarchy: Submission, Servitude and Escape*, Maria Jaschok and Suzanne Miers, editors, pp. 221–237. Hong Kong Univ. Press, Hong Kong.

1995   *A Sense of History: Studies in the Social and Urban History of Hong Kong*. Hong Kong Educational Publishing Co., Hong Kong.

Sokoloff, Valentin A.
1982   *Ships of China*. Museu e Centro de Estudos Maritimos de Macau, Macau.

Spence, Jonathan D.
1996   *God's Chinese Son: The Taiping Heavenly Kingdom of Hong Xiuquan*. W.W. Norton, New York, NY.

Starbuck, Alexander
1969   *The History of Nantucket*. Charles E. Tuttle Co., Rutland, VT. Originally published 1924.

Stauffer, John
2002   *The Black Hearts of Men: Radical Abolitionists and the Transformation of Race*. Harvard Univ. Press, Cambridge, MA.

Sterling, Dorothy
1991   *Ahead of Her Time: Abby Kelley and the Politics of Anti-Slavery*. W. W. Norton & Co., New York, NY.

Stevens, Judith Sargent [Constantia]
1784   Desultory Thoughts upon the Utility of encouraging a degree of Self-Complacency, especially in Female Bosoms. *Gentleman and Lady's Town & Country Magazine*. Oct. 1784.

Stowe, H.B.
  1868   *Men of Our Times; or Leading Patriots of the Day, Being Narratives of the
            Lives and Deeds of Statesmen, Generals, and Orators including Biographical
            Sketches and Anecdotes.* Hartford Publishing Co. Hartford, CT.

Tiffany, Osmond, Jr.
  1849   *The Canton Chinese or the American's Sojourn in the Celestial
            Empire.* James Munroe, Boston, MA.

Trevor-Roper, Hugh
  1978   *Hermit of Peking: The Hidden Life of Sir Edmund Backhouse,* rev. ed. Penguin
            Books, New York, NY. Originally published 1976 as *A Hidden Life:
            The Enigma of Sir Edmund Backhouse,* Macmillan, London, England.

Vaille, F. O., and H. A. Clark
  1875   *The Harvard Book: A Series of Historical, Biographical, and Descriptive Sketches,*
            Vol. 1. Welch, Bigelow, and Co., Univ. Press, Cambridge, MA.

Varley, James F.
  1996   *Lola Montez: The California Adventures of Europe's Notorious
            Courtesan.* Arthur H. Clark Co., Spokane, WA.

Walkowitz, Judith R.
  1982   *Prostitution and Victorian Society: Women, Class and the State.*
            Cambridge Univ. Press, Cambridge, England.

Walpole, Horace
  1903–1905 *The Letters of Horace Walpole: Fourth Earl of Orford.*
            Clarenden Press, Oxford, England.

Wang, Shuo
  2004   The Selection of Women for the Qing Imperial Harem. In *The
            Chinese Historical Review* 11(2):212–222. [See also, Shuo Wang's
            presentation at "Chinese Historians in the United States" panel at
            the 2003 annual meeting of the American Historical Association in
            Chicago, IL: Women's Roles in Late Imperial and Modern China.
            Newsletter of the Chinese Historians of the United States, Inc XVI(1):6.]

Waters, Thomas Franklin
  1916   *Augustine Heard and His Friends.* Ipswich Historical Society, Ipswich, MA.

White, G. Edward
  1993   *Justice Oliver Wendell Holmes: Law and the Inner Self.*
            Oxford Univ. Press, New York, NY.

Whitehill, Walter Muir, and Lawrence W. Kennedy
   2000   *Boston: A Topographical History*, 3rd ed. The Belknap
            Press of Harvard Univ. Press, Cambridge, MA.

Wigglesworth, Mary C. D.
   1918   Only Glimpses, Nothing More [typescript, 82 pp., with
            numerous unnumbered pages of photographs]. Privately
            held by Constance Holden, Cambridge, MA.

Wigglesworth, Mary C. D. (editor)
   1907   *Epes Sargent Dixwell, An Autobiographical Sketch: Unfinished and Unrevised,*
            Begun for his Children and Found Among Some Papers Which After Came into
            My Hands After his Death. Geo. E. Ellis Co., Printers, Boston, MA.

Wilder, Thornton
   1957   *Three Plays: Our Town, The Skin of Our Teeth, The*
            Matchmaker. Harper, New York, NY.

Wilkie, Frank B.
   1858   *Davenport Past and Present.* Luse, Lane & Co., Davenport, IA.

Williams, Alicia Crane (editor)
   1990   *Chase-Wigglesworth Genealogy: The Ancestors and Descendants*
            of Philip Putnam Chase and his wife Anna Cornelia
            Wigglesworth. Gateway Press, Inc., Baltimore, MD.

Wollstonecraft, Mary
   1792   *A Vindication of the Rights of Woman with Strictures on Political and*
            Moral Subjects. Joseph Johnson, London, England. Reprinted
            1992 by Penguin Classics, Harmondsworth, England.

Worcester, G. R. C.
   1948   *The Junks and Sampans of the Yangtze.* Statistical Dept. of the
            Inspectorate General of Customs, Shanghai. Reprinted
            1971 by U. S. Naval Institute, Annapolis, MD.

Wyman, Morrill
   1872   *Autumnal Catarrh (Hay Fever) with Three Maps.*
            Hurd and Houghton, New York, NY.

Yourcenar, Marguerite
   1985   *Oriental Tales.* Farrar Straus Giroux, New York, NY. Originally published
            1938 as *Nouvelles Orientales*, Librairie Gallimard, Paris, France.

Zacks, Richard
   1994   *History Laid Bare: Love, Sex and Perversity from the Ancient Etruscans*
            to Warren G. Harding. Harpercollins, New York, NY.

APPENDIX A

The Other Eurasians

Throughout this book we have followed the Eurasian children of George Dixwell's China trade colleagues: James Bridges Endicott, William C. Hunter, and George Tyson. Following is a brief summary of what became of some of them.

The Endicott lineage

During the mid-1860s, Henry Bridges Endicott, the son of James Bridges Endicott and Ng Akew, became head of coastal shipping for Augustine Heard & Co. in Shanghai. When the Heard Company began to fail in 1873, Henry joined Butterfield and Swire, where, with his facility in the Chinese language, he became the highest-paid employee outside of senior management (Marriner & Hyde 1967:74–75). Henry married a Chinese woman, fathered a son named Henry, Jr., and died at the age of 51 on Jan. 5, 1895 (*North China Herald* 11 Jan. 1895 [28]:2). Only a few weeks before his father's death, Henry, Jr., a second-form student at Shanghai Public School, shared an academic prize with two other boys (*North China Herald and Supreme Court Gazette* 28 Dec. 1894:1056–1057).

Henry, Jr., later married a Chinese woman. In about 1920, he attempted to contact the American Endicotts, only to have his query ignored. This incident is described in Robert Endicott's note to William C. Endicott [the family genealogist]. "This Henry Bridges Endicott is the illegitimate son of an illegitimate son of James Bridges Endicott, half brother of my father and own brother to Uncle William. He knows of his own parentage, his mother was a Chinese woman and so was his grandmother" (New England Historic Genealogical Society, Endicott Genealogy File).

We do not know what became of Henry, Jr. He may well have lived into the 1970s and have grandchildren living today.

The Hunter lineage

The Endicott and Hunter lineages were joined in 1863 when Anna Rosa Hunter (daughter of William C. Hunter and a Tanka-Chinese woman) married John Endicott Gardner (nephew of James Bridges Endicott). Their son, John Endicott Gardner, Jr. (1863–1943), moved from Canton, China, to Australia in 1878, together with his mother and stepfather, the Rev. Daniel Vrooman. The family then moved to Oakland, California, in 1882, where John (then known as John Vrooman) began work as an interpreter for the U.S. Customs Bureau. In 1884, John moved to British Columbia to become official translator for the Canadian government. When that job was abolished, John (having resumed his birth name, John Endicott Gardner, Jr.) became superintendent of the Chinese M.E. (Methodist-Episcopal) churches and missions throughout the province. He married Bertha Burgess in 1887. Their daughter Rose and son John were born in 1888 and 1890, respectively. Gardner returned to San Francisco in the mid-1890s and worked first as interpreter and inspector at the U.S. Chinese Bureau (~1897–1905) and later as inspector at the U.S. Commission of Immigration (~1906–1915).

Gardner enjoyed a remarkable public career in San Francisco as the resident expert on all things Chinese. His activities were often the subject of feature articles in local newspapers. On Jan. 3, 1897, the San Francisco *Call* described his already 13-year project to translate "the imperial or official history of the Chinese people" as well as to complete his Chinese dictionary of 11,071 characters.

Unfortunately, the manuscript of Gardner's history and his library met a tragic end in the 1906 San Francisco earthquake and fire. The *Call* reported (14 May 1906 [1]:7):

> "Dr. J. E. Gardner of the Chinese immigration bureau was a heavy loser in the recent conflagration. His home was destroyed by the flames, but his deepest grief is over the loss of his library, the most complete of its kind in the world. Before the fire Dr. Gardner owned about 4,000 volumes ... . Of all his treasures the only one Dr. Gardner saved was the manuscript of a Chinese-English dictionary upon which he had been working for many years."

Shortly before Gardner's retirement in 1915, the San Francisco *Chronicle* celebrated him as a "Notable Californian" in its "Golden Jubilee and Exposition Edition" (6 Jan. 1915 [7]:1–2). The article noted Gardner's recent completion of his Chinese dictionary and key for searching out its characters; his extension class in Chinese at the University of California; the phonograph recordings of his voice that enabled him to extend that class across the country; his long campaign to end the trade in Chinese slave girls and his courageous rescues of more than 50 of these women.

Gardner's mother Anna Rosa (1839–1923) lived in San Francisco until about 1921, when she moved to Hawaii to live with her daughter, Dr. Lucy Vrooman Cooper. Dr. Cooper was a University of California trained medical doctor who, together with her husband, operated the Cooper Ranch Inn at Hauula (Dr. R. Gary Tiedemann, 2007, pers. comm.).

The Tyson lineage

In 1866, when George Tyson (1831–1881) married Sarah Anthony and started his American family, he asked his Chinese family not to continue using the Tyson surname. Tyson had originally named his eldest son by Lam Fong Kew (1842–1871) George Bartou Tyson. Then, in 1869 when his American son was born, the elder Tyson gave that son the name George, and his Chinese son became Chan Kai Ming. Tyson saw to it that Chan Kai Ming (1859–1919) was well educated, and he eventually became one of the most successful Hong Kong merchants of his generation. His obituary listed him as managing director of several Hong Kong banks and a mercantile company, as well as vice-chairman of the Chinese Chamber of Commerce. Among his many philanthropies were several medical buildings for the University of Hong Kong (*South China Morning Post* 12 Dec. 1919). I thank Wilfred Tyson of Hong Kong, Chan Kai Ming's grandson, for sending me the obituary and explaining the history of the Tysons in Hong Kong. For a full listing of George Tyson's Chinese descendants, see Hall (1992).

THE DIXWELL FAMILY

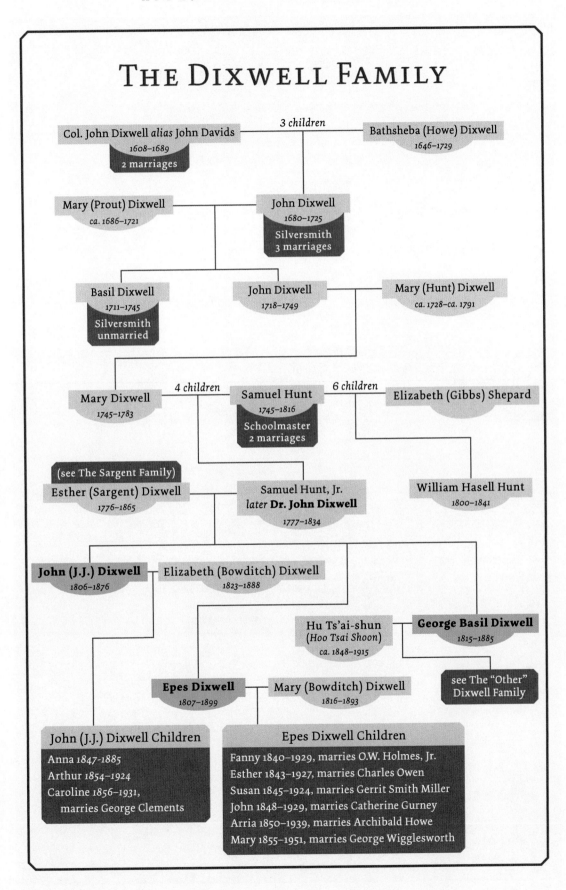

Col. John Dixwell *alias* John Davids
1608–1689
2 marriages

— 3 children —

Bathsheba (Howe) Dixwell
1646–1729

Mary (Prout) Dixwell
ca. 1686–1721

John Dixwell
1680–1725
**Silversmith
3 marriages**

Basil Dixwell
1711–1745
**Silversmith
unmarried**

John Dixwell
1718–1749

Mary (Hunt) Dixwell
ca. 1728–ca. 1791

Mary Dixwell
1745–1783

— 4 children —

Samuel Hunt
1745–1816
**Schoolmaster
2 marriages**

— 6 children —

Elizabeth (Gibbs) Shepard

(see The Sargent Family)
Esther (Sargent) Dixwell
1776–1865

Samuel Hunt, Jr.
later **Dr. John Dixwell**
1777–1834

William Hasell Hunt
1800–1841

John (J.J.) Dixwell
1806–1876

Elizabeth (Bowditch) Dixwell
1823–1888

Hu Ts'ai-shun
(*Hoo Tsai Shoon*)
ca. 1848–1915

George Basil Dixwell
1815–1885

Epes Dixwell
1807–1899

Mary (Bowditch) Dixwell
1816–1893

see The "Other"
Dixwell Family

John (J.J.) Dixwell Children

Anna *1847-1885*
Arthur *1854–1924*
Caroline *1856–1931*,
   marries George Clements

Epes Dixwell Children

Fanny 1840–1929, marries O.W. Holmes, Jr.
Esther 1843–1927, marries Charles Owen
Susan 1845–1924, marries Gerrit Smith Miller
John 1848–1929, marries Catherine Gurney
Arria 1850–1939, marries Archibald Howe
Mary 1855–1951, marries George Wigglesworth

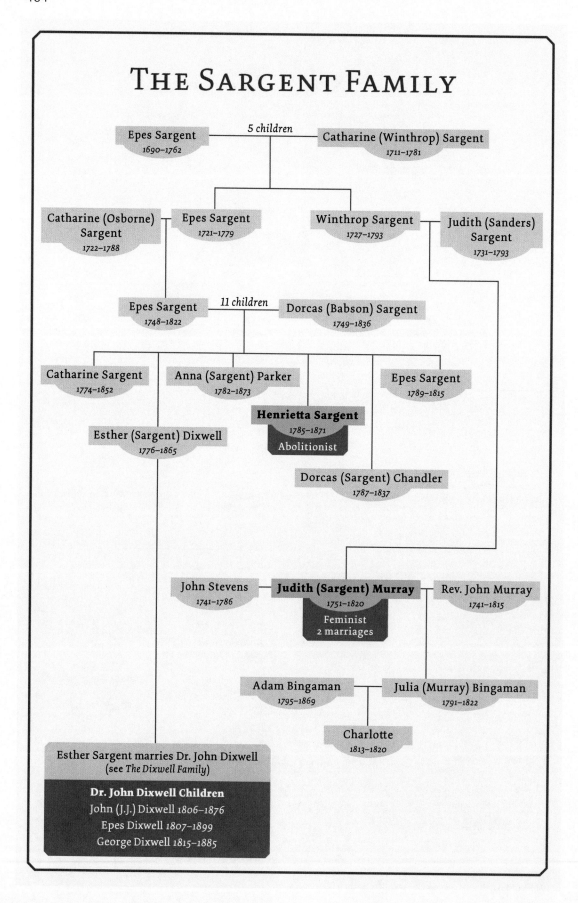

THE SARGENT FAMILY

Epes Sargent
1690–1762

— 5 children —

Catharine (Winthrop) Sargent
1711–1781

Catharine (Osborne) Sargent
1722–1788

Epes Sargent
1721–1779

Winthrop Sargent
1727–1793

Judith (Sanders) Sargent
1731–1793

Epes Sargent
1748–1822

— 11 children —

Dorcas (Babson) Sargent
1749–1836

Catharine Sargent
1774–1852

Anna (Sargent) Parker
1782–1873

Epes Sargent
1789–1815

Esther (Sargent) Dixwell
1776–1865

Henrietta Sargent
1785–1871
Abolitionist

Dorcas (Sargent) Chandler
1787–1837

John Stevens
1741–1786

Judith (Sargent) Murray
1751–1820
Feminist
2 marriages

Rev. John Murray
1741–1815

Adam Bingaman
1795–1869

Julia (Murray) Bingaman
1791–1822

Charlotte
1813–1820

Esther Sargent marries Dr. John Dixwell
(see *The Dixwell Family*)

Dr. John Dixwell Children
John (J.J.) Dixwell *1806–1876*
Epes Dixwell *1807–1899*
George Dixwell *1815–1885*

The "Other" Dixwell Family

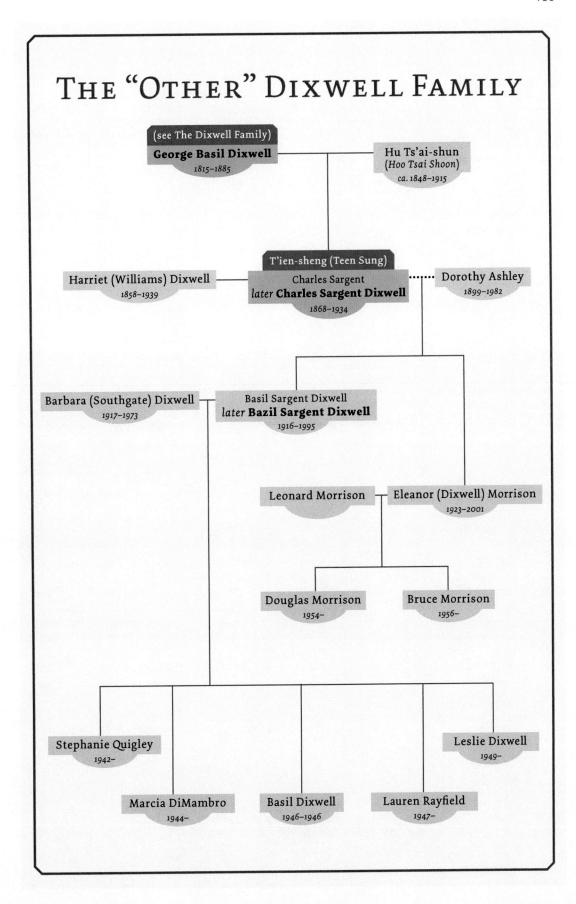

(see The Dixwell Family)
George Basil Dixwell
1815–1885

Hu Ts'ai-shun
(*Hoo Tsai Shoon*)
ca. 1848–1915

T'ien-sheng (Teen Sung)
Charles Sargent
later **Charles Sargent Dixwell**
1868–1934

Harriet (Williams) Dixwell
1858–1939

Dorothy Ashley
1899–1982

Barbara (Southgate) Dixwell
1917–1973

Basil Sargent Dixwell
later **Bazil Sargent Dixwell**
1916–1995

Leonard Morrison

Eleanor (Dixwell) Morrison
1923–2001

Douglas Morrison
1954–

Bruce Morrison
1956–

Stephanie Quigley
1942–

Leslie Dixwell
1949–

Marcia DiMambro
1944–

Basil Dixwell
1946–1946

Lauren Rayfield
1947–

Made in the USA
Middletown, DE
21 April 2021